AN IMPOSSIBLE
FRIENDSHIP

RELIGION, CULTURE, AND PUBLIC LIFE

RELIGION, CULTURE, AND PUBLIC LIFE

SERIES EDITOR: ELEANOR B. JOHNSON (2024–)
MATTHEW ENGELKE (2018–2024)

The Religion, Culture, and Public Life series is devoted to the study of religion in relation to social, cultural, and political dynamics, both contemporary and historical. It features work by scholars from a variety of disciplinary and methodological perspectives, including religious studies, anthropology, history, philosophy, political science, and sociology. The series is committed to deepening our critical understandings of the empirical and conceptual dimensions of religious thought and practice, as well as such related topics as secularism, pluralism, and political theology. The Religion, Culture, and Public Life series is sponsored by Columbia University's Institute for Religion, Culture, and Public Life.

Moral Atmospheres: Islam and Media in a Pakistani Marketplace, Timothy P. A. Cooper

Karma and Grace: Religious Difference in Millennial Sri Lanka, Neena Mahadev

Samson Occom: Radical Hospitality in the Native Northeast, Ryan Carr

Perilous Intimacies: Debating Hindu-Muslim Friendship After Empire, SherAli Tareen

Baptizing Burma: Religious Change in the Last Buddhist Kingdom, Alexandra Kaloyanides

At Home and Abroad: The Politics of American Religion, edited by Elizabeth Shakman Hurd and Winnifred Fallers Sullivan

The Arab and Jewish Questions: Geographies of Engagement in Palestine and Beyond, edited by Bashir Bashir and Leila Farskah

Modern Sufis and the State: The Politics of Islam in South Asia and Beyond, edited by Katherine Pratt Ewing and Rosemary R. Corbett

German, Jew, Muslim, Gay: The Life and Times of Hugo Marcus, Marc David Baer

The Limits of Tolerance: Enlightenment Values and Religious Fanaticism, Denis Lacorne

The Holocaust and the Nakba, edited by Bashir Bashir and Amos Goldberg

Democratic Transition in the Muslim World: A Global Perspective, edited by Alfred Stepan

The Politics of Secularism: Religion, Diversity, and Institutional Change in France and Turkey, Murat Akan

Holy Wars and Holy Alliance: The Return of Religion to the Global Political Stage, Manlio Graziano

Faithful to Secularism: The Religious Politics of Democracy in Ireland, Senegal, and the Philippines, David T. Buckley

For a complete list of books in the series, please see the Columbia University Press website.

AN IMPOSSIBLE FRIENDSHIP

Group Portrait, Jerusalem Before and After 1948

SONJA MEJCHER-ATASSI

Columbia University Press
New York

Publication of this book was made possible in part by funding from the Institute for Religion, Culture, and Public Life at Columbia University.

Columbia University Press
Publishers Since 1893
New York   Chichester, West Sussex
cup.columbia.edu

Copyright © 2024 Columbia University Press
All rights reserved

Library of Congress Cataloging-in-Publication Data
Names: Mejcher-Atassi, Sonja, author.
Title: An impossible friendship : group portrait, Jerusalem before and after 1948 / Sonja Mejcher-Atassi.
Other titles: Group portrait, Jerusalem 1946
Description: New York : Columbia University Press, [2024] | Series: Religion, culture, and public life | Includes bibliographical references and index.
Identifiers: LCCN 2023053868 | ISBN 9780231214742 (hardback) | ISBN 9780231214759 (trade paperback) | ISBN 9780231560443 (ebook)
Subjects: LCSH: Melen ha-Melekh David (Jerusalem) | Intellectuals—Jerusalem—Biography. | Authors—Jerusalem—Biography. | Jerusalem—Intellectual life—20th century. | Palestine—History—1929–1948. | Transnationalism.
Classification: LCC DS109.93 .M357 2024 | DDC 956.94/4050922—dc23/eng/20240129
LC record available at https://lccn.loc.gov/2023053868

Printed and bound by CPI Group (UK) Ltd, Croydon, CR0 4YY

Cover design: Milenda Nan Ok Lee
Cover photo courtesy of Walid Khalidi

*"To Racha, Sally, Waleed and Wolf
Once together, now by cruel chance dispersed"
And to Jabra, who wrote these words,
in memory of an impossible friendship.*

CONTENTS

Acknowledgments ix
Note on Translation and Transliteration xvii

Prologue: The King David Hotel Bombing, Jerusalem, July 22, 1946   1

Introduction: Reading an Impossible Friendship Through a Group Portrait   11

PART I: THE TIME BEFORE 1948

1 "Changing Jerusalem: A New Panorama of the Holy City"   31

2 Walid Khalidi: A Jerusalemite "in the Byronic Tradition"   51

3 Rasha Salam Khalidi: "A Non-Conformist Moslem Arab Woman"   85

4 Wolfgang Hildesheimer: Belated Surrealist and "Exclusive Geheimtyp"   102

5 Jabra Ibrahim Jabra: "Spark-Plug" of the YMCA Arts Club   138

PART II: THE TIME BEYOND

6 Border Crossing   177

7 Public Engagement in Worlds Apart   202

Epilogue: Late Correspondence   225

Notes 239
Bibliography 301
Index 335

ACKNOWLEDGMENTS

Writing *An Impossible Friendship* would not have been possible without the friendship, support, and generosity of many people in many places. I am grateful to Wendy Lochner, publisher at Columbia University Press, and Matthew Engelke, the editor of the press's Religion, Culture, and Public Life series, for having given my book such a wonderful home. Their personal enthusiasm and professional support since I shared my first complete draft with them in 2021 were key in turning my manuscript into this book. I had the pleasure of working with Lowell Frye, associate editor, and the entire team at Columbia University Press, all of whom were of tremendous help. I am particularly indebted to the three anonymous readers in two rounds of reviews for their generous feedback and helpful criticism. I especially thank the reviewer who suggested I use a few lines of Mahmoud Darwish's poetry referred to in the body of my text as an epigraph—they have become two, one for each part of my book—and for pushing me to think through the new possibilities my book is opening for our political present. I hope we can continue the conversation, if in different capacities.

I received generous institutional support that freed me from teaching and administrative service to focus on my research and find both time and space to write. The American University of Beirut has provided me with a rich trajectory of professional and personal growth. Afforded with a senior research faculty grant as well as long-term and short-term faculty grants, I was able to travel abroad to participate in conferences and visit archives, a University Research Board grant made possible extended archival research. In 2017-2018, the Wissenschaftskolleg, Institute for Advanced Study, in Berlin opened its doors to me and my family, where I spent one of the most intellectually stimulating years in my life. Fellows from diverse disciplinary backgrounds and several different countries of origin breathed new life into my research. I am indebted not only to the Wissenschaftskolleg and its fabulous team of researchers and staff but also to the former homeowners of the beautiful Villa Jaffé in Berlin Grunewald, which housed my office. Emmy and Georg Braun greeted me daily from the two *Stolpersteine* in their memory on the sidewalk in front of the villa that bear their names and the dates and places of birth and death. Both were born in Berlin and fled Nazi Germany to Shanghai in 1940, where Georg passed away a year later. Emmy died in the ghetto in Shanghai in 1943. Their tragic deaths evoke political realities here and there, past and present, and their entanglements.

Many individuals at both institutions have contributed in various ways to this book making the journey from an idea to an actual object that you can now hold in your hands and read. At the Wissenschaftskolleg, I am indebted to the institute's former and current rectors, of whom I have had the pleasure to meet Wolf Lepenies, Luca Giuliani, and Barbara Stollberg-Rilinger, its head of academic programs Daniel Schönpflug, whose encouragement and friendship are very dear, and the amazing library team, led by Anja Brockmann, whose help in finding books was nothing short of magical. Among my cohort, I would like to thank in particular Yassin al-Haj Saleh, Anna Kathrin Bleuler, Pascale Cancik, Manu Goswani, Mohammad Hanif, Carola Lentz, Isidore Lobnibe, Pawel Machcewicz, Charles S. Maier, Kris Manjapra, Stanislas Meda Bemile, H. Glenn Penny, Viktoriya Sereda, and James Simpson. I also thank Georges Khalil from the Forum Transregionale Studien.

At the American University of Beirut, my thanks go to my home department, the Department of English, for the collegial, inspiring, and safe space it has afforded me in times often described in Arabic as *inhiyar* (collapse). Although the 2019 uprising in Lebanon offered glimmers of hope, the country's political and economic disintegration, topped by the 2020 Beirut port explosion, not to mention the Covid-19 pandemic, have all wreaked havoc and almost extinguished those hopes. With dreams of an Arab Spring crushed, particularly in the war in neighboring Syria, unfathomable loss and one of the world's worst refugee crises has taken hold of our lives. In the midst of all this, our department provided a safe haven, gently steered by its chairpersons, Syrine Hout and David Currell, with the assistance of our administrative angel Marwa El Roz Ramadan. I thank every member in the department—those who stayed and those who left—and in particular my colleagues in creative writing, theater, and film, Doyle Avant and

Robert Myers, who have inspired me to free myself from some of the shackles of academic writing and who have generously read earlier versions of this book's opening chapters. I have also been fortunate to teach a range of courses closely related to my research: our capstone seminar for literature majors focused on literary biography, another undergraduate course dealt with the translation of life writing, and a graduate course on global modernism explored some of the texts touched on in this book. I thank my students in these courses for many insightful discussions. In particular, I thank the graduate assistants with whom I have had the pleasure to work: Iman Al Kaisy, Xena Amro, Lyne Jradi, Fatima Kassem Moussa, Deema Nasser, and Dana Shahbary. Four of them have been accepted at top universities abroad to pursue their doctorates, and the other two are on their way. You cannot imagine how proud I am of you; you have taught me so much more than I will ever be able to teach you. Other colleagues at the American University of Beirut have in manifold ways enriched my life and work on this book: the late Abdulrahim Abu-Husayn, Hala Auji, Rula Baalbaki, Hayat Bualuan, Samer Frangie, Lina Ghaibeh, Zeina H. Halabi, Sari Hanafi, Safaa Ibrahim, Rana Issa, Maher Jarrar, Tarif Khalidi, Rami Khuri, John Meloy, Sara Mourad, Cynthia Myntti, Nadine Panayot, Bilal Orfali, Walid Sadek, Aliya Saidi, Kirsten L. Scheid, the late Richard Smith, Tariq Tell, Fawwaz Traboulsi, Livia Wick, and Huda Zurayk. Special thanks are due to our University Libraries and Archives and Special Collections Department, to Carla Chalhoub, Fatme Charafeddine, Shaden Dada, Samar Kaissy Mikati, Mervat Kobeisy, and Lokman Meho. I also thank Rami Zurayk and his team at the Palestine Land Studies Center, Abed al Kareem Yehia and Ghada Dimashk, who found in their archive the map of Jerusalem, published by the Survey of Palestine in 1937, that is reproduced in this book. For their support, and the interest they have taken in my research, I extend my thanks to the former deans of the Faculty of Arts and Sciences, Patrick Mc Greevy, Nadia El Cheikh, and Saouma Boujaoude, and our current Dean Fares El Dahdah, Provost Zaher Dawy, President Fadlo R. Khuri, and Trustee Philip S. Khoury. Philip kindly shared his 1998 Middle East Studies Association Presidential Address with me in which he recalls his student days at the American University of Beirut, and specifically a class he took with Walid Khalidi in 1969–1970.

Another institution has greatly supported me, the Alexander von Humboldt Foundation, which in 2021 awarded me the Reimar Lüst Award for International Scholarly and Cultural Exchange. I am grateful to Friederike Pannewick, who kindly nominated and hosted me at the Center for Near and Middle East Studies at the Philipps University of Marburg, for our collaboration and friendship dating back many years, and I look forward to more collaborative work in the years to come.

The Moving Biography Summer School, a cooperation of the American University of Beirut with the Orient-Institut Beirut and the Global (De)Center in June 2022 provided another inspiring platform. I thank my co-organizers Nadia von Maltzahn, Kirsten L. Scheid, and Peggy Levitt for their input and friendship as well as the Volkswagen Foundation for its generous support. I am indebted to what I have learned from our speakers, Marilyn Booth, Tarif Khalidi, Lina Majdalani, Jean Said Makdisi, Daniel Schönpflug, Sherene Seikaly, and Salim Tamari, as well as from our participants, among them Yvonne Albers and Sarah Sabban whose research journeys I am grateful to have been able to follow closely. Two other very enriching venues of academic exchange opened with the Arab-German Thought Initiative and the workshop on "Memoirs of the Colonized and the Colonizer," organized by Mada al-Carmel: Arab Center for Applied Social Research in Haifa. I thank Islam Dayeh, Jens Hanssen, Somar Al Mahmoud, and Nahed Samour for asking me to join the former, and Qasam Alhaj, Nadim Rouhana, and Salim Tamari for inviting me to participate in the latter.

Research is indeed like a journey; it takes you places not only in your mind but also in the physical world where it leads to myriad encounters with archival material as well as with extraordinary people past and present. Some have devoted their lives and careers to building archives, to collect, preserve, and curate the papers, photographs, and ephemera that serve as building blocks of our writing. I wish to express my gratitude to those who opened their archives, institutions, homes, and hearts to me, and those who generously granted permission to include some of their archival material and quote from unpublished personal papers. At the Wolfgang Hildesheimer Archive at the Academy of Arts in Berlin, I thank Franka Köpp and Bettina Köhler who kindly helped me with accessing Hildesheimer's personal papers. I extend my thanks to Christa Geitner and Inge Geitner-Thurner who kindly responded to my questions and granted permission to include Wolfgang Hildesheimer's illustrations for Jabra Ibrahim Jabra's poems as well as a drawing of their artist mother, Sylvia Dillmann Hildesheimer, which Wolfgang Hildesheimer sent along one of his letters to Rasha Salam Khalidi. I am thankful to the Suhrkamp Verlag to grant permission to quote from Wolfgang Hildesheimer's published and unpublished correspondence, preserved in the Wolfgang Hildesheimer-Archiv. At Cambridge, I thank Professors Hero

Chalmers and John Cleaver of Fitzwilliam College for their hospitality in spring 2018 and for granting me access to the college's archives where I was able to locate a wealth of documents pertaining to Jabra's studies at Cambridge in the early 1940s. At Oxford, I thank Debbie Usher, Archivist of the Middle East Centre Archive at St Antony's College, and the team of alumni relations at St John's College for hosting me. It's always a very special treat to be back.

I am indebted to Walid Khalidi who opened his home in Cambridge, Massachusetts, to me. As the only member of the group of friends at the heart of this book who is still with us, his memories are precious, and I am forever grateful for the time and care he took to discuss what I came to term an *impossible friendship* with me, while situating it in the specific historical context of Palestine under the British Mandate. The photographs and documents he shared from his personal archive have greatly enriched this book. I extend my thanks to his daughter, Karma Khalidi, and their warm and gracious house manager-cum-secretary, Lydia Cristobal, for their hospitality. My thanks also go to Walid's classmate, Suhail Bulos, who attended Saint George's School in Jerusalem with him, before he pursued his studies at the American University of Beirut where he would later work as an orthopedic surgeon. I cherish the many hours we spent over coffee at the café of the American University of Beirut Medical Center as he took me through his memories back to Jerusalem. Profound thanks also go to Tarif Khalidi, who, over many long coffees in Mahatma Gandhi Street close to his house in Hamra, has played a key role helping me piece together some of the puzzles of my research but has also wisely offered sage advice on issues beyond my book. Laila Shahid, too, has been most generous in sharing personal recollections, helping me to bring my subjects to life in the pages of this book, as did the memoirs of her Jerusalemite mother, Sirene Husseini Shadid. In Montreal, the late Professor Issa J. Boullata welcomed me into his house, offering answers to my many questions about Jabra, once his teacher in Jerusalem. I extend my thanks to Sadeer and Yasser Jabra and to Matthew Pruen who generously shared valuable information about their respective parents, Jabra and Sally, and granted me permission to include some of their artwork. I thank my former professor Angelika Neuwirth, an internationally renowned Quranic scholar and advocate for interreligious dialogue, for drawing my interest to modern Palestinian literature.

I had the opportunity to present some of my work in progress at different conferences and workshops and sincerely thank the organizers for inviting me and the respective audiences for engaging with my research. I presented an early talk, entitled "In Search of Jabra Ibrahim Jabra: A Life in Literature and Art Between Palestine and Iraq," at the Wissenschaftskolleg / Institute for Advanced Study in Berlin, when I was a fellow in residence there in 2017–2018, and I thank Manu Goswani for generously agreeing to moderate it. Next, I participated in a workshop, also in Berlin, organized by Khaled Saghieh and Rasha Salti on behalf of the Arab Fund for Arts and Culture in June 2018 on "Imagining the Future: The Arab World in the Aftermath of Revolution." In Beirut, I was invited to give a paper at a conference on "The Archive: Visual Culture in the Middle East," at the Lebanese American University in April 2019, organized by Yasmine Nachabe Taan and Melissa Plourde Khoury. I gave another talk on my book in the making in the framework of the workshop on "Memoirs of the Colonized and the Colonizer" at the University of Amsterdam in July 2022. In October 2022, I participated at a conference organized jointly by the Institute for Palestine Studies and Birzeit University in Ramallah on "Reassessing the British Mandate in Palestine," at the kind invitation of Hana Sleiman.

I thank other friends and colleagues in different places who have accompanied my research and writing, some listened to my ideas, some read chapters of the manuscript in the making, offered encouragement, criticism, or suggestions for further reading, and some were simply there as friends: Hala Abdallah, Azza Abo Rebieh, Ruth Abou Rached, Refqa Abu-Remeileh, Walter Armbrust, Salma Atassi, Azza Barazi, Bashir Bashir, Sybille Bikar, Doerte Bischoff, Marilyn Booth, Dominique Eddé, Tarek El-Ariss, Ulrike Freitag, Stathis Gourgouris, Beatrice Grunedler, Ghassan Hage, Sune Haugbolle, Brigitte Herremans, Fady Joudah, Samar Kanafani, Elias Khoury, Verena Klemm, Christian Lange, Wolf-Dieter Lemke, Victoria Lupton, Khalid Lyamlahy, Lydia Liu, Zeina Maasri, Ziad Majed, Ussama Makdisi, Khaled Mansour, Farouk Mardam-Bey, Adey Mohsen, Yasser Munif, Muhsin al-Musawi, Tania Nasser, Tamara Rifai, Eugene Rogan, Joude Roukbi, Rula Roukbi, Amro Saadeddine, Suja Sawafta, Abdelhay Sayed, Kinda Sayed, Sherene Seikaly, Rosemary Sayigh, Jenny Siegel, Lina Sinjab, Lukas Spinner, Rania Stephan, Petra Stienen, Simone Susskind, Salim Tamari, Stefan Tarnowski, Lindsay Whitfield, Elsa Wiehe, Salaam Yousif, and Afaf Zurayk. Two book recommendations, albeit set in different times and places, were influential in transforming a group of friends into the protagonist of my book. In 2019, David Damrosch invited me with some of his colleagues and students to dinner at his house. Hearing about my book project, he suggested I read his brother Leo Damrosch's newly published book, *The Club: Johnson, Boswell, and the Friends*

Who Shaped an Age (2019), which I have since used in teaching. In a later email exchange with Anton Shammas—the author of *Arabesques* (1986), a novel about the Nakba that was originally written in Hebrew and has just been newly reissued in its English translation by Vivian Eden—advised I read Nicholas Delbanco's *Group Portrait: Joseph Conrad, Stephen Crane, Ford Madox Ford, Henry James, and H. G. Wells* (1982).

Special thanks are due to Nicholas Davies for his thoughtful and thorough editing. He read each chapter and the complete manuscript in close back and forth exchange and provided most helpful suggestions that empowered my writing to take form. I thank Rasha Salti for kindly putting us in touch.

I thank the "Beirut gang," a circle of friends my husband, Mohammad Ali Atassi, and I have spent many happy hours with, turning to weekly lunches during the lockdown: Livia Wick, Samer Jabbour, Rabia Barazi, and Fouad Mohamad Fouad. They and their children Ramla, Naji, Yamen, and Leen and Ghadi, have become our extended family, making life in Beirut livable and lovable despite the *inhiyar*.

I also thank my family back in Hamburg, and in particular Opa and Oma: my father, Helmut Mejcher, a historian of the modern Middle East, and his wife, Marianne Schmidt-Dumont, an Arabist, who has spent many years of her life in different countries in the Middle East, but that is another story. I am grateful to Teta, my mother-in-law, Salma Hassibi, who with the Syrian Revolution turned war has moved from Damascus to Beirut, where she expresses her love through exquisite Damascene dishes that nourish us and everyone around her. Last but not least, I thank my partner in life, Mohammad Ali Atassi, a documentary filmmaker, whose critical eyes and love, not least for the poetry of Mahmoud Darwish, permeate every page of this book and have informed its title. To our children, Nour and Karim, their mother's friends (Rasha, Sally, Walid, Wolfgang, and Jabra) have become part of their childhood memories in Beirut as they set out to find their own paths in life. I thank them for the joy they have brought into my life.

Beirut, August 2023

NOTE ON TRANSLATION AND TRANSLITERATION

Unless otherwise noted, all translations into English are mine. English translations of Arabic book and article titles are provided in square brackets in the bibliography.

The transliteration of Arabic words follows a simplified version based on the guidelines of the *International Journal of Middle East Studies*. I have omitted diacritical marks but have retained the Arabic letter 'ayn and marked it with a backward apostrophe ('); the hamza is marked with an apostrophe ('). Arabic personal names are written according to how the respective individuals spell their names in English, or they follow the common spelling in English. Differences may occur in how a name is written if that name is transliterated differently in a source I quote, especially if this source makes use of diacritics in its transliteration. Arabic words widely used in English, such as Nahda, Nakba, and Quran, are left in their familiar form.

AN IMPOSSIBLE FRIENDSHIP

PROLOGUE

The King David Hotel Bombing, Jerusalem, July 22, 1946

AN ECUMENICAL CIRCLE OF FRIENDS

A group of friends strolls through the magnificent lobby of the King David Hotel, Jerusalem's first five-star property, a palatial, six-story structure built of locally quarried pink limestone on an elevated site overlooking the Old City and Mount Zion. The elegantly dressed young men and women walk toward the bar on the ground floor. There, they ensconce themselves in plush leather chairs and are joined by a tall young man, his longish hair falling over his cheeks and light-colored eyes, a pipe in his hand. He sits down next to a woman, her dark curly hair cropped short. The bar stools are mostly occupied by British Army officers and civil servants working for the British Mandate for Palestine and Transjordan. Reflecting the gentle twilight of early evening, the large, beveled mirror over the bar makes the luxurious, Tudor-style room appear even larger than it is. The officers trade jokes, laughing at a volume that betrays colonial entitlement. The friends order drinks—lager, Scotch, or Campari soda, perhaps—from the Sudanese waiter, who sports his customary white robe with a red sash. They discuss a reading of English Romantic poetry they attended a few days earlier at the Young Men's Christian Association (YMCA), which is located just across the street in an equally spectacular building. As the conversation drifts inevitably toward politics, the friends exchange worried glances and hopeful smiles, then rise out of their comfortable chairs and continue the evening at La Régence, a swank restaurant in the hotel's basement. There, they toast Walid and Rasha Salam Khalidi's first wedding anniversary and bid the couple farewell, as the Khalidis will soon depart for Beirut.

The celebration included a group of friends that Walid Khalidi, many years later—in an article about Albert Hourani, who worked at the Arab Office in Jerusalem after World War II, before he went on to become an acclaimed Oxford historian—would refer to as "a small 'ecumenical' circle of friends which met regularly in Jerusalem at its 'headquarters,' the bar of the King David Hotel."[1] In the same article, Khalidi also recalls "an evening in Lulie [Abul-Huda]'s flat where we all sat around on the floor listening to Albert [Hourani] read T. S. Eliot's *Wasteland* by candlelight."[2] Khalidi's use of the term *ecumenical* in his description of the group indicates its members' diverse religious backgrounds—a coming together of Christianity, Islam, and Judaism. Ussama Makdisi employs the same word, ecumenical, tracing its etymology from the Greek word *oikoumenē*, which denotes the whole of the inhabited world, both Christian and Islamic usages of the term draw from. He goes on to outline an "ecumenical frame" with which to reevaluate "a new kind of intimacy and meaningful solidarity that cut across Muslim, Christian, and Jewish religious lines" within the Middle East, refuting accounts of both continuous sectarian strife and overidealized coexistence as communal harmony.[3]

Such an ecumenical framing is crucial to understanding what allowed these young men and women to come together, as depicted in the photograph on this book's cover: Walid Khalidi, Sally Kassab, Wolfgang Hildesheimer, Rasha Salam, and Jabra Ibrahim Jabra. The "small 'ecumenical' circle" (as I shall henceforth designate them) recalled by Khalidi in his article on Hourani is grounded in what Makdisi refers to as an age of coexistence. Yet the friends came together not in the "golden" years of that coexistence but toward its end, when coexistence was under threat by war and combating national aspirations and political ideologies, in the specific historical context of Palestine under the British Mandate and Jerusalem in the early 1940s in particular. Their friendship was also subject to what Kris Manjapra refers to as an age of entanglement,[4] one of transnational circulation and encounter that was contingent on British colonial rule. Seen in this context, the ecumenical circle intersected closely with notions of race, class, and educational opportunity that set this group of friends apart from other segments of society in Mandate Palestine as an intellectual elite, enmeshed in a cosmopolitanism of affluence, as I illustrate in chapter 1.

As an instance of literary circulation, Eliot's "The Waste Land" resonated with the ecumenical circle in Jerusalem as it did with lovers of modernist poetry across Europe and well beyond. As Eliot's poem aptly puts it, the world they had known—and with it their means of epistemic representation—was being transformed into "a heap of broken images." As Jabra suggests, "Arab poets responded so passionately to 'The Wasteland' [sic] because they, too, went through an experience of universal tragedy, not only in World War II, but also, and more essentially, in the Palestine debacle and its aftermath."[5]

The celebration of the Khalidi's first wedding anniversary was the last time the ecumenical circle came together. The next day—July 22, 1946—life in Jerusalem would be shaken to its core by a momentous terrorist attack. The King David Hotel bombing was part of a series of Zionist attacks against the British Mandate authorities, which started in 1944 and saw the assassination in Cairo of Lord Moyne, the British Minister Resident in the Middle East, the killing of British policemen and soldiers, and attacks on major railroad and highway bridges across Palestine. The first such attacks were carried out by the Lohamei Herut Yisrael (Freedom Fighters of Israel), known as Lehi or Stern Gang, and the Irgun Zva'i Leumi (National Military Organization), known as Irgun. The Haganah—the paramilitary organization of the Yishuv, as the Jewish population in Mandate Palestine had come to be called—joined forces with its militant offshoots as the United Resistance Movement, within which each group retained its independent existence, only after the end of World War II.[6]

The King David Hotel bombing killed more than ninety people in a human-made avalanche of rubble. Thurston Clarke provides a minutely detailed description of how the Irgun prepared the bombing, while life in the hotel went on as usual until 12:37 p.m., when more than 750 pounds of TNT brought down the entire south wing of the building, in whose upper floors the offices of the British government's army headquarters and chief secretariat were housed. The explosives were concealed in milk churns, which the Irgun terrorists, disguised as Arab workers—one of them wearing the uniform of a Sudanese waiter—had moved into the kitchen of La Régence and placed next to the pillars that supported the floors above. Another bomb was planted in the street outside the hotel; it was to be detonated first to block the road and create a diversion that would allow sufficient time to light the fuses on the explosives inside the hotel. Once the explosives were all in place, the terrorists placed a number of telephone calls to evacuate the hotel. The adequacy of these warnings has caused controversy; as Clarke suggests, the calls were either ignored or considered to be a false alarm, or else they came too late.[7] Those injured in the first explosion outside the hotel—among them passengers on a bus coming up Julian's Way, mostly Arab women en route from the Old City to the western neighborhoods—were helped into the hotel, thereby increasing the number of casualties from the attack inside the hotel. Clarke lists, according to government announcement, the final toll: "91 dead and 46 injured. Of these 91 dead there were 21 first-rank government officials, 13 soldiers, 3 policemen, and 5 members of the public. The remaining 49 were second-rank clerks, typists, and messengers, junior members of the Secretariat, employees of the hotel, and canteen workers. By nationality there were two Armenians killed, one Russian, a Greek, an Egyptian, twenty-eight Britons, forty-one Arabs, and seventeen Jews."[8]

Clarke provides us with an idea of the wide range of the victims, but his list of the dead by rank of "importance" is unseemly, and his breakdown of the dead by nationality misleading, given that "Arabs" and "Jews" did not figure as nationalities in Palestine (yet). Jews and Arabs very well may have been among the "twenty-eight Britons," and the "seventeen Jews" may have been of different nationalities, some of them perhaps citizens of Palestine, like most but not necessarily all of the "forty-one Arabs." Representations of Arabs and Jews as disparate and opposed communities are not carved in stone; rather, they are recent developments, generated first and foremost by European colonialism and in particular by British imperial policy in the Middle East following the collapse of the Ottoman Empire at the end of World War I, before which Arabs and Jews were just as likely to be aligned with each other as they were with other common if complex identities, such as Ottoman, Syrian, Iraqi, or Palestinian, with all of these categories in a dynamic process of transformation.[9]

The bombing left its mark on Jerusalem well beyond the numbers of dead and wounded. While "a plume of billowing smoke rose skyward, marking high above the city the site of Palestine's most legendary explosion," as Thomas Abowd writes, "the bombing would be etched in the memory of thousands of Jerusalemites."[10] The rescue effort went on for two days, and the work of clearing the site continued much longer, as more bodies were pulled from beneath the rubble.

> Postmaster-General Gerald Kennedy had been walking down the Secretariat path to the turnstile. The blast tossed him into the air, blew him a hundred and fifty yards across the street and smacked him against the wall of the YMCA. His body slid to the pavement, leaving behind a bloody silhouette.... In the building itself, six floors of reinforced concrete slapped against one another and pancaked to the ground with a crash.... In that split second after 12:37, thirteen of those who had been alive at 12:36 disappeared without

a trace. The clothes, bracelets, cufflinks and wallets which might have identified them exploded into dust and smoke. Others were burned to charcoal, melted into chairs and desks or exploded into countless fragments.[11]

"TIME PRESSES"

The consequences of the bombing in the fracturing of both the political landscape and the historiography of Palestine are evident in contemporary newspaper coverage. Tracking the different representations of the event across different publications illustrates how a hardening of differences would foreclose ecumenical possibilities. The bombing sent shock waves across Palestine and indeed around the world, as international headlines document (figure P.1). High Commissioner Alan Cunningham was in London at the time and returned to Jerusalem by air the following day. Acting High Commissioner Sir John Shaw was in his office on the third floor in the southeastern corner of the King David but managed to escape with minor injuries. He assumed charge of the rescue work and the search for the terrorists, placing the entire municipality of Jerusalem under curfew. The British authorities strongly condemned the attack.

In a statement to the House of Commons, Prime Minister Clement Attlee called it an "insane act of terrorism" and expressed "horror [at] the brutal and murderous crime," asserting that the British government would "not be diverted by acts of violence in their search for a just and final solution of the Palestine Problem."[12] U.S. President Truman, however, voiced concern that the bombing might slow the peace efforts.[13] Time now emerged as a key factor in deciding the future of Palestine, as was expressed in an article titled "Time Presses" in London's *Daily Telegraph* on July 24, 1946: "For Time is now of the essence of the question whether the wreckage of the King David Hotel does or does not symbolize the wreckage of all hopes for a better future of the Holy Land."[14] In an article titled "Lesser Evils," published on the day of the bombing, the same newspaper had said that the "vision of an unitary Palestinian State is proving impossible of fulfilment," while "partition on the lines recommended by the Peel Commission, though not necessarily with the same boundaries, might offer a practicable solution with some historical justification."[15] In defense of British policy in Palestine and of Operation Agatha, a wide-ranging search for arms and documents that saw numerous arrests of Zionist leaders and the headquarters of the Jewish

P.1 *Illustrated London News*, August 3, 1946.

Agency in Jerusalem raided, the *Times* also reported on the Anglo-American talks in its coverage of the bombing. It explained that British policy was not in opposition to the Yishuv or the hope for a national home in Palestine for the Jewish people, but it mentioned no word of Palestine's indigenous Arab population, subsuming it instead—in line with Zionist terminology—under the term "non-Jews": "The moment selected for this latest outrage is peculiarly unfortunate, since the Anglo-American committee now sitting in London is engaged in formulating proposals for an agreed policy aiming at peace and justice in Palestine. The position of the Jewish community in that country is in no way menaced; the recent action of the mandatory Power was not directed against the National Home, but against those extremist elements in the population who were endeavouring to impose their own policy by violence upon Jews and non-Jews alike."[16]

The Jewish Agency and the Va'ad Leumi—the Jewish National Council—condemned the bombing in a joint statement, expressing "their horror at the dastardly crime perpetrated by the gang of desperadoes."[17] Chaim Weizmann—who in 1920 had assumed the leadership of the Zionist Organization and went on to serve as Israel's first president—delivered an address to the British Zionist Federation at the Palace Theater in London, saying "nothing can excuse so abominable and brutal an act," while at the same time pointing out that lamentable actions had also been taken against the Yishuv by the British authorities, notably the raid on the Jewish Agency.[18] Similar positions were voiced in the *Palestine Post*.[19] In contrast, the liberal Hebrew-language newspaper *Haaretz* called for the resignation of the executive of both the Jewish Agency and the Va'ad Leumi, stating it could not "face the future under leadership responsible for such failures."[20] After much controversy, it emerged that the Haganah had given its approval of the bombing "in general, if not specific, terms as an action of the United Resistance Movement."[21]

The Irgun assumed responsibility for the attack in a communiqué the day after the bombing, in which it also blamed the British authorities for not evacuating the hotel: "The tragedy was not caused by Jewish soldiers, who carried out their duty courageously and with self-sacrifice. It was caused by the British themselves, who disregarded a warning and refused to evacuate the building."[22] According to the Irgun, its "soldiers," and not terrorists, had "attacked centers of the British occupation Government as a battle with the British Army and police forces."[23] In this communiqué, as elsewhere, the Palestinian Arab population goes unmentioned. The *Illustrated London News* offered a reward of two thousand pounds sterling for the capture of Menachem Begin, who had emerged as the Irgun's leader after the death of Ze'ev Jabotinsky. A founding member of the Haganah, Jabotinsky had launched the Revisionist movement in 1925 from which a number of right-wing paramilitary movements emerged, among them the Lehi and the Irgun.[24]

Although the international press reported on the various Jewish responses to the bombing, notably in an article in the *New York Times* by Anne O'Hare McCormick, the first woman to win a Pulitzer Prize for journalism,[25] reports about Arab responses were scarce. "If the underground forces in Palestine are out of control, this is all the more reason for attacking the fundamental issue before the whole situation gets out of hand," writes McCormick, adding that "it is no longer either an isolated or merely triangular conflict. The United States is involved, Russia is interested, the whole area is in dangerous ferment."[26] With the Cold War on the horizon,[27] the future of Palestine morphed into an international issue. It was increasingly linked to the fate of Jewish Holocaust survivors in European refugee camps. In defense of a Jewish national home, concerned not with the lives lost in the bombing but rather with a potential decrease in political and moral support for Zionism, McCormick refers to the Irgun as "the greatest enemy of Zion." She concludes, "it is the worst way to win backing for a Zionist state which might be controlled by such elements, and the best way to help the case of the Arabs, who have played an astutely quiet role in all this turmoil."[28] The *Times* mentioned an "Arab Manifesto" issued by the Arab Higher Committee (AHC)—the central political organ of the Palestinian Arabs—condemning the bombing. It also reported that Jamal Husseini, in his capacity as the AHC's acting chair, had warned the British government "that unless immediate action is taken to terminate terrorism, we shall call upon Arabs to undertake themselves the protection of their lives and interests, holding your Government responsible for all consequences."[29]

The Arab press strongly condemned the bombing, seeing it not as an isolated crime committed by extremists or a "gang of desperadoes," as the Jewish Agency and the Va'ad Leumi had phrased it in their joint statement, but rather as part and parcel of a firmly entrenched Jewish terrorist movement that British policy had failed to suppress (figure P.2). Palestine's largest and most influential Arabic-language newspaper, *Filastin* [Palestine] opens its lead article from its special correspondent in Jerusalem on July 22 thus: "Today, the Jewish terrorists committed a crime that exceeds in atrocity, the large number of victims, and, through its long-term impact, all the crimes they have committed in the country before . . . the government of Palestine has not yet been able to eradicate this terrorist movement and crush the evil heads behind it. And perhaps the origin

P.2 *Filastin*, July 23, 1946.

of this negligence is the London government's inability to put a definitive end to Jewish terrorism."[30]

Filastin was founded in the port city of Jaffa—known at the time as "the gateway to Palestine" and "a thriving center of Arab modernity"[31]—in 1911 by the renowned journalist 'Isa al-'Isa and his cousin Yusuf al-'Isa.[32] *al-Difa'*, which was founded in Jaffa in 1934 by Ibrahim al-Shanti from Jaffa, Sami al-Siraj from Homs, and Khayr al-Din al-Zirikli from Damascus, also covered the bombing.[33] Close to the Palestinian Independence Party, which drew inspiration from the Indian Congress Party in its attempt to present an alternative to the rivalry, instigated by the British, among Palestine's notable families who dominated the Palestinian national movement throughout the Mandate years,[34] *al-Difa'* emerged as a leading daily newspaper that attracted many young educated Palestinians with its pan-Arab views. *Filastin* and *al-Difa'* also reported on what was written in British newspapers about the Anglo-American talks in London and the partition of Palestine as a possible outcome, with *al-Difa'* pointing out that British newspapers neither knew nor cared much about the Palestinian cause.[35]

After the bombing, Jerusalem became "a city of gloom as the funeral processions of some of the dead wound their way to the Protestant, Catholic, Jewish, and Moslem cemeteries."[36] In her memoirs, Hala Sakakini recalls the many daily funerals, "at least five or six, as the seriously wounded died and more corpses were discovered under the debris." She had witnessed the bombing from the veranda of her family's house in the Western neighborhood of Qatamon, when she saw "a huge cloud of dust rising just beyond the German Colony," and waited anxiously for her father, the renowned educator Khalil al-Sakakini, to return home for lunch. At the time of the bombing, he "was sitting with some friends on the terrace of the Piccadilly, his favorite coffeehouse, about three hundred metres from the King David Hotel."[37] She recalls the deep shock everyone felt, explaining that "these 'modern' methods of terror used by the Jews were still new to us," while the British authorities began to divide Jerusalem into security zones; "there were three or four zones, each surrounded by barbed wire. In order to move about in Jerusalem, one had to have an identity card, which stated in which zone one was residing, and permits to the other zones."[38]

The bombing literally blew apart the very ground that brought together the ecumenical circle, and more precisely the individuals at the heart of this book, from under their feet. It figures as the event—anticipating more violent events to come—that rendered their continued friendship impossible and as a metaphor of its dissolution as they were dispersed around the globe.

INTRODUCTION

Reading an Impossible Friendship Through a Group Portrait

METHODOLOGICAL CONSIDERATIONS

An Impossible Friendship brings to life an extraordinary group of young men and women, some of whom went on to become internationally acclaimed writers, artists, and intellectuals. Who were these young men and women who took their cultural communion at the King David Hotel bar and read Eliot's poetry aloud late into a Jerusalem summer's night? What brought them together? What were their social backgrounds and class alliances? What were their political and cultural affiliations? What sense did they have of belonging to Jerusalem? What role did religion play in their lives? What were their everyday lives like and how did they imagine their futures would unfold? And what were their hopes and expectations for the future of Palestine?

To reconstruct all of this in full is, of course, impossible. We can, however, recover bits and pieces of the individual lives that intersected in this ecumenical circle. No matter how fragmentary the picture remains, its pieces provide us with insight into the complexities of their lives and the dreams they harbored, both as individuals and as members of imagined communities in the throes of formation and transformation.[1] By including imaginary futures in this book, or *futures past*, as suggests the title of Reinhart Koselleck's book on the semantics of historical time—that is, what was experienced and expected to take place in the sense that it was considered possible and was once an anticipated future[2]—I set out not only to excavate and reimagine past everyday lives and dreams but also to envision alternatives to the impasse of identity politics both past and present. There is an urgency to this task as the individual lives depicted in this group portrait are being lost, even from memory—literally disappearing from visibility against the background of current developments in the Middle East, where diversity is dealt with as a threat and ideologies of one religion, one people, and one language dominate the politics of the day. Today, the separation wall that runs through the very fabric of the land, sealing the Palestinian territories off from the world, has profoundly transformed people's everyday life experiences and expectations for the future, restricting the very movement of Palestinians. Some people have argued that the politics of visibility in the Occupied Territories has reached its threshold, as documentaries, testimonials, and other audiovisual material that aim to make visible the plight of Palestinians have increased significantly with the growth of local and international media agencies on the ground since the Second Intifada,[3] but much remains at stake. The Israeli raids on Palestinian civil society organizations in the West Bank on August 18, 2022, which resulted in their closure and the confiscation of their archives, and the killing of iconic Palestinian-American journalist Shireen Abu Akleh, who was hit by a bullet to the head fired by an Israeli soldier while she was wearing a clearly marked bulletproof press vest and reporting on the Israeli raids in Jenin on May 11, 2022, are but two recent cases in point.

Grounded in archival research, *An Impossible Friendship* draws on literary studies and the social sciences, and more specifically on microhistory and biography, to bring the ecumenical circle to life, while also addressing some of the political and ethical questions this raises. As has been argued since the linguistic, or the cultural, turn, history is not free of fiction by its very claim to representation. Microhistory, however, uses stories and people as devices, as Jill Lepore writes,[4] whereas biography as a literary genre is more prone to storytelling. Biography may be as old as the study of history, yet it explicitly— and increasingly self-consciously—draws on the imagination to bring its subjects to life. Over the past few decades, life writing not only has gained in popularity but also has emerged as a subfield of cultural and social history.[5] Much debate has centered on how biography is to bridge world and word— that is, historical reality and its representation in the fiction of history. Out of this debate has developed "the view of biography as a kind of 'third way' between fact and fiction,"[6] or of biography as "grounded in historical data that we can trust."[7] This grounding in historical data, however, is a complex undertaking, especially when it comes to the modern history of Palestine. In particular, I draw on literary biography, with its attention to the intellectual output of the individuals it studies. As Edward W. Said reminds us in "The Return to Philology," "literature provides the most heightened example we have of words in action and therefore is the most complex and rewarding—for all sorts of reasons—of verbal practices."[8] The consideration of works of fiction in this book is inspired by the fact that a number of its subjects were aspiring writers and artists in Jerusalem before 1948, and two of them—Wolfgang Hildesheimer and Jabra Ibrahim Jabra—gained international recognition in the field of literature after 1948 with a range of publications, among them novels, plays, poetry, essays, and autobiographical and biographical narratives. I want to give readers insight into the writing produced by the individuals at the heart of the ecumenical circle: reading this book, you will also be meeting texts written by Hildesheimer, Jabra, Walid Khalidi, and Rasha Salam Khalidi.

With the publication of an increasing number of autobiographies and memoirs, real-life narratives of Jerusalem before 1948 have increased in prominence.[9] At the same time, the role of "social biographies in making sense of history" has gained ground,[10] and intercommunal practices of sociability in Palestine have come into sharper focus.[11] A contemporary of the ecumenical circle, Virginia Woolf writes in her fictional biography of Orlando: "she had a great variety of selves to call upon, far more than we have been able to find room for, since a biography is considered complete if it merely accounts for six or seven selves, whereas a person may well have as many thousand."[12] The effort to bring the ecumenical circle to life in the pages of a book has its limits. Woolf describes biography as "something betwixt and between," blurring as it does the boundaries between craftsmanship and artwork,[13] what we may compare to a convergence of academic and creative writing. In the end, I also want to tell a good story, one that is here told for the first time: the story of an impossible friendship in Jerusalem, which I have derived from "historical data that we can trust."[14] Storytelling matters. It connects us as human beings across time and space, and it puts names and faces to a history that all too often has been reduced to numbers that tell us very little. Good stories move us. Here, I use the verb "to move" in its double sense: first, as shifting our perspectives away from the great events that make history, usually written by the winners, to include a multitude of perspectives, specifically from the standpoint of its victims; and, second, as stirring our emotions and setting free feelings of empathy and practices of solidarity in a world we share.

By pursuing an interdisciplinary approach, I contribute to a more complex, inclusive, transnational, entangled, and, at the same time, personalized picture of what we know from international headlines and history books as the Israeli-Palestinian conflict. Words matter. The terminology used to speak and write about Palestine and Israel has its own histories full of facts and fictions. "The Israeli-Palestinian conflict" seems to suggest two equal sides, whereas, in fact, nothing is equal about it.

Not attempting to recover the ecumenical circle in its entirety but rather exploring gaps and silences in the archive, I set out to decenter historical accounts and biographical narratives alike and touch on the boundaries between historiography and fictionality, objectivity and subjectivity. I draw in particular on what Saidiya Hartman calls "critical fabulation"—"it is a history of an unrecoverable past; it is a narrative of what might have been or could have been; it is a history written with and against the archive."[15] Hartman's approach to reading the Atlantic slave trade is useful in reading the Israeli-Palestinian conflict, as both have been mostly reduced to single storylines that offer few glimpses into the entangled stories of people dispossessed and of lives broken and taken. In recuperating and redrawing storylines running counter to the one storyline across the pages of history, I want to conjure different perspectives, draw more complex pictures, and devise new possible pathways for the future. In writing a counterhistory to the conventional histories written about the Israeli-Palestinian conflict, I embrace biographical writing—and, with it, fiction—to think about past, present, and future in genuinely new ways that take into consideration the (hi)stories of those who have not made it onto the pages of history—"the subaltern, the dispossessed, and the enslaved"[16]—while also respecting the gaps and silences in the archive, which urge us not to rush to a closure where none exists.

As Palestinian filmmaker Larissa Sansour, known for her interdisciplinary artwork that incorporates elements of science fiction, says, "I feel that work that attempts to be rationally grounded with facts and documentation fails to deliver an adequate and genuine picture of the surreal, absurd atrocities on the ground."[17] In fictionalizing reality, she posits "fiction as a stepping stone for a future reality on the ground, rather than the other way around."[18] It is in a similar resort to fiction that the title of my book alludes to the Palestinian poet Mahmoud Darwish and his love for a Jewish woman known as Rita, who appears in Darwish's poetry on several occasions, notably in "Rita wal-bunduqiyya" ("Rita and the Rifle"), which was set to music and rendered popular across the Arab world in the late 1960s.[19] Darwish returns to Rita many years later in "Shita' Rita" ("Rita's Winter").[20] As Tamar Ben-Ami, the real-life Rita, says, "There's something about *that impossible love* that is . . . beyond wars and perhaps because of them at times" (my emphasis).[21] *An Impossible Friendship* argues that what brought the ecumenical circle together in Jerusalem was more than mere historical coincidence; it was *beyond* wars but, paradoxically, also *because* of them. An impossible friendship is a certain kind of friendship, not a friendship that is impossible, and as such, it has a historical presence built on dreams and aspirations, futures past, that hold manifold possibilities for the future.

In part I, I reconstruct in fragments a world forever lost, reimagining what brought the ecumenical circle together in Jerusalem before 1948. Foregrounding the power and beauty of friendship in the midst of political turmoil and war, I do not brush aside the messy contradictions that all biographies entail but instead open new and compelling perspectives on the complexities of real-life stories and everyday intimacies. Through them, I aim to contribute to writing the social and cultural history of Jerusalem—aware of the shortcomings entailed in directing the spotlight on an intellectual elite. In part II, I trace the ecumenical circle's afterlives—to borrow a term coined by another contemporary of the group of friends, the German-Jewish writer Walter Benjamin[22]—in this case, the afterlife of friendship, as the individuals at the center of this book carried their camaraderie across and beyond borders, and as they reconnected in different geographical and temporal settings and under new historical circumstances, giving renewed life to their friendship primarily through correspondence.

In using a group portrait as the starting point of my book, I partake in microhistorical writing. As Lepore tells us, historians need to strike a balance between intimacy and distance: historians who get too close to their subjects—who "love too much"—run the danger of not being taken seriously as historians and trespassing into biography. As a literary scholar and a cultural historian, I am not afraid of trespassing into biographical writing, and embrace the danger of loving too much, getting too close to my book's subjects. I thus refer to this group of friends by their given names, as we turn to the individual lives at the heart of the ecumenical circle in the pages that follow and the story of that impossible friendship they cast in Jerusalem.

THE INDIVIDUAL LIVES AT THE HEART OF THE ECUMENICAL CIRCLE

The true protagonist of this book is the ecumenical circle, and more precisely Walid, Sally, Wolfgang, Rasha, and Jabra. In examining the individual lives at the heart of this circle, *An Impossible Friendship* focuses on people whose dreams and aspirations were in the cultural field—in modern art, literature, and intellectual thought. At first glance, the differences in their religious and social backgrounds seem so great that it is perhaps surprising they ever ended up sitting together; however, when we look at them as a group, they display a remarkable resemblance to one another in social habits, literary and artistic preferences, and political (world)views.

Furthermore, situating its members within wider networks of interpersonal relations, ranging from professional ties to family connections, to intimate friendship and romance, also sheds light on each individual's life. The coming together of young talent and like-minded artists, writers, and intellectuals in a particular place and time is intriguing and has gained some attention, notably with the Bloomsbury Group, the Bauhaus, and the circle of Gertrude Stein in early twentieth-century Europe. But more often than not it has gone unnoticed, especially when the place of encounter was not in the Western hemisphere, and when its individual members ended up in social groups and cultural worlds apart, as was the case with our ecumenical circle.

Wolfgang Hildesheimer (1916–1991), seated in the center of the group portrait, his legs crossed, hands placed one on top of the other on his knees, was the only Jewish member of the ecumenical circle.[23] He was born in Hamburg into a middle-class German family who left Germany for Palestine in 1933, when the Nazis came to power. He trained in stage and graphic design but was to gain recognition in postwar German literature as a playwright, novelist, biographer of Mozart, and member of the influential literary circle Gruppe 47. Wolfgang is flanked by Sally and Walid to his right and by Rasha and Jabra to his left.

Sally Kassab (also known as Selwa Pruen; 1920–1998), was born to Greek Orthodox parents in Beirut, but grew up with her mother's family, the Hananias, in Jerusalem and in England. Tall and good-looking and with a friendly demeanor (as those who can still remember the group of friends did not fail to point out to me),[24] she had a presence that caught the eye but somehow left few tangible traces of her life in Jerusalem. Although Sally and Wolfgang were known in the ecumenical circle as a couple, she would later marry a British diplomat and Wolfgang would wed a German painter.

Seated next to Sally, at the far left of the group portrait, is Walid Khalidi (1925–), his hands folded in his lap, a pipe in his mouth. He hails from an old and distinguished Jerusalemite Muslim family. His father, Ahmad Samih al-Khalidi, was the principal of the Government Arab College, on whose premises the group portrait was taken, and which until 1948 was the highest Arab educational institution in Palestine. Walid has become a world-renowned historian of modern Palestine and a public intellectual, and at the time of this writing, is the only one in the picture who is still alive.

Walid married Rasha Salam (1922–2004), seated between Wolfgang and Jabra, her unruly hair cut short, who was from one of the main political families of Lebanon who championed Arab nationalism and women's emancipation. Her elder sister Anbara's memoirs are referred to in foundational works on the modern Middle East, including in Albert Hourani's *A History of the Arab Peoples*, and ascribe to her a prominent role in the emancipation of Arab women, which is made explicit in the title of their English translation, *Memoirs of an Early Arab Feminist: The Life and Activism of Anbara Salam Khalidi*.[25] Unlike Anbara, Rasha did not step into the public spotlight and her memoirs, which Walid kindly gave to me, remain unpublished.

Seated at the right end of the group portrait is Jabra Ibrahim Jabra (1919–1994), wearing, like the other men in the portrait, a suit and tie, a pipe in his left hand. He was born into a Syriac Christian family in the region of Adana, from where his family fled to Palestine during the Franco-Turkish War of 1922, when he was barely three years old. He grew up in poverty in Bethlehem but enjoyed significant social mobility through education as a Palestinian student, having obtained scholarships that enabled him to study at the Government Arab College in Jerusalem and then at the University of Exeter and the University of Cambridge. After 1948, he played a major role in Baghdad's cultural life and the formation of Arab modernism as a literary writer, art critic, and translator of Shakespeare, Beckett, and Faulkner, among others.

Wolfgang and Jabra have been studied within the confines of national literary traditions—German and Arabic (both Palestinian and Iraqi), respectively[26]—but not in terms of their connection to one another and to transnational circuits of modern art, literature, and intellectual thought. Walid has not been studied in relation to either of these other writers; his name is not usually associated with modern art or literature, although he was well versed in English Romantic poetry and published some of his own verses as a young man. Although he is an influential public figure whose books constitute key references in Palestinian historiography, his life and work have rarely been the subject of study.[27] Documenting, on the one hand, Palestinian Arab national aspirations and, on the other, foreign—particularly British and American—support for political Zionism, Walid has for decades challenged Zionist narratives of Palestine as "a country without a people for a people without a country."[28] This he has detailed in numerous articles and in the groundbreaking volumes he has edited: *From Haven to Conquest: Readings in Zionism and the Palestine Problem until 1948* (1971), *Before Their Diaspora: A Photographic History of the Palestinians, 1876–1948* (1984), and *All That Remains: The Palestinian Villages Occupied and Depopulated by Israel in 1948* (1992). His work resonates strongly with Israel's revisionist historians, also referred to as new historians, among them Benny Morris, Ilan Pappé, and Avi Shlaim, who have come to the fore since the late 1980s, when they gained access to declassified documents in Israeli state archives. With these archives, they, too, began to challenge the myths that until then had shrouded the establishment of the State of Israel and the First Arab-Israeli War.[29]

With no publications to their names, Rasha and Sally, like so many other women the world over, have sadly and silently slipped through the cracks of history. This book cannot fully bring them back to life, but it does sketch experiences and expectations past, which may enable us to imagine, albeit in fragments, their lives in Jerusalem. While archival research has allowed me to glimpse into Rasha's life and devote a chapter to her name, Sally comes into the picture only here and there because I was not able to uncover enough "historical data that we can trust" to enable me to sketch a more detailed picture of her life in Jerusalem. The absence of a chapter devoted to Sally underlines the silence we often encounter in archives as well as the gendered nature of this silence.

THE SPATIAL AND TEMPORAL SETTING

A battle emerges between "seemingly incompatible memories" when it comes to Palestine before 1948, writes Aleida Assmann, and "a more complex and inclusive transnational memory of the entangled history of 1948" is still very much in the making.[30] The establishment of the State of Israel in 1948 and the First Arab-Israeli War of 1948–1949 are referred to in Arabic as the Nakba (which translates as "catastrophe" or "disaster"), as they went hand in hand with the expulsion and dispossession of an estimated 750,000 Palestinians from their homeland. "After the post–World War I partition of the Middle East," writes Eugene Rogan, "the Palestine disaster stands as the most important turning point in twentieth century Arab history. We are still living its consequences today."[31] The term *nakba* was coined by Constantine Zurayk in 1948,[32] but, in recent years, it has undergone a shift—against the backdrop of the failed Oslo Accords and the Second Intifada—from denoting a past event to describing an ongoing process. As Shir Alon explains, the ongoing Nakba is "a historiographic narrative through which to comprehend decades of Zionist settler colonialism and Palestinian dispossession."[33] This reconsidered understanding of the Nakba not only offers a new perspective onto the past but also is "not history to be remembered but a present threatened by interpretation," according to the Lebanese novelist Elias Khoury.[34] As Khoury relates, he had to rethink the Nakba when he collected memories of it in Palestinian refugee camps in Lebanon for his novel *Bab al-shams* (1998), translated into English by Humphrey Davies as *Gate of the Sun* (2005).[35] "The Nakba is not a past event that 'happened' seventy years ago but is a continuing, painful journey that began in 1948 but endures to this day," writes Khoury in his foreword to *The Holocaust and the Nakba: A New Grammar of Trauma and History* (2019).[36] In placing the Holocaust and the Nakba in conversation, with all the difficulties that this entails, the volume's editors, Bashir Bashir and Amos Goldberg, envision "an alternative language of history, in which the syntax and grammar of memory and suffering would not be based on exclusive, hostile, and violent identities but, on the contrary, would help to create more historically complex and politically or even ethically constructive national narratives. . . . a language of historical reconciliation between the two peoples."[37] Although such historical reconciliation can draw on an age of coexistence past, it is oriented not toward the past but the future. As such, it holds political implications, calling for justice and equality, as it comes to terms with historical inequalities and injustices and imagines alternative pasts, presents, and futures. As Bashir outlines, historical reconciliation is essential to moving forward and devising new concepts, such as egalitarian binationalism, which he and others promote in lieu of a two-state solution, recognizing the existence of two national groups with equal rights to self-determination.[38] His view echoes Edward W. Said's standpoint:

"In the tradition of thinkers such as Hannah Arendt, Judah Magnes and Martin Buber, who argued between the wars for the creation of a two-nation state, Said took up the cause of the one-state solution in the 1990s."[39] He concludes his famous essay entitled "The One-State Solution" writing, "The alternatives are unpleasantly simple: either the war continues (along with the onerous cost of the current peace process) or a way out, based on peace and equality (as in South Africa after apartheid) is actively sought, despite the many obstacles. Once we grant that Palestinians and Israelis are there to stay, then the decent conclusion has to be the need for peaceful coexistence and genuine reconciliation. Real self-determination. Unfortunately, injustice and belligerence don't diminish by themselves: they have to be attacked by all concerned."[40]

In view of the settler-colonial context in which the ongoing Nakba is unfolding, Nadim N. Rouhana proposes, that such "reconciliation, although difficult to achieve in the near future, should be pursued as decolonization within a framework of transitional justice."[41]

The Holocaust has long been perceived as being separate from processes of decolonization. Michael Rothberg suggests a shift in perspective: considering memory to be multidirectional, he reads Holocaust memory as having "always been intertwined with ongoing processes of decolonization."[42] Although he focuses on the Algerian War of Independence, in his epilogue, he refers also to the struggles of Indigenous peoples around the world and the Israeli-Palestinian conflict as cases in which "conflicts of memory converge with contests over territory."[43] Despite the ferocity with which such conflicts are being fought, on the battlefield as well as through the media, he holds that "the uncomfortable proximity of memories is also the cauldron out of which new visions of solidarity and justice must emerge."[44]

In reading an impossible friendship through the lens of a group portrait and telling the story of the ecumenical circle, this book contributes to such "a language of historical reconciliation" and "new visions of solidarity and justice"—and, with them, to a shared, multifaceted social and cultural history of Jerusalem.[45] It thus asserts, as outlined by Rashid Khalidi, "the possibility of a multidimensional narrative that would reproduce all of Jerusalem's ambiguity and the overlapping traditions it represents, instead of reducing the complexity of the city's history to a single dimension."[46]

The life trajectories of the individuals at the heart of the ecumenical circle intersected in Jerusalem during a time that was witnessing a rapid surge of anti-Semitism in Europe, decisive transformation across the Middle East, and dramatic change in Palestine. It "was a time of deep crisis, which exposed long-festering realities," says Sherene Seikaly, but by no means a time of political or social stagnation; in fact, Palestine was enmeshed in the social, economic, and political changes in the wider Arab world that had accelerated significantly since the Nahda, the Arab awakening of the nineteenth and early twentieth centuries.[47] In Hourani's *Arabic Thought in the Liberal Age, 1798–1939* (originally published in 1962), the Nahda is described as "the liberal age," but in his preface to the 1983 reissue of the book, the author expresses dissatisfaction with this term because of its emphasis on individual rather than national rights.[48] These latter rights figure more prominently in George Antonius's *The Arab Awakening: The Story of the Arab National Movement* (1938).[49] As Tarif Khalidi informs us, Antonius was one of a number of lawyer-historians who turned to modern history to make the case for the historical legitimacy of the Arabs of Palestine, aware that British support for Zionism was literally writing them out of history by subsuming them under the category of "the non-Jewish communities in Palestine," who were to be granted civil and religious but not national rights.[50]

Aspirations for Arab national independence found encouragement in U.S. President Woodrow Wilson's principle of self-determination, which he outlined in his Fourteen Points in preparation for the 1919 Paris Peace Conference.[51] But these aspirations were disappointed when the Arab provinces of the Ottoman Empire were separated into mandates granted to France and Britain by the newly formed League of Nations. Based on the Sykes–Picot Agreement of 1916, which had secretly divided the Ottoman provinces into British and French spheres of influence and control, and the Balfour Declaration of 1917, which promised British support for the establishment of a national home in Palestine for the Jewish people, the British Mandate for Palestine closely aligned British imperial interests in the Middle East with the Zionist movement, thereby setting Palestine apart among the League of Nations mandates.[52] As political tensions in Palestine rose among its Palestinian Arab population, the British Mandate authorities, and the Yishuv, new geopolitical realities enforced—and at times imposed—new national identities, thereby widening the divide between Arabs and Jews. Tensions culminated in the 1936–1939 Great Revolt, the popular Arab uprising against British colonial rule and increased Jewish immigration to Palestine. It started with a general strike but became violent when the Peel Commission recommended the partition of Palestine into Arab and Jewish states in 1937, having reached the conclusion that "an irrepressible conflict has arisen between two national communities within the narrow bounds of one small country" and that "their national aspirations are incompatible."[53] Britain's brutal repression of the uprising is well documented. While Britain supported, trained, and armed the Haganah, Palestinian Arabs were disarmed and persecuted, several thousand were killed, and many more wounded, while their leadership was sent into exile. As a result, Palestinian Arabs emerged from the revolt politically and economically weakened.[54]

In response to the Great Revolt, the UK government issued the White Paper of 1939, which signaled a shift in British policy as it recognized the need to align Jewish immigration to Palestine with Palestinian Arab national interests. Hence, it sought to restrict the number of Jewish immigrants to Palestine while also retaining the idea of a national home for the Jewish people. World War II temporarily overshadowed political tensions in Palestine, but they returned violently to the fore as the war drew to its end, and an ever-increasing number of nations and international organizations—notably the United States and the United Nations—intervened in the Middle East, and a series of Zionist terrorist attacks rocked the country. Half a year after the King David Hotel bombing, the British government transferred the question of Palestine to the United Nations—an "inexperienced UN, just two years old," as Ilan Pappé points out—which "entrusted the future of Palestine's fate into the hands of a Special Committee for Palestine, UNSCOP, none of whose members turned out to have any prior experience in solving conflicts or knew much about Palestine's history."[55] UNSCOP recommended partition, as the Peel Commission had done a decade earlier. On November 29, 1947, the UN General Assembly, dominated by the United States and Russia, passed Resolution 181, which stipulated that the British Mandate for Palestine would be terminated and that "independent Arab and Jewish States and the Special International Regime for the City of Jerusalem [would] come into existence in Palestine two months after the evacuation of the armed forced of the mandatory Power [had] been completed."[56] While Britain fixed the date for its withdrawal from Palestine as midnight on May 14, 1948, following a precedent it had recently set in India,[57] Resolution 181 drove Palestine further into war. As Rashid Khalidi writes in *The Hundred Years' War on Palestine*, "the resolution was another declaration of war, providing the international birth certificate for a Jewish state in most of what was still an Arab-majority land, a blatant violation of the principle of self-determination enshrined in the UN Charter."[58] The unilateral proclamation of the State of

Israel on May 14, 1948, the day before the termination of the British Mandate for Palestine came into effect, set the stage for the First Arab-Israeli War.

THE QUESTION OF ARCHIVES

Unraveling the complexities of real-life stories, practices of sociability, and everyday intimacies is not an easy task, particularly when it comes to Jerusalem before 1948. The very character of the city as the site of Christian, Jewish, and Muslim religious pilgrimage, the center of British mandatory rule, and a battlefield of conflicting national struggles, complicates the picture. In addition, "current debates on Jerusalem have been so mystified by the nature of ideological claims put forth by Israelis, Palestinians and the world community, that we forget that before the war there was an 'ordinary' city called Jerusalem," as Salim Tamari writes. "Fundamentally unrecognizable today," he explains, it was "a city of considerable social mobility, of ethnic diversity, and of communal conflict . . . tempered by a fair amount of mutual dependence and local solidarities. . . . an evolving and vibrant city whose life was cut short."[59]

Research into that city has been obstructed by the destruction, looting, and displacement of Palestinian archival material, some of it expropriated into the Israeli State Archives and the National Library of Israel.[60] As Angelos Dalachanis and Vincent Lemire remark, "Jerusalem is an extraordinary city that can be understood only with the greatest possible use of the most ordinary tools of social, political, and cultural historical research," yet "Jerusalem's local history can only be reconstructed by reference to archives often located in faraway places," including those of the former colonial powers and private collections of Palestinians in the diaspora.[61]

The question of archives, and in particular the material inaccessibility of postcolonial state archives as a result of the impact of authoritarian regimes or war and its lingering methodological implications, has been a focus of Middle East historiography,[62] but it comes with a further subset of questions in Palestinian historiography. As Lila Abu-Lughod explains, "what archives are or should be in this case of a dispersed people with no state archive, no less a state, a majority of whom live in exile or under occupation and have had their 'proper' archive destroyed, seized, or sealed in inaccessible colonial archives belonging to those who dispossessed them and still rule over them with force, are tough questions."[63]

These "tough questions" pose challenges but also offer political possibilities. Having been a key player in widening the consideration of archives to include not only their content but also their form "as cultural artefacts of fact production,"[64] Ann Laura Stoler draws on Jacques Rancière's formulation that "politics is dissensus" to imagine an archive "that fissures the fictions of power politics, one that taps the veins of unarticulated sensibilities, sensibilities that are the substance of how Palestinian dispositions have been shaped, where contemporary conditions have forestalled what were once more open, mixed, and not separatist alliances."[65] Archival research, then, is not necessarily oriented toward the past as detached from present and future concerns; rather, it engages in unearthing and imagining new political possibilities. Examining how contemporary artists and writers make use of the archive to imagine a future of Palestine, Gil Z. Hochberg argues that "to archive for the future we must abandon our attachment to history and the redemptive hopes of messianic delivery in favor of a more radical imagination that breaks away from the past towards new becomings: unknown, uncertain, but potentially more just."[66]

It is in search for new political possibilities and a potentially more just future that I set out to bridge microhistorical and biographical writing. While I am all for "radical imagination," I do think it matters that it be "grounded in historical data that we can trust"—we cannot abandon our attachment to history because history is not a fixed entity in some distant past.[67] There is too much at stake in today's world. To bring the individual lives at the heart of the ecumenical circle to life in the pages of this book, I make use of not only historical newspapers and magazines but also private papers, among them diaries, correspondences, and photographs, many hitherto unpublished, and other ephemera. As I have outlined, I also rely on my protagonists' writings, including works of fiction. In addition, I draw on memory, as it is documented in autobiographical narratives and in personal interviews I conducted, with Walid Khalidi and with other people who still have memories of the individuals at the heart of the ecumenical circle.

MY OWN STORY WITH THE ECUMENICAL CIRCLE

All biographical writing is partly autobiographical; we choose to write about certain lives because they matter to us. At times, we may define ourselves with or against them, feel bonds of friendship or love, and contemplate resemblances or things we have in common. It is no surprise, then, that I have my own story with the ecumenical circle that takes me back to earliest childhood.

I grew up hearing myriad stories about the Arab world and the Israeli-Palestinian conflict—in particular from my father, Helmut Mejcher, a historian of the Middle East who studied with Hourani at Oxford.[68] I grew up in Germany, however, where these stories found little resonance outside my immediate family. At school, history classes focused squarely on Europe, and in particular Germany. If the Middle East was mentioned at all, it was with respect to Israel, or as a hotbed of wars since 1948 from which Europe seemed miraculously to have distanced itself. Alexander Schölch, a close friend and colleague of my father who passed away too early, published an article shortly after the watershed 1982 chapter of the Lebanon War. He argues that Germany, trying to come to terms with its history, has accepted its obligations toward the State of Israel as a result of the Holocaust. However, it has been reluctant to deal with one of the immediate consequences in the Middle East of the establishment of the State of Israel, especially given the mass expulsion of the Palestinians from their homeland, and to assume, as Schölch writes, "a shared responsibility for the Palestine conflict in its entirety as a historical legacy."[69] What the journalists of *al-Difaʿ* observed in 1946, following the King David Hotel bombing, remains true to some extent: a familiarity with, and genuine interest and concern in, the Palestinian cause is lacking despite increased media coverage and influential books, such as Edward W. Said's *The Question of Palestine*, first published in 1979.

The Lebanese Civil War (1975–1990), the background against which Said wrote *The Question of Palestine*, has played a key role in my life from earliest childhood, as my father was in Beirut when the war started. The Israeli invasion and siege of Beirut in 1982, which forced the Palestine Liberation Organization (PLO) out of Lebanon and saw the Sabra and Shatila Massacre, coincided with my growing political awareness. As I came of age, the First Intifada, which erupted in 1987, brought the Palestinian cause to the world's attention, and the Gulf War of 1991, the first conflict televised in real time, brought war onto hundreds of millions of television screens for the entire world to see that peace in the Middle East had not been achieved.

When I moved to Lebanon as a student in the mid-1990s to study Arabic and later became a professor of Arabic and comparative literature at the American University of Beirut, childhood stories met with real-life experiences. I visited Jerusalem for the first time in December 1995, and I stood in Manger Square in

Bethlehem when Israeli control of the city was passed to the Palestinian Authority as part of the Oslo Accords. Twenty-five years later, the euphoria of that moment has been completely lost; with Israel's settlement enterprise ongoing, a two-state solution seems to have lost all viability.

My research has not been without surprises and challenges. Living and working in Beirut, I was investigating the life trajectories of the individuals who came together as the ecumenical circle in Jerusalem in the early 1940s, but each life took me in different directions; many had their beginnings in different locations, and all continued out of Palestine after 1948.

One day, I was walking across the American University of Beirut's beautiful campus overlooking the Mediterranean, when I ran into my colleague Tarif Khalidi, who is the author of *Images of Muhammad: Narratives of the Prophet in Islam Across Centuries*, among many other books, which opens with critical reflections on the genre of biography, referred to in Arabic as *sīra*, a path through life, a word also used to refer to the life of Muhammad.[70] When I told him I was researching Jabra, he was excited and told me I should meet his half-brother, Walid, who had been friends with Jabra in Jerusalem. When Walid came to Beirut the next time, my husband, Mohammad Ali Atassi, and I invited him to our house. Over dinner one spring evening in 2014, Walid told me how he used to meet with Jabra, Wolfgang, Sally, and Rasha at the King David Hotel bar. He recalled other friends on the fringes of the ecumenical circle, some of whom are mentioned in this book, and he referred me to the article he had written about Hourani.

A few years later, when I was on sabbatical in Berlin, I decided to look more closely into this group of friends and visited the Wolfgang Hildesheimer Archive at the Academy of Arts. This archive turned out to be a treasure trove of documents pertaining not only to Wolfgang's life but also to the ecumenical circle. There, I came across the lithographs Wolfgang had produced as illustrations to some of Jabra's early poetry written in English—part of a joint book project, as I found out later, that never saw the light of day and that are brought together in this book in fragments for the first time—and read the late correspondence between Rasha and Wolfgang.

Having embarked on writing this book, I visited Walid in Cambridge, Massachusetts, in 2018, 2019, and again in 2022 and 2023, after the Covid-19 lockdown and the Beirut port explosion, to conduct further interviews. I arrived at his house, which looks over the Fresh Pond Golf Course, on the outskirts of Cambridge on a sunny morning, the trees a fiery splendor of autumnal color, as the days were becoming shorter and temperatures were cooling at night. Invited into the house by Lydia Cristobal, Walid's warm and gracious house manager, who, as I found out later, is the one who responds to emails and types out Walid's handwritten notes, I felt the warmth of hospitality and booklined walls. Pictures of Jerusalem and family members, in particular Walid's late wife Rasha, filled the house. When Walid entered the living room, leaning on a walking stick, he invited me to sit down next to the fireplace, which was already lit.

As he went into great detail explaining the historical circumstances of what I came to call an impossible friendship, he referred to books, documents, and photographs, and we eventually moved to his study, where we looked at some of this material together. We passed through the dining room and kitchen into another, smaller sitting room; from there, we entered his study, transformed from a garage into a spacious yet cozy room with three desks at which Walid works on his various projects. It was at one of these desks that I would spend the next three days, from morning until after lunch, which Lydia, together with Karma, Walid's daughter, kindly prepared. As the four of us sat down to eat in the dining room, our conversations turned to more contemporary issues. Showing no signs of fatigue, Walid would then withdraw to the upper rooms of the house for his afternoon nap, a book in his hands, as I went back to my notes and papers. Increasingly, my discussions with Walid became private tutorials on the modern history of Palestine—a format we were both familiar with, he from his years as an Oxford don in the early 1950s, me from my student years at Oxford. As Philip S. Khoury, who took a class with Walid on "The Military in Arab Politics and Society" at the American University of Beirut in 1969/70, writes, "To many, Walid Khalidi is a caricature of the Oxford don that he once was: articulate, erudite, and somewhat eccentric, which in America translates as 'absent-minded.' How many people have come up to me over the years to ask: 'Can this man really be a Palestinian? He seems so British, so Oxonian, so aristocratic.' My response is always: 'Well, he is an Oxonian and he is aristocratic, and I can assure you that every day Walid Khalidi wakes up a Palestinian.' "[71]

Intersectionality is after all not restricted to individuals or groups in America. I will be forever grateful for Walid's generosity, trust, and friendship, and cherish what I learned in these tutorials, as Walid looked back at his lengthy life through the eyes of a historian used to applying "reasoned analysis based on sound evidence."[72] Was this why, I wondered, he had postponed writing his memoirs over and again? I was surprised to learn that he had not read Jabra's first autobiography, *The First Well*, which so lovingly captures its author's boyhood in Bethlehem; hoping to encourage Walid to rekindle memories of his childhood and include them in his memoirs, I gave him Jabra's book when I visited again in spring 2019, his garden now glorious with cherry blossoms. He read it closely, paying particular attention to Jabra's Assyrian background, and I draw on things he pointed out in my discussion of Jabra later. While Walid stopped short of talking about his personal life, he entrusted me with Rasha's unpublished memoirs, which have proved invaluable in allowing me to sketch a picture of her in this book, and at the same time have provided me with insight, through her eyes, into his everyday life in Jerusalem as a young man. It is also Walid who gave me the picture that came to serve as an empirical index of the lens through which this book examines an impossible friendship in Jerusalem before 1948 and beyond.

Having inscribed my own story in *An Impossible Friendship*, the lives at the heart of the ecumenical circle take center stage in the pages that follow. But before we turn to them, let us return to the King David Hotel bar and explore the larger urban context in which their friendship unfolded as Jerusalem was transformed from a former Ottoman *mutasarrifate* into a center of British imperial policy in the Middle East and the scene of conflicting national struggles in Palestine.

PART I
THE TIME BEFORE 1948

بين ريتا وعيوني . . بندقيه
. . .
بيننا مليون عصفور وصوره
ومواعيد كثيره
أطلقت ناراً عليها . . بندقيه

Between Rita and my eyes . . . is a rifle
. . .
Between us are a million sparrows and a picture
And many a rendezvous
Fired at her . . . a rifle

—Mahmoud Darwish, "Rita and the Rifle"

CHAPTER 1

"CHANGING JERUSALEM: A NEW PANORAMA OF THE HOLY CITY"

A COSMOPOLITANISM OF AFFLUENCE

The King David Hotel opened its doors in 1931. It was founded by the Mosseris, a wealthy Jewish banking family from Cairo and Alexandria who owned Egyptian Hotels Limited. This chain of luxury properties includes holdings such as the Mena House Hotel, which affords views of the Great Pyramid of Giza; Shepheard's Hotel in Cairo; the Old Cataract Hotel in Aswan; and the Winter Palace, which stands along the Nile in Luxor. In 1921, the Mosseris founded Palestine Hotels Limited, and in 1929, they purchased eighteen dunams (approximately 4.5 acres) of land west of Jerusalem's Old City from the Greek Orthodox Church to build the King David. (figure 1.1) Most of the shareholders of Palestine Hotels were Egyptian Jews,[1] but the company was also a subsidiary of the Palestine Economic Corporation (PEC), which had been established in New York City in 1925 "to facilitate investment in Palestine by American Jews and others interested in fostering the economic development and resettlement of the Jewish homeland."[2] Other shareholders included Justice Louis Brandeis and the banker and philanthropist Felix Warburg, both closely associated with the PEC; Baron Edmund de Rothschild, who in 1924 had established the Palestine Jewish Colonization Association; and Sir Alfred Mond, the Lord Melchett, a British industrialist and liberal minister of parliament with strong Zionist leanings.[3]

As was the case with many of Jerusalem's modern landmarks, the plans for the King David were commissioned from foreign architects, namely Emil Vogt and his Swiss compatriot, the interior designer Gustave-Adolphe Hufschmid who was renowned for his eclectic historicism, a trademark of the grand hotel. To oversee the construction, Vogt in turn hired Benjamin Chaikin, a Russian-born

1.1 Map of Jerusalem. Survey of Palestine, 1937. Palestine Land Studies Center, American University of Beirut.

Jewish immigrant who had close ties to Britain, having studied architecture at the prestigious Architectural Association School of Architecture in London and served in the British Army's Royal Engineers during World War I. Chaikin also oversaw the construction of the Hebrew University in Jerusalem, which was designed by Patrick Geddes in partnership with his son-in-law Frank Mears.[4] A product and a proponent of the British colonial era, Geddes work in Palestine aligned closely with Orientalist imaginaries of pilgrimage to the Holy Land as well as with Zionist interests in foregrounding the country's biblical heritage.[5] When the Hebrew University was formally established in 1918, the British Zionist Federation, headed since 1917 by Chaim Weizmann, commissioned Geddes to design the university's first campus on Mount Scopus. His plan was only partially implemented but includes the domed library, mirroring the Dome of the Rock, which today houses the Faculty of Law and has become one of the university's most distinctive features.[6] The university was inaugurated in 1925 with a celebration presided over by Sir Herbert Samuel, the first high commissioner for Palestine and Transjordan; Hayim Bialik, a pioneer of modern Hebrew literature;[7] and Rabbi Abraham Kook, the first Ashkenazi chief rabbi of Mandate Palestine,[8] thus bringing together key representatives of political, cultural, and religious Zionism. The guest speaker was former UK Prime Minister Arthur James Balfour, who, during his tenure as secretary of state for foreign affairs in the government of David Lloyd George, had authored the Balfour Declaration. The invitation of Balfour to address the audience triggered widespread protest from the Arab population of Palestine, who were referred to in the declaration in the negative, subsumed under the non-Jewish communities of Palestine.

The imposing palatial structure of the King David on an elevated site signaled change and opened up to "a new panorama of the holy city," as the headline of the London *Times* stated on January 17, 1931 (figure 1.2):

> The development of Julien's Way has made possible this new panoramic view of the western side of Jerusalem, which has just reached London. It was taken from the roof of the recently completed King David Hotel, one of many buildings to be built on Julien's Way. The view includes the Mount of Olives and Mount Zion, with the Valley of Hinnom on the right. On the left can be seen Jaffa Gate and the Citadel and, on the skyline, the Kaiserin Augusta Hospice, formerly used as Government House, and the Russian Tower. On the right are the Church of the Dormition and David's Tomb with a glimpse of the Dead Sea and the Mountains of Moab in the distance.[9]

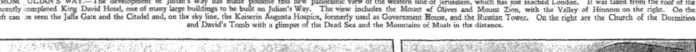

34 THE TIME BEFORE 1948

1.2 "Changing Jerusalem: A New Panorama of the Holy City," *Times*, January 17, 1931.

Featuring modern conveniences such as hot and cold running water, and, in addition to its grand lobby, resplendent with facilities ranging from a rose garden and a tennis court to two restaurants, a banquet hall, an Arab salon, and a bar, the King David boasted about two hundred rooms and sixty bathrooms. It attracted the affluent from near and far: royalty, politicians, celebrities, and an increasing number of tourists on Mediterranean cruises, who were visiting Egypt and the holy sites of Christianity, Islam, and Judaism in Palestine. Like its sister properties in Egypt, the King David welcomed its guests into a world of luxury, where ancient motifs and elements of Middle Eastern decor came together with state-of-the-art contemporary architecture.[10] Writing about the hotel's design, Daniella Ohad Smith notes that "the hotel's high ceilings, spacious public spaces, white shimmering marble floors, rich cedar paneling [imported from Lebanon], and gilt surfaces all conveyed royalty and magnificence."[11] The hotel also became "a meeting place for English, Arabs, and Jews who could afford its prices and cared to participate in the lively society of its celebrated bar and dining rooms."[12] Its inauguration was a major social event, attended by religious representatives of Jerusalem, officials of the British Mandate, European consuls, and members of the Palestinian and Egyptian elite.[13]

Although the hotel's opening received much praise in the international press as the "best hostelry in the Near East" and for its "historic location" looking over "biblical territory,"[14] local Arab newspapers sounded the alarm. The short-lived, midsize *al-Hayat*, which was founded in Jerusalem in 1930 by Adel Jabre and Khalid Duzdar and gave voice to a young, politicized generation, ran a short but scathing notice about the luxuriousness of the hotel, unequaled in the world's finest and richest cities.[15] *Filastin*, Palestine's largest and most influential Arabic-language newspaper, which we quoted in our prologue, sharply criticized the hotel in an article titled "King David Hotel: A Network of Zionist Networks to Eliminate Arabs Economically." As its authors, Marqus 'Isa and George Sahhar, explain, the King David participated in Zionist strategies intended to deprive Arabs of economic power and job opportunities in a sector of significant growth and capital. In particular, they accused Palestine Hotels of employing Arabs to carry out unskilled, menial work, such as attending to the night watch or washing dishes, rather than in prime positions.[16] They identified a crucial point: the Histadrut—established as a trade union of Jewish workers in the first year of the British Mandate—had become one of the most powerful institutions of the Yishuv. In the late 1920s and early 1930s, the union launched a campaign to promote Jewish labor by excluding Arabs from working for Jewish-owned enterprises, whereby it gave economic strength to an autonomous structure put in place by political Zionism with the support of British Mandate authorities and powerful individuals, among them Lord Melchett, who is named in the article.[17] In 1932, the Histadrut established the Palestine Labor League, by which it "foreclosed any possibility that Arab workers would be allowed to become full and equal members of a transformed, non-Zionist Histadrut."[18]

As was the case in Egypt, management expertise at the King David was imported from Switzerland. The hotel manager as of 1937 was Max Hamburger, who had previously been the assistant manager of Shepheard's Hotel in Cairo. Palestinian Arabs and Jewish immigrants were employed in administrative positions and as laborers. At the bottom of the employment ladder were Sudanese migrant workers, who were housed in the hotel's dormitory annex. There are few accounts in which the lives of these latter are told; if mentioned at all, they are couched in exoticist representation and racist prejudice as part of the decor. "The waiters were towering black Sudanese athletes in tight-fitting, red jackets who circulated among the guests, offering them whiskey and coffee from golden trays," writes Tom Segev, falling in line with Orientalist depictions of Jerusalem, to which the King David evidently catered.[19] The hotel's former bandleader, Izhak Mendelbaum, a Jewish immigrant from Poland who arrived in Palestine in 1935, describes the Sudanese employees as "very, very tall, black-like-chocolate people, very nice, with white dresses [with] a red stripe on them." He recalls one waiter named Salah, who was shot in the street by British soldiers during the Great Revolt. He also remembers the Sudanese were paid two pounds a month, whereas he made seventeen; that they worked twenty-four hours a day; and that they were treated "like slaves."[20] Might we compare Salah's story to that of Venus in the archive of Atlantic slavery, which Saidiya Hartman set out to tell by pointing to the inherent impossibility of its telling, given "the limits of fact, evidence, and archive, even as those dead certainties are produced by terror"?[21] Was Salah shot in the street because he was seen, in the eyes of British soldiers, as an enemy Arab in the Great Revolt? If yes, then how do the stories of Black lives intersect with the stories of Palestinian Arabs, and, more specifically, with the group of friends who came together at the King David Hotel bar? To investigate Salah's story further is beyond the scope of this book; however, recognizing its absence and the precariousness of his life, may cast light on the social and political conditions from which the Great Revolt turned against the British Mandate in anticolonial struggle.

Palestine under the British Mandate included not only Arabs and Jews—categories that, as we have seen, were in dynamic transformation—but also small communities of other ethnic origins that have garnered little attention, among them men, women, and children of African descent—some newly arrived, and others with a long history in Palestine, who have come to identify as Afro-Palestinians. Most of the latter trace their origins either to Muslim pilgrims who came to Jerusalem on their own free will or to victims of the slave trade.[22] Palestine has an intricate history of relations with Sudan as well as a shared experience of British colonial rule. With the Anglo-Egyptian Condominium, which established British control over Sudan in 1899 and was in place until 1956, many Sudanese moved to Cairo and Alexandria in search of a living. As Eve M. Troutt Powell writes, they "became an active part of the increasingly diverse mosaic of the Egyptian population."[23] Some were hired by Egyptian Hotels and subsequently by Palestine Hotels. At the same time, the British government employed Arab Christians from *Bilad al-Sham*, known as Greater Syria in English, which encompassed historic Palestine/Israel and the Occupied Palestinian Territories, Jordan, Lebanon, and Syria. Many of these colonial employees were educated at the Syrian Protestant College, which later was renamed the American University of Beirut, or its French counterpart, the Université Saint-Joseph, to work in the Sudan Medical Department, later renamed the Sudan Medical Service, which "would be crucial to the categorizing, mapping, and policing of Sudan as a racial state in which white rule dominated."[24] In this capacity, they became "partner[s] in the British and Egyptian colonization of Sudan," as Sherene Seikaly writes, drawing on the archive "full of details and silences" of her great-grandfather, Naim Cotran, who worked for the Sudan Medical Department in Omdurman during World War I.[25] As Seikaly shows, three decades later, "the British colonial authorities he emulated would be the agents of his subordination and ultimate dispossession" in Palestine.[26]

Obstructing as they do the power dynamics and inequality in play at the King David, neither colonial binaries of the global versus the local nor nostalgic invocations of a bygone cosmopolitanism properly capture the varying life trajectories—which, silenced as they are in colonial archives, appear contradictory today if indeed they are mentioned at all—that intersected there. More often than not, the adjective *cosmopolitan* is used to describe the social elite, and it has been applied rather uncritically in Middle Eastern contexts, in particular to port cities in the nineteenth and early twentieth centuries, with Alexandria serving as the cosmopolitan city *par excellence*.[27] Referring to the title of Silviano Santiago's contribution to *Cosmopolitanisms*, a collection of essays that posits a plurality of cosmopolitanisms, we might propose that the Sudanese workers partook in a *cosmopolitanism of the poor*.[28] As such, their lives have remained invisible. Their contours in the pages of this book cannot bring them to life, but they hint at an existence beyond the King David's sumptuous decor, one sentenced to propagate precarious lives left undocumented in imperial records. Although their paths crossed with those of the ecumenical circle in the halls of the hotel, social and racial discrimination excluded them from the "extraterritorial cultural center in which Arabs, Jews, and English participated," as Wolfgang Hildesheimer describes Jerusalem in rather nostalgic terms from the spatial and temporal distance of his resumed life in Europe after World War II.[29] The cosmopolitanism the ecumenical circle partook in was a cosmopolitanism of affluence. Notwithstanding their diverse religious and social background, the friends who came together in the King David Hotel bar were part of the intellectual elite in Palestine, which—not unlike Seikaly's grandfather—was steeped in British colonial lifestyles. Although this may have caused less of a problem for Wolfgang, it would lead to bitter disappointment for his Arab friends.

Across the street from the King David, the Young Men's Christian Association (YMCA) opened its doors in 1933, on land also purchased from the Greek Orthodox Church. A spectacular building with a bell tower rising to a height of more than 160 feet, it was designed by the U.S. architect Arthur Loomis Harmon, who also developed the Empire State Building.[30] Its opening was presided over by Humphrey E. Bowman, director of education in Mandate Palestine from 1920 to 1936. He kept the leaflet from the opening ceremony in his "confidential journal," which has also preserved other illuminating ephemera, brochures, and flyers from events attended during his time of service, and which is archived at the Middle East Centre at St Antony's College, University of Oxford (figure 1.3). General Edmund Allenby, who during World War I had led the conquest of Palestine, and entered the holy city through the Jaffa Gate in 1917 on foot (in marked contrast to Kaiser Wilhelm II of Germany, who had part of the city walls removed to allow him to enter Jerusalem triumphantly on horseback in 1898), delivered the opening address. While Allenby gave his address, Matiel E. T. Mogannam, a leading figure of the Palestinian women's movement, delivered a speech from the minbar of the al-Aqsa Mosque in the Old City, giving voice to Palestinian national aspirations.[31]

The King David Hotel and the YMCA stood out as beacons of global modernity on Julien's Way in Mamillah, the central commercial district of the New City of Jerusalem in the vicinity of the Jaffa Gate that featured municipal offices, the general post office, banks, private businesses, and cinemas. Jerusalem, at the time, was not divided into west and east neighborhoods; rather, as in other Arab cities of the former Ottoman provinces, distinctions were made between the poverty-ridden Old City, on the one hand, and the New City, which had begun its expansion beyond the city walls in the late nineteenth century, on the other.[32] Jerusalem's leading families, among them the Alamis, Dajanis, Husseinis, Khalidis, Nashashibis, and Sakakinis, along with the rising middle classes, had moved out of the old town, building sumptuous homes surrounded by gardens in the new, which accommodated their contemporary lifestyles. A number of

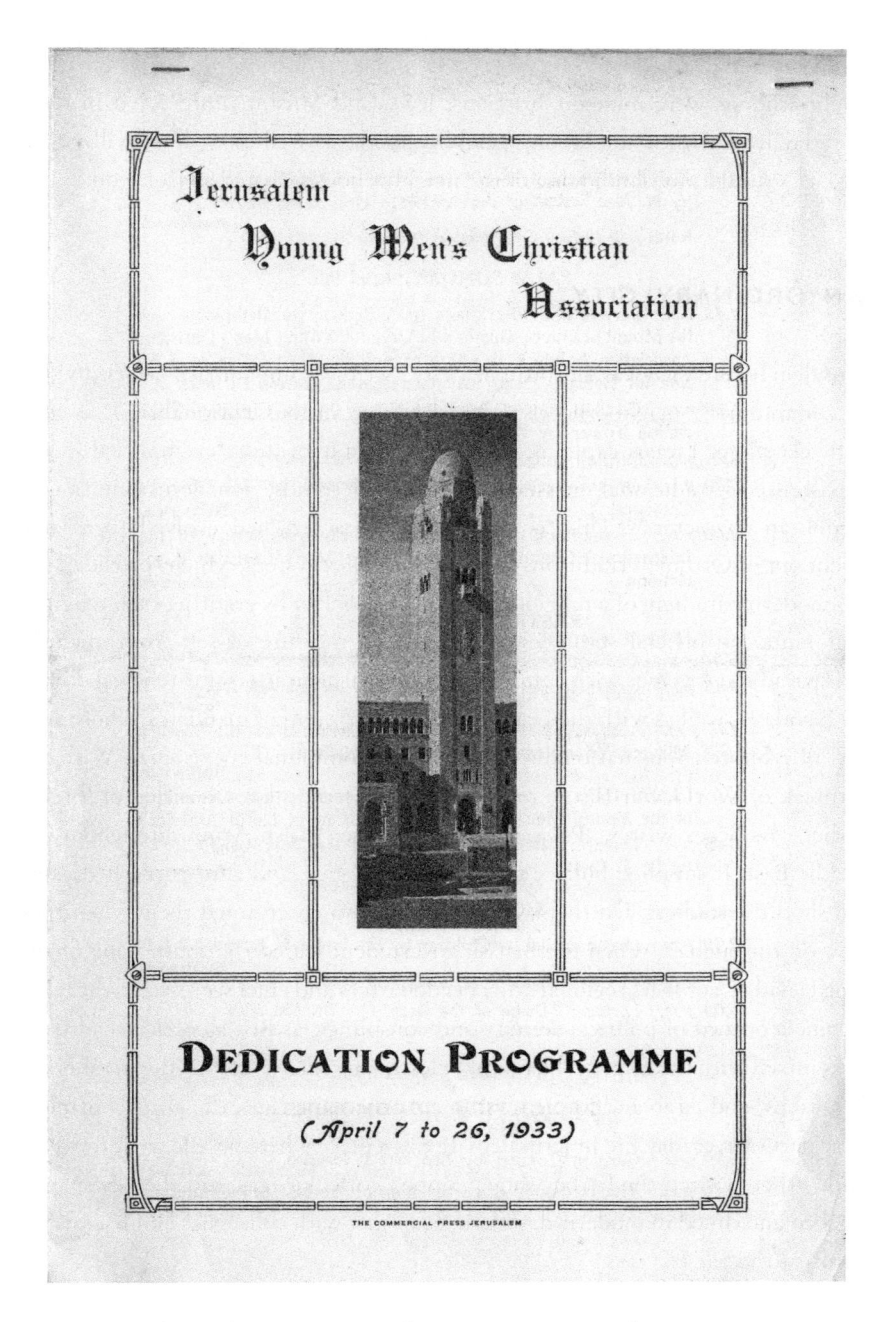

1.3 Brochure of Jerusalem Young Men's Christian Association Dedication Programme (April 7 to 26, 1933).

Humphrey E. Bowman, "Confidential journal," April 16, 1933, Middle East Centre Archive, St Antony's College, University of Oxford, Bowman, Box 4B.

neighborhoods were mixed: Christians, Jews, and Muslims interacted in their everyday lives within and among neighborhoods, as well as with the villages in the city's rural hinterland; none of the neighborhoods existed in isolation.[33]

"AN 'ORDINARY' CITY"

Jerusalem before 1948 was "an 'ordinary' city," writes Salim Tamari, "a city divided by communities, neighborhoods, ethnicities (of various nationalities), as well as by class." As Tamari explains, the city's ethnic hybridity, "exemplified in the coexistence of traditional, messianic, and secular trends," lent Jerusalem "a cosmopolitan character."[34] This "cosmopolitan character" had evolved to a large extent out of Ottoman traditions—namely the *millet* system, which "provided the pre-modern paradigm of a religiously pluralistic society by granting each religious community an official status and a substantial measure of self-government."[35] This paradigm was met with cultural and political aspirations for renewal during the Nahda, as well as with the League of Nations system of mandates, whose support of ethnoreligious nationalisms threatened communal coexistence. With the outbreak of World War II, the region saw a hitherto unknown influx of foreign soldiers. As Segev writes, "Palestine equipped the British Army throughout the Middle East. It supplied bullets and mines, fuel, tires, and auto parts. It dressed and shod the soldiers, fed them, housed them, and entertained them when they were on furlough."[36] When the British government leased the south wing of the King David to house its regional army headquarters and chief secretariat, the hotel became a hotbed of political activity and conspiracy, as British officials and soldiers mixed with the upper echelons of Palestinian society, well-to-do members of the Yishuv, and Arab and foreign visitors. At the same time, the hotel continued to be part of everyday life in Jerusalem. It was a place where people went to work, while others visited the barber shop,[37] sipped coffee or tea, read the newspaper, lunched and dined in modern-day settings, or met with colleagues and friends for drinks at the bar.

The ephemera retained in Humphrey E. Bowman's journal include the program of a farewell dinner for Major Alan Saunders, hosted by the Government of Palestine on December 7, 1935, at La Régence, the King David's prestigious restaurant. Perhaps the menu was not always as extravagant as the one served on this occasion, but a closer look at the program is telling for a number of reasons (figures 1.4 and 1.5). The "Sole de Jaffa Meunière" and "Dinde de Palestine à la

1.4 Brochure cover for the farewell dinner for Major Alan Saunders at the King David Hotel, December 7, 1935.

Humphrey E. Bowman, "Confidential journal," December 29, 1935, Middle East Centre Archive, St Antony's College, University of Oxford, Bowman, Box 4B.

MENU

Cocktail Luisiane

Petite Marmite Bouchère

Sole de Jaffa Meunière

Dinde de Palestine à la Brocke
Bouquet de Primeurs

Asperges de Californie
Sauce Sylvette

Bombe Aida
Mignardises

Corbeille d'eve

Tasse Orientale

TOASTS

THE KING

MAJOR SAUNDERS.

Proposed by the Chairman.

Seconded by E. Mills, Esq., C.B.E.

The Guest of Honour will reply.

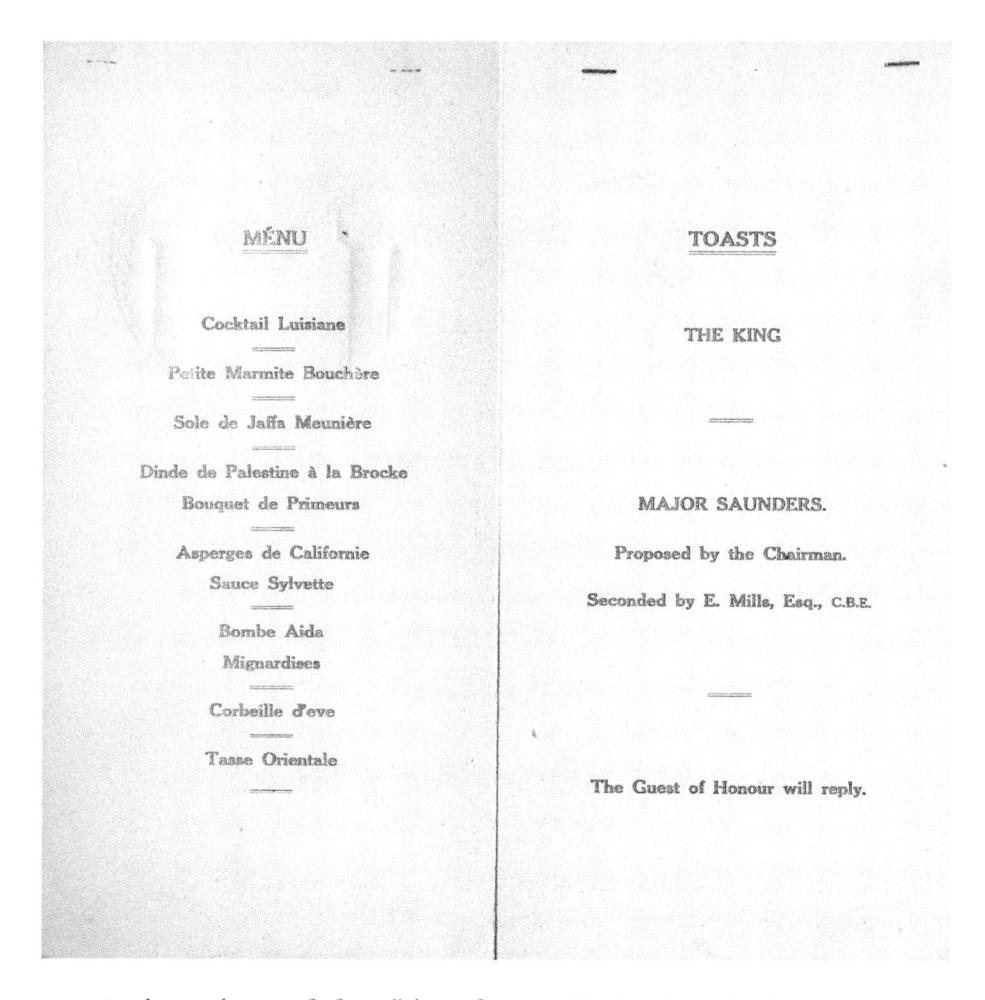

1.5 Brochure with menu of a farewell dinner for Major Alan Saunders at the King David Hotel, December 7, 1935.

Brocke," with their local and regional renown, along with dishes that circulated globally, such as a "Petite Marmite Bouchère," "Asperges de Californie" with "Sauce Sylvette," and a "Bombe Aida" with "Mignardises," evince not only the variety of culinary traditions prepared at La Régence but also an age of entanglement in which Jaffa and Palestine figure as part of a global modernity. Begun with a "Cocktail Luisiane" and finished with a "Corbeille d'eve" and a "Tasse Orientale," the menu stands out for its bridging of Western and Eastern culinary traditions. At the same time, the program features numerous signifiers of social distinction—not only in the choice of dishes but also in its very wording, which, next to the English, appears in both French and Latin, but not in Arabic or Hebrew. A quote from Horace, *Caelum non animum mutant qui trans mare current* (They change their sky, not their soul, who rush across the sea), reaffirms the "Guest of Honour" and a sense of belonging to the British Empire.

As is noted in the program, Saunders had most recently served as deputy inspector general of the Palestine Police Force and Prisons Services from 1926 through 1935. His service was part and parcel of the institutionalized manner in which Britain controlled Palestine, drawing on prior experience in her older colonies and her violent crackdown on the Irish Rebellion of 1919–20.[38] Before serving in France, Flanders, and Palestine during World War I, Saunders had been with the Indian Police starting in 1908. He would go on to the post of inspector general of the Nigeria police, and then returned to Palestine in 1937 as inspector general of police and prisons, a post he held until 1943. In this capacity, he played a key role in Britain's brutal response to the Great Revolt, which placed Palestine under martial law,[39] and the construction of fortified police stations or fortresses across Palestine and a barbed-wire fence, or rather wall, along its northern frontier—named after Sir Charles Tegart, an Irishman who had risen to prominence in the colonial police force in Calcutta and closely advised Saunders during two extended visits to Palestine.[40] Only two weeks before Saunders's farewell dinner, on November 20, 1935, the British police had killed Sheikh Izz al-Din al-Qassam—after whom the Izz al-Din al-Qassam Brigades, the military wing of Hamas, are named. Al-Qassam was a popular leader of armed rural resistance against the British Mandate. Born in Jabla, south of the Syrian city of Latakiya, he was educated at al-Azhar University in Egypt. He had gained wide support in Islamic circles for his promotion of fundamentalist ideas of jihad, as well as among those Arab farmers who had lost their livelihood when the land they held as tenants in Upper Galilee was purchased by the Jewish National Fund (JNF). Driven into poverty, the farmers had migrated in search of work north to the port city of Haifa, where they lived in slum-like environs and formed new political alliances with fellow Palestinian Arabs.[41]

The JNF was proposed at the constituent congress of the Zionist Organization (ZO) founded by Theodor Herzl—generally regarded as the father of modern political Zionism—in Basel in 1897, and came into existence at the Fifth Zionist Congress in Basel in 1901 as the primary instrument for the purchase of land in Palestine.[42] It initially had its headquarters in Vienna, then Cologne (1907), the Hague (1914), and eventually Jerusalem (1922). It made its first land purchases in 1905 in Kefar Hittim (northwest of Tiberias), Hulda (south of Ramle), and Ben Shemen (east of Lydda).[43] To oversee Jewish settlement of the acquired lands, the ZO decided at the Eighth Zionist Congress in the Hague in 1907 to open a Palestine Office in Jaffa, which started to operate under Arthur Ruppin's direction in 1908. JNF acquisitions were modest until 1920, when the British Mandate for Palestine came into effect and Sir Herbert Samuel was appointed as the first high commissioner for Palestine and Transjordan. His administration issued a Land Transfer Ordinance, which facilitated the transfer of land ownership, and registered the JNF "as a foreign company authorized to engage in business, specifically the purchase and development of land in Palestine. As a consequence JNF holdings began to increase steadily, from 22,363 dunums [5,526 acres] in 1920 . . . to 936,000 [231,290 acres] by May 1948."[44] Despite this significant rise, "Jewish land ownership in the whole of Mandate Palestine in 1948 totaled 1.7 million dunams" only, as Walid Khalidi points out, whereas the area designated for the Jewish state by the United Nations General Assembly (UNGA) partition resolution of November 27, 1947, was fifteen million dunams (thirty-seven million acres).[45]

As the Zionist movement increasingly clashed with the national aspirations of the Palestinian Arabs, the British embarked on what Anbara Salam Khalidi remembers in her memoirs as "an endless cavalcade of commissions," although no one really believed that these "would result in any good, restore peace to the country or put an end to the ongoing injustice."[46] As Walid Khalidi explains in his introduction to *From Haven to Conquest*,

> Under the Mandate, there was no constitutional redress for the Arabs. . . . British policy in practice, and for obvious reasons, was never to accept the principle of one-man-one-vote in Palestine, and no self-governing institutions were ever developed for the country at large. To be sure, the Arabs could air their grievances before the Permanent Mandates Commission of the League of Nations, but the terms of reference of this Commission precluded the questioning of the provisions of the Mandate. The circle was Kafkaesque in its completeness. Arab resistance, therefore, escalated from delegations, petitions, demonstrations and strikes, to riots and violent clashes with the British security forces and the Zionist colonists.[47]

Such violent clashes had already occurred, notably in the 1929 riots that took place at what is known in Arabic as the Buraq Wall, in Hebrew as the Western Wall, and commonly in English as the Wailing Wall, which, according to Hillel Cohen, contributed significantly to the formation of the Yishuv, since they drew Jewish settler communities in Palestine closer to the Zionist movement.[48] "Following a century or so of waves of Jewish immigration under the protection of foreign powers and almost fifty years of organized Zionist activity," writes Cohen, "the Jews were no longer merely refugees seeking shelter but settlers taking possession of land and seeking sovereignty."[49] Arab resistance took a more comprehensive form in the Great Revolt under the direction of the Arab Higher Commission (AHC), which had come into existence in 1936 to coordinate a general strike. The AHC was presided over by Hajj Amin al-Husseini, who had risen to significant power since his appointment by Palestine's first high commissioner, Sir Herbert Samuel, to the new post of Mufti of Jerusalem.[50] Its membership included representatives of the main political parties and community leadership. When it rejected the Peel Commission's July 1937 proposal to partition Palestine, the AHC was outlawed by the British authorities, while the Palestine Police Force and Prisons Services, directed by Saunders, cracked down brutally on the revolt. Key Palestinian leaders were arrested. Some were exiled to the Seychelles, among them Dr. Hussein Fakhri al-Khalidi, Walid Khalidi's uncle, who had served as Jerusalem's mayor from 1934 to 1937—he was the last mayor to be freely elected by both Arab and Jewish inhabitants of Jerusalem, as Walid Khalidi pointed out to me.[51] He was also a founding member of the Palestinian Arab Reform Party. Others were already out of Jerusalem or managed to elude arrest and find exile in other Arab countries. Among the exiles were Hajj Amin; Jamal al-Husseini, who led the Palestinian Arab Party; 'Awni 'Abd al-Hadi, who led the Palestinian Independence Party; Ragheb al-Nashashibi, who led the National Defense Party; and Musa Alami, who was not associated with any political party but would go on to represent Palestine at various international conferences, notably the St James's Palace Conference in London, convened by the government of Neville Chamberlain, which resulted in the White Paper of 1939.[52]

Recognizing as it did the need to align Jewish immigration to Palestine with Palestinian Arab national interests, the White Paper—its rejection by the Palestinian leadership notwithstanding—signaled a shift in British policy. Its publication, however, coincided with the severe deprivation of civil liberties of Germany's Jewish population under Nazi rule, the outbreak of World War II, and the growing awareness that greater conflict was on the horizon in Europe, all of which worked against it.[53] Considerations of Arab-Jewish relations in Palestine during World War II have been overshadowed by their focus on Hajj Amin, whose sympathies with Fascist Italy and Nazi Germany and whose stay in Berlin from 1941 to 1945 are well documented.[54] As Gudrun Krämer explains, "Arab sympathies with Germany, both under Wilhelm II and under Hitler . . . were largely premised on Germany's perceived competition with, and antagonism toward, Britain and France as the principal colonial powers in the Middle East ('my enemy's enemy is my friend'). It was thus primarily based on political and strategic considerations rather than ideological affinity."[55] After the war, Hajj Amin did not return to the Arab world as a leading politician but instead as a "politically failed existence" used as an ineffectual pawn in the political rivalries of various Arab regimes.[56] His positions did not represent the Palestinian national movement, which is documented by the Alexandria Protocol at the foundation of the Arab League in 1945, drafted by Alami in his role as representative of Palestine. It reads: "The Committee also declares that it is second to none in regretting the woes which have been inflicted upon the Jews of Europe by European dictatorial states. But the question of these Jews should not be confused with Zionism, for there can be no greater injustice and aggression than solving the problem of the Jews of Europe by another injustice, that is, by inflicting injustice on the Palestine Arabs of various religions and denominations."[57]

Alami, one of the first Palestinians educated at the University of Cambridge, had worked as a legal adviser in the British Mandate government and as private secretary for Arab affairs to High Commissioner Arthur Wauchope in the 1930s. Together with George Antonius, the author of *The Arab Awakening* about whom more will be said shortly, Alami had drafted the June 30, 1936, Memorandum of Arab Senior Government Officials to the High Commissioner in support of the Palestinian national demands as they had been formulated by the AHC: "the formation of a national government responsible to a representative assembly, the prevention of the transfer of Arab lands to the Jews, and the stoppage of Jewish immigration."[58]

In response to the White Paper, the Yishuv, under the leadership of David Ben-Gurion, who would go on to become Israel's first prime minister, increasingly turned to the United States for support. As chair of the Jewish Agency, the operative branch of the ZO that had been established as the Palestine Office by Arthur Ruppin in Jaffa in 1908, Ben-Gurion was determined to create a Jewish state in Palestine at any cost.[59] Accordingly the Biltmore Program, drafted in May 1942 at an extraordinary Zionist conference at the Biltmore Hotel in New York City, called for unrestricted Jewish immigration to Palestine and "that the gates of Palestine be opened . . . . and that Palestine be established as a Jewish Commonwealth integrated in the structure of the new democratic world"[60]—that is, that a Jewish state be established throughout Palestine, taking into account that this would involve armed conflict.[61] This shift toward more radical currents, and the departure of the Zionist movement from its former reliance on the United Kingdom, coincided with the rise of American economic interests in the Middle East. In March 1942, the United States joined the Middle East Supply Center, a British enterprise that had been founded in Cairo in 1941 to coordinate the supply and transport of goods across the Middle East in support of the Allied war effort. The Allies defeated German and Italian troops in El Alamein, Egypt, in November 1942, cutting off Axis access to the Suez Canal and Middle Eastern oil fields. Around the same time, Saudi Arabia emerged as a key regional player when the Arabian-American Oil Company (Aramco) was founded in 1944 and the Trans-Arabian Pipeline project, with termini in Qaisumah, Saudi Arabia, and Sidon, Lebanon, increased in importance in both postwar planning and American security policy, especially with the onset of the Cold War.[62]

Against this background, Palestinians were left with but one hope, writes Walid Khalidi: "British adherence to the 1939 White Paper in conjunction with active support from the newly created Arab League,"[63] which was formed in Cairo in March 1945 and initially included six members: Egypt, Iraq, Transjordan (renamed Jordan in 1949), Lebanon, Saudi Arabia, and Syria. This—in addition to the cultural affinities of the British-educated Palestinian elite—partly explains the closeness of Arab-British ties in Palestine, prior rebellion and recurrent disappointment notwithstanding, and provides the general context for the ecumenical circle. Put another way, it was at this crucial historical juncture that the ecumenical circle came into existence in Jerusalem.

"YEARS OF FRAGILE TRANQUILITY"

In the end, "Jerusalem was a small town," writes Albert Hourani, who would join the ecumenical circle occasionally when in Jerusalem, accompanied by Lulie Abul-Huda (also known as Velia Abdel-Huda), who was one of the first Arab women to have graduated from Oxford.[64] Hourani came to Jerusalem to work as director of research at the Arab Office.

In 1945, the newly established Arab League, founded in Alexandria in 1944, authorized Alami to set up the Arab Office as an organization to further the cause of the Arabs of Palestine, with financial support from Iraq, and offices in Jerusalem, London, Paris, and Washington, D.C., thereby providing Palestinian Arabs with diplomatic representation abroad for the first time. The Arab Office "served as the unofficial Palestinian foreign and information ministry, albeit with the most modest of resources."[65] Well connected to the political leadership in Palestine and across the Arab world, notably in Egypt and Iraq, yet not affiliated with any one political party, Alami was known as an intellectual and an honest man committed to the Palestinian cause. He was a "magnet to younger people," remembers Yusif Sayigh, who worked for the Arab Office as an external economics specialist.[66] The Arab Office in Jerusalem was headed by Ahmad Shukeiri, a member of the Arab Independence Party. He later became the first chair of the Palestine Liberation Organization, before Yasser Arafat.

Walid Khalidi, who would work as one of Hourani's research assistants at the Arab Office, recalls that he first met Hourani in 1944 "in a booklined room overlooking Jerusalem from the north," when the latter was a guest at Karm al-Mufti, the home of Katy Antonius.[67] The mansion was situated above the Old City on the slopes of Mount Scopus in Sheikh Jarrah, one of the first neighborhoods built outside the city walls north of Bab al-Zahira (Herod's Gate), where a number of Jerusalem's leading Muslim families built extravagant homes. Karm al-Mufti was built by Hajj Amin for himself and then was rented and later purchased by the Antoniuses. Katy was a prominent figure of Jerusalem's social elite renowned for her hospitality and her salon, which brought together "British officials, Arab notables and intellectuals, and occasional non-Zionist Jews."[68] The famed Druze singer Amal al-Atrash, better known as Asmahan, who rose to fame in Cairo but who died young in a car accident in 1944, is said to have entertained Katy's guests.[69] Katy was married to Cambridge-educated George Antonius who passed away a few years after the publication of his influential book, *The Arab Awakening*, "a gentle frustrated man and my friend," as Freya Stark, the Anglo-Italian writer who traveled the Middle East, remarks in her autobiography.[70] Antonius was repeatedly passed over for leading positions in the Department of Education in Mandate Palestine, while British subordinates were promoted.[71] At his burial in the Orthodox cemetery on Mount Zion, Palestinian educators Ahmad

Samih al-Khalidi—Walid's father—and Khalil al-Sakakini delivered eulogies. His epitaph reads: "Tanabbahu wa-istafiqu ayyuha al-'arab" (Awake oh Arabs and arise), which was taken from the title of a well-known poem by the Nahda writer Ibrahim al-Yaziji.[72]

Born in Manchester, where his father had established himself as a successful merchant, Hourani was educated at the University of Oxford. His parents were from Marjayoun, a village in southern Lebanon that had close ties to Palestine.[73] After graduating from Oxford, Hourani taught at the American University of Beirut. When World War II broke out, he was hired by the Royal Institute of International Affairs, later Chatham House, in London, where he worked with the acclaimed historian and international affairs specialist Arnold J. Toynbee and the Alexandria-born Laudian Professor of Arabic at Oxford, Sir Hamilton A. R. Gibb. From that post, he was sent by the Foreign Office on a fact-finding mission to the Middle East and then was hired as assistant adviser on Arab affairs to the Office of the British Minister of State Resident in Cairo, Brigadier Sir Iltyd Nicholl Clayton. Hourani's younger brother Cecil—who, like Albert, was an Oxford graduate—had joined the British Army in World War II and worked at General Headquarters in Cairo. Albert and Cecil rented a room in the house of their friend, the Czech-born Jewish Arabist Paul Kraus.[74] Both Albert and Cecil would visit Jerusalem frequently, where their eldest brother, George Hourani, trained as a classicist at Oxford, was teaching Latin at the Arab College.

It was in Cairo that Albert and Cecil met Musa Alami who, after the war, would hire Cecil to work at the Washington, D.C., branch of the Arab Office,[75] and Albert to direct research at the Arab Office in Jerusalem and prepare the Arab case for the Anglo-American Committee of Inquiry. The formation of this joint committee was proposed by the British Foreign Secretary Ernest Bevin in the House of Commons after the Potsdam Conference of 1945 "to examine the question of European Jewry and to make a further review of the Palestine problem in light of that examination,"[76] whereby the future of Palestine was formally linked to the fate of European Jewry after the Holocaust, and as Walid Khalidi explains, "Britain transformed its mandate into a condominium, with the United States as the senior partner."[77] After assembling in Washington, D.C., and London in January 1946, the committee moved to Vienna, where its members visited a Jewish displaced persons camp and interviewed Holocaust survivors. It then continued to Cairo to take into consideration Arab perspectives, and from there, it arrived in Jerusalem in March, where it held hearings with Arab and Jewish representatives, among them Hourani and Shukeiri as representatives of the Arab Office, before it debated its findings in Lausanne in April. Its report recommended that Europe's displaced Jewish persons be authorized to enter Palestine, while Palestine be neither Arab nor Jewish and the British Mandate extended. In May 1946, Albert returned to the United Kingdom, where he directed the London branch of the Arab Office. "A year later, in June 1947, he resigned, a disappointed man,"[78] as the political situation in Palestine deteriorated further. At the request of Gibb, he returned to Oxford, where he would become one of the most acclaimed historians of the Arab world.[79] He would later recall Jerusalem as "a special place for only a limited number, for that group that gathered there due to the war and the circumstances of those years of fragile tranquility. I had no doubt that it would end in tragedy. For us Jerusalem was a dream. It was too good to go on."[80] This dream did become a reality in the coming together of aspiring artists, writers, and intellectuals across religious lines in Jerusalem in the early 1940s, a coming together that challenged notions of the possible and the impossible at a time when World War II was coming to an end and the future of Palestine seemed to still be open.

As we revealed, what brought the ecumenical circle together and made their friendship possible was *beyond* wars but, paradoxically, also *because* of them. Despite a diversity in terms of religious background, the young men and women who made up this group of friends were a rather homogeneous group, differences in their individual social backgrounds notwithstanding. Partaking as they did in a cosmopolitanism of affluence, facilitated by English as their lingua franca, they were part of the British educated elite and had accumulated significant social, cultural, and economic capital. Although the Arab members were subject to colonial subjugation, not unlike the Sudanese workers employed by the King David, their social habitus set them apart not only from the Sudanese waiters but also from their fellow Palestinian Arabs, who did not have access to similar educational opportunities. This disconnect from the daily lives and worries of their fellow citizens may have been one of the profoundest tragedies of their lives, as their lifestyles and tastes—not least their habit of smoking the pipe—aligned them closely with their British friends in the hotel bar as the "years of fragile tranquility" in Jerusalem came to an end.[81]

CHAPTER 2

WALID KHALIDI

A Jerusalemite "in the Byronic Tradition"

POLITICAL AWARENESS

Born in Jerusalem on July 16, 1925, Walid Khalidi was the youngest member of the ecumenical circle. His Jerusalemite family traces its origins back to Khalid ibn al-Walid, a companion of the Prophet Muhammad and the commander of the Muslim conquest of Jerusalem in 636, after whom Walid Khalidi was named.[1] Through the ages, the family has played an important role in Islamic jurisprudence, political leadership, and education. His family background not only gave Walid connections that were useful to him in later life, writes his cousin, Rashid Khalidi, himself a renowned historian of the Middle East, but "also helps to explain his conservative, indeed almost patrician, outlook and his strong sense of duty and public responsibility."[2] Although this description may befit Walid as we know him—today, he is among the most influential historians of modern Palestine—it provides scant information about him as a youth. Walid was a recent graduate when the ecumenical circle came together. He was raised by German, French, and Russian nannies in his early childhood along with his two-years-older sister Sulafa, and then was schooled at private institutions. The American Friends School in Ramallah, founded by American Quakers in 1869, which he and Sulafa attended as boarders, provided his elementary education. He moved on to secondary studies at the Anglican Saint George's School in Jerusalem's neighborhood of Sheikh Jarrah, north of the Old City, which had also been his father's school. Instruction at the American Friends School in Ramallah was in Arabic, but at Saint George's School, it was in English.

    Walid's father, Ahmad Samih al-Khalidi, who had obtained a master's degree in education from the Syrian Protestant College, now the American University of Beirut, was the principal of the Arab College in Jerusalem from 1925 until its forced closure in 1948.³ Although Jewish government and private schools were granted a great degree of autonomy in Mandate Palestine, the Arab College, founded in 1918 as the Teachers' Training College, was closely supervised by the Department of Education, as were other Arab educational institutions. Yet, it was a unique institution. In tune with Nahda ideas, the curriculum of the Arab College was known for its emphasis on both Arab-Islamic heritage and Western classical and liberal traditions—the latter including American and European influences. Many of the college's teachers, like al-Khalidi, were graduates of the American University of Beirut. Inspired by progressive European educators, such as Maria Montessori and Johann Heinrich Pestalozzi, al-Khalidi was the author of a number of school textbooks, such as *Arkan al-tadris* (Foundations of teaching) in which he voiced his support for educational reform and his conviction that "the hands of the teacher, more than any other person, hold the future of the nation, its progress, and the development of its culture and literature."⁴ The college housed a library that "contained 250 [books] in 1923 and 7,122 in 1946," according to the principal's report in 1946,⁵ and it published an influential journal, *Majallat al-kulliyyah al-'arabiyya* (Journal of the Arab College).⁶ It brought together the best Arab students from across Palestine and played an important role in the Palestinian national struggle.⁷ As Jabra, who graduated from the Arab College in 1938, remembers, al-Khalidi, with his "stentorian voice" and "strong presence, . . . turned his educational theories into a way of life and so would accept nothing from his students but the pursuit of knowledge and distinction as a relentless patriotic tenet. At the new site of the college on Mount al-Mukabbir which was open to all the world's ideas blown there on the four winds, we read and studied with passion and perseverance all day long, and then all night to the point of sickness."⁸

Walid did not attend the Arab College, but its educational vision and the social network it afforded nevertheless played an important role in his life. He was tutored privately by two of its faculty members, the historian Nicola Ziyadeh and Abdul Rahman Bushnaq, who taught English literature, both graduates of the Arab College, and he made friends with some of the college's students, notably with Jabra and Nimr Tuqan. Nimr, who was a brother of the acclaimed Palestinian poets Ibrahim and Fadwa Tuqan, would go on to become a successful pathologist at the American University of Beirut until his sudden death in a plane crash along with Emile Boustani, a Lebanese entrepreneur and politician.

After his father's second marriage to Anbara Salam in 1929, Walid and his sister Sulafa were raised by their Lebanese stepmother alongside their half-siblings: Usama, Randa, Tarif, and Karma, the latter of whom died in childhood. In her memoirs, Anbara says that she had no difficulty at all in adopting Walid and Sulafa as her own, having had significant experience with her younger siblings, and especially Rasha whom she had "taken on as a real daughter." She describes Walid as "conspicuous by his intelligence and quickness of mind, with a distinct character all his own, despite his young age, and . . . a strong personality that attracted everyone's attention."[9] Ahmad Samih al-Khalidi's marriage to Anbara Salam closely aligned two notable families, one from Jerusalem and the other from Beirut. As Ziyadeh, who would go on to become an acclaimed professor of history at the American University of Beirut, says, it also brought together "the scholarship [*'ilm*] of Ahmad Samih with the refinement [*adab*] of Anbara,"[10] who according to Albert Hourani, shared "the life and misfortunes of the Palestinian Arabs, while playing her own part in the emancipation of Arab women" (figure 2.1).[11] After having been trained at a Quranic school, where she became a *hafiza*, having memorized the Quran at age ten, she received a modern education at the Makassed School for Girls in Beirut, directed by the well-known educator Julia Tuma Dimashqiyya, which was part of the Makassed Philanthropic Islamic Association, founded in Beirut in 1878, that her father presided over. In addition, she was tutored privately by Shaikh Abdullah al-Bustani, one of the most distinguished Arab linguists of his time who had translated Homer's *Iliad* from Greek into English and compiled a comprehensive Arabic-Arabic dictionary in two volumes. As a young woman, she was briefly engaged to 'Abd al-Ghani al-'Uraysi, the editor of Beirut's *Mufid* newspaper for which she used to write from time to time, signing one of her early articles *Fatat Beirut* (a girl from Beirut). In her articles, she called for women's education to fully participate in the rising Arab national sentiment. al-'Uraysi was among a group of young Arab nationalists accused of treason and publicly hanged by Jamal Pasha, the Ottoman governor of Syria and military leader during World War I, in Damascus and Beirut on May 6, 1916. In Beirut, these executions were carried out in al-Burj Square, which later became known as Martyr's Square. They earned Jamal Pasha the name "al-Saffah" (the blood shedder), as Anbara does not fail to point out in her memoirs.[12]

In the mid-1920s, Anbara spent two years with her father in London. She went on to play an important role in the women's movement: in one instance, she removed her veil at a lecture she delivered in public upon her return to

2.1 Anbara Salam Khalidi and Ahmad Samih al-Khalidi, Jerusalem, 1929.
Salam Collection, American University of Beirut/Library Archives.

Beirut, which caused a stir in the city's then predominantly traditional society, as she recalls.[13] In Jerusalem, Anbara participated in women's petitions and demonstrations against the British Mandate for Palestine and its support of the Zionist movement. In her first year in Jerusalem, she participated alongside Wahida al-Khalidi, the wife of Hussein Fakhri al-Khalidi, and Matiel Mogannam, two of the leading figures of the Palestinian women's movement, in the first women's conference held in Jerusalem. After the conference, the women organized a protest in the form of a car convoy across the city, including more than eighty vehicles, passing by foreign consulates until they reached the British High Commissioner's home.[14] Anbara also gave talks on Palestine Broadcasting Service, mainly on women's issues. As she recalls, "some broadcasts were recorded for the BBC Arabic Service in London."[15] Humphrey E. Bowman's journal, whose ephemera, as we have seen, contain a wealth of information, includes a list of "Recordings for BBC-Arabic" that names one Mrs. Anbara Khalidi as giving a talk titled "The Position of the Arab Woman in Modern Civilization" on July 20, 1939.[16] Her translations of Homer and Virgil from Alfred J. Church's renditions in English, which are used in schools across the Arab world, were published in Cairo in 1945 with a foreword by the Nahda's figurehead Taha Hussein, renowned for his three-volume *al-Ayyam* (*The Days*), a landmark of Arabic autobiography, and his study *Fil-shi'r al-jahili* (On pre-Islamic poetry), which caused much controversy as it argued that a portion of "pre-Islamic" poetry was fabricated after the coming of Islam.

Alongside this overall modern and secular education, Walid was particularly influenced by his paternal grandfather, Hajj Raghib al-Khalidi, who played a key role in familiarizing him with Arabic and Islamic thought. As a child, Walid often visited his grandfather. Hajj Raghib lived in a *bayyara*, a house with a well (*bi'r*), in an orange orchard outside the Arab village of Tal al-Rish near Jaffa. Walid felt particularly drawn to his grandfather after having lost his mother, Ihsan Aql, the daughter of an influential lawyer from Jaffa.[17] As I sat down with Walid in his study in Cambridge and our conversation turned to his mother, there was a moment of silence, and my eyes wandered over the map of Jerusalem facing his main desk. I reproduced this same map in chapter 1 (see figure 1.1) to enable my readers to trace the paths that the individuals at the heart of the ecumenical circle would take across the city and also to see the Jerusalem I was looking at with Walid. This map, which shows the old as well as the new city all the way south to where the Arab College was located, was published by the Survey of Palestine in 1937. From its inception in 1920, the Survey of Palestine had the status of a full government department responsible for the survey and mapping of Palestine during the British Mandate. Its rationale has its roots in the Balfour Declaration, which had "raised the question of defining and determining lands on which the Jewish national home was to be established."[18] From the map, my eyes moved to family pictures and other historical documents hung up between bookcases. In particular, two family portraits taken outside of Hajj Raghib's home caught my attention. One of the portraits depicts the men of the family—Hajj Raghib with his sons, in the company of Anbara's father, Salim Ali Salam—whereas another portrait includes some of the female members: Hajj Raghib's wife Amira Khalili, known as Um Hasan, the descendent of a famous eighteenth-century Sufi scholar from Hebron, Muhammad al-Khalili; their daughters, daughters-in-law, and grandchildren; and, among them, Anbara, newly wed to Ahmad Samih, holding four-year-old Walid in her arms as Sulafa stands next to her grandfather. In both pictures, Hajj Raghib is seated in the middle. His white beard, traditional dress, and turban set him apart from the other family members, who wear Western attire and no headwear, with the exception of Um Hasan, whose hair is held back with a scarf. Hajj Raghib was an acclaimed religious scholar and a judge in the Sharia courts of Palestine. He supported the Ottoman constitutionalist movement opposed to Sultan Abdul Hamid II's autocratic rule. Having studied at the Haram al-Sharif in Jerusalem and al-Azhar University in Cairo, he embraced educational reform as a member of Jerusalem's Ottoman Education Department and sent his sons to Saint George's School, which was run by Anglican missionaries.[19] He served as the deputy director between 1915 and 1917 of Jerusalem's short-lived Kulliyya al-Salahiyya, an educational institution devoted to Islamic theological studies, which was conceived as a counterpoint to al-Azhar.[20] In 1900, he assisted his mother, Khadija al-Khalidi, in establishing the Khalidi Library as a family *waqf* (religious endowment) in Jerusalem, where it is housed in a thirteenth-century Mamluk building on Bab al-Silsila Street, the neighborhood in the Old City inhabited by the al-Khalidi family for centuries.[21] The Khalidiyyah, as the library is known in Arabic, constitutes one of the most important private Palestinian collections of books, whose ownership has been handed down through the generations and remains with the family to this day. Walid was introduced to the Khalidiyyah at an early age as he and his sister Sulafa were instructed in reading the Quran by Sheikh Amin al-Ansari, whom Hajj Raghib had charged with taking care of the library. Later in life, Walid would contribute significantly to the preservation of the library, in particular through the Friends of the Khalidi Library, an association he incorporated in Massachusetts in the late 1980s.

On my return to Beirut from my visits to Cambridge, I met with Walid's half-brother, Tarif Khalidi, born in Jerusalem in 1938, the only one of Walid's siblings still alive. He explained that he did not have much contact with Walid and his friends in Jerusalem, given the age difference between the half-brothers. He did, however, remember that the ecumenical circle used to meet at the King David Hotel bar and would also come together in the Khalidis' garden. In particular, he recalled Wolfgang's extraordinary knowledge of music and quiet, precise English as well as Sally's friendly demeanor and good looks. "There was this business of the pipe," he added, "which Walid took over from Lord Oxford—Julian Asquith—who was an imposing figure. . . . I think they were all pretending to be British intellectuals." Equipped with a sonorous voice and an impeccable Oxford accent, Walid had a strong presence among his friends, Tarif explained: "He had already developed a kind of persona, as if he had decided that he was going to be an important figure; he had what Ibn Khaldun calls *hadra*—presence. I once asked [Lebanese historian] Kamal Salibi what Walid was like as a young man, because he knew him as a young man, and he said exactly as he is today."[22]

Julian Asquith, the second earl of Oxford and Asquith, known simply as Oxford, was assistant district commissioner in Palestine from 1942 to 1948. He and the woman he was to marry, Anne Palairet, knew Albert Hourani from the University of Oxford. The daughter of a diplomat, Paris-born Palairet was widely traveled and served in the British Army's Women's Auxiliary Air Force (WAAF) in Palestine.[23]

In reporting on Walid's marriage to Rasha Salam on July 18, 1945, the *Palestine Post*, the main English-language newspaper in Palestine added the title *effendi*, bestowed in Ottoman times upon men of high education or social standing, to Walid's name: "The marriage took place yesterday of Walid eff. Khalidi, son of Ahmed Samih Khalidi, Principal of the Government Arab College, to Miss Rasha Salam of Beirut. The couple intend to leave for England to study at London University."[24]

According to Tarif, the marriage was "subterraneously arranged by his mother, Anbara," whom he described as a great schemer; "she encouraged Rasha and Walid to come together; she was glad to see the children of her husband's first marriage, Walid and Sulafa, marry into the Salam family."[25] After Tarif's father died prematurely in 1951, Walid became a substitute father. Tarif remembers him as "a very stern older brother, who instilled in me a number of things, in particular devotion to Palestine, and a sense of duty: Don't waste time, time is very precious."[26]

Ahmad Samih and Anbara Salam al-Khalidi lived with their children in the principal's residence of the Arab College in the neighborhood of Bab al-Zahira north of the Old City until 1935, when they moved to the new premises of the Arab College on Jabal al-Mukabbir in the southern outskirts of Jerusalem. Known in English as the Hill of Evil Counsel, Jabal al-Mukabbir has a different meaning in Arabic; it translates verbatim into the "Hill of the Glorifier," a reference to 'Umar ibn al-Khattab, a senior companion of the Prophet Muhammad and the second caliph of the Rashidun Caliphate. al-Khattab significantly expanded the caliphate and conquered Jerusalem in 638, granting Christians, Jews, and Muslims access to the holy city—in the Byzantine Empire, Jews had been banned from entering Jerusalem. 'Umar ibn al-Khattab traveled to Jerusalem from the south, his first view of the city was from the hill thereafter named Jabal al-Mukabbir, where he glorified God, exclaiming "Allahu Akbar" (God is great) in awe. "It was a beautiful area on the road to the British High Commissioner's residence" (Government House), remembers Rasha, and "the view overlooking the Judean hills was breathtaking, with hill upon barren hill going down all the way to the Dead Sea."[27]

The Khalidis' two-story house was located immediately behind the Arab College and was surrounded by a beautiful garden lined with pine and cypress trees. Both the college building and the house were designed by British architect Austen St Barbe Harrison, a graduate of McGill University in Montreal and the School of Architecture at University College London. The chief architect in the Department of Public Works in the civil administration of Mandate Palestine, Harrison also designed the high commissioner's residence and the Rockefeller Foundation in Jerusalem, which stand out for drawing inspiration from Islamic art and architecture. Close friends with the Egyptian architect Hassan Fathy and well connected in Arab circles in Palestine, Harrison was outraged by the British administration's brutal handling of the Great Revolt and resigned from his position in 1937.[28]

In my conversations with Tarif, he recalled the sheltered life he spent as a child growing up on the beautiful Arab College campus, overlooking the Old and the New City and the Jordan Valley, all the way to the Dead Sea which on moonlit nights shimmered from afar. From this vantage point, he added, upon climbing to the top of one of several pine trees, Jerusalem appeared to him as if painted by David Roberts, who is known for his Orientalist depictions of the Holy Land produced from sketches he made during his travels to the region in the late 1830s. For Tarif, at the time, it was his universe; the horizon of his world.[29] Despite its remote location, the Arab College was deeply affected by the ongoing political turmoil of the time. Both of the college's previous directors, Khalil al-Sakakini and Khalil Totah, had resigned following political disputes with the British authorities: al-Sakakini in 1920 to protest the appointment of Herbert Samuel, an avowed Zionist, as Britain's first high commissioner for Palestine and Transjordan; Totah in the wake of demonstrations in 1925 that were triggered by the invitation of Arthur Balfour to speak at the opening of the Hebrew University, in which a significant number of the college's students participated.[30]

Walid dates the formation of his political awareness to the Great Revolt, when he was twelve years old. In his introduction to *From Haven to Conquest*, he recalls—referring to himself in the third person singular in his capacity as the editor of the book—"the breathless incredulity, with which he, as a boy, first saw the proposed map" of the Peel Commission, which in 1937 had recommended the partition of Palestine.[31] As we have already seen, his uncle, Dr. Hussein Fakhri al-Khalidi, was among the Palestinian political leadership sent into exile to the Seychelles by the British authorities the same year.[32] His arrest most certainly affected Walid, who recalls close relations with his uncle and the correspondence he kept up with him throughout the doctor's exile, supplying him with his favorite reading—cowboy novels. These he used to purchase at the Standard Stationery bookshop, which was owned by Edward W. Said's uncle, on Jaffa Street between the Jaffa Gate and Barclays Bank, which today houses the Jerusalem Municipality.[33] As Walid recalls, he used to traverse Jerusalem's neighborhoods "on foot, bicycle, school bus, taxi, private car, and motorbike (both piggyback and sidecar)."[34] The means of transportation across Palestine increased rapidly as he came of age—when he was born in 1925, there had been only about four hundred private cars; by 1937, there were well over six thousand, with motorized vehicles, including commercial vehicles, taxis, buses, and motorbikes, totaling close to sixteen thousand.[35] To reach Saint George's School at the other end of town, Walid would take the school bus. When transportation broke down because of the general strike, he would occasionally catch a ride on the back of Henry Knesevich's motorbike (Knesevich was the bursar at the Arab College)[36] or in a sidecar, and then would use his bicycle. In my conversations with Walid, he vividly recalled seeing, on his way to school, an Arab man, a villager wearing a white *kufiya* with a black *aqeel* probably picked by British soldiers at random from the train station in Jerusalem, chained to the front of a train to deter Arab guerilla fighters from acts of sabotage, which gained prominence during the Great Revolt.[37]

The Arab College had to temporarily relocate to the Bab al-Zahira neighborhood when British troops were stationed on its premises. Anbara Salam Khalidi recalls British soldiers breaking into the Arab College and her family's home several times.[38] In our conversations, Walid, remembered one of these occasions: early one morning in the summer of 1938, the entire family, still in their pajamas, was forced out of the house by British soldiers. "There was not actual violence, but they pushed us and shouted 'Out!' 'Out!' 'Out.'"[39] The soldiers kept the members of the household in an enclosure behind barbed wire throughout the day while they searched the premises of the college for arms. It was not until Director of Education Jerome Farrell was notified and came to the college that they were released, remembered Walid. He added that it was perhaps then that Farrell took pity on him or felt guilty, because he offered to tutor him a few years later. The Khalidis' only immediate neighbor on Jabal al-Mukabbir was a Jewish agricultural school for girls. As Walid remembered, it was "run by Mrs. Ben-Zvi, whose husband, Yitzhak Ben-Zvi, was to become the second president of Israel after Chaim Weizmann. . . . When the Arab College was attacked by Zionist paramilitary groups in August 1948, these attacks were carried out from this school."[40]

Until 1948, the Khalidis' spacious salon on the ground floor of their home served as a cultural and intellectual meeting place for Palestinian Arabs and Jews, as well as other Arab and Western visitors.[41] Ahmad Samih al-Khalidi had a number of Jewish friends, among them Judah Leon Magnes. Magnes, a well-known "American Jewish nonconformist,"[42] had obtained his doctorate in philosophy from the University of Heidelberg in Germany and was a strong advocate of a binational state in Palestine. He played an important role in the Brit Shalom (Alliance for Peace), which he had cofounded in 1925 along with Samuel Hugo Bergmann, a former member of the Prague intelligentsia; Martin Buber, a prolific scholar of Austrian background renowned for his philosophy of dialogue; Salman Schocken, an influential publisher and entrepreneur from Germany; and Gershom Scholem, a philosopher of German origin, professor of Jewish mysticism at the Hebrew University, and close friend of Walter Benjamin.

Seeking peaceful coexistence among Jews and Arabs in Palestine, Brit Shalom has been associated with a spiritual trend in Zionism.[43] Originally, it also included Arthur Ruppin, the mastermind of Zionist settlement in Palestine, but he left the society following the 1929 riots, after which he worked instead toward the establishment of an independent Jewish state.

Magnes contributed significantly to the foundation of the Hebrew University and served as its first chancellor from 1924 to 1935, leading the university as its first president until 1948. In line with the Balfour Declaration, the British Mandate had recognized Hebrew along with English and Arabic as the official languages of Palestine,[44] and assisted with plans for the foundation of the Hebrew University. It considered providing similar assistance to the Arabs of Palestine, possibly by transforming the Arab College into a university, but plans to do so did not materialize.[45] As Tarif Khalidi recalls, a new building was under construction in early April 1948 when, given the fierce fighting in and around Jerusalem, he and his sister Randa were sent to Beirut. They were joined shortly afterward by their parents with their older siblings.[46] Questions of how professional ties and a personal friendship between Ahmad Samih al-Khalidi and Judah Leon Magnes might have developed in a binational state as the respective presidents of Arab and Jewish universities are lost in the possibilities of history—those futures past that did not emerge from potentiality into actuality.

Magnes left Palestine for New York City in April 1948, where he lobbied to impose a truce on the First Arab-Israeli War. In conversations with the Egyptian diplomat Mahmoud Fawzi and the representative of the Jewish Agency to the United Nations, Mordecai Eliash, Magnes proposed plans for "a federal structure called the United States of Palestine," under which two sovereign states would coexist with a common defense and foreign policy and Jerusalem as their shared capital. He sent the proposal to Robert McClintock from the U.S. State Department's Bureau of International Organization Affairs to pass it on to Count Folke Bernadotte, who had been assigned to the post of UN Security Council mediator in Palestine in line with Resolution 186, whose intent it was to "promote a peaceful adjustment of the future situation of Palestine."[47] A few months into his appointment, Bernadotte was assassinated by members of the Stern Gang, a radical offshoot of the Haganah. Hannah Arendt had fled Nazi Germany first to Paris and then to the United States—following the same route Walter Benjamin had taken a year earlier, ending his life in Port

Bou—where she would gain recognition as a political philosopher with the publication of *The Origins of Totalitarianism* in 1951. In New York, Arendt voiced her opinion in a regular column "This Means You!" in *Aufbau*, a periodical for German-speaking Jews around the globe.[48] Just days before the proclamation of the State of Israel, she published an article in *Commentary* titled "To Save the Jewish Homeland: There Is Still Time" in support of Magnes's efforts at establishing Arab-Jewish cooperation, drawing on lost traditions of council democracy in Europe.[49] She also made revisions to Magnes's federation plan, which he had shared with her.[50] Magnes suffered a stroke and died the same year in New York and was thus not able to pursue his efforts to ameliorate Arab-Jewish coexistence further. Although his vision of a United States of Palestine may sound like science fiction today, it was grounded in a lived experience in British Mandate Palestine.

As Walid told me, "Magnes visited [the] house at Jabal al-Mukabbir several times.... I have a book autographed by Magnes, which he gave to my father," he added, "about the Hebraic roots of Islam by a German orientalist."[51] The title escaped his memory, but it was perhaps Carl Brockelmann's *History of the Islamic Peoples*, published in German in 1937 and translated into English by Joel Carmichael and Moshe Perlmann in 1947, which starts with a chapter on "Arabia before Islam."[52] The friendship between Magnes and al-Khalidi has largely been forgotten. Magnes is usually studied in the context of American Jewish and Israeli history, and al-Khalidi is referred to in the context of Palestinian history, detached from each other, as if these histories were not connected. Daniel P. Kotzin's biography of Magnes does not reference al-Khalidi; however, the two men were not only colleagues but also engaged in friendly gift and intellectual exchange. In addition, they may have done more than is known to advance alternative futures. In *Educating Palestine: Teaching and Learning History Under the Mandate*, Yoni Furas quotes al-Khalidi who wrote to Magnes in the early 1930s that "the friendship of the Arab should be in the long run more precious to Jews than obtaining millions of dunams or introducing thousands of immigrants."[53] Furas also refers to a personal report about al-Khalidi written by the Haganah's intelligence unit Shai responsible for collecting intelligence on the Arab population in Palestine, which "mentions that in March 1942, he was approached by the British to serve as a mediator between the two peoples, but he refused, although the report also mentions that in September a meeting between Magnes and 'Awni 'Abd al-Hadi was held in his home."[54]

As Walid explained to me, friendship between Arabs and Jews in Palestine became more limited in his generation.[55] The growing number of Jewish immigrants in Mandate Palestine resulted in increased encounters between Arabs and Jews in but a few places—namely, Jerusalem, Jaffa, and Haifa in particular. In most cities and towns, as well as in the villages, the influx limited any engagement with the Palestinian Arab population because it went hand in hand with Zionist efforts to build a society of its own and, as such, was met by widespread protest, which culminated in the Great Revolt. The generations of his parents and grandparents, and their parents before them, Walid continued, had had more amicable and intimate relations with Jews in Jerusalem. This included the tradition of foster-brothers, according to which children of different families born nearby at around the same time were linked in kinship as a result of the practice of engaging a common wet nurse, but such relations became increasingly rare after the 1917 Balfour Declaration.[56] Walid remembered in particular Mordechai Weingarten, the *mukhtar* of the Old City's Jewish Quarter from 1935 to 1948, who like his father and grandfather before him had been a tenant of the Khalidis and maintained friendly relations with them. He also told me about Friedrich Rosen, German Orientalist and politician born to the Prussian consul in Jerusalem in 1856, and about Georg Rosen, and his wife, Serene Moscheles, who had been tenants of the Khalidis.[57] In his memoirs, Rosen recalls his milk-brother, Ismail Khalidi.[58] In addition, Walid referred to two of his ancestors, Yusuf Diya and Ruhi al-Khalidi—both contemporaries of Hajj Raghib, the former an elected member of the first Ottoman Parliament of 1877, the latter of the Ottoman Parliament of 1908—to underline the tangled histories of Arabs and Jews in Palestine as well as the dawning awareness that the Zionist movement was promoting a form of ethnoreligious nationalism that threatened peaceful coexistence.

ANCESTORS AND ROLE MODELS: YUSUF DIYA AND RUHI AL-KHALIDI

The Ottoman Empire was known for the diversity of its religious, ethnic, and linguistic composition. When the Jews of medieval Spain had to flee persecution, many found refuge in North African and Ottoman lands.[59] Outside Jerusalem, the Jewish population of Palestine remained relatively small until the 1880s, when Jewish immigration to Palestine increased because of the pogroms in Russia.

In his groundbreaking study *Before Their Diaspora*, Walid writes that the "population of the three Palestinian districts [Jerusalem, Nablus and Acre] was c. 600,000, about 10 percent of whom where Christians and the rest mostly Sunnite Muslims. The Jews numbered about 25,000; the majority were deeply religious, devoting themselves to prayer and contemplation and deliberately eschewing employment in agricultural activity."[60]

In the early phases of Jewish immigration to Palestine, financial support was provided mainly by Jewish philanthropists, such as the Rothschilds, and by the Alliance Israélite Universelle, which had been founded in Paris in 1860. This immigration took on a new dimension in 1897 when the constituent congress of the Zionist Organization (ZO, which was renamed the World Zionist Organization [WZO] in 1960), founded by Theodor Herzl, was held in Basel—the event Walid regards as the starting point of the Palestine tragedy.[61] The program of the congress opens with the words "Zionism strives for the establishment of a publicly and legally secured home in Palestine for the Jewish people" and names concrete means by which this aim might be attained, among them "the appropriate promotion of colonization with Jewish agricultures, artisans and tradesmen" and "the promotion of Jewish national feeling and consciousness."[62] The former outlines Zionism as a settler colonial movement, aligning it with European imperialism; the latter places it within the rise of nationalism worldwide, which laid the grounds for defining Jewishness as an ethnoreligious and national identity.

The son of al-Sayyid Muhammad 'Ali al-Khalidi, a deputy judge of the Jerusalem Sharia court, Yusuf Diya al-Khalidi (1829–1907) received a traditional Islamic education in Palestine. He continued his education first at a British missionary school in Malta, then in Istanbul at the Imperial Medical College, and then at the newly opened Robert College, which was founded by American missionaries in 1863, just as the Syrian Protestant College in Beirut would be in 1866. He subsequently served as Ottoman consul in the Russian (now Georgian) city of Poti on the east coast of the Black Sea, governor of Kurdistan, and three-time mayor of Jerusalem.[63] Having traveled across Europe and having taught Oriental languages at the Imperial Academy in Vienna,[64] he experienced firsthand both a contemporary surge of European anti-Semitism and the formation of Zionism as a political movement. On March 1, 1899, he sent a letter to Zadoc Kahn, chief rabbi of France (who, in that capacity, was the religious and spiritual counterpart of the Rothschilds, who had taken charge of social and political affairs in the Jewish community), with the understanding that Kahn would pass it on to Herzl.

In the letter, Yusuf Diya al-Khalidi draws attention to the fact that Palestine was already "inhabited by others"; that the Zionist movement would have a negative impact on the friendly relations that existed in Palestine across Christian, Jewish, and Muslim religious lines; and that it thus should find another location for the implementation of its aims. "In the name of God," he writes, "let Palestine be left alone."[65] Herzl responded promptly on March 19, 1899, saying that the Zionist idea was for "the well-being of the entire country" and that should "His Majesty the Sultan . . . not accept it, we will search and, believe me, we will find elsewhere what we need."[66] His letter seeks the approval of the Ottoman government and not the approval of the indigenous Arab population of Palestine, which he refers to in passing only as "the non-Jewish population of Palestine."[67] This representation—or, better, nonrepresentation—of Palestinian Arabs, echoed in the Balfour Declaration, speaks of the epistemic, and thus the historical and political, connection between Zionism and European imperialism in their view of resident natives, as is discussed by Said in *The Question of Palestine*.[68]

Ruhi al-Khalidi (1864–1913) was educated at various religious, government, and private institutions, including the Alliance Israélite Universelle in Jerusalem, which attracted a number of Christian and Muslim students from the upper classes;[69] the Sultaniyya in Beirut; the Mekteb-i Mülkiye in Istanbul; and the École des Hautes Études in Paris. Like his uncle Yusuf Diya al-Khalidi, in Istanbul, Ruhi al-Khalidi frequented the circle of Jamal al-Din al-Afghani, whose thoughts on Muslim unity and civilization made him a key representative of the Nahda while he ended his life "a virtual prisoner" of Sultan Abdul Hamid II.[70] Ruhi al-Khalidi was appointed consul in Bordeaux and, in 1908, was elected as a representative for Jerusalem in the Ottoman Parliament, which in turn elected him in 1912 as its vice president. He was a prolific and polyglot scholar who ventured into fields ranging from linguistics and comparative literature to Islamic history, international politics, and studies on Zionism and was also a close friend of the Palestinian educator Khalil al-Sakakini.[71] Before World War I, he wrote the first substantive Arabic-language study of Zionism, *al-Sayunizm aw al-mas'ala al-saahiyuniyya* (Zionism or the Zionist question), which remained unfinished and was published only in 2020, more than a century after he died.[72] Walid had published an article about this study in 1988[73] and was editing the complete manuscript for publication and writing an introduction to it when I visited him in Cambridge. It describes the biblical and Talmudic religious roots of Zionism as well as the rise of anti-Semitism across Europe, in particular in Tsarist Russia, as compared with the historical tolerance of Islam, and documents the extent and diversity of the Zionist movement in Palestine. It shows an early awareness of the threat that the Zionist movement posed to the Ottoman Empire, its Arab provinces, and Palestine, in particular. al-Khalidi saw in the Second Constitutional Era of the Ottoman Empire a new beginning, which was made possible after the 1908 Young Turk Revolution, which had forced Abdul Hamid II to restore the constitutional monarchy and allowed, for the first time in the empire's history, the formation of political parties. The Ottoman Empire, he concluded, was capable of limiting Zionist activity in Palestine, especially given that the majority of Jews from Russia preferred the United States, which was still open to mass immigration, over Palestine as a destination.

Poetic Affinities: Breton, Césaire, and Kafka in Jerusalem

Given that Walid was part of the generation born after the 1917 Balfour Declaration, his contact with Jews in Palestine was infrequent. At Saint George's School, the majority of students were Christian and Muslim Palestinians; there were a few Jewish students, with whom relations were friendly but limited to school, as Walid recalled.[74] Walid did not sit for the Palestine matriculation examination there, opting instead to take the University of London matriculation examination, which was administered by the Department of Education in Mandate Palestine. In preparation, he was tutored in private by Jerome Farrell, who was director of education after Bowman, from 1936 to 1946, a classicist by training and a Cambridge graduate. Instead of heading north to Bab al-Zahira, where Saint George's was located, Walid was now going three or four times a week to Farrell's house in the German Colony. The neighborhood, set up by the German Templars in the 1860s in the southwestern part of the New City, close to the railway station, housed the Sporting Club, which featured a swimming pool and tennis courts, and was popular with British officials.[75] *The Palestine Post* lists Walid among the successful candidates of the First Division in August 1943.[76] As Walid explained to me, the fact that he was in the First Division (the equivalent of honors) is deceptive because this was his second attempt. "You will be amused to know that I passed my second try only because my father (who had been furious at my earlier failure) had sent me to a brilliant young Rabbi who thoroughly tutored me in Math starting with such basics as 2 + 2 = 4. The Rabbi, unfortunately I can't remember his name, was recommended by a Mr. Bloom, a senior Jewish colleague of my father at the Mandatory Department of Education," remembered Walid. "I used to go to his house in West Jerusalem for private lessons in his small book-lined dining room several times a week."[77]

Walid continued to study for his bachelor's degree in Greek and Roman history and Latin from the University of London, administered by the Department of Education in Mandate Palestine, because travel to the United Kingdom was impossible during World War II. Upon finishing school, he briefly taught history at al-Ummah, a Palestinian private school in Upper Baq'a, a mixed Christian and Muslim neighborhood south of the German Colony. The school was run by one of his former teachers at Saint George's School, Shukri Harami. According to a family anecdote related to me by Tarif,[78] who also attended al-Ummah, Walid arrived for his first day of teaching wearing shorts. Given that some of his students were not much younger than he was, they mistook their new teacher for one of their cohort—among them Katy Antonius's daughter Soraya, also known as Tutu, who would later write two novels set in Mandate Palestine.[79]

At around the same time, in the fall of 1943, Jabra Ibrahim Jabra returned from his studies at the University of Cambridge, where he had obtained a bachelor's degree in English literature. Jabra knew Walid as the son of the principal of the Arab College who had selected him for a scholarship to study abroad.[80] Six years Jabra's junior, Walid was at the time immersed in English literature, in part due to his having failed his mathematics exam the previous year, which meant he had to study all his subjects, including English, again. Walid recalls reading Shakespeare's plays as well as Byron, Keats, Milton, Shelley, Spencer, and Wordsworth. At the same time, he was studying Latin with Farrell.[81] He read Cicero, Horace, and Ovid, but was riveted by Virgil, and translated "Dido's Passion," part of Book IV of the *Aeneid* from Latin into English in hexameter. At Farrell's suggestion, he took it to *Forum*, an English-language magazine issued by the Public Information Office in Jerusalem for publication.[82] As Walid explained to me, the publication of his translation "coincided with Jabra's return from the UK. My name would immediately have identified me as the son of . . . 'Abu Walid' [which translates as 'the Father of Walid']—his principal at the Arab College. We must have met soon after. . . . Wolfgang [Hildesheimer] would most likely have read the poem about this time and this also helps in dating the beginning of our relationship."[83]

The same year, in 1943, Wolfgang Hildesheimer started to work for the Public Information Office where, among other tasks, he was charged with editing *Forum*, in which he also published some of his own writing. *Forum* was directed primarily at British soldiers and administrative staff and their families stationed in the Middle East during World War II, but it was also read by Arabs and Jews educated in English. It mainly reproduced material published in London but occasionally included texts by local writers.

In April 1944, Walid published "A Little Site," another of his own poems, in *Forum*—

> Where hang the threats of mossy walls,
> And there where brooding, slowly, tide-like falls
> The grisly shadow of appalling Night,
> Where flit the breasted bats at eve, and calls
> Of screeching owls thrill through the shrouded light;
> Thither my soul in melancholy flight,
> Goes through the sadness of that ancient gate,
> And, lingering, hovers o'er one little site,
> And weeps and weeps, my darling Karma, at thy fate.[84]

The poem is about the tragic death of his youngest half-sister Karma who "died in a harrowing and tragic accident, when, at age eighteen months, she slipped into the garden unnoticed by anyone and there fell into a small ornamental pond," as Anbara Salam Khalidi recalls with a heavy heart in her memoirs.[85] Jabra had experienced a similar loss—that of his only sister, Susan, who had died at the age of nine in 1938, and whose death he describes in his autobiography as coinciding with a new stage in his life, when he was on the threshold of becoming a writer.[86] Having already published literary translations from English into Arabic as well as a number of English-language poems of his own, he must have related strongly to Walid's attempts at poetry. To Jabra and Wolfgang, as well to other members of the ecumenical circle in the early 1940s, Walid was known as a young man whose mind was buzzing with literature—a side of him not much known today (figure 2.2).

These poetic affinities developed in pressing political circumstances. The front covers of the two issues of *Forum* in which Walid had his translation of Virgil and his poem published announce a lecture series on British Traditions by "Major A. S. Eban" that Walid remembers attending at the British Council (figure 2.3).[87] Born Aubrey Solomon Meir Abban in Cape Town, South Africa, Abba Eban was a Cambridge graduate in Oriental languages and classics and a

2.2 Wolfgang Hildesheimer, Walid Khalidi, and Rasha Salam, Judean Hills, 1945. Academy of Arts, Berlin, WHA 1437.

2.3 *Forum* 7, no. 17 (April 14, 1944), cover page.
Courtesy of Walid Khalidi.

committed Zionist. During World War II, he worked for Chaim Weizmann at the ZO in London and then served as assistant adviser on Jewish affairs—Albert Hourani's counterpart—to the Office of the British Minister of State resident in Cairo, where he met both Albert and Cecil Hourani.[88] Eban subsequently pursued a career in diplomacy, serving as liaison officer with the UN Special Committee on Palestine in 1947, playing a key role in attaining approval of Resolution 181 in favor of partition and, later, as Israel's foreign minister from 1966 to 1974.[89] Walid's and Eban's paths crossed again in the aftermath of the 1967 War, when Walid addressed the Fifth Emergency Special Session of the UN General Assembly.

Jabra captures some of these historical circumstances in his first novel, *Surakh fi layl tawil* (*Cry in a Long Night*),[90] which he wrote in Jerusalem in 1946 in English. The novel has never been published in its original English version, and the original manuscript is likely lost. While on a fellowship at Harvard in the early 1950s, Jabra translated it into Arabic,[91] and it was published in a first edition in Baghdad in 1955, and in a second edition in Beirut in 1988. Jabra meant to dedicate his novel to "Racha, Sally, Waleed and Wolf/Once together, now by cruel chance dispersed," as he wrote in a letter to Wolfgang from Harvard in 1952, to which we shall return.[92] This dedication, however, does not appear neither in the first nor in the novel's second edition.

Cry in a Long Night, like much of Jabra's writing, is interspersed with autobiographical elements. Like Jabra, its protagonist, Amin Samma', is a Christian Arab who grew up in poverty in a Palestinian village. His encounter with "the town"—Jerusalem is never mentioned by name—is marked by mixed feelings, a blend of attraction and disgust, as he affirms his sense of belonging to "the town." Bashir Abu-Manneh reads *Cry* as Jabra's "revolutionary-artistic manifesto," declaring "the birth of a new artistic project" in which redemption is achieved "in-and-through this emergent agency."[93] Abu-Manneh recognizes the book as "the first artistically compelling Palestinian novel," but points to "the total absence of both Palestine and the colonial threat" in it.[94] Although I agree with the significance of Jabra's novel as an early expression of literary modernism in Palestine, I do not see a complete absence of Palestine or the colonial threat in it—quite the contrary. As Jabra's rendering of the title as *Cry in a Long Night* suggests, it is reminiscent of André Breton's cry for freedom from societal restraints in his *Manifestoes of Surrealism* and Aimé Césaire's cry of poverty and revolt in his *Cahier d'un retour au pays natal* (*Notebook of a Return to the Native Land*), with which Césaire embraced black identity and culture and laid the foundations of the Négritude movement against colonialism.[95] However, just as Jerusalem is referred to only as "the town," the references to the historical circumstances in which the novel is enmeshed come in disguise, similar to hidden truths revealed in dreams in Surrealist fashion. Considered in the specific context of the social milieu Jabra moved in after his return from the University of Cambridge in 1943—namely the ecumenical circle in Jerusalem—its scathing critique of Palestinian society and the political turmoil it faced in the last years of the British Mandate are striking. *Cry* opens with a reference to a policeman checking the narrator's identity card, a practice increasingly common as Jerusalem was divided into different security zones by the British authorities as the "years of fragile tranquility," as Albert Hourani had phrased it, came to an end. The description in *Cry* of the Al Yasser family and its obsession with its family history is a caricature of the Palestinian political elite, whose longstanding notable families were failing to live up to the demands of the present.

> My sister loved the history of her family. My whole life, I haven't known anyone like her—someone who sacrifices themself and erases their personality in order to live in the glory of their ancestors. Ever since she gained awareness of her own existence—more than thirty years ago—I cannot recall her thinking of anything else but the Al Yasser family: the Al Yassers and the Fatimids, the Al Yassers and the Ottomans, the Al Yassers and Napoleon, the Al Yassers and Mohammad Ali Pasha, the Al Yassers here, the Al Yassers there . . . she doesn't love anything more than the secrets of their lives, the dirty laundry that filled the house.[96]

The depiction of the two sisters, Inayat and Rakzan Al Yasser, draws on real figures, perhaps among them Anbara and Rasha Salam Khalidi who, like the Al Yasser daughters, were separated by a significant age difference. In the prologue to her memoirs, Anbara relates that she destroyed many of her private papers when her father was "twice arrested and taken to the military tribunal which the Turkish authorities had set up during the First World War in the town of Aley, Lebanon, to try Arab nationalists."[97] Jabra may very well have heard this story directly from Anbara or her sister. In *Cry*, Rakzan burns the family's precious library and papers in an attempt to live in the present and not the past, as the protagonist is set free to determine his own life as an artist. The novel culminates in his walking the streets of "the town" at the end of a long night and the beginning of a new life. It echoes ideas of renewal as expressed by T. S. Eliot—particularly in his essay "Tradition and the Individual Talent" (1919). Eliot was introduced to an Arabic-speaking audience by Louis Awad in January 1946 in *al-Katib al-misri* (The Egyptian writer).[98] One of the first Arabic-language postwar journals, published between 1945 and 1948 by the Egyptian Press and Publishing House owned by the Jewish al-Harari family,[99] *al-Katib al-misri* was edited by Taha Hussein. Known as a promoter of cultural exchange and new talent, he included translations of world literature and literary criticism by authors such as T. S. Eliot, James Joyce, Franz Kafka, and Jean-Paul Sartre, alongside works by promising Arab writers.[100] Drawn to Eliot, Jabra would later argue to "take from heritage what is alive and leave what is dead to the academics, about whom Rimbaud said that they were more dead than any fossil. Heritage has a power that we assume but we must add to it a new power so that modernity may shoot forward like an arrow and not in a circular, self-sufficient way."[101]

Furthermore, Jabra would depict Arab poets as "voices crying in an intellectual desert," as he called for a rebirth of Arabic culture and anticipated some of the self-criticism Arab intellectuals were to voice after the Arab defeats of 1948 and, in a more pronounced way, after the 1967 War.[102] The explosions described at the end of *Cry*, caused by Rakzan's setting fire to the family's palace and library, reads like dystopian fiction, but it is grounded in a lived experience, namely what Jabra and his contemporaries experienced when the King David Hotel was blown up, when the first explosion was followed by another even larger blast: "At that moment, I heard a loud explosion. It made my teeth chatter. The ground started to shake under my feet. I looked out the window; it was bright daylight. . . . Shortly after there was the sound of another explosion. The earth shook again, and a column of smoke rose on the horizon—behind the houses and the trees I saw from my window—from which a huge blaze tore through the sky."[103]

Jabra spent much time at the Khalidis' house on the premises of his former college, where he read parts of his novel in the making to his friends. Walid also visited Jabra at his house, which we will look at in greater detail later. Walid does not recall having ever visited Wolfgang at home, nor having met his family. Wolfgang, however, did introduce Walid to some of his Jewish friends—Walid recalled meeting Wolf Rosenberg and Max Brod.[104]

74 THE TIME BEFORE 1948

Rosenberg was one of Wolfgang's oldest friends; they knew each other from their schooldays in Germany. He and Wolfgang shared a deep interest in music; like Wolfgang, he was at odds with the Zionist movement and would return to Germany after World War II.[105] Brod, the renowned literary executer, biographer, and friend of Franz Kafka who had not followed the author's instructions to burn his manuscripts, and instead published them after Kafka's death, had emigrated from Prague to Palestine in 1939, after Nazi Germany occupied Czechoslovakia. He subsequently worked at the Habimah in Tel Aviv, which was to become Israel's national theater.

As Walid remembered, he read Kafka's *The Trial*, published posthumously by Brod in 1925 and translated into English in 1937, on Wolfgang's suggestion, and he later recommended the novel to his colleagues at the American University of Beirut.[106] Kafka has received significant attention in the Arab world since the 1930s, when his texts circulated in francophone Surrealist circles in Cairo, with readers identifying strongly with their themes of alienation, persecution, and injustice; however, this reception has only recently made its way into global Kafka studies.[107] Jens Hanssen explains: "Around the time that Arendt carried Kafka's and Benjamin's legacies to America, [Egyptian Surrealist writer Georges] Henein, who had studied at the Sorbonne in Paris, took Kafka eastwards to Egypt,"[108] where Taha Hussein played an important role in making his works accessible in Arabic translation, notably in *al-Katib al-misri*.[109] Brod and Hildesheimer, too, can be said to have carried Kafka eastward to Mandate Palestine, where he was read not only in German-Jewish circles but also by Wolfgang's Arab friends, and Walid in particular.

Battles over who "owns" Kafka have repeatedly made headlines, significantly in a trial at the Supreme Court of Israel in 2016, which ruled that Brod's estate, including Kafka's manuscripts (which Brod's heirs had wanted to sell to Germany's National Literature Archive in Marbach) must be handed over to the National Library of Israel in Jerusalem.[110] Brod's biography of Kafka was published in 1937, a few years after Benjamin's influential "Franz Kafka: On the Tenth Anniversary of His Death."[111] Although Benjamin set out to read Kafka as a universal writer, on par with other modernist authors, Benjamin's friend Scholem argued that Kafka had no position in the continuum of German literature but rather belonged "in the continuum of Jewish literature."[112] Scholem arranged a meeting between Benjamin and Magnes in Paris in 1927 in an attempt to convince Benjamin to move to Jerusalem and join the newly established School of Humanities at the Hebrew University as a university lecturer of German and French literature, a prospect Benjamin considered over many years. Benjamin received funding from Magnes to study Hebrew in Berlin, but he never took up Hebrew in earnest and kept postponing his trip to Jerusalem.[113] He eventually admitted to Scholem that he had "come to know living Judaism in absolutely no form other than you."[114] Scholem's conception of Kafka as belonging to Jewish literature was shared by Brod in his biography of Kafka and was a decisive element in the ruling of Israel's Supreme Court. Unlike Brod and Scholem, Wolfgang read Kafka along Benjamin's lines—as part and parcel of a global modernism. He contributed a translation of Kafka's "Eleven Sons" to Fred Marnau's *New Road: Directions in European Art and Letters*, which was published in London in 1946,[115] and he would later name Kafka as one of the major influences on his own writing.[116] Meanwhile, political tensions in Palestine escalated into armed conflict at the end of World War II. As the Anglo-American Committee of Inquiry was formed to consider the question of European Jewry and its impact on the Palestine Question, an eerie calm reminiscent of Kafka's fictional worlds filled Jerusalem's streets.

THE ARAB OFFICE AND THE ANGLO-AMERICAN COMMITTEE OF INQUIRY

The Anglo-American Committee of Inquiry convened in Jerusalem in March 1946. It comprised six British and six American members in addition to research assistants and secretaries.[117] Its meetings with representatives of both the Arab and Jewish political leadership took place behind closed doors at the Young Men's Christian Association (YMCA), while "British soldiers with tommy guns guarded the entrances and exits, and the streets outside were patrolled by armed tanks," as Bartley C. Crum, one of the committee's American members, writes in *A Personal Account of Anglo-American Diplomacy in Palestine and the Middle East*, published in 1947.[118] In the King David Hotel across the street, where Crum and his colleagues were housed, life went on seemingly undisturbed. "After two days in Jerusalem," writes Crum, he "felt like a character in a Hollywood mystery film . . . in the center of an extraordinary socio-political ferment."[119] His report includes brief summaries of the Arab and Jewish testimony given before the committee. The Arab representatives included Hourani and Shukeiri from the

Arab Office, along with Jamal Husseini and 'Awni 'Abd al-Hadi of the Arab Higher Committee (AHC). The representatives of the Jewish side included Moshe Sharett, the head of the Jewish Agency's political department, who would later serve as Israel's first foreign minister and second prime minister; Golda Meir, a leading figure of the Histadrut who replaced Sharett as head of the Jewish Agency's political department when he was detained during Operation Agatha and who later served as Israel's second foreign minister and fourth prime minister; Chaim Weizmann; David Ben-Gurion; and Judah Leon Magnes.

Crum refers to Hourani as "Mrs. Antonius' outstanding protégé, Director of the Arab Office in Jerusalem, a friend of Beeley and one of Crossman's former students," and recalls that he "made an extremely competent summation of the Arab case."[120] Sir Harold Beeley was the secretary of the Anglo-American Committee of Inquiry. Like Hourani, Beeley was born into a Mancunian merchant family and had studied modern history at Oxford. At the outbreak of World War II, he worked with Arnold J. Toynbee at Chatham House. He later pursued a career in diplomacy. Richard Crossman was a professor of classics at Oxford before he moved into politics and served as a member of the Anglo-American Committee of Inquiry. In *Palestine Mission: A Personal Record*, which, like Crum's account, was published in 1947, Crossman describes the atmosphere of the King David Hotel as "terrific, with private detectives, Zionist agents, Arab sheikhs, special correspondents, and the rest, all sitting about discreetly overhearing each other."[121] With Zionist agents and Arab sheikhs, the dichotomies between modern intelligence agencies and traditional modes of governance are all laid out, as foreign correspondents and British private detectives à la Sherlock Holmes assume the role of objective observers. Seeing, after all, is an act of choice. Crossman's description is representative of what the British and American members of the committee wanted to see as they dealt with Palestine. As Edward W. Said argues in *The Question of Palestine*, the country in question has "always played a special role in the imagination and in the political will of the West,"[122] while the multifaceted act of "making statements about it, authorizing views of it, describing it, teaching it, settling it, ruling over it," is a central feature of what Said defines as Orientalism.[123] Crossman's personal record also includes a few lines about Hourani, who was formerly his student at Oxford, and a reference to the ecumenical circle. In a manner similar to that of his portrayal of Arabs and Jews at the hotel, these lines are not free of prejudice: they reduce women to their beautiful appearance, while the young men Crossman met are set apart from Arab society at large as "westernized":

> To-night I dined in an Arab restaurant with Albert Hourani, the beautiful Luli Abu[l] Huda, and some of their friends. We talked until 2 a.m. Hourani seems to be in charge of preparing the case to be presented by the Arab Office. . . . He and his friends are highly critical in a tolerant sort of way of the present Arab leadership and its methods of propaganda. These young men have understood Britain and grasped that the most effective propaganda is contacts in the right places, combined with quiet documentation which conceals the fact that it is propaganda. But they are actually more intransigent in their policy than the old leaders. Partly, I suppose, because they are westernized and so compensate for any western bias by an excess of nationalism. But even more, because they realize that the present social structure won't last long and that the new political movements will be ultra-nationalistic.[124]

Crum, too, recalls "the young Arab intellectuals [he] had met at the King David," who, he adds, "were conspicuously absent" at the committee hearings.[125] Although the committee convened behind closed and guarded doors, its informal meetings with Hourani, Abul Huda, and their young Arab intellectual friends, as well as with Jewish men and women in Jerusalem, Tel Aviv, and on the kibbutzim they visited during their stay, proved to be just as important. If Jerusalem had indeed once been an ordinary city of cosmopolitan character, by the middle of 1946, it had become "a center of postwar intrigue and the King David Hotel its epicenter," while the hotel bar served as "the Best Informed Bar in Jerusalem."[126]

Having recently obtained his degree from the University of London, Walid may very well have been among Hourani's "young Arab intellectual friends" who met with Crum. He was hired as Hourani's research assistant, along with Burhan Dajani, who had graduated from the American University of Beirut in economics. Wasfi Tell was another young man at the office.[127] Walid describes him as "a handsome swarthy young man in his mid-twenties of ramrod posture with a crew cut, wearing a British Army uniform with the rank of captain," who "seemed to act as Musa [Alami]'s aide-de-camp, carrying his briefcase and opening the car door for him," but he then ran away with Alami's Damascene

78   THE TIME BEFORE 1948

wife, Saadiyah Jabiri.[128] He later served as prime minister of Jordan a number of times, until he was assassinated by Palestinians in Cairo in 1971 for his role in Black September in 1970. After the West Bank and East Jerusalem were occupied by Israel in the 1967 War, Jordan had become the main base for the Palestine Liberation Organization (PLO). As tensions increased between the PLO and its fedayeen on one side and the Jordanian Armed Forces on the other, thousands of Palestinian refugees were expelled from Jordan and the PLO's leadership decamped to Lebanon.

The early 1940s were formative years for Walid. His work at the Arab Office provided him with professional experience in institution building, on which he would draw years later in Beirut when he cofounded the Institute for Palestine Studies.[129] Too young and inexperienced in 1946 to have been directly involved in the hearings convened by the Anglo-American Committee of Inquiry in Jerusalem, he contributed to compiling the appendixes of the report the Arab Office prepared under Hourani's directorship, which was published by the Arab Office in London in 1947 as *The Future of Palestine*.[130] Some of Walid's research would also result in articles he was to publish in Lebanese newspapers, notably "Fi filastin 15 hizban siyasiyyan yahudiyyan" (In Palestine: 15 Jewish political parties), which was published in four parts in *Beirut al-masa'* in 1948.[131] In addition, he was charged with building up the office's library, which led him to bookshops across Arab and Jewish neighborhoods in Jerusalem, and with communicating with representatives of Western news media, "which meshed in very nicely," he writes, "with my beat at the King David Hotel bar."[132]

The ecumenical circle continued to meet at the bar despite increased political tensions. Walid vividly remembers the last time they all came together for a belated celebration of his twenty-first birthday and the first anniversary of his and Rasha's marriage, the evening before the King David Hotel bombing: "After dinner, we walked out into the corridor, Afif [Bulos] was singing Auld Lang Syne, a sentimental song. It was a long corridor from which you could go up to the ground floor, but the corridor also led to the outside, to a side street of the hotel. The Irgun terrorists came from the opposite direction the next day, they came by car from this side street, then entered the corridor, carrying cans of milk full of explosives."[133]

Afif Bulos was a talented singer immersed in both Arab and Western musical traditions.[134] Socially outgoing and openly gay, in such a natural and fluid way that everyone around him forgot that homosexuality was not commonly accepted at the time,[135] Afif was friends with a number of British civil servants in Palestine and always ready to entertain his companions with some singing. He compiled a number of travel guides together with Stephan Hanna Stephan, an ethnographer who worked at the library of the Palestine Archaeological Museum and at the Khalidiyyah.[136] With titles such as "This Is Palestine" and "Palestine by Rail and Road," these travel guides assert Palestinian agency in the representation of Palestine to an audience of anglophone travelers, primarily British and Commonwealth civil servants and soldiers stationed in the Middle East during World War II.[137] As Jabra recalls in *Princesses' Street*,

> throughout 1944 and 1945, Jerusalem teemed with British soldiers, a faceless group that was difficult to distinguish one from the other, and one was not concerned to distinguish them. But some high-ranking British officers intentionally wanted to meet as many educated Arabs as possible. My friend Afif Boulus wanted to meet these educated officers too, and he invited some of them to parties at his elegant home in al-Baqa neighborhood, along with a select group of Arab men and women. He believed at that time that many of those Englishmen would soon have high positions in English political life, and we had to influence them so that they might know that we were a civilized people and rather distinguished, contrary to what the European Jews who often mixed with them suggested.[138]

Among the British friends Jabra made at Afif's house were Lawrence Durrell, who would become famous for his *Alexandria Quartet* (1957–1960), and Michael Clark, whom he would meet again in Baghdad. Clark was also friends with Walid, recalls Jabra, who then was "deeply knowledgeable about English poetry" and "amazingly fluent in English, although he had not yet gone to study at Oxford."[139] Afif was the oldest of six brothers. Their father, David Bulos, had studied medicine at the Syrian Protestant College. Like Naim Cotran (mentioned in the introduction), he was recruited by the British colonial authorities into the Sudan Medical Department. Appointed to medical positions in Acre, Haifa, and Gaza after World War I, he served the British as senior medical officer in the Department of Health in Jerusalem.[140] Of the other Bulos brothers, or "the Buloi," as Walid referred to them, Suhail and Nassib would also join the ecumenical circle from time to time. Suhail, the youngest, was Walid's classmate at Saint George's School in Jerusalem before he left to study medicine at the American University of Beirut. He later continued his medical training abroad and became a successful orthopedic surgeon at the American University of Beirut. After 1948, Suhail stayed in touch with the Khalidis and Sally in Beirut, where he was joined by his mother and brothers after his parents' forced expulsion from their home in Jerusalem's western neighborhood of Upper Baq'a and his father's premature death.[141] Nassib was a graduate of the Jerusalem Law School and the University of London,[142] and he became a successful lawyer in Beirut. In his memoirs, he recalls his political ambitions and journalistic work for *al-Difa'*, by then the leading Palestinian newspaper. Nassib boasts that a certain Katy Antonius embraced his political ambitions and "had developed a 'tendre' " for him that he "was more than ready to reciprocate."[143] Nassib describes Walid as "tall, good looking in the Byronic tradition, and in manner and dress, consciously or unconsciously, he modelled himself on the romantic English poets, was it Shelley perhaps?"[144] Jabra, too, compares Walid to Shelley, mentioning "the ethereal fire that was always burning in Shelley's eyes and voice, as it was in Walid's eyes and voice at the time."[145]

Next to Afif, Walid recalls that F. W. G. Blenkinsop joined them at the bar the evening before the King David Hotel bombing. Another Oxford graduate, he was a senior official in the British administration and had his office in the King David. A memorandum he circulated on "2 November (Balfour Day) 1944" that railed against "that fateful mental aberration known to history as the Balfour Declaration" is archived in the Middle East Centre at St Antony's College, University of Oxford.[146] The next afternoon, Blenkinsop was buried under the debris of the hotel's southern wing. The *Manchester Guardian* listed him as the last British victim found dead, with twenty people, almost all Arabs, still missing on July 30, 1946.[147] He was laid to rest on Mount Zion.[148]

A number of other British friends would sometimes join the ecumenical circle at the bar, among them John Sheringham, the British Vice-Consul in Jerusalem and a trained Hebraist. He was married to George Hourani's sister-in-law, Yvette Haddad, "who was a francophone Egyptian Copt, a poet and journalist."[149] As Walid related to me in our conversations, he told him about Rabbi Zvi Yehuda Kook who along his father Rabbi Abraham Isaac Kook—whom we have come across as a keynote speaker next to High Commissioner Herbert Samuel and Hebrew poet Hayim Bialik at the inauguration of the Hebrew University—played a key role in the foundation of religious Zionism, aligning non-Zionist Orthodox Jews with the secular Zionist leadership. Kook became the spiritual leader of the Gush Emunim, the right-wing settler colonial movement that gained ground in the occupied West Bank, Gaza Strip, and the Golan Heights after the 1967 War. In addition, Richard Chichester, John Briance, and Richard Catling would come to the King David Hotel bar for drinks, small talk, and insider views on the future of Palestine. Chichester was the aide-de-camp to Alan Cunningham, the high commissioner for Palestine and Transjordan, while Briance and Catling worked as intelligence officers for the Criminal Investigation Department. Briance was in charge of anti-Arab terrorism and Catling was in charge of anti-Jewish terrorism, as Walid recalls.[150] A number of these friends at the fringes of the ecumenical circle figure in a group portrait taken in the Khalidis' garden around the time of Walid and Rasha's marriage (figure 2.4).

2.4 Photograph in the garden of the Khalidis' house, Arab College, Jerusalem, 1945; back row: Nassib Bulos, Salma Salam, Assem Salam, Sulafa Khalidi, John Briance; front row: Afif Bulos, Albert Hourani, Suhail Bulos, Haifa Salam, F. W. G. Blenkinsop, Jabra Ibrahim Jabra, John Sheringham; seated: Walid Khalidi and Rasha Salam.
Courtesy of Walid Khalidi.

FOLLOWING THE EVENTS IN PALESTINE FROM BEIRUT

Walid and Rasha left Jerusalem for Beirut shortly after the King David Hotel bombing. As Rasha relates in her memoirs, because Walid did not get along with Shukeiri, who was now in charge of research at the Arab Office in Jerusalem, he resigned and accepted a job at the U.S. legation in Beirut "in the hope that he could help in conveying to his superiors the real state of feelings among Arabs to[ward] Truman's pro-Zionist policies."[151] The legation had opened in Beirut in 1943, after Lebanon achieved independence; it was eventually granted embassy status in 1952 and served as regional headquarters for a number of U.S. agencies until the Lebanese Civil War.[152] In addition to working at the legation, Walid taught English at the Makassed and wrote articles on Palestinian and Arab affairs for Lebanese newspapers.[153] He had come a long way since the days, only a few years earlier, when he was consumed by English literature, translating Virgil, and trying his own hand at writing poetry. In October 1948, Rasha gave birth to the Khalidis' first child, whom they named Ahmad Samih, after Walid's father.

While Walid and Rasha followed the events in Palestine from Beirut, Walid's father remained in Jerusalem, where he opened the Arab College to Palestinian families who had fled Jerusalem's western neighborhoods, among them David Bulos and his wife,[154] and placed it under the protection of the Red Cross Delegation. Given the deteriorating situation in and around Jerusalem, he and Anbara had sent their youngest children to stay with Walid and Rasha. In April 1948, they, too, eventually fled to Beirut with their elder children, temporarily, or so they thought.[155] On the night of August 16, a skirmish broke out close to Government House, formerly the British high commissioner's residence, between the Egyptian Army and Jewish forces under the command of Moshe Dayan. The Jewish forces withdrew to the Jewish Agricultural School, located next to the Arab College. From there, they launched an attack on the Arab College the next day. The remaining staff of the college, including its bursar, Henry Knesevich, and the families who had found temporary refuge there, were forcibly removed. When the United Nations restored the status quo of the security zone, Knesevich was able to return to the college in the company of UN observers and Arab and Jewish commanders. He found the premises severely damaged, looted, and vandalized, as he wrote in a detailed "report on the violation of the Government Arab College by Jewish armed forces," addressed to Ahmad Samih al-Khalidi and dated September 21, 1948.[156] Today, the Arab College premises are used as a Jewish Agency immigration center.

Walid's uncle, Dr. Hussein Fakhri al-Khalidi, general secretary of the AHC, remained in Jerusalem.[157] When, in April 1948, Zionist troops attacked the city's western neighborhoods, which had been shelled repeatedly since the bombing of the Semiramis Hotel in January, he played a key role in safeguarding the Sheikh Jarrah neighborhood north of the Old City, sending numerous appeals to the British, who were still stationed in the country and officially in charge, as well as reports to Hajj Amin in Cairo, through telegrams that were often intercepted by Zionist intelligence and that today are kept in Israeli state archives.[158] Throughout 1948, Walid worked from Beirut as his uncle's private secretary. Hussein Fakhri al-Khalidi later served as the custodian and supervisor of the Haram al-Sharif under Jordanian rule. He became Jordan's minister of foreign affairs and was briefly its prime minister in 1957.

Walid's grandfather, Hajj Raghib, stayed in Palestine until his death in 1952. As Tarif Khalidi writes,

> in 1948, living alone and stubbornly refusing all offers to leave, Hajj Raghib was bundled out [of his house in Tal al-Rish near Jaffa,] by force by a Jewish platoon and tossed onto the street. A Jewish photographer came by and took a picture of this dignified old man sitting on a chair in the middle of nowhere. . . . the Hajj feebly waving the photographer away with his hand. Later the photographer, no doubt thinking it exotic, put it in his shop window where it was eventually bought by a family friend who was passing by and distributed it here and there among family members. The Palestinian *Nakba* personified.[159]

Hajj Raghib eventually left Jaffa with the help of the Red Cross in July 1948 and joined his son in Beirut. Jaffa had been "earmarked in the 1947 United Nations Partition Plan as an Arab enclave in the Jewish dominated Coastal Plain," but in April 1948 the Irgun "launched what was to be its major offensive of the war—the assault on Jaffa," described in detail by Benny Morris.[160] "A once thriving center of Arab modernity, Jaffa has since become a monument of loss, and a memory of what could have been," writes Nadi Abusaada.[161] All that remains has become part of a southern suburb of Tel Aviv. A photograph taken in late 1948 or early 1949, which caught my attention when I visited Walid in his house in Cambridge, Massachusetts, shows Walid in Beirut with his firstborn son, his father, and his grandfather. Hajj Raghib would later return to Palestine to live in Nablus in the northern part of what became known as the West Bank, which between 1948 and 1967 was under Jordanian control, with one of Walid's uncles, Dr. Hassan Shukri al-Khalidi, who had served as medical officer in Jaffa during the British Mandate. Hajj Raghib died in 1952. He was buried in the family enclosure in the Muslim cemetery under the eastern wall of the Old City of Jerusalem, outside the Gate of Mercy, facing the Mount of Olives.

CHAPTER 3

RASHA SALAM KHALIDI

"A Non-Conformist Moslem Arab Woman"

"JERUSALEM WAS JOY"

"Rasha was very much a child of Anbara. She inherited Anbara's liberal outlook, she was even more liberal than Anbara," remembers Tarif Khalidi.[1] The youngest of thirteen children, Rasha was born to Salim Ali Salam and Kalsum Barbir in Beirut on March 15, 1922. A "leading citizen" of the populous quarter of Museitbeh at the south-western end of the city, Salim Ali Salam, also known as Abu Ali and, in official contexts, as Salim Bey, was "a successful merchant and an active public figure."[2] With his spacious mansion in the heart of Museitbeh, overlooking the harbor, he set the Salam family apart as notables. Having attended both Muslim and Christian schools, he sent his sons to study at the Syrian Protestant College which later became the American University of Beirut, and actively promoted modern education, in particular as a member, and for some years the president, of the Makassed Philanthropic Islamic Association.[3] His marriage to the daughter of the Barbirs and the Aghars, Beirut's leading families of Sunni Muslim clerics, provided him considerable acceptance among the traditional urban elite.[4] "Elegant in manner and possessed of a noble bearing," as the Lebanese-Palestinian historian and journalist Samir Kassir describes him, "in public [he] always dressed in the European style wearing the Ottoman tarboush."[5] "He had a powerful personality," recalls his daughter Anbara, "and was a well-respected and prominent figure in his community, with friends of every religious sect."[6] He was a deputy of the Vilayet of Beirut in the Ottoman Parliament and a loyal Ottoman citizen; at the same time, as he relates in his memoirs, which cover the final ten years of Ottoman rule, he was involved in the Arab nationalist movement, the Fatat, and supported the Arab Revolt against the Ottoman Empire, which took place between 1916 and 1918 under the leadership of Hussein ibn Ali al-Hashimi, sharif of Mecca.[7] He subsequently became a staunch opponent of the French Mandate for Syria and Lebanon, which led to his repeated arrest and put the Salams under financial constraints. Under his guidance, however, the family emerged as a powerful political force, renowned for their Arab nationalist stance and pioneering role in the emancipation of women.[8]

In her unpublished memoirs, written in the mid-1980s and titled "A Non-Conformist Moslem Arab Woman: A Century of Evolution (1873–1976)," Rasha Salam Khalidi recalls a very close relationship with her father as well as with her elder siblings, Anbara and Saeb, from whom she was separated by a generation. In 1925, at the age of three, she accompanied them to London, where their eldest brother, Ali, was studying agriculture, and their father was involved in legal battles over the drainage concessions he had obtained in Palestine's Huleh Valley during the years of Ottoman rule. The family rented a "an elegant little family pension" in Richmond, an affluent suburb bordering the River Thames.[9] A number of pictures from this stay show Rasha with Anbara, Saeb and their father, in addition to King Faisal I of Iraq, strolling through Richmond Park (figure 3.1). Salim Ali Salam had developed a close friendship with the king. A descendent of the Prophet Muhammad and third son of Sharif Hussein, King Faisal had played a key role in the Arab Revolt, accompanied by Thomas Edward Lawrence (i.e., Lawrence of Arabia), who had worked as British intelligence staff in Cairo before joining Faisal in the Arab Revolt and advising him during the Paris Peace Conference. Faisal's short-lived Syrian Arab Kingdom (March 8 to July 25, 1920), a constitutional monarchy that encompassed the *Bilad al-Sham* from the Mediterranean to the west, the Syrian desert to the East, and the Taurus Mountains in Anatolia to the north and the Red Sea in the south, was brutally crushed by France. The British and French refused to recognize an independent Syrian state, formally dividing the region into British and French mandates ratified by the League of Nations in the San Remo Conference.[10] Faisal subsequently became king of Iraq (1921–33) with British backing.

In her memoirs, Rasha, remembers her father's, and her own as a little girl, close friendship with King Faisal. Anbara, too, recalls King Faisal in her memoirs, asking what she thought about the English girl. She answered that "frankly, Your Majesty, the first thing that comes to my mind as I look at her enjoying all the pleasure of life is to ask myself: What favor has she won with God to deserve this freedom? And what sin have I, the Arab Girl, committed in God's sight

3.1 Rasha Salam with her father, Salim Ali Salam, her siblings, Anbara and Saeb, and King Faisal in Richmond Gardens, London, October 5, 1925.
Salam Collection, American University of Beirut/Library Archives.

to deserve as punishment a life filled with repression and denial?" The king is reported to have turned to her father and advised him to "keep a sharp eye on that daughter of [his]. In her heart she carries a revolution."[11] As Anbara's son, Tarif, relates in his acknowledgments to his translation into English of her memoirs, "the two years she spent in England (1925–27) had a formative influence on her activism [as an early Arab feminist], allowing her to observe first hand the role that English women were beginning to play in public life."[12]

In Beirut, Rasha recalls sharing a room with Anbara and their being inseparable. She dates the end of her childhood to 1929, when Anbara, newly wed to Ahmad Samih al-Khalidi, left Beirut for Jerusalem.[13] Rasha attended the Syrian National School, now the Ahliah School, at the elementary level, then the Lycée de Jeunes Filles (Mission Laïque Française) and the Lycée de Garçons in Beirut, because the girls' school did not provide baccalaureate classes. She traveled frequently with her family to Palestine, visiting Anbara in Jerusalem. She writes about her "love affair with Jerusalem" from the time she was seven and first visited Anbara and her new family, until she was twenty-five, when newly wed to Walid Khalidi, and having just given birth to their first child in Beirut, she witnessed the establishment of the State of Israel and the First Arab-Israeli War:

> From the very beginning, Jerusalem exercised a bewitching, hypnotic effect on me. . . . No other city in the world, not Venice, not my beloved Beirut of the old days, ever had that effect. There was a mystique about Jerusalem, that neither Beirut nor Venice had. Jerusalem was joy. Joy was what I experienced as I got my first view of it. Joy at the magnificence of the city itself, and joy at the prospect of being soon with my beloved sister and much later at the prospect of being with the love of my life, the man I was to marry.[14]

Rasha also used to accompany the Khalidis to Jaffa to visit her sister's in-laws, among them Hajj Raghib, who had played such an important role in Walid's upbringing, and to visit Ain-Zhalta and Souk el-Gharb in the mountains of Lebanon, where the Salams used to spend their summers. Close in age to Ahmad Samih al-Khalidi's children from his previous marriage, Rasha was particularly drawn to Walid from the beginning. She recalls how they used to play together as children. "On one of my visits," she writes, "Walid, who had a bicycle, offered to teach me how to ride. We went to a dirt road next to the house and I sat on the saddle. The road was full of boulders and pebbles, and it was on an incline. So Walid gave me one push and I went down the road, falling straight off, bruising myself badly. As I walked back home, bloody and crying, my brother-in-law took Walid to his office and gave him a sound thrashing."[15]

The bicycle was a present from Rasha's father; it had red handles and a clinking bell, remembers Walid.[16] A few years later, Abu Ali would give Rasha a bicycle of her own, much to her mother's disdain. A picture I found in the archives at the American University of Beirut shows her happily riding her bike in Mount Lebanon (figure 3.2). While her sister Anbara had stirred social outrage in Beirut in the late 1920s for removing her veil in public, by the late 1930s, Rasha was riding to school on her bicycle, which would have been unthinkable a generation before, earning her the reputation of being a tomboy.[17] Rasha recalls cycling trips

3.2 Rasha Salam riding her bicycle, Barouk, Mount Lebanon, 1935.
Salam Collection, American University of Beirut/Library Archives.

with friends to the outskirts of Beirut as well as outings to the Patisserie Suisse at Bab Idriss, a popular destination where two tramway lines intersected at the western gateway to downtown Beirut until 1975, when the Lebanese Civil War tore the city apart.[18] Like Anbara, Rasha had the support of their loving and powerful father, "a man of remarkably modern outlook," as Salibi remarks.[19] "My father and later my brother Saeb who became my guardian," after Abu Ali had passed away, says Rasha, "never insisted on my wearing the veil," and her mother, who continued to wear the veil, came to accept the fact that neither her daughters nor her daughters-in-law did.[20]

THE HULEH VALLEY

Salim Ali Salam had close ties with Palestine well before the several marriages between his family and the Khalidis—after his daughter Anbara's nuptials, his son Mohammad wed Fatima al-Khalidi, one of Ahmad Samih al-Khalidi's sisters; his youngest daughter Rasha married Walid; and his grandson Assem married Sulafa, Walid's sister. In similar fashion to other notable families of the former Ottoman provinces of the *Bilad al-Sham*, the Salams had invested in the agricultural sector of Palestine, notably in the Huleh Valley in the district of Safad in northern Galilee, which extends like a panhandle from Lake Tiberias north toward Lebanon. Salim Ali Salam had been in charge of the Syrian-Ottoman Agricultural Company, which had been granted concessions to drain the marchland of the Huleh by the Ottoman authorities in 1914. When the British and French mandates came into effect in the aftermath of World War I, numerous legal disputes ensued, while the Jewish Agency exerted significant pressure on the British government to transfer the concessions to it.[21] Initially the Salams had partnered with other Beiruti notables, among them the Beyhums, the Sursuqs (also Sursocks), and the Pharaons;[22] however, when these parties withdrew from the project, the Salams were left alone without sufficient capital to effectively drain the lands. Anbara briefly writes about the legal disputes that ensued, mentioning her father's extended travels to London to negotiate with British companies, as well as the cases raised against him in the law courts in Safad.[23] With a population of some 13,300 inhabitants, of whom about 20 percent were Jews, Safad served as the administrative, economical, and cultural capital of the subdistrict that carried its name.[24]

Rasha also writes about the Huleh Valley in her memoirs, albeit from a different perspective, as she recalls the happy days she spent as a child during winter and spring holidays with her family in the marchlands, where she learned swimming, horseback riding, boating, and angling. The lake and its surrounding marches not only attracted migratory birds but also served its inhabitants for fishing; harvesting papyrus, which was woven into mats and baskets as well as burnt to be used as fertilizer for the ground; herding water buffalo and sheep; and cultivating a limited number of crops.[25] For the Salams, it promised economic agricultural productivity, but it was also a site of leisure for boat trips and picnics, setting them apart as urban notables from the Bedouins and peasants, originally from various parts of the region but often subsumed under the label of the Ghawarna tribe, who inhabited the marchlands. The archives of Salim Ali and Saeb Salam, recently donated to the American University of Beirut, contain a wealth of photographs of the Huleh Valley, depicting the Salam family's endeavors as well as the marchlands' physical environment, indigenous population, and close-knit ecosystem. These photographs are in stark contrast to the landscapes produced by Omar Onsi, one of Abu Ali's nephews and a pioneer in Lebanon's modern art movement, who would sometimes accompany the Salams to the Huleh Valley. In 1934, the year the Salams gave up the concessions, he left a lasting imprint of the valley in oil on canvas. Originally titled *le Lac de Houlé*, the painting reproduced in the exhibition catalog of Onsi's 1997 retrospective at the Nicholas Sursock Museum in Beirut as *Houlé*, recasts the valley as a *paysage* devoid of the social fabric it sustained and the politics at stake in its impending transformation.[26]

In her memoirs, Rasha mentions Rosh-Pinna on the shores of Lake Huleh, one of the first modern Jewish agricultural settlements in Palestine founded under the patronage of the Rothschilds in 1882 after the pogroms in Russia. Rasha recalls the problems that arose between her family and the Jewish settlers and that she did not understand at the time.[27] Among these settlers was Arna Mer-Khamis, who was born in Rosh-Pinna in 1929. Her father, Gideon Mer, was a Russian-born physician and malariologist trained in Italy, the Netherlands, and France. Under his direction, the Hebrew University had established the Rosh Pina Malaria Research Station in 1927.[28] While the indigenous Arab population of the Huleh Valley was struggling with malaria, it was not the disease, spread to humans through the bites of infected mosquitoes, that defined its perception of the marchlands but the marchlands' greatest asset as one of the oldest freshwater resources in the world. Accordingly, they "named the area 'watering place' (*al Sheriat al Kebira*)."[29] In contrast, Zionist pioneers described the lands—but not its people—in need of healing, which "was not only intended for the ideological purpose of Jewish redemption but also for the practical corollary of settlement extension and more immigration."[30]

Mer not only fought malaria but also would later fight with the Palmach, the Haganah's elite fighting force. The Palmach had been established during World War II with the support of the British Army to fight, on the one hand, the advance of the Axis powers in the Middle East and, on the other, to defend Jewish settlements.[31] Rasha may have been too young to be fully aware of the changes that took shape, yet she was a witness to a world that is now lost, albeit captured in some of the Salams' family photographs now housed at the American University of Beirut. Rasha and Arna never met, but their life trajectories were intricately interwoven as the world around them, the very landscape of places once dear and familiar, was violently transformed. What would Rasha and Arna's encounter have looked like, had they been given the chance to meet in Palestine before 1948, or after? Arna later married Saliba Khamis, an Arab member of Maki, the Israeli Communist Party, and became a political activist, notably through her work with Palestinian children orphaned in the First Intifada in 1987. This activism is documented by her son Juliano Mer-Khamis and Danniel Danniel in their film *Arna's Children* (2004).[32]

The Salams eventually had to give up the drainage concessions in the Huleh Valley and accepted compensation. The British government transferred the concessions from the Syrian-Ottoman Agricultural Company headed by the Salams to the Palestine Land Development Company (PLDC), which had been founded by the Zionist Organization (ZO) under the leadership of Arthur Ruppin and Otto Warburg in 1909. After 1948, the PLDC became the Israeli Land Development Company, under which name it continues to operate as "the oldest . . . and one of the leading real estate companies in Israel."[33] The Salams were severely criticized, notably by the renowned Lebanese journalist and literary writer Amin al-Rihani who questioned Abu Ali's standing as a true Arab leader, asking whether he was "one of those who prefers money to the nation?"[34] Years later, after the outbreak of the Lebanese Civil War, Abu Ali's son, Saeb Salam, felt compelled to issue a book against such enduring charges.[35] As Anbara points out in her memoirs, her father "did not leave the lands of Huleh before stipulating that all lands drained as a result of the building of the dam and the diversion of the course of the lake should revert to the Arab inhabitants of the region."[36] When the final transfer took place in 1934, protections were given to Arab tenants who had been living in the area; however, these were "continually manipulated and changed to allow for forms of compensation (monetary and land) to stand in for allowing tenants to remain on the land."[37] Once the PLDC was in possession of the concession rights, the Huleh Valley saw a rapid increase of Jewish land purchases and settlements, despite the concurrent Great Revolt. The valley's strategic importance—it is located at Palestine's northeastern border, along the Golan Heights and in reach of the Jordan and Yarmouk Rivers—was considerable. It was part of the N-shaped region between Jaffa and Lake Tiberias that Ruppin had recommended for Jewish land purchases as early as 1907, which, by the time the United Nations Special Committee on Palestine recommended partition in 1947, had become a reality.[38] Ruppin listed the acquisition of the Huleh concessions in his diary as one of the major achievements of 1934:

> The year 1934 is drawing to a close. With the arrival of 50,000 Jewish immigrants, the acquisition of the Huleh concessions, the agreement for the £500,000 loan [from Lloyds Bank] and the continuing prosperity in Palestine, it has been a very successful year for Zionism, the most successful we have ever had . . . I am convinced that the Arabs will not be content to watch our progress passively and that will one day experience serious disturbances in the country. It is important that we become strong before then.[39]

Referred to as "the father of Zionist settlements and the father of Jewish sociology,"[40] Ruppin is less known for his views on "racial purity,"[41] which have triggered controversy among historians.[42] As his diary entry shows, Ruppin was well aware of the fact that Palestine was not "a country without a people for a people without a country," as Zionist propaganda described it abroad, and he did not expect its Arab population to look on passively as the Zionist movement progressed, anticipating "disturbances in the country" on the eve of the Great Revolt. The Jewish population of Palestine had risen from 18 percent in 1932 to more than 31 percent in 1939, in part a reflection of the Nazi Party's adoption of anti-Semitic persecution as official policy. As Rashid Khalidi points out, the increase in Jewish immigration to Palestine "provided the demographic critical mass and military manpower that were necessary for the ethnic cleansing of Palestine in 1948."[43]

In his groundbreaking 1992 study, *All That Remains: The Palestinian Villages Occupied and Depopulated by Israel in 1948*, Walid Khalidi documents more than seventy Palestinian villages that were seized by Israel in the district of Safad alone.[44] The settlement of Rosh-Pinna, mentioned by Rasha in her memoirs, was established on the southeast site of an Arab village called al-Ja'una and soon expanded well beyond the land purchased by its founders.[45] As Benny Morris writes, al-Ja'una was occupied and purged of its Arab population when Zionist forces, in this case the Palmach, made it their objective to take over the city of Safad before the British evacuation of Palestine in May 1948. News of the Deir Yassin Massacre on April 9, 1948—an Arab village in the vicinity of Jerusalem, where the Irgun and Lehi had murdered hundreds of civilians, among them women and children—and of the fall of Tiberias and Haifa, sent shockwaves across Palestine. Terrified, the majority of Safad's Arab population fled. Its remaining Arab inhabitants, along with the inhabitants of other villages, were forcibly expelled and transferred southward, to the interior of Galilee.[46] The Huleh Valley came to be closely associated with the image of the Zionist pioneer, exemplified in Gideon Mer.

The Huleh drainage project was completed in 1958; it has been "heralded as one of the chief wonders of the Zionist project"[47] despite the well-known ecological damage it wrought, destroying "an ecology seen by ecologists in retrospect as being in a climax state of equilibrium, as much as the swamp produced the society that depended upon it. They had grown up in relation to one another. Yet these relations were simultaneously influenced by the larger geopolitical and economic changes that were occurring at the time."[48] Although the official Zionist historical narrative of healing the land has remained strong, some criticism has been raised by Israeli social scientists since the mid-1980s about the necessity to drain the valley, which suggest, "perhaps, tiny cracks in conventional Zionist understandings that are beginning to make room for critical re-assessment."[49]

FROM HAIFA TO CAIRO BY TRAIN

A year after the Salams gave up the drainage concessions in the Huleh Valley, in 1935, Rasha traveled with her parents and her brother Saeb to Cairo. They took the train from Haifa, where the family had invested in real estate—"a spacious and innovatively designed mansion in which Haifa's first elevator was installed."[50] Built in the new international style that had been introduced primarily by Jewish architects of European origin, some previously affiliated with the Bauhaus, the Salams' building, located in Haifa's commercial zone, was designed by the architect Benjamin Orell. It was later sold, possibly through middlemen, to Jewish buyers.[51]

Haifa was a burgeoning city that had seen significant development since Ottoman times as a crossroads of transportation. The Hejaz Railway had opened its headquarters there in 1905, turning the city into a major port by connecting it not only to the Ottoman capital of Constantinople and to the Hejaz in Arabia, the site of the holiest cities of Islam (i.e., Mecca and Medina) but also accelerating regional transportation to Beirut, Damascus, and Cairo, as well as within Palestine, to Tulkarm, Lydda, Jaffa, and Jerusalem. Haifa's rapid growth continued during the British Mandate, with the Colonial Office investing heavily in infrastructure. The city advanced as Britain's principal naval base and one of the most modern and best-equipped deep seaports in the Eastern Mediterranean. It became the "gateway to the Middle East" and India, especially after the Iraq Petroleum Company opened its refinery northeast of the city as a terminal for its pipeline from the Kirkuk and Mosul oilfields, which would supply British and U.S. forces with fuel during World War II.[52] The Palestine Electric Corporation, founded by Pinhas Rutenberg, who, along with Ze'ev Jabotinsky, was a founding member of the Haganah and became one of the Yishuv's most influential businessmen, supplied the city with electricity from the hydroelectric power stations it built at the confluence of the Jordan and the Yarmuk.[53] All of this attracted significant capital from both Arab and Jewish communities and from a range of industries, among them the largest Zionist industrial projects—the Shemen edible oil factory, the Nesher cement factory, and the Grands Moulins flour mills.[54] Between 1931 and 1939, Haifa's population more than doubled; the proportion of its Jewish residents rose from about a quarter to almost half.[55] In 1934, Britain established Haifa Airport as Palestine's first international airport—an addition to the Qalandiya airfields between Jerusalem and Ramallah, which opened in 1920, and the Lydda airfields, a short distance from Tel Aviv, which opened in 1936. Rutenberg founded Palestine Airways, which operated from 1937 to 1940 under the aegis of British Imperial Airways, the latter later merged with the British Overseas Airways Corporation (BOAC) before it became British Airways.

Signifying imperial power and modernity, Haifa's new infrastructure profoundly affected people's everyday lives and dreams in the region. As the indigenous Arab population of Upper Galilee was driven into poverty by the land purchases of the Jewish National Fund (JNF), many sought employment in the growing labor market opened by Haifa's new industries, where they joined forces with Sheikh Izz al-Din al-Qassam, mentioned in chapter 1, and his followers in opposition to British rule and Zionist land purchases. At the same time, Rasha traveled with her parents and her brothers Fuad, Malik, and Saeb from Haifa in luxurious wagons across the Sinai Desert to al-Qantara on the eastern side of the Suez Canal, a twelve-hour journey (figure 3.3). From al-Qantara, they took a connecting train, arriving three-and-a-half hours later in Cairo. They stayed at the Shepherd's Hotel, which was one of the most celebrated hotels at the time that had served as a model of the King David in Jerusalem. Rasha notes: "It was my first visit to a big, cosmopolitan city (I do not remember much of my visit to London). Cairo's large avenues, orderly traffic, huge department stores, parks, hotels, bridges, the Nile, everything in it was bewildering, especially the fact that

3.3 Rasha Salam at the train station in Haifa with her father, Salim Ali Salam, her siblings, to her left: Fuad, to her right: Mohammad, Saeb, and Malik, and their mother, Kalsum Barbir, looking out of the train from a window, February 25, 1935.
Salam Collection, American University of Beirut/Library Archives.

cars stopped at traffic lights. We visited museums, theaters, the Pyramids, the Sphinx, and took a ride on the Nile in a felucca."[56]

Rasha's description of the family's visit to Cairo offers glimpses into the leisure and lifestyle made possible by the transfer of capital in the interwar period. It clearly indicates Western conceptions of order and modes of representation, which played a key role in the colonization of Egypt, as Timothy Mitchell has shown, with Cairo and other Middle Eastern cities standing out as symbols of modern economic and political transformation.[57] Rasha's mention of Cairo's large avenues and orderly traffic differs significantly from her descriptions of Jerusalem which, in comparison, appears like a small town. It also differs from her experience of the same city not much later, in the early 1940s, when she returned to study at King Fuad I University, this time arriving by plane from Beirut. Misr Airwork, which later became Egypt Air, had just started service to Beirut as well as to Haifa and Lydda. Rasha writes, "I arrived at Cairo airport and the first thing that struck me was a kind of poverty I was not accustomed to. Beirut was not at that time the rich, flourishing city it was to become later, but we did not in Lebanon know the degree of poverty you encountered in Egypt."[58]

Beirut's airport opened in 1938 but, during World War II, air travel in Lebanon was limited and controlled by the French. It grew in popularity after Lebanon gained its independence in 1943 and was transformed into the "Switzerland of the Orient," especially when, with the support of BOAC, Middle East Airlines was founded by Rasha's brother Saeb and his friend Fawzi el-Hoss. "By splitting off Grand Liban from its natural hinterland the French not only confirmed the financial and commercial hegemony of Beirut over the mountain," writes Roger Owen, "but also strengthened a pattern of economic activity in which agriculture and industry had become more and more subordinate to banking and trade."[59] This tendency remained in place after independence, triggering further migration to Beirut, which was poorly prepared for such rapid growth.

Educated in French, Rasha did not feel comfortable pursuing her studies at the American University of Beirut, and the only choice available for French-language higher education in Beirut at the time was the Law School of the Université Saint-Joseph, in which she had no interest. Her life in Beirut had become stifling after her father's death in 1938, and she was looking for a way out. Encouraged by Mahmoud Fawzi, the Egyptian consul in Jerusalem,[60] who was on friendly terms with Ahmad Samih and Anbara Salam Khalidi and often visited their house,

Rasha decided to study history at King Fuad I University. Walid, by now a young adult whom she was helping with his math as he was preparing for his matriculation exams, may also have influenced her. For a few years, Rasha lived as a boarder in a girls' hostel in the affluent neighborhood of Dokki on the western bank of the Nile, where she met a wide range of young female students of upper- and middle-class backgrounds from across Egypt, Lebanon, Palestine, and Syria, and who, like her, set out to break free from the traditional roles ascribed to women in their societies (figure 3.4).

3.4 Rasha Salam early 1940s.
Salam Collection, American University of Beirut/Library Archives.

"RELATIONSHIPS ARE SO COMPLEX"

Rasha's visits to Jerusalem became more frequent as her friendship with Walid transformed into a love affair. "How do two people who have known each other almost the whole of their lives as childhood friends and members of the same family suddenly come to be gripped by this mental and physical passion that was not there before?" she asks in her memoirs, "And why do you suddenly come to look at another person with completely different eyes?" Unable to find an answer, she writes, "relationships are so complex, so full of contradictions."[61] In Beirut, every day Rasha would pass by the post office, "a small, old Turkish building, located in downtown Beirut in the heart of the business center" to pick up the family's mail, hoping for a letter from Walid, but "the mail from Palestine took over two weeks in those days as the war was still on."[62] Traveling to Jerusalem, she would arrive by taxi in the early evening, the city coming into view from the Ramallah Road, and rush into Walid's arms, burying her face in his Harris Tweed jacket.

In the summer of 1944, while on a family visit to Sofar, a buoyant summer resort in Mount Lebanon, she and Walid became engaged. Rasha recalls the engagement party at which the whole Salam family came together to celebrate, as well as the "beautiful black and pink taffeta dress with black sequins" her mother gave her for the occasion. During the following Christmas holidays, Walid visited Rasha in Cairo, arriving from Jerusalem by train. They spent a few days, some of the happiest days of her life at the Mena House Hotel—which she describes as one of the most beautiful hotels of the time, with its neo-pharaonic design, extensive grounds, rose garden, and splendid views of the Pyramids—where they were soon joined by her brother Ali and his wife in the company of Anbara, who did not express the slightest surprise at her staying together with Walid at the hotel. This broad-mindedness would puzzle Rasha for the rest of her life. Rasha did not return to her studies in Cairo. A year later, on Walid's twentieth birthday, the couple were married in Jerusalem, where they remained for another year.[63]

Accompanying her fiancé and then husband Walid to the King David Hotel bar, Rasha soon became part of the ecumenical circle that met there. She in particular recalls Wolf, as Wolfgang was known among his friends, and Jabra:

Both had charm and wit, but Wolf's wit surpassed anything I had ever come across. He was the funniest, most charming person I had ever met, exceptionally warm and sympathetic. Both were older than Walid and myself, but we soon became inseparable. We did not only talk philosophy and literature, but often discussed our personal problems. Wolf talked about his wife whom he had just divorced and of whom he still seemed to be fond. Jabra talked about the beautiful girl he had left behind in England as well as the novel he was writing.... Wolf's interest in music and his knowledge of it was bewildering: he only had to listen to two notes of a piece to tell you what it was. He entered competitions and always won. He hated Beethoven and made us hate him too, he loved Mozart and made us love him (years later he was to write one of the best books on Mozart). And Jabra I so often remember him humming the first movement of Mozart's 39th symphony.

Jabra and Wolf were very different physically. Jabra was thin, dark, with frizzy hair, pointed nose and thin lips. Wolf was medium built, fair, with a full face and blue pale eyes, short-sighted but refusing to wear glasses, a full nose and lips, an impish smile and an impish way of talking which made you always wonder how serious he was.[64]

Both Jabra and Wolfgang often visited the Khalidis' home to see Walid and Rasha. As Rasha recalls in her memoirs, they would sit in the garden, or spend the evening in Walid's room. She felt especially drawn to Wolfgang, whom she would sometimes meet on her own for morning coffee at the Viennese Coffee House down Mamillah Road, exchanging timid embraces in a world full of uncertainties, as World War II was coming to an end. At the same time, Walid was experiencing significant professional growth, having obtained his bachelor's degree from the University of London and joined the Arab Office in Jerusalem, while moving in ever-expanding social circles and gaining attention in particular from "an attractive WAAF in blue and grey uniform," Anne Palairet, who would later marry Julian Asquith, as Nassib Bulos recalls in his memoirs.[65] As Rasha remembers, Wolfgang did not attend her wedding to Walid in Jerusalem on July 18, 1945, as work kept him in Haifa. However, he picked up the newlyweds at the port in Haifa in early August when they returned from their honeymoon in Cyprus, deeply shocked by the atomic bombings of Hiroshima and Nagasaki, and they resumed their friendship. He sent a painting he had done as a wedding present, an accordion player in dark oil, which remained with the Khalidis until 1982, when their apartment in Beirut was shelled by the IDF during Israel's invasion of Lebanon and siege of Beirut. Rasha's description of the painting is reminiscent of another of Wolfgang's works, this one of a bandoneon player that is dated by his sister to 1946 and that is reproduced in the critical edition of his letters to his parents, which inform much of our look at Wolfgang in the next chapter.[66] The gift might very well have been an earlier version of this painting.

Rasha was drawn to Wolfgang at a time when her relationship with Walid was in its early stages, and not free of obstacles. Years later, from the spatial and temporal distance from her exile in Cambridge, Massachusetts, where the Khalidis lived after the Israeli invasion of Lebanon, she once again breaks free of social constraints, musing in her memoirs: "I have often wondered whether I would have married Wolf had Walid and I separated. I think I might have. I was very much attracted to him, both physically and intellectually. The fact that he was Jewish would not have stood in the way, in spite of the objections of my family. I knew how bitter he was about Zionism and what was happening to the Arabs of Palestine."[67]

Rasha's personal reflections capture the bliss she felt visiting Jerusalem but also the anxiety she experienced about her own future as well as that of Palestine and, closely entwined with it, of Lebanon and the Arab world at large, as prospects of a shared life of Arabs and Jews in Palestine progressively faded into a future past.

CHAPTER 4

WOLFGANG HILDESHEIMER

Belated Surrealist and "Exclusive Geheimtyp"

MODERN ORTHODOX JUDAISM, ZIONISM, AND PROGRESSIVE EDUCATION IN GERMANY

Wolfgang Zewi Hildesheimer was born in Hamburg on December 9, 1916, the second child of Arnold and Hanna Hildesheimer (née Goldschmidt). The family lived between the northern and southern branches of the Elbe River in Hamburg-Wilhelmsburg, an industrial area that was not yet part of the city of Hamburg, in one of the *Direktorenhäuser* (directors' houses) on the premises of the trans-fat factory of H. Schlinck and Cie. AG, where Wolfgang's father worked. Drafted into the Imperial German Army during World War I as a chemist, Arnold Hildesheimer invented a substitute for the ricin oil used to make gas masks airtight, his patent was later purchased by the German chemical and pharmaceutical conglomerate IG Farben.[1] Given the political and economic instability in Germany after World War I, he left Schlinck and accepted a position with Van den Bergh Margarine Works, a Jewish Dutch family business that was a prominent European margarine and soap manufacturer in the early twentieth century. In 1929, Van den Bergh merged with another Dutch family business to form Margarine Unie, which in turn merged with the British company Lever Brothers in 1929 to form Unilever, a British-Dutch multinational consumer goods company that continues to operate on a global scale. The consolidation of these family businesses allowed the new conglomerate to emerge from the Great Depression in a strong position. The Hildesheimers moved away from Hamburg, first to Berlin, then to Kleve, Nijmegen, and Mannheim, where Arnold worked as technical director of Estol AG,[2] one of the biggest producers of the Rama margarine brand (known as Blue Band outside Germany) started by Van den Bergh.[3]

It is partly due to his having lived in several cities across Germany and the Netherlands, suggests Henry A. Lea, that Wolfgang was disposed to identify himself as cosmopolitan, rather than as an émigré, when he arrived in Palestine, after a brief stop in London.[4] Later, having returned to Europe, Wolfgang would explain his sense of homelessness in artistic terms:

> I emigrated to Palestine with my parents in 1933—Israel did not even exist as a dream at the time—but when the state was founded, I was back in Europe, where I belonged then and still belong now. So, to a certain extent, I have spurned my homeland at the expense of that homelessness that, viewed from the outside, is a characteristic of the Jew and symbolizes for me—that is, from the inside—that homelessness in which we, Jews or otherwise, are all at home. It is the source of all my creative activity. I do not want to have a homeland [*Heimat*] on Earth: perhaps my Judaism will reveal itself at last in this refusal. However, in contrast to the pious Jews, I do not want *Heimat* in heaven either.[5]

Wolfgang's mother's family was part of Hamburg's educated elite and was very much engaged in the city's cultural life. His maternal grandfather, Salomon Goldschmidt, was a playwright, and his brother Jehuda, known as Leon Goldschmidt, was a founding member of the city's Literary Society and its People's Theater, which "promoted regional and local authors and became one of Hamburg's largest publishers of North German *Heimat* literature," an expression of provincial modernity.[6] One of Wolfgang's mother's sisters was part of the influential George Circle, which had formed around the poet Stefan George in the late nineteenth century and a number of whose followers later became adherents of Nazism.[7] The Goldschmidts lived in the Grindelviertel in the Rotherbaum neighborhood, which was the center of Jewish life in Hamburg and at one time housed the city's main synagogue. As Wolfgang remembers, however, they felt only "vaguely Jewish, they never went to worship service, the traditional cultural heritage was German, was literature, especially Schiller."[8]

By contrast, Arnold was from "an old family of rabbis"[9]—an understatement, as Lea points out, because the Hildesheimers were one of central Europe's most prominent families of Orthodox rabbis and Talmudic scholars.[10] The family's reputation in Orthodox circles traces back to Esriel Hildesheimer (1820–1899), Wolfgang's great-grandfather. A native of Hildesheim, he was the first rabbi of

Adass Jisroel, a Jewish congregation established in Berlin in 1869, whose goal was "to unite an Orthodox lifestyle with an openness for culture, education, and art. Emancipation and the active participation in society were encouraged, whilst maintaining Jewish traditions."[11] In 1870, Esriel cofounded the Orthodox German weekly *Die Jüdische Presse* and, in its first issue, announced the formation of the Society of Palestinian Affairs (*Verein für Palästinensische Angelegenheiten*), whose intent was to provide financial aid for Jews in Jerusalem. As David Ellenson says, Esriel viewed Jerusalem in religious rather than secular-nationalistic terms: he "was not a modern Zionist."[12] Rather, he "attempted to mediate between the pull of tradition and the demands of modernity," argues Ellenson; "his efforts make him a paradigmatic practitioner of the dialectical interplay between tradition and change that characterizes modern Orthodoxy."[13] In 1873, he founded the Berlin Rabbinical Seminary, which became the most important training school for Orthodox rabbis across Central Europe.[14]

Esriel's eldest son, Hirsch Hildesheimer, Wolfgang's grandfather, obtained his doctorate under the renowned German classicist Theodor Mommsen in 1880; he subsequently taught Jewish history at the Berlin Rabbinical Seminary and the University of Leipzig, and authored *Beiträge zur Geographie Palästinas* (Contributions to the geography of Palestine, 1886), a book about Palestine's geography, which he had never seen. In 1883, he became editor-in-chief of *Die Jüdische Presse*. In 1884, he was one of a group of young men who founded the association Esra, Sammelbüchse für Palästina (a combination of the Hebrew for "help" and the German for "collecting tin for Palestine"). "The national element in this effort was not overt," says Jehuda Reinharz, "yet it must be counted as one of the first manifestations of Jewish nationalism in Germany."[15] In 1888, Esriel was a founding member of Lema'an Zion (for the sake of Zion). As Reinharz explains, "its character, aims and organizational framework differed from those of the 'Esra.' The board of this association consisted of Jews opposed to the *Halukah* system—the organized collection of funds in the diaspora for distribution among needy Jews in Palestine—hitherto prevalent. It encouraged self-sufficiency among Palestinian Jewry, fought against missionary activities, and tried to settle Jews in Arab villages and towns."[16]

Lema'an Zion was not an isolated initiative. Against the background of anti-Jewish pogroms in the Russian Empire and the rise of anti-Semitism across Europe, a range of new associations emerged in the 1880s, which signaled a shift from the philanthropic practice of supporting fellow Jews so they might devote themselves to a religious life in Palestine to Zionist methods of acquiring land to further Jewish settlements in Palestine.[17] Esriel may not have been a "modern Zionist," but his civic engagement with the *Hovevei Zion* (Lovers of Zion), as the new Zionist associations were collectively called, aligned him more closely with political Zionism than had his religious and scholarly duties at the Berlin Rabbinical Seminary.[18] His son Hirsch had agreed to meet with Theodor Herzl in Cologne in 1896, but Herzl was not able to attend the meeting.[19] When his efforts to win over representatives of Jewish Orthodoxy in Germany in support of his proposed Jewish state failed, Herzl transferred the location of the first Zionist Congress, initially planned to take place in Munich, to Basel, where it was held from August 29 to 31, 1897. A brief notice in *Die Jüdische Presse* on May 5, 1897, informs readers that its editor, Hirsch Hildesheimer, had envisaged giving a talk in Munich on "the tasks of Jewish charity in Palestine," but canceled his participation when he found out his address was to be part of a congress devoted not to "the manifold tasks of the Palestinian relief organization [in German, *das palästinensische Hilfswerk*]" but instead to the "discussion of 'Zionist' theories and plans for the future," which were not only fundamentally different from Orthodox standpoints but, in his eyes, would "cause severe damage and threaten to compromise and seriously damage more immediate and realizable efforts."[20]

Arnold Hildesheimer broke with his family's tradition of involvement in Modern Orthodox Judaism and pursued a secular career. As Wolfgang remembers, his father turned his back on his forefathers' religiosity as well as their frivolity—the latter expressed in their preference of "the operetta over the opera, the cabaret over the concert"—and became an "a-religious Zionist."[21] In 1909, he obtained his doctorate in chemistry from the Humboldt University of Berlin, where he had joined the Verein Jüdischer Studenten Maccabaea (VJSt, Jewish student fraternity), founded in Berlin in 1895, and met Kurt Blumenfeld, Felix Rosenblüth (also known as Pinchas Rosen), and Julius Rosenfeld, who played important roles in the Zionist movement in Germany and, later, in Palestine, and who would remain close family friends.[22]

After the Zionist Congress in Basel, the Zionistische Vereinigung für Deutschland (ZVfD, the Zionist Federation of Germany) was founded in Cologne in 1897, and a number of Jewish student fraternities, organized in the Kartell jüdischer Verbingungen (KJV, the umbrella organization of Jewish university student fraternities), brought to the fore a new generation of German Zionists committed "to include emigration to Palestine in their life plan."[23] Blumenfeld was one of the leaders of this new generation; he "was the typical representative of what he named 'post-assimilation Zionism,' Zionism that did not stem directly from Jewish tradition but sought to return to Jewishness out of assimilation."[24] Not familiar with Palestine, Blumenfeld would accompany Ruppin, who before opening the Palestine Office of the Zionist Organization (ZO) in Jaffa in 1908 headed the Berlin Bureau for Jewish Statistics and Demography, on some of his travels.[25] Nahum Goldman—who in 1942 would call for the extraordinary Zionist Congress in New York City that led to the Biltmore Program—credits Blumenfeld with having "managed to give Zionism a basis of common humanity, link it with every great cultural movement of our time and give it a tremendous openness to the world," in addition to having drawn prominent people into the Zionist movement, among them Albert Einstein and Paul Warburg, who were to play important roles in the American Jewish community.[26] Blumenfeld was also good friends with Hannah Arendt.[27] Before emigrating to Palestine in 1933, he served as Secretary-General of the ZO from 1911 to 1914, and as chair of the ZVfD from 1924 until 1933.

Rosenblüth also served as chair of the ZVfD, from 1920 to 1923. He emigrated to Palestine in 1926 and is credited with having laid the foundations of Israel's judiciary. He was among the signatories of the Declaration of the Establishment of the State of Israel on May 14, 1948, and he served as Israel's first minister of justice under David Ben-Gurion.[28] Blumenfeld, Rosenblüth, and Rosenfeld were instrumental, along with Ruppin, in the Hitachduth Olej Germania (HOG, the association of immigrants from Germany), which had been established in Tel Aviv in 1932, opened branches in Haifa and Jerusalem, and later became the Central European Immigration Association. "The establishment of the HOG, before and independent of Hitler's rise to power," writes Lilo Stone, "is perhaps the real importance of the early German Zionist immigration. It is hard to imagine how the large numbers of immigrants from Germany after 1933 would have fared without the experience and dedication of these early immigrants."[29] About sixty thousand German Jews arrived in Palestine between 1933 and 1939 in the framework of the Haavara Agreement, which was signed by the ZVfD, the Anglo-Palestine Bank (under the directive of the Jewish Agency), and the Third Reich's Ministry of Economics in August 1933, which allowed the transfer (in Hebrew, *ha'avara*) of capital to British Mandate Palestine in exchange for goods manufactured in Germany, the controversy the agreement triggered within the Zionist leadership notwithstanding.[30]

Given Arnold Hildesheimer's connections in German Zionist circles, it is not surprising that he had considered emigrating to Palestine before 1933: once when confronted with anti-Semitic attitudes in Hamburg's political and economic circles—plans that went unrealized with the outbreak of World War I, as Hanna Hildesheimer remembers[31]—and again in 1929, as Wolfgang recalls, mentioning neither the factors that triggered his father's renewed plans, nor the reasons the family remained in Germany.[32] It is possible that these were linked to the transfer of ownership of the Shemen edible oil factory in Haifa, which had been established by the Wilbushewitz brothers and other Russian Jewish men of capital during the early years of the British Mandate, to Unilever,[33] where his father, now based in Mannheim, worked. It is also possible that the Hildesheimers stayed in Germany because of the political unrest in Palestine the same year.

The year 1929 also saw Wolfgang's thirteenth birthday and with it his bar mitzvah, which he describes in retrospect as the last time religion played any significant role in his life.[34] While keeping the image of his rabbinical forefathers alive, his parents found "their spiritual home" in Zionism, but refrained from influencing him in that direction, he says.[35] In 1923, the Hildesheimers had taken up residence in a spacious Mannheim apartment on Kantstraße, looking over Luisenpark, which is named for the Grand Duchess Luise von Baden, the daughter of Kaiser Wilhelm I. Their home became a meeting place for Mannheim's Jewish—and Zionist—intelligentsia. Arnold headed the ZVfD's Mannheim branch.[36] As Hanna recalls, they held a "big banquet" for Chaim Weizmann, "at which [the Jewish philosopher Martin] Buber gave an unforgettably beautiful poetic speech."[37] Along with Blumenfeld and Rosenblüth, oft-seen friends included Georg Landauer, who had studied law and economics in Bonn and Cologne. He was very active in the Zionist youth movement Blau-Weiss (blue-white) and the KJV, as well as the ZVfD, and would go on to become the director of the Berlin Palestine Office. He emigrated to Palestine in 1934, where he became director of the Jewish Agency's Central Bureau for the Settlement of German Jews, and a member of the Jewish National Council (JNC, the Va'ad Leumi). Like Ruppin, Landauer had been a member of the Brit Shalom, but unlike Ruppin—and Rosenblüth, with whom Landauer cofounded the Aliya Hadassah (new immigration) Party in 1942—Landauer was "a convinced pacifist" and "believed until the end of his life that a Jewish state could not survive without integration into the Arab world."[38] Opposed to the Biltmore Program, he regarded the establishment of a Jewish state "at the price of an endless war with the Arabs" as "the downfall of Zionism."[39] Whereas Rosenblüth steered Aliya Hadassah to accept the 1947 UN partition plan, Landauer resigned from the party. Disillusioned with Israel, he left for New York City in 1953 and was soon forgotten, despite his contribution to the juridical negotiations that led to the reparations paid by the Federal Republic of Germany under its first chancellor, Konrad Adenauer, to the immediate survivors of the Holocaust.[40]

Until 1930, Wolfgang had attended the Karl-Friedrich Gymnasium in Mannheim, but he now joined the Odenwaldschule, a boarding school located in Heppenheim in the Odenwald. Founded by Paul and Edith Geheeb in 1910 during the vanguard of the progressive education movement, the Odenwaldschule introduced Wolfgang to a community characterized by an openness to different social backgrounds, which were brought together in a "process-oriented and individualized approach to learning."[41] He wholeheartedly embraced the school's vision, and he would stay in touch with the Geheebs well into his adult life. Having developed a liking for the theater, Wolfgang participated in a number of the school's productions: as Vorwitz (Emanation) in Hugo von Hofmannsthal's *Das Salzburger große Welttheater* (The great Salzburg theater of the world); a bailiff in Shakespeare's *Twelfth Night, or What You Will*; Truffaldino in Carlo Goldino's *The Servant of Two Masters*; and, in Shakespeare's *A Midsummer Night's Dream*, Bottom—the classic comic fool whose head is transformed into that of a donkey, for which Wolfgang designed his own mask.[42] He did not finish his education at the Odenwaldschule, however. After Adolf Hitler's appointment as chancellor of Germany on January 30, 1933, the Hildesheimers' emigration to Palestine became a reality. In March 1933, men of the Nazi Sturmabteilung (Storm Detachment, more commonly known as storm troopers), seized control of the Odenwaldschule, a number of teachers were replaced with *Nationalsozialistische Deutsche Arbeiterpartei* (NSDAP, National Socialist German Workers' Party) sympathizers.[43] Having obtained a passport for their son from the Mannheim police headquarters, Wolfgang's parents sent him to England, shortly after the school's staging of *A Midsummer Night's Dream* in July 1933. In Farnham, Surrey, he attended the Frensham Heights School, which operated an exchange program with the Odenwaldschule.[44]

Wolfgang's parents, sister, and maternal grandmother arrived in London in October 1933, as the Reichstag fire trials were being broadcast on the radio. In the wake of the Reichstag fire on February 27, 1933, the NSDAP had established itself as the only political party in Germany, while all forms of political opposition were banned and the rights of individuals were suspended. In London, Arnold Hildesheimer negotiated with Unilever to explore the market for its consumer goods and establish a factory in Palestine, as is documented in the Central Zionist Archives.[45] As Hanna Hildesheimer wrote to Paul Geheeb, the family's stay in London was temporary.[46] Wolfgang's report card from the Odenwaldschule, issued at Hanna's request by Geheeb to be forwarded to his new school in Palestine,[47] describes Wolfgang as "gifted in music as well as in the fine arts; particularly interested in stage decoration and architecture; has a feeling for space. He is also technically adept and not clumsy, has worked hard in the woodworking shop. . . . In German he sometimes does very well, especially when dealing with drama; he has also proved to be highly articulate. He was particularly interested in ancient languages and history; also satisfactory in French and English. He was less attuned to mathematics and the natural sciences."[48]

JERUSALEM, 1933–1937

In December 1933, the Hildesheimers departed England for Palestine.[49] The family rented an apartment on Ben Maymon Avenue in Rehavia, an upscale German Jewish neighborhood in Jerusalem bordering on the busy Mamillah and the more residential, primarily Arab Christian neighborhood of Talbiya, not far from the Old City. Established in the 1920s on land that once belonged to the Greek Orthodox Church and that had been purchased by the Palestine Land Development Company (PLDC)—which a decade later would obtain the drainage concessions previously held by the Salams for the Huleh Valley— Rehavia was planned by the German Bauhaus architect Richard Kaufmann as a garden city modeled after Berlin Grunewald.[50] It featured the headquarters of the Jewish Agency, and a number of prominent private villas, notably those of Ruppin, Schocken, and Scholem. It was referred to as Neues Berlin (new Berlin), remembers Leila Mantoura Canaan, it "was all German Jews, and you would not hear much Hebrew. They were discussing Schiller and Goethe and Beethoven and Mozart."[51] After 1933, immigrants from Germany were greeted with suspicion and prejudice by the Yishuv, who questioned their commitment to Hebrew culture and Zionist motivations for immigration. Referred to as "Hitler Zionists" or, less harshly but derogatorily, as *yekkes*—a term derived from German or Yiddish that relates either to their more Western style of dress

(*Jacke*) or the biblical name Jacob (*Yekkef*)—they were regarded as "conservative, blockheaded, and cold."[52]

Wolfgang learned some Hebrew, but he never became fluent.[53] Many German immigrants continued to speak German among themselves. More than anything else, writes Tom Segev, "their inability—sometimes their refusal—to learn Hebrew" put them in "deep and painful conflict with the Zionist ethos of the Yishuv."[54] The Hildesheimers, however, moved comfortably in their new environs, a result of their many contacts within German Zionist circles.[55]

Wolfgang briefly attended the Ben Shemen Youth Village, an agricultural boarding school located between Jerusalem and Tel Aviv. This choice of school, likely taken by his parents while still in Germany, as Hanna's request for a report from the Odenwaldschule suggests, may have been related to Arnold's professional ties and connections to Zionist circles. Ben Shemen was one of the Jewish National Fund's (JNF's) first holdings in Palestine, where Nahum Wilbush, one of the Wilbushewitz brothers, had been involved in the founding of Atid, the first Jewish factory for edible oil and soap production, in 1905. Atid collapsed early in World War I, but it was revived with the support of the ZO in London as the Shemen edible oil factory in Haifa after the war.[56] Founded in 1927 by Siegfried Lehmann, who had previously established similar schools in Germany and Lithuania and had close ties with the Brit Shalom, Ben Shemen "would gain great importance for the absorption of German Jewish youth after 1933."[57] In 1940, Lehmann would be convicted, along with other Ben Shemen teachers, by the Jerusalem Military Court "on the charge of being jointly in possession of bombs, rifles, machine-guns, ammunition and explosives," as was reported in the *Palestine Post*, but his sentence of seven years' imprisonment was commuted to a fine of four hundred Palestine pounds and he was released along with his colleagues.[58]

At Ben Shemen, Wolfgang was introduced to the Haganah, the Yishuv's main paramilitary organization, which would constitute the core of the Israel Defense Forces (IDF). As he said in "an offhand manner" in a conversation with Hadara Lazar: " 'We were trained in a village between Jerusalem and Haifa, and I remember one night we were in the mountains, six of us. The night watch was divided, and I was woken up to guard for two hours with my rifle. I fell asleep, and when I woke up it was seven. I wasn't really capable of these things. My career in the Haganah was not very heroic.' He gave a hint of a smile."[59]

After Ben Shemen, Wolfgang learned carpentry in Jerusalem; interested in interior design, he completed his training with a chair designed for Schocken's villa in Rehavia.[60] His first stay in Palestine clearly set him on the path of the Zionist movement's "promotion of colonization with Jewish agriculture, artisans, and tradesmen," as outlined in the program of the ZO's constituent congress. As Wolfgang stated, his father was a proponent of the idea of a national home for Jews in Palestine, envisioning some form of binational state.[61] This was a position for which German immigrants were known, as Segev explains: "They advocated all kinds of arrangements, such as autonomy and cantonization. But in the main they supported a binational society and rejected the various plans for dividing the country into two independent states."[62]

Taking a stance against Zionism, Wolfgang would later say: "I had never been a Zionist, and I found most Jews of my own age too nationalistic, too provincial. My sister was different, she had been a Zionist, she was an officer in the Haganah."[63] However, it was only during his second stay in Palestine that he developed this more critical position. In a letter to his sister from London in 1938, he writes, "I am looking forward to seeing you and the country, although I don't think I can ever enter it again without a certain discontent, because next to such people, like Jakob Berger, I feel so ridiculous and insignificant, because I am afraid for my life, which after all means a lot to me. You have to be a hero in Palestine, but I am not a hero. That's bad enough, but many people in Palestine are not heroes either, and that's even worse."[64]

As this letter suggests, Wolfgang's involvement in the Haganah would be more extensive than he would later admit. Jakob (also known as Jaakov) Berger, a leading figure of the Haganah, trained Zionist youth in Jerusalem. Of Polish origin, he had gained a reputation as a member of the Hashomer Hatzair (Hebrew for "the young guard"), a socialist Zionist movement that formed its own federation of kibbutzim and constituted a key component of the future United Workers' Party of Israel (MAPAM).[65] He was fatally injured by Arab villagers when Kibbutz Hanita was erected as a strategic location in the Western Galilee on the border with Lebanon, after the Peel Commission recommended the partition of Palestine.[66] At the time of the Great Revolt, Zionist settlers engaged in a tower-and-stockade campaign, whose method consisted of assembling guard towers surrounded by fences; these illicit land claims were then expanded into fortified agricultural settlements with the tacit approval of the

British authorities. Kibbutz Hanita was one such settlement; the battle to establish it was led by Yitzhak Sadeh, one of the founders of the Palmach and the IDF. It also figured Moshe Dayan, who would go on to become the commander of the Jerusalem front in the First Arab-Israeli War, chief of staff of the IDF in the 1956 Suez War, and minister of defense in the 1967 War. Whether Wolfgang or his sister knew Berger personally is uncertain, but Wolfgang in his letter to his sister depicts him as a heroic role model, ready to fight and give his life for Eretz Yisrael (Land of Israel/Greater Israel), a sacrifice Wolfgang himself felt incapable of making—for personal and political reasons, as he became increasingly critical of Zionism.

In 1936, the Hildesheimers acquired Palestinian citizenship, issued by the British Mandate government. They gave up their German citizenship at a time when Germany, in the wake of the Nuremberg Race Laws, moved to persecute its Jewish population in a systematic way.[67] At around the same time, Wolfgang's parents moved to Haifa, where his father was to open a new factory for Unilever. Unilever's archives include records of an "agreement with Dr. A. Hildesheimer on October 8, 1937, regarding the manufacture and sale of margarine in Palestine and the use of Unilever trademarks."[68] The *Palestine Post* published an article entitled "Margarine Made in Palestine," on December 1938, in which it informs its readers that, "Palestine Edible Products was founded by Distributors and Transporters Ltd., of London, Shemen Ltd., Haifa, and Dr. Hildesheimer, a margarine expert who came several years ago from London. The Company has acquired from Messrs. Van den Bergh, London, the right to market its margarine under the well-known trademark, 'Blueband'."[69] In Wolfgang's 1965 short story "Die Margarinefabrik" (The margarine factory), a first-person narrator says,

> I know margarine factories; my father was a chemist in a margarine factory in Hamburg, directed one in Mannheim, and opened a third one in Haifa. While it was praised emphatically, the product did not come on the table at our house, but it provided a certain secure prosaic background against which the foreground of an animated intellectuality had reasonably easy play. I have often watched the production process, a completely unromantic but appetizing and immaculately hygienic process ("untouched by human hands"), a fascinating interlocking of mechanical arms and fingers, which finally dissolves into an assembly-line flow, everything surrounded by white-tiled walls that were constantly being scrubbed. It would have seemed inconceivable to me that all of this could happen in places like this, even if my imagination

covered the splintering, rough, gaping wooden walls with a few strokes of white paint. It is not the place for margarine, neither the air nor the landscape, the factual preconditions are missing, and even if ships could dock here to transport Ohlens margarine across the seas, it was still a bad speculation.[70]

What remains unsaid in this narrative—remarkable as it is for its precision of modern means of production detached from human hands and the environment into which it is transferred—is that the "secure prosaic background" provided by the margarine factory came at an expense, namely "the exclusive employment of Jewish immigrants and workers in building the factory and in production,"[71] in line with Zionist calls for Jewish labor voiced in the Histadrut. Moreover, the product was "to be used instead of *samna*, the traditional Arab cooking fat," and the local soap industry, traditionally centered in Nablus, was badly hit by competition from the Shemen works in Haifa.[72] Under British protection, Shemen pursued "a separate route from the older Palestinian oil and soap industries and commerce," as the country's Arab population was factored out, and, consequently, set out to join forces in the General Strike, which soon turned into the Great Revolt.[73]

LONDON, 1937–1939

Equipped with his new passport, Wolfgang left Palestine for London in March 1937 to study interior and stage design at the Central School of Arts and Crafts (today Central Saint Martin's College of Arts and Design at the University of the Arts London). From this time until the early 1960s, he sent letters in German to his parents almost every week, and these provide a wealth of illuminating insight into his daily life.

He was fascinated by London's metropolitan society, which had surpassed Paris and New York City since the 1920s with a multicultural and cosmopolitan reputation "rife with contradictory connotations," as "xenophobic stereotypes still lingered in [the] popular culture of the time."[74] In his letters to his parents, Wolfgang describes London as "big, foggy, hazy, dirty—but beautiful," and goes on to inform them about his courses, which included "life and freehand drawing, design and detailed drawing of furniture, textile design and weaving, and mosaic," adding that "the students, mostly girls, give a very cultured impression.

114 THE TIME BEFORE 1948

There are many foreigners, Indians, also Negroes, etc."[75] He met people from various British colonies, among them Palestinian Arabs. In June 1937, he attended an "Artist-Bottle Party," where he met "two very nice Palestinian girls" and "played Ping-Pong with Mrs. Husseini and lost."[76] This reference is most likely to Nimati al-Alami al-Husseini, the wife of Jamal al-Husseini, but may have been her eldest daughter Sirine,[77] who had accompanied Jamal al-Husseini to London, where he, along with other members of the Arab Higher Committee (AHC), were invited by the Colonial Office to negotiate an end to the General Strike in Palestine. While in London, Jamal al-Husseini "tried to persuade the mandatory government to recognize the Palestinian leadership's passionate opposition to immigration, especially illegal immigration;" concurrently, he tried to negotiate with "non-Zionist Jewish groups in the United States and the Brit Shalom group in Palestine to support voluntary Jewish restrictions on immigration and land purchase."[78] Against this background, it is not surprising that he and his wife, or their daughter, socialized with Jews in London at a time when contacts among Arabs and Jews in Palestine were becoming less common. Nimati was the sister of Musa Alami, who had graduated from the University of Cambridge and, in the 1930s, was working as Private Secretary for Arab Affairs to High Commissioner of Palestine and Transjordan Arthur Wauchope. In 1946, Alami would open the Arab Office in Jerusalem, as we have seen earlier. It is probable that neither Nimati nor Wolfgang knew much about each other when they played a game of table tennis. The AHC was outlawed in September 1937 because of its opposition to the Peel Commission's recommendation of the partition of Palestine. Unlike its representatives who were exiled to the Seychelles—and who had been invited to London along with him—Jamal al-Husseini and his family managed to escape Jerusalem for Beirut.

Wolfgang led a bohemian life. He became engaged to a fellow student, Pauline May Tilbury, but the engagement did not last long. He immersed himself in the city's cultural life, visiting art exhibitions, the opera, and the theater.[79] In July 1937, he traveled to Austria to attend the Salzburg Festival, established in the aftermath of World War I, where he participated in a summer academy given by the pioneer of Expressionist stage design, Emil Pirchan. He also spent time in Cornwall in the company of another fellow student, Anthony Froshaug, who was to become a renowned typographer. Wolfgang drew stage designs for Hofmannsthal's *Everyman* and Shakespeare's *As You Like It*, *Hamlet*, and *Macbeth*,[80] and he read widely, in particular Auden, Joyce, T. S. Eliot, Aldous Huxley, and

D. H. Lawrence. Exposed to European avant-garde and modernist art, he was especially drawn to Surrealism. London's art scene was bursting with life, as the founding in 1938 of the *London Bulletin*, a journal dedicated to Surrealist and abstract art, illustrates.[81] Concurrently, the art world in Germany was increasingly dominated by Nazi ideology, as books were burned, and artworks stolen and destroyed. The spectacular *Entartete Kunst* exhibition was organized by Adolf Ziegler—Hitler's favorite painter—and the Nazi Party in Munich in November 1937 to showcase the perceived degeneracy of modern art. Wolfgang followed the political events in Germany from afar. After Kristallnacht, which saw hundreds of Jews killed and thousands arrested and incarcerated in concentration camps while Jewish homes, schools, and synagogues were attacked, vandalized, and destroyed across Germany, Wolfgang writes on November 12, 1938: "What do you say about the pogroms in Germany? Here, people are honestly outraged but that does not help much. *I already begin to doubt the Jews' right to exist.* Sometimes, I feel ashamed that all these problems occupy me so little, but I can't help it" [my emphasis].[82] The mention of doubt suggests in Wolfgang a seemingly tortured attempt to keep painful existential questions at bay—questions that demonstrate his acute awareness of the gravity of events in Germany, which bring to mind Heinrich Heine's words: "Where they burn books, they will ultimately burn men as well."[83]

Wolfgang did not mix much with German-speaking émigrés. He refers to having met the Austrian filmmaker Berthold Viertel, a pioneer of the silent film who played an important role in German and British cinema before working for the booming Hollywood film industry. Through his friend, the painter Lucian Freud, Wolfgang also met Sigmund Freud, the founder of psychoanalysis and Lucian's grandfather, whom he described as already visibly ill.[84] On June 30, 1939, two months before the outbreak of World War II, Wolfgang writes, "I suppose there will soon be a war, although I cannot really imagine it."[85] "Of course fascism cannot last long," he adds in another letter on August 22, 1939, "but before it goes down, it will still grow, I am strongly convinced of that."[86]

At the same time, Wolfgang was also following the political developments in Palestine, deliberated in the British Empire's capital at the London Conference, which the British government held with Arab and Jewish delegations in February and March 1939 to reach an agreement on the end of its mandate in, and the future of, Palestine. Among the members of the Arab delegation were Musa Alami, George Antonius, and Hussein Fakhri al-Khalidi,

Walid Khalidi's uncle; Chaim Weizmann and David Ben-Gurion were part of the Jewish delegation. The conference resulted in the White Paper issued by Prime Minister Neville Chamberlain, whom Wolfgang, in a letter dated October 1, 1938, referred to as "one of the biggest bastards of world history."[87] Writing again, on February 22, 1939, he remarks, "I am following the Palestine Conference in the papers. It seems to me that the Arabs are making unbelievable demands and are getting more outrageous. Here, however, no one seems to be interested and it does not matter. If there were no detailed broadcasts on the radio, no one would know about it."[88]

Wolfgang's political views, as expressed in these and other of his letters from London, were consistent with his father's overall Zionist leanings. His observation that people in Britain were not interested in the London Conference, nor, by extension, in the political developments in British Mandate Palestine, is telling, as it gives us a sense of the relative insignificance of Palestine in people's everyday lives in Europe on the eve of World War II.

With the outbreak of war, Wolfgang returned to Palestine with reluctance. He had gained a foothold in London's cultural circles, compared to which life in Palestine—as he had experienced it during his first stay there—seemed dull.[89] He sailed from Southampton to Saint-Malo and continued by train to Switzerland to see the Geheebs, who had by this time opened the École d'Humanité in Versoix, close to Geneva. In an undated letter, probably written from Versoix, he voices feelings of guilt for escaping the war: "I strongly feel that I am somehow dodging the war. Of course, that's not possible. A year ago, I would have thought it was none of my business. But it concerns us all, fascism must be defeated. And in my opinion, it is worth fighting against it. But I don't want to fight for Palestine, and I would rather join an organization in England or France than one like the Haganah in Palestine."[90]

In Versoix, he met Wolf Rosenberg, his friend from the Odenwaldschule, who was taking musical directing courses in Zürich with the German conductor and composer Hermann Scherchen, an advocate of contemporary and atonal music who had left Germany in protest against the Nazis's rise to power in 1933.[91] Together with Rosenberg, who like him was waiting for the necessary papers to continue his journey to Palestine, Wolfgang worked on an opera titled *Pansuun* and published a poem of the same name in German, giving voice to Surrealist experimentation.[92]

JERUSALEM WITH BELLA SOSKIN, 1939–1942

Wolfgang returned to Palestine by sea from Venice at the end of 1939. The world he encountered was markedly different from the one he had lived in just a few years earlier. The political situation had changed significantly with the White Paper of 1939 and Britain's stated goal of aligning Jewish immigration to Palestine with the national interests of its Arab population. At the same time, despite its opposition to the White Paper, the Yishuv was drawing closer to Britain because of the escalating conflict in Europe. Wolfgang's parents were now living in Haifa, which had emerged as the hub of industrial development in the region. On December 4, 1941, the *Palestine Post* announced that "Dr. A Hildesheimer, Managing Director of Palestine Edible Products Ltd., was yesterday admitted as a new member of the Haifa Rotary Club."[93] In 1939, Wolfgang's sister Eva had married Ernst Teltsch, who had emigrated to Palestine from Vienna and would go on to succeed his father-in-law as director of the Shemen factory in Haifa. His family had founded the Teltsch House Hotel and Pension, which was designed by the Austrian-born architect Leopold Krakauer in 1936 as a Jewish "national mission" and a "showcase of Zionism."[94] Intended to cater to the increasing number of Zionist tourists visiting Palestine, the hotel was located on Mount Carmel, where the Hildesheimers rented a house. Mount Carmel looked over the sand dunes of Haifa Bay, where the Shemen factory was built just above the expanding Jewish neighborhood of Hadar HaCarmel. The latter was a strategic location used by the Carmeli Brigade, a division of the Haganah Field Corps (HISH), on April 21 and 22, 1948, in an all-out attack on Haifa's Arab neighborhoods. This aggression was carried out in collusion with the British Army as "part of a new, general military offensive to establish a Jewish state in Palestine by force of arms in the wake of the UNGA partition recommendation and in anticipation of the end of the British Mandate on 15 May 1948," as Walid Khalidi shows in his 1959 article "The Fall of Haifa."[95] The name of this offensive was unknown to Walid in 1959, but a few years later, he uncovered its name and details: Plan Dalet, which aimed to expand Jewish areas in Palestine beyond those allocated to the proposed Jewish State by the UN Partition Plan.[96]

In a letter to his parents written in May 1940, Wolfgang expressed a general feeling of malaise at being back in Palestine. Struggling to make a living, he voiced dismay at prospects of continuing to work for Epstein—referring to Eliyahu Epstein-Eilat from the Jewish Agency, as Eva Teltsch told Volker Jehle, the editor of Wolfgang's letters to his parents.[97] This work for Epstein is not described further but probably had to do with advertising, as Wolfgang went on to say, "to make myself happy I would have to throw the stuff at Epstein's feet. Advertising is interesting. I can also draw well, but it is difficult to regurgitate things that have already been pre-chewed and spit them out exactly as the person who digested them wanted them to be."[98] It may also have been linked to the Tel Aviv, Haifa, and Jerusalem offices of the Jewish Agency, which launched an ad campaign to recruit Jewish soldiers into the British Army, as Jehle suggests.[99] "As the German army overran Europe and North Africa," writes Segev, "it appeared possible that it would conquer Palestine as well. In the summer of 1940, in the spring of 1941, and again in the fall of 1942 the danger seemed imminent."[100] Epstein, who had immigrated from the Ukraine to Palestine in 1924, was a committed Zionist from his early teens. Dedicated to the idea of Hebrew labor, he worked as a construction worker with the local Bedouins in Ma'an and Salt in Transjordan and later studied Arabic at the School of Oriental Studies at the Hebrew University and the American University of Beirut. Having acquired an intimate knowledge of Arabic and established ties with Arab intellectuals, he was recruited by the Political Department of the Jewish Agency to file reports on his contacts, and from 1934 to 1944, he headed the Department's Near East Section.[101] After World War II, he became the Jewish Agency's representative in Washington, D.C., and it was in this capacity that he signed the letter to President Harry S. Truman on May 14, 1948, to inform him "that the state of Israel has been proclaimed" and to remind him of the "deep bond of sympathy which has existed and has been strengthened over the past thirty years between the Government of the United States and the Jewish people of Israel."[102] He subsequently served as Israel's first ambassador to the United States, Israel's ambassador to the United Kingdom, and president of the Hebrew University, a position Judah Leon Magnes had held before 1948, when a binational state and peaceful coexistence between Arabs and Jews in Palestine still seemed possible.

In another letter to his parents, Wolfgang refers to the HOG and reiterates his aversion to continuing to work for Epstein.[103] In the same letter, he singles out Jerusalem as "the only place where one can live" in Palestine, adding, "I am sick and tired of Tel Aviv too."[104] Wolfgang increasingly distanced himself from the German Zionist networks to which his family background linked him, seeking refuge instead in British circles in Jerusalem, and it was through these connections that he came in touch with Arab intellectuals.

Together with Reginald (Reggie) Weston, who had grown up in Egypt and arrived in Palestine in 1936, Wolfgang opened an advertising agency in Jerusalem. Weston was both a journalist and an artist. He held one of the first exhibitions of abstract art in Jerusalem at the Schlosser-Glasberg Cabinet of Arts in Ben Yehuda Street, north of Julian's Way, in 1939,[105] and devoted himself entirely to painting when he moved to Paris in the late 1940s.[106] The *Palestine Post* published a number of ads for the agency, HW, describing Hildesheimer and Weston as "commercial artists" (figure 4.1)[107] As part of his work as a commercial artist, Wolfgang designed advertisements for Blue Band margarine. In a signed advertisement in the *Palestine Post*, he lists "the Hebrew word 'margalith', the Arabic 'marjan' and the Greek 'margaritis', all meaning pearl" as the source words from which the English *margarine* is derived. To connect this product with its new environment, another advertisement depicts "the flowers of Palestine," such as the anemone, in a series to "cut out and collect . . . for the children who will love them—Just as they love Blue Band, the margarine, the old household favorite" (figures 4.2 and 4.3).[108]

More aspiring artist than writer at this time, Wolfgang had planned a solo exhibition in London in 1939 but, because of the outbreak of war and his return to Palestine, the exhibition took place instead in Jerusalem in the early 1940s, at Schlosser-Glasberg Cabinet of Arts. The exhibition featured drawings, collages, and illustrations for Baudelaire's *Fleurs du mal*, which Th. F. M. (a pseudonym of Edward J. Ezra Sperling), who had reviewed Weston's earlier exhibition, derided in the *Palestine Post* as "belated surrealism."[109] The exhibition catalog, which included a text by André Breton, is lost.[110] Wolfgang and Weston also participated in

4.1 "HW Advertising and Commercial Artists," *Palestine Post*, August 20, 1941.

4.2 "1869," Wolfgang Hildesheimer's advertisement for Blue Band, *Palestine Post*, June 7, 1940.

a number of group exhibitions at the Habimah Art Gallery and the Katz Gallery in Tel Aviv and again at the Cabinet of Arts in Jerusalem.[111] The latter gained significant attention in the press. It was opened on December 20, 1942, by R. D. (Reggie) Smith, who worked for the Palestine Broadcasting Service and later for the BBC in London and was known for his communist leanings, and reviewed by his wife, the British writer Olivia Manning, in an article for the *Palestine Post* titled "Five Modern Artists."[112] The exhibition also showed works by William Gear,[113] Marcel Janco,[114] and Rudolf (Rudi) Lehmann.[115]

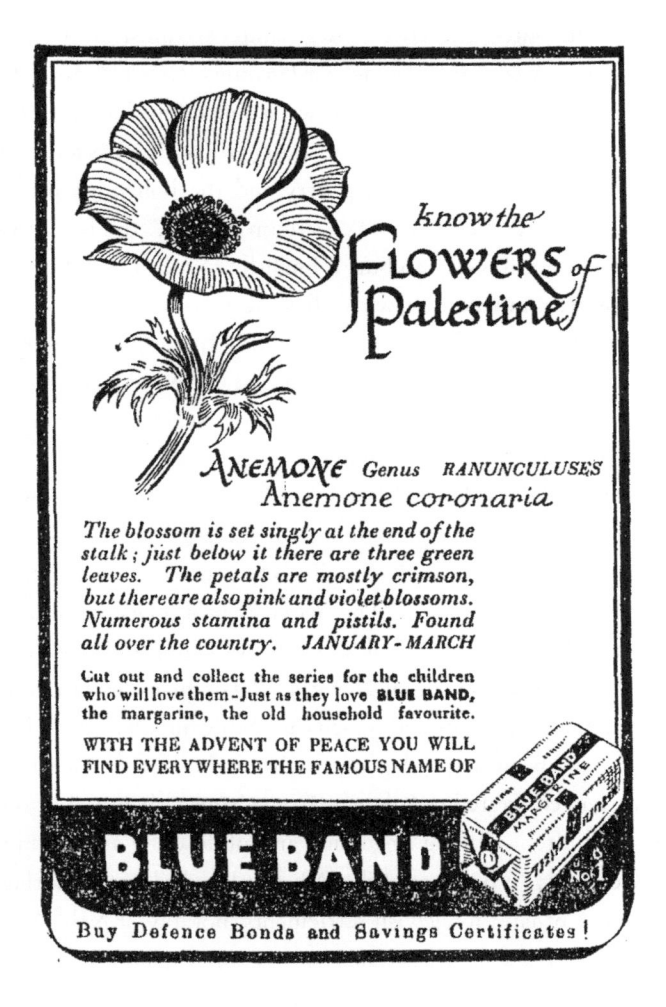

4.3 "Know the Flowers of Palestine," Wolfgang Hildesheimer's advertisement for Blue Band, *Palestine Post*, February 16, 1945.

Around the same time, between 1940 and 1941, Wolfgang underwent psychoanalysis, meeting as many as six times a week with Margarete Brandt, who worked at the Palestine Psychoanalytical Association. The association had been founded in Jerusalem in 1934 by Max Eitington, a close friend of Sigmund Freud and the former president of the Berlin Psychoanalytical Polyclinic.[116] Wolfgang's resolve to become a writer was taken up later but, in retrospect, he considered his psychoanalysis to be a central step toward that end, saying that without that experience he would not have been able to write any of his longer prose works.[117]

Wolfgang contributed the cover image and two illustrations to Manfred Vogel's 1941 volume *Ariel—ein Almanach für Literatur—Graphik—Musik* (Ariel—an almanac for literature, graphics, and music), a collection that brought together the work of German writers in Palestine, among them Else Lasker-Schüler, who was renowned for her Expressionist poetry and the bohemian life she led in Berlin. It also included Wolfgang's "Perpetuum Mobile," the lone poem in the anthology written not in German but in English.[118] Wolfgang did not mix much with German writers in Palestine, with a few exceptions, among them Max Brod whom he would later introduce to Walid Khalidi. In German literary circles in Palestine, Wolfgang was known as an "exclusive Geheimtyp[!]"—in German, a play on words between an insider tip (*Tipp*) and a secretive person (*Typ*)—and a proponent of dandyism in the company of an "exotic, extraordinary, dark beauty," a description not devoid of racist and sexist connotations, which could have been aimed at either Bella Soskin or Sally Kassab.[119]

Wolfgang was briefly married to Bella. Their marriage was announced in the *Palestine Post* on May 6, 1942: "The marriage took place yesterday between Wolf, only son of Dr. and Mrs. A. Hildesheimer, of Haifa, and Bella, only daughter of Dr. and Mrs. S. E. Soskin, of Nahariya."[120] The marriage lasted less than a year. From the few references about Bella in Wolfgang's letters to his parents, it appears to have been a failed prospect from the start.[121] Her father, Selig Eugen Soskin, had emigrated to Palestine from Crimea, then part of the Russian Empire, in 1896, after studying agronomy and philosophy at the University of Rostock in Germany. As director of the JNF, he played a key role in the purchase and development of land for Jewish settlements, notably of Nahariya, north of Acre on the Mediterranean coast. Nahariya was built on land the JNF purchased in the early 1930s from the Tueinis, a Greek Orthodox Christian family from Beirut who, in 1933, founded *An-Nahar*, which remains one of Lebanon's largest newspapers. The settlement was in proximity to a number of Arab villages along the road that linked Tarshiha to Acre, namely al-Ghabisiya, al-Kabri, al-Nahr, al-Tall, and Umm al-Faraj—villages that were demolished as part of the Haganah's Plan Dalet. Their destruction was closely linked to the fall of the seaport of Acre, renowned for its walls and fortifications, on May 17, 1948, three days after the establishment of the State of Israel.[122]

In the 1930s, Soskin sought to develop Nahariya as an agricultural settlement in the image of Monte Algaida on the eastern rim of the Mediterranean; when this proved difficult, he contributed to transforming Nahariya into a European-style seaside resort. In its early days, it attracted mainly British officers and their families stationed in Khartoum and Abadan, key theaters of war in the East African Campaign of 1940–1941 and the 1941 Anglo-Soviet invasion of Iran, with which the Allies managed to secure important oil supply lines. After the White Paper of 1939, the Nahariya coast became the main entry point for illegal immigration to Palestine.[123] Soskin supported the Revisionist movement of Jabotinsky, which formed the basis of a number of right-wing Zionist paramilitary organizations, among them the Irgun.[124] Jehle identifies Soskin as "one of the most famous personalities of the Zionist movement" in his edition of Wolfgang's letters to his parents, whereas Wolfgang himself refers to Soskin only as a *"Pflanzenzüchter"* (plant breeder), while remaining silent about his politics.[125]

JERUSALEM WITH SALLY KASSAB, 1943–1946

In a letter to Rasha Salam Khalidi written from Poschiavo, Switzerland, on April 8, 1984, in response to her request to help her remember their time together in Palestine as she was starting to write her memoirs, Wolfgang gives a description of Haifa's Mount Carmel. He recalls the many pine trees and the beautiful old houses in the nearby German Colony, an upper-class, predominantly Arab Christian neighborhood, where he met Sally Kassab in the home of one of his architect friends, George Rais, a graduate of the Bartlett School and the Architectural Association School of Architecture in London.[126]

Sally and George were second cousins—his mother was Wadad Rais (née Kassab),[127] a cousin of Aziz S. Kassab, Sally's father, a merchant from Beirut who had close ties to Palestine, in particular Haifa. As we have seen, Haifa witnessed a rapid process of urbanization during the British Mandate and stood out as a mixed city. In *A Survey of Palestine*, a three-volume report prepared by the Government of Palestine in December 1945 and January 1946 for the Anglo-American Committee of Inquiry, Rais's father, the entrepreneur Raja Rais (also known as Rayyis), is listed as a representative of Haifa's Arab Landlords Association on the government's Housing Advisory Committee.[128] He built a number of projects in Haifa together with the renowned Lebanese architect Antoine Tabet. Notably, a housing complex on the edge of the German Colony was constructed to house employees of Haifa's new refinery and was planned in conjunction with the same Benjamin Chaikin who had overseen the construction of the King David and the Hebrew University.[129]

George ran an architecture office in Haifa with Theo Canaan, a graduate of the University of Cambridge. Theo was also friends with Wolfgang. He was the son of Tawfiq Canaan, a pioneering physician, scholar, and ethnographer of Palestine,[130] who was married to Margot Eilender, the daughter of a German tradesman living in Jerusalem. Most likely, Theo and Wolfgang spoke German together.[131] Both George and Theo were friends with Assem Salam, who had also studied architecture at Cambridge and would marry Sulafa Khalidi, Walid's sister.[132]

Sally is mentioned in a few letters written by Wolfgang to his sister Eva, which confirm that he had strong feelings for her; their love affair probably started in 1943, when Wolfgang became part of the ecumenical circle, as Sally was also close friends with Jabra, Walid, and Rasha (figures 4.4 and 4.5). In a letter written to his sister Eva at his return to London in 1946, Wolfgang says that he was glad they, his sister and her husband, liked Sally and that she had liked them too, and suggests they see her again when they come to Jerusalem.[133]

4.4 Sulafa Khalidi, Assem Salam, Wolfgang Hildesheimer, Sally Kassab, and Rasha Salam in the garden of the Khalidis' house, Arab College, Jerusalem, 1945.
Courtesy of Walid Khalidi.

4.5 Wolfgang Hildesheimer and Sally Kassab in the garden of the Khalidis' house, Arab College, Jerusalem, 1945.
Courtesy of Walid Khalidi.

After her parents' divorce, Sally had grown up with her mother, Malvina Hanania, and her British stepfather, Richard L. Moon, in England, where she attended Saint Mary's Hall in Brighton, a boarding school for girls. When her mother's second marriage failed, she returned with her mother to Jerusalem.[134] This coincided with the outbreak of World War II. Sally's maternal grandfather, the Reverend Sotiri Hanania, was a respected member of the Greek Orthodox clergy in Jerusalem.[135] A few ink on paper drawings Sally did as a young woman in Jerusalem have survived with her son, Matthew Pruen, in England, and give us a sense of her artistic leanings. They depict a magnolia, possibly from a tree in the Hanania's garden in Jerusalem, a flower she would paint often throughout her life. Sally would meet John Belassis Pruen, whom she married in Amman in 1951 (figure 4.6).[136]

In addition to his work in advertising, Wolfgang made a living by teaching English at the British Council. Among his students, he remembers, were Polish

4.6 Sally Kassab, *Magnolia*, ink on paper, 29, 7 × 42 cm, June 4, 1940. Courtesy of Matthew Pruen.

officers and their wives who had found temporary refuge in Palestine, but most of his students were Arabs.[137] In the spring of 1943, he designed stage sets and costumes for plays by Ibsen, Shakespeare, and Wilde that were produced by the Jerusalem Dramatic Society at the Young Men's Christian Association (YMCA) in collaboration with the British Council.[138] The same year, he was recruited by Christopher Holme to work for the Public Information Office (PIO), which had its headquarters in the David Building at the roundabout a mere two hundred meters south of the YMCA and the King David Hotel. *A Survey of Palestine* describes the PIO as "Press Bureau," and informs us that, since April 1939,

> the Public Information Office has paid increasing attention to what is now generally known as public relations work and has developed rather on the lines of a link and medium of contact between Government and the press than as an instrument for the control of the press, in accordance with modern democratic practice. With the establishment of the British Ministry of Information on the outbreak of the war, the Public Information Office in Palestine undertook the performance of certain additional services on behalf of His Majesty's Government in connection with spreading knowledge of the Allied war effort and securing the goodwill and cooperation of the inhabitants of Palestine in this war effort. This services gradually expanded during the war years to include the operation of rural cinema caravans, the display of posters, the organization of press advertising, the publication of magazines and other publicity material.[139]

Holme was an Oxford graduate in classics and an acclaimed journalist who had covered the Berlin Reichstag fire trial and the Spanish Civil War, notably the bombing of Guernica carried out by the Luftwaffe on April 26, 1937, at the behest of General Franco.[140] In "Pieces of Poetical Reporting on Spain," published posthumously, Holme writes,

> The world ended tonight.
> There in that unreal desolation
> Of molten tunnel, flame-arched passageway,
> House-hung setpieces dripping cement and bricks,
> A handful of dim creatures
> Are scratching for fragments of their slaughtered world.[141]

The Spanish Civil War provided a bitter foretaste of the catastrophes that were soon to engulf all of Europe and the Middle East. Wolfgang and Holme did not socialize much in Palestine; their friendship "developed later, when the colonial constellation was over. One could be friends in England," remembers Wolfgang.[142]

In an undated letter to his parents, Wolfgang refers to World War II as "possibly not our war but more my war than yours," marking a difference between his identification with Britain's war effort against Nazi Germany and that of his parents.[143] Wolfgang's work at the PIO may have enabled him to engage in the war, but this was met with reservations by his parents, given the Yishuv's strained relations with Britain since the White Paper of 1939, as an undated letter he wrote to them, probably in September 1943, suggests. In the letter, he describes his tasks at the PIO and says he spoke with Georg Landauer, a close friend of his parents from their days in Mannheim and a member of the JNC, who said that it was indeed compatible with the Yishuv's interests.

> The work consists of arranging exhibitions (for example there is one now at the YMCA about the war in Italy [the Allies landed on mainland Italy on September 3, 1943]), compiling and selecting the photographic material, drawing maps or having them drawn, writing labels, designing exhibition cases.... I talked about it with Landauer, who not only thought that it was harmless but also advised me to accept the job offer. He said it was part of the war effort (he is correct) and had nothing to do with domestic political issues. No part of the Jewish population would resent such work; on the contrary, official bodies might even welcome it.[144]

Not much more is known about Wolfgang's work for the PIO.[145] A brochure published in Germany in the early 1960s for a production of one of his plays, a biographical sketch, possibly written by Wolfgang, notes that he was going back and forth between Jerusalem and Haifa "with a briefcase that said 'His Majesty's Service' but without a uniform."[146] Another brochure, published when he was awarded the Bremen Literature Prize in 1966, says that he spent "an interesting war" as an English information officer in Palestine.[147] In the German TV series *Zeugen des Jahrhunderts* (Witnesses of the century), he would describe the PIO as "a kind of Ministry of Information ... designed to influence the Arab and Jewish populations along British lines."[148] In conversations with Jehle, he said that "he put together display cases in Palestine, Syria and Lebanon, with propaganda for the English, that is to say against the establishment of the state of Israel."[149] At the YMCA in Jerusalem, he curated a number of exhibitions. A photograph shows him in one of the exhibition halls at the YMCA, leaning against the wall with a book under his arm; in the background hangs a picture of the future Queen Elizabeth II, who made her first solo public appearances as heir presumptive in support of Britain's war effort in 1943; to its left are posters of General Barker and Winston Churchill; and to its right, posters of Chiang Kai-shek, Churchill, and Franklin D. Roosevelt—the exhibition probably took place at the time of their meeting in Cairo in November 1943 (figure 4.7).

The PIO had three publications, one in Arabic, another in English, and a third in Hebrew; the English-language *Forum* was edited by Reggie Smith.[150] On May 3, 1946, the *Palestine Post* announced that "M. W. Hildesheimer, previously in charge of the PIO sub-office in Haifa," had joined the PIO in Jerusalem as acting editor of *Radio Week*,[151] as *Forum* was renamed in 1946. The same rubric also refers

4.7 Wolfgang Hildesheimer at a PIO exhibition at the YMCA.
Academy of Arts, Berlin, WHA 1329.

130   THE TIME BEFORE 1948

to a concert given at the Antonian Hall in Jaffa by the Jerusalem Orpheus Choir with Johannes Garabedian (tenor) and Afif Bulos (baritone). *Radio Week*'s first issue featured Wolfgang's essay "On James Joyce."[152]

It was probably through his work at the PIO, but possibly at the YMCA or with British friends at the bar of the King David, that Wolfgang met Jabra and Walid, both of whom had published some of their poetry in *Forum* between 1943 and 1946. Wolfgang would later say: "When I think about this period in Jerusalem, I remember the people I saw daily were Arabs. Walid el-Khalidi and his sister Sulafa, his wife Rasha was Lebanese, born Salaam, her cousin Asid [Assem] Salaam was an architect in Beirut who came often to Jerusalem because he was engaged to Sulafa. Those were my greatest friends."[153]

His "greatest friends," however, knew little about his life in Germany, about the Zionist circles his family background had placed him in during his first stay in Palestine, or about his work for the PIO, not to mention the Holocaust, which even Wolfgang knew little about at the time, following news from Germany from a distance.[154] In conversations with Walid, I asked if he and Wolfgang had spoken about politics: he recalled that Wolfgang would at times warn him about how dangerous the mood was in the Yishuv and its leadership, which was preparing for war, suggesting that the Arab side may not have been fully aware of the seriousness of the situation; however, all in all, they did not discuss politics much.[155] In conversations with Hadara Lazar, Wolfgang said he did not speak with Walid about his work for the PIO. He also referred to Jabra and to the dream of a cosmopolitan way of life, which he shared with his Arab friends but was not able to find in Jewish circles: "Do you speak Arabic?" Lazar asked;

"No, no," [Wolfgang] protested, "we spoke English, of course. Walid and Rasha spoke perfect English.". . . . Another Arab friend was Gabriel Jabra," he went on. "He came from a Christian sect, I believe. He was very gifted and studied in Cambridge and wrote poetry which I thought was very good in those days, and which I illustrated". . . . "I am not a *Homo politicus*. I am a great pessimist, and I think that before the next century is at an end men will have left this planet and this will also solve the Palestine problem. Even now," he went on, "I find myself absolutely impartial. I can't say that I am for Israel or for the Arabs. My father always said it was a question of right against right, and he belonged to the German Zionists who fought for a national home, but not for a Jewish state. . . . It's about time we admitted that these people, especially the Arabs I mixed with, dreamt of a cosmopolitan way of life, which the Jews did not. The Jews had Zionistic ideas. The Arabs were in Palestine anyway."[156]

Wolfgang's use of the word *cosmopolitan* denotes open-mindedness and worldliness, reaching out from Palestine to the world, as opposed to a Zionist-driven closing in on Palestine. Grounded in European conceptions that would lead to a world citizen movement centered in Paris after World War II, which Wolfgang was to join with enthusiasm (as is elaborated on later), his notion of cosmopolitanism turns a deaf ear to his Arab friends' aspirations to attain national self-determination. Despite the poetic affinities he shared with his Arab friends, with whom he was able to discuss Shakespeare, English Romantic literature, Joyce, Kafka, or Surrealist art, Wolfgang showed little interest in, and remained an outsider to, many of the political and intellectual issues that preoccupied them—partly because he neither knew, nor made any effort to learn, Arabic, which was, after all, Palestine's primary language and remained one of its official languages even when English and Hebrew were introduced as additional official languages under the British Mandate. Had he spoken Arabic, Wolfgang would have been able to engage in more depth in discussions of Arabic language and literature and its aesthetic and political sensibilities with his friends, but these remained as foreign to Wolfgang as did German language and literature to Walid and Jabra. Their common preoccupation was with English letters, which later were to have a significant impact on Wolfgang and Jabra's respective literary output in German and Arabic.

Wolfgang remembers an evening at the Moghanams' (also known as Mogannam) house in the elegant neighborhood of Talbiya, where he gave a poetry recital introduced by Walid.[157] Mogannam Elias Mogannam was a well-known, U.S.-educated Jerusalemite lawyer who was from an Arab Christian Orthodox family that had converted to Protestantism. His wife, Matiel E. T. Mogannam, was of Lebanese American background. As had Anbara Salam Khalidi, she had come to Palestine with her husband and fully embraced the Palestinian cause, standing out as a leading figure in women's emancipation. As we have already seen, she delivered a speech from the minbar of the al-Aqsa Mosque in the Old City while General Allenby gave his address at the opening of the YMCA in 1933. A few years later, her book *The Arab Woman and the Palestine Problem* was published in London.[158] In conversations with Lazar, Wolfgang also mentions Katy Antonius: "I can't say I was friends with Katy Antonius . . . but I was invited to her parties. . . . She was violently anti-Zionist . . . but of course when a man like Arthur Koestler came, he was a guest in her house. He was at his best when he had a public, the public at Katy Antonius' house. There were always people I don't know, but one met Christopher [Holme] and Reggie Smith and his wife, Olivia Manning, the novelist. All sorts of intellectuals and my Arab friends."[159]

Perhaps best known for his 1940 novel *Darkness at Noon*, Arthur Koestler was a controversial figure who flirted with various political movements, from communism to liberalism and including Zionism.[160] His ties to the Zionist movement, in particular to Jabotinsky, are well documented. While he was a guest at Katy Antonius's salon during his stay in Palestine from January to August 1945, he was, with the approval of Chaim Weizmann, also meeting with Menachem Begin of the Irgun and Nathan Yellin-Mor (Friedman) of Lehi, to "talk to those mad friends of yours," as Weizmann wrote to him, "and try to convince them that Partition is our only chance."[161] Although Koestler did not succeed in influencing the underground Zionist leaders, whose members he describes as belonging "to a different [younger] generation—hard, bitter, and fanatical," he was influenced by them, suggests Louis A. Gordon. He describes Koestler's 1946 novel *Thieves in the Night: Chronicle of an Experiment* as "a penance to Jabotinsky, not only in its dedication (which is in Jabotinsky's memory) but also in the story itself," which chronicles the conflict between Arabs and Jews in Mandate Palestine, and which was read by members of the 1947 United Nations Palestine Commission before making recommendations for the partition of Palestine.[162]

Asked about the King David Hotel, Wolfgang recalls, "the atmosphere was amazing, and the bar, especially the bar of the King David, was something absolutely magnificent. It didn't have the glamour of the great places in the world, but it was unique, a center of intellectual small talk."[163] The King David Hotel bombing—carried out by Irgun terrorists who are portrayed through heroic gestures and biblical references as "thieves in the night" by Koestler—is neither mentioned in Wolfgang's conversations with Lazar, nor in his letters, nor in any other available documents.

FROM JERUSALEM TO LONDON, CORNWALL, AND NUREMBERG

In love with England and certain that his place was in Europe, as he explained in later letters to his parents,[164] Wolfgang returned to London after the end of World War II, leaving Palestine shortly before the King David Hotel bombing, on July 1, 1946, possibly along with his mother and father, with whom he attended the Glyndebourne Festival Opera later that month.[165] In a letter to his sister Eva and her husband, postmarked in London on July 18, 1946, he refers to his illustrations for a collection of poems to be published by Nicolson and Watson—likely those he drew to accompany several poems by Jabra, a collaboration about which more is said in the next chapter.[166]

In my conversations with Walid, he remembered Wolfgang as being among the group of friends who celebrated the Khalidis' wedding anniversary at the King David Hotel on the evening before the bombing, with which we opened this book. Memory is known to fail and to play tricks. This raises questions about the place of testimony—autobiographical accounts of past events in oral conversation or written form—in historical research, while at the same time shedding light on the complex relationship between reality and fiction. It is indeed possible that the celebration dinner took place earlier, at a further distance in time from the bombing, but it is also possible that Wolfgang did not attend this dinner but came to Walid's mind because he had been part of so many other gatherings of the ecumenical circle at the King David.

After visiting Glyndebourne with his parents, Wolfgang traveled with Anthony Froshaug, a friend from his student days at the Central School of Arts and Crafts, and other artists to Cornwall.[167] A month after the King David Hotel bombing—as if nothing had happened—on August 23, 1946, the *Palestine Post* published his travel report, "Cornish Summer: Holiday-Makers Paradise," along with one of his illustrations.[168] Wolfgang would return to Cornwall in actual travel as well as in travel writing, namely in *Zeiten in Cornwall*, published in 1971. Questioning conventions of autobiographical writing, the book opens as an unnamed first-person narrator moves forward "in a labyrinth" as he reflects on avant-garde art and the time he spent in Cornwall and London. Caught between memory and writing as an act of storing past experiences (in German, he writes *ad acta legen*), his narrative blurs the lines between reality and fiction with the aim of drawing a truer picture of Cornwall than conventional travel writing could possibly provide. This approach is in line with the conceptions of literature Wolfgang developed more clearly in "The End of Fiction" (1975), namely that "the function of literature is not to turn truth into fiction but to turn fiction into truth: to condense truth out of fiction."[169] The narrative ends with a reference to Hamlet's final words, "the rest is silence," rendered as "the intangible rest consists of that material that does not find expression in words" (in German, Der ungreifbare Rest besteht aus jenem Stoff, der nicht zur Sprache kommt).[170]

In London, Wolfgang had resumed the bohemian life of his student days. Wolfgang's letters to his parents tell of financial difficulties as he sets out to make a living as a graphic artist. His life took an unexpected turn when a friend told him that the American Embassy in London was hiring people to conduct simultaneous translation at the Nuremberg trials.[171] Wolfgang took an exam to qualify as an interpreter and, in January 1947, returned to Allied-occupied Germany, where he worked with Siegfried Ramler, a pioneer of simultaneous translation who first implemented his system at Nuremberg. Ramler had escaped Vienna shortly after Kristallnacht in 1938 on a kindertransport to London.[172] Some of the most prominent journalists and acclaimed writers were sent to Nuremberg to cover the trials, among them John Dos Passos, Ilja Ehrenburg, Martha Gellhorn, Erich Kästner, Erika Mann, Elsa Triolet, Rebecca West, and Anne O'Hare McCormick, the Pulitzer Prize winner who had reported about the King David Hotel bombing the same year for the *New York Times*. It was "a media event of the first order," transmitted to a world public in English, Russian, German, and French, rendered possible by new innovations made available by the American multinational technology corporation IBM.[173] Wolfgang had published a few articles in English before, notably in *Forum* back in Jerusalem, but he was not yet known as a writer. It was only in subsequent years that he turned away from visual art, and from writing in English, to literary work in the German language. What he was to witness at the trials deeply affected him—and his later writing. He arrived in Nuremberg after the trials of major war criminals by Justice Robert H. Jackson, when most of the celebrity writers had left. Under Jackson's successor, Telford Taylor, he worked as an interpreter in the Subsequent Nuremberg Proceedings, specifically the

Schutzstaffel (SS)-Einsatzgruppen Trial of Otto Ohlendorf, which brought to the fore the involvement of the German leadership, ranging from medical doctors to judges, industrials, SS and police commanders, military personnel, state officials, and diplomats, in the Nazi crimes.[174]

For the next two years, from 1947 to 1949, Wolfgang lived as a member of the occupation forces in Nuremberg, first in the confiscated castle of the stationery manufacturers Faber-Castell on the outskirts of town, which served as an international press camp, and then in a room in the Grand Hotel in proximity of Nuremberg's central station. Here, he transformed his room into an atelier to distract himself from "the horrors of these extensively recapitulated processes" by painting.[175] In a letter to his sister written in the spring of 1947, he describes Germany as "hopeless. Everything is in ruins..... At night you see all kinds of strange, sinister creatures [in German, he writes *finstere Gestalten*] in the railway stations, displaced persons from Poland, who don't really belong anywhere."[176] He read about the events in Palestine in the English and German press but only sporadically referred to the "troubling news" in letters to his parents.[177] In a letter written from Nuremberg on August 5, 1947, he explains this distance with his dislike of all nationalism and offers a glimpse into the political differences between his parents and himself with respect to the future of Palestine:

> It is not the first time that you—the Other—are making this accusation. That I should like to have a state or a country full of artists, or at least of people like myself, is out of the question. That could only lead to disaster. But I don't think you can build a country through stubbornness and chauvinism alone. Perhaps it's right, perhaps not. In any case, I think this narrow-mindedness, as it prevails—in cultural matters—in Palestine is unnecessary and unworthy—and what is unworthy for the individual is also unworthy for the general public. I hate all nationalism. Again, that doesn't mean I don't fully understand Jewish nationalism. Because under the prevailing circumstances—nationalism in other countries, anti-Semitism, etc.—this was bound to arise. But it still means injustice—and not only in Palestine but in the entire world. That's why I prefer to disassociate [in German, he writes *absondern*] myself, at least until I stumble across [it] myself. After all, it is possible this will never happen.[178]

In another letter to his parents, Wolfgang remarks that "the Palestine problem is of no importance to the German population. They have other worries. The Americans I know, as far as they are interested at all—and Americans are not interested in much—are all pro-partition."[179] On December 7, 1947, he writes that "according to the newspapers, real war has broken out in Palestine," but while he considers the recommendation of partition, as stipulated in Resolution 181, to be a great success, he is worried about losing his Palestinian passport should it come into effect.[180] In the midst of the fighting, on April 17, 1948, he refers to the desolate situation in Palestine, pointing out that things are not much better in Europe given that the Soviet Union left the Allied Control Council for Germany in protest against the London Six-Power Conference, to which it was not invited following the Soviet-backed communist takeover of Czechoslovakia. Despite all this, he says, "What worries me most right now is that I shall apparently be stateless from [!] 15 May."[181] On May 18, 1948, he congratulates his parents on the declaration of the State of Israel: "I congratulate you on the establishment of the new state, it is great whatever it may look like at the moment. The Israeli (?) army must be heroic, I follow the newspapers with amazement and pride. The American newspapers are full of it and what they say about the reactions of the European countries is quite satisfactory."[182]

Although Wolfgang congratulated his parents, he refrained from requesting Israeli citizenship, as a letter sent on April 15, 1949 from London by John B. S. Jardine, preserved in the Academy of Arts in Berlin, suggests. Jardine, who worked at the British Council in Palestine, seems to be responding to Wolfgang's inquiries about British nationality, but he also tells him about Jerusalem—"it's torn now, rubble heaped, wounded"—and shares news from mutual friends, among them, Katy Antonius, Sally Kassab, and the Khalidis:

> I quite understand that you may have strong feelings about getting an Israeli passport and so nationality. But having got it, you can at least travel about and move and get visas. With it you could get a visa for England. Once in, then you pull strings to remain and could then, after whatever number of years it is, apply for British Nationality.
>
> My news? I loved Jerusalem and my house and the county and the views. I was very happy. Then came the end of the Mandate. All around me was war and ugliness; the shops were closed; most of my Arab staff had fled or been bereaved; the post office was shut and no water or light. I could not

communicate with the outside world. The Terrorists were very close, just down the street. So I went. Over to Amman, to wait and see if wisdom and reason would win. They didn't. My house was looted. . . . Now some Jewish army unit have the house and the spoils. . . . I shall see Katie Antonius in Jerusalem, God bless her (she fought physically and spiritually very hard, even firing Sten guns from her garden—she has of course lost all she had in her house). Sally? I think she is in Cairo. The Khalidis in the Lebanon, very depressed and miserable. Their world, like [that of] so many others, has gone.[183]

CHAPTER 5

JABRA IBRAHIM JABRA

"Spark-Plug" of the YMCA Arts Club

A CHILDHOOD IN BETHLEHEM: ACTUAL AND IMAGINED

Jabra Ibrahim Jabra might be described as one of the last men of the Nahda. He was influenced by that generation of Arab writers and educators, who were entrenched in social reform and cultural modernization. Jabra committed himself to playing an active part in this sea of change by continuing to formulate ideas of Arab awakening and rebirth and carrying them forward to new generations of cultural practitioners in Jerusalem, Beirut, Baghdad, and other cities in the Arab world. Issa J. Boullata was, in the early 1940s, a student at Jerusalem's De La Salle College (commonly called the Frères' or Brothers' College), where Jabra taught English literature upon his return to Palestine after completing his studies at the University of Cambridge. Boullata recalls that Jabra introduced him to Shakespeare and the Romantic poets and singles him out not only as "the most acclaimed literary figure" among his former teachers but also as "a window onto modernity."[1]

Jabra wrote two autobiographies toward the end of his life, both of which Boullata, who went on to become a professor of Arabic literature at McGill University in Montreal, translated into English: *al-Bi'r al-ula* (1987) as *The First Well: A Bethlehem Boyhood* (1995), and *Shari' al-amirat* (1994) as *Princesses' Street: Baghdad Memories* (2005). Despite these masterly written accounts, Jabra's life remains poorly documented. As I have argued elsewhere, this has to do with the legacies of European colonialism in the Middle East, and in particular in Palestine, Jabra's social background, and, possibly, with commonly held conceptions of (auto)biographical writing.[2] In general, it is the wealthy and educated who leave behind documents that are handed down from one generation to the next and that are preserved as collectibles in private and public archives. Jabra, however, grew up in poverty; as a result, few documents evince his early life in Palestine. Both of his parents, Ibrahim and Maryam, were illiterate. According to the 1931 general census of Palestine conducted under the British Mandate, literacy among sedentary Arabs in Palestine was 20 percent; by the end of the mandate, it had reached 27 percent.[3] In addition, the Nakba led to a violent rupture between Jabra's past in Palestine and his future in Iraq, with only a small number of personal belongings from the former carried over into the latter. Those few books, papers, and other personal effects that did survive this rupture were lost a decade and a half after Jabra's death in 1994, when his home in Baghdad was destroyed in 2010. In the aftermath of the Iraq War, a series of car-bomb attacks targeted foreign embassies; in one such attack, a vehicle containing explosives was parked in the driveway of Jabra's house, which was located next door to the embassy of Egypt. Jabra's personal library, private papers, and collections of musical records and modern Iraqi art, as well as many of his own paintings were lost as a result of the explosion (figure 5.1). This destruction has been mourned by Arab intellectuals

5.1 Jabra Ibrahim Jabra's destroyed house in Baghdad.
Courtesy of Holly Pickes © 2010 *New York Times*.

as his ultimate death in "the ruins of the second well"[4]—a pointed reference to the title of Jabra's first autobiography—or, as Anthony Shadid writes, "an epitaph of sorts, the end of eras in Iraq and the Arab world and the eclipse, in war and strife, of the ideal he represented."[5]

As Jabra says in the opening lines of his preface to *The First Well*, "I wanted at first to write a complete autobiography, especially because I had often asked the writers of my generation to write their memoirs and to record the experiences of change, growth, and conflict that gave flavor and meaning to their lives, the lives of each one of us, even to life as a whole in our age."[6] Faced with the challenges of autobiographical writing, Jabra mentions gaps, the large number of documents, particularly letters, dispersed around the globe or lost, and the fallibility of memory. Despite these odds, his autobiographies provide us with intimate views into his life and age. Yet "childhood stories," he goes on to explain, "are stories of events which have become a blend of memory and dream, of existential intensity and poetic trance;" bringing them together in one coherent story requires a "fictional stratagem."[7] One such stratagem starts with Jabra's date and place of birth. Although these are not specified in his writings, it is generally accepted that he was born in Bethlehem on August 28, 1919, or 1920. However, Jabra's year and place of birth are indicated as 1919, Adana, in applications seeking admission to Fitzwilliam House (today Fitzwilliam College), University of Cambridge, in 1940, and a fellowship at Harvard University from the Rockefeller Foundation in 1952, which I found in the Fitzwilliam College archives on a visit to the University of Cambridge and in the Rockefeller Archive Center in New York City (figures 5.2 and 5.3). This corresponds to an observation made by the Palestinian poet Ahmad Dahbour, who once saw Jabra's Iraqi passport and remarked that it indicated his birthplace as Turkey, which struck Dahbour as odd.[8]

In the aftermath of World War I, France took over the Ottoman vilayet of Adana, then known as French Cilicia, but withdrew from the region in early 1922 following the end of the Franco-Turkish War. This withdrawal resulted in a new wave of Christian minorities fleeing Anatolia for Iraq, Lebanon, Palestine, and Syria. This, as Benny Morris and Dror Ze'evi have shown, was part of a history of violence spanning three decades, from the reign of Sultan Abdul Hamid II, to the Young Turks, to Mustafa Kemal and the Nationalists.[9] This period saw the Armenian and the Assyrian genocides, which did not evolve in isolation from global currents but rather in conjunction with "the stream—the violent stream—of modern European and near-European history."[10] Jabra's family most

FITZWILLIAM HOUSE, CAMBRIDGE
FORM OF APPLICATION FOR ADMISSION

(To be returned to The Censor, Fitzwilliam House, Cambridge, with the Candidate's Testimonials)

(1) Candidate's name in full (block letters): JABRA IBRAHIM JABRA

(2) Date and place of Birth: Adana (Turkey), 28th August 1919.

(3) Name, address and occupation of Father, and whether alive or deceased: IBRAHIM JABRA, P.O.B. 453, Jerusalem (Palestine) Retired, alive.

(4) Name, address and signature of person responsible for the payment of fees: The British Council, 3 Hanover Street, London, W.1.

(5) Place or places of Education (complete list with dates):
Rachidiya Secondary School, Jerusalem, till July 1935,
Government Arab College, Jerusalem till July 1938,
University College of the South West, Exeter, Nov. 1939 – June 1940.

(6) Nationality: Palestinian. Race: Arab.

(7) Religion: Christian.

(8) Further reference to character: The British Council

(9) Course of Reading: Honours, Pass Degree or otherwise, and subjects: English Tripos

(10) Claims for exemption from the whole or part of the University Previous Examination (Certificates must be sent): Palestine Matriculation (1937), Diploma of Elementary Education (1938, Jerusalem), Proficiency in English (Exeter 1940).

(11) Date (term and year) when it is desired to begin residence: Michaelmas Term 1940.

(12) Has application been made elsewhere for admission? If so to what College: No.

Signature of Candidate: J. I. Jabra

Date: 8.10.40

N.B. *It is not sufficient to leave any of these spaces blank, or any of these questions unanswered.*

5.2 "Fitzwilliam House, Cambridge: Form of Application for Admission," Jabra Ibrahim Jabra, October 8, 1940, 1/4.
Courtesy of Fitzwilliam College, University of Cambridge.

THE ROCKEFELLER FOUNDATION

PERSONAL HISTORY AND APPLICATION FOR A FELLOWSHIP IN HUMANITIES

(Note: Please type or print all entries in English)

Field of Special Interest: English Literature

Date: 5th March, 1952

Name in Full: Jabra Ibrahim JABRA   Sex: Male

Present Address: College of Arts and Sciences, Baghdad, IRAQ.
(Street and Number) (City) (State or Country)

Permanent Address: Star Street, Bethlehem, JORDAN
(Street and Number) (City) (State or Country)

Place of Birth: Adana   Year: 1919   Month: August   Day: 28th

Citizenship: Jordanian (ex-Palestinian)

Single, married, widowed, divorced: Single   Wife's name: _____
(Form of customary legal signature)

Date of marriage: _____   Number of Children: _____   Age and Sex: _____

Other dependents: _____

Present Position: Lecturer in English, College of Arts and Sciences.   Annual Salary: ID. 816 plus about ID. 310 for extra lectures.

Other sources of family income: None

What part of salary and other income will be continued if a fellowship is granted? (Attach official letter giving assurance of continued salary): None

Have you at any previous time filed an application with The Rockefeller Foundation or the General Education Board? No   If so, give details: _____

Have you at any time held a fellowship from any other American institution or agency or are you now an applicant for one? No   If so, give details: _____

FORM 434

5.3 "The Rockefeller Foundation: Personal History and Application for a Fellowship in Humanities," Jabra Ibrahim Jabra, March 5, 1952, 1/4. Jabra, Jabra Ibrahim, Box 297, Folder 4634.
Courtesy of Rockefeller Archive Center.

likely came to Bethlehem seeking refuge from this "history of violence." In 1922, Bethlehem had a population of 6,600 inhabitants, compared with the 62,500 people living in Jerusalem. It was a predominantly Christian town, housing various old monasteries with adjacent schools and hospices that offered shelter.[11] Jabra's family name was originally Chelico;[12] as Boullata explained to me, "his name is Jabra, his father's name is Ibrahim, and his grandfather's name is Jabra, but his grandfather was named Jabra Chelico, which is a Syriac name. . . . Jabra Ibrahim Jabra is an Arabized name, which was used when Jabra registered in government-run schools."[13]

Jabra is very much a product of his education, in particular a result of the years he spent at the Arab College in Jerusalem, which has literally overwritten his Assyrian origins, his name, and his date and place of birth. It is likely that he elided this information in his autobiographies as he embarked on a writerly project of *ars vitae poetica*, as Angelika Neuwirth has argued, carving out a portrait of the artist as a young man in Palestine before 1948 and of the Palestinian exile as writer after 1948.[14] In *The First Well*, the portrayal of the self/artist as a young man coincides with the portrayal of Palestine, lost but redeemed in the act of writing and in art. Jabra held fast to his Palestinian identity at a time when, like other national identities across the Middle East, it was still in the making, enmeshed in "several overlapping senses of identity . . . senses that have not necessarily been contradictory for the Palestinians themselves, but can be misunderstood or misinterpreted by others," as Rashid Khalidi has shown, especially as that identity came under attack by the Zionist movement.[15]

In searching for Jabra, then, we find we are faced with multiple Jabras: the historical figure, a person whose identity papers fix his date and place of birth as 1919, Adana, and who died in Baghdad in 1994; and the literary persona, whose identity was carved into his autobiographies and numerous characters of his novels, who was born around 1920 in Bethlehem and who expired in Baghdad in 2010, along with his home, personal library, artworks, and private papers in an "end of eras in Iraq and the Arab world." I presented some of this research at a conference organized by the Arab Fund for Arts and Culture (AFAC) in Berlin in 2018, following which William Tamplin published an article in which he refers to Jabra's application to Fitzwilliam as proof that Adana was Jabra's place of birth and highlights his "lifelong concealment" of his family history.[16] In investigating Jabra's Assyrian background, Tamplin assumes an objective history devoid of "fictional stratagem," one in which gaps and silences can be filled unabashedly, a historiographical method called into question since the linguistic turn. Rather than making room for messy contradictions, Tamplin essentializes Jabra, disregarding the complexities of life narratives and national identities, as well as Jabra's trials and tribulations as a modernist writer. I suggest that a more interesting approach does not attempt to prove either of the two Jabras, person and persona, true or false; but rather draws attention to overlapping senses of identity and the complexities related to personhood, which are difficult to find room for in the pages of a biography, as Virginia Woolf—quoted in the introduction to this book—aptly said about Orlando. Jabra is a multifaceted literary writer who contributed in myriad ways to global modernism, and he should be read on par with other modernist writers, such as T. S. Eliot, James Joyce, Fernando Pessoa, or Virginia Woolf. The historical Jabra was not able to remember his birth in Adana, he was not more than three years old when he arrived in Palestine. He and his literary personae were born in Palestine metaphorically, as it was in Palestine that his consciousness, identity, and memory were formed. Jabra grew up and studied in Palestine, and it was from Palestine that he was displaced.

Jabra makes a number of references to his family's Assyrian background in *The First Well*, which Walid Khalidi opened my eyes to when discussing Jabra's autobiography with me.[17] Jabra recalls, for instance, that his father used to tell stories "about the hardships of his childhood and boyhood," and was "deprived of his land for about twenty years."[18] He also relates that his "mother's first husband, and her twin and only brother, Yusuf, were both killed on the same day in 1909 in tragic circumstances,"[19] which are not further described but suggest the 1909 massacre of Armenians and Assyrians in Adana by Muslim forces loyal to Abdul Hamid II. Between twenty and thirty thousand Armenians, in addition to more than one thousand Assyrians, are reported to have been killed in the Adana Massacre.[20] Jabra further recalls his mother's saying that "the war" came and took his father away and asking him what the history books he and his brother were reading at school said about "the woes of the days of yore."[21] Further references to Jabra's Assyrian background appear in his novel *al-Baḥth 'an Walid Mas'ud* (1978), translated into English by Adnan Haydar and Roger Allen as *In Search of Walid Masoud* (2000)—here, they are written into the first pages of the protagonist's autobiography, titled "The Well."

Jabra grew up in "a [region] society ravaged and impoverished by war and famine," as Rashid Khalidi describes Palestine after World War I.[22] The Jericho earthquake of 1927, which figures in both *The First Well* and *In Search of Walid Masoud*, added to the precariousness of life, as did the political turmoil that broke out in the 1929 riots and in the Great Revolt. As Jabra recalls, his parents struggled to make ends meet and moved homes frequently. His family—including his parents and maternal grandmother; brothers Murad, Yusuf, and Isa; and sister Susan—is said to have lived in several different houses in the vicinity of the Syriac Orthodox Church in Bethlehem's Star Street, likely as tenants of the church.[23] Most of the time, they shared a single room, which offered only rudimentary shelter. His father was a day laborer, yet Jabra describes him as closely connected, physically in touch with the historic legacy of Palestinian stonemasonry.

> He carried building stones on his back, taking them to the mason after the chiseler had finely dressed their surface with the chisel and carefully shaped their angles. He was paid five or six piasters per day, and he gave what he earned to my mother to spend as her wisdom and experience dictated. Yet, however wise and experienced she was in spending the money, she knew she had to feed us and, in addition, to sew our clothes by hand, patch them, and make do with the few fabrics available to her, which were often parts of older clothes. When winter came, matters were more complicated. Construction work was hard to find, and my father spent days going from one construction site to another looking for work, and he returned home exhausted and hungry.[24]

As did most of the other children he played with as a youngster in Bethlehem, Jabra went barefoot. A story about a pair of boots he was given as a Christmas gift at the monastery he attended for after-school activities provides a telling illustration of the dire social circumstances in which he lived, and also marks his first encounter with Jerusalem. As Jabra remembers, he rushed home, overjoyed with his new boots, but his mother persuaded him to put them aside, since Orthodox Christmas came about two weeks after the Christmas of the Western calendar. She sold the new boots for fifteen or twenty piasters, writes Jabra, to provide her family with a Christmas dinner. She then took her son to the Jewish Quarter in Jerusalem's Old City to buy a pair of used boots that cost no more than two piasters. They took a horse-drawn carriage from the Square of the Church of Nativity in Bethlehem to "Jaffa Gate, crowded with people and animals," where Jabra marveled at "the wonderful city" with its "arched narrow alleyways" in which people spoke "the dialect of the Jews of the Maghrib," which he did not understand, while his mother negotiated the price of "the miserable pair of shoes."[25] "For many years afterward, whenever Christmas came," he writes, "I remembered those boots which I never wore. But I soon forgot them in the overwhelming joys of the feast—or in the overwhelming sorrows which it cruelly brought with it in some years, without mercy."[26]

A STUDENT AT THE ARAB COLLEGE IN JERUSALEM, 1932–1938

The cruelty of the years leading up to the Nakba offered one outlet: education. In Bethlehem, Jabra went to a Syriac Orthodox school in which boys of all ages attended class together. He remembers their only teacher, Jiryis, and the Syriac texts he taught, which were, "for the most part, very old devotional lyrics and hymns which the early Church Fathers in Antioch, Damascus, Jerusalem, Edessa, and the cities of Mesopotamia had composed and set to music."[27] Standing in a circle around the lectern with the other boys of the children's chorus, he learned Syriac without really understanding it, praying in a language that was "mostly closed to us, in spite of the fact that we could read it right side up, sideways, or upside down, in the light or in no light at all."[28] This training added little to his overall reading capacity, but it illustrates his familiarity with the liturgical texts and ceremonies of the Syriac Orthodox Church, which played an important role in the worshippers' lives and experiences of time, as it structured the course of their year.[29] As Jabra explains, "Latin and Greek remained the ritual languages used, next to Arabic, in many of the major monasteries, likewise, Syriac continued to be used with Arabic, as it had been for over one thousand years."[30] Father Anthony's Monastery, which Jabra went to in the afternoons and on holidays, provided more worldly knowledge, as it introduced the boys to the arts, music, theater, and cinema. Jabra recalls "some of the most delightful hours" of his life watching "silent movies with fascination while the projector whirred away in the back of the hall."[31]

In 1929, Jabra followed his brother Yusuf to attend Bethlehem's National School, an event that marked the beginning of a new life. Jabra's account of his schooldays provides valuable information on the schoolbooks circulating in Palestine at the time, among them Muhammad Is'af al-Nashashibi's Arabic poetry textbook *al-Bustan* (The garden) and Muhammad Izzat Darwaza's *Durus al-tarikh al-mutawassit wal-hadith* (Studies in medieval and modern history), both published in Cairo; Louis Cheikho's *Kitab 'ilm al-adab* (Book of literature) and *Majani al-adab fi hada'iq al-'arab* (Harvests of literature in the gardens of the Arabs), published by the Jesuit Press in Beirut; and S. S. Pugh's *Tales of Heroes and Great Men of Old* translated into Arabic by Ya'qub Sarruf, one of the cofounders of the influential Nahda journal al-*Muqtataf*, and published by the American Press in Beirut.[32] In addition, he mentions Daniel Defoe's *Robinson Crusoe*, which was translated into Arabic by Butrus al-Bustani, who had worked closely with Cornelius Van Dyck of the American Protestant Mission in Beirut on translating the Bible into Arabic, and Hafiz Naguib's popular detective stories *Johnson and Milton Top*, which were published in Cairo in the 1920s. He also recalls reading excerpts of the Bedouin romance *Sirat 'Antar ibn Shaddad* (*Antar, A Bedouin Romance*) and of *Alf layla wa-layla* (*One Thousand and One Nights*). Jabra remembers a number of his teachers at the National School in Bethlehem, in particular one named Faheem, who was a graduate of the Teachers' Training College (later the Arab College) in Jerusalem. In addition, he mentions inspectors from the department of education who visited the school, among them Khalil al-Sakakini, who had served as the first director of the Arab College; Muhammad Is'af al-Nashashibi, an acclaimed professor of Arabic at Rashidiyya Secondary School in Jerusalem; Shaykh Hussam al-Din Jarallah, who had been the opponent of Hajj Amin in the elections for mufti in 1921 and was appointed grand mufti of Jerusalem by Emir Abdallah I, after Jordan formally annexed East Jerusalem in 1948; and an Irishman, Jerome Farrell, who would later serve as director of education and whom we met in chapter 2 in his capacity as Walid's tutor. As Jabra recalls in *The First Well*, upon one of his visits, Farrell recorded Jabra's name in his notebook.[33]

An outstanding student, Jabra obtained Mandate government scholarships to continue his studies in Jerusalem, first at Rashidiyya, and then at the Arab College, where he was among the few students selected to be sent abroad to attend university. The expectation was that these students would return to Palestine to play an active role in the education of their fellow countrymen. Farrell played an important role in Jabra's education, following his studies at the University of Cambridge closely, as documents I found at Fitzwilliam College attest. Education spread rapidly in Palestine—whereas in 1922–1923, only about 20 percent of Arab school-age children were in school, in 1947, almost

50 percent were enrolled. A significant gap in attendance, however, was evident between urban and rural areas. "In the towns in 1945–46, 85 percent of boys and 65 percent of girls were in school; the problem was in the countryside," explains Rashid Khalidi, "where only 65 percent of boys and 10 percent of girls were in school, a problem caused in part by the fact that only 432 of about 800 villages had schools."[34] The Mandate government "never achieved its goal of universal education," writes Rochelle Davis, arguing that "a fundamental reassessment of the conception of the British as the providers of education to the Palestinian Arabs is necessary."[35] Jabra's trajectory, however, stands out as a success story.

When Jabra started his studies at Rashidiyya in 1932, his family moved to Jerusalem. His brothers Murad and Yusuf, accompanied by their grandmother, had already left for Jerusalem to seek out a living. Jabra worked at a foundry during the summer holidays. Located just outside Herod's Gate, Rashidiyya was one of the few secondary schools started under Ottoman rule that were developed under the British Mandate. When Jabra returned to teach at the school after having obtained his bachelor's degree at Cambridge, it had become "a full secondary school with two years of literary and scientific sides of post-secondary education leading to the Higher School certificate."[36] Jabra continued his education at the Arab College, where acceptance was strictly on merit. About two-thirds of the college's students came from rural areas. Although their education, as in Jabra's case, brought social, economic, and cultural mobility, it also led to their estrangement from their families and village background.[37] The college prepared students for the Palestinian matriculation examination which "was conducted under the supervision of the Council of Higher Education . . . composed of British, Arab, and Jewish experts, and was headed by the general director of British education."[38] "Students wore college uniforms consisting of a green jacket, with the motto of the college on its left side pocket, and grey woolen pants, a white shirt, and a green tie," as Sadiq Ibrahim 'Odeh, a student at the college in the early 1940s, remembers.[39] The college badge, a falcon clutching an inkhorn, was designed by Jalal Badran, a renowned artist who had trained in Cairo and London, and who was Jabra's art teacher at the college. A picture of the class of 1938 shows Jabra standing at the far left in the last row, wearing the college uniform, with the college's principal, Ahmad Samih al-Khalidi—Walid's father—seated in the middle of the first row among the teachers (figure 5.4). 'Odeh writes, "College life was

5.4 The Jabra Ibrahim Jabra, last row left, among the students; Ahmad Samih al-Khalidi, first row middle, among the faculty, Arab College, Jerusalem, 1938. Walid Khalidi, *Before Their Diaspora*, 173 (Plate 227).
Courtesy of Walid Khalidi.

formal for the most part," but included extracurricular activities and other entertainment:

> The location of the college protected it from the noise of the city and provided an excellent atmosphere for study. Extracurricular activities were a must. The mandatory sports activities were soccer and basketball, which were played by all students. ... As to other entertainment, there was a gramophone or a phonograph with its black records, which used to be started by hand, not by electricity. It had a small copper plaque on it that said it was a gift from Arthur Wakhoub [Wauchope], the British high commissioner during 1931–1937. ... In a hut east of the college there was a radio and a tennis table. Students used to go there during free time to play and to listen to the radio, which mostly had news of the Second World War.[40]

The Palestine Broadcasting Service had started to broadcast daily in three languages—Arabic, Hebrew, and English—in 1936, with loudspeakers set up in public spaces in villages for the transmission of government announcements, as radios were not yet widely owned.[41] That same year, Palestine's Arab population came together in the Great Revolt. Jabra was not actively involved in the revolt, but recalls its impact on his political consciousness, adding to an existential malaise: "long walks, the tireless hikes for miles every day, which we took because our homes were not capable of holding our endless, explosive discussions, which even the whole wide world could hardly contain."[42] He spent what little money he had on books. Newspapers and journals circulated well beyond the number of their subscribers at the time, because they were passed on from hand to hand and read aloud to those who could not read, as Jabra recalls in his short story "al-Ghramufun" (The Gramophone), written in Jerusalem before 1948 but not published until 1956 in Beirut.[43] In his essay "Shakespeare and I," published much later, he traces his passion for Shakespeare back to these days, when as a student of the Arab College—possibly influenced by Abdul Rahman Bushnaq, a Cambridge graduate, who was his English teacher—he was contemplating "the impossible task of making Arabic versions of Shakespeare which carried the same verbal charge, the same evocative imagery and sustained metaphors, the same diversity of rhythm, tone, eloquence, word-play, etc."[44] Jabra would become one of the most important translators of Shakespeare into Arabic. Starting with *Hamlet*, he translated and wrote critical introductions to Shakespeare's major plays and sonnets; in addition, he translated key texts in Shakespearean criticism.[45] Jabra is listed among the "Successful 'Metric' Candidates of the Palestine Matriculation Examination" in *The Palestine Post* on August 18, 1937.[46]

Jabra's early publications date back to these years in Jerusalem. Poetry dominated the literary field, but narrative fiction was gaining in prominence.[47] Jabra wrote a number of short stories with which he participated in what his contemporary Ishaq Musa al-Husseini would describe as *adab maqalat* (periodical literature), rather than *adab mu'allafat* (book-form literature).[48] Al-Husseini, who had obtained his doctorate from the University of London under the supervision of Hamilton A. R. Gibb, was teaching at Rashidiyya and the Arab College. In 1945, he established the Arab Cultural Committee which organized the first Arabic book fair in Jerusalem in October 1946. The committee had big plans for the future of Palestinian literature, such as publishing a magazine, opening an archive/library, and founding a publishing house, but these initiatives were cut short by the Nakba.[49]

Similar to other modernist writers the world over and the Nahda figures who preceded him in Palestine and the Arab world, translation played a major role in Jabra's life.[50] Fresh out of school, he published an Arabic translation of Emile Zola's "La Fée amoureuse" in *al-Hilal*.[51] An influential cultural journal founded by the Lebanese writer Jurji Zaydan in Cairo in 1892, *al-Hilal* played an important role in familiarizing readers across the Arab world with Western literature. Also in 1938, Jabra published a translation of André Maurois's *Ariel ou la vie de Shelley* in serialized form in *al-Amali*, a Beirut-based weekly magazine for culture.[52] He started translating Percy Shelley's *Prometheus Unbound* at around the same time but did not publish it until forty years later.[53] Translations of the works of Oscar Wilde and George Moore followed.[54] The same year, in 1938, two years after the Anglo-Egyptian treaty that made Egypt a de jure independent nation, Taha Hussein—who wrote a foreword to Anbara Salam Khalidi's translations of Homer and Virgil—published his influential *Mustaqbal al-thaqafa fi Misr* (*The Future of Culture in Egypt*). It argued for both Egyptian nationalism and the adaptation of European models, with Europe—and France in particular—standing out for its humane culture, civic virtues, and democracy: the modern world of which Egypt must become a part.[55] Hussein's idealized view of Europe stood in stark contrast to the political realities in play both there and in the Middle East on the brink of World War II. Moreover, it ascribed a special role to Egyptian nationalism based on Egypt's Pharaonic and not its Arab past, a move that advocates of Arab nationalism strongly criticized. Among these critics was Sati' al-Husri, who had followed King Faisal from Syria to Iraq, where he made a lasting impression on politics and culture before taking up a position in the Cultural Directorate of the Arab League in Cairo.[56] Jabra shared Hussein's admiration of Western culture; at the same time, he embraced Arab nationalism, as promoted by al-Husri, based on linguistic ties and cutting across regional as well as religious differences. In "Arab Language and Culture," a general background article in *The Middle East: A Handbook*—which also includes "an historical outline to the present" by the British historian Arnold J. Toynbee and an article on Arabic music by Afif A. Bulos—Jabra writes that "not even the strong bonds of Islam between the Ottomans and the Arabs were to weaken the national bonds of the language itself, which kept the nation psychologically and culturally united and distinct."[57] He elaborates, expressing his sense of cultural belonging, that "Arabic then is at the essence of Arab culture today, exactly as it was a thousand years ago. A man who speaks Arabic as his own language could not help normally feeling as an Arab: for the verbal miracle is at work within him, unconsciously fusing him with 100 million others who speak the same language and who, therefore, share the same cultural experience."[58]

A STUDENT AT THE UNIVERSITY OF CAMBRIDGE, 1939–1943

Jabra left Palestine in September 1939, shortly after the outbreak of World War II. In the company of Hilmi Samara and Hamid Attari, two other students from the Arab College who, like Jabra, had received competitive fellowships from the British Council to pursue their studies abroad, he traveled by train from Haifa to Egypt, first to El Qantara and then Port Said, where the trio boarded a Japanese ship that took them to Naples and Marseille, and then through the Strait of Gibraltar and northward to the English Channel to dock at Dover.[59] In preparation for entry to the University of Cambridge, he spent one year at the University of Exeter, and, in the summer of 1940, he attended a course in English language and literature organized by the British Council at Sommerville College at the University of Oxford.[60] As the assistant keeper of the Oxford University Archives informed me, "no records survive concerning attendees at the 1940 course, nor any documentation regarding its organization or content. I have been able to find, however, a report of it in the [Extra Mural] Delegacy [Department of Continuing Education, as it is called today]'s annual report for 1939–40. . . . The report notes the various countries from which students came to attend the course, one of which was Palestine. Unfortunately, we are unable to confirm that Jabra Ibrahim Jabra did attend this course; but the evidence suggests that he may have done."[61]

From Oxford, Jabra continued to Cambridge, where he was admitted to Fitzwilliam House (since 1966 Fitzwilliam College), a noncollegiate student board that provided those students who could not afford the college fees with access to the university and admitted many students from abroad.[62] Jabra read for the English Tripos, as the honors bachelor's program is known at Cambridge, under the supervision of Helena Mennie Shire, a lecturer of medieval English literature who later specialized in Scottish court poetry in comparative perspective with English, French, and Italian literature.[63] He also came under the influence of F. R. Leavis and I. A. Richards, and developed a profound interest in literary criticism. As part of the Tripos, Jabra had to study Latin and Anglo-Saxon, which caused him significant difficulty, as Jerome Farrell's correspondence with the college on his behalf illustrates.[64] Despite the war years, which saw part of the university transformed into a military hospital and a significant number of faculty and students drafted into the army, Jabra graduated with a bachelor's degree on June 22, 1943, and obtained his master's degree in absentia on October 30, 1948.[65]

In his second autobiography, *Princesses' Street*, Jabra recalls World War II, the Battle of Dunkirk, young men leaving university when they were conscripted for military service, and the air raids on British cities by German bombers.[66] He also recalls his first encounters with love. Like *The First Well*, *Princesses' Street* has to be read with an eye on its "fictional stratagem." Chapters 2 and 3, titled "Hamlet, Ophelia, and I" and "The Lady of the Lakes," in which Jabra describes his visits to Shakespeare's birthplace, Stratford-upon-Avon, and the Lake District, where the Romantic movement started, are especially telling. Following the footsteps of the poets he admired, Jabra finds himself in the midst of tragedy in Stratford. Gladys Newby, a fellow student from the north of England, joins him only to bid him farewell, as she is to marry another man. As Jabra wanders into the Lake District, a young woman in a long white dress appears seemingly out of nowhere. Upon hearing he was from Jerusalem, had grown up in Bethlehem, and spoke not only Arabic but also a bit of Aramaic—the language of Jesus whose written form is an antecedent of the Arabic, Hebrew, and Syriac abjads—she sees in him a vision of Christ.[67] Whatever the truth of this story, it certainly adds to Jabra's playful self-fashioning as a Christ figure in his autobiography.

BACK IN JERUSALEM: FROM THE ASSYRIAN QUARTER TO QATAMON

Jabra returned to Jerusalem in the summer of 1943, with World War II ongoing but the Allies having obtained a firm hold in North Africa and the Middle East having successfully defeated the Axis forces in El Alamein the previous year. He taught at Rashidiyya, his former secondary school, and the College des Frères, where, as we have seen, Boullata was one of his students. He very likely paid a visit to Farrell and to Ahmad Samih al-Khalidi, his former principal at the Arab College. It may very well have been through one of them that Jabra met Walid Khalidi. Six years Jabra's junior, Walid had just passed his matriculation examination, and his mind was brimming with Latin and English literature. Their paths also crossed at the Young Men's Christian Association (YMCA) and the King David Hotel bar across the street, where they were to become regulars as part of the ecumenical circle.

Since moving from Bethlehem to Jerusalem in 1932, Jabra's family lived in Jawrat al-'Unnab (Jujube Pit), a Christian shanty town not far from the Sultan's Pool, which Jabra describes in *The First Well* as "an area below the level of the main road, just before reaching Jaffa Gate. Above it and above the road, the western wall of the city rose majestically with David's Citadel and the minaret of the citadel Mosque."[68] In my conversations with Walid, he recalled visiting Jabra and referred to the area as "al-hayy al-syriani" (the Assyrian quarter),[69] whose inhabitants were mainly Assyrian refugees who had fled Iraq after the country's de facto independence in 1932 and the Simele Massacre that followed.

In the aftermath of World War I, the British Army in Iraq employed Assyrians—who had been forced out of the Hakkari mountains in the vilayet of Van, which, as was the case with the vilayet of Adana, was to become part of modern Turkey—and conscripted them into the Iraq Levies, an Iraqi military force established by the British and staffed primarily by minorities—Assyrians, Kurds, and Iraqi Turkmen—to fight against the anticolonial resistance of the predominantly Muslim Iraqi population. When Britain ended its mandate in Iraq, the Assyrians called on the League of Nations to grant them autonomy in northern Iraq.[70] Having set the Assyrian minority against Iraq's national majority, Britain did little to protect them. What has been belittled as "the Assyrian Affair" ended in the brutal Simele Massacre, which was led by Bakr Sidqi al-Askari, an Iraqi military general of Kurdish descent. About six thousand Assyrians, many of them refugees from the Armenian and Assyrian genocides that had taken place in the final years of the Ottoman Empire, were murdered. The massacre went hand in hand with the rise of the Iraqi Army as the guardian of the nation and a "militarization of society that would ultimately disfigure politics in the postcolonial Arab world," as Ussama Makdisi remarks in *Age of Coexistence*.[71] King Faisal, who had aimed at Arab unity across religious lines, saw in the events "the outcome of his own policies. He recognized the high cost of collaborating with Britain and the need to secure Arabs' true independence through solidarity."[72] Suffering complications of heart disease, he underwent treatment in Switzerland and died on September 8, 1933, in Bern. Jabra may not have paid much attention to these events upon arriving in Jerusalem from Bethlehem and settling with his family in the Assyrian Quarter, but he was to come into close contact with the history of violence that had led to his neighbors' expulsion from Iraq when he married al-Askari's niece, Lami'a Barqi al-Askari in 1952.

To Walid, it appeared that Jabra's family was newly arrived in Jerusalem from Iraq. He remembers their home as makeshift; it consisted of a single room on the ground floor divided into two sections—one where Jabra's parents lived, and a second, with bookcases, some paintings, armchairs, and a gramophone, where Jabra lived.[73] Tarif Khalidi vaguely remembers accompanying Walid and either Sulafa or Rasha to Jabra's house, where "one descended a number of steps down to his house, almost below street level; it was a hovel rather than a house, very poor."[74] The differences in social background between Jabra and the Khalidis did not go unnoticed but were not an obstacle to friendship.

Shortly after his return from Cambridge, now gainfully employed as a teacher, Jabra moved with his parents to the New City between Mamillah Road and the Shamma'a Quarter, before renting an apartment in Qatamon, a well-to-do predominantly Arab Christian neighborhood south of the Jewish neighborhood of Rehavia.[75] This was where al-Sakakini, who had visited Jabra's school in Bethlehem as a governmental inspector, lived with his family, and from where his daughter, Hala, had witnessed the King David Hotel bombing. Next to a number of grocer's shops, a dressmaker, two tailors, a telegraph office, the Church of Saint Therese, a bakery, and a butcher shop, all remembered by her,[76] the neighborhood was also the site of the Semiramis Hotel, which was to be the scene of another fateful terrorist attack early in January 1948.

THE YMCA ARTS CLUB

Jabra immersed himself in Jerusalem's cultural life. At the YMCA, he founded the Arts Club, which organized public lectures, poetry readings, music recitals, and art exhibitions. Despite growing political tensions, the YMCA managed to bring people together across religious lines, as is documented in the Records of YMCA International Work in Palestine and Israel:

> In spite of the tensions and changes in staff leadership, the Jerusalem Association thrived. In 1936 it had nearly 1,500 members. . . . The building was a meeting ground of Jews and Arabs and was popular with the soldiers stationed in the region. In 1944, membership rose to 1,927. Activities continued throughout 1946 in spite of the bombing of the King David Hotel just across the street from the building. . . . In the total membership, 32 nations were represented; two-thirds were Christians (including Protestants, Catholics, Orthodox, and Armenians), a little over a sixth were Jews, and slightly less than a sixth were Muslims.[77]

As Hala Sakakini remembers, "a stranger passing by [the YMCA] at any time of the day might have thought it was a university building, so many young people would be going up or coming down the wide front steps or just hanging about in small groups on the terrace."[78] A social and cultural hub, the YMCA featured a number of sports facilities, including a soccer field, tennis courts, and a heated outdoor swimming pool, in addition to a large auditorium, a library, and a reading hall; the latter is described by Ami Ayalon as "a lavishly furnished and amply lit hall [where] silence was a strict requirement."[79] The library initially included some three thousand books, which increased to about twenty-five thousand in the 1940s, most of them in European languages.[80] The Arts Club run by Jabra is remembered by a number of his contemporaries.[81] It is also listed in the report of the YMCA's Annual General Meeting of January 29, 1945, submitted by Alvah Leslie Miller, senior secretary from 1935 to 1950, who describes Jabra as "the spark-plug of this club":

> Arts Club: Our newest club has taken the high-browish title of "The Arts Club", and already they have proven worthy of this name. Their purpose is to promote the creation and appreciation of music, painting, and poetry among the members of the Y.M.C.A. and, when possible, the community. Mr. G. I. Jabra is the spark-plug of this club, but he certainly is ably assisted by his follow-members. Already they have given several programmes open to Association members, and each one has been outstandingly successful. The club demonstrates what can be done by a group with an idea, enthusiasm and well-directed effort.[82]

The report lists a number of events organized by the club, such as "recorded poetry and music, including poems by Shakespeare, Shelley, Keats, Lord Tennyson, and music by Tchaikowski, Moussorgski, Debussy, and Suppé," and "Nocturnes in music (Beethoven, Mozart, Chopin, Field, Debussy, Moussorgski), pictures (Tintoretto, Rubens, Watteau, Crome, Daumier, Van Gogh, Beardsley, Pissaro, Manet, Toulouse-Lautrec, Dulac, etc.) and poetry (Shakespeare, Merrick, Gray, Wordsworth, Coleridge, Shelley, Keats, Eliot, etc.)." These events provide a glimpse into the global circulation of European writers, composers, and artists, and the familiarity of people in Jerusalem—across religious lines—with their work. In October 1946, the *Palestine Post* announced that "the Jerusalem Y.M.C.A. Evening School is beginning a new course of 20 lectures on English literature, covering in the main contemporary poetry and fiction. The lecturer is Mr. Gabriel Jabra, B. A. (Cantab)."[83]

Whereas Jabra signed his works written in Arabic as Jabra Ibrahim Jabra, he used the name Gabriel Jabra for his works authored in English. In 1944, he published a poem entitled "Song" in *Poetry London*, a cutting-edge periodical edited by Thurairajah Tambimuttu, a modernist writer of Tamil background who was at the core of avant-garde literary circles in London and New York City.[84] Celebrating spring as "a new beginning," "Song" opens with the lines,

> When in the year's decay I hear
> The breath of a new beginning
> I long for a tree's existence among the trees.
> What falls from me will never return,
> Return, return, ah sweet return
> Of spring![85]

Reminiscent of "The Dying God," the title of part four of James Frazer's *The Golden Bough: A Study in Comparative Religion*, which Jabra started to translate into Arabic in Jerusalem,[86] "Song" anticipates themes of rebirth and redemption that played a key role in modernist poetry across the Arab world. Jabra participated in this modernist movement as both a "Tammuzi poet"—a term he coined in reference to the Mesopotamian god Tammuz to denote the beginnings of a new life in a review of modern Arabic poetry published in the literary journal *Shi'r* (Poetry) in Beirut[87]—and a promoter of new talent.

In *The First Well*, Jabra mentions the Cairene poet and playwright Ahmed Shawqi and his influential play *Majnun Layla* (Mad about Layla), when writing

158   THE TIME BEFORE 1948

about the loss of his sister. Shawqi—along with the works of Eliot and Frazer—played an important role in Jabra's recourse to myth to denote themes of a new life in spring. It was the Palestinian poet Ibrahim Tuqan who introduced him to Shawqi's play, probably in its 1931 reprint.[88] Tuqan was Jabra's teacher at Rashidiyya, where he "used to transform the Arabic class into an hour of magic with his poetic sensibility, tenderness, and good sense of irony."[89] Born in Nablus and educated at Saint George's School in Jerusalem and the American University of Beirut, Tuqan came to fame during the Great Revolt while working for the Arabic section of Palestine Broadcasting Service, with poems directed against both the British Mandate and the Zionist movement, the most famous being "Mawtini" (My homeland), which became the de facto Palestinian national anthem.[90]

Themes of rebirth and redemption were also expressed in Jabra's visual art. Some of his paintings dating to before 1948 were recently rediscovered in Bethlehem; they place him among the pioneers of modern art in Palestine. Jabra started sketching in pencil and watercolors in Bethlehem and Jerusalem, and then picked up painting with oils in Cambridge. Unlike Jamal Badran, his art teacher at the Arab College who was known for his geometric abstractions inspired by Islamic art,[91] Jabra's experiments with abstraction were closely linked to European modernism. Although he was "practicing his art in Jerusalem during the 1940s, expressing familiarity with radical trends," as Palestinian artist Samia A. Halaby writes, "the majority of artists, critics, and historians worldwide had not yet recognized the importance of abstraction. The Abstract Expressionists of New York were just then beginning to form their ideas."[92] In *The First Well*, Jabra describes anemones—the same "flowers of Palestine" that Wolfgang refers to in his graphic work—recalling the Feast of the Resurrection in springtime, which reads like a description of Jabra's 1946 painting *Field of Anemones* (figure 5.5).[93] Jabra writes, "The neglected, terraced plots turned green, dotted with flowers of all kinds, which we simply called *hannoun*, anemones. There were yellow anemones, blue anemones, violet anemones. And there were those anemones of deep red that have the color of blood: poppies, which lifted their heads to the sun, their petals shining with dew. They shot up through rocks, thorns, and horrid weeds. They even raised their heads proudly from under the stone walls over which the cacti spread."[94]

In Jabra's painting, the deep red of the poppies is matched by that in the blouse and lips of the young woman seated on a terraced plot of land turned

5.5 Jabra Ibrahim Jabra, *Field of Anemones*, oil on canvas, 44 × 29.5 cm, 1947. Courtesy of Sadeer Jabra.

green, set against the earthen tones of an olive grove and a profound blue sky. The woman bears a resemblance to Jabra's recollection of his sister, "her long maroon hair flowing on her shoulders and chest like that of the angels, and her skin which resembled rose petals on a dewy morning."[95] The young woman and Palestine's landscape—which Jabra was deeply familiar with given the long walks he took with his friends across the Judean hills—merge into one as they are brought to life on his canvas and redeemed in art. Despite the poverty Jabra experienced in his childhood, he depicts Palestine in both his writings and his paintings "in its still unmutilated pre-1948 shape, the unblemished image of paradise on earth" (figure 5.6).[96]

AN UNFINISHED BOOK COLLABORATION

Having gained a reputation as a graduate of Cambridge, an engaged teacher of English literature, and "the spark-plug" of the YMCA's Arts Club, Jabra was a known figure in Jerusalem's cultural life. As part of his job at the Public Information Office, Wolfgang was frequenting the YMCA and may very well have met Jabra there when attending some of the events organized by the Arts Club. Wolfgang and Jabra both belonged to minority communities, each burdened by their respective histories of persecution in Europe and the Middle East, yet both were educated outside communal confines in distinctively secular and progressive schools (the Odenwaldschule in Germany and the Arab College in Palestine, respectively) that centered on the individual, and both were aspiring artists and writers. As such, they shared a number of interests, namely their love of English literature, classical music, and avant-garde art.

Although Jabra's works in Arabic were not accessible to Wolfgang, his poetry written in English was. As Wolfgang recalls in his conversations with Lazar, he thought highly of Jabra's writing and illustrated some of his poems. These illustrations consist of six ink drawings dating to 1945, which survive in the Wolfgang Hildesheimer Archive at the Academy of Arts in Berlin (figure 5.7).[97] They may well have been intended as part of a collaborative book project, as a letter Wolfgang wrote to his sister and her husband from London on July 18, 1946, indicates; in it, he mentions illustrations for a collection of poetry to be published by Nicholson and Watson.[98] Jabra may very well have planned to publish a volume of poetry with Nicholson and Watson or with Editions

5.6 Jabra Ibrahim Jabra with Sally Kassab, Richard Chichester, and Afif Bulos, on a walk across the Judean Hills close to the village of Ayn Karim, ca. 1946.
Courtesy of Suhail Bulos.

5.7, 1–6 Wolfgang Hildesheimer's illustrations of Jabra's poems, six lithographs. Academy of Arts, Berlin, WHA 1636.

5.7, 1–6 (*Continued*)

5.7, 1–6 (Continued)

5.7, 1–6 (*Continued*)

5.7, 1–6 (*Continued*)

5.7, 1–6 (Continued)

Poetry London, a publishing house run by Tambimuttu that was supported by Nicholson and Watson.[99] Tambimuttu is known to have had a liking for poetry illustration and to have encouraged submissions from young and aspiring artists and writers.[100] Jabra had already published "Song" in *Poetry London* and, as the journal's archives, housed in the British Library, show, he also had submitted another poem, titled "Fluctuations," for publication.[101] The copy in *Poetry London*'s archives features marginalia, minor editorial notes, added most likely by Tambimuttu. They read, " 'I like this & wd have printed it but unfortunately 2 sections are missing' (the text in the file is wanting parts VII and VIII)."[102] The poem was never published, and I have not found other documents pertaining to possible further exchanges between Jabra and Tambimuttu that would confirm Jabra was indeed planning to have Editions Poetry London publish his collection of poetry accompanied by Wolfgang's illustrations. At Cambridge University Library, however, I found a typescript of poems, titled "Fluctuations" and written by Jabra in English between 1946 and 1949, which not only sheds light on Jabra's early, largely unpublished, literary output in English but also allows us to unite, at least in part, what was produced in the literary/artistic collaboration between these two friends.

Four of the six illustrations Wolfgang executed to accompany Jabra's poems incorporate words that reflect the titles of poems in the typescript, namely "Fluctuations," "The Foam Dressed Riders," "The House of Shadows," and "The Annals of Love."[103] Wolfgang's illustration for "Fluctuations" depicts a man and a woman, both nude, their bodily contours roughly outlined, walking or floating as if in a dream through a deserted, lunar landscape, engulfed on one side in darkness, exposed in daylight on the other. The illustration bears a distinctly Surrealist imprint, characteristic of Wolfgang's exhibitions reviewed in the *Palestine Post*, a style from which he later departed.[104] Placed alongside Jabra's poem, it gives expression to the existential anxieties experienced by Jabra and Wolfgang as they took long walks across the Judean hills or met over early evening drinks at the King David Hotel bar. Jabra's poem consists of sixteen numbered sections; its first section reads:

> From post to post and land to land,
> From hope to hope, we plod an endless way,
> And interlocked ambitions stand
> Like merging oceans, inviting to destroy.

Where should we pause, refuse to go
Forward, further? The murderous mermaids call
Enchantingly, and though we know
The song, we cannot resist the driving gale.
Love may hold us sweetly content
To save us, but the mighty power
It gathers soon will not relent:
When all ambitions, reduced to fragile wishes,
Flee the impact of love's fulfilling hour:
The maelstrom only may compass love's intent.[105]

Two of Wolfgang's illustrations are untitled. One of these figures on the book cover of the second edition of Jabra's novel, *Surakh fi layl tawil* (*Cry in a Long Night*), discussed in chapter 2, which was published by Dar al-Adab, one of Lebanon's leading publishers of modern Arabic literature, in 1988 (figure 5.8).[106] It shows two figures: to one side, a man dressed in a suit, his eyes closed as though he were dreaming; to the other, farther in the background, a nude woman. They are separated by a signpost, which points in two directions but offers no place names. The book does not provide any information about the image; the illustration might well have been intended to accompany the novel. As Rasha recalls in her memoirs, Jabra used to tell his friends about the novel he was writing. Wolfgang might very well have read parts of Jabra's work, which, in Joycean manner, depicts the artist in the making, and he might have given his illustration to Jabra in a friendly and intellectual gift exchange.

In a letter written from Nuremberg in 1947, Wolfgang mentions "the Jabra illustrations," asking his mother to send three or four copies of each to him in Germany.[107] The letter suggests a certain familiarity of Wolfgang's family with Jabra's name as the author of the poems Wolfgang illustrated, while the real person, Jabra, disappears behind this attribute. It is unlikely that Wolfgang knew about the later use of his work on the cover of Jabra's novel; there is no mention of it in his papers. Its reappearance in 1988, more than forty years later, on the cover of a publication in Beirut, is striking, and it sheds light on the mobility and circulation of texts and objects across geographical and temporal boundaries. The illustration may very well have been in the "battered suitcase full of books and papers"[108] that Jabra carried over from his past in Jerusalem to his future in Baghdad, and all that remained of his friendship with Wolfgang,

5.8 Jabra Ibrahim Jabra, *Surakh fi layl tawil*, 2nd ed. (Beirut: Dar al-Adab, 1988), book cover. Courtesy of Dar al-Adab.

similar to the way he was reduced to a ghostlike figure in the attribute Wolfgang used to refer to his "Jabra illustrations."

Jabra's book of modernist poetry with illustrations by Wolfgang remains incomplete. Placing the extant illustrations next to fragments of poetry gives a sense of lost possibilities, of futures past, of what was once an anticipated future, a shared project: the coming together of young, like-minded writers and artists, across religious lines and diverse social backgrounds, ready to take part in global modernism from the common ground they found in Jerusalem in the early 1940s. Then, despite growing political tensions, "an 'ordinary' city" of "cosmopolitan character," as Tamari writes, was "an evolving and vibrant city whose life was cut short."[109]

Jabra and his family stayed in Jerusalem until the bombing of the Semiramis Hotel in the Qatamon neighborhood carried out by the Haganah on the night of January 5, 1948. As Jabra recalls, "We had to leave our house in Jerusalem for the invaders, the morning after they had blown up the Semiramis Hotel—almost next door to us—in the small hours of a cold stormy night, killing so many people, some of whom I knew personally, including one of my dearest friends. Innocently, we thought we were leaving our house for a mere two or three weeks."[110]

Along with other terrorist attacks in Jaffa and Haifa, some of which were carried out by the Haganah, others by the Irgun and Lehi, the Semiramis Hotel bombing contributed significantly to the flight of Qatamon's predominantly Arab Christian population.[111] It killed dozens of people, among them almost every member of the Abu Suwan family, who, along with the Lorenzo family, owned the hotel, as well as the Spanish vice-consul, who was staying there as a guest. "The whole front of the two-storey building" was turned into "a mass of powdery rubble," reported the *Palestine Post*,[112] bringing back memories of the attack on the King David Hotel.

On April 30, 1948, the Sakakinis were one of the last Palestinian families to leave Qatamon.[113] Ilan Pappé quotes Itzhak Levy, the head of the Haganah's intelligence in Jerusalem, who later wrote that "while the cleansing of Qatamon went on, pillage and robbery began. Soldiers and citizens took part in it. They broke into the houses and took from them furniture, clothing, electric equipment and food."[114] Pappé resumes, "All in all, eight Palestinian neighbourhoods and thirty-nine villages were ethnically cleansed in the Greater Jerusalem area, their population transferred to the eastern part of the city. The villages are all gone today, but some of Jerusalem's most beautiful houses are still standing, now inhabited by Jewish families who took them over immediately after their eviction—silent reminders of the tragic fate of the people who used to own them."[115]

The Sakakinis fled to Cairo, and Jabra's family took refuge in Bethlehem, where they rented "a couple of small rooms on top of an old ramshackle house."[116] "Within the universal tragedy of dispossession, dislodgment and massacre engulfing a whole people," Jabra writes, "every one of us had, of course, his own personal sorrows in the violent loss of friends and relatives.... One kept picking up bits of news about one's friends: killed, scattered, lost."[117]

Jerusalem became "a phantom city."[118] As Pappé has shown, the Zionist movement began ethnic-cleansing operations with attacks on Arab villages and neighborhoods as early as December 1947; these were branded as retaliation for Arab protests against partition.[119] Then followed, in March 1948, Plan Dalet, the "master plan of the conquest of Palestine," as reads the title of Walid Khalidi's article.[120] Plan Dalet openly carried out the depopulation and destruction of Palestinian villages, accompanied by a number of massacres, notably that of Deir Yassin. As we have seen, the Deir Yassin Massacre contributed significantly to the demoralization of Palestine's indigenous Arab population and their mass exodus to neighboring Arab countries.[121]

The Arab League authorized the Arab Liberation Army (ALA; in Arabic, *jaysh al-inqath al-'arabi*, which literally translates as Arab Rescue Army) to enter Palestine. Its first battalions arrived in December 1947.[122] An Arab volunteer force under the command of Fawzi al-Qawuqji, a former officer in the Ottoman Army who had emerged as a leading military figure of Arab nationalism,[123] the ALA was poorly trained and badly equipped. Moreover, it competed with Palestinian paramilitary groups, in particular those of Abd al-Qadir al-Husayni—who died in battle in the village of al-Qastal, a strategic location on the hilltops around Jerusalem on April 9, 1948, the same day as the Deir Yassin Massacre—and Hasan Salama, who had been appointed by Hajj Amin to lead the Army of the Holy War (in Arabic, *jaysh al-jihad al-muqaddas*).[124] As Pappé shows, the ALA's arrival in Palestine in late 1947 provided the Zionist leadership with a welcome pretext to escalate further the Haganah's operations, which were already underway.[125] What ensued after May 14, 1948, is known as the First Arab-Israeli War and involved the regular armies of the new State of Israel and its Arab neighbors—Egypt, Iraq, Syria, and Transjordan—with the former significantly better equipped and organized than the latter, themselves relatively young states under considerable

European dominance.[126] The Gaza Strip along Palestine's southern coast was set apart and placed under Egyptian administration and Jordan annexed the West Bank, while Jerusalem was divided between Israel and Jordan.[127]

In a letter to William Sutherland Thatcher, the censor of Fitzwilliam House at the University of Cambridge, sent from Bethlehem via Egypt on July 8, 1948, Jabra writes: "Before the British left Palestine, I had intended to write to you and enquire what I was to do in order that I might be given the M.A. degree. But in the confusion and erratic fighting that soon spread all over the country, postal services broke down. I had to leave Jerusalem for Bethlehem (almost as a refugee), and tens of thousands of the city's inhabitants have suffered dislodgement and terrible losses of all kinds."[128]

Jabra also tells Thatcher about prospects of his employment with United Nations Educational, Scientific and Cultural Organization (UNESCO) in Paris, which then had plans to open an international university in Europe. He briefly mentions how grateful he was to hear that Assem Salam, referred to in the letter as Mr. Salaam, was admitted to Fitzwilliam. He signs his letter "G. J. I. Jabra." In another letter to Thatcher, written shortly after he arrived in Baghdad on October 11, 1948, from the Baghdad Hotel, al-Rashid Street, as is indicated in the letterhead, Jabra refers to his earlier letter and says further that he had sent another on July 26, 1948, in which he asked Thatcher for a letter of recommendation to UNESCO in Paris, which had offered him a job: "Towards the end of August, however, I discovered that although *some* letters did go out of our part of the country towards their destination, practically no letters whatever came in, which meant that we were almost entirely cut off from the outside world. Whereupon I left Palestine for Syria to look for a job, since for months everything at home had come to a terrifying standstill, all employment had ceased and all sources of income had disappeared, and it looked as if matters were getting worse, and starvation was not very far off."[129]

Jabra's letter from July 26, 1948, did not make it to Cambridge, and Jabra did not hear back from UNESCO. In Damascus, he learned that the Iraqi Embassy was hiring teachers; he applied and was offered a job. He traveled back to Amman and from there embarked on a new life in Baghdad. In another letter to Thatcher sent from Baghdad, this time from Towjihiya College, Adamiya, as is indicated in the letterhead, on December 1, 1948, he thanks Thatcher for his recommendation and the master's degree, and writes about Palestine, expressing his disappointment with the United Nations and his belief that "no congregation of men in the world can make injustice look just":

> Although most people in the Middle East are disheartened, in fact almost on the verge of despair, they still hope that matters will finally be set right. I for one have not much confidence in the United Nations anymore: it is anything but a forum of free opinion. Unless something is done soon enough to create confidence in the hearts of men everywhere in this body of conflicting members, it will eventually go the same way as its predecessor the League. Where Palestine is concerned, the Arabs in all their various states feel that no congregation of men in the world can make injustice look just. And it is not yet certain that they will accept injustice for good.[130]

PART II
THE TIME BEYOND

ماذا تقول؟
لا شيء يا ريتا، أقلد فارساً في أغنية
عن لعنة الحب المحاصر بالمرايا . . .
عني؟
وعن حلمين فوق وسادةٍ يتقاطعانِ ويهربان
فواحِد يسثل سكينا وآخر يودع الناي الوصايا
لا أدرك المعنى، تقول
ولا أنا، لغتي شظايا

—What are you saying?
—Nothing, I mimic the horseman in a song
about the curse of a love besieged by mirrors . . .
—About me?
—And about two dreams on the pillow, they intersect and escape so one
draws out a dagger and another entrusts the commandments to the flute
—I don't get the meaning
—Nor do I, my language is shrapnel

—Mahmoud Darwish, "Rita's Winter" (translated by Fady Joudah)

CHAPTER 6

BORDER CROSSING

JABRA'S SUITCASE AND HILDESHEIMER'S IDENTITY CARD

In "The Palestinian Exile as Writer" (1979), in a passage reminiscent of Hannah Arendt's essay "We Refugees" (1943), Jabra Ibrahim Jabra expresses fury at being referred to as a refugee:

> If anyone used the word "refugee" with me, I was furious. I was not seeking refuge. None of my Palestinian co-wanderers were seeking refuge. We were offering whatever talent or knowledge we had, in return for a living, for survival. We were knowledge peddlers pausing at one more stop on our seemingly endless way. When in the autumn of 1948 the customs men asked me upon arrival in Baghdad to open my luggage for inspection, I offered them a battered suitcase full of books and papers, a small box full of paints and brushes. And half a dozen paintings on plywood. I was not a refugee, and I was proud as hell.[1]

Conceiving of himself and his Palestinian co-wanderers as "knowledge peddlers" on a "seemingly endless way," Jabra's description of a border crossing falls within the parameters of what Rashid Khalidi refers to as "the quintessential Palestinian experience" in his book *Palestinian Identity*: it "takes place at a border, an airport, a checkpoint: in short, at any one of those many modern barriers where identities are checked and verified."[2] Jabra is a literary writer, identifying himself as a Palestinian exile who gives voice to the Palestinian exile as writer. Exactly what he carried in his luggage we do not know. Just as, despite speculation by philosophers the world over, we do not know what Walter Benjamin was carrying in his briefcase[3] when, in September 1940, after Nazi Germany had invaded France, he attempted to cross the French-Spanish border at Port Bou. Benjamin was on his way out of Europe to join his colleagues Theodor W. Adorno and Max Horkheimer at the Institute for Social Research in New York, which originally was part of the University of Frankfurt and was moved back to Germany after World War II. Benjamin killed himself when the crossing was denied. As Gershom Scholem points out, he had "repeatedly reckoned with the possibility of his suicide and prepared for it. He was convinced that another world war would mean a gas war and bring with it the end of all civilization."[4] Arthur Koestler—whom we have come across as one of the guests at Katy Antonius's lavish garden parties—remembered that Benjamin had carried morphine with him since leaving Germany in 1933 and left Marseille, where through the efforts of Adorno and Horkheimer he had obtained an emergency visa for the United States, with enough morphine "to kill a horse."[5]

What does "a battered suitcase full of books and papers, a small box full of paints and brushes" represent if not the tools of modernist expression Jabra had acquired as a young man in Palestine? He spent his life returning to in his writing in search of a better future. Just as the crossing of borders has become "the quintessential Palestinian experience," so too has the suitcase morphed into a symbol of that experience. In his 1970 poem "Yawmiyyat jurh filastini" (Diary of a Palestinian wound), Mahmoud Darwish asserts, "My homeland is not a suitcase/I am not a traveler/I am a lover and the land is my beloved!"[6] (The poem is dedicated to the Palestinian poet Fadwa Tuqan—the sister of Ibrahim Tuqan, who had been Jabra's Arabic teacher at Rashidiyya Secondary School in Jerusalem.) An exile in his own homeland, or, according to Israel's Emergency Regulations Laws of 1948 and the Absentees' Property Laws of 1950, a "present absentee," Darwish would return to the trope of the suitcase a decade later in his long documentary poem "Madih al-zill al-'ali" (In praise of the high shadow), following the 1982 Israeli invasion of Lebanon and siege of Beirut. Embracing exile, he writes, "My homeland is a suitcase/My suitcase is my homeland,"[7] as he bears in mind al-Andalus—a beacon of learning and tolerance at a time when the major Abrahamic religions were practiced side by side in harmony on the Iberian Peninsula—which he carries like Palestine from one exile into another. Likewise, Jabra carried his childhood memories but also his first artistic and literary trials as a young man in Palestine with him in his luggage to Baghdad and other cities east of the Mediterranean, notably Beirut. Jabra opens his 1978 essay "The Palestinian Exile as Writer" with "the Wandering Palestinian having replaced the Wandering Jew. A historical horror, which over the centuries had acquired the force of a myth, seemed after 1948 to come alive again. It was ironic that the new wanderers should be driven into the wilderness by the old wanderers themselves."[8]

Jabra's thoughts are in line with those expressed by Edward W. Said in his "Reflections on Exile," written from New York City in 1984. "Palestinians feel that they have been turned into exiles by the proverbial people of exile, the Jews," says Said, drawing a comparison between Jewish and Palestinian exilic experiences, adding that, at the same time, the Palestinian's "own sense of national identity has been nourished by the exile milieu."[9] Said defines the terms *refugees* and *exiles* discretely, describing the former as "large herds of innocent and bewildered people requiring urgent international assistance" and the latter as possessing "a touch of solitude and spirituality." According to him, despite the terrible loss it entails, exile makes possible originality of vision: "Most people are principally aware of one culture, one setting, one home; exiles are aware of at least two, and this plurality of vision gives rise to an awareness of simultaneous dimensions, an awareness that—to borrow a phrase from music—is contrapuntal."[10] Along similar lines, writing from exile in Baghdad in the 1970s, Jabra describes the exilic Palestinian intellectual as a harbinger of change: "One was uprooted as a person, and uprooted as a group, and both seemed to float away by a mysterious impulsion. Palestinians as individuals had become wanderers. . . . Palestinian intellectuals were suddenly everywhere: writing, teaching, talking, doing things, influencing a whole Arab society in most unexpected ways. They were coping with their sense of loss, turning their exile into a force, creating thereby a mystique of being Palestinian."[11] He refers to Arnold J. Toynbee, who compared the Twelve Apostles and the Greek thinkers and artists expelled from Byzantium in 1453 to the indigenous Palestinians, who likewise were released into the world after 1948 as "a force of radical change."[12]

In her essay, written from exile in New York in the early 1940s, Arendt outlines the condition of the refugee as a new historical consciousness, arguing that "refugees expelled from one country to the next represent the avant-garde of their people."[13] While Jabra turned to literature, regaining Jerusalem in writing and reckoning with his new identity as a Palestinian exile as writer in Baghdad, he "wrote letters in every direction," trying to keep track of his friends "tossed about like flotsam on a violent sea . . . where no sea could bring them back together again, except in imagination."[14]

At the same time, Wolfgang Hildesheimer was back in Germany, working as a simultaneous interpreter at the Nuremberg trials, where he would come face to face with his Jewish identity. He had read about the Holocaust in the English press when he was in Palestine, but it was only now that he became a witness, as the horrendous extent of the Holocaust was rolled out before his eyes. In his essay "Mein Judentum" (My Judaism), published in 1978, he explains:

> I was confronted with Judaism in its cruelest meaning, with racial identity, foreign race and all the other terms of this vocabulary, only when I became a simultaneous interpreter at the Nuremberg trials; there, systematically and schematically, a story unfolded—one that, in the years during which it actually occurred, I had known of only from reports and rumors. The story was terrible, but it belonged to a past that, in the end, it was *not* my task to come to terms with. I left the question of guilt or collective guilt to my unconscious and waited for the decision from within. For three years I lived as a member of the occupying forces in a large room in the Grand Hotel in Nuremberg, which I had set up as a studio in order to distract myself from the horrors of these extensively recapitulated processes while drawing and painting, which I succeeded in doing. I even succeeded in differentiating, with respect to the former enemy, the Germans, among the good, the half-good and the bad.[15]

As Wolfgang makes clear, he returned to Germany "as a member of the occupying forces," setting himself apart from his compatriots, in whose ranks he had grown up until 1933 and with whom he shared a mother tongue. Questions of guilt—not his own, but collective German guilt as discussed by the German philosopher Karl Jaspers in a lecture series at Heidelberg University in 1946 and Jasper's former student Hannah Arendt[16]—were to preoccupy him, even if, for the time being, he found distraction in art and was able to overcome his aversion to the former enemy, unlike many of his colleagues at the military tribunal, as he remarks.[17] In conversation with Hans Helmut Hillrichs for the German television series *Zeugen des Jahrhunderts* in 1989, Wolfgang singles out his experience as an interpreter at the Nuremberg trials as his most important testimony, specifically his being confronted by "war criminals and potential war criminals, the tremendous variety of people. . . . From destructive to constructive, without passing [moral] judgement. Of course, this is good versus evil, one might say, but I mean the possibilities inherent in man, the diversity, the characteristics given to man. This tremendous plurality was probably what marked me most and what, in the end, provided me with material to write. All these experiences are in one way or another dealt with [in my writing]; through many hallways and doors they come back to daylight."[18]

What he witnessed at the Nuremberg trials kept Wolfgang silent for many years, as he sought refuge in avant-garde art, first in Surrealism and then in the Theater of the Absurd, and its exploratory use of language that seemingly falls to pieces before opening up new horizons. This lengthy period of silence between Wolfgang's exposure to and his writing about the crimes of the Holocaust is explained by Henry A. Lea in terms of the task of the simultaneous interpreter: one "clings so intensely to the wording that one fails to take notice of the content.... Only years later, in a very slow, gradually progressing process of discovery or awakening, does one become aware of the full content and its meaning."[19] Lea had met Wolfgang as a fellow translator in Nuremberg and would later become a professor of Germanic Languages and Literatures at the University of Massachusetts Amherst, authoring a number of studies on Wolfgang's literary works. This content and its meaning found expression in words in *Tynset*, published in 1965, for which Wolfgang received the Bremen Literature Prize and the Georg Büchner Prize.[20]

Tynset is delivered in the form of an interior monologue, a literary device associated with modernist writers from Djuna Barnes to Samuel Beckett to James Joyce.[21] Wolfgang refused to call it a novel, describing it instead in musical terms as a rondo.[22] During a sleepless night, its first-person narrator returns over and again to the terrible past in Germany he can neither forget nor put into words, despite having found refuge in Switzerland, as he picks up a Norwegian railway guide and randomly picks the village of Tynset as his destination. *Tynset* is published together with *Masante* (1973) in the second volume of Wolfgang's collected works, titled *Monological Prose*. Both texts are permeated with autobiographical elements and have been read as major contributions to German Jewish exile literature and the Holocaust novel.[23] *Masante*, named after a house in Italy that the narrator describes as "das Ziel einer Flucht" (the destination of an escape), elaborates on the memories and trauma that cause its narrator a sleepless night before he quite literally disappears into the desert—from an outpost at the edge of the desert called Me'ona. The narrator describes it as "the southernmost and easternmost escape and counter point to Masante,"[24] but its exact location is not further specified. As Lea points out, there is in fact a place called Me'ona in Israel near the Lebanese border;[25] its name is taken from the words of Moses in the Book of Deuteronomy: "The eternal Lord is your place of refuge" (in Biblical Hebrew, *me'ona* means "place of refuge").[26] The settlement of Me'ona was built in 1949—not in the desert but on fertile land that belonged to the Arab villages of al-Kabri or Tarshiha (renowned for their springs, which made them one of the main sources of fresh water in Palestine and allowed the villagers to grow fig, olive, pomegranate, mulberry, and apple trees), of which all that remains today are "crumbled walls and stone rubble, overgrown with thorns, weeds, and bushes."[27] Whether Wolfgang had in mind this specific location, which was established after his departure from Mandate Palestine in 1946 and the establishment of the State of Israel in 1948, is questionable, but references to "Oriental" imaginaries—such as camels, a caravanserai, hummus (described as "an archaic dish from the Orient [in German, he says *Morgenland*]"[28]), and arak—point to the country he and his family found refuge in when they fled Nazi Germany in 1933.

Trains permeate Wolfgang's work, writes Hillrichs in the introduction to his conversations with Wolfgang, as a constant reminder of "the trains to Auschwitz and the ghost train of so-called technical progress."[29] Auschwitz is not referred to directly in any of Wolfgang's literary texts. In a manner comparable to that of Adorno, he was "never able to speak directly about what happened in [Auschwitz and the other death camps], and yet at the same time it was, if not an eloquent theme, at least a 'never-ending task' of his thinking."[30] In his 1967 Lectures in Poetics at the Goethe University Frankfurt, Wolfgang takes Adorno's oft-quoted—and -misrepresented—saying, "To write poetry after Auschwitz is barbaric," and inverts it. After Auschwitz, Wolfgang argues, *only* poetry is possible and not the novel—with the exception of absurdist prose, which he regards as closely related to poetry. "Auschwitz and similar places have expanded human consciousness; they have added a dimension that hardly existed before as a possibility," he writes—a dimension, he claims, the novel cannot express, whereas reality [*Wirklichkeit*] is no longer thinkable without it.[31] His views align with Giorgio Agamben's notion that "the poetic word is the one that is always situated in the position of a remnant and that can, therefore, bear witness."[32]

Wolfgang's long silence about the Holocaust might be read along similar lines as those suggested by Shoshana Felman in her discussion of Benjamin's silence in the aftermath of World War I—not as "a state of noiselessness or wordlessness," but as an event in its own right.³³ Felman focuses her consideration of Benjamin's silence on his autobiographical *Berlin Chronicle* and two theoretical essays, "The Storyteller" (1936) and "Theses on the Philosophy of History" (1940). In "The Storyteller," Benjamin depicts storytelling as an art lost to the trauma of World War I: "With the World War a process began to become apparent which has not halted since then. Was it not noticeable at the end of the war that men returned from the battlefield grown silent—not richer, but poorer in communicable experience.... A generation that had gone to school on a horse-drawn streetcar now stood under the open sky in a countryside in which nothing remained unchanged but the clouds, and beneath these clouds, in a field of force of destructive torrents and explosions, was the tiny, fragile human body."³⁴

In "Theses on the Philosophy of History," says Felman, "the story of the silence of narration—the story of the First World War—is again narrated but this time interpreted as a theory of history" against the backdrop of World War II. Referring to Benjamin's iconic reading of Paul Klee's *Angelus Novus* (1920), a storm blowing from Paradise caught in his wings as he turns toward the past and "the pile of debris before him grows skyward,"³⁵ she adds, "the angel of history is mute: his mouth is speechlessly open, as he is helplessly pushed back toward the future, pushed back from the Second World War to the speechless experience of the First."³⁶ In similar ways, Wolfgang perceives a continuation of catastrophes of a political and increasingly environmental nature that, in his eyes, may very well result in the world's coming to an end. Falling silent recurs throughout his writing, until he departs from writing altogether later in life, turning once again to visual art, in particular collage, as a means of expression.

In his first years back in Germany after World War II, Wolfgang was preoccupied with questions of citizenship. In 1936, Wolfgang gave up German citizenship to obtain a Palestinian passport and was left without valid travel documents after the establishment of the State of Israel in 1948. In a letter to his parents written from Nuremberg, he considers emigrating to the United States but then emphatically writes, "I want to stay in Europe until it perishes. Having been away for 7 years, I never want to leave it again."³⁷ As Volker Jehle suggests, Wolfgang was not serious about going to the United States; he entertained this idea primarily to please his parents, who had mixed feelings about his return to Germany.³⁸ As we have seen, he also considered going back to London and acquiring British nationality, and he was thinking about working for UNESCO in Paris.³⁹ Paris in the late 1940s, figured "both in France and throughout the world as the capital of a republic having neither borders nor boundaries," as Pascale Casanova writes: "a universal homeland exempt from all professions of patriotism, a kingdom of literature set up in opposition to the ordinary laws of states, a transnational realm whose sole imperative are those of art and literature: the universal republic of letters. 'Here,' wrote Henri Michaux with reference to Adrienne Monnier's bookshop, one of the chief places of literary consecration in Paris, 'is the homeland of [all] those free spirits who have not found a homeland.' Paris therefore became the capital of those who proclaimed themselves to be stateless and above political laws: in a word, artists."[40]

In January 1949, former U.S. bomber pilot Garry Davis founded the International Registry of World Citizens in Paris, which gained the support of renowned French intellectuals, among them Albert Camus and Jean-Paul Sartre, and registered more than 750,000 individuals.[41] In Germany, too, registration offices were set up and more than 160,000 people gave their names.[42] In a letter to his parents written from Nuremberg in February 1949, Wolfgang proudly announces: "In the meantime, I am also registered as a citizen of the world, have a provisional identity card and I firmly believe in it. My friends in Munich and I went to the newly founded registration office and all of us registered. Then we organized a "Citizen's Breakfast" in which we addressed each other as 'Citizen of the World.'"[43]

His enthusiasm did not last long. In July 1949, he writes about his "escape into the imagination because reality [*Wirklichkeit*]—one can safely say—is unbearable."[44] He again invokes the possibility of emigration to the United States and says that taking Israeli citizenship would be inappropriate and would amount to pure opportunism given that he left Palestine voluntarily in 1946, did not fight for Israel, and played no part in its establishment.[45]

In October 1949, Wolfgang left Nuremberg for Ambach on Lake Starnberg, a region close to Munich that had emerged as a kind of artists' colony in the late nineteenth century.[46] For some time, he shared a sparsely furnished apartment with Wolf Rosenberg, his friend from the Odenwaldschule who, like Wolfgang, had gone to Palestine but could not identify with Zionism and returned to Germany after the war to pursue his career as a musical composer. In Ambach, Wolfgang immersed himself in literature. He read Camus's *The Myth of Sisyphus* (1947) and Sartre's *What Is Literature?* (1947), both of which had just been translated into German.[47] In a letter to his parents, he mentions "the new discovery of his narrative talent" and refers to the "French (atheist!) existentialist philosophers" as "a revelation," which helped him to make the decision to become a writer rather than a visual artist.[48] He published his first literary texts, primarily short prose and plays in German, which were also broadcast on radio. In May 1951, Wolfgang was invited to a meeting of the literary circle Gruppe 47 in Bad Dürkheim, at the invitation of Hans Werner Richter. As he explained to his parents, it was not "a gang of storming and stressing avant-gardists" but "a loose group of around 30 writers, critics, editors, artistic directors and teachers between 30 and 60 years old," some of them rather conservative.[49] Started by Richter in 1947 as a platform to renew German-language literature after the war, Gruppe 47 emerged as an influential literary forum in West Germany and convened regularly until 1967. Among others, its members included Ilse Aichinger, Ingeborg Bachmann, Heinrich Böll, Paul Celan, Günter Eich, Erich Fried, Günter Grass, Peter Handke, Walter Jens, Marcel Reich-Ranicki, and Peter Weiss.[50] Wolfgang was regularly seen at the group's meetings. Gruppe 47 presented him with a sense of homecoming and an intellectual environment he embraced, but he had difficulty explaining this to his parents.[51] After the group's meeting in Bad Dürkheim, Wolfgang at last told his parents that he intended to remain in Germany and request German citizenship. Explaining his choice, he criticizes not so much their perception of postwar German society but rather the society in which they live in Israel: "The question is, which society you still feel comfortable in. This is not meant in a defamatory way. I am afraid that in Israel for various reasons—not least due to resentment—one loses the preconditions for a reasonable coexistence and an exchange of ideas with other groups of people and peoples. I see in this a terrible danger for future generations."[52]

In other letters, he says he finds politics disgusting and hates nationalism,[53] and adds "I am primarily concerned with aesthetic, not political, issues."[54] As Wolfgang was gaining recognition as a German writer, he also settled down in his personal life. After a number of half-hearted love relationships,[55] in 1952, he married the German painter Silvia Dillmann (1917–2014), having moved into her apartment in the Waldschlössel, a castle-like house with a tower room looking over Lake Starnberg. Having decided during his first marriage to Bella Soskin in Jerusalem that he did not want children of his own,[56] he now had a family that included Christa and Inge, Silvia's daughters from her previous marriage.[57] Despite his renewed sense of belonging to Europe, and more precisely to German-language literature, Wolfgang embraced the concept of homelessness. In a manner similar to that of Jabra and Said, who ground originality of vision in the experience of exile, Wolfgang describes homelessness as "the source of all his creative activity."[58]

A LETTER FROM EXILE AND NOTES FROM ISRAEL

At the end of 1952, Wolfgang received a letter from Jabra written from Harvard, "this so-called Cambridge of America," where Jabra was staying as a special student on a Rockefeller Foundation fellowship (figure 6.1). Dated November 9, 1952, and addressed to "My dear Wolf," the letter abounds with intimate

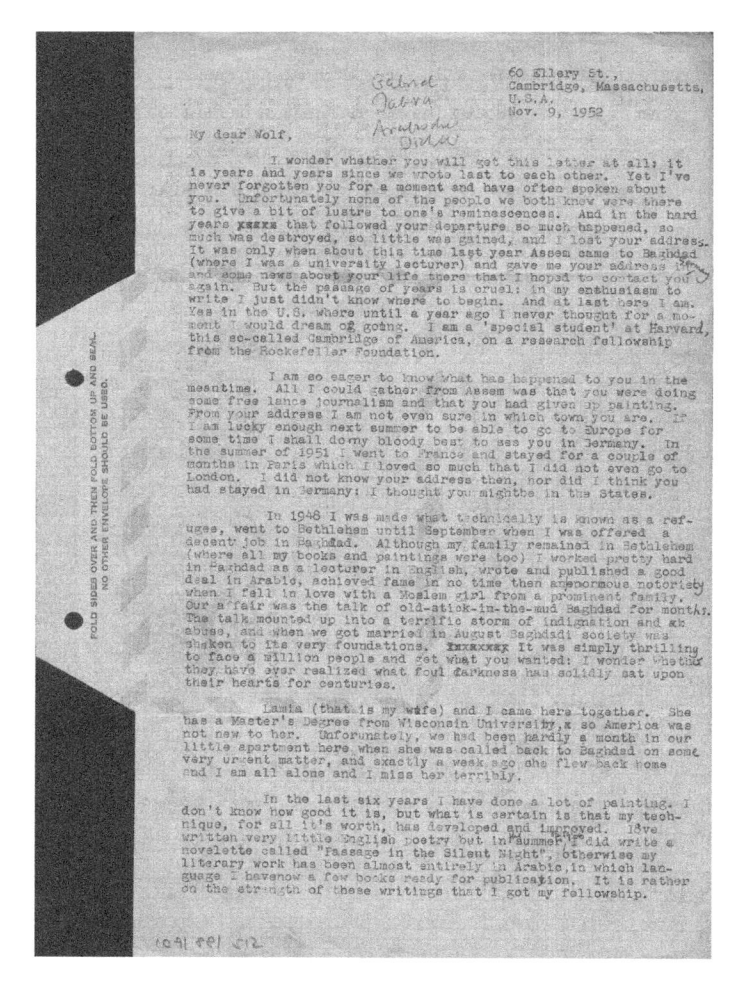

6.1 Gabriel Jabra's [Jabra Ibrahim Jabra] letter to Wolfgang Hildesheimer from Harvard, November 9, 1952.
Academy of Arts, Berlin, WHA 478.

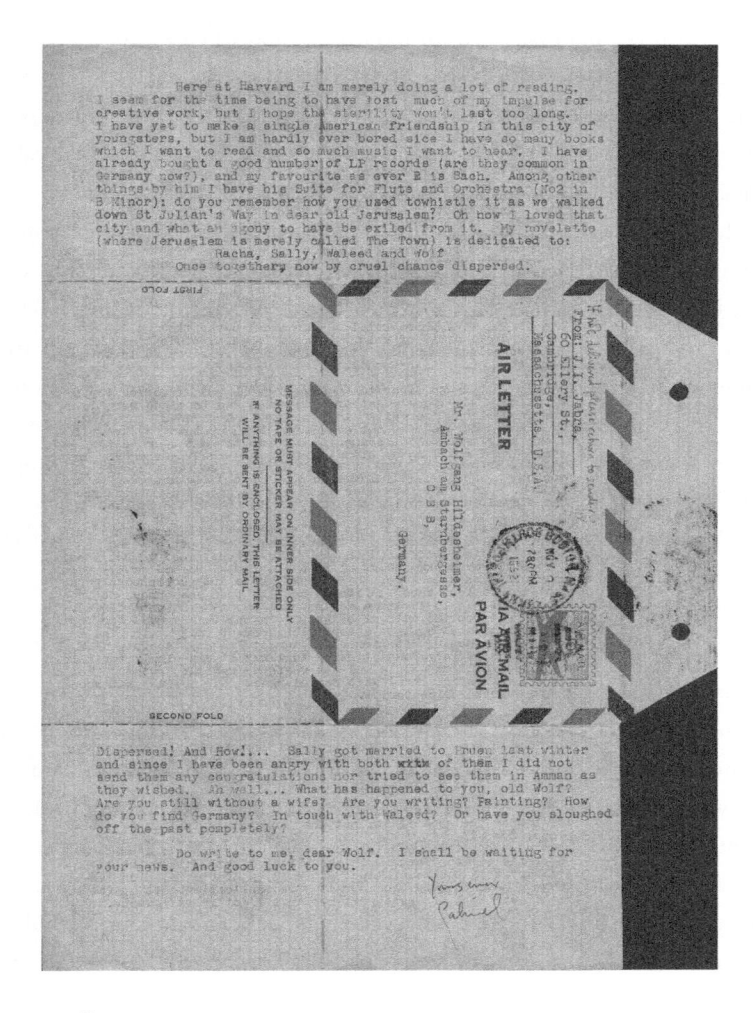

6.1 (*Continued*)

reminiscences of their shared life in Jerusalem. At the same time, it provides the reader with news about Jabra's new life in exile:

> In 1948 I was made what technically speaking is known as a refugee, went to Bethlehem until September when I was offered a decent job in Baghdad. . . . I worked pretty hard in Baghdad as a lecturer in English, wrote and published a good deal in Arabic, achieved fame in no time . . . when I fell in love with a Moslem girl from a prominent family. Our affair was the talk of

188   THE TIME BEYOND

old-stick-in-the-mud Baghdad for months . . . and when we got married in August Baghdadi society was shaken to its very foundation. . . .

In the last six years I have done a lot of painting. . . . I've written very little English poetry but, in the summer of 1946, I did write a novelette called "Passage in the Silent Night". . . .

Here at Harvard I am merely doing a lot of reading. . . . I have yet to make a single American friendship in this city of youngsters, but I am hardly ever bored since I have so many books which I want to read and so much music I want to hear. I have already bought a good number of LP records (are they common in Germany now?), and my favorite as ever is Bach. Among other things by him I have his Suite for Flute and Orchestra (No. 2 in B Minor): do you remember how you used to whistle it as we walked down St Julien's Way in dear old Jerusalem? Oh how I loved that city and what an agony to have been exiled from it. My novelette (where Jerusalem is merely called The Town) is dedicated to:

    Racha, Sally, Waleed and Wolf
    Once together, now by cruel chance dispersed.[59]

We have already encountered Jabra's novel and its scathing critique of the Palestinian political elite. As Jabra says in *Princesses' Street*, he translated it into Arabic while at Harvard, around the same time that he was writing his letter to Wolfgang. Neither of the two editions of the novel in Arabic translation, *Surakh fi layl tawil* (*Cry in a Long Night*), include the dedication cited in Jabra's letter. As we discussed in chapters 2 and 5, however, the novel's second edition, published in Beirut in 1988, features one of Wolfgang's illustrations on its book cover, but it neither provides any information about the image nor mentions the artist's name. We do not know if Wolfgang ever replied to Jabra's letter; there is no further correspondence between the two in the Wolfgang Hildesheimer Archive in Berlin.

Similar to Wolfgang, Jabra was not a *homo politicus*; unlike Wolfgang, however, he was not a pessimist. "While distancing himself from the revolutionary left," writes Bashir Abu-Manneh, Jabra "nonetheless celebrated a romantic form of rebellion and challenge,"[60] quoting his essay "The Rebels, the Committed and Others: Transitions in Arabic Poetry Today," where Jabra writes, "the rebel remains an undigested element: his concern remains with individual dignity and freedom whenever threatened, regardless of the source of such a threat."[61]

Jabra placed his hope not in politics but in cultural practices, turning his "exile into a force," as he says in "The Palestinian Exile as Writer." Although both he and Wolfgang conceive of their wanderings as a source of creativity, Jabra's exile differs significantly from Wolfgang's homelessness. While Wolfgang did not leave Germany by his own choosing in 1933, he departed Palestine voluntarily in 1946, and returned to Europe, first to London and from there to Nuremberg and Munich—to another Germany after the Holocaust, in which Jewish life is best represented by "the physical emptiness that resulted from the expulsion, destruction, and annihilation of Jewish life in the Shoah, which cannot be refilled after the fact,"[62] as the voids that cut through Daniel Libeskind's Jewish Museum, opened in Berlin in 2001, have been described. While Wolfgang hated nationalism and registered as "a citizen of the world," opting for "that homelessness in which we—Jews or not—are all at home,"[63] Jabra's sense of national belonging to Palestine increased during his exile, as it did for many other Palestinians, especially after the 1967 War.[64] Jabra held on to his Palestinian identity throughout his life, insisting "If I were not Palestinian, I would be nothing."[65]

Also unlike Wolfgang, Jabra did not leave Palestine voluntarily. The new geopolitical realities he describes in his letter to Wolfgang are reflected in the application form Jabra submitted to the Rockefeller Foundation for a fellowship at Harvard, in which his permanent address is recorded as "Bethlehem, Jordan" and his citizenship as "Jordanian (ex-Palestinian)," whereas in his application form to Fitzwilliam House, Cambridge, a decade earlier, he had indicated his nationality as "Palestinian," race, "Arab," and religion, "Christian."[66]

As Jabra mentions, he married "a Moslem girl from a prominent family" in Iraq. This was Lami'a Barqi al-Askari, who had earned a master's degree from the University of Wisconsin at Madison and was a professor at the Teachers' Training College in Baghdad. Mixed marriages were not common in Iraq, and Jabra converted to Islam in order to marry Lami'a. The marriage was met with outrage. Lami'a hailed from a family of army officers; her father was Muhammad Barqi al-Askari, a member of the Iraqi parliament and a former brigadier general of the Iraqi Army, and her uncle was Bakr Sidqi al-Askari, a general in the Iraqi Army and "the first person in modern Arab history to stage a military coup d'état," as Jabra points out in *Princesses' Street*. Underlining Bakr Sidqi's loyalty to Arab nationalism, Jabra adds: "in 1936 he rose in support of the man he loved and revered, King Ghazi, son of Faisal I, giving his life as a price less than a year after the coup when he was assassinated."[67] What remains unsaid by Jabra is that Bakr Sidqi was responsible for the Simele Massacre, carried out by the nascent Iraqi Army in 1933 against the Assyrian population in northern Iraq, and was believed to be behind the assassination of Ja'far Pasha al-Askari during the 1936 coup. Ja'far Pasha al-Askari had served twice as prime minister of Iraq under the British Mandate and played a key role in the formation of the Iraqi Army along with Nouri al-Said, his brother-in-law, who was one of the most influential politicians in Iraq's modern history; he served as prime minister of Iraq under the British Mandate and then of the Hashemite Kingdom of Iraq until his assassination during the overthrow of the British-backed monarchy in the 1958 Iraq Revolution. Lami'a joined Jabra at Harvard but "was called back to Baghdad on some very urgent matter," as Jabra writes to Wolfgang. Fadhil Jamali, a member of the Iraqi delegation at the United Nations in New York City, wrote to the Rockefeller Foundation that "Mrs. Jabra was not recalled because of her mother's illness, but because of Moslem annoyance at her marriage to her Christian husband (who, of course, turned Moslem to marry her)."[68]

At Harvard, Jabra studied with Archibald MacLeish, and he met again with two of his friends from Jerusalem who, like him, had received fellowships from the Rockefeller Foundation: the poet Tawfiq Sayigh, another graduate of the Arab College, and the literary scholar Mounah A. Khouri, who had been Jabra's colleague at De La Salle College.[69] Like them, he wanted to study for a doctorate. As he specifies in his application form to the Rockefeller Foundation, he intended to work on "the transition from the Classical Age to Romanticism" in English literature.[70] He also considered employment at Princeton and Harvard, as well as at the American University of Beirut, and was discussing work for the BBC's Arabic department, as John Marshall says in reports of the Rockefeller Foundation. Eventually Lami'a was able to rejoin Jabra at Harvard, and they returned together to Baghdad in early 1954. Jabra obtained Iraqi citizenship and was offered jobs at the College of Arts and Sciences and in the public relations department of the Iraqi Petroleum Company (IPC), a British-chartered company, as the editor of its journal *al-'Amilun fi al-naft* (Workers in petroleum).[71] The Jabras had two sons, Sadeer and Yasser, who today live in New Zealand and the United States.

Now writing almost exclusively in Arabic, Jabra continued his literary career, contributing to cultural journals across the Arab world, in particular to *Shi'r*. Founded in Beirut in 1957 by Yusuf al-Khal, *Shi'r* was known for its modernist stance and openness to foreign literature. Along with al-Khal, the *Shi'r* group included, among others, a number of writers who today figure among the most renowned of Arab poets—Adonis, Unsi al-Hajj, Muhammad al-Maghout, Tawfiq Sayigh, and Badr Shakir al-Sayyab. Despite its importance, the group has only recently received attention in studies in global modernism in the English-speaking world.[72] *Shi'r* was a product of its time and place—Beirut's modernist moment—but also of late modernism, in which artistic modernism had lost its earlier rebellious stance and was promoted globally as a weapon in the Cold War. *Shi'r* was not funded by the Congress of Cultural Freedom (CCF), which had been established by the Central Intelligence Agency with the aim of strengthening anti-Communist trends. However, its focus on issues of aesthetics rather than politics brought the group close to the liberal values fostered by the Congress, as exemplified in the 1961 Rome Conference on modern Arabic literature, sponsored by the CCF, in which many of the *Shi'r* poets, among them Jabra, participated.[73] Jabra also frequently contributed to *Hiwar*, which was published out of Beirut between 1962 and 1966 as part of a CCF-funded global network of literary journals and edited by his friend, the Palestinian poet Tawfiq Sayigh.[74] Walid Khalidi, too, would be duped, as Elizabeth Holt suggests, to publish an article in *Hiwar*. Dismantling the Zionist rhetoric of "rescuing the land" as "propaganda for gathering support from abroad," his article focuses on the West's positions on the Palestinian cause.[75] The CIA's role in the CCF was revealed in a series of articles in the *New York Times* in April 1966, while suspicion was raised in the Arabic press earlier, notably by Palestinian writer Ghassan Kanafani. Kanafani was known in particular for his 1963 novel *Rijal fil-shams* (*Men in the Sun*), which the Egyptian filmmaker Tewfiq Salih turned into a feature film in 1972 titled *al-Makhdu'un* (*The Dupes*), as well as for his 1966 study *Adab al-muqawama fi Filastin al-muhtalla 1948–1966* (Resistance literature in Occupied Palestine). Kanafani was the official spokesperson of the Popular Front for the Liberation of Palestine (PFLP)and was assassinated by the Mossad, Israel's intelligence agency, in Beirut in 1972.[76]

In a different manner from *Shi'r*, two other cultural journals in Beirut took a decidedly political stance: *al-Adab* in favor of Arab nationalism and *al-Tariq* in favor of Communism. Founded in 1953 by Suhayl Idris, a graduate of the Sorbonne, *al-Adab* espoused Sartre's notion of literary engagement (referred to in Arabic as *iltizam*). *al-Adab* celebrated Sartre for the position he took on the Algerian War of Independence, in which he voiced support for Algerians in their struggle against colonization, but fell out with him after the 1967 War, in which

Sartre sided with Israel.[77] In the 1950s, Beirut was emerging as the Arab world's economic and cultural hub, attracting publishers, writers, and artists from across the region. Palestinians in particular contributed to the city's intellectual life. Already before 1948, the American University of Beirut had attracted some of the best minds among its students and faculty but, with the Nakba, a whole wave of Palestinians turned into knowledge peddlers, as Jabra says. They were to be joined by Egyptians, Syrians, Iraqis, and other Arabs who sought refuge in Beirut from the increasingly authoritarian regimes backed by the militaries of their respective countries. Beirut's economic boom was closely tied to the loss of competition from Palestinian cities—particularly Haifa, which had seen much development and emerged as a strategic port in the Eastern Mediterranean under British mandatory rule, but was now cut off from the Arab world at large.[78]

In 1959, Jabra's first collection of poetry written in Arabic and titled *Tammuz fil-madina* (Tammuz in the city) was published by *Shiʿr*'s publishing house in Beirut.[79] It abounds with notions of death and rebirth reminiscent of T. S. Eliot's *The Waste Land*, which, as we have seen, Albert Hourani had read aloud to the ecumenical circle in Jerusalem, a decade before it would be translated by Adonis and Yusuf al-Khal into Arabic as *al-Ard al-kharab*.[80] Other allusions are to James Frazer's *The Golden Bough*, which Jabra had started to translate into Arabic in Jerusalem and later circulated among poets in Iraq, where it was to leave its mark in particular on al-Sayyab.

In addition to the novella mentioned in his letter to Wolfgang, Jabra published six novels. For the most part, these novels are set in Baghdad, taking their readers back to Palestine as the country of origin of a number of the characters, who were exilic Palestinian intellectuals like Jabra. "The quintessential Palestinian experience" of crossing borders figures prominently. In *al-Safina* (1970, The Ship), excerpts of which were published in *Hiwar*, a group of Arab intellectuals on a cruise in the Mediterranean discuss world literature from Camus to Dostoevsky to Kafka, modern art, and music, as a series of flashbacks draws them back to the land: Wadi Assaf, a Palestinian businessman, recalls the fighting in Jerusalem in 1948, while Issam Salman, an Iraqi architect, tries to run away from his family, after his father kills another man in a dispute over land.[81] The protagonist of his most-acclaimed novel *In Search of Walid Masoud*—which we have drawn on previously for its autobiographical references—goes missing in a no-man's land between borders, about fifty miles west of Rutba, a strategic location on the Amman-Baghdad highway in the Mesopotamian heartland.

As his friends in Baghdad set out to reconstruct Walid's life, his fate remains unresolved, his life suspended, and rumors spread that he emigrated to Canada or Australia, was killed like his son Marwan who had joined the fedayeen in Lebanon, or went back to Occupied Palestine.[82] A tape left in his car provides a recording of a long stream-of-consciousness monologue, reminiscent of modernist writing from Joyce to Faulkner, in which Walid recalls his life in Palestine as he drives out into the desert toward the Iraqi-Jordanian border. In a string of catastrophes—bringing to mind Benjamin's reading of Klee's *Angelus Novus*—previous disasters from before the Nakba, inherited from his parents, enter his mind,[83] from "my father who before he died was lying on the floor like a huge oak felled by the wind and he knew many stories about acorn bread during the days of the Ottoman War banishment and famine I was born after the famine the road sped away with us we were in a truck along a white road wound through the dust fleeing away from us from me and the hills fleeing away and the stones the stone kilometer landmarks which I learned to read after I grew older and I was able to read the calendar on which 1927 was written."[84]

This dreamlike vision, of being in a truck speeding along a white road, might well be one of Jabra's earliest childhood memories of leaving the hills around Adana for Bethlehem with his family,[85] here recalled as his historical self and literary persona collide in Walid Masoud as he disappears into the desert. The hills may denote the mountainous area that is today in southern Turkey and northern Syria in which Jabra was born (as his university records document). Given how difficult it is for a child less than three years old to remember, however, it is more likely that these hills are the Judean hills around Jerusalem, where Jabra used to take long walks as a student of the Arab College (as he recalls in *The First Well*). The stone kilometer landmarks mentioned by the novel's protagonist are a clear index of Palestine. Jabra saw a devastating earthquake in 1927, which he recalls in both *The First Well* and *In Search of Walid Masoud*, in which the natural disaster is followed by a reference to political conflict (i.e., the 1929 riots). The figure of the "fighter" (*al-thawar*) appears on the horizon in a novel that has been read as documenting a shift from "the Palestinian intellectual wandering in exile" to "the Palestinian freedom fighter rooted in the refugee camp."[86] Like a black hole into which the novel's protagonist disappears along with the hopes and dreams attached to the role of the exilic Palestinian intellectual as an agent of change, the border crossing in the middle of nowhere figures as the antipode of the lost homeland described as a colorful paradise on Earth: "the olive trees and the red soil and the shady caves where we could eat figs and grapes hanging down in huge clusters from the vines."[87]

The disappearance of Jabra's protagonist shows striking similarities with the fate of the narrator in Wolfgang's *Masante*, in which the narrator disappears into the infinitude of the desert. But whereas *Masante* is located in postwar German literature, *In Search of Walid Masoud* is part of a body of works of modern Palestinian literature and film,[88] in which the theme of disappearance, namely that of the Palestinian from and in their homeland, figures prominently. The odyssey of Jabra's absent protagonist does not end in a homecoming but in a no-man's-land. *In Search of Walid Masoud* makes possible multiple readings—*al-bahth*, translated in the novel's English title as "search," can be understood as "both the product of intellectual inquiry and its process, as it takes as its object knowledge, the intellectual, and the very project of intellectual production itself."[89] Humanistic inquiry, then, offers the only way forward as we try to make sense of the life of Walid, the exilic Palestinian intellectual described in the novel as "one of those exiles who'll use that vantage point to shake the *Arab* world into reexamining everything it's ever thought or made."[90] Walid Masoud shares many characteristics with Jabra, but he also serves as a mirror in which "the other characters are merely reflecting on aspects of themselves, creating ambiguity with respect to authorial identity."[91] *In Search of Walid Masoud* can accordingly be read as "the polyphonic portrait of the exilic Palestinian intellectual, one that reveals this figure's many contributions to the overall modernist project in the Arab world," and, at the same time, as "a portrait of the Iraqi intelligentsia at a particular moment in history—specifically, in the aftermath of the 1967 defeat."[92] Focusing in particular on Wisal, Walid's youngest lover and herself a poet, Emily Drumsta offers yet another reading of the novel, one that foregrounds not its function as a mirror of society but rather its celebration of the poetic word "as a recurring thematic motif and as a formal conceit" to overcome absence and loss.[93] Wisal's name translates as a "bond of love," here the communion of the exilic Palestinian intellectual with a new generation of revolutionary voices, as he and Wisal read Shakespeare alongside al-Mutanabbi—"Shakespeare is Mutanabbi's brother, they're both masters of words"—and confirm that words matter just as much as deeds, which in their lives means political action, "words are everything."[94]

As Tarif Khalidi suggested to me, Jabra may have named his protagonist after Walid Khalidi, who became an important public figure in Arab and Palestinian affairs in the 1960s and 1970s, as we shall see. Jabra and Walid did not meet again after 1948, but Jabra used to visit Walid's sister Sulafa in Beirut. Their amicable friendship seemed to be based on genuine love, recalls Tarif, who would meet Jabra again at Sulafa's house in Hamra Street.[95] Sulafa also appears in one of Jabra's novels, *Hunters in a Narrow Street*, written in English and first published in 1960.[96] This Sulafa is a beautiful Muslim woman from one of Baghdad's leading families with whom the protagonist, like Jabra an Arab Christian from Jerusalem with a degree in English literature from Cambridge University, called Jameel Farran, falls in love. Whereas the real Sulafa would have been unattainable for Jabra—who, like his protagonist in *Cry*, was new to "the town" and considered a nobody before building a reputation as a graduate of the Arab College and Cambridge University—Jabra married Lami'a, after having gained recognition as a "Palestinian exile as writer" across the Arab world. Tarif remembers Jabra as a man of "enormous charm and kindness—that's the impression I still have of him, always a sweet smile on his face, a very generous human being, seductive, beautiful, with a slightly nasal voice, precise English, superb Arabic, a bit like Yusuf al-Khal, the Ezra Pounds of their respective cities, al-Khal of Beirut, Jabra of Baghdad, discoverers and promoters of literary and artistic talent."[97]

Having previously tried his hand at painting in Jerusalem, Jabra continued to paint in Baghdad but soon became better known as an art critic. Together with the Iraqi artists Jewad Selim and Hassan Shakir Al Said, he founded the Baghdad Group for Modern Art in 1951.[98] He also authored a number of studies on modern art in Iraq, notably *Jawad Salim wa-nasb al-hurriyya* (Jewad Selim and the Monument of Freedom), in which he reads the Monument of Freedom from right to left, like a verse of Arabic poetry. The monument commemorates the 1958 Iraq Revolution in fourteen bronze sculptures mounted on a mural—reminiscent of Assyrian bas-relief, Arabic calligraphy, and Picasso's *Guernica* all at once—and is raised six meters above the ground at Baghdad's Tahrir Square, where it still stands.[99] Jabra's deep interest in modern art is reflected in his literary work. In *'Alam bila khara'it* (1982, A world without maps), a novel he coauthored with 'Abd al-Rahman Munif,[100] dreams and reality are deliberately blurred as its characters investigate the murder of Najwa, which recall André Breton's iconic work of Surrealist fiction *Nadja* (1928). *'Alam bila khara'it* has been described as "a novel on the art of the novel,"[101] and, in a similar manner to *In Search of Walid Masoud*, it signals a shift in modern Arabic literature after the Arab defeat in the 1967 War, which led to rigorous self-critique and a "constant questioning with no pretense to ready answers."[102]

Jabra started his literary career as a translator and would translate numerous books from English into Arabic. His translations of Shakespeare's plays and sonnets have had a tremendous influence on the reception of Shakespeare across the Arab world, but he also translated Beckett's *Waiting for Godot*, Faulkner's *The Sound and the Fury*, and many other works of literature and literary criticism. His translation of Faulkner into Arabic, published in Beirut in 1961, has been considered one of the best.[103] However, it has met with criticism in recent years, partly because of its omission of "dialectic elements and polyphonic configurations," which can be explained by the preference of Standard Arabic over Arabic dialects at the time of translation,[104] and partly because of its entrenchment in American cultural diplomacy during the Cold War.[105] Faulkner was introduced in the Middle East through Franklin Book Programs, which—like the CCF—was funded by the U.S. Department of State and covertly by the CIA.[106] Muhammad Yusuf Najm, a former student of the Arab College and professor of Arabic at the American University of Beirut, was in charge of Franklin in Beirut. He had suggested Jabra, who in 1954 had published a critical analysis of *The Sound and the Fury* in *al-Adab*, for the translation.[107] As Hilary Falb Kalisman argues, Jabra along with other Palestinian diaspora intellectuals in the 1950s "fused a conservative acceptance of state authority and avoidance of radical politics with a liberal understanding of nationalism and of scholarship that emphasized freedom, secularism, and objectivity informed by, as they put it, Western culture and norms."[108] Literary modernism in the Arab world coalesced with a boom in the oil industry in which Iraq was a key sponsor of cultural production. As Jabra mentions in *Princesses' Street*, he met again in Baghdad some friends he had made among British officers in Jerusalem, notably Michael Clark who introduced him to "the world of filmmaking industry."[109] Jabra worked on the Arabic text of Clark's 1952 film *The Third River*, produced by the IPC. The film's title refers to the "huge pipeline from Kirkuk in Iraq to the Syrian port of Banyas on the Mediterranean Sea" that the IPC was constructing in the land between two rivers, the Tigris and the Euphrates.[110]

After the IPC's nationalization in 1972, Jabra was in charge of publications at the Iraqi National Oil Company and was the editor of its journal *al-Naft wal-'alam* (Oil and the world). In 1977, he was made a counselor of the Iraqi Ministry of Culture and Information, an appointment tantamount to a state fellowship. He may not always have been able to stay out of politics as much as he would have liked to, as we shall see in the epilogue, living in a country that would see the rise to power of the Ba'th Party and Saddam Hussein, the Iran-Iraq War, and the Gulf War of 1991, and its ugly aftermath of economic sanctions and U.S.-British led airstrikes, which culminated in the 2003 Iraq War. Unlike Edward W. Said, Jabra was not the celebrated Palestinian intellectual in exile who would find his place, out of place, in Western academia.[111] Whereas Said was able to engage in dialogue with Daniel Barenboim to "search for alternative approaches to a political solution" in the Middle East, and join forces in bringing together young Arab and Israeli musicians first in the West-Eastern Divan Orchestra in Weimar, and then in the Barenboim-Said Akademie in Berlin,[112] Jabra's intellectual communion with Wolfgang has been forgotten. The two gained renown in different literary fields, respectively, as members of Gruppe 47 in Germany and the *Shi'r* Group in the Arab world, which offered few points of contact, despite both writers' attempts at breaking out of the limitations imposed by verbal expression. Along with their unfinished book collaboration, the ecumenical circle and the age of coexistence, which had made an impossible friendship possible in Jerusalem before 1948, both vanished.

After finding a new home in literary circles in postwar Germany, Wolfgang married a German artist, regained German citizenship, and traveled to Israel and Greece in early 1953, returning to Jerusalem for the first time since he had left Mandate Palestine for London in 1946. With "Times in Cornwall," published in the *Palestine Post* shortly after the King David Hotel bombing, he had already gained some experience in travel writing, a genre he would now explore further. Upon his return to Germany, he wrote a vivid travelogue, which he read at the meeting of Gruppe 47 in October 1953 at Bebenhausen Castle close to Tübingen in the Swabian Alps. The reading was a success, he wrote to his literary colleague and friend Heinrich Böll, whom he sent a copy of the typescript along with two of his early poems in English and two of his "Jabra illustrations," saying, "it is quite possible that it will shed light on me—even if only in parts—from a different angle."[113] As travel writing often does, Wolfgang's notes from Israel say as much about their author as they do about the places he visited. They were broadcast on German radio and published in a range of German newspapers under various titles: "Palästina und Griechenland" (Palestine and Greece), "Auf einer Bank in Askalon" (On a bench in Ashkelon), "Zwischen Florenz und Tel Aviv" (Between Florence and Tel Aviv), "Reise durch Griechenland und Israel" (Journey through Greece and Israel), and "Aufzeichnungen aus Israel" (Notes from Israel).[114] The name "Palestine," mentioned in the first broadcast in 1953, is absent from later broadcasts and publications.

Wolfgang opens his narrative with a late afternoon's walk along Jaffa Road, "the central traffic artery which formerly led to the big square in front of Jaffa Gate," whose name, he says, he has forgotten.[115] It was Allenby Square, named after General Edmund Allenby, who led the British conquest of Jerusalem in 1917.[116] Wolfgang describes Jaffa Gate as "the entrance of the walled Old City and the bazaar-like center of Oriental Jerusalem," and inserts,

> I knew Jerusalem when it was still the capital of the British Mandate, knew it well; not a big city but a cosmopolitan one [Weltstadt] in which three nations—the many sects and minorities not considered—clashed day after day, and then forgot, or with more or less diplomatic skills set aside, the politics of the day, evening after evening, at receptions, concerts, and large colonial-style social events. A city of unparalleled charm—then—like no other; with generous villa suburbs, magnate palaces—neo-Moorish or colonial baroque, bazaars filled with all kinds of fragrances and mud huts painted blue to protect their inhabitants against the evil eye. A city in whose major streets American limousines dodged camel caravans, where exotic figures offered sunflower seeds and sweet juice shimmering in a poisonous green color in front of elegant fashion boutiques; with French, Italian, and German monasteries and churches, with colossal synagogues and mosques, with Viennese cafés, English tea rooms, American bars and spacious Arabic coffee houses where you could comfortably smoke your water pipe and spend the afternoon playing trick track. Cocktail time was spent in the bar of the colossal King David Hotel, whose second floor housed the British headquarters during the war. Here officers of Allied nations met with newspaper correspondents and members of the government, and young native intellectuals explained to Western writers traveling through Jerusalem the essence of European culture. ("As a cubist Braque is much greater than Picasso!"—"Do you really believe Eliot will outlast Auden?")[117]

As Wolfgang recalls the city he left behind in 1946, he caters to European fantasies of the Orient; he evokes camel caravans and licorice syrup sellers in its streets, while at the same time outlining its modern features—the voices of his Arab friends ringing in his ears, as they manifest their familiarity with avant-garde literature and art. The last lines of this quote, ascribed to "young native intellectuals," are left in English in a travelogue addressed to a German-speaking public; they sound indeed as if they come straight from the mouths of Wolfgang's Arab friends, possibly Jabra—the "spark-plug" of the YMCA Arts Club—whose letter from exile had reached Wolfgang only weeks before his departure. Yet nowhere in the travelogue does Wolfgang refer to Jabra and his Arab friends explicitly. Jaffa Road no longer leads to the square whose name, he repeats, he has forgotten. A busy central node of the city until the First Arab-Israeli War, now the square had been transformed into a no-man's-land of barbed wire, ruined buildings, broken walls, and a penetrating silence, dividing West Jerusalem from East Jerusalem, one side guarded by the Israel Defense Forces (IDF) and the other by the Jordanian Arab Legion. Wolfgang's description of divided Jerusalem and two Jordanian legionnaires "armed to their teeth" might have been intended to remind his German readers of Berlin, which was not yet separated by its wall but rather was divided into zones with Soviet soldiers drawing its eastern part into the Soviet orbit.[118]

Having contrasted the Oriental and at the same time cosmopolitan character of Jerusalem in its former days with its current state of desolation, Wolfgang takes his readers on a journey to the archaeological ruins of Ashkelon in the south of Israel where, he explains, the border is disputed with Egypt. "The street ends in the yellow sand of an Arab village destroyed and devastated in the Israeli-Arab war"; only a few dark brown mud walls—traces of a former Arab presence—are still standing, behind which he and his travel companions park their car to avoid being spotted by enemy soldiers. Wolfgang pays no further attention to the remains of this Arab village. Instead, he is drawn to "the remains of buildings, column shafts and capitals" of Byzantine origin, contemplating the romantic character of antique ruins in nature, like the Temple of Zeus at Olympia covered with daisies in bloom, which he visited on his return to Europe. "Nothing is a richer breeding ground for rampant nature than a few layers of dilapidated civilization," he concludes.[119] That these layers included only recently the Arab town of Majdal and its surrounding villages, one of them Al-Sawafir al-Gharbiyya, which was known for its "archaeological remains, such as pieces of marble and the shafts and capitals of ancient columns,"[120] goes unmentioned, as does the name of the Arab village.

The IDF defeated the Egyptian Army on Israel's southern front in October 1948 with air raids that caused "despair among the local inhabitants," as an Israeli intelligence officer said, adding that "it was a surprise for [the Arab villagers] to see squadrons of Jewish aircraft rule the skies."[121] Left without shelter under the open sky, the villagers fled to the dunes and beaches; those who attempted to return to their homes were "sealed off with barbed wire and IDF guards in a small, built-up area commonly known as the 'ghetto' " in Majdal, after which they were transferred to the Gaza Strip, then under Egyptian control.[122] The use of the term *ghetto*, with its Holocaust connotation, for the detention of Palestinian refugees inside the newly created State of Israel was part and parcel of Jewish Israeli consciousness in the late 1940s and early 1950s, but it fell into oblivion as the Holocaust and the Nakba "gradually became competitors for memory and victimhood."[123]

Unearthing these recent "layers of dilapidated civilization" for a German audience may have been unthinkable at the time—not only because this audience knew very little about the recent history of Palestine but also because criticism of the newly established State of Israel was out of the question in Germany, where the horrors of the Holocaust had come into full view only with the Nuremberg trials. Under Chancellor Konrad Adenauer, Germany pursued a "forgive and forget" policy, allowing former Nazis to occupy important positions well into the 1960s, when mass student protests would eventually impose change.[124] In addition, Palestine's recent history—and with it its native Palestinian Arab inhabitants—were obstructed from sight, denied visibility, and erased as Israel "perpetuated the legacy of repression established by Britain in Mandate Palestine," and institutionalized the state of emergency "under the thinly veiled pretext of security in order to dispossess, remove, and concentrate Palestinian populations that remained in Israel," as Noura Erakat writes.[125] The Absentees' Property Law of 1950 not only enforced new realities on the ground but also introduced a new vocabulary: in a Kafkaesque twist the approximate 750,000 Palestinian refugees, whom Israel denied the right of return to their homeland, were described as "absentees," and those who were internally displaced within Israel as "present-absentees," while the law placed their movable and immovable property (e.g., their lands) under the custody of the State of Israel.[126]

Wolfgang's travelogue displays an acute awareness of the rupture caused in 1948 by the establishment of the State of Israel and the First Arab-Israeli War and can be read as a farewell to the country in which he and his family had found a place of refuge, Palestine under the British Mandate, when the Nazis came to power in Germany.[127] In remembering Jerusalem, the voices of his Arab friends haunting him in his resumed life back in Europe, and in contemplating the flowers—daisies in Greece, and anemones in Palestine—covering "a few layers of dilapidated civilization," Wolfgang cannot conceal his gnawing disillusionment with Israel. At the same time, Jabra was developing themes of rebirth and redemption—which would see the flowers of Palestine reemerge not only as "objects of beauty in their own right" but also as "symbolic expressions of aesthetic and cultural values related to identity and belonging" in Palestinian embroidery.[128]

CHAPTER 7

PUBLIC ENGAGEMENT IN WORLDS APART

VISITS IN AMBACH AND OXFORD AS THE KHALIDIS AND HILDESHEIMER REUNITE

"And then my Arabs will come soon," writes Wolfgang Hildesheimer to his parents from Ambach in late July 1951. He goes on in early August to specify that "on Sunday, Waleed and Rasha are coming to visit me, and next week Patsy, Cantacuzino, Assem and Sulafa."[1] Wolfgang knew Patsy (Patricia) Wood, from Nuremberg, where, like him, she had worked at the Military Tribunal; at one point, he had considered marrying her.[2] Having decided otherwise, he wrote to his sister, Eva Teltsch, "Besides, to be honest, I never loved her as much as I did Sally [Kassab] or Ann [possibly Anne Palairet, who became Anne Oxford after her marriage to Julian Asquith], for whom I would have done much more."[3] Wolfgang met Sherban Cantacuzino through Assem Salam who had befriended him at the University of Cambridge, where both Assem and Cantacuzino were studying architecture. Of Romanian aristocratic background, Cantacuzino was born in Paris and educated in England, deprived of returning to the land of his ancestors because of the Soviet-backed Communist takeover of Romania at the end of World War II. He would become a renowned architecture historian and critic.[4] Still a student in the early 1950s, he left a deep impression on Wolfgang.[5] Wolfgang's reference to "my Arabs" recurs in his letters to his parents.[6] Conceived as part of a private communication between him and his parents, it may have been meant endearingly, as a friendly and jovial expression of affection, but read against the background of the ongoing Nakba it assumes a patronizing tone. Wolfgang was enchanted by the reunion and "having a very good time" with his friends, as he inserts in English in another letter that was written, as was all his correspondence with his parents, in German: "Rasha and Waleed arrived on Sunday and are sitting next to me on the couch reading. They are wonderful and the connection was there again immediately. Rasha is studying mathematics and Waleed was offered a lectureship at Oxford this spring. They are staying with me. Cantacuzino slept in my room, Patsy is coming on Sunday, Rasha and Waleed stay until Thursday and at the end of next week Assem and Sulafa are coming for ten days. *I am having a very good time* [emphasis added], because I had almost forgotten such sophistication."[7]

In the same letter, Wolfgang says he has just received "a letter from Julian and Ann Oxford, who, if they can arrange it, plan to visit in September."[8] Later the same month, he writes that Assem and Sulafa are traveling across Europe "wherever there is architecture to see," describing them as very open-minded, but adding "they are not as profound as Waleed and Rasha. Waleed is brilliant."[9]

In her memoirs, Rasha also recalls this visit to Ambach, when she marveled at the rapid reconstruction of Germany and at how little of the destruction caused by World War II was apparent. On their journey to visit Wolfgang, the Khalidis traveled from Oxford to Paris, leaving their son with Assem and Sulafa in Cambridge, and then continued to Munich:

> We arrived in Munich utterly exhausted and were met by Wolf at the station. He had not changed since the Jerusalem days, the same wry smile, the same twinkling eyes and the same ironic humor. It was as if we had never parted. We did not drive directly to Ambach where Wolf was staying. We were starving as we had had nothing to eat on the train. So we sat in a sidewalk café and talked about all the things that had happened since our parting in Jerusalem: the establishment of the state of Israel to which Wolf was bitterly opposed, our life in Lebanon and England, his life in England and Germany, our mutual friends, etc., etc.[10]

Rasha's description of the friends' reunion is as passionate as Wolfgang's. As she recalls, they talked about all the things that had happened since their parting in Jerusalem, referring explicitly to Wolfgang's opposition to the establishment of Israel. Wolfgang, however, would later say in conversations with Hadara Lazar that his Arab friends from Jerusalem came to see him in Ambach but that they "never talked about what had happened in 1948."[11] This aligns with Walid's memory that they avoided talking about politics.[12]

The enthusiasm Wolfgang had expressed toward his parents in congratulating them on the establishment of the new state in his letter of May 18, 1948, quoted in chapter 4, might have been exaggerated and meant to please his parents, but it might also reveal true—if conflicted—feelings about which he remained silent with his Arab friends.

During this visit in Ambach, the Khalidis met Patricia Highsmith, the American author of psychological thrillers whose first novel, *Strangers on a Train* (1951), was adapted by Alfred Hitchcock for the screen the same year. *The Talented Mr. Ripley*, her first in a series of crime novels featuring Thomas Ripley as the titular protagonist, was published in 1955, and has led to a range of film adaptations. Highsmith was traveling back and forth from the United States to Europe at the time and was friends with Wolfgang. Upon becoming fascinated by Highsmith's books, Rasha struck a correspondence with her in the late 1980s, when Highsmith was living in Switzerland.[13]

Having left Beirut for London in 1949, Walid had pursued postgraduate studies at Oxford and obtained his master's degree in 1951 under the supervision of Hamilton A. R. Gibb. Walid wrote his thesis on Sufism in the late seventeenth and eighteenth centuries and its conception of Jerusalem, focusing on the Damascene scholar Abd al-Ghani al-Nabulsi. Deeply influenced by Ibn Arabi, the Arab-Andalusian poet-cum-philosopher, al-Nabulsi was a strong proponent of religious tolerance. Walid based his thesis on manuscripts housed in the Khalidi Library that chronicle Nabulsi's visits to Palestine in 1690 and 1693–1694.[14] Gibb offered Walid a position as lecturer in Arabic studies at Oxford and, when Gibb left for Harvard in 1955, he entrusted Walid with teaching his courses. Walid's interest in both history and mystical Islam, and the special place it accords to Jerusalem, did not divert his attention from politics. Alongside his research and teaching, he wrote a number of letters to the editor of the *Times*, intervening in public debates, which he signed Walid A. S. El Khalidi, University College, Oxford.[15]

On September 27, 1951, in Beit Meri, a summer resort in the mountains that looks over Beirut, Walid's father, Ahmad Samih al-Khalidi, died, having suffered a stroke. His wife Anbara and their children Randa and Tarif were visiting Rasha and Walid in Oxford at the time, but he had stayed behind to finish some writing. "It was as if an arrow had pierced my heart," writes Anbara, "I could not for a moment believe that he had really died nor can I begin, even today, to describe the utter misery that filled my life thereafter."[16] Al-Khalidi left behind his memoirs, which were published in weekly installments in *Beirut al-masa'* between January and May 1950 as "Filastin fi nusf qarn: Ra'aytuha tanhar" (Palestine in half a century: I saw her disintegrate), but they remain unpublished in book form and have largely been forgotten. He was buried in the Iman al-Awza'i cemetery on the southern outskirts of Beirut. Anbara had an imposing tomb built for him out of pinkish stone, which Henry Knesevich, al-Khalidi's right hand at the Arab College, helped her to import from Jerusalem. Knesevich had worked for the United Nations Relief and Works Agency for Palestine Refugees (UNWRA) as director for the Hebron and Jerusalem areas in the 1950s. Anbara would be buried next to her husband in a simple white tomb when she passed away in 1986.[17]

In Oxford, Walid and Rasha rented an apartment from Walid's college at 19 Banbury Road that was spacious enough to house family and friends. After their father's death, Walid's half-siblings Randa and Tarif stayed with them. While Randa attended Oxford High School, Tarif was sent to Jerome Farrell, the former director of education in Palestine who had tutored Walid in Latin. Farrell had retired to the village of Castletownshend in County Cork in the south of Ireland, where he would prepare Tarif for the Common Entrance Exam so he could be admitted to Haileybury College, the English public school Farrell had attended.[18] In Oxford, Walid and Rasha saw a great deal of Albert and Cecil Hourani, who had played important roles in the Arab Office, Albert in Jerusalem and Cecil in Washington, D.C. While Cecil would make his name as a political adviser to Habib Bourguiba, Tunisia's first president, who held that office from 1957 to 1987, Albert embarked on an academic career at Oxford, where he founded and directed the Middle East Centre at St Antony's College. Rasha revived an old passion and began attending classes in mathematics at Oxford, as Wolfgang mentions in his letter to his parents, but in 1952 the Khalidis had a second child, Karma, whose health deteriorated soon after her birth and thus demanded Rasha's full attention. In the midst of this, Wolfgang visited the Khalidis in the summer of 1955.[19] As Rasha recalls, "Wolf came with his new wife Silvia and his two step-daughters whom he was trying to get into Oxford. Somehow, it did not feel right to see Wolf in these surroundings, and the meeting was not as warm as expected. That was the last time we ever saw Wolf."[20]

Christa Geitner and Inge Geitner-Thurner, Silvia's daughters from her previous marriage, recall the warmth with which they were received at the Khalidis' home but do not recall any specific memories of the visit.[21] Tarif Khalidi, who would visit from Haileybury, remembers that the Khalidis' friendship with Wolfgang had frayed. "Not that they were arguing, but Wolfgang's positions were not as clearly anti-Zionist as they had been back in Palestine."[22]

In letters to his mother written from Munich, where he and Silvia had settled in 1953, Wolfgang refers only briefly to his visit in Oxford, writing that he "visited some of Oxford's colleges from inside, having drinks with two philosophy professors from University College in their faculty lounge" (likely Walid and his colleague Peter Strawson, at the time a tutorial fellow of philosophy with whom Wolfgang got along well, as Walid recalls) and saw "the charming Khalidis" again.[23] Wolfgang visited a number of other friends in England, among them Reggie Smith and Olivia Manning,[24] and possibly also Julian and Anne Oxford at Mells Manor, their sixteenth-century estate in Somerset. Julian would appear many years later in *Nachlese* (Supplement, 1987), a collection of prose fragments from Wolfgang's note box that he had drafted over the years but that had gone unused and that resemble diary entries and aphorisms: "When we pulled up at Julian's castle in Somerset, he came out of his garden and said: 'I am sorry I am so dirty, but I only have one gardener left.' "[25]

Wolfgang also saw the actor and playwright Peter Ustinov, whom he had asked to translate one of his plays.[26] Christopher Holme, Wolfgang's former director at the Palestine Information Office, was not in London at the time.[27] Holme now worked for the BBC Third Programme and would translate a number of Wolfgang's works into English, notably his story "A World Ends," which was broadcast in 1957. Wolfgang did meet with Christopher Hugh Sykes, who also worked for the BBC Third Programme and who, along with Holme, had joined the literary Gruppe 47 at its meeting in Berlin in May 1955 at Wolfgang's invitation.[28] As Wolfgang relates to his mother, Sykes had visited Israel, was interested in Zionism, and was close friends with Vera Weizmann, Israel's first First Lady.[29] In a letter to his sister and her husband, written on March 6, 1955, Wolfgang mentions reading about the "worrying border incidents" between Egypt and Israel and recalls a conversation he had with Sykes. Having traveled through Israel with the writer Evelyn Waugh, Sykes told Wolfgang, "We couldn't help feeling—although it's an awful thing to say—that the UN should not have interrupted the war just then. It would have given Israel the chance to conquer a wider territory and get a proper shape."[30] Wolfgang recalls these words in English in his letter, which is otherwise, written in German. He adds that Sykes called the Arab leaders "unbelievable fools," which would not be so bad if they were not also "scoundrels." The position expressed by Wolfgang in referring to Sykes has gained notoriety in the wake of the Second Intifada, notably through Benny Morris, previously a vocal representative of Israel's new historians. In an instantly infamous interview published in *Haaretz* in 2004, marking a radical shift in his thinking, Morris made an attempt to justify the ethnic cleansing of Palestine, saying that David Ben-Gurion, who became known as "Israel's founding father" and served as its first prime minister, "made a serious historical mistake" in 1948 by not doing "a complete job." If he "had carried out a large expulsion and cleansed the whole country—the whole Land of Israel, as far as the Jordan River. . . . If he had carried out a full expulsion—rather than a partial one—he would have stabilized the State of Israel for generations."[31] What Wolfgang leaves unsaid about Sykes is that he was the son of Mark Sykes, the coauthor of the Sykes-Picot Agreement, who had played a key role in negotiating the Balfour Declaration. Like his father, the junior Sykes embarked on a career with the British Foreign Office and served as a UK special operations executive officer under diplomatic cover as second secretary at the British Legation in Tehran, in the aftermath of the Anglo-Soviet invasion of Iran in 1941. On not finding success in a career as a diplomat, he turned to writing. He is known today primarily for his biography *Evelyn Waugh* (1975) but he also wrote *Cross Roads to Israel: Palestine from Balfour to Bevin* (1965), in which he examines British policy in Palestine from the genesis of the Balfour Declaration to the creation of the State of Israel during Ernest Bevin's tenure as the UK's foreign secretary.

Wolfgang also visited Sydney James van den Bergh at Unilever House. Van den Bergh had agreed to finance an English translation of Arnold Hildesheimer's book, *Die Welt der ungewohnten Dimensionen* (The world of unfamiliar dimensions), which sought to explain modern physics and its philosophical implications to a lay audience, and which Wolfgang had suggested for publication to Weidenfeld and Nicolson.[32] On August 8, 1955, Wolfgang's father died while on a visit to Switzerland. He was buried in the Jewish cemetery in Zurich.[33] A memorial was held for him in Haifa about a month later, at which Felix Rosenblüth (also known as Pinchas Rosen) gave a speech. One of Arnold Hildesheimer's closest friends from his student days in the Association of Jewish Students (the Jewish student fraternity in Berlin), Rosenblüth had become Israel's first minister of justice under Ben-Gurion.[34]

FROM THE SUEZ CRISIS TO THE 1967 WAR

The Khalidis traveled to Beirut in the summer of 1952 and again in 1954, when Walid accompanied his brother-in-law Saeb Salam, who served as prime minister of Lebanon six times between 1952 and 1973, on visits to Egypt and Iraq. Walid had acquired Lebanese citizenship. He went back to then-Jordanian-controlled East Jerusalem for the first time in 1952 and would return several times, traveling by plane from Beirut to Qalandia Airport, which between 1948 and 1967 functioned as a civilian airport, or by car via Amman. He has not been back since 1967, however: "on principle," he says, "I cannot ask the Israelis for permission."[35] In Cairo, he and Saeb Salam met with Gamal Abdel Nasser, Egypt's charismatic new president, who had come to power in the 1952 Revolution of the Free Officers, which had overthrown the British-backed monarchy of King Farouk. Like many of his contemporaries, Walid saw in Nasser the possibility of challenging the balance of power in the region.[36] Known for his Arab nationalist stance, Salam attempted to mediate between Egypt and Iraq amid growing political tensions. While Iraq would be drawn closer to its Western allies with the signing of the 1955 Baghdad Pact, a military agreement between Iran, Iraq, Pakistan, Turkey, and the United Kingdom that aimed to halt Soviet expansion in the Middle East, Egypt under Nasser pursued a policy of neutrality.

In July 1956, Nasser nationalized the largely British- and French-owned Suez Canal Company. That October, Israel partnered with the region's former colonial powers, France and the United Kingdom, and attacked Egypt in what is known in the Arab world as the Tripartite Aggression and in Israel as the Sinai War, which is also referred to as the Second Arab-Israeli War. Under pressure from the Soviet Union, the United States, and the United Nations, the British and French troops withdrew from Egyptian territory later the same year. The IDF followed suit in March 1957. The Suez Crisis signaled, at least symbolically, the decline of British and French dominance in the Middle East, and more broadly the impending end of their respective empires. In the context of Cold War reckonings between the United States and the Soviet Union, however, it led to heightened Arab-Israeli hostility and profound political changes across the Middle East: Nasser emerged as an iconic figure of anticolonial struggle and of Arab unity, especially after the establishment of the short-lived union of

Egypt and Syria as the United Arab Republic (UAR), while the British-backed monarchy in Iraq was overthrown in the July 14 Revolution. Also known as the 1958 Iraq Revolution, it brought to power a group of army officers with strong leftist leanings who withdrew Iraq from the Baghdad Pact, which continued as the Central Treaty Organization (CENTO) until the 1979 Iranian Revolution.[37] Throughout the Sinai crisis, the Israeli-Jordanian border had remained quiet. Hours before the Tripartite Aggression was launched against Egypt on October 29, 1956, however, the Israeli government and military imposed a curfew on the villages of the Triangle, an area transferred from Jordan to Israel in the 1949 armistice agreement between the two countries. Israeli border policemen on orders from Israeli military commanders shot close to fifty civilians, including women and children, in the Palestinian village of Kafr Qasim, when the villagers—all citizens of Israel—returned to their homes from work in the early evening, unaware of the sudden movement restriction. As Adel Manna has shown, this massacre was part of "a plot to terrorize the inhabitants [of the Triangle] and force them to leave;" it "reminded Palestinians of the trauma of killing and expulsion in 1948," the Deir Yassin and other massacres.[38] The plan did not work. The villagers stayed. The Kafr Qasim Massacre "represented a turning point in relations between Israel and its Arab citizens, reminding them that the Nakba had not ended with the war of 1948."[39]

In protest against the Tripartite Aggression, Walid resigned from his position at Oxford. The *Daily Mirror* reported on November 26, 1956, that the British politician and broadcaster "Woodrow Wyatt will be seen in a filmed interview [on the BBC Television current affairs program *Panorama*] with Walid Khalidi, who resigned his post as lecturer in Arabic Studies at University College, Oxford, because of events in the Middle East."[40]

The Khalidis moved back to Beirut, where Walid joined the faculty of the American University of Beirut. He built strong connections to faculty and students, having previously collaborated with Issam Yusuf Ashour and Burhan Dajani, both professors of economics, on the publication of *Israel: Khatar iqtisadi wa-askari wa-siyasi* (Israel: An economic, military, and political danger). The book, published by the Chamber of Commerce, Agriculture and Industry in Beirut in 1952, is likely the first critical study in Arabic about the new state in the Middle East. As its authors, not mentioned in the publication, say in the introduction, it aims to resist the Zionist threat, setting out to "understand our enemy as much as he understands us."[41]

With the installation in 1957 of the Eisenhower Doctrine, which pledged U.S. financial and military aid to combat the spread of communism in the Middle East, Lebanon saw increased U.S. interference in support of President Camille Chamoun, who sought a change in the Lebanese constitution to enable his reelection. This move was widely perceived as a threat to Lebanon's unwritten National Pact, which was based on the division of constitutional powers along sectarian lines. Chamoun's pro-Western stance was strongly opposed by Sunni and Druze representatives of the Lebanese government, among them Kamal Jumblatt, Rashid Karami, and Saeb Salam, who looked favorably on Arab unity. As fighting broke out between Beirut's mainly Maronite Christian and Muslim communities, the former predominantly in favor of Chamoun and the latter against, the Salam family mansion in West Beirut's Museitbeh neighborhood was besieged by government troops. Salam emerged as the most powerful Sunni *za'im*—a powerful leader within Lebanon's elaborate democratic political system of confessional checks and balances—in Beirut.[42] Working as a political adviser to Salam, Walid was injured; some British newspapers went so far as to report that he had been killed.[43] As Lebanon plunged into civil war, U.S. Marines, spurred on by the events in the revolution in Iraq, landed in Beirut on July 15, 1958. With the election of General Fouad Chehab, the commander of the Lebanese Army from the country's independence in 1943 to 1958, to the Lebanese presidency in September 1958, sectarian hostilities were pacified, and a new national reconciliation government was formed.

Having returned to Beirut and a social environment that provided the protection and warmth of an extended family at the forefront of Lebanon's political elite, Rasha recalls the years between 1958 and the renewed outbreak of civil war in 1975 as "the best of memories, the best of life."[44] The Khalidis lived in Ghazir, a suburb in the south of Beirut. Like many well-to-do families, they rented a summer house in Shemlan, a small village in Mount Lebanon looking over the Mediterranean, where Walid devoted much time to writing. This resulted in a number of influential articles, such as "Why Did the Palestinians Leave?" (1959), "The Fall of Haifa" (1959), and "Plan Dalet: The Zionist Master Plan for the Conquest of Palestine" (1961),[45] which refuted Israeli claims that Arab leaders had ordered the Palestinians to leave their country in 1948 and found much resonance with Israel's new historians. The 1950s through the 1970s not only marked Beirut's modernist moment, expressed in various cultural and political periodicals, but those decades were also a time described by the Lebanese sociologist Samir Khalaf as "Lebanon's golden/gilded age."

> The brief interlude between the relatively benign civil war of 1958 and the protracted cruelties of 1975 stands out as a perplexing often anomalous epoch in Lebanon's eventful political history. It is a period marked by sustained political stability, economic prosperity, and swift societal transformations, the closest the country ever got to a "golden age" with all the outward manifestations of stupendous vitality, exuberance, and rising expectations. But these were also times of growing disparities, cleavages, neglect, portends perhaps of a more "gilded age" of misdirected and uneven growth, boisterous political culture, conspicuous consumption, and the trappings of frivolous life-styles masking creeping social tensions and other ominous symptoms of political unrest.[46]

The Khalidis spent the 1960–61 academic year at Princeton University. There, they met again with Yusif Sayigh, who had worked for the Arab Office in Jerusalem and who would become an influential economist. They also were introduced to his British-born wife Rosemary Sayigh, who would gain recognition as a scholar of Middle East history, in particular of the oral history of Palestinian refugees in Lebanon.[47]

In Beirut in 1963, Walid, along with two of his colleagues—the historian Constantine Zurayk from Damascus and the political economist Burhan Dajani from Jaffa—cofounded the Institute for Palestine Studies (IPS), which later opened offices in Washington, D.C. (in 1982); Jerusalem (1995–2000); and Ramallah (in 2000). As Walid points out, "it was at the Arab Office in Jerusalem that the Institute for Palestine Studies had its roots. . . . When the three of us established the Institute in 1963, Musa [Alami]'s example was before us. While determined not to repeat his mistakes in terms of dependency, we embraced his vision."[48]

In contrast to the Arab Office, which was supported by the Arab League and Iraq, the IPS was intent on maintaining independence from other institutions—particularly from the Palestinian National Liberation Movement (Fatah), which had been founded in 1959, and the Palestine Liberation Organization (PLO), which was established in 1964, as well as from the governments of Arab nations. The IPS would soon be joined by another Beirut-based Palestinian research institution: the PLO Research Center, headed first by Fayez and then by his brother Anis Sayigh. Fayez had been a member of the first PLO executive under Ahmad Shukeiri, Walid's former supervisor at the Arab Office, who was replaced as chair of the PLO by Yasser Arafat in 1969. Anis, similar to their brother Tawfiq, had close ties to the Congress of Cultural Freedom (CCF) through which he published three books, among them an Arabic translation of one of Boris Pasternak's novels, as he writes in his memoirs, probably *Dr. Zhivago*, whose instrumentalization by the Central Intelligence Agency (CIA) in the Cold War is well documented.[49] As their brother, the economist Yusif Sayigh points out, the IPS was "the brain child of Walid Khalidi" who "accepted all along the role of a dignified adviser, *in camera*, to Arafat, but he never entered into open association, never attended a single National Council meeting."[50] Were there a group portrait featuring Walid among the founding fathers of the IPS and the broader circle of Palestinian intellectuals in Beirut in the 1960s and early 1970s, it would doubtless show Walid in a very different light: gone were the days of Shelleyan demeanor and poetic affinities with Jabra and Wolfgang, as Walid emerged as a towering figure in scholarship, institution building, politics, and diplomacy.[51] The IPS's English-language academic publication, the *Journal of Palestine Studies*, published its first issue in 1971—just four years after Israel had gained control over the whole of historical Palestine in addition to territory from Egypt and Syria in the 1967 War. This journal has played a key role in the struggle for narrative sovereignty, writes Sherene Seikaly, as it materialized as a leading platform to "articulate the question of Palestine" against "a landscape of erasure, denial, and urgency."[52]

In the meantime, Wolfgang continued to attract renown as a writer in postwar Germany and began work on a biography of Mozart, which saw various forms, developing out of an essay and eventually becoming a book. It was published by Suhrkamp in 1977 and has been translated into several languages. A major literary success, it does not focus on Mozart's musical genius but rather depicts him as a complex, flawed human being. From Europe, Wolfgang continued to follow political events in the Middle East, but he refrained from commenting on them publicly until the 1967 War. During the Suez Crisis, he reassured his mother of the pro-Israel stance of West German public opinion: "above all the radio and press commentaries are on the side of Israel," he wrote, "but that of course does not reduce the impending danger of a world war."[53] In another letter, he writes: "public opinion changed a little when it became clear that it was a prearranged affair [in German, *ein abgekartetes Spiel*] with the United Kingdom and France, which, in strict terms, waged a war of aggression. Had Israel invaded Egypt in a spontaneous reaction to a particular provocation it would of course have been better from a moral point of view. The general mood is now against England and France, and the only thing that can be justified is that Nasser is a villain and a kind of Hitler."[54]

Aware of the moral bankruptcy in Israel's waging "a war of aggression," Wolfgang justified the Tripartite Aggression by comparing Nasser to Hitler. Such depictions of Nasser prevailed in the British and French press at the time.[55] Nasser's authoritarian leadership style and human rights violations are well documented.[56] His depiction as "a kind of Hitler," however, is a misrepresentation of Middle Eastern politics and symptomatic of the way in which the Arab world became stigmatized as Israel's new enemy.

In 1957, Wolfgang and Silvia moved to the remote southeastern Swiss village of Poschiavo in the Engadin, an Alpine valley connected to the outside world only by the Bernina Pass and Railway between the Swiss resort of Saint Moritz and the Italian town of Tirano. To his mother, Wolfgang cites climatic reasons for leaving Munich, where air pollution had significantly increased because of coal-fired power production, but his growing political engagement and disappointment in postwar Germany, particularly its failure to investigate its Nazi past from a critical standpoint, likely played a role.[57] Wolfgang had tried to draw a positive picture of postwar German society in his earlier letters to convince his parents of his decision to return there. His letters in the late 1950s, however, indicate increasing concern, not only with West Germany's new army and its acquisition of nuclear weapons—he mentions signing Hans Werner Richter's 1958 political resolution "Kampf dem Atomtod" (Struggle against atomic death)—but also with "Germany becoming fascist again, maybe this time without anti-Semitism and concentration camps, but bad enough."[58]

In 1962, Wolfgang drafted an article describing his reasons for having left West Germany, stating clearly that when he returned to Germany in 1947, he had been under the impression that the guilty were in the minority and occupied no positions of authority, political or otherwise, but that he came to realize he had been mistaken.[59] Wolfgang's article was motivated in part by the political scandal of the 1962 *Spiegel* affair, which had been triggered when West Germany's Minister of Defense Franz Josef Strauss gave the order to search the Hamburg offices of *Der Spiegel*, West Germany's leading news magazine. This order led to the arrest of its owner and editor-in-chief Rudolf Augstein as well as two of its journalists, who were accused of divulging military secrets. The journalists were not convicted, but Strauss was forced to resign in what came to be perceived as a watershed moment for democracy and press freedom in West Germany.[60] Wolfgang withdrew his article from publication after Strauss stepped down.[61]

Also in 1962, Wolfgang visited Israel to see his mother, who died in May of that year. Upon his return to Poschiavo, he wrote the one-act play *Nachtstück* (Nightpiece) and the short narrative *Vergebliche Aufzeichnungen* (Records in vain), which starts with the words, "Mir fällt nichts mehr ein" (I cannot think of anything [to narrate] anymore), uttered by its protagonist, a writer like himself, who sets out on one last journey before putting down his pen.[62] Premiered at the Kammerspiele Düsseldorf in 1963, *Nachtstück* features a solitary protagonist who is haunted by memories and fears, which he tries to suppress with sleeping pills. While he remains sleepless, an intruder enters his room and winds up seated on his bed, eating a sandwich for breakfast, as if there were nothing unusual about it. As Wolfgang said in an interview, his protagonist's sleeplessness was his own: "whenever I read the papers, I am struck by insomnia. Who can sleep when reading about Germany. . . . he [the intruder] could be playing the piano while Jews are hunted outside. You can meet him everywhere, in the streets, [on] the trains; going about his daily business [in German he says, "er funktioniert"].[63]

With this allusion to the nineteenth-century German poet Heinrich Heine's well-known lines "Denk ich an Deutschland in der Nacht/Dann bin ich um den Schlaf gebracht" (Thinking of Germany in the night/I lie awake and sleep takes flight), Wolfgang outlined a theme—sleeplessness—that, as we have seen, he would develop further in his monological prose works *Tynset* and *Masante*.

Wolfgang changed publishers in 1963, moving from Günther Neske to the Suhrkamp Verlag, which, under Siegfried Unseld's direction, emerged as the leading publisher of twentieth-century German literature. Neske was one of a group of German writers known as "inner emigrants"—those who opposed Nazism but remained in Germany.[64] Neske was also the publisher of Martin Heidegger, whose 1933 inaugural address as the rector of Freiburg University, generally regarded as evidence of his endorsement of Nazi ideology, had just come to light.[65] In the late 1950s, Wolfgang translated Djuna Barnes's 1936 novel *Nightwood* into German. His version was published in 1959 by Neske, who had acquired the rights for the translation from Faber and Faber, which had become the foremost publisher of literary modernism under T. S. Eliot's direction. The novel took Wolfgang back to his early fascination with avant-garde art and literature—back to the years he spent as a student at the Central School of Arts and Crafts in London and as an aspiring graphic artist in Jerusalem during World War II. As he says in his afterword to the second edition of his translation, published by Suhrkamp in 1971, *Nightwood* was written in Paris in the late 1920s and early 1930s, when the city emerged as "the chosen home of American, English, and Irish writers."[66] While Barnes had remained an insider tip, he places her on equal footing with Joyce, in that she reaches for "the limits of the possibilities of linguistic expression."[67] He describes the novel's general theme as "the night side of human existence" and "the night around us and within us"[68]—a theme he would develop in *Nachtstück* as well as in *Tynset*, as we have seen—and its characters, from Nora, Robin, and Jenny ("the three lesbians," as Wolfgang affectionately refers to them) to the protagonist Felix Volkbein, as "archetypes of psychological insight."[69] He likens Volkbein to Leopold Bloom—to whom he would return in "The Jewishness of M. Bloom," his Bloomsday Dinner Speech at the Ninth International James Joyce Symposium in 1984—explaining that they share more than their Jewishness, as he draws a portrait of the artist as rooted in feelings of alienation. Wolfgang would further develop this notion conceiving of homelessness as "the source of all my creative activity" in his 1978 essay "Mein Judentum" (My Judaism),[70] which we have already compared to Jabra's "The Palestinian Exile as Writer" and Said's "Reflections on Exile."

Having embraced his identity as a writer who, akin to Volkbein and Bloom, draws inspiration from "that homelessness in which we—Jews or not—are all at home,"[71] Wolfgang increasingly intervened in public debates in the German press and signed a number of political resolutions. Notably, he signed an open letter to André Malraux, the French minister of culture, which was written by Max Frisch and Alfred Andersch at the meeting of the Gruppe 47 in Aschaffenburg in November 1960. The letter voiced support for the Manifesto of the 121, signed by French intellectuals, among them Simone de Beauvoir and Jean-Paul Sartre, which called on the French government to recognize the Algerian War as a legitimate struggle for independence and denounced the use of torture by the French army.[72] Wolfgang's engagement in support of the French Left was partly grounded in personal experience: his stepdaughter Christa was studying in Paris, where she became friends with Micheline Pouteau. Pouteau was sentenced to ten years in prison for having been a member of the circle of activists around the French philosopher Francis Jeanson. This group was referred to as *les porteurs de valises* (the suitcase carriers)—a reference to the French resistance during World War II—as they had assisted the Algerian Front de Libération Nationale (FLN) by carrying money or documents in suitcases to avoid detection by the French authorities. Wolfgang mentions his support of these French intellectuals to his mother, describing Christa as not being "pro-Arab," as his mother feared, "in the sense of being anti-Israeli; rather," he explains, "she is interested in the developing countries and in decolonization."[73] Wolfgang also signed a resolution against German chancellor Konrad Adenauer's establishment of *Das freie Deutsche Fernsehen*, which was widely perceived as an instrument of state propaganda, and an open letter addressed to the United Nations secretary-general a few weeks after the construction of the Berlin Wall in August 1961, requesting a prompt and peaceful solution to the German question.[74] It was the Eichmann Trial in Jerusalem in 1961 and the Mulka Trial in Frankfurt in 1963, however, that marked a turning point in his political engagement as a writer.[75]

Questions of memory, namely how (West) Germany was coming to terms—or not—with its Nazi past, and of German collective guilt would take center stage in Wolfgang's work. Concurrently, he turned for reassurance to two fellow literary colleagues of the Gruppe 47: Ingeborg Bachmann and Paul Celan. Having obtained her doctorate from the University of Vienna in 1949 with a thesis expressing disillusionment with Heidegger's conception of existentialism, Bachmann gave the prestigious Lectures in Poetics at the Goethe University Frankfurt in 1959–1960, in which she discussed the role of the writer in search of a new language in a postwar society. Born to a German-speaking Jewish family in Romania, Celan had emerged as one of the most important of the European modernist poets. In 1960, however, he was unjustly accused by Claire Goll of having plagiarized the poetry of her deceased husband, Yvan Goll—an accusation that would trouble Celan for the rest of his life and that possibly drew Wolfgang closer to him in solidarity.[76] "Celan's poems want to speak of the most extreme horror through silence," writes Theodor W. Adorno in his posthumously published *Aesthetic Theory*.[77] In Bachmann's search for a new language and Celan's poetics of silence, Wolfgang discovered like-minded attempts at finding words and literary forms that would express what he had witnessed in Nuremberg.

Since Richter had invited Wolfgang to join the Gruppe 47 in Dürkheim in 1951, Wolfgang had participated regularly in the group's meetings. When, on the group's behalf, Richter accepted an invitation to hold one such meeting in the Swedish town of Sigtuna in 1964, accompanied by cultural events in Stockholm,

Wolfgang distanced himself from the group. Richter explained that the hospitality of the Swedes was directed at "the other Germany"—Germany in its postwar period—but it was precisely the fact that the group seemed to have taken on the role of representative of this "other Germany" that Wolfgang rejected.[78] He would be confronted with the Nazi background of some Gruppe 47 members later, as claims that postwar Germany had made a new beginning, detached from its Nazi past, were exposed as a myth, and *Vergangenheitsbewältigung*—investigating and learning from the past with a critical eye—emerged as a key theme in postwar German literature. Responding to "the question [as to] whether my friends were Nazis," Wolfgang would later say that such a question "implies a past continuous, which defies any evaluation. It needs to be reformulated: Were Nazis my friends? The response is categorically and clearly: no."[79] Nevertheless, Wolfgang did not participate in the group's annual gatherings again until October 1967, when they met in the Pulvermühle, a guesthouse near Waischenfeld in Upper Franconia, which would prove to be the last meeting of the Gruppe 47. The meeting was interrupted by students from nearby Erlangen University who were protesting against the Springer Press, and particularly its tabloid *Bild-Zeitung*, which had strongly condemned the student movement. The students accused Gruppe 47 of maintaining an apolitical stance. Although some members reacted angrily, others, among them Wolfgang, sought to enter into dialogue with the students, but the gap between the old and the new generations proved too wide to bridge. The latter would make history as part of the May 68 movement with chants like "Unter den Talaren Muff von tausend Jahren" (The mustiness of a thousand years under academic gowns), revolting against stifling social norms and the lack of public debate about Germany's Nazi past, while demanding political change on a global scale in the context of the Vietnam War.[80]

Wolfgang had shown solidarity with the Algerian War of Independence—if indirectly through his support of the French intellectuals who stood with the FLN—but, in a manner similar to Beauvoir and Sartre, he took a different position with respect to the 1967 War, referred to in Arabic as the *naksa* (setback) or *hazima* (defeat) and in Hebrew as *milhemet sheshet hayamim* (the Six-Day War).

In February 1967, Walid and Rasha met Sartre and Beauvoir during the latter pair's visit to Egypt, when they were accompanied by the French filmmaker Claude Lanzmann, who would go on to gain international acclaim with the Holocaust documentary *Shoah* (1985). Like many of their Arab contemporaries, Walid and Rasha were disappointed with these French intellectuals' pro-Israeli stance. Rasha recalls, "Jean-Paul Sartre and Simone de Beauvoir were visiting Cairo at the time at the invitation of Hassanein Haikal, editor of *al-Ahram* newspaper and a close friend and adviser of Nasser. Walid received an invitation from Haikal to meet Sartre and I decided to go with him. After spending almost a week in frustrating waiting, the meeting took place at the Ahram in an overcrowded, smoke filled room. Sartre was arrogant and condescending and dealt in an offhand manner with any question concerning Israel, ignoring many of them, categorically refusing to admit that the Israelis could be considered colonizers."[81]

On June 5, 1967, Israel launched a number of airstrikes against Egypt, which had mobilized forces along the Israeli border. Egypt, along with Jordan and Syria, was defeated within days, as Israel occupied the West Bank and East Jerusalem in addition to the Gaza Strip, the Golan Heights, and the Sinai Peninsula. "Of the four most traumatic experiences of our lives," writes Rasha, "I don't know which was the most horrendous, the war of 1948, 56, 67, or (later) 1982. The day East Jerusalem fell was the worst. We left the dinner table as we heard the news and went out to sit on the steps in our house in Zarif. The three of us, Walid, Ahmad and myself, burst out in sobs as the triumphalist sound of the horn was blown by the chief rabbi of the Israeli army, relayed by the BBC radio station, in celebration of the Israeli conquest."[82]

In 1956, Wolfgang had shared his political views only in private, but in 1967, he stated his position publicly. Having gained renown in German literary circles, notably with his novel *Tynset*, he responded to a letter published by his friend and literary colleague Peter Weiss in the Swedish press and translated into German for the Swiss left-wing magazine *Die Tat*. Weiss, who had gained international acclaim with his 1963 play *Marat/Sade*, was a member of the Gruppe 47. Born near Berlin to a Jewish father and a Christian mother, he had left Nazi Germany for London with his family in 1935; then moved to Prague; and, when Germany occupied Czechoslovakia in 1938, fled to Stockholm. In "Der Sieg, der sich selbst bedroht" (The victory that poses a threat to itself), Weiss accuses Israel's aggressive military tactics of threatening peace in the Middle East by disguising its attack as defensive and draws a parallel to U.S. involvement in the Vietnam War.[83] Wolfgang's response, published in the German weekly *Die Zeit*, titled "Denken auf eigene Gefahr" (Thinking at your own risk), is concerned primarily with unmasking a pro-Soviet stance in Weiss's reasoning. The title of Wolfgang's response can be read as a reference to Hannah Arendt's *Eichmann in Jerusalem: A Report on the Banality of Evil*. In her observations from the trial of

Adolf Eichmann, which she depicts as a "show trial," Arendt explains Eichmann's inability to express feelings of guilt as an "inability to think, namely to think from the standpoint of somebody else," as he relied on "officialese" (*Amtssprache*) as his only language and, in his words, did his duty in obeying orders and the law.[84] Arendt's book caused much controversy. After fierce criticism, Gershom Scholem ceased all communication with Arendt, ending their more than two decades-long correspondence, which Arendt had started in 1939 when she was working in Paris for Youth Aliyah, which assisted Jewish children to escape from Nazi Germany and settle in Palestine.[85] As we have seen, Arendt had a complicated relationship with Zionism, and then with Israel; however, she unambiguously took sides with Israel in the 1967 and 1973 wars.[86]

Wolfgang agrees with Weiss's depiction of Israeli Minister of Defense Moshe Dayan as a fascist, but rejects his description of the Israelis as a *Herrenvolk* (master race), arguing that Dayan "was needed in this situation, not only in the way that, unfortunately, every state needs its generals—whose attributes are probably more or less the same everywhere—in order to win a war, but, in this case, to avoid the danger of extinction," adding that "Israel is not equal to Dayan!"[87] He condemns Weiss for not criticizing the Arab political leaders, in particular Nasser, and finds fault with his suggesting a connection to Vietnam. He closes his response with the words, "The West is not your political home. Neither is it mine. Unlike you, I have no political home."[88] In a personal note to Weiss, he writes that he would have shown his response to Weiss before publishing it in *Die Zeit*, had Weiss been available, and adds, "How dare you say, Israel should not forget that it is living among Arab neighbors . . . as if Israel had ever been given the opportunity to forget this."[89]

Wolfgang's response brought him much sympathy, in particular from Adorno, who wrote to him saying that he had read his open letter with much enthusiasm. "I am in the rare situation of identifying myself with every word," wrote Adorno, "one is [after all] not so alone as one might think."[90] Thanking him, Wolfgang responded, "often one is horror stricken with respect to one's own friends."[91] But Wolfgang's public response to Weiss was also met with criticism, notably from Erich Fried, another member of the Gruppe 47 who was renowned for his political and love poems as well as for his translations of Shakespeare. Born to Jewish parents in Vienna, Fried fled to London after his father was murdered by the Gestapo when Nazi Germany annexed Austria in March 1938. Fried published a letter to the editor titled "Held wider Willen" (Hero against one's will) in *Die Zeit*, in which he called Wolfgang politically naive and unobjective, criticizing him in particular for justifying Israel's reliance on fascist figures like Dayan, given Germany's Nazi past.[92] Wolfgang responded in a letter to the editor titled "Ist Nasser kein Faschist?" (Is Nasser not a fascist?) in *Die Zeit*. Dismissing both Weiss and Fried for not knowing what they are talking about, he refers to his experience in Palestine. He goes on to denounce the warmongering in the Arab, and especially the Egyptian, press, and argues that Israel could not be expected to have an objective point of view because the war was about its very existence.[93] Wolfgang's assumption, shared by Weiss and Fried, that Israel was indeed fighting for its very existence has been revoked by Israel's new historians, who have shown that the balance of power in the 1967 War—as already in the First Arab-Israeli War in 1948–1949—was in favor of Israel and that the war was not one of self-defense.[94]

While Wolfgang was engaging in debates about the 1967 War in the West German press, Walid was a political adviser to the Iraqi delegation to the United Nations. In this capacity, he addressed the UN General Assembly Special Emergency Session on July 14, 1967, when he refuted Israel's position on Jerusalem as put forward by its foreign minister Abba Eban. Walid knew Eban from the time Eban had worked as Albert Hourani's counterpart as assistant adviser on Jewish affairs to the Office of the British Minister of State resident in Cairo. As we have seen, Eban's name figures prominently on the issues of *Forum* in which Walid published his translation of Virgil's poetry and his own work in 1943 and 1944. In his speech at the United Nations, Walid dismissed the Israeli allegation that the Arab governments had refused access to the Holy Places, unmasking the annexation of Jerusalem (celebrated as "unified" Jerusalem) as Israel's "strategic key" to the West Bank.[95] "The Arab defeat of June 1967," writes Rashid Khalidi, "represented a watershed for Walid as for many other Palestinians."[96] It "was a turning point in many different ways," explains Hourani.

> The conquest of Jerusalem by the Israelis, and the fact that Muslim and Christian holy places were now under Jewish control, added another dimension to the conflict. The war changed the balance of forces in the Middle East. It was clear that Israel was militarily stronger than any combination of Arab states, and this changed the relationship of each of them with the outside world. What was, rightly or wrongly, regarded as a threat to the existence of Israel aroused sympathy in Europe and America, where memories of the Jewish fate during the Second World War were still strong; and the swift Israeli victory

also made Israel more desirable as an ally in American eyes. For the Arab states, and in particular Egypt, what had happened was in every sense a defeat which showed the limits of their military and political capacity; for the USSR it was also a kind of defeat, but one which made the Russians more resolute to prevent their clients from incurring another defeat of the same magnitude. At a very deep level, the war left its mark on everyone in the world who identified himself as either Jew or Arab, and what had been a local conflict became a worldwide one.[97]

Jerusalem, in particular, would represent this global conflict. "The one place where all these divisions, partitions, inequalities, and symbolic demarcations come into play all at once," writes Gil Z. Hochberg "is Jerusalem."[98] During the first week of the war, Israel razed the Mughrabi (Moroccan) Quarter in the southeast corner of the Old City to create a large public square. The Mughrabi Quarter was established as an Islamic *waqf*, a religious endowment, as an extension of the Muslim Quarter more than seven hundred years earlier. An oil painting of its old houses in Walid's living room in his house in Cambridge, Massachusetts, bears witness to a world forever gone. The painting is dated 1945 and signed by Ludwig Blum, the Moravian-born Israeli painter who had emigrated to Palestine in 1923 where he became known as "the painter of Jerusalem." The demolition of the Mughrabi Quarter hearkens back to the master plan for Jerusalem developed in Mandate Palestine by Patrick Geddes, the British architect who designed the Hebrew University and who was mentioned in chapter 1. As Nazmi Jubeh points out, "Israel did not wait long to implement Geddes' plan and remove the Mughrabi quarter: bulldozers tore down the quarter in June 1967, even before the war was over."[99]

"Truthfully speaking, Jerusalem was never unified," writes Hochberg. "Once it was partitioned in 1948 it remained so, despite (or maybe due to) the repeated declaration of its unification." What is celebrated as "unified" Jerusalem, she concludes, is "the militarized presence of Israel all over East Jerusalem: in the gates to the Old City, in the alleys, by the train, by the universities and schools. What is celebrated in other words, is the Occupation."[100] With Israel's militarized presence throughout East Jerusalem and the rise of the military in its neighboring countries, the "age of coexistence," in which Arabs and Jews were able to find common ground and to build friendships in Jerusalem as well as in other cities across the Arab world, was not only over but also forgotten and, indeed, erased.

In the aftermath of the 1967 War, Rasha cofounded the Arab Women's Information Committee (AWIC) in Beirut, which later merged with several other organizations to form the Lebanese Association for Information on Palestine (LAIP). The committee issued a brochure, titled *Facts*. In her memoirs, Rasha recalls a number of articles and pamphlets she wrote, among them *The Big Lie*, *the Story of the Boots*, *Israel at the UN*, and *The ABCs of the Palestine Problem*. She remembers that Arafat and other leaders of the PLO commended her for her work, and that Arafat, often accompanied by Salah Khalaf (also known as Abu-Iyad), a prominent PLO leader who was assassinated in 1991, visited Walid on numerous occasions to confer with him on the activities of the Palestinian resistance in Lebanon. Given Walid's good relations with the Palestinian leadership as well as with Lebanese, Egyptian, and Jordanian politicians, he would play an important "role of behind-the-scenes-mediator and facilitator," even after he and Rasha left Lebanon for the United States.[101] Throughout the 1960s, Walid was a regular speaker at the Arab Cultural Club, founded in Beirut in 1944. After the 1967 War, the student movements in Egypt and Lebanon brought to the fore a new generation of leftist intellectuals who increasingly called for armed resistance, voicing support for the *fedayeen*. With the outbreak of the Lebanese Civil War in 1975, however, sectarian politics gained the upper hand and the student movement splintered. "Never a populist or an advocate of 'people's war' or guerrilla tactics, even when these ideas were highly fashionable among Palestinians and other Arabs in the 1960s and 1970s," as Rashid Khalidi writes, Walid was "a firm believer in the importance of power in politics" and convinced "that the United States was the stronger of the two superpowers, and that it was imperative for the Palestinians and Arabs to recognize this and act accordingly."[102]

With his 1978 article "Thinking the Impossible: A Sovereign Palestinian State," Walid advanced the idea of a two-state solution, a sovereign Palestinian state within the frontiers of 1967, including East Jerusalem, the West Bank, and the Gaza Strip.[103] "There is no monopoly in history or common sense for any one of the three great monotheistic faiths over the fate or future of Jerusalem," he writes. "A partition solution does not mean the erection of a wall"—contrary to what we have seen since the early 2000s. Instead, not giving up hope, he envisions that "the frontiers could remain open between the capital of Israel in West Jerusalem and the capital of Arab Palestine in East Jerusalem. . . . It would be supremely fitting if both capitals could be demilitarized in part or wholly. . . . Only some such solution for Jerusalem is likely to capture the imagination of the world and stamp out for all time the ugly embers of holy wars. Only by some such solution would Jews, Christians and Muslims translate their veneration of Jerusalem from rhetoric to the idiom of accommodation and love."[104]

At around the same time, Wolfgang was deliberating "the end of fiction," as reads the title of a lecture he gave at Trinity College Dublin in 1978, in which he refers to Joyce as "the greatest prose writer of them all" and to *Finnegans Wake* as his "masterpiece . . . unequaled in 'passionate imagination,' in beauty and—excuse my pathos—eternal truth."[105] Joyce fascinated Wolfgang throughout his life—from his essay "On James Joyce," published in *Radio Week* in Jerusalem in 1946, to his translation and interpretation of "Anna Livia Plurabelle," the eighth chapter of *Finnegans Wake*, and his Bloomsday Dinner Speech.

After *Tynset* and *Masante*, Wolfgang had started to work on another novel, inspired by Shakespeare's *Hamlet*, but in the process of writing, the conventional form of the novel collapsed for him, and he aborted the project.[106] Wolfgang subsequently turned away from fiction toward the literary genre of biography, first with his book on the life of Mozart (1977), and then with *Marbot* (1981), a biography of a fictitious character—a person "who never existed, but who could have," as Wolfgang writes. He weaves this story into the cultural history of early nineteenth-century Europe, where all the other characters, among them Goethe and Schopenhauer, existed in actuality.[107] *Marbot* allowed him to explore "the stages in the process of discovering what it is that moves and actuates the creative genius, its pressures and repressions,"[108] but also to blur the lines between *Wirklichkeit* and *Realität*, both of which are rendered in English as *reality*. *Wirklichkeit* was derived by thirteenth-century German theologian-cum-philosopher Meister Eckhart from the Latin word *actualitas*, whereas *Realität* encompasses what T. S. Eliot expressed in his line "What might have been and what has been/Point to one end, which is always present," as Wolfgang explains.[109] *Marbot*'s protagonist shares a number of characteristics with its author, from his passion for English literature, in particular Shakespeare, to his interest in art and music, while his dandyism is reminiscent of Wolfgang's time in London and Jerusalem. Interspersed with autobiographical elements, *Marbot* reminds us of the vast range of possibilities found in real life. Wolfgang describes Marbot as "one of those complex beings whose qualities cannot simply be classified in positive or negative categories," writing that "biography too is beset by 'these terrible simplifications', which draw lopsided and therefore false pictures, or take care that they are perpetuated in intensified form."[110] Reminiscent of

Hamlet's soliloquy, Marbot chooses between life and death, or to be more precise between "to be or not to be." Deciding on "not to be" [*Nichtsein*] over "to be" [*Sein*], he disappears, as "it would be unseemly to stage [his death] and more dignified to vanish without a trace," indeed "that he should never be found was part of the plan."[111] *Marbot* not only exposed the difficulties of biographical writing, in a playful yet "dead serious" way, as Wolfgang writes in a letter to Christopher Holme on September 3, 1981.[112] It "ultimately also revealed the limitations of language's ability to convey truth," as Mary Cosgrove concludes,[113] resulting in Wolfgang's renewed silence and return to visual art.

"Each person is a microcosm," says Wolfgang in *Zeugen des Jahrhunderts*, which "prevents one from writing biographies—as biographers generally do—in which characteristics come to light that in reality are one's own projected onto others."[114] Like his protagonist in *Vergebliche Aufzeichnungen*, he concludes that

> There are no more stories to tell. I am left speechless. I would have to dive back into the past, but there is no figure left who fascinates me today, or about whom I am able to write: and to write about the present would be impossible for me, because the present that we are experiencing today is not the real present. If you ask a genetic engineer or an astrophysicist what his present looks like, it is very different from the one we write about. We write about love, while in reality the world is ending, changing, everything is developing into doom and ruin.[115]

Quoting the last lines of "The Hollow Man" (1925), written by Eliot in the aftermath of World War I, Wolfgang concludes, "'This is the way the world ends, not with a bang but with a whimper.'"[116] Disillusioned and depressed, Wolfgang would not again engage publicly in political debate, but he became a strong supporter of the nongovernmental environmental organization Greenpeace.

Returning to Eliot, whose poetry Albert Hourani read aloud by candlelight to the ecumenical circle on a Jerusalem summer's night in the immediate aftermath of World War II, seems apt for a book that tells that circle's story. We may be tempted to conclude that with the 1967 War their impossible friendship ended once and for all. After a few attempts at reviving it across borders—with the grounds that had made friendship across religious lines in Jerusalem possible hurled into a past that few people remember—the tapestry of a life in common frayed. Walid, Sally, Wolfgang, Rasha, and Jabra were now living in worlds apart.

EPILOGUE

Late Correspondence

"YES, WE SHOULD MEET, BEFORE WE ALL DIE"

Following the King David Hotel bombing, and the subsequent ongoing Nakba, the group of friends strolling through the lobby of the King David Hotel at the beginning of this book was dispersed around the globe. Although they exchanged letters and paid visits to one another in an attempt to carry their friendship across borders in the years that passed, the 1967 War firmly entrenched them in opposing political camps. We might conclude that their impossible friendship had indeed become impossible—were it not for the renewed dialogue triggered by a correspondence between Rasha and Wolfgang dating to the 1980s, when Rasha was working on her memoirs. This correspondence has survived in the Wolfgang Hildesheimer Archive at the Academy of Arts in Berlin as well as among Walid Khalidi's private papers in Cambridge, Massachusetts.[1] Reading these letters today allows us to imagine a different outcome, as Rasha and Wolfgang recall their shared lives in Jerusalem, reminding us of a time when the future of Palestine was still open and when so much seemed possible. This was a time we have described with Ussama Makdisi as an "age of coexistence," and with Kris Manjapra as an "age of entanglement" under British colonial rule, when Ahmad Samih al-Khalidi and Judah Leon Magnes would engage in collegial ties and gift/book exchange while the ecumenical circle was coming together for drinks and intellectual conversation at the bar of the King David.

Having read the English translation of Wolfgang's biography of Mozart, which was published in 1982 and reviewed in the *New York Review of Books*,[2] Rasha decided to get in touch with Wolfgang, not having heard from him for more than thirty years. She and Walid had moved to the United States in the aftermath of the Israeli invasion of Lebanon in 1982. That same year Walid accepted a position as senior research associate at the Center for International Relations and the Center for Middle East Studies at Harvard University, with which he had been affiliated since 1976.

The letter with which Rasha renewed her contact with Wolfgang has been lost. The earliest extant letter is from Wolfgang, written in Poschiavo on November 10, 1983. After noting how touched he was to have heard from Rasha and Sulafa, he continues:

> I should very much like to meet you, and Waleed of course—I mean Walid!—but he might not want to speak to me, as I was in Israel twice with Silvia, the last time twenty-one years ago, when I swore that I would never go again. Do you ever come to Europe?* Because I shall never go to the States. To England for instance? We might go in spring again. And possibly to Paris in November. But I suppose you cannot dispose of your time just like that? What about coming here? It is beautiful, high up in the mountains and comparatively quiet, except during the summer season. Incidentally, when was it that we came to Oxford to see you? And were Silvia's two daughters with us? And when was it that we played this unspeakably intellectual game at Albert's? There was an Egyptian there, with his Jewish girl friend, do you remember? Sometimes I wonder how many lives we live, I mean consecutively. Simultaneously I live one which is quite enough. Love, Wolf
>
> * We went to see my parents. My father WAS a "Zionist," but he never DREAMT of a Jewish state, all he wanted was a National Home.[3]

Trying to remember when they last saw each other, and wondering about the "many lives we live consecutively," Wolfgang seeks to position himself politically, having both Rasha and Walid in mind as intended readers. Mentioning that he visited Israel twice but swore never to return, he explains in an afterthought that his father was a Zionist and dreamed of a national home, not a Jewish state. In his introduction to *From Haven to Conquest*, Walid contests this idea of a national home, which is inscribed in the Balfour Declaration, as a "deliberate obfuscation" of Zionist aims.[4] Nevertheless, he was convinced that "the only way out of the deepening tragedy of Palestine is the start of self-examination by liberal Jews through whom, in spite of all that has happened, a bridge may yet be built between perhaps the two closest peoples on earth—the Arabs and the Jews."[5] Despite their irreconcilable positions in the 1967 War, and the opposite poles their forefathers inhabited—Esriel, Hirsch, and Arnold Hildesheimer at one end, and Yusuf Dia, Ruhi, and Hussein Fakhri al-Khalidi at the other—Walid was receptive to Wolfgang's conciliatory tone,[6] but he did not engage in a correspondence with Wolfgang.

In a letter from Poschiavo a few months later, Wolfgang apologizes for not having written sooner, telling Rasha about his depression as he draws a rather bleak picture of the future, concerned not with old age but with the growing environmental crisis: "I haven't written for so long because I have the greatest difficulties in writing. Depressions. Not about my age but about the state of the earth. In Germany and Switzerland trees are dying rapidly, and a team of German scientists has predicted that in twenty years' time, there will be no trees left. I myself am convinced that in three to four generations man will have left the earth."[7]

In the only surviving letter from Rasha from January 24, 1985, she replies:

Although your letters are so short, it is always a pleasure to receive them, I can't even remember when I last wrote to you as I don't keep notes when I write by hand. Maybe it was some time before Christmas. Anyway, I, for your information, am not a *prospective* grandmother, as the enclosed picture will show you. The girl's name is Anbara, after my sister (if you remember her in Jerusalem) and she is a real sweetie, and I think, very beautiful. . . . This is another reason why I hate living here, it is so far from England where my son and his family live now. I don't know whether I told you that Ahmad married a Scottish girl two years ago and that they live in London, and that my daughter . . . lives with us.[8]

She closes with a reference to Patricia Highsmith, all of whose thrillers, she says, she has read, and with whom she began to correspond at around the same time, trying to remember whether she and Walid had met Highsmith at Wolfgang's home on their visit to Ambach in 1951. From this letter from Rasha and those written by Wolfgang, we can sense an intimate friendship. They exchange news about their respective lives in the United States and in Switzerland and share memories of Jerusalem before 1948. They recall a number of mutual friends:

Theo Canaan, Albert Hourani, Sally Kassab, George Rais, and Assem Salam are mentioned—but not Jabra. Jabra's disappearance from the Khalidis' and Wolfgang's lives—other than the one letter written by Jabra from Harvard in 1952, which we discussed along with Wolfgang's travelogue about his first return to Jerusalem (see chapter 6), and occasional references in Wolfgang's letters to his parents about his "Jabra illustrations"—raises questions: Why did neither Wolfgang nor Rasha mention Jabra in their correspondence, whereas they recalled other common friends from Jerusalem days? Was he mentioned in other letters that have not been preserved? Or were letters addressed to him destroyed along with Jabra's house in the aftermath of the 2003 Iraq War? How many lives are we able to trace, given that in a biography we usually do not account for more than six or seven of the parallel lives of our characters, although they may have lived many more, as Woolf says in *Orlando*? And when we are faced with the silences of archives, what kind of evidence do we base our conclusions on?

In a postcard showing "the Spires of Oxford from the west," sent to Rasha during a visit to Oxford in 1984, Wolfgang recalls that he and Silvia last saw Rasha and Walid there and sends "many thanks to Walid for the book which I read with great concern and sympathy. It is a very good book."[9] The copy of Wolfgang's letter shows marginalia, a note in pencil possibly added by Silvia, who kept her husband's private papers before passing them on to the Academy of Arts in Berlin. It reads, "Eva [Wolfgang's sister] says, W. did not read the book but gave it to her, she found it despicable and, I believe, she destroyed it."[10] There is no mention of the book's title. It was most likely one of Walid's most recent publications, possibly *Conflict and Violence in Lebanon: Confrontation in the Middle East*, published in 1983 by the Harvard University Press's Harvard Studies in International Affairs Series. That book focuses on the genesis, development, and aftermath of the first round of the Lebanese Civil War in 1975–1976, the interplay of internal Lebanese and external factors, and the impact of the Israeli invasion of southern Lebanon in March 1978. It opens with an epigraph from Lucretius: "Tantum religio potuit suadere malorum" (To such heights of evil are men driven by religion).[11] Walid would later, in a book dedicated to Albert Hourani, describe himself as "one for whom the twin agonies of Palestine and Lebanon constitute in equal measure the greater part of what T. S. Eliot calls 'the damage of a lifetime.'"[12]

The marginalia add to the complexities of archival research, as they open onto another story that remains untold. Whether or not Wolfgang read the book is not of primary concern; what matters is that he passed it on to his sister, whom he describes in his conversations with Hadara Lazar as having been a Zionist and an officer in the Haganah. We can surmise that Wolfgang thought the book might interest Eva, and thus that he had at least some idea what it was about. She, however, was so outraged by the book that she destroyed it—suggesting that she must have read at least some of it. The story evoked in a third-party note in pencil is one of dissent within Wolfgang's immediate family, and by extension the Yishuv and, after 1948, Israeli society—a story that revolves around the silencing of the Palestinian narrative, which "has never been officially admitted to Israeli history, except as that of 'non-Jews,'" as Edward W. Said says in his essay "Permission to Narrate."[13] As outlined in the introduction to *An Impossible Friendship*, a battle exists between "seemingly incompatible memories" when it comes to Palestine before 1948. As the understanding of an ongoing Nakba makes clear, however, a battle also exists over the varying narratives of the Israeli-Palestinian conflict, and indeed the employment of that very term, its impact on the Middle East at large, and in this case Israel's involvement as an external belligerent in the Lebanese Civil War.

Wolfgang was able to break the silence about what he had witnessed at Nuremberg and contributed significantly to *Vergangenheitsbewältigung* in postwar German literature in an attempt at critical investigation of a past that caused his protagonists—and himself—sleepless nights, as noted in our discussions of *Tynset* (chapter 6) and *Nachtstück* (chapter 7). He remained silent about the Nakba, however, with the exception of scattered references in his literary works and his interventions in the West German press in defense of Israel in the 1967 War. Given his experience as a member of the ecumenical circle in Jerusalem and his intimate friendships with Arabs, among them prominent Palestinian artists, writers, and intellectuals, we may conclude that Wolfgang was in a position to break this silence.

On March 20, 1984, Wolfgang writes to Rasha, "I am trying to set a friend to found a Society of Jewish Enemies of Israel. I don't know whether he will. He wrote that today you might as well establish a Society of Israeli Enemies of Israel. But this is another subject" (figure E.1).[14] As these lines suggest, Wolfgang's critical views of nationalism and his gnawing disillusionment with Israel, expressed in his letters to his parents as well as in his travelogue from his first visit back to Jerusalem in 1953, had at this point in his life—after the Israeli invasion of Lebanon and siege of Beirut in 1982—given way to an oppositional stance,

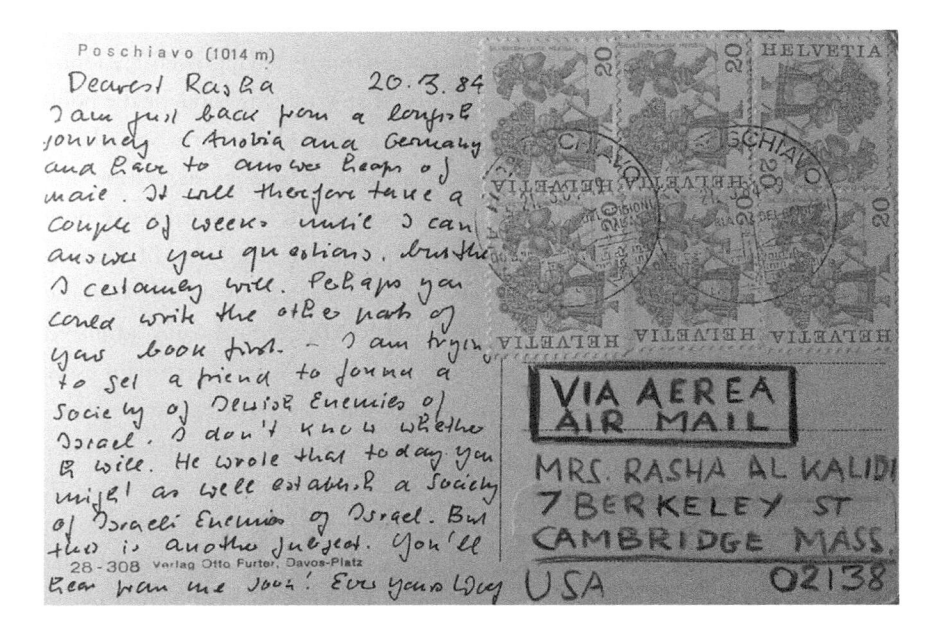

E.1 Wolfgang Hildesheimer's postcard to Rasha Salam Khalidi, Poschiavo, March 20, 1984. Academy of Arts, Berlin, WHA 1642.

even if he refrained from explicit public criticism of Israeli policies. His words foreshadow some of the criticism Israel's new historians would come to voice since the late 1980s, inspired partly by Walid's writing. In a letter dated April 8, 1984, referenced in chapter 4, Wolfgang shares his memories of Haifa, a response to Rasha's request that he help her remember the past, and shows understanding for her hatred of politics: "I do understand your hatred for everything. But I have given up concerning myself with politics, I have become the perfect escapist with considerable success. I don't write anymore, as in about two generations nobody will be able to read, and—I am certain—in four generations man will have left this earth, perhaps only in five, but certainly by the end of next century."[15]

A "great pessimist," as he describes himself elsewhere, Wolfgang was convinced humanity was coming to an end. With *Mitteilungen an Max über den Stand der Dinge* (1986, Messages to Max about the state of affairs), a semi-autobiographical text expanded from a birthday greeting in honor of his Swiss literary colleague Max Frisch, Wolfgang bade writing farewell. The text expresses the senselessness of language and is accompanied by a glossary and eight of Wolfgang's own pen-and-ink drawings, with which he returned to abstract art. Notwithstanding the affection apparent in the correspondence between Rasha and Wolfgang, feelings of melancholy permeate Wolfgang's letters as he suggests they meet again, but prospects of such a meeting are repeatedly, if kindly, deferred (figure E.2). In his last letter to Rasha preserved in the archives, dated March 12, 1988, written by

E.2 Wolfgang Hildesheimer's letter to Rasha Salam Khalidi, Poschiavo, March 12, 1988, drawing Silvia Hildesheimer.
Academy of Arts, Berlin, WHA 1642, drawing courtesy of Inge Geitner-Thurner.

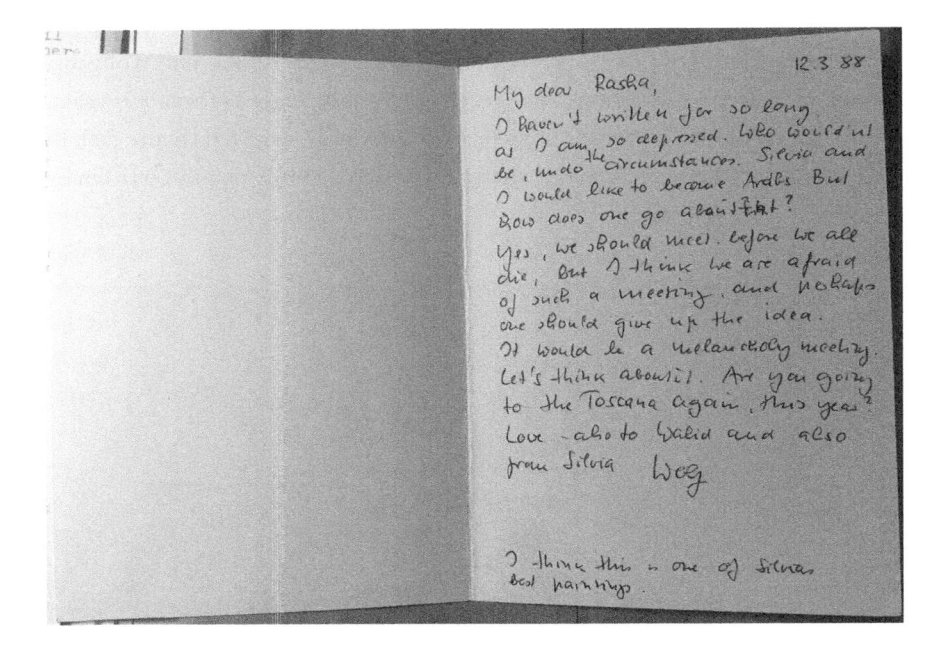

E.2 (*Continued*)

hand on a card along with a drawing by Silvia of Poschiavo. which he notes that he considered among Silvia's best, Wolfgang writes:

My dear Rasha,

I haven't written for so long as I am so depressed. Who wouldn't be, under the circumstances? Silvia and I would like to become Arabs. But how does one go about that?

Yes, we should meet, before we all die, but I think we are afraid of such a meeting, and perhaps one should give up the idea.

It would be a melancholy meeting. Let's think about it. Are you going to the Toscana again this year?

Love—also to Walid and from Silvia

Wolf[16]

In declaring "Silvia and I would like to become Arabs," Wolfgang expresses empathy and solidarity one year into the First Intifada led by the "children of the stones" in defiance of the Israeli occupation of Palestinian territories seized in the 1967 War—a war he had defended publicly in the West German press. His words remind us of the close ties between Arabs and Jews, categories seemingly ossified as polarized identities by European colonial intervention. Despite his depression and the seemingly hopeless political situation more than fifty years later, Wolfgang retains a shimmer of hope that the friends might see one another again.

"THIS TERRIBLE WAR"

Wolfgang was awarded the Bundesverdienstkreuz—the Order of Merit of the Federal Republic of Germany—in 1983, one year after he became naturalized in Switzerland and renounced his German citizenship. In a ceremony—held, at his request, not in the West German capital of Bonn but in Chur, the capital of the Swiss canton of Graubünden, to which Poschiavo belongs—he expressed his gratitude at receiving the honor. At the same time, he voiced subtle criticism, as he returned to his chosen identity as a citizen of the world, which he had first embraced upon his return to Germany after World War II:

> I thank the President of the Federal Republic of Germany for the honor shown to me, which has been extended to me as a German writer. As I am now a Swiss citizen, I would be inclined to regard this honor as a parting gift, if it were given to me to think in terms of nationalities. But it is not given to me. I have never wanted to settle on this earth in such orderly, safe and calm ways, because I have always found that a great charm in life consists in its multi-layered and varied transience. Some say that we are only guests on this earth, but I do not know who the host would be in my case.[17]

After referring to Germany as his "former homeland" [*ehemaliges Heimatland*] and Graubünden as his "new home" [*neue Heimat*], he ends his brief speech thanking Graubünden for having "actively accepted me as a human being [*Mensch*] in its community."[18] Given his wariness of nationalism and the subtle criticism aimed at his "former homeland," which had honored him as a "German writer [*deutschen Schriftsteller*]," it is not surprising that Wolfgang viewed the reunification of Germany with great concern, as he writes to his sister on January 14, 1990.[19] Nevertheless, he accepted an invitation from the president of the Federal Republic of Germany, Richard von Weizsäcker to open a series of cultural events at Schloss Bellvue in Berlin on March 30, 1990. He read from *Marbot*.[20] Wolfgang knew Weizsäcker from the Ministries Trial in the Subsequent Nuremberg Proceedings—where Richard von Weizsäcker defended his father, Ernst von Weizsäcker—and held him in high esteem, specifically his 1985 speech on the fortieth anniversary of the end of World War II. Weizsäcker had spoken boldly of that end as a "day of liberation" for his country, too, as he called on it to confront the Nazi past.[21] By the early 1990s, however, Wolfgang had retired from public life and refrained from commenting on political events.

In a letter to Christopher Holme, his former boss at the Public Information Office in Jerusalem, Wolfgang refers to "this terrible war" on January 31, 1991,[22] and in a letter to his German literary colleague Fritz Raddatz on April 28, 1991, he writes: "Regarding the Gulf War: I didn't know that Günter [Grass] had even commented on it. No, of course, one could not let Saddam continue on his rampage. I sympathized with [Wolf] Biermann. Unfortunately, the US only went half-way."[23] Günter Grass, renowned for his 1959 novel *Die Blechtrommel* (*The Tin Drum*), had spoken out against the U.S.-led bombardment of Iraq, whereas the former East German dissident and singer-songwriter Wolf Biermann supported the war, seeing in Saddam Hussein another Hitler figure—comparable to Wolfgang's former depiction of Nasser.[24]

After Iraq invaded and annexed oil-rich Kuwait in early August 1990, a U.S.-led coalition of thirty-five nations waged war against Iraq, which culminated in Operation Desert Storm from January 17 to February 28, 1991. In an unsuccessful attempt at widening the war in the Middle East, Iraq launched a number of missile attacks against Israel. The Gulf War resulted in the liberation of Kuwait but caused near-apocalyptic damage and loss of life in Iraq, as a UN report documents.[25] Saddam Hussein, however, remained in power. The war also "resulted in one of the worst setbacks for the Palestinians," after the PLO failed to condemn Iraq's invasion of Kuwait.[26] Many Palestinians who had found work in Kuwait fled during the invasion; more were forcibly expelled after the Gulf War, reducing the Palestinian community in Kuwait to less than 10 percent of its number before the conflict began. Moreover, as Philip Mattar writes, "Gulf financial and diplomatic backing that had sustained the Palestine Liberation Organization (PLO) for two decades had been withdrawn, international endorsement for Palestinian self-determination had declined, and the Arab consensus established in the Alexandria Protocol of 1944 in support of the Palestinian cause had been damaged."[27]

A few prominent voices in the Palestinian diaspora, among them Walid Khalidi and Edward W. Said, criticized the PLO for not taking a clear stance against the invasion.[28] "The principles violated by Saddam in his invasion of Kuwait," wrote Walid, "were the very principles from which the Palestinian cause drew its moral strength . . . a UN stand led by the United States against the aggression of an occupier was precisely the phenomenon that the PLO should itself be seeking."[29] The Gulf War caused deep rifts within the PLO and saw the death of Salah Khalaf (also known as Abu Iyad). Khalaf had been critical of Saddam Hussein and was assassinated in Tunis on January 15, 1991, by members of the Abu Nidal Organization, a militant Palestinian splinter group that had close ties to Iraq but is also said to have been infiltrated by the Mossad.[30] After the Gulf War, the U.S. administration put forward a proposal to resolve the Israeli-Palestinian conflict, which resulted in the Madrid Conference of 1991, bilateral negotiations between Israel and the PLO, and the subsequent signing of the Oslo Accords in a public ceremony on September 13, 1993, in Washington, D.C. At the ceremony, Prime Minister of Israel Yitzak Rabin and PLO Chair Yasser Arafat shook hands—a handshake that won Arafat and Rabin, along with Shimon Peres, the Israeli foreign minister, the 1994 Nobel Peace Prize but that cost Rabin his life the following year when he was assassinated by an Israeli right-wing extremist.

There is no mention in Wolfgang's letters of the people living in Iraq, among them Jabra, literally under the falling bombs, while "this terrible war" in the cradle of civilization was broadcast live on CNN into the remotest corners of Switzerland. Throughout his life, Jabra tried to stay out of politics as much as possible, says Issa J. Boullata; he never joined a political party, neither in Palestine, nor in Iraq.[31] With his screenplay *al-Malik al-shams* (Sun king, 1986) about the Babylonian king Nebuchadnezzar II, however, he may have participated in what Kanan Makiya decries as "*turath*-as-kitsch," the employment of heritage (*turath*) under Ba'athist rule.[32] Apart from a short sequence showing the king at age twenty-five, Jabra focused his screenplay on the year 586 BCE, when Nebuchadnezzar destroyed Jerusalem and King Solomon's Temple, causing the Babylonian Exile described in the Book of Daniel.[33] Commissioned by Iraq's

General Organization for Cinema and Film, *al-Malik al-shams* was turned into a stage production and performed by the Iraqi National Troupe at the Babylon Festival in 1987. This reconstruction of Babylon—or rather, the transformation of an archaeological site into a colossal Disneyland-esque palace meant to celebrate the regime's glory and to promote the image of Saddam Hussein as a modern Nebuchadnezzar—was brought to a close in the midst of the Iran-Iraq War.[34] In 1988, the same year that Naguib Mahfouz was awarded the Nobel Prize in Literature, Jabra was awarded the Saddam Literature Award. Asked about this award and his relation to the Iraqi president in a televised film on "Saddam's Iraq," Jabra abounds in praise for Saddam Hussein.[35] His testimony, however, may say more about the American film director, Jeff B. Harmon, who asked him about his "love" for the president and whether he would die for him, than it does about the interviewee, who searches for words trying to explain that the word "love" is misplaced, turning the conversation to "the independence and dignity of this nation." Jabra may have truly admired Saddam Hussein's Arab nationalist stance, despite his repressive dictatorship, but he could hardly have been expected to voice political dissent in front of Western media inside Saddam's "Republic of Fear."[36]

Read alongside Wolfgang's letter to Raddatz, Jabra's praise for Saddam Hussein enables us to visualize the former friends in worlds apart. With "this terrible war," Wolfgang was confronted not with a war in some faraway country but with a war that haunted him in his "place of refuge" (*me'ona*) in Switzerland, a war with which it became clear to the entire world that the Middle East had not arrived at peace. What are the possibilities of peaceful coexistence between Arabs and Jews, and how can we rethink the "history of 'Europe' in its relation to *both* Jew *and* Arab,"[37] as Gil Anidjar invites us to do, as we set out to read the story of an impossible friendship from what remains, archival traces and a late correspondence?

Most of our protagonists are gone. Wolfgang suffered a first heart attack upon finishing *Marbot*; after a second, he died in Poschiavo on August 21, 1991. Jabra died of heart failure a few years later, on December 10, 1994, in Baghdad. Sally died in Winchester in 1998. Among her papers she kept Wolfgang's biography of Mozart, translated into English in 1983, and a copy of Wolfgang's obituary in *The Independent*.[38] Rasha passed away in Cambridge, Massachusetts, on October 12, 2004, after a lengthy battle with cancer. Walid is the only one of the group of friends still alive.

As a Palestinian from Jerusalem who lived outside the Occupied Territories and had close ties to the PLO, Walid would have been excluded from the 1991 Madrid Peace Conference based on the conditions imposed by Israel on the PLO's involvement in the conference. "US Secretary of State James Baker and his assistants," however, "negotiated the inclusion of a Palestinian from Jerusalem in the Jordanian part of the delegation, over which Israel could not exercise a veto," explains Rashid Khalidi, and "in filling this role, [Walid] Khalidi was thus the thin edge of a wedge that ultimately led to Israel's negotiating directly with the PLO."[39] The question of Jerusalem, in particular, would continue to absorb Walid. In response to the Jerusalem Embassy Act passed by the U.S. Congress in 1995, which recognized Jerusalem as the capital of Israel and called for relocating the Embassy of the United States to Jerusalem from Tel Aviv, he published a special report. Titled "The Ownership of the U.S. Embassy Site in Jerusalem," it provided evidence that "at least 70 percent of the site is refugee private property, of which more than a third is Islamic *waqf* (trust)."[40] In 2009, he delivered a keynote presentation on the question of Jerusalem at the United Nations in his capacity as general-secretary of the Institute for Palestine Studies (IPS) on the occasion of the commemoration of the International Day of Solidarity with the Palestinian People, identifying Jerusalem as "the key to peace." Walid withdrew as general-secretary of the IPS in 2016, but he remains connected to Jerusalem through his scholarly work and the Friends of the Khalidi Library. A picture of Wolfgang in his early seventies, sent along with one of his letters to Rasha, bears silent witness to an impossible friendship in Jerusalem among the many pictures of family members, political figures, and friends on the bookshelves of Walid's house in Cambridge, Massachusetts. With their late correspondence, Rasha and Wolfgang renewed their dialogue and breathed new life into their friendship (despite their shared pessimism and hatred for everything), showing us that inscribed in the impossibility of that impossible friendship is the possibility of friendship.

Writing about *Marbot*, Wolfgang refers to Paul Klee's famous passage from "Creative Confessions" (1920) that "Art does not reproduce the visible [*das Sichtbare*]; rather it creates visibility [*macht sichtbar*]." Wolfgang applies this notion to literature, saying, "Literature does not reproduce experience [*das Erfahrene*]; rather it creates experience [*macht erfahrbar*]." A literary writer does not transform reality into fiction, he explains, but fiction into reality; "the biographer, however, presents—usually involuntarily—what could have been as what has been, and this is what I have done, voluntarily."[41]

The set of characters in *An Impossible Friendship* are all real: there is no fictitious Marbot or Orlando among the ecumenical circle. In imagining what their everyday lives, dreams, and futures past looked like in Jerusalem before 1948 and tracing the afterlives of an impossible friendship—acknowledging gaps and silences in the archive, as Saidiya Hartman has motivated us to do—I have drawn on both microhistory and biography, literary studies, and the social sciences to write this book. Although the individual lives at the heart of this ecumenical circle and that impossible friendship which came together before the bombing of the King David Hotel cannot be recovered in full, they can be recast in fragments. In the end, it is these stories that enable us to create and re-create experience—in all its complexities and contradictions. In so doing we search for a "language of historical reconciliation" and "new visions of solidarity and justice" that might allow us to carve out a space for an impossible friendship in Jerusalem before 1948 and beyond in the pages of history, from which we may derive a glimmer of hope for the future, no matter how faint it appears in the present.[42]

NOTES

PROLOGUE

1. Walid Khalidi, "On Albert Hourani, the Arab Office, and the Anglo-American Committee of 1946," *Journal of Palestine Studies* 35, no. 1 (September 2005): 61.
2. Khalidi, "Albert Hourani," 61.
3. Ussama Makdisi, *Age of Coexistence: The Ecumenical Frame and the Making of the Modern Arab World* (Oakland: University of California Press, 2019), 2.
4. Kris Manjapra, *Age of Entanglement: German and Indian Intellectuals Across Empire* (Cambridge, MA: Harvard University Press, 2014).
5. Jabra Ibrahim Jabra, "Modern Arabic Literature and the West," *Journal of Arabic Literature* 2 (1971): 83.
6. Camille Mansour, "Zionist Operations Against the British Mandate Authorities 1944–1947," *Interactive Encyclopedia of the Palestine Question*, accessed June 23, 2023, https://www.palquest.org/en/overallchronology?nid=139&chronos=139. See also Eugene Rogan, *The Arabs: A History* (New York: Basic Books, 2009), 247–50; Gudrun Krämer, *History of Palestine: From the Ottoman Conquest to the Founding of the State of Israel*, trans. Graham Harman and Gudrun Krämer (Princeton, NJ: Princeton University Press, 2008), 297–304; and David A. Charters, *The British Army and Jewish Insurgency in Palestine, 1945–47* (New York: Palgrave Macmillan, 1989), 42–53.
7. Thurston Clarke, *By Blood and Fire: The Attack on the King David Hotel* (New York: Putnam, 1981), 254.
8. Clarke, *By Blood and Fire*, 254.
9. Rashid Khalidi, *Palestinian Identity: The Construction of Modern National Consciousness*, 2nd ed. (New York: Columbia University Press, 2010), 19–20. The entangled histories of Arabs and Jews have gained renewed academic interest since Edward W. Said's *The Question of Palestine* (New York: Vintage, 1992), especially chapter 2, "Zionism from the Standpoint of Its Victims," 56–114. See especially Avi Shlaim, *Three Worlds: Memoirs of an Arab-Jew* (London: One World, 2023); Ella Shohat, "On Orientalist Genealogies: The Split Arab/Jew Figure Revisited," in *The Arab and Jewish Questions: Geographies of Engagement in Palestine and Beyond*, ed. Bashir Bashir and Leila Farsakh (New York: Columbia University Press, 2020), 89–121; Orit Bashkin, *New Babylonians: A History of the Jews in Modern Iraq*

(Stanford: Stanford University Pres, 2012); Gil Z. Hochberg, *In Spite of Partition: Jews, Arabs, and the Limits of Separatist Imagination* (Princeton, NJ: Princeton University Press, 2007); Gil Anidjar, *The Jew, The Arab: A History of the Enemy* (Stanford, CA: Stanford University Press, 2003); and Ammiel Alcalay's *After Jews and Arabs: Remaking Levantine Culture* (Minneapolis: University of Minnesota Press, 1993).

10. Thomas Abowd, " 'Diverse Absences': Remembering and Forgetting Arab-Jewish Relations in the Jerusalem of the British Empire," in *Jerusalem Interrupted*, ed. Lena Jayyusi (Northampton, MA: Olive Branch, 2015), 249.
11. Clarke, *By Blood and Fire*, 222.
12. Quoted in "Palestine Outrage 'Insane Act of Terrorism,' " *Manchester Guardian*, July 24, 1946. See also "A Senseless Outrage," *Times*, July 23, 1946; and "Action to Cope with Terrorists," *Times*, July 24, 1946.
13. "Bomb Attack May Retard Peace Efforts," *Washington Post*, July 24, 1946.
14. "Time Presses," *Daily Telegraph*, July 24, 1946.
15. "Lesser Evils," *Daily Telegraph*, July 22, 1946. See also "Anglo-U.S Talks Progress," *Daily Telegraph*, July 23, 1946; and "Federal Plan for Palestine," *Daily Telegraph*, July 25, 1946.
16. "A Senseless Outrage," *Times*, July 23, 1946.
17. Quoted in "39 Killed in Jerusalem Headquarters," *Times*, July 23, 1946. See also "Government and Army H.Q. Blown Up: Palestine's Worst Outrage," *Manchester Guardian*, July 23, 1946.
18. "Dr. Weizmann Warns Jews," *Daily Telegraph*, July 29, 1946.
19. For instance, in "Leaders in Jail—Lunatics in Charge," *Palestine Post*, July 24, 1946.
20. Quoted in Clifton Daniel, "Palestine Paper Attacks Zionists: Hebrew Journal Says Boards Should Resign," *New York Times*, July 25, 1946. Founded in Jerusalem in 1918, *Haaretz* was published solely in Hebrew until 1997, when an English-language edition was established alongside the Hebrew one.
21. Charters, *British Army and Jewish Insurgency*, 58–59. See also Clarke, *By Blood and Fire*, 83–85 and 96–101.
22. Quoted in "Responsibility for the Outrage," *Manchester Guardian*, July 24, 1946. See also Clifton Daniel, "Terrorist Zionists Say They Set Bomb: Denouncing British," *New York Times*, July 24, 1946, and "British Are Blamed for Ignoring Warning," *Washington Post*, July 24, 1946.
23. Quoted in "Responsibility for the Outrage."
24. Begin eventually served as Israel's sixth prime minister from 1977 to 1983. He signed the 1979 Egypt-Israel Peace Treaty, which resulted from the 1978 Camp David Accords, for which he and Anwar Sadat were jointly awarded the Nobel Peace Prize, but he also authorized the 1982 Israeli invasion of Lebanon and siege of Beirut. Edward W. Said mentions Begin as an example to illustrate how Zionism has concealed its own history, not only in Israel but also abroad "at the expense of Palestinian Arab silence in the Western 'marketplace of ideas.' " Said, *Question of Palestine*, 57–58.
25. Anne O'Hare McCormick, "Abroad: The Crisis of Palestinian Leadership," *New York Times*, July 24, 1946.
26. McCormick, "Abroad."
27. The bombing of the King David Hotel figures prominently in Victor Sebestyen's *1946: The Making of the Modern World* (New York: Macmillan, 2014), 294–97.

28. McCormick, "Abroad."
29. "Arab Manifesto," *Times*, July 24, 1946, and "Death Roll of 123 Feared in Jerusalem," *Times*, July 25, 1946.
30. "al-Irhabiyun al-yahud yaqtarifun jarima wahshiyya . . . ," *Filastin*, July 23, 1946.
31. Nadi Abusaada, "Jaffa: The Rise and Fall of an Agrarian City," Institute for Palestine Studies, September 20, 2000, https://www.palestine-studies.org/en/node/1650539. See also Mahmoud Yazbak, "Jaffa Before the Nakba: Palestine's Thriving City, 1799–1948," in *The Social and Cultural History of Palestine: Essays in Honour of Salim Tamari*, ed. Sarah Irving (Edinburgh: Edinburgh University Press, 2023), 8–25.
32. On *Filastin*, see Rashid Khalidi, *The Iron Cage: The Story of the Palestinian Struggle for Statehood* (Boston: Beacon, 2006), 94–103; Ami Ayalon, *The Press in the Arab Middle East: A History* (Oxford: Oxford University Press, 1995), 98–99; and Yousef Khuri, ed., *al-Sihafa al-'arabiyya fi Filastin 1876–1948* (Beirut: Institute for Palestine Studies, 1976), 20.
33. "Tatawwur fil-janayat," *al-Difa'*, July 23, 1946.
34. On *al-Difa'*, see Khalidi, *Iron Cage*, 83–86; Ayalon, *Press*, 99; and Khuri, *al-Sihafa*, 75.
35. "al-Wizara al-britaniyya tabhath mushkilat Filastin . . .," *Filastin*, July 23, 1946; "al-suhuf al-britaniyya tanshuru al-maqalat haul al-taqsim li-ma'rifat al-sadaha" and "Iqtirah irsal lajna wizariyya ila Filastin li-dars al-mawqif," *al-Difa'*, July 23, 1946.
36. As reported in *Manchester Guardian*, July 24, 1946.
37. Hala Sakakini, *Jerusalem and I: A Personal Record* (Jerusalem: Habesch, 1987), 81–82.
38. Sakakini, *Jerusalem*, 90.

INTRODUCTION

1. Benedict Anderson, *Imagined Communities: Reflections on the Origin and Spread of Nationalism* (London: Verso, 1983).
2. Reinhart Koselleck, *Futures Past: On the Semantics of Historical Time*, trans. with an introduction by Keith Tribe (New York: Columbia University Press, 2004).
3. See, for instance, Gil Hochberg, *Visual Occupations: Violence and Visibility in a Conflict Zone* (Durham, NC: Duke University Press, 2015).
4. Jill Lepore, "Historians Who Love Too Much: Reflections on Microhistory and Biography," *Journal of American History* 88, no. 1 (2001): 144.
5. Edward Saunders, "Introduction: Theory of Biography or Biography of Theory?," in *Biography in Theory: Key Texts with Commentaries*, ed. Wilhelm Hemecker and Edward Saunders (Berlin: De Gruyter, 2017), 7.
6. Saunders, "Introduction," 5.
7. Michael Benton, *Towards a Poetics of Literary Biography* (New York: Palgrave Macmillan, 2015), 140.
8. Edward W. Said, "The Return to Philology," in *Humanism and Democratic Criticism* (New York: Columbia University Press, 2004), 60.
9. See Terri De Young, "The Disguises of the Mind: Recent Palestinian Memoirs," *Review of Middle East Studies* 51, no. 1 (February 2017): 5–21; and Rochelle Davis, "Growing Up Palestinian in Jerusalem Before 1948: Childhood Memories of Communal Life, Education, and Political Awareness," in *Jerusalem Interrupted: Modernity and Colonial Transformation 1917–present*, ed. Lena Jayussi (Northampton, MA: Olive Branch, 2015), 187–210.

10. As reads the title of Mark LeVine and Gershon Shafir's introduction to their edited volume, *Struggle and Survival in Palestine/Israel* (Berkeley: University of California Press, 2012), 1–20, largely inspired by *Struggle and Survival in the Modern Middle East*, ed. Edmund Burke III and David N. Yaghoubian, 2nd ed. (Berkeley: University of California Press, 2006). Salim Tamari and Beshara Doumani, in particular, have made use of social biography as a tool, as part of a global microhistory, in examining the modern history of Palestine and the wider Eastern Mediterranean. See Salim Tamari, *Mountain Against the Sea: Essays on Palestinian Society and Culture* (Berkeley: University of California Press, 2009); Beshara B. Doumani, *Family Life in the Ottoman Mediterranean: A Social History* (Cambridge: Cambridge University Press, 2017), *Rediscovering Palestine: Merchants and Peasants in Jabal Nablus, 1700–1900* (Berkeley: University of California Press, 1995); and Beshara Doumani, ed., "My Grandmother and Other Stories: Histories of the Palestinians as Social Biographies," *Jerusalem Quarterly* 30 (Spring 2007): 3–9.

11. See, for instance, Abigail Jacobson and Moshe Naor, *Oriental Neighbors: Middle Eastern Jews and Arabs in Mandatory Palestine* (Waltham, MA: Brandeis University, 2016); Jonathan Marc Gribetz, *Defining Neighbors: Religion, Race, and the Early Zionist-Arab Encounter* (Princeton, NJ: Princeton University Press, 2015); Menachem Klein, *Lives in Common: Arabs and Jews in Jerusalem, Jaffa and Hebron* (New York: Hurst, 2014); and Michelle Campos, *Ottoman Brothers: Muslims, Christians, and Jews in Early Twentieth-Century Palestine* (Stanford, CA: Stanford University Press, 2011).

12. Virginia Woolf, *Orlando: A Biography*, ed. with an introduction and notes by Michael H. Whitworth (Oxford: Oxford University Press, 2015), 179.

13. Virginia Woolf, "The Art of Biography (1939)," in *Biography in Theory*, 129.

14. Benton, *Towards a Poetics*, 140.

15. Saidiya Hartman, "Venus in Two Acts," *Small Axe* 12, no. 2 (June 2008): 12. See also Saidiya Hartman, *Lose Your Mother: A Journey Along the Atlantic Slave Road* (New York: Farrar, Strauss and Giroux, 2008).

16. Hartman, "Venus in Two Acts," 12.

17. Wafa Gabsi, "'Fiction and Art Practice': Interview with Larissa Sansour 'A Space Exodus,'" *Contemporary Practices* 10 (2012): 115.

18. Gabsi, "'Fiction and Art Practice,'" 117.

19. The poem is part of a series of poems addressed to Rita in *'Ashiq min Filastin* (1966) and *Akhir al-layl* (1967) in *Diwan Mahmud Darwish*, 10th ed. (Beirut: Dar al-'Awda, 1983), 77–163 and 165–248.

20. First published in Mahmoud Darwish, *Ahad 'ashara kawkaban* (Beirut: Dar al-Jadid, 1992), 42–55; see also Mahmoud Darwish, *If I Were Another*, trans. Fady Joudah (New York: Farrar, Straus and Giroux, 2009), 88–93.

21. Quoted in Ibtisam Mara'ana's documentary film *Sajil ana 'arabi / Write Down, I Am an Arab* (Israel/Palestine: Ibtisam Films, 2014).

22. In Walter Benjamin, "The Task of the Translator," *Illuminations*, ed. with an introduction by Hannah Arendt, trans. Harry Zorn (New York: Pimlico, 1999), 70–82.

23. Hadara Lazar, *Out of Palestine: The Making of Modern Israel*, trans. Marsha Pomerantz (New York: Atlas, 2011), 80.

24. Tarif Khalidi in conversations with the author, Beirut, January 14, 2019; and Suhail Bulos in conversations with the author, Beirut, January 22, 2019.

25. Anbara Salam Khalidi, *Jawla fil-dhikrayat bayn lubnan wa-filastin* (Beirut: Dar An-Nahar, 1997), translated as *Memoirs of an Early Arab Feminist: The Life and Activism of Anbara Salam Khalidi*, trans. Tarif Khalidi (London: Pluto, 2013). See also "Anbara Salam Khalidi," *Interactive Encyclopedia of the Palestine Question*, accessed May 28, 2023, https://www.palquest.org/en/biography/9714/anbara-salam-khalidi.

26. On Hildesheimer, see in particular Stephan Braese, *Jenseits der Pässe: Wolfgang Hildesheimer. Eine Biographie* (Göttingen: Wallstein, 2017); Henry A. Lea, *Wolfgang Hildesheimers Weg als Jude und Deutscher* (Stuttgart: Hans-Dieter Heinz, 1997); and Volker Jehle, *Wolfgang Hildesheimer: Werkgeschichte* (Frankfurt: Suhrkamp, 1990). On Jabra, see Faisal Darraj, *Jabra Ibrahim Jabra: wujuh al-muthaqqaf al-rumansi* (Doha, Qatar: Hamad Bin Khalifa University Press, 2018); and Bashir Abu-Manneh, *The Palestinian Novel: From 1948 to the Present* (Cambridge: Cambridge University Press, 2016), 33–70.

27. An interesting exception is John Docker, "Dissident Voices on the History of Palestine-Israel: Martin Buber and the Bi-National Idea, Walid Khalidi's Indigenous Perspective," in *Sovereignty: Frontiers of Possibility*, ed. Julie Evans et al. (Honolulu: University of Hawaii Press, 2016), 1–29. There are of course numerous reviews of his books in various languages. For brief biographical sketches, see Rashid Khalidi, "Khalidi, Walid," *Encyclopedia of the Palestinians*, ed. Philip Mattar (New York: Facts on File, 2005), 280–84; and Mahdi Abdul Hadi, ed., *Palestinian Personalities: A Biographic Dictionary*, 2nd ed. (Jerusalem: Palestinian Academic Society for the Study of International Affairs, 2006), 113. See also *Walid Khalidi: A Biographical Summary* (Tunis: Arab League of Education, Culture and Sciences Organization, 2002); and Bayan Nuweihid al-Hout, "Walid al-Khalidi wal-ta'rikh lil-nakba," in *Mi'at 'am 'ala tasrih Balfour: al-thabit wal-mutahawwil fi al-mashru' al-kulunyali iza' Filastin*, ed. Maher Charif (Beirut: Institute for Palestine Studies, 2019), 7–26. .

28. The slogan was coined by Israel Zangwill in "The Return to Palestine," *New Liberal Review* 2 (December 1901): 627. A few years later, aware that "Palestine proper has already its inhabitants," Zangwill dismissed the idea of colonizing Palestine and broke with the Zionist movement. Israel Zangwill, *The Voice of Jerusalem* (London: Heinemann, 1920), 88, quoted in Hani A. Faris, "Israel Zangwill's Challenge to Zionism," *Journal of Palestine Studies* 4, no. 3 (1975): 85.

29. See Eugene L. Rogan and Avi Shlaim eds., *The War for Palestine: Rewriting the History of 1948* (Cambridge: Cambridge University Press, 2001), 3. Morris later turned away from revisionist historical positions, as is elaborated in chapter 7.

30. Aleida Assmann, "One Land and Three Narratives: Palestinian Sites of Memory in Israel," *Memory Studies* 11, no. 3 (July 2018): 287. See also Nadim N. Rouhana and Areej Sabbagh-Khoury, "Memory and the Return of History in a Settler-Colonial Context: The Case of the Palestinians in Israel," in *Israel and Its Palestinian Citizens: Ethnic Privileges in the Jewish State*, ed. Nadim N. Rouhana and Sahar S. Huneidi (Cambridge: Cambridge University Press, 2017), 393–432; Nur Masalha, *The Palestine Nakba: Decolonising History, Narrating the Subaltern, Reclaiming Memory* (London: Zed Books, 2012); Motti Golani and Adel Manna, *Two Sides of the Same Coin: Independence and Nakba 1948. Two Narratives of the 1948 War and Its Outcome*, trans. Geremy Forman, English-Hebrew ed. (Dordrecht: Republic of Letters, 2011); Gilbert Achcar, *The Arabs and the Holocaust: The Arab-Israeli War of Narratives* (London: Saqi, 2010); and Ahmad H. Sa'di and Lila Abu-Lughod, *Nakba: Palestine, 1948, and the Claims of Memory* (New York: Columbia University Press, 2007).

244 INTRODUCTION

31. Rogan, *Arabs*, 275.
32. Constantine Zurayk, *Ma'na al-nakba* (1948) in *al-A'mal al-kamila* (Beirut: Markaz al-dirasat al-wahda al-'arabiyya, 1994), translated as *The Meaning of the Disaster*, trans. B. Winder (Beirut: Khayat's CollegeBook Cooperative, 1956).
33. Shir Alon, "No One to See Here: Genre of Neutralization and the Ongoing Nakba," *Arab Studies Journal* 27, no. 1 (2019): 946.
34. Elias Khoury, "Rethinking the *Nakba*," *Critical Inquiry* 38, no. 2 (2012): 262. The text was originally written in Arabic and published as "al-Nakba al-mustamirra," *Majallat al-dirasat al-filastiniyya* 89 (2012): 37–50. On the concept of the Nakba and its contemporary understanding as an ongoing Nakba, see also Anaheed Al-Hardan, "al-Nakbah in Arab Thought: The Transformation of a Concept," *Comparative Studies of South Asia, Africa and the Middle East* 35, no. 3 (2005): 622–38.
35. Khoury, "Rethinking the *Nakba*," 266.
36. Elias Khoury, "Foreword," in *The Holocaust and the Nakba: A New Grammar of Trauma and History*, ed. Bashir Bashir and Amos Goldberg (New York: Columbia University Press, 2019), xv.
37. Bashir and Goldberg, "Introduction," in *The Holocaust and the Nakba*, 8.
38. Bashir Bashir, "Interrogating Modernity and Egalitarian Binationalism in Palestine/Israel," *Contending Modernities* (blog), University of Notre Dame, August 26, 2021, https://contendingmodernities.nd.edu/theorizing-modernities/interrogating-modernity-egalitarian-binationalism.
39. Dominique Eddé, *Edward Said: His Thought as a Novel*, trans. Trista Selous and Ros Schwartz (London: Verso, 2019), 161.
40. Edward W. Said, "The One-State Solution," *New York Times Magazine*, 10 January 1999.
41. Nadim N. Rouhana, "Decolonization as Reconciliation: Rethinking the National Conflict Paradigm in the Israeli-Palestinian Conflict," *Ethnic and Racial Studies* 41, no. 4 (2018): 655.
42. Michael Rothberg, *Multidirectional Memory: Remembering the Holocaust in the Age of Decolonization* (Palo Alto, CA: Stanford University Press 2009), 309. His reading builds on Hannah Arendt's *The Origins of Totalitarianism*, first published in 1951, which reads the rise of anti-Semitism across Europe against the history of Imperialism.
43. Rothberg, *Multidirectional Memory*, 311.
44. Rothberg, *Multidirectional Memory*, 313.
45. Bashir and Goldberg, "Introduction," 8; Rothberg, *Multidirectional Memory*, 313.
46. Rashid Khalidi, *Palestinian Identity*, 18.
47. Sherene Seikaly, *Men of Capital: Scarcity and Economy in Mandate Palestine* (Stanford, CA: Stanford University Press, 2015), 3. See also Ilham Khuri-Makdisi, *The Eastern Mediterranean and the Making of Global Radicalism, 1860–1914* (Berkeley: University of California Press, 2013); Issa Khalaf, *Politics in Palestine: Arab Factionalism and Social Disintegration 1939–1948* (New York: SUNY Press, 1991); Alexander Schölch, *Palestine in Transformation, 1856–1882: Studies in Social, Economic and Political Development*, trans. William C. Young and Michael C. Gerrity (Washington, DC: Institute for Palestine Studies, 2006).
48. Albert Hourani, *Arabic Thought in the Liberal Age, 1798–1939* (Cambridge: Cambridge University Press, 1983), iv. See also Jens Hanssen and Max Weiss, "Introduction," in *Arabic*

Thought Beyond the Liberal Age: Towards an Intellectual History of the Nahda (Cambridge: Cambridge University Press, 2016), 12–13. On the modern history of the term Nahda, see Hannah Scott Deuchar, "'Nahda': Mapping a Keyword in Cultural Discourse," *Alif: Journal of Comparative Poetics* 37, no. 37 (2017): 50–84.

49. George Antonius, *The Arab Awakening: The Story of the Arab National Movement* (London: Hamish Hamilton, 1938).
50. Tarif Khalidi "Palestinian Historiography: 1900–1948," *Journal of Palestine Studies* 10, no. 3 (Spring 1981): 75–76.
51. As Gudrun Krämer says, Wilson "used guarded language, speaking somewhat vaguely of 'security' and 'autonomous development,' not of sovereignty, with regard to the 'nationalities' under Turkish rule." Gudrun Krämer, *A History of Palestine: From the Ottoman Conquest to the Founding of the State of Israel*, trans. Graham Harman and Gudrun Krämer (Princeton, NJ: Princeton University Press, 2008), 154.
52. See Rashid Khalidi, *Iron Cage*, 32–38; Rogan, *Arabs*, 197. See also Salim Tamari, *The Great War and the Remaking of Palestine* (Berkeley: University of California Press, 2017); and Walid Khalidi, "The Arab Perspective," in *The End of the Palestine Mandate*, ed. William Roger Louis and Robert W. Stookey (Austin: University of Texas Press, 1986), 104–36.
53. For the full text of the Peel Report, see United Nations, accessed May 8, 2020, https://www.un.org/unispal/document/auto-insert-196150/.
54. See Matthew Hughes, *Britain's Pacification of Palestine: The British Army, the Colonial State, and the Arab Revolt, 1936–1939* (Cambridge: Cambridge University Press, 2019); Matthew Hughes, "The Banality of Brutality: British Armed Forces and the Repression of the Arab Revolt in Palestine, 1936–39," *English Historical Review* 124, no. 507 (April 2009): 314–54; and Ted Swedenburg, *Memoirs of Revolt: The 1936–39 Rebellion and the Struggle for a Palestinian National Past* (Minneapolis: University of Minnesota, 1995). As Rashid Khalidi points out, "the repression of the revolt had an impact not only on the populace, but also on the Palestinians' ability to fight thereafter, and on the already fractured capabilities of their national leadership," which played a key role in the outcome of events in 1948. Rashid Khalidi, *Iron Cage*, 108.
55. Ilan Pappé, *The Ethnic Cleansing of Palestine* (Oxford: Oneworld, 2006), 31.
56. "Resolution 181 (II): Future Governance of Palestine," United Nations, November 29, 1947, https://documents-dds-ny.un.org/doc/RESOLUTION/GEN/NR0/038/88/PDF/NR003888.pdf?OpenElement.
57. Albert Hourani, *A History of the Arab Peoples* (London: Faber and Faber, 1991), 359.
58. Rashid Khalidi, *The Hundred Years' War on Palestine: A History of Settler Colonialism, 1917–2017* (New York: Metropolitan Books, 2020), 71–72.
59. Salim Tamari, "Introduction," in *Jerusalem 1948: The Arab Neighbourhoods and Their Fate in the War* (Jerusalem: Institute for Jerusalem Studies and Badil Resource Center, 1999), 2.
60. Rashid Khalidi, *Palestinian Identity*, 89. See also Rona Sela, "The Genealogy of Colonial Plunder and Erasure—Israel's Control over Palestinian Archives," *Social Semiotics* 28, no. 2 (2018): 201–9; Hannah Mermelstein, "Overdue Books: Returning Palestine's 'Abandoned Property' of 1948," *Jerusalem Quarterly* 47 (2011): 46–64; and Amit Gish, "Ownerless Objects? The Story of the Books Palestinians Left Behind in 1948," *Jerusalem Quarterly* 33 (2008): 7–20.

61. Angelos Dalachanis and Vincent Lemire, "Introduction: Opening Ordinary Jerusalem," in *Ordinary Jerusalem 1840–1940: Opening New Archives, Revisiting a Global City* (Leiden, Netherland: Brill, 2018), 1.
62. Omnia El Shakry, "'History Without Documents': The Vexed Archives of Decolonization in the Middle East," *American Historical Review* 120, no. 3 (June 2015): 920–34; Sonja Mejcher-Atassi and John Pedro Schwartz, ed., *Archives, Museums and Collecting Practices in the Modern Arab World* (Farnham, UK: Ashgate, 2012); Yoav Di-Capua, *Gatekeepers of the Arab Past: Historians and History-Writing in Twentieth-Century Egypt* (Berkeley: University of California Press, 2009); and Anthony Gorman, *Historians, State, and Politics in Twentieth Century Egypt: Contesting the Nation* (London: Routledge, 2003).
63. Lila Abu-Lughod, "Palestine: Doing Things with Archives," Doing Things with Archives, Special Issue, *Comparative Studies of South Asia, Africa and the Middle East* 38, no. 1 (May 2018): 3. See also Sherene Seikaly, "How I Met My Great-Grandfather: Archives and the Writing of History," Doing Things with Archives, Special Issue, *Comparative Studies of South Asia, Africa and the Middle East* 38, no. 1 (May 2018): 6–20.
64. Ann Laura Stoler, "Colonial Archives and the Arts of Governance: On the Content in the Form," in *Refiguring the Archive*, ed. Carolyn Hamilton et al (New York: Springer, 2002), 8, and *Along the Archival Grain: Epistemic Anxieties and Colonial Common Sense* (Princeton, NJ: Princeton University Press, 2008).
65. Ann Laura Stoler, "On Archiving as Dissensus," Doing Things with Archives, Special Issue, *Comparative Studies of South Asia, Africa and the Middle East* 38 no. 1 (May 2018): 48.
66. Gil Z. Hochberg, *Becoming Palestine: Toward and Archival Imagination of the Future* (Durham, NC: Duke University Press, 2021), xi.
67. Hochberg, *Becoming Palestine*, xi; Benton, *Towards a Poetics*, 140.
68. His DPhil was supervised by Elizabeth Monroe and Roger Owen, and published as *Imperial Quest for Oil: Iraq, 1910–28* (London: Ithaca, 1976).
69. Alexander Schölch, "Das Dritte Reich, die zionistische Bewegung und der Palästina-Konflikt," *Vierteljahreshefte für Zeitgeschichte* 30, no. 3 (1982): 646 and 673. Examining the negotiations that took place between West Germany and Israel to reach a reparations agreement between the two countries, Ian S. Lustick suggests that similar negotiations between Israel and the Palestinians over the Palestinian refugee problem could contribute to negotiating truth. See Ian S. Lustick, "Negotiating Truth: The Holocaust, *Lehavdil*, and al-Nakba," in *Exile and Return: Predicaments of Palestinians and Jews*, ed. Ann M. Lesch and Ian S. Lustick (Philadelphia: University of Pennsylvania Press, 2005), 106–30.
70. Tarif Khalidi, *Images of Muhammad: Narratives of the Prophet in Islam Across the Centuries* (New York: Doubleday, 2009).
71. Philip S. Khoury, "Lessons from the Eastern Shore: (1998 MESA Presidential Address)," *Review of Middle East Studies* 33, no. 1 (1999): 7–8.
72. Khoury, "Lessons from the Eastern Shore," 9.

1. "CHANGING JERUSALEM: A NEW PANORAMA OF THE HOLY CITY"

1. Among them Minister of Finance Joseph Cattawi Bey, Sir Victor Harari Pasha and his son Colonel Ralph Harari, and Barons Felix and Alfred Manasca of Alexandria. See Daniella Ohad Smith, "Hotel Design in British Mandate Palestine: Modernism and the Zionist Vision," *Journal of Israeli History* 29, no. 1 (2010): 117.

1. "CHANGING JERUSALEM: A NEW PANORAMA OF THE HOLY CITY"

2. Palestine Economic Corporation (PEC) Records, 1921–1944, The New York Public Library: Manuscript and Archives Division, May 1993, http://archives.nypl.org/mss/2326#overview. See also Joseph B. Glass, *From New Zion to Old Zion: American Jewish Immigration and Settlement in Palestine, 1917–1939* (Detroit, MI: Wayne State University Press, 2002), 286.
3. Smith, "Hotel Design," 117.
4. Samuel D. Albert, "Egypt and Mandatory Palestine and Iraq," in *Architecture and Urbanism in the British Empire*, ed. G. A. Bremner (Oxford: Oxford University Press, 2016), 446; and Diana Dolev, *The Planning and Building of the Hebrew University, 1919–1948: Facing the Temple Mount* (London: Lexington, 2016), 63–66.
5. Nazmi Jubeh, "Patrick Geddes: Luminary or Prophet of Demonic Planning," *Jerusalem Quarterly* 80 (2019): 23–40; and Noah Hysler-Rubin, "Geography, Colonialism, and Town Planning: Patrick Geddes' Plan for Mandatory Jerusalem," *Cultural Geographies*, 18, no. 2 (2011): 231–48.
6. Jubeh, "Patrick Geddes," 28–29.
7. Born in Ivnitsa, then part of the Russian Empire, in 1873, Bialik received a traditional Jewish religious education before studying Russian and German literature at Odessa and embarking on a career of Yiddish and Hebrew publishing in Berlin. In 1924, he moved to Tel Aviv, where he soon became a celebrated literary figure, bridging secular and traditional Jewish identities. See Avner Holtzman, *Hayim Nahman Bialik: Poet of Hebrew* (New Haven, CT: Yale University Press, 2017).
8. Born in Grive, then part of the Russian Empire, in 1865, Kook immigrated to Palestine in 1904. Regarded as the founding father of religious Zionism, he became one of the most influential rabbis in Palestine. See Yehuda Mirsky, *Rav Kook: Mystic in a Time of Revolution* (New Haven, CT: Yale University Press, 2014).
9. "Changing Jerusalem: A New Panorama of the Holy City," *Times* (London), January 17, 1931.
10. Kobi Cogen-Kattab and Shoval Noam, *Tourism, Religion, and Pilgrimage in Jerusalem* (New York: Routledge, 2014), 57–58.
11. Smith, "Hotel Design," 104.
12. A. J. Sherman, *Mandate Days: British Lives in Palestine 1918–1948* (Baltimore, MD: Johns Hopkins University Press, 1997), 163.
13. Cogen-Kattab and Noam, *Tourism, Religion, and Pilgrimage*, 57–58.
14. See, for instance, "$1,000,000 Jerusalem Hotel Overlooks Biblical Territory," *New York Times*, December 21, 1930.
15. "Funduq al-malik dawud," *al-Hayat*, December 21, 1931. On *al-Hayat*, see Yousef Khuri, ed., *al-Sihafa al-'arabiyya fi Filastin 1876–1948* (Beirut: Institute for Palestine Studies, 1976), 54.
16. Marqus 'Isa and George Sahhar, "Funduq al-malik dawud: shabaka min shibak al-suhyuniyyin," *Filastin*, December 20, 1931, 5.
17. See Zackary Lockman, *Comrades and Enemies: Arab and Jewish Workers in Palestine, 1906–1948* (Berkeley: University of California Press, 1996), 47–57; Musa Budeiri, *The Palestine Communist Party 1919–1948: Arab and Jew in the Struggle for Internationalism* (London: Ithaca, 1979); and Steven A. Glazer, "Picketing for Hebrew Labor: A Window on Histadrut Tactics and Strategy," *Journal of Palestine Studies* 30, no. 4 (2001): 39–54, and "Language of Propaganda: The Histadrut, Hebrew Labor, and the Palestinian Worker," *Journal of Palestine Studies* 36, no. 2 (July 2007): 25–38.

18. Lockman, *Comrades and Enemies*, 197.
19. Tom Segev, *One Palestine, Complete: Jews and Arabs Under the British Mandate*, trans. Haim Watzman (London: Little, Brown, 2000), 7.
20. "King David Hotel," YouTube, September 10, 2014, https://www.youtube.com/watch?v=QRaTKGiWjCk.
21. Saidiya Hartman, "Venus in Two Acts," *Small Axe* 12, no. 2 (2008): 9.
22. Susan Beckerleg, "The Hidden Past and Untold Present of African Palestinians," in Kwesi Kwaa Prah, ed., *Reflections on Arab-led Slavery of Africans* (Cape Town: Center for the Advanced Studies of African Society, 2005), 193–207, and "African Bedouin in Palestine," *African and Asian Studies* 6 (2007): 289–303. See also Charmaine Seitz, "Pilgrimage to a New Self: The African Quarter and Its People," *Jerusalem Quarterly* 16 (2002): 43–51.
23. Eve M. Troutt Powell, *A Different Shade of Colonialism: Egypt, Great Britain, and the Mastery of the Sudan* (Berkeley: University of California Press, 2003), 69.
24. Sherene Seikaly, "The Matter of Time," *American Historical Review* 124, no. 5 (December 2019): 1681.
25. Seikaly, "Matter of Time," 1681, 1687.
26. Seikaly, "Matter of Time," 1681.
27. Will Hanley, "Grieving the Cosmopolitanism in Middle Eastern Studies," *History Compass* 6, no. 5 (September 2008): 1346–67; and Hala Halim, *Alexandrian Cosmopolitanism: An Archive* (New York: Fordham University Press, 2013).
28. Silviano Santiago, "The Cosmopolitanism of the Poor," in *Cosmopolitanisms*, ed. Bruce Robbins and Paulo Lemos Horta (New York: New York University Press, 2017), 21–39.
29. Wolfgang Hildesheimer, "Mein Judentum," in *Gesammelte Werke in sieben Bänden* [hereafter *GW VII*], ed. Christiaan Lucas Hart Nibbrig and Volker Jehle (Frankfurt: Suhrkamp, 1991), 163.
30. Ruth Kark and Michal Oren-Nordheim, *Jerusalem and Its Environs: Quarters, Neighborhoods, Villages 1800–1948* (Jerusalem: Hebrew University Magnes Press, 2001), 183–84.
31. Ellen L. Fleischmann, "Mogannam, Matiel," in *Encyclopedia of the Palestinians*, ed. Philip Mattar (New York: Facts on File, 2005), 323, and *The Nation and Its "New" Women: The Palestinian Women's Movement, 1920–1948* (Berkeley: University of California Press, 2003), 199.
32. Rochelle Davis, "The Growth of the Western Communities, 1917–1948," in *Jerusalem 1948: The Arab Neighborhoods and Their Fate in the War*, ed. Salim Tamari (Beirut: Institute for Palestine Studies, 2002), 59.
33. Davis, "The Growth of the Western Communities," 38–51; Salim Tamari, "The City and Its Rural Hinterland," in *Jerusalem 1948*, 74–91; Kark and Oren-Nordheim, *Jerusalem and Its Environs*, 285–93.
34. Tamari, "Introduction," 2.
35. Abdulaziz Abdulhussein Sachedina, *The Islamic Roots of Democratic Pluralism* (New York: Oxford University Press, 2001), 96–97.
36. Tom Segev, *The Seventh Million: The Israelis and the Holocaust*, trans. Haim Watzman (New York: Holt, 2000), 68.
37. Ragheb al-Nashashibi, Mayor of Jerusalem from 1920–1934, had "a great affection" for the hotel and "always had his hair cut there," recalls Nasser Eddin Nashashibi in *Jerusalem's Other Voice: Ragheb Nashashibi and Moderation in Palestinian Politics, 1920–1948* (Exeter, NH: Ithaca, 1990), 15.

1. "CHANGING JERUSALEM: A NEW PANORAMA OF THE HOLY CITY"   249

38. On the latter, see in particular Richard Cahill, "The Image of 'Black and Tans' in late Mandate Palestine," *Jerusalem Quarterly* 40 (2009): 43–51.
39. Noura Erakat, *Justice for Some: Law and the Question of Palestine* (Stanford, CA: Stanford University Press, 2019), 26 and 41.
40. Richard Cahill, "Sir Charles Tegart: 'The Counterterrorism Expert' in Palestine (Part 1)," *Jerusalem Quarterly* 74 (2018): 57–66, and "The Tegart Police Fortresses in British Mandate Palestine: A Reconsideration of Their Strategic Location and Purpose (Part 2)," *Jerusalem Quarterly* 75 (2018): 48–61.
41. Rashid Khalidi, *Palestinian Identity: The Construction of Modern National Consciousness*, 2nd ed. (New York: Columbia University Press, 2010), 115. On al-Qassam, see also Mark Sanagan, *Lightning through the Clouds: 'Izz al-Din al-Qassam and the Making of the Modern Middle East* (Austin: University of Texas Press, 2020); Ted Swedenburg, " Al-Qassam Remembered," *Alif: Journal of Comparative Poetics* 7 (Spring 1987): 7–24; Abdullah S. Schleifer, "Izz al-Din al-Qassam: Preacher and Mujahid," in *Struggle and Survival in the Modern Middle East*, ed. Edmund Burke III and David N. Yaghoubian (Berkeley: University of California Press, 2006), 137–51; Gilbert Achcar, *The Arabs and the Holocaust: The Arab-Israeli War of Narratives*, trans. G. M. Goshgarian (London: Saqi, 2011), 131–33; Philip Mattar, "al-Qassam, Izz al-Din," in *Encyclopedia of the Palestinians*, 408–09; "Izzeddin al-Qassam," *Interactive Encyclopedia of the Palestine Question*, accessed May 28, 2023, https://www.palquest.org/en/biography/9837/izzeddin-al-qassam.
42. Walter Lehn, "The Jewish National Fund," *Journal of Palestine Studies* 3, no 4 (1974): 74–96.
43. Lehn, "The Jewish National Fund," 81.
44. Lehn, "The Jewish National Fund," 85.
45. Walid Khalidi, "The Hebrew Reconquista of Palestine: From the 1947 United Nations Partition Resolution to the First Zionist Congress of 1897," *Journal of Palestine Studies* 39, no. 1. (2009): 26.
46. Anbara Salam Khalidi, *Jawla fil-dhikrayat bayn lubnan wa-filastin* (Beirut: Dar An-Nahar), translated as *Memoirs of an Early Arab Feminist: The Life and Activism of Anbara Salam Khalidi*, trans. Tarif Khalidi (London: Pluto, 2013), 137.
47. Walid Khalidi, ed., *From Haven to Conquest: Readings in Zionism and the Palestine Problem until 1948* (Beirut: Institute for Palestine Studies, 1971), xxxix.
48. Outlining differing Jewish and Arab narratives of the riots, he shows how they unfolded and were experienced differently across Palestine. Hillel Cohen, *Year Zero of the Arab-Israeli Conflict 1929*, trans. Haim Watzman (Waltham, MA: Brandeis University Press, 2015).
49. Cohen, *Year Zero*, 255.
50. Ilan Pappé, *The Rise and Fall of a Palestinian Dynasty: The Husaynis 1700–1948*, trans. Yael Lotan (Berkeley: University of California Press, 2010), 212–45.
51. Walid Khalidi in conversations with the author, Cambridge, MA, October 30, 2018.
52. Michael R. Fischbach, "Arab Higher Committee," in *Encyclopedia of the Palestinians*, 28–29. See also Bayan Nuweihid al-Hout, "The Palestinian Political Elite During the Mandate Period," *Journal of Palestine Studies* 9, no. 1 (Winter 1979): 85–111, and *al-Qiyadat wal-mu'assasat al-siyasiyya fi Filastin 1917–1948* (Beirut: Mu'assasat al-dirasat al-filastiniyya, 1986).

53. Alexander Schölch, "Das Dritte Reich die zionistische Bewegung und der Palästina -Konflikt," *Vierteljahreshefte für Zeitgeschichte* 30, no. 4 (1982): 657.
54. Pappé, *Rise and Fall*, 304–41. See also Achcar, *The Arabs and the Holocaust*, 128–31 and 140–67; René Wildangel, *Zwischen Achse und Mandatsmacht: Palästina und der Nationalsozialismus* (Berlin: Klaus Schwarz Verlag, 2007); Gerhard Höpp, ed., *Mufti-Papiere: Briefe, Memoranden, Rede und Aufrufe Amin al-Husainis aus dem Exil, 1940–1945* (Berlin: Klaus Schwarz Verlag, 2002); and Philip Mattar, *The Mufti of Jerusalem: Al-Hajj Amin al-Husayni and the Palestinian National Movement* (New York: Columbia University Press, 1988), and "al-Husayni, Amin," in *Encyclopedia of the Palestinians*, 213–18.
55. Gudrun Krämer, "Anti-Semitism in the Muslim World: A Critical Review," Anti-Semitism in the Arab World, Special Issue, *Die Welt des Islams: International Journal for the Study of Modern Islam* 46, no. 3 (January 2006): 259–60. See also Gudrun Krämer, *A History of Palestine: From the Ottoman Conquest to the Founding of the State of Israel*, trans. Graham Harman and Gudrun Krämer (Princeton, NJ: Princeton University Press, 2008), 261–69; and Alexander Flores, "Judeophobia in Context: Anti-Semitism Among Modern Palestinians," Anti-Semitism in the Arab World, Special Issue, *Die Welt des Islams: International Journal for the Study of Modern Islam* 46, no. 3 (January 2006): 307–30.
56. Schölch, "Das Dritte Reich," 673.
57. Quoted in Schölch, "Das Dritte Reich," 671.
58. Walid Khalidi, ed., *Before Their Diaspora: A Photographic History of the Palestinians 1876–1948*, 4th ed. (1984; repr., Washington, DC: Institute for Palestine Studies, 2010), 197 and 204–06. On Alami, see Geoffrey Furlonge, *Palestine Is My Country: The Story of Musa Alami* (London: Murray, 1969); Albert Hourani, "Musa 'Alami and the Problem of Palestine, 1933–1949," in *Studia Palaestina: Studies in Honor of Constantine K. Zurayk/Dirasat filastiniyya: majmu'at abhath wudi'at takriman lil-duktur Qustantin Zurayk*, ed. Hisham Nashabeh (Beirut: Institute for Palestine Studies, 1988), 23–41; Bernard Wasserstein, *The British in Palestine: The Mandatory Government and the Arab-Jewish Conflict 1917–1929*, 2nd ed. (London: Basil Blackwell, 1991), 191–95; and "Musa Alami," *Interactive Encyclopedia of the Palestine Question*, accessed May 28, 2023, https://www.palquest.org/en/biography/29920/musa-alami.
59. As the title of Tom Segev's biography suggests, *A State at Any Cost: The Life of David Ben-Gurion*, trans. Haim Watzman (New York: Farrar, Straus and Giroux, 2018).
60. Quoted in Khalidi, ed., *From Haven to Conquest*, 497.
61. Rashid Khalidi, *The Hundred Years' War on Palestine: A History of Settler Colonialism, 1917–2017* (New York: Metropolitan, 2020), 60; and James L. Gelvin, *The Israel-Palestine Conflict: One Hundred Years of War* (Cambridge: Cambridge University Press), 122.
62. Albert Hourani, *A History of the Arab Peoples* (London: Faber and Faber, 1991), 355–57; Helmut Mejcher. *Der Nahe Osten im Zweiten Weltkrieg* (Paderborn: Ferdinand Schöningh, 2017), 33–70; and Martin W. Wilmington, *The Middle East Supply Centre* (Albany, NY: SUNY Press), 1971.
63. Walid Khalidi, "The Arab Perspective," in *The End of the Palestine Mandate*, ed. William Roger Louis and Robert W. Stookey (Austin: University of Texas Press, 1986), 107.
64. She was the granddaughter of Abul-Huda al-Sayyadi, who headed the Rifa'iyya Sufi order in Aleppo before serving as religious adviser to Sultan Abdul Hamid II in Istanbul. Her father, Hasan Abul-Huda, served as prime minister in Transjordan. In Palestine, she

played an important role in the women's movement, notably with the Women's Social Endeavor Society, which had been founded with British support. She left for London after World War II, in early 1946, and later married Prince Omer Fevz, a grandson of Mehmed V, the last Ottoman sultan, and became an influential figure in the London art world. See B. Abu-Manneh, "Sultan Abdulhamid II and Shaikh Abulhuda al-Sayyadi," *Middle Eastern Studies* 15, no. 1 (May 1979): 131–53; Ellen L. Fleischmann, *The Nation and Its "New" Women: The Palestinian Women's Movement, 1920–1948* (Berkeley: University of California Press, 2003), 194–95; and Alan Rush, "Princess Lulie Abul-Huda Fevzi Osmanoglu (1919–2012)," *al-Ahram Weekly*, December 26, 2012.

65. Rashid Khalidi, "Khalidi, Walid," in *Encyclopedia of the Palestinians*, 281.
66. Yusif Sayigh, *Arab Economist, Palestinian Patriot: A Fractured Life Story*, ed. Rosemary Sayigh (Cairo: AUC Press, 2015), 184.
67. Walid Khalidi, "State and Society in Lebanon," in *State and Society in Lebanon*, ed. Leila Fawaz (Cambridge, MA: Tufts University, 1991), 29. Walid Khalidi in conversations with the author, Cambridge, MA, October 30, 2018.
68. Wasserstein, *The British in Palestine*, 187. Katy's father was Faris Nimr, who, along with Ya'qub Sarruf, had founded the influential Beirut- and later Cairo-based Nahda journal *al-Muqtataf*.
69. Suhail Bulos in conversations with the author, Beirut, January 22, 2019.
70. Freya Stark, *Dust in the Lion's Paw: Autobiography, 1939–1946* (London: John Murray, 1961), 129.
71. See Rashid Khalidi, *The Iron Cage: The Story of the Palestinian Struggle for Statehood* (Boston, MA: Beacon, 2006), 39.
72. "George Antonius," *Palestinian Journeys*, accessed May 9, 2020, https://www.paljourneys.org/en/biography/6571/george-antonius. On Antonius, see also Susan Silsby Boyle, *Betrayal of Palestine: The Story of George Antonius* (Boulder, CO: Westview, 2001); and William L. Cleaveland, "The Worlds of George Antonius: Identity, Culture, and the Making of an Anglo-Arab in the Pre-World War II Middle East," in *Auto/Biography and the Construction of Identity and Community in the Middle East*, ed. Mary Ann Fay (Berkeley: California University Press, 2001), 125–38.
73. His father's story is told by Cecil and Zelfa Hourani in *Fadlo Hourani: The Quiet Merchant of Manchester* (Beirut: Antoine, 2020).
74. Kraus was working at King Fuad I University—founded in 1908 as the Egyptian University, it became Cairo University after the 1952 Revolution—with the influential Egyptian intellectual Taha Hussein. In 1944, Kraus was found dead in this house, having allegedly committed suicide, while his family claimed he was assassinated. Joel L. Kraemer, "The Death of an Orientalist: Paul Kraus from Prague to Cairo," in *The Jewish Discovery of Islam: Studies in Honor of Bernard Lewis*, ed. M. Kramer (Tel Aviv: Moshe Dayan Center, 1999), 181–205; Thomas F. Glick, "From the Sarton Papers: Paul Kraus and Arabic Alchemy," *Cronos* 2, no. 2 (1999): 221–44.
75. In Washington, he worked under Khulusi al-Khayri, who in the 1950s would serve as Jordan's Minister of Foreign Affairs. Cecil later worked as adviser to Tunisian President Habib Bourguiba. Cecil Hourani, *An Unfinished Odyssey* (London: Weidenfeld and Nicolson, 1984), and *An Unfinished Odyssey Books I and II* (Beirut: Antoine, 2012).

76. *A Survey of Palestine: Prepared in December 1945 and January 1946 for the Information of the Anglo-American Committee of Inquiry*, 2 vols. and supplement (Jerusalem: Government Printer, 1946–47; reproduced facsimile of vol. 1, Washington, DC: Institute for Palestine Studies, 1991), 1:82.
77. Walid Khalidi, "On Albert Hourani, the Arab Office, and the Anglo-American Committee of 1946," *Journal of Palestine Studies* 35, no. 1 (2005): 70. See also Jens Hanssen, "Albert's World: Historicism, Liberal Imperialism and the Struggle for Palestine, 1936–48," in *Arabic Thought Beyond the Liberal Age: Towards an Intellectual History of the Nahda*, ed. Jens Hanssen and Max Weiss (Cambridge: Cambridge University Press, 2016), 80; and Michael J. Cohen, "The Genesis of the Anglo-American Committee on Palestine, November 1945: A Case Study in the Assertion of American Hegemony," *Historical Journal* 22, no. 1 (March 1979): 185–207.
78. Khalidi, "On Albert Hourani," 77–78.
79. Abdulaziz A. Al-Sudairi, *A Vision of the Middle East: An Intellectual Biography of Albert Hourani* (Oxford: Center for Lebanese Studies, 1999); and Leila Fawaz, "Albert Hourani (1915–1993)," *Middle East Studies Association Bulletin* (Summer 2002), https://web.archive.org/web/20060218221244/http://fp.arizona.edu/mesassoc/Bulletin/36-1/36-1HouraniBio.htm.
80. Hadara Lazar, *Out of Palestine: The Making of Modern Israel*, trans. Marsha Pomerantz (New York: Atlas, 2011), 96.
81. Hourani quoted in Lazar, *Out of Palestine*, 96.

2. WALID KHALIDI: A JERUSALEMITE "IN THE BYRONIC TRADITION"

1. Tarif Khalidi, "A Family's History," accessed January 2, 2021, http://www.khalidilibrary.org/en/Article/56/A-Family's-History—By-Tarif-Khalidi); and Johan Büssow, *Hamidian Palestine: Politics and Society in the District of Jerusalem 1872–1908* (Leiden: Brill, 2011), 382.
2. Rashid Khalidi, "Khalidi, Walid," in *Encyclopedia of the Palestinians*, ed. Philip Mattar (New York: Facts on File, 2005), 281.
3. On Ahmad Samih al-Khalidi, see Kamal Moed, "A Memorable Educator from Palestine: Ahmad Samih al-Khalidi (1896–1951)," *Jerusalem Quarterly* 89 (2022): 78–87; and "Ahmad Samih al-Khalidi," *Interactive Encyclopedia of the Palestine Question*, accessed May 28, 2023, https://www.palquest.org/en/biography/9833/ahmad-samih-al-khalidi. As Wasserstein says, al-Khalidi's name already came up for the post of assistant director of education in 1922 but Britain's first high commissioner, Herbert Samuel, advised by the director of education, Humphrey E. Bowman, favored a British citizen, Jerome Farrell. Al-Khalidi's appointment as principal of the Arab College was at first also opposed by the Colonial Office; this time, however, Bowman supported him. In Bernard Wasserstein, *The British in Palestine: The Mandatory Government and the Arab-Jewish Conflict 1917–1929*, 2nd ed. (London: Basil Blackwell, 1991), 173–74.
4. Ahmad Samih al-Khalidi, *Arkan al-tadris* (Jerusalem: Maktabat Bayt al-maqdis, 1934), 23, quoted in Kamal Moed, "A Memorable Educator from Palestine: Ahmad Samih al-Khalidi (1896–1951)," *Jerusalem Quarterly* 89 (2022): 81–82. In 1942, al-Khalidi opened another school, the Deir 'Amr Agricultural School for boys from rural areas who had been orphaned in the Great Revolt of 1936–39. A similar school was also started for girls.

Walid Khalidi, ed., *All That Remains: The Palestinian Villages Occupied and Depopulated by Israel in 1948* (Washington, DC: Institute for Palestine Studies, 1992), 266–90 and 301–22.

5. Quoted in A. L. Tibawi, *Arab Education in Mandatory Palestine: A Study of Three Decades of British Administration* (London: Luzac, 1956), 98.
6. Kamal Moed, "College Journals, Educational Modernism, and Palestinian Nationalism in Mandate Palestine: *Majallat al-Kulliyyah al-'Arabiyya*," *Journal of Holy Land and Palestine Studies* 20, no. 2 (2021): 180–98.
7. Marco Demichelis, "From Nahda to Nakba: The Government Arab College of Jerusalem and Its Palestinian Historical Heritage in the First Half of the Twentieth Century," *Arab Studies Quarterly* 37, no. 3 (Summer 2015): 264–71; Rochelle Davis, "Commemorating Education: Recollections of the Arab College in Jerusalem, 1918–1948," *Comparative Studies of South Asia, Africa, and the Middle East* 23, nos. 1–2 (2003): 190–204. On the Arab College, see also Muhammad Yusuf Najm, ed., *Dar al-Mu'allimin wal-kulliya al-'arabiyya fi Bayt al-Muqaddas* (Beirut: Dar Sadir, 2007); Sadiq Ibrahim 'Odeh, "The Arab College in Jerusalem, 1918–1948: Recollections," *Jerusalem Quarterly* 9 (2000): 48–58; *Khamsa wa-saba'un sana 'ala ta'sis al-kulliyya al-'arabiyya fil-Quds* (Amman: al-Bank al-'arabi, 1995); and Walid Khalidi, ed., *Before Their Diaspora: A Photographic History of the Palestinians 1876–1948*, 4th ed. (1984; repr., Washington, DC: Institute for Palestine Studies, 2010), 172–73, 181.
8. Jabra Ibrahim Jabra, *al-Bi'r al-ula: Fusul min sira dhatiyya*, 2nd ed. (Beirut: al-Mu'assasa al-'arabiyya lil-dirasat wal-nashr, 1993), 269, translated as *The First Well: A Bethlehem Boyhood*, trans. Issa J. Boullata (Fayetteville: University of Arkansas Press, 1995), 185. This corresponds to Ihsan Abbas' description of al-Khalidi as strict but humane in his autobiography *Ghurbat al-ra'i: sira dhatiyya* (Amman: Dar al-shuruq, 2006), 135.
9. Anbara Salam Khalidi, *Jawla fil-dhikrayat bayn lubnan wa-filastin* (Beirut: Dar An-Nahar, 1997), translated as *Memoirs of an Early Arab Feminist: The Life and Activism of Anbara Salam Khalidi*, trans. Tarif Khalidi (London: Pluto, 2013), 154.
10. Nicola Ziyadeh, "Ahmad Samih al-Khalidi (1896–1951): tarikh wa-dhikrayat," in *Dar al-Mu'allimin wal-kulliya al-'arabiyya*, ed. Muhammad Yusuf Najm (Beirut: Dar Sadir, 2007), 196.
11. Albert Hourani, *A History of the Arab Peoples* (London: Faber and Faber, 1991), 344.
12. Anbara Salam Khalidi, *Memoirs*, 51–64.
13. Anbara Salam Khalidi, *Memoirs*, 104–14. See also Tarif Khalidi, "Unveiled: Anbara Salam in England 1925–1927," in *The Arabs and Britain: Changes and Exchanges* (Cairo: The British Council, 1999), 378–88.
14. See Islad Jad, "From Salons to the Popular Committees: Palestinian Women, 1919–89," *The Israel/Palestine Question: A Reader*, ed. Ilan Pappé, 2nd ed. (London: Routledge, 2007), 188; and Mahasen Nasser-Eldin, *The Silent Protest: 1929 Jerusalem*, documentary film, Creative Interruptions/AHRC, 2019, https://vimeo.com/552065327?.
15. Anbara Salam Khalidi, *Memoirs*, 147.
16. Humphrey E. Bowman, "Private Journal January 1939–June 1940," Middle East Centre Archive, St Antony's College, University of Oxford, Bowman, Box 4B. See also Anbara Salam Khalidi, *Memoirs*, 134–35 and 142–44; Ellen L. Fleischmann, *The Nation and Its "New" Women: The Palestinian Women's Movement, 1920–1948* (Berkeley: University of California Press, 2003), 177, 293.

17. Walid Khalidi in conversations with the author, Cambridge, MA, October 30, 2018.
18. Dov Gavish, *A Survey of Palestine Under the British Mandate, 1920–1948* (London: Routledge, 2005), 22.
19. Yoni Furas, *Educating Palestine: Teaching and Learning History Under the Mandate* (Oxford: Oxford University Press, 2020), 26.
20. Martin Strohmeier, *al-Kullīya as-salāhīya in Jerusalem: Arabismus, Osmanismus und Panislamisumus im 1. Weltkrieg* (Stuttgart: Deutsche Morgenländische Gesellschaft/Franz Steiner Verlag, 1991), 38.
21. On the Khalidi Library, see also Ami Ayalon, *Reading Palestine: Printing and Literacy, 1900–1948* (Austin: University of Texas Press, 2004), 46–47 and 94–96; Khalidi, *Before Their Diaspora*, 73 (Plate 65); "Other Khalidis," Khalidi Library in Jerusalem, accessed on May 8, 2020, http://www.khalidilibrary.org/otherse.html.
22. Tarif Khalidi in conversations with the author, Beirut, January 14, 2019.
23. "The Earl of Oxford and Asquith," *Telegraph*, January 17, 2011; and John Jolliffe, "Obituary: The Countess of Oxford and Asquith," *Independent*, September 6, 1998.
24. "Social and Personal," *Palestine Post*, July 18, 1945.
25. Tarif Khalidi in conversations with the author, Beirut, January 14, 2019.
26. Tarif Khalidi in conversations with the author, Beirut, January 14, 2019.
27. Rasha Salam Khalidi, "A Non-Conformist Moslem Arab Woman: A Century of Evolution (1873–1976)," c. 1986, unpublished memoirs.
28. He would later work on Nuffield College, Oxford, the planning of Valetta, Malta, and the University College of the Gold Coast, now the University of Ghana. Ron Fuchs and Gilbert Herbert, "Representing Mandatory Palestine: Austen St Barbe Harrison and the Representational Buildings of the British Mandate in Palestine, 1922–37," *Architectural History* 43 (2000): 281–333.
29. Tarif Khalidi in conversations with the author, Beirut, October 24, 2020.
30. Davis, "Commemorating Education," 193–94.
31. Walid Khalidi, ed., *From Haven to Conquest: Readings in Zionism and the Palestine Problem Until 1948* (Beirut: Institute for Palestine Studies, 1971), xli; the map is reproduced as Map 7, 337.
32. Like his brother, Amad Samih al-Khalidi, Hussein Fakhri al-Khalidi was educated at Saint George's School and the American University of Beirut, from which he graduated in medicine. He served in the Ottoman Army in World War I and subsequently in Emir Faisal's army in Aleppo, where he worked as a medical doctor, before returning to Mandate Palestine to work in the Department of Health. See Ya'qub al-'Awdat, *Min a'lam al-fikr wal-adab fi Filastin* (Jordan: Jam'iyyat 'ummal al-matabi' al-ta'awuniyya, 1976), 150–52; and Michael R. Fischbach, "Khalidi, Husayn Fakhri," in *Encyclopedia of the Palestinians*, 279.
33. Walid Khalidi, "On Albert Hourani, the Arab Office, and the Anglo-American Committee of 1946," *Journal of Palestine Studies* 35, no. 1 (2005): 75. See also Hussein Fakhri al-Khalidi, *Exiled from Jerusalem*, ed. Rafiq Husseini, with a foreword by Rashid Khalidi (London: Tauris, 2020).
34. Khalidi, "On Albert Hourani," 76.
35. As documented in the appendix of Helmut Mejcher, *Der Nahe Osten im Zweiten Weltkrieg* (Paderborn: Ferdinand Schöningh, 2017), 335, reproduced from *Economic Organization of Palestine*, ed. S. B. Himadeh (Beirut: American University of Beirut Press, 1938), 332.

36. He was the son of Alexander Anton Knesevich who had served as the British honorary consul in Gaza. An Austrian subject of Croatian descent, Alexander Knesevich had grown up in Lebanon, and was fluent in Arabic and Turkish. On Alexander Knesevich, see Dotan Halevy, "Marginal Diplomacy: Alexander Knesevich and the Consular Agency in Gaza, 1905–1914," *Jerusalem Quarterly* 71 (2017): 81–93.
37. Walid Khalidi in conversations with the author, Cambridge, MA, October 29, 2018.
38. Anbara Salam Khalidi, *Memoirs*, 139. In 1939, the British Army occupied the college for a number of months, taking out its entire equipment, as depicted in photograph in *Khamsa wa-saba'un sana*, 34.
39. Walid Khalidi in conversations with the author, Cambridge, MA, April 23–25, 2019. This incident is also conveyed by Rasha Salam Khalidi in her memoirs.
40. Walid Khalidi in conversations with the author, Beirut, May 20, 2014. In *O Jerusalem* (New York: Simon and Schuster, 1972), Larry Collins and Dominique Lapierre say that Ahmad Samih al-Khalidi and Anbara Salam Khalidi had to take a number of precautions before leaving for Beirut, such as moving their chairs in their book-lined library away from the window and changing their bedroom, as "their daughter sorrowfully noted the disappearance of the family's rose garden, dug up to fill the sandbags that now marked the boundary between her father's Arab College and the Ben-Zvi Agricultural School with which it shared its Judean hilltop. On its grounds she could see the students who used to toss her back a missing balloon or ball with a shy '*Shalom*' digging slit trenches, young people like her father's students trained for leadership but condemned to war" (215).
41. Rashid Khalidi, "Khalidi, Walid," 281; Ziyadeh, "Aḥmad Sāmiḥ al-Khālidī," 196.
42. Daniel P. Kotzin, *Judah L. Magnes: An American Jewish Nonconformist* (Syracuse, NY: Syracuse University Press, 2010), 1.
43. Shalom Ratzabi, *Between Zionism and Judaism: The Radical Circle in Brith Shalom 1925–1933* (Leiden: Brill, 2001).
44. As announced in the *Official Gazette of Palestine* on October 1, 1920, quoted in Liora R. Halperin, "Hebrew Under English Rule: The Language Politics of Mandate Palestine," in *The Routledge Handbook of the History of the Middle East Mandates*, ed. Cyrus Schayegh and Andrew Arsan (London: Routledge, 2015), 337.
45. Rochelle Davis, "Growing Up Palestinian in Jerusalem Before 1948: Childhood Memories of Communal Life, Education, and Political Awareness," in *Jerusalem Interrupted: Modernity and Colonial Transformation 1917–Present*, ed. Lena Jayyusi (Northampton, MA: Olive Branch, 2015), 428n45. Among Bowman's papers in the archives of the Middle East Centre at St Antony's College, University of Oxford, there is a folder on the "Proposed Scheme for the Creation of a British University in Palestine at the Palestine Royal Commission of 8 January 1937." It includes evidence provided by Bowman, saying that "it would be a tremendous advantage to the young Arabs to get a British university education instead of the American university education which they are getting at present. They are not taught anything about the British Empire there; in fact, I have been told, although I have never had it proved, that at Beirut there is a certain amount of anti-British propaganda" (Bowman, Box 2, File 2).
46. Tarif Khalidi in conversations with the author, Beirut, October 24, 2020.
47. "Appointment and Terms of Reference of a United Nations Mediator in Palestine," May 14, 1948, accessed June 6, 2020, https://digitallibrary.un.org/record/210013?ln=en.

48. *Aufbau* was founded in New York in 1934 by the German-Jewish Club, later renamed the New World Club. It became an important venue of the German press in exile, speaking out against Nazi Germany. It was relaunched in Switzerland in 2004.
49. The article was first published in *Commentary* 5 (1948), and republished in Hannah Arendt, *The Jewish Writings*, ed. Jerome Kohn and Ron H. Feldman (New York: Schocken, 2007), 388–401. See also Susie Linfield, *The Lions' Den: Zionism and the Left: From Hannah Arendt to Noam Chomsky* (New Haven, CT: Yale University Press, 2019), 37–38; Enzo Traverso, *The End of Jewish Modernity*, trans. David Fernbach (London: Pluto Press, 2016), 67–70; Jens Hanssen, "Translating Revolution: Hannah Arendt in Arab Political Culture," HannahArendt.Net 7, no. 1 (2013): 4–5, https://doi.org/10.57773/hanet.v7i1.301; and Seyla Benhabib, *The Reluctant Modernism of Hannah Arendt*, revised ed. (Lanham, MD: Rowman and Littlefield, 2003), 42.
50. See Richard Bernstein, *Hannah Arendt and the Jewish Question* (Cambridge, MA: MIT Press, 1996), 102–5; Amnon Raz-Krakotzkin, "Binationalism and Jewish Identity: Hannah Arendt and the Question of Palestine," in *Hannah Arendt in Jerusalem*, ed. Steven E. Aschheim (Berkeley: University of California Press, 2001), 165–80; and Kotzin, *Judah L. Magnes*, 315–25.
51. Walid Khalidi in conversation with the author, Cambridge, MA, April 23–25, 2019.
52. Carl Brockelmann, *Geschichte der islamischen Völker und Staater* (Munich: Oldenbourg, 1939), translated as *History of the Islamic Peoples with a Review of Events, 1939–1947*, trans. Joel Carmichael and Moshe Perlmann (New York: Putnam, 1947).
53. Furas, *Educating Palestine*, 66.
54. Personal report on Ahmad Samih al-Khalidi, File 2/B Series/175, Shai Archive, Truman Institute, Hebrew University of Jerusalem, quoted in Furas, *Educating Palestine*, 67.
55. Walid Khalidi in conversations with the author, Cambridge, MA, April 23–25, 2019.
56. Walid Khalidi in conversations with the author, Cambridge, MA, October 29, 2018. This corresponds to accounts of Musa Alami about the tradition of foster-brothers recorded in Geoffrey Furlonge, *Palestine Is My Country: The Story of Musa Alami* (London: Murray, 1969): "The custom took no account of the religion or social status of the two families, but only of the times of birth and propinquity. Musa recalls that the child who became his own foster-brother was the son of the Jewish grocer down the street, and that for the next thirty years the two families used to visit each other, to exchange presents on each other's feast days, and to proffer congratulations or condolences as occasions demanded, until in the 1920's militant Zionism began to frown on such contacts between Jews and Arabs and brought the relationship to an end" (6). See also Wendy Pullan, "Moments of Transformation in the Urban Order of Jerusalem," in *Routledge Handbook on Jerusalem*, ed. Suleiman A. Mourad, Naomi Koltun-Fromm, and Bedross Der Matossian (London: Routledge, 2019), 226.
57. On Rosen, see Amir Theilhaber, *Friedrich Rosen: Orientalist Scholarship and International Politics* (Berlin: De Gruyter, 2020).
58. Friedrich Rosen, *Oriental Memories of a German Diplomat* (New York: Dutton, 1930), 268, quoted in Theilhaber, *Friedrich Rosen*, 41.
59. Jewish-Muslim relations have a long history, as outlined in *A History of Jewish-Muslim Relations: From the Origins to the Present Day*, ed. Abdelwahab Meddeb and Benjamin Stora, trans. Jane Marie Todd and Michael B. Smith (Princeton, NJ: Princeton University Press, 2013). See also Maria Rosa Menocal, *The Ornament of the World: How Muslims,*

Jews and Christians Created a Culture of Tolerance in Medieval Spain (New York: Little, Brown, 2002).
60. Khalidi, *Before Their Diaspora*, 32.
61. Khalidi, ed., *From Haven to Conquest*, xxi–xxii. See also Walid Khalidi, *al-Sahyuniyya fi mi'at 'am: min al-bika' 'ala al-atlal ila al-haymana 'ala al-mashriq al-'arabi (1897–1997)* (Beirut: Dar An-Nahar, 1998).
62. Khalidi, ed., *From Haven to Conquest*, 89.
63. On Yusuf Diya al-Khalidi, see Alexander Schölch, "Ein palästinensischer Repräsentant der Tanzimat Periode." *Der Islam* 57 (1980): 311–22, and "A Palestinian Reformer: Yusuf al-Khalidi," in *Palestine in Transformation, 1856–1882: Studies in Social, Economic and Political Development* trans. William C. Young and Michael C. Gerrity (Washington, DC: Institute for Palestine Studies, 2006), 241–52; Rashid Khalidi, *The Hundred Years' War on Palestine: A History of Settler Colonialism, 1917–2017* (New York: Metropolitan Books, 2020), 2–4, and *Palestinian Identity: The Construction of Modern National Consciousness*, 2nd ed. (New York: Columbia University Press, 2010), 63–88; and Adel Manna, *A'lam Filastin fi awakhir al-'ahd al-'uthmani (1800–1918)* (Beirut: Institute for Palestine Studies, 2008), 77.
64. According to papers at the Austrian State Archive, the Haus-, Hof- und Staatsarchiv in Vienna, Yusuf Diya al-Khalidi [Yusuf Zia al-Chalidi] was teaching Oriental languages at the academy until 1875, when he had to return to Jerusalem "to sort out family matters." Signature: ÖStA HHStA MdÄ AR Fach 8, Karton 292, Orientalische Akademie, Lehrpersonal Korrepetitoren.
65. Quoted from the English translation of Yusuf Diya al-Khalidi's letter, originally written in French, in Khalidi, *Before Their Diaspora*, 41.
66. Quoted from the English translation of Herzl's letter, originally written in French, in Khalidi, ed., *From Haven to Conquest*, 91–93.
67. Khalidi, ed., *From Haven to Conquest*, 92.
68. Edward W. Said, *The Question of Palestine* (New York: Vintage, 1992), 83.
69. Rashid Khalidi, *Palestinian Identity*, 60.
70. Albert Hourani, *Arabic Thought in the Liberal Age 1798–1939*, 9th ed. (1962; repr., Cambridge: Cambridge University Press, 1993), 112.
71. Muhammad Ruhi al-Khalidi, *Muhammad Ruhi al-Khalidi al-Maqdisi (1864–1913): Kutubuhu wa-maqalatuhu wa-muntakhabat min makhtubatihi*, ed. with introduction Mariam Saeed El-Ali, 2 vols. (Beirut: Institute for Palestine Studies, 2021). Three of Ruhi al-Khalidi's works have been translated into English by Tarif Khalidi and are available in the online digital library of the Khalidi Library at https://www.khalidilibrary.org/en/Category/11/online-digital-library (last accessed January 8, 2021). On Ruhi al-Khalidi, see Rashid Khalidi, *Palestinian Identity*, 63–88; Yaseen Noorani, "Translating World Literature Into Arabic and Arabic Into World Literature: Sulayman al-Bustani's al-Ilyadha and Ruhi al-Khalidi's Arabic Rendition of Victor Hugo," in *Migrating Texts: Circulating Translations around the Ottoman Mediterranean*, ed. Marilyn Booth (Edinburgh: Edinburgh University Press, 2019), 236–65; Haifa Saud Alfaisal, "Liberty and the Literary: Coloniality and Nahdawist Comparative Criticism of Rūḥī Al-Khālidī's History of the Science of Literature with the Franks, the Arabs, and Victor Hugo (1904)," *Modern Language Quarterly* 77, no. 4 (December 2016): 523–46; Nur Masalha, *Palestine: A Four Thousand Year History* (London: Zed Books, 1999), 283–84; Khairieh Kasmieh, "Rūḥī al-Khālidī 1864–1913: A Symbol of the Cultural Movement in Palestine Towards the End of Ottoman Rule,"

in *The Syrian Land in the 18th and 19th Century: The Common and the Specific in the Historical Experience*, ed. Thomas Philipp (Stuttgart: Franz Steiner Verlag, 1992), 123–46; H. Al-Khateeb, "Rūḥī al-Khālidī: A Pioneer of Comparative Literature in Arabic," *Journal of Arabic Literature* 18, no. 1 (1987): 81–87; Nasir al-Din al-Asad, *Muhammad Ruhi al-Khalidi ra'id al-bahth al-tarikhi fi Filastin* (Cairo: Ma'had al-buhuth al-'arabiyya, 1970); "Muhammad Ruhi al-Khalidi," *Interactive Encyclopedia of the Palestine Question*, accessed May 28, 2023, https://www.palquest.org/en/biography/9839/muhammad-ruhi-al-khalidi; Manna, *A'lam Filastin*, 78. Ruhi al-Khalidi figures in *1913: Seeds of Conflict, Early Encounters between Jewish and Arab Nationalism*, documentary film directed by Ben Loeterman (Israel: Loeterman Productions, 2014).

72. Muhammad Ruhi al-Khalidi, *al-Sayunizm aw al-mas'ala al-sahyuniyya: Awwal dirasa 'ilmiyya bil-'arabiyya 'an al-sahyuniyya*, ed. with introduction Walid Khalidi (Beirut: Institute for Palestine Studies, 2020).

73. Walid Khalidi, "Kitab al-Sayunizm aw al-mas'ala al-sahyuniyya li-Muhammad Ruhi al-Khalidi," in *Studia Palaestina: Studies in Honor of Constantine K. Zurayk/Dirasat filastiniyya: majmu'at abhath wudi'at takriman lil-duktur Qustantin Zurayk*, ed. Hisham Nashabeh (Beirut: Institute for Palestine Studies, 1988), 37–81.

74. Walid Khalidi in conversations with the author, Cambridge, MA, October 29, 2018. Suhail Bulos recalls that one of the Jewish boys was named Moshe Russo; he was born in Jerusalem and spoke Arabic like any other Arab boy. Suhail Bulos in conversations with the author, Beirut, January 22, 2019.

75. During World War II, the German Templars considered enemy aliens by the British were interned and then expelled from Palestine; their properties were seized and later sold to the JNF. Helmut Mejcher, "The Plight and Relief of God's Nation," in *The Struggle for a New Middle East in the 20th Century*, ed. Camilla Dawletschin-Linder and Marianne Schmidt-Dumont (Münster: Lit Verlag, 2007), 383–90.

76. "London Matric Passes," *Palestine Post*, August 13, 1943.

77. Walid Khalidi in conversations with the author, Cambridge, MA, April 23–25, 2019.

78. Tarif Khalidi in conversations with the author, Beirut, October 24, 2020.

79. Soraya Antonius, *The Lord* (London: Hamish Hamilton, 1986) and *Where the Jinn Consult* (London: Hamish Hamilton, 1987).

80. Jabra, *The First Well*, 185.

81. Walid Khalidi in conversations with the author, Cambridge, MA, April 23–25, 2019.

82. *Forum* VI, no. 49 (26 November 1943): 4.

83. Walid Khalidi in conversations with the author, Cambridge, MA, April 23–25, 2019.

84. *Forum* VII, no. 17 (April 14, 1944): 4; his name here is misspelled 'Wahud al Khalidi.'

85. Anbara Salam Khalidi, *Memoirs*, 155.

86. Jabra, *The First Well*, 185.

87. Walid Khalidi in conversations with the author, Cambridge, MA, April 23–25, 2019.

88. Cecil Hourani, *An Unfinished Odyssey: Lebanon and Beyond* (London: Weidenfeld and Nicolson, 1984), 45 and 58. Cecil Hourani remembers being on friendly terms with Eban and attending his wedding to Suzy Ambache who was of Russian-Jewish descent but grew up in Cairo. In conversations with the author, Beirut, January 3, 2020.

89. Abba Eban, *An Autobiography* (London: Weidenfeld and Nicolson, 1978).

90. Bashir Abu-Manneh translates the title as *Screams in a Long Night* in *The Palestinian Novel*; however, it is rendered, most likely by Jabra himself, as *Cry in a Long Night* in Najman Yasin's interview with Jabra, "On Interpoetics" published in *The View from Within: Writers and Critics on Contemporary Arabic Literature. A Selection from Alif: Journal of Comparative Poetics* (Cairo: American University in Cairo Press, 1994), 208, as well as in Jabra's biographical notice accompanying his essay, "Arab Language and Culture," in *The Middle East: A Handbook*, ed. Michael Adams (New York: Praeger, 1971), 178. This title is also the title of William Tamplin's translation published by Darf in 2022.

91. Jabra Ibrahim Jabra, *Shari' al-amirat: Fusul min sira dhatiyya*, 2nd ed. (1994; repr., Beirut: al-Mu'assasa al-'arabiyya lil-dirasat wal-nashr, 1999), 260, translated as *Princesses' Street: Baghdad Memories*, trans. Issa J. Boullata (Arkansas: University of Arkansas Press, 2005), 179. As Jabra says, his novel was initially entitled Passage in the Silent Night, and he wrote an earlier unpublished novel, Echo and the Pool. The manuscripts of these early works written in English are lost.

92. Jabra Ibrahim Jabra, Letter to Wolfgang Hildesheimer, Harvard, November 9, 1952, WHA 478, in Wolfgang Hildesheimer, *"Alles andere steht in meinem Roman": Zwölf Briefwechsel*, ed. Stephan Braese with Olga Blank and Thomas Wild (Frankfurt: Suhrkamp, 2017), 488–93.

93. Abu-Manneh, *The Palestinian Novel*, 44.

94. Abu-Manneh, *The Palestinian Novel*, 44.

95. Breton's manifestoes were first issued in 1924 and 1930. Césaire's *Cahier* was first published in 1939, then revised by Césaire in its 1947 and 1956 editions, which are introduced with an essay by Breton entitled "Un grand poete noir" (A Great Black Poet).

96. Jabra, *Surakh fi layl tawil*, 2nd ed. (Baghdad: Matba'at al-'ani, 1955; repr., Beirut: Dar al-Adab, 1988), translated as *Cry in a Long Night and Four Stories*, trans. William Tamplin (London: Darf, 2022), 76.

97. Anbara Salam Khalidi, *Memoirs*, 2.

98. Louis Awad, "T. S. Eliot," *al-Katib al-misri* 4, no. 1 (January 1946): 557–68.

99. As pointed out in chapter 1, the family also owned shares in Palestine Hotels Limited, which built the King David Hotel. Having immigrated from Lebanon to Cairo in the mid-nineteenth century, the Hararis were closely associated with British interests and involved in the Zionist movement. After Sir Victor Harari Pasha (1858–1945), his son Ralph (1893–1969), who served as an officer in the British Army in both World War I and II, was in charge of the family's holdings. Uri M. Kupferschmidt, "Harari, Sir Victor Pasha and Ralph," *Encyclopedia of Jews in the Islamic World*, accessed May 7, 2020, https://referenceworks.brillonline.com/entries/encyclopedia-of-jews-in-the-islamic-world/harari-sir-victor-pasha-and-ralph-SIM_0009300.

100. May Hawas, "Taha Hussein and the Case for World Literature," *Comparative Literature Studies* 55, no. 1 (2018): 66–92; Yoav Di-Capua, "Changing the Arab Intellectual Guard: On the Fall of the *udaba'*, 1940–1960," in *Arabic Thought Against the Authoritarian Age: Towards an Intellectual History of the Present*, ed. Jens Hanssen and Max Weiss (Cambridge: Cambridge University Press, 2018), 45–46.

101. Elias Khoury, "Hiwar ma'a Jabra Ibrahim Jabra," *Shu'un filastiniyya* 77 (1978); republished as "Min al-furu' ila al-jusur," in Jabra Ibrahim Jabra, *Yanabi' al-ru'ya: Dirasat naqdiyya* (Beirut: al-Mu'assassa al-'arabiyya lil-dirasat wal-nashr, 1979), 142.

102. Jabra Ibrahim Jabra, "Mulahathat 'an al-adab wal-thawra al-filastiniyya," in *al-Nar wal-jawhar: Dirasat fil-shi'r*, 3rd ed. (Beirut: al-Mu'assassa al-'arabiyya lil-dirasat wal-nashr, 1982), 157.
103. Jabra, *Surakh fi layl tawil*, 99–100.
104. Walid Khalidi in conversations with the author, Cambridge, MA, October 30, 2018.
105. In 1950, he accepted a lectureship at the newly founded College of Music in East Berlin but, accused of being a Zionist agent, he moved back to West Germany, where he became a renowned music critic and composer. Christiane Niklew, "Wolf Rosenberg," *Lexikon verfolgter Musiker und Musikerinnen der NS-Zeit*, ed. Claudia Maurer Zenck, Peter Petersen, and Sophie Fetthauer (Hamburg: Hamburg University, 2015), https://www.lexm.uni-hamburg.de/object/lexm_lexmperson_00003149.
106. Walid Khalidi in conversations with the author, Cambridge, MA, October 30, 2018. *The Trial* was originally published in German as *Der Prozess* by Verlag Die Schmiede in Berlin in 1925. The English translation by Willa and Edwin Muir was published by Gollancz in London in 1937.
107. Jens Hanssen, "Kafka and Arabs," *Critical Inquiry* 39, no. 1 (2012): 167–97; Atef Butros, *Kafka: Ein jüdischer Schriftsteller aus arabischer Sicht* (Wiesbaden: Reichert, 2009).
108. Hanssen, "Kafka and Arabs," 175.
109. Taha Hussein, "Franz Kafka," *al-Katib al-misri* 5, no. 18 (March 1947): 197–213.
110. Benjamin Balint, *Kafka's Last Trial: The Case of a Literary Legacy* (New York: Norton, 2018). See also Judith Butler, "Who Owns Kafka?," *London Review of Books*, March 3, 2011, https://www.lrb.co.uk/the-paper/v33/n05/judith-butler/who-owns-kafka.
111. Max Brod, *Franz Kafka: Eine Biographie (Erinnerungen und Dokumente)* (Prague: Mercy, 1937); and Walter Benjamin, "Franz Kafka: On the Tenth Anniversary of His Death," in *Illuminations*, ed. Hannah Arendt, trans. Harry Zorn (New York: Pimlico, 1999), 108–35.
112. As expressed in a letter to Benjamin on August 1, 1931, quoted in Gershom Scholem, *Walter Benjamin: The Story of a Friendship*, trans. Harry Zohn (New York: New York Review Books, 2003), 215–20.
113. Howard Eiland and Michael W. Jennings, *Walter Benjamin: A Critical Life* (Cambridge, MA: Belknap Press of Harvard University Press, 2014), 284–85 and 307–08. See also Hannah Arendt, "Introduction: Walter Benjamin: 1892–1940," in *Illuminations*, 32 and 40.
114. Quoted in Eiland and Jennings, *Walter Benjamin*, 338.
115. Fred Marnau, ed., *New Road: Directions in European Art and Letters* no. 4 (London: Grey Walls, 1946), 102–06.
116. Wolfgang Hildesheimer, *"Ich werde nun schweigen": Gespräch mit Hans Helmut Hillrichs in der Reihe "Zeugen des Jahrhunderts,"* ed. Ingo Hermann (Göttingen: Lamuv, 1993), 83.
117. The British members were Justice John E. Singleton (co-chair); Major Manningham-Buller, Conservative MP; W. F. Crick, adviser to the Midland Bank; R. H. S. Crossman, Labor MP; Sir Frederick Leggett, deputy secretary in the Labor Ministry; and Lord R. Morrison, Labor peer. The U.S. members were Justice Joseph C. Hutcheson (co-chair); Dr. Frank Aydelotte, director of Princeton's Institute for Advanced Studies; Frank W. Buxton, editor of the *Boston Herald*; Bartley C. Crum, a San Francisco lawyer; J. G. McDonald, the League of Nations High Commissioner for Refugees; and William Phillips, diplomat. See Khalidi, "On Albert Hourani," 74.

118. Bartley C. Crum, *Behind the Silken Curtain: A Personal Account of Anglo-American Diplomacy in Palestine and the Middle East* (New York: Simon and Schuster, 1947), 167.
119. Crum, *Behind the Silken Curtain*, 163–64.
120. Crum, *Behind the Silken Curtain*, 254. Hourani's testimony was published as a historical document, "The Case Against a Jewish State in Palestine: Albert Hourani's Statement to the Anglo-American Committee of Enquiry 1946," *Journal of Palestine Studies* 35, no. 1 (2005): 80–90.
121. Richard Crossman, *Palestine Mission: A Personal Record* (London: Hamish Hamilton, 1947), 127.
122. Said, *The Question of Palestine*, 9.
123. Edward W. Said, *Orientalism* (London: Penguin, 2003), 3.
124. Crossman, *Palestine Mission*, 134.
125. Crossman, *Palestine Mission*, 174.
126. Thurston Clarke, *By Blood and Fire: The Attack on the King David Hotel* (New York: Putnam, 1981), 48.
127. In addition, Khalidi mentions Ruhi Khatib, Nasr al-Din Nashashibi, Wadi' Tarazi, and Abdul Hamid Yasin, who also worked at the Arab Office. In Khalidi, "On Albert Hourani," 76.
128. Khalidi, "On Albert Hourani," 77.
129. Khalidi, "On Albert Hourani," 78.
130. *The Future for Palestine* was published by the Arab Office in London in 1946 and republished with an introduction by Alami in Beirut in 1970. The text does not mention authorship. According to Walid Khalidi, it was written primarily by Albert Hourani and reviewed by Musa Alami. Its appendixes were compiled by Burhan Dajani, Walid Khalidi and outside specialists, in particular Yusif Sayigh and Charles Issawi. Khalidi, "On Albert Hourani," 73–76.
131. On November 1, 1948; December 6, 1948; December 13, 1948; and December 20, 1948.
132. Khalidi, "On Albert Hourani," 76.
133. Walid Khalidi in conversations with the author, Beirut, May 20, 2014.
134. Because of World War II, Afif was not able to continue his musical training abroad. He later obtained a doctorate in linguistics from Princeton University, and taught in the Department of English at the American University of Beirut. He founded the Beirut Orpheus Choir, with which he gave concerts across the Arab world. Afif died in Beirut in 1982; he was shot in his own flat during the Israeli invasion of Lebanon. He recorded a number of albums and published a handbook of Arabic music. He is also the author of *Hajjeh Hilaneh: Stories from Palestine and Lebanon* (Beirut: Librarie du Liban, 1975), a collection of short stories that features a foreword by Edward W. Said, and of *The Arabic Triliteral Verb: A Comparative Study of Grammatical Concepts and Processes* (Beirut: Khayats, 1965), and *Handbook of Arabic Music* (Beirut: Librarie du Liban, 1971). Two of his records were reissued by Smithsonian Folkways Recordings in 2007: *Afif Bulos Sings Songs of Lebanon, Syria and Jordan* (1961); and *Classical Arabic Music: A Recital of Muwashahat with Afif Bulos and His Ensemble* (1976).
135. Tarif Khalidi in conversations with the author, Beirut, October 23, 2020.
136. On Stephan Hanna Stephan, see Sarah Irving, " 'A Young Man of Promise': Finding a Place for Stephan Hanna Stephan in the History of Mandate Palestine," *Jerusalem Quarterly* 73 (2018): 42–62.

137. Sarah Irving, "'This Is Palestine': History and Modernity in Guidebooks to Mandate Palestine," *Contemporary Levant* 4 (2019): 64–74. Stephan Hanna Stephan and Afif Bulos published three guidebooks together: *This Is Palestine: A Concise Guide to the Important Sites in Palestine, Transjordan and Syria* (Jerusalem: Bayt-ul-Makdes, 1942); *Palestine by Road and Rail: A Concise Guide to the Important Sites in Palestine and Syria* (Jerusalem: Ahva Co-op, 1942); and *This Is Palestine: A Concise Guide to the Important Sites* (Syria: Modern Press, 1947).
138. Jabra, *Princesses' Street*, 153.
139. Jabra, *Princesses' Street*, 153.
140. The brothers' paternal grandfather, Suleiman Bulos, had converted from Orthodoxy to Protestantism in Kafr Yasif, a village northeast of Acre in Upper Galilee, where his family, originally from the Hauran, owned olive groves and built a church and school that exist to this day. Suhail Bulos, *The Church Bell on Sunday: A Memoir* (Beirut: Dar Nelson, 2016), 19–21.
141. Next to his memoirs, Suhail Bulos published two collections of short stories, *Rue du Mexique and Other Stories* (Nicosia: Rimal, 2010) and *Seminar and Other Stories* (Beirut: Dar Nelson, 2018), in addition to a novella, *Land of Dreams* (Beirut: Dar Nelson, 2016).
142. On the Jerusalem Law School, see Assaf Likhovski, *Law and Identity in Mandate Palestine* (Chapel Hill: University in North Carolina Press, 2006).
143. Nassib Bulos, *A Palestinian Landscape* (Beirut: Arab Institute for Research & Pub., 1998), 30 and 58. He also published a novel: Nassib Bulos, *Jerusalem Crossroads* (Beirut: Dar An-Nahar, 2003).
144. Bulos, *A Palestinian Landscape*, 48.
145. Jabra, *Princesses' Street*, 154.
146. Middle East Centre Archive, St Antony's College, University of Oxford, Blenkinsop, GB 165–0030, 6 folios.
147. "More Illegal Immigrants: The Largest Load Greater Tension in Palestine," *Manchester Guardian*, July 30, 1946.
148. "Two Funerals on Mt. Zion," *Palestine Post*, July 31, 1946.
149. Edward Hughes, "Michael Sheringham Obituary," *Guardian*, February 12, 2016.
150. Walid Khalidi in conversations with the author, Cambridge, MA, October 29, 2018. Both are mentioned in David A. Charters, *The British Army and Jewish Insurgency in Palestine, 1945–47* (New York: Palgrave Macmillan, 1989), 91 and 156–57.
151. Rasha Salam Khalidi, "A Non-Conformist."
152. A series of attacks on Multinational Forces and the U.S. Embassy in Beirut in 1983 and 1984 led to the closing of the embassy in 1989. "History of the U.S. and Lebanon," U.S. Embassy in Lebanon, accessed June 6, 2020, https://lb.usembassy.gov/our-relationship/policy-history/io/.
153. Some of these articles were reprinted in "Khams maqalat 'an Filastin ashiyyat intiha' al-intidab al-britani," in *Majallat al-dirasat al-filastiniyya* 133 (2018): 32–44.
154. As related to me by Suhail Bulos in conversations in Beirut, January 22, 2019.
155. Anbara Salam Khalidi, *Memoirs*, 160.
156. Walid Khalidi kindly showed me a copy of this report in Cambridge, MA, 31.10.2018.
157. Benny Morris, *The Birth of the Palestinian Refugee Problem Revisited* (Cambridge: Cambridge University Press, 2004), 607; Rashid Khalidi, *Hundred Years' War*, 57.

158. Ilan Pappé, *The Ethnic Cleansing of Palestine* (Oxford: Oneworld, 2006), 98–99 and 273. As Pappé notes, fourteen of these telegrams are quoted in Gershon Rivlin and Oren Elhanam, *The War of Independence: Ben-Gurion's Diary* (Tel Aviv: Ministry of Defense, 1982).
159. I thank Tarif Khalidi for sharing his unpublished memoirs, "Have I Seen This Movie Before? A Memoir" (Beirut, 2020), with me, and for granting me permission to quote this passage.
160. Morris, *The Birth of the Palestinian Refugee Problem*, 95.
161. Nadi Abusaada, "Jaffa: The Rise and Fall of an Agrarian City," Institute for Palestine Studies, September 20, 2000, https://www.palestine-studies.org/en/node/1650539.

3. RASHA SALAM KHALIDI: "A NON-CONFORMIST MOSLEM ARAB WOMAN"

1. Tarif Khalidi in conversations with the author, Beirut, January 14, 2019.
2. Kamal Salibi, "Beirut Under the Young Turks, as Depicted in the Political Memoirs of Salīm 'Alī Salām (1868–1938)," in Jacques Berque and Dominique Chevalier, ed., *Les Arabes par leurs archives (XVIe–XXe siècles)* (Paris: Centre national de la recherche scientifique, 1976), 193.
3. Salibi, "Beirut Under the Young Turks," 193.
4. Jens Hanssen, *Fin de Siècle Beirut: The Making of an Ottoman Provincial Capital* (Oxford: Oxford University Press, 2005), 77.
5. Samir Kassir, *Histoire de Beyrouth* (Paris: Fayard, 2003), 244. Kassir, an outspoken advocate of democracy and opponent of Syria's military presence in Lebanon, was assassinated in Beirut in 2005 in a series of political assassinations that rocked Lebanon.
6. Anbara Salam Khalidi, *Jawla fil-dhikrayat bayn lubnan wa-filastin* (Beirut: Dar An-Nahar, 1997), translated as *Memoirs of an Early Arab Feminist: The Life and Activism of Anbara Salam Khalidi*, trans. Tarif Khalidi (London: Pluto, 2013), 4.
7. Salibi, "Beirut Under the Young Turks," 194. His memoirs were published by Hassan Hallaq as *Mudhakkirat Salim 'Ali Salam (1868–1938) ma'a dirasat lil-'alaqat al-uthmaniyya—al-'arabiyya wal-'alaqat al-firansiyya—al-lubnaniyya* (Beirut: Dar al-nahda al-'arabiyya, 2013).
8. Hanssen, *Fin de Siècle Beirut*, 74; Marwan Buheiry, *Beirut's Role in the Political Economy of the French Mandate 1919–39* (Oxford: Center for Lebanese Studies, 1986), 16 and 18.
9. Anbara Salam Khalidi, *Memoirs*, 109.
10. Elizabeth F. Thompson, *How the West Stole Democracy from the Arabs: The Syrian Arab Congress of 1920 and the Destruction of Its Historic Liberal-Islamic Alliance* (New York: Atlantic Monthly, 2020). A draft of the Syrian constitution, titled "The Constitution of the United States of Syria," was submitted in 1919 to the King-Crane Commission, the American section of the Inter-Allied Commission. Probably drafted by the Syrian Union Party in Cairo, which included notables from Beirut, Mount Lebanon, Damascus, Aleppo, Homs, Jaffa, and Jerusalem, advocating unity across religious lines in a federal state, it is an interesting precedent in the region to Magnes's 1948 call for a "United States of Palestine," briefly mentioned in chapter 2.

11. Anbara Salam Khalidi, *Memoirs*, 109–10.
12. Tarif Khalidi, "Translator's Acknowledgments," in Anbara Salam Khalidi, *Memoirs*, xiii.
13. Rasha Salam Khalidi, "A Non-Conformist Moslem Arab Woman: A Century of Evolution (1873–1976)," unpublished typescript, n.d.
14. Rasha Salam Khalidi, "A Non-Conformist."
15. Rasha Salam Khalidi, "A Non-Conformist."
16. Walid Khalidi in conversations with the author, Cambridge, MA, October 31, 2018.
17. Kassir, *Histoire de Beyrouth*, 378.
18. Rasha Salam Khalidi, "A Non-Conformist."
19. Salibi, "Beirut Under the Young Turks," 193.
20. Salibi, "Beirut Under the Young Turks," 193.
21. See W. P. N. Tyler, "The Huleh Lands Issue in Mandatory Palestine, 1920–34," *Middle Eastern Studies* 27, no. 3 (1991): 343–73, and "The Huleh Concession and Jewish Settlement of the Huleh Valley, 1934–48," *Middle Eastern Studies* 30, no. 4 (1994): 826–59. As Dov Gavish points out, it was only in April 1924 that the Huleh Valley had been "included definitively within the territory of the Palestine Mandate" and that "the northern frontier was finally demarcated to form the Huleh Salient (the 'Finger of Galilee')," after which "the Survey Department added five new points to the major triangulation net, and forty-three to the secondary net of third-order triangulation so as to cover the 'newly acquired territory' by the survey." Dov Gavish, *A Survey of Palestine Under the British Mandate, 1920–1948* (London: Routledge, 2005), 69.
22. The question of absentee landlords in Palestine and land sales to the JNF is discussed by Rashid Khalidi in *Palestinian Identity: The Construction of Modern National Consciousness*, 2nd ed. (New York: Columbia University Press, 2010), 111–14. The best-known example of absentee landlords is that of the Sursuq family in Beirut. Alexander Schölch, *Palestine in Transformation, 1856–1882: Studies in Social, Economic and Political Development* trans. William C. Young and Michael C. Gerrity (Washington, DC: Institute for Palestine Studies, 2006), 112–17; W. F. Abboushi, *The Unmaking of Palestine* (Boulder, CO: Rienner, 1985), 44–45.
23. Anbara Salam Khalidi, *Memoirs*, 101–03.
24. Michael R. Fischbach, "Safad," *Encyclopedia of the Palestinians*, ed. Philip Mattar (New York: Facts on File, 2005), 430.
25. Glenna Anton, "Blind Modernism and Zionist Waterscape: The Huleh Drainage Project," *Jerusalem Quarterly* 35 (2008): 82.
26. Kirsten L. Scheid discusses landscape painting in Lebanon, and Omar's *le lac de Houlé*-cum-Houlé in particular, and how it partook in what Glenna Anton calls "blind modernism," overlooking what was there to bring into view a *paysage*, in Kirsten L. Scheid, *Fantasmic Objects: Art and Sociality from Lebanon, 1920–1950* (Bloomington: Indiana University Press, 2022), 143–91. The original painting, *le Lac de Houlé*, is owned by Tammam Salam, Saeb Salam's eldest son, who served as prime minister of Lebanon between 2014 and 2016, and generously bequeathed the personal archives of his father and grandfather to the American University of Beirut.
27. Rasha Salam Khalidi, "A Non-Conformist."

28. Sandra M. Sufian, *Healing the Land and the Nation: Malaria and the Zionist Project in Palestine, 1920–1947* (Chicago: University of Chicago Press, 2007), 204 and 208.
29. Anton, "Blind Modernism," 83.
30. Sufian, *Healing the Land*, 112.
31. Mer had served as a medical officer in the Jewish Legion, a unit of the British Army, in World War I in Gallipoli, Palestine, Syria, and Turkey. During World War II, he joined the British forces as malaria adviser of Middle East Command in Iraq, Iran, and Burma. See "Obituary: Gideon Mer, M.D.," *British Medical Journal* 2 (July 29, 1961): 315.
32. Juliano Mer-Khamis and Danniel Danniel, dirs., *Arna's Children* (Netherlands: Pieter Van Huystee Film and Television, 2004). The film traces some of the children Arna worked with when she established the Freedom Theater in Jenin refugee camp during the First Intifada. Juliano Mer-Khamis was assassinated by masked men in Jenin in 2011.
33. "Israeli Land Development Company," accessed May 16, 2020, https://www.ildc.co.il/en/category/company-profile.
34. Amin al-Rihani quoted in Hallaq, *Mudhakkirat Salim 'Ali Salam*, 74. See also Scheid, *Fantasmic Objects*, 180.
35. Saeb Salam, *Qissat Imtiyaz al-Hula, 1914–1934* (Beirut: Saeb Salam, 1976).
36. Anbara Salam Khalidi, *Memoirs*, 103.
37. Anton, "Blind Modernism," 86. See also Gavish, *A Survey of Palestine*, 117.
38. Penny Sinanoglou, "British Plans for the Partition of Palestine, 1929–1938," *Historical Journal* 52, no. 1 (2009): 136.
39. Arthur Ruppin, *Memoirs, Diaries, Letters*, ed. with an introduction by Alex Bein, trans. Karen Gershon, with an afterword by Moshe Dayan (New York: Herzl, 1971), 269.
40. "Arthur Ruppin (1876–1943)," Jewish Virtual Library, accessed May 14, 2020, https://www.jewishvirtuallibrary.org/arthur-ruppin.
41. As expressed in Arthur Ruppin, "Die Auslese des Menschenmaterials für Palästina," *Der Jude. Eine Monatschrift* 3 (1918–19): 373–83.
42. Etan Bloom aligns them with anti-Semitic and, more specifically, Nazi ideologies, Amos Morris-Reich situates them in the historical context of Ruppin's exchange of ideas with "German, sometimes wildly anti-Semitic writers" in the early twentieth century, when German *Rassenkunde* (roughly, "race knowledge") proliferated. See Etan Bloom, *Arthur Ruppin and the Production of Pre-Israeli Culture* (Leiden: Brill, 2011), and "What 'The Father' Had in Mind: Arthur Ruppin (1876–1943), Cultural Identity, Weltanschauung, and Action," *History of European Ideas* 33, no. 3 (2007): 330–49. Amos Morris-Reich, "Ruppin and the Peculiarities of Race: A Response to Etan Bloom," *History of European Ideas* 34, no. 1 (2008): 118.
43. Rashid Khalidi, *The Hundred Years' War on Palestine: A History of Settler Colonialism, 1917–2017* (New York: Metropolitan Books, 2020), 8.
44. Walid Khalidi, ed., *All That Remains: The Palestinian Villages Occupied and Depopulated by Israel in 1948* (Washington, DC: Institute for Palestine Studies, 1992), 426–511.
45. Khalidi, *All That Remains*, 458–59.
46. Benny Morris, *The Birth of the Palestinian Refugee Problem Revisited* (Cambridge: Cambridge University Press, 2004), 223 and 511–12.
47. Anton, "Blind Modernism," 77.

48. Anton, "Blind Modernism," 83.
49. Anton, "Blind Modernism," 91. See also Sufian, *Healing the Land*, 346.
50. Waleed Karkabi and Adi Roitenberg, "Arab-Jewish Architectural Partnership in Haifa during the Mandate Period: Qaraman and Gerstel Meet on the 'Seam Line,'" in *Haifa Before and After 1948: Narratives of a Mixed City*, ed. Mahmoud Yazbak and Yfaat Weiss (Dordrecht: Institute for Historical Justice and Reconciliation and Republic of Letters Publishing, 2011), 49.
51. May Seikaly, *Haifa: Transformation of an Arab Society 1918–1939*, with a foreword by Walid Khalidi (London: Tauris, 1995), 125, 131n11.
52. Seikaly, *Haifa*, 5. See also Jacob Norris, "The 'City of the Future' Haifa, Capital of British Palestine," in *Land of Progress: Palestine in the Age of Colonial Development, 1905–1948* (Oxford: Oxford University Press, 2013), 99–138.
53. Frederik Meiton, *Electrical Palestine: Capital and Technology from Empire and Nation* (Oakland: University of California Press, 2019), 53–57.
54. Seikaly, *Haifa*, 86.
55. Seikaly, *Haifa*, 47–51; Meiton, *Electrical Palestine*, 57.
56. Rasha Salam Khalidi, "A Non-Conformist."
57. Timothy Mitchell, *Colonising Egypt* (Oakland: University of California Press, 2007).
58. Rasha Salam Khalidi, "A Non-Conformist."
59. Roger Owen, "The Political Economy of Grand Liban, 1920–1970," in *Essays on the Crisis in Lebanon*, ed. Roger Owen (London: Ithaca, 1976), 24.
60. He served as foreign minister under Gamal Abdel Nasser from 1952 to 1964, and as prime minister and vice president of Egypt in the early 1970s.
61. Rasha Salam Khalidi, "A Non-Conformist."
62. Rasha Salam Khalidi, "A Non-Conformist."
63. Rasha Salam Khalidi, "A Non-Conformist."
64. Rasha Salam Khalidi, "A Non-Conformist."
65. Nassib Bulos, *A Palestinian Landscape* (Beirut: Arab Institute for Research & Pub., 1998), 48.
66. Wolfgang Hildesheimer, *"Die sichtbare Wirklichkeit bedeutet mir nichts": Die Briefe an die Eltern*, ed. Volker Jehle, 2 vols. (Frankfurt: Suhrkamp, 2016), 1:272 and 2:1488.
67. Rasha Salam Khalidi, "A Non-Conformist."

4. WOLFGANG HILDESHEIMER: BELATED SURREALIST AND "EXCLUSIVE GEHEIMTYP"

1. Hanna Hildesheimer, "Vier Generationen," unpublished typescript, WHA 1639, 13. See also Stephan Braese, *Jenseits der Pässe: Wolfgang Hildesheimer. Eine Biographie* (Göttingen: Wallstein, 2017), 37–39.
2. *International Biographical Dictionary of Central European Émigrés 1933–1945*, ed. Werner Röder and Herbert A. Strauss (Munich: Saur, 1999), 295.
3. Henry A. Lea, *Wolfgang Hildesheimers Weg als Jude und Deutscher* (Stuttgart: Hans-Dieter Heinz, 1997), 1.
4. Lea, *Wolfgang Hildesheimers Weg*, 2 and 13.

5. Wolfgang Hildesheimer, "Mein Judentum," in *Mein Judentum*, ed. Jürgen Schultz, (Stuttgart: Kreuz, 1978), in *Gesammelte Werke in sieben Bänden* [hereafter *GW I–VII*], ed. Christiaan Lucas Hart Nibbrig and Volker Jehle (Frankfurt: Suhrkamp, 1991), *GW VII*, 160. See also Manfred Durzak, "Ich kann über nichts anderes schreiben als über ein potentielles Ich: Gespräch mit Wolfgang Hidlesheimer," in *Gespräche über den Roman: Formbestimmungen und Analysen* (Frankfurt: Suhrkamp, 1976), 272.
6. Jennifer Jenkins, *Provincial Modernity: Local Culture and Liberal Politics in Fin-de-Siècle Hamburg* (Ithaca, NY: Cornell University Press, 2003), 129. In 1884, Leon Goldschmidt purchased the bookstore M. Glogau Jr. and set up a publishing house under the same name. He is known in particular as the publisher of Johann Kinau, known under the pen name Gorch Fock, a popular writer of regional literature. See also Hildesheimer, *"Die sichtbare Wirklichkeit bedeutet mir nichts": Die Briefe an die Eltern 1937–1962*, ed. Volker Jehle, 2 vols. (Frankfurt: Suhrkamp, 2016), 1:13.
7. Hildesheimer, "Mein Judentum," 161.
8. Hildesheimer, "Mein Judentum," 161.
9. Hildesheimer, "Mein Judentum," 160.
10. Lea, *Wolfgang Hildesheimers Weg*, 5.
11. "About Us," Adass Jisroel, Jewish Congregation Adass Yisroel, Berlin, accessed May 20, 2020, http://www.adassjisroel.de/en/. As was the case for all Jewish congregations in Germany, Adass Jisroel was deprived of its legal rights when it was included in the new Reich Association of Jews established by the Nazis in 1939. It was reinstated in 1989 and is today housed in its former location in Berlin.
12. David Ellenson, *Rabbi Esriel Hildesheimer and the Creation of a Modern Jewish Orthodoxy* (Tuscaloosa: University of Alabama Press, 1990), 108–09. See also Esriel Hildesheimer, "Die Palästinafrage und ihre Geschichte (ein Vortrag)," in *Rabbiner Dr. Israel Hildesheimer, Gesammelte Aufsätze*, ed. Meier Hildesheimer (Frankfurt: Verlag Hermon, 1923), 180–217.
13. Ellenson, *Rabbi Esriel Hildesheimer*, x.
14. See Eliav Mordechai and Esriel Hildesheimer, *Das Berliner Rabbinerseminar: Seine Gründungsgeschichte, seine Studenten*, ed. Chana Schütz and Hermann Simon, trans. Jana C. Reimer (Berlin: Hentrich and Hentrich, 2008).
15. Jehuda Reinharz, "Ideology and Structure in German Zionism, 1882–1933," *Jewish Social Studies* 42, no. 2 (1980): 122. See also Jehuda Reinharz, "The Esra Verein and Jewish Colonisation in Palestine," *Yearbook of the Leo Baeck Institute* 24 (1979): 261–89.
16. Reinharz, "Ideology and Structure," 122.
17. Abigail Green, "Rethinking Sir Moses Montefiore: Religion, Nationhood, and International Philanthropy in the Nineteenth Century," *American Historical Review* 110, no. 3 (2005): 631–58.
18. A street in today's Jerusalem located in what used to be the German Colony is named after Esriel (also Azri'el) Hildesheimer. Ronald L. Eisenberg attributes this to Hildesheimer's foundational role in Modern Orthodox Judaism, namely through the Berlin Rabbinical Seminary, as well as the Hovevei Zion (Lovers of Zion), who were instrumental in building the Batei Mahse (shelter for the needy) in the Jewish Quarter of Jerusalem's Old City. Ronald L. Eisenberg, *The Streets of Jerusalem: Who, What, Why* (Jerusalem: Devora Publishing, 2006), 200–01.

4. WOLFGANG HILDESHEIMER

19. Theodor Herzl, *The Complete Diaries of Theodor Herzl*, ed. Raphael Patai, trans. Harry Zohn (New York: Herzl, 1960), 2:447, https://archive.org/details/TheCompleteDiaries OfTheodorHerzlEngVolume3OCR/TheCompleteDiariesOfTheodorHerzlEngVolume1. See also Lea, *Wolfgang Hildesheimers Weg*, 8.
20. "Correspondenzen," *Jüdische Presse*, May 5, 1897. The article gives the title of his talk in German as "Die Aufgaben der jüdischen Wohltätigkeit in Palästina." See also Lea, *Wolfgang Hildesheimers Weg*, 8; Mordechai Breuer, *Jüdische Orthodoxe im deutschen Reich 1871–1918: Sozialgeschichte einer religiösen Minderheit* (Frankfurt: Jüdischer Verlag bei Athenäum, 1986), 328–30.
21. Hildesheimer, "Mein Judentum," 161.
22. Hanna Hildesheimer, "Vier Genrationen," 13. See also Lea, *Wolfgang Hildesheimers Weg*, 10; Braese, *Jenseits der Pässe*, 33; Central Zionist Archives, A231\227-27p, accessed May 20, 2020, http://www.zionistarchives.org.il/en/Pages/ArchiveItem.aspx?oi=09001e158143e565 &ot=cza_photo.
23. Lilo Stone, "German Zionists in Palestine Before 1933," *Journal of Contemporary History* 32, no. 2 (1997): 172. See also Miriam Rürup, *Ehrensache: Jüdische Studentenverbindungen an deutschen Universitäten 1886–1937* (Göttingen: Wallstein Verlag, 2008), 67–70.
24. Etan Bloom, *Arthur Ruppin and the Production of pre-Israeli Culture* (Leiden: Brill, 2011), 127.
25. Bloom, *Arthur Ruppin*, 121.
26. Nahum Goldman quoted in Bloom, *Arthur Ruppin*, 128.
27. Hannah Arendt and Kurt Blumenfeld, *In keinem Besitz verwurzelt: Die Korrespondenz*, ed. Ingeborg Nordmann and Iris Pilling (Berlin: Rotbuch Verlag, 1995).
28. Pnina Lahav, *Judgement in Jerusalem: Chief Justice Agranat and the Zionist Century* (Berkeley: University of California Press, 1997), 80.
29. Stone, "German Zionists in Palestine," 186.
30. Tom Segev, *The Seventh Million: The Israelis and the Holocaust*, trans. Haim Watzman (New York: Holt, 2000), 24–34; Gudrun Krämer, *A History of Palestine: From the Ottoman Conquest to the Founding of the State of Israel*, trans. Graham Harman and Gudrun Krämer (Princeton, NJ: Princeton University Press, 2008), 242.
31. Hanna Hildesheimer, "Vier Genrationen," 13.
32. Hildesheimer, "Mein Judentum," 162.
33. On the transfer of ownership of the Shemen factory, see Mustafa Abbasi and David de Vries, "Commodities and Power: Edible Oil and Soap in the History of Arab-Jewish Haifa," in *Haifa Before and After 1948: Narratives of a Mixed City*, ed. Mahmoud Yazbak and Yfaat Weiss (Dordrecht: Institute for Historical Justice and Reconciliation and Republic of Letters Publishing, 2011), 99.
34. Wolfgang Hildesheimer, "Wer zweifelt nicht," *Publik Forum* 34, quoted in Braese, *Jenseits der Pässe*, 47.
35. Hildesheimer, "Mein Judentum," 161.
36. Lea, *Wolfgang Hildesheimers Weg*, 11.
37. Hanna Hildesheimer, "Vier Generationen," 14.
38. Stone, "German Zionists in Palestine," 179.
39. Segev, *The Seventh Million*, 62.
40. Other guests on Kantstraße included Leo Motzkin, a key figure of the Jewish delegation to the 1919 Paris Peace Conference, and Paul Eppstein, a graduate of Heidelberg

University and a renowned sociologist who would become an elder in the Theresienstadt Ghetto, established by the Schutzstaffel (SS, Protection Squadron), the paramilitary troops of the *Nationalsozialistische Deutsche Arbeiterpartei* (NSDAP, National Socialist German Workers' Party), in German-occupied Czechoslovakia as both a ghetto and a concentration camp. Eppstein was shot in Theresienstadt in 1943, and his wife, Hedwig, was deported to and murdered at Auschwitz. The economist Samuel Paul Altmann and his wife, the acclaimed economist Elisabeth Altmann Hottheiner, who was one of the first women to become a university lecturer in Germany and a vocal advocate of women's rights, frequently visited the Hildesheimers in Mannheim, as did Julius Moses, a social democrat and member of the Reichstag of the Weimar Republic, who was the Hildesheimers's family doctor; he would be deported to and killed in the Theresienstadt Ghetto in 1942. See Braese, *Jenseits der Pässe*, 41.

41. Dennis Shirley, *The Politics of Progressive Education: The Odenwaldschule in Nazi Germany* (Cambridge, MA: Harvard University Press, 1992), 1 and 46. See also Edward Diller, "With Paul Geheeb from the 'Odenwaldschule' to the 'Ecole d'Humanité,'" *Journal of Educational Thought (JET)/Revue de la Pensée Éducative* 17, no. 1 (1983): 23–28.

42. A photo album containing pictures of these school productions, some with brief descriptions, is archived at the Academy of Arts in Berlin, but the pictures of *A Midsummer Night's Dream* are missing. See Hildesheimer, "*Die sichtbare Wirklichkeit*," 1:28–29; Braese, *Jenseits der Pässe*, 53.

43. Shirley, *The Politics of Progressive Education*, 78.

44. Donald K. Jones, "Book Review: *Frensham Heights, 1925–1949: A Study in Progressive Education*, by Peter Daniel, Frensham Heights, 1986," *History of Education* 18, no. 2 (2006): 167–69, https://www.tandfonline.com/doi/pdf/10.1080/0046760890180206.

45. Central Zionist Archives, A449\6, accessed May 20, 2020, http://www.zionistarchives.org.il/en/Pages/ArchiveItem.aspx?oi=0b001e158043b004&ot=cza_tik.

46. Hanna Hildesheimer to Paul Geheeb, October 7, 1933, unpublished correspondence, WHA 891.

47. Hanna Hildesheimer to Paul Geheeb, July 27, 1933, unpublished correspondence, WHA 891.

48. Quoted in Hildesheimer, "*Die sichtbare Wirklichkeit*," 1:29–30.

49. Hildesheimer, "*Die sichtbare Wirklichkeit*," 1:30; Lea, *Wolfgang Hildesheimers Weg*, 16; Braese, *Jenseits der Pässe*, 60. Two of Arnold Hildesheimer's siblings also emigrated to Palestine with their families: Henriette Hildesheimer, who would later leave a testimony about her life in Germany, published as "Erinnerungen an meine Jungend," in *Jüdisches Leben in Deutschland*, vol. 2, *Selbstzeugnisse zur Sozialgeschichte im Kaiserreich*, ed. Monika Richarz (Stuttgart: Deutsche Verlags-Anstalt, 1979), 77–86; and Esriel Erich Hildesheimer, who had been the head librarian at the Berlin Rabbinical Seminary and managed to move its library with him to Palestine in 1939. The library is today part of the Rambam (Maimonides) Library at Beit Ariela Shaar Zion Library, Tel Aviv's central public library.

50. On Rehavia, see Thomas Sparr, *Grunewald im Orient: Das deutsch-jüdische Jerusalem* (Berlin: Berenberg Verlag, 2018); Ruth Kark and Michal Oren-Nordheim, *Jerusalem and Its Environs: Quarters, Neighborhoods, Villages 1800–1948* (Jerusalem: Hebrew University Magnes Press, 2001), 168–73.

270   4. WOLFGANG HILDESHEIMER

51. Quoted in Hadara Lazar, *Out of Palestine: The Making of Modern Israel*, trans. Marsha Pomerantz (New York: Atlas, 2011), 20–21.
52. Segev, *The Seventh Million*, 34 and 50.
53. Lazar, *Out of Palestine*, 85–86.
54. Segev, *The Seventh Million*, 53.
55. Hanna Hildesheimer. "Vier Generationen," 14; Braese, *Jenseits der Pässe*, 64–65.
56. Abbasi and de Vries, "Commodities and Power," 104–05; May Seikaly, *Haifa: Transformation of a Palestinian Arab Society 1918–1939* (London: Tauris, 2002), 87 and 95.
57. Stone, "German Zionists in Palestine," 181.
58. "Fine for School Heads: ben shemen sentences commuted or reduced," *Palestine Post*, May 7, 1940; and "Farm School Heads Released: dr. Siegfried lehmann and colleagues," *Palestine Post*, May 9, 1940.
59. Quoted in Lazar, *Out of Palestine*, 86. Lazar's book was first published in Hebrew as *ha–Mandatorim: Erets Yisra'el, 1940–1948*, 2nd ed. (1990; repr., Jerusalem: Keter, 2003). Her conversations with Hildesheimer took place in English; they were then translated into Hebrew. They were translated back into English by Marsha Pomerantz and published by arrangement with the Institute for the Translation of Hebrew Literature. The English publication differs from the Hebrew text, which is quoted by Volker Jehle, based on an English transcript provided by the Institute for the Translation of Hebrew Literature titled "In and Out of Palestine, 1940–1948," in his critical edition of Hildesheimer's letters to his parents, "*Die sichtbare Wicklichkeit*," 1:37.
60. Wolfgang Hildesheimer, "*Ich werde nun schweigen*": *Gespräch mit Hans Helmut Hillrichs in der Reihe "Zeugen des Jahrhunderts*," ed. Ingo Hermann (Göttingen: Lamuv, 1993), 22–23.
61. Hildesheimer, "Mein Judentum," 160.
62. Segev, *The Seventh Million*, 61.
63. Lazar, "In and Out of Palestine," 58, quoted in Hildesheimer, "*Die sichtbare Wirklichkeit*," 1:228. See also Lazar, *Out of Palestine*, 86.
64. Wolfgang Hildesheimer, Letter to Eva Teltsch, London, 1938, WHA 661.
65. As Areej Sabbagh-Khoury argues, "Hashomer Hatzair maintained a vague commitment to the idea of binationalism," notwithstanding, it played an important "role as a colonizing force." Areej Sabbagh-Khoury, *Colonizing Palestine: The Zionist Left and the Making of the Palestinian Nakba* (Stanford, CA: Stanford University Press, 2023), 25–26. See also Joel Beinin, *Was the Red Flag Flying There? Marxist Politics and the Arab-Israeli Conflict in Egypt and Israel 1948–1965* (Berkeley: University of California Press, 1990), 24–31; Elkana Margalit, "Social and Intellectual Origins of Hashomer Hatzair Youth Movement," *Journal of Contemporary History* 4.20 (1969): 25–64.
66. Eisenberg, *The Streets of Jerusalem*, 62.
67. Hildesheimer, "*Die sichtbare Wirklichkeit*," 1:37; Lea, *Wolfgang Hildesheimers Weg*, 12; Braese, *Jenseits der Pässe*, 67.
68. "Legal Worldwide file 'Agreement with Dr. A. Hildesheimer,'" GB1752.UNI/GF/LG/1/4/120, accessed May 20, 2020, http://unilever-archives.com/Record.aspx?src=CalmView.Catalog&id=GB1752.UNI%2fGF%2fLG%2f1%2f4%2f120&pos=7. *Progress*, the magazine of Unilever, "Dr. A. Hildesheimer . . . joined the company in 1911 and held appointments, primarily connected with the production side of the margarine business,

with associated companies in Germany and Holland until 1933, in which year he went to Palestine. He is now in charge of the Unilever company, Palestine Edible Products Limited, with which he has been concerned since its formation in 1938" (*Progress* 41, no. 226 (Spring 1950): 2).

69. "Margarine Made in Palestine," *Palestine Post*, December 14, 1938.
70. Wolfgang Hildesheimer, "Die Margarinefabrik," in *GW I*, 307.
71. Abbasi and de Vries, "Commodities and Power," 104.
72. Seikaly, *Haifa*, 94 and 107.
73. Abbasi and de Vries, "Commodities and Power," 105.
74. Christina Hink, "Where East Meets West: Cultivating a Cosmopolitan London in the 1920s," *Altre Modernitsa/Otras Modernidades/Autres Modernités/Other Modernities* 20 (November 2018): 50.
75. Hildesheimer, "*Die sichtbare Wirklichkeit*," letter 5 [London, April 6, 1937], 1:40.
76. Hildesheimer, "*Die sichtbare Wirklichkeit*," letter 20 [London before June 29, 1937], 1:78.
77. Sirine Husseini Shahid, *Jerusalem Memories*, with a foreword by Edward W. Said (Beirut: Naufal, 1990).
78. Ilan Pappé, *The Rise and Fall of a Palestinian Dynasty: The Husaynis 1700–1948*, trans. Yael Lotan (Berkeley: University of California Press, 2010), 279.
79. Hildesheimer, "*Die sichtbare Wirklichkeit*," 1:131–32; Braese, *Jenseits der Pässe*, 71–74.
80. Hildesheimer, "*Die sichtbare Wirklichkeit*," letter 24 [Salzburg August 7 and 10, 1937], 1:88; letter 25 [London, after September 27, 1937], 1: 92; letter 27 [London, fall 1937], 1: 96; letter 28 [London, November 18, 1937], 1: 97; letter 31 [London, January 9, 1938], 1: 104; letter 49 [London, December 21, 1938], 1: 140.
81. Hilde Strobl, "Hildesheimers 'Zeiten in England' im Kontext des Surrealismus," in *Wolfgang Hildesheimer und England: Zur Topologie eines literarischen Transfers*, ed. Rüdiger Görner and Isabel Wagner (Bern: Peter Lang, 2012), 54. See also Braese, *Jenseits der Pässe*, 68–87.
82. Hildesheimer, "*Die sichtbare Wirklichkeit*," letter 46 [November 12, 1938], 1:130.
83. From Heine's 1821 tragedy *Almansor*, set in Granada after the fall of the Moorish Emirate to the Catholic monarchs of Spain.
84. Hildesheimer, "*Ich werde nun schweigen*," 65. See also Lea, *Wolfgang Hildesheimers Weg*, 16; Brease, *Jenseits der Pässe*, 75.
85. Hildesheimer, "*Die sichtbare Wirklichkeit*," letter 73, June 30 [1939], 1:189.
86. Hildesheimer, "*Die sichtbare Wirklichkeit*," letter 81, [August 22, 1939], 1:207.
87. Hildesheimer, "*Die sichtbare Wirklichkeit*," 1:121. In German, he writes, "Chamberlain hat sich als seiner der größten Scheisskerle der Weltgeschichte erwiesen."
88. Hildesheimer, "*Die sichtbare Wirklichkeit*," letter 60, [February 22, 1939], 1:164.
89. Hildesheimer, "*Die sichtbare Wirklichkeit*," letter 78, [August 1939], 1:201.
90. Hildesheimer, "*Die sichtbare Wirklichkeit*," letter 78, [September 1939], 1:210.
91. Christiane Niklew, "Wolf Rosenberg," and Sophie Fetthauer, "Hermann Scherchen," in *Lexikon verfolgter Musiker und Musikerinnen der NS-Zeit*, ed. Claudia Maurer Zenck, Peter Petersen, and Sophie Fetthauer (Hamburg: University of Hamburg, 2006), https://www.lexm.uni-hamburg.de/object/lexm_lexmperson_00001158.
92. Published in Hildesheimer, *GW VII*, 547. See also Braese, *Jenseits der Pässe*, 84–85.

93. "Social and Personal," *Palestine Post*, December 4, 1941.
94. Daniella Ohad Smith, "Hotel Design in British Mandate Palestine: Modernism and the Zionist Vision," *Journal of Israeli History* 29, no. 1 (2010): 109.
95. Walid Khalidi, "The Fall of Haifa Revisited," *Journal of Palestine Studies* 37, no. 3 (2008): 30–58. The article was originally published in *Middle East Forum* in 1959. See also Benny Morris, *The Birth of the Palestinian Refugee Problem Revisited* (Cambridge: Cambridge University Press, 2004), 197.
96. Walid Khalidi, "Plan Dalet Master: Plan for the Conquest of Palestine," *Journal of Palestine Studies* 18, no. 1 (1988): 4–33. The article was originally published in *Middle East Forum* in 1961.
97. Hildesheimer, "*Die sichtbare Wirklichkeit*," letter 88, [24 May 1940], 1:218–20.
98. Hildesheimer, "*Die sichtbare Wirklichkeit*," letter 88, [24 May 1940], 1:219.
99. Hildesheimer, "*Die sichtbare Wirklichkeit*," letter 88, [24 May 1940], 1:220.
100. Segev, *The Seventh Million*, 68.
101. Yoni Furas, *Educating Palestine: Teaching and Learning History Under the Mandate* (Oxford: Oxford University Press, 2020), 73–74.
102. "Correspondence Between Eliahu Epstein, Chaim Weizmann, and Harry S. Truman, with related material, May 14, 1948. Confidential file, Truman Papers," Harry S. Truman Library and Museum, Presidential Libraries, U.S. National Archives and Records Administration, accessed May 20, 2020, https://www.trumanlibrary.gov/library/research-files/correspondence-between-eliahu-epstein-chaim-weizmann-and-harry-s-truman.
103. Hildesheimer, "*Die sichtbare Wirklichkeit*," letter 89, [1940/1941], 1:223.
104. Hildesheimer, "*Die sichtbare Wirklichkeit*," letter 89, [1940/1941], 1:222. In German, he says, "Auch Tel Aviv habe ich zum Kotzen satt."
105. Reviewed by Th. F. M. under the title "The Judean Landscape" in *Palestine Post*, December 27, 1939.
106. "Reginald Reggie Weston," Historica Accents, accessed May 20, 2020, https://historicaccents.com/products/10129-vtg-reginald-regie-weston-watercolor-abstract-israeli-french-british-modernism.
107. These ads appeared in the *Palestine Post*, August 20, 1941.
108. *Palestine Post*, June 7, 1940, and February 16, 1945, published in Hildesheimer, "*Die sichtbare Wirklichkeit*," 1:247 and 1:261. As Jehle points out, the name "Wolf" is written in the shading of the woman's left shoulder, next to the year 1869.
109. Th. F. M., "Chartres in Jerusalem," *Palestine Post*, January 17, 1940.
110. Hildesheimer, "*Die sichtbare Wirklichkeit*," 1:222.
111. Sperling also reviewed one of these exhibitions, this time positively. Th. F. M., "Subjective Painting," *Palestine Post*, July 2, 1941.
112. Olivia Manning, "Five Modern Artists," *Palestine Post*, December 23, 1942. See also Hildesheimer, "*Die sichtbare Wirklichkeit*," 1:266.
113. Gear (1915–1997) was a Scottish abstract painter who served with the Royal Corps of Signals in Egypt, Palestine, Syria, and Cyprus, before participating in the Allied invasion of Italy. "Artist Biography: William Gear," Tate, accessed May 20, 2020, https://www.tate.org.uk/art/artists/william-gear-1146.
114. Before leaving his native Romania for Palestine in 1941, Janco (1895–1984) had gained significant recognition for his contributions to a range of avant-garde movements, from

Art Nouveau to Futurism, Cubism, Expressionism, Constructivism, and Dadaism, and as a founding member, along with Hans Arp, Hugo Ball, and Tristan Tzara, of the Cabaret Voltaire in Zurich. Tom Sandqvist, *Dada East: The Romanians of Cabaret Voltaire* (Cambridge, MA: MIT Press, 2005).

115. Lehmann (1903–1977), who had left Berlin for Haifa in 1933, worked primarily in wood sculpture and ceramics. A former Haganah fighter, he founded, along with Janco and other Jewish artists, the Ein Hod Artist Village, which was established in 1953 in the southern Carmel hills on the ruins of Ayn Hawd, an Arab village that had been depopulated when the Haganah attacked Haifa's Arab quarter. "Rudolf (Rudi) Lehmann," The Israel Museum, accessed May 20, 2020, https://web.archive.org/web/20140813195201/http://www.imj.org.il/artcenter/default.asp?artist=280437; and "Ayn Hawd and 'the Unrecognized Villages,'" *Journal of Palestine Studies* 31 (2001/2002): 39, https://oldwebsite.palestine-studies.org/jps/abstract/40984.

116. Hildesheimer, "*Ich werde nun schweigen*," 64–65. Brandt had studied medicine in Berlin, Freiburg, and Heidelberg, and then trained in psychotherapy with Eitington in Berlin. Like Eitington, she left Germany for Palestine in 1933. Braese, *Jenseits der Pässe*, 95.

117. Hartmut Buchholz, "... ich wäre mir ohne sie gar nicht denkbar": Wolfgang Hildesheimer und die Psychoanalyse," *Luzifer-Amor: Zeitschrift zur Geschichte der Psychoanalyse* 41 (2008): 142.

118. Manfred Vogel, ed., *Ariel—ein Almanach fuer Literatur-Graphik-Musik* (Jerusalem: Junge Dichtung, 1941), 38; Hildesheimer, *GW VII*, 547.

119. In German, it reads "erötisch außergewöhnlich dunkel Schönen," in Walter Lovis Arie Sternheim Goral, *Um Mitternacht* (Hamburg: Neue Presse, 1983), 81, quoted in Hildesheimer, "*Die sichtbare Wirklichkeit*," 1:232.

120. "Social and Personal," *Palestine Post*, May 6, 1942.

121. Hildesheimer, "*Die sichtbare Wirklichkeit*," 1:244. Bella Soskin later married a British officer with whom she moved to Nairobi and then England.

122. Walid Khalidi, ed., *All That Remains: The Palestinian Villages Occupied and Depopulated by Israel in 1948* (Washington, DC: Institute for Palestine Studies, 1992), 13, 19, 28, 32, 34; Morris, *The Birth of the Palestinian Refugee Problem*, 252–54; and Mustafa Abbasi, "The Fall of Acre in the 1948 Palestine War," *Journal of Palestine Studies* 39, no. 4 (2010): 1–22.

123. "Nahariya's Early Years 1934–1949," Lieberman House—Museum of the History of Nahariya, accessed May 20, 2020, http://museum.rutkin.info/en/node/27.

124. "Soskin, Selig Eugen," *Encyclopaedia Judaica*, ed. Joseph Ben-Shlomo and Michael Denman, accessed May 20, 2020, https://www.encyclopedia.com.

125. Hildesheimer, "*Die sichtbare Wirklichkeit*," 1:244. Braese echoes Hildesheimer's silence, referring to Soskin's agricultural projects but not the politics that went hand in hand with them in *Jenseits der Pässe*, 106–07.

126. Wolfgang Hildesheimer, Letter to Rasha Khalidi, Poschiavo, April 8, 1984, WHA 1642.

127. See "George Rais," MyHeritage, accessed October 12, 2023, https://www.myheritage.com/names/george_rais.

128. *A Survey of Palestine: Prepared in December 1945 and January 1946 for the Information of the Anglo-American Committee of Inquiry*, 2 vols. and supplement (Jerusalem: Government Printer, 1946–47; reproduced facsimile, Washington, DC: Institute for Palestine Studies, 1991), 2:1056.

4. WOLFGANG HILDESHEIMER

129. See in particular Waleed Karkabi and Adi Roitenberg, "Arab-Jewish Architectural Partnership in Haifa During the Mandate Period: Qaraman and Gerstel Meet on the 'Seam Line,'" in *Haifa Before and After 1948: Narratives of a Mixed City*, ed. Mahmoud Yazbak and Yfaat Weiss (Dordrecht: Institute for Historical Justice and Reconciliation and Republic of Letters, 2011), 49.

130. Tawfiq Canaan (1882–1964) was at the center of what Salim Tamari calls "Canaan's circle," a group of Palestinian Arab nativist anthropologists that included Stephan Hanna Stephan, Afif Bulos's coauthor of travel guides. Salim Tamari, "Lepers, Lunatics and Saints: The Nativist Ethnography of Tawfiq Canaan and His Circle," in *Mountain Against the Sea: Essays on Palestinian Society and Culture* (Berkeley: University of California Press, 2009), 93–112. See also Vera Tamari, "Tawfik Canaan—Collectionneur par Excellence: The Story Behind the Palestinian Amulet Collection at Birzeit University," in *Archives, Museums and Collecting Practices in the Modern Arab World*, ed. Sonja Mejcher-Atassi and John Pedro Schwartz (Farnham: Ashgate, 2012), 71–90; Philippe Bourmoud, "'A Son of the Country': Dr. Tawfiq Canaan, Modernist Physician and Palestinian Ethnographer," in *Struggle and Survival in Palestine/Israel*, ed. Mark LeVine and Gershon Shafir (Berkeley: University of California Press, 2012), 104–24; Khaled Nashef, "Tawfiq Canaan: His Life and Work," *Jerusalem Quarterly* 16 (2002): 12–26; Ya'qub al-'Awdat, *Min a'lam al-fikr wal-adab fi Filastin* (Jordan: Jam'iyyat 'ummal al-matabi' al-ta'awuniyya, 1976), 547–50; and "Tawfiq Canaan," *Interactive Encyclopedia of the Palestine Question*, accessed May 28, 2023, https://www.palquest.org/en/biography/14283/tawfiq-canaan.

131. Braese, *Jenseits der Pässe*, 115.

132. In 1955, Assem Salam, Theo Canaan and Georges Rais designed the Pan-American building, a landmark of modernist architecture in Beirut. Canaan died young, but Salam and Rais became famed architects in Lebanon who for many years taught at the American University of Beirut. See "Rayes, George," al-Hakawati, A Digital Public Library of Arab and Islamic Culture, accessed February 18, 2019, http://al-hakawati.net/en_architectures/ArchitectureDetails/272/Rayes,-Georges.

133. Hildesheimer, "*Die sichtbare Wirklichkeit*," 1:275.

134. After the war, Malvina married a third time—the American diplomat Malcolm P. Hooper, with whom she lived in Italy and the United States, before retiring in England.

135. Wasif Jawhariyyeh lists him among other of Jerusalem's well-known figures who attended a musical evening he hosted, recalling a photograph of the group "showing an intoxicated Reverend Hanania who has taken off his cap and placed it beside him on the table." In Wasif Jawhariyyeh, *The Storyteller of Jerusalem: The Life and Times of Wasif Jawhariyyeh, 1904–1948*, ed. Salim Tamari and Issam Nassar, trans. Nada Elzeer (Northampton, MA: Olive Branch, 2014), 111.

136. Pruen had served as a soldier in World War II, and then joined the British Colonial Service in Palestine. The couple moved to Beirut, where Pruen worked as director of personnel and administration at the United Nations Relief and Works Agency for Palestine Refugees until the outbreak of the Lebanese Civil War in 1975, when he and Sally left for Amman, and then Winchester, England. Email correspondence with Emma and Matthew Pruen, April 2 and 3, 2021.

137. Hildesheimer, "*Die sichtbare Wirklichkeit*," 1:239.
138. Hildesheimer, "*Die sichtbare Wirklichkeit*," 1:266–67. See also Sperling's review of "Macbeth in Jerusalem" *Palestine Post*, May 5, 1943; May 28, 1943; and June 2, 1943.
139. *A Survey of Palestine*, 2:876.
140. Holme worked as Public Information Officer in Palestine from 1938 to 1946. See his obituary in *The Times*, July 13, 1991; see also Mitchel Roth, ed., *Encyclopedia of War Journalism*, 2nd ed. (London: Grey House, 2010), 171–72.
141. H. Christopher Holme, *Portrait* (Oxford: Text and Graphica, 1992), 12. Taylor Institution Library, University of Oxford, Box MS.Fol.G29.
142. Quoted in Lazar, *Out of Palestine*, 58.
143. Hildesheimer, "*Die sichtbare Wiklichkeit*," letter 88, [after May 24, 1940], 1:219.
144. Hildesheimer, "*Die sichtbare Wiklichkeit*," letter 90, [1943], 1:240. Jehle dates the letter to 1940/1941, but given its reference to the war in Italy, I think it was written in or after September 1943. See also Braese, *Jenseits der Pässe*, 109–10.
145. My inquiries at the UK National Archives in Kew led to no results.
146. In the brochure of the premiere of his play *Die Verspätung* (The delay) at the Kammerspiele Düsseldorf in 1961/1962, quoted in Hildesheimer "*Die sichtbare Wirklichkeit*," 1:239.
147. In the brochure of the Bremen Literature Prize awarded to Hildesheimer for his novel *Tynset* in 1966, Taylor Institution Library, University of Oxford, Box MS.Fol.G29.
148. Hildesheimer, "*Ich werde nun schweigen*," 24.
149. Quoted in Hildesheimer, "*Die sichtbare Wirklichkeit*," 1:239–40.
150. Hildesheimer, "*Ich werde nun schweigen*," 24. See also Hildesheimer's letter to German writer Heinrich Böll, written in 1953, in Wolfgang Hildesheimer, *Briefe*, ed. Silvia Hildesheimer and Dietmar Pleyer (Frankfurt: Suhrkamp, 1999), 39.
151. "Social and Personal," *Palestine Post*, May 3, 1946.
152. *Radio Week*, May 3, 1946, in *GW VII*, 273–275. Other publications included a translation of Stefan George's poem "Das Jahr der Seele" (*Forum*, March 17, 1944) and reviews of concerts, exhibitions, and plays, written between August and November 1946 from London, listed in Hildesheimer, "*Die sichtbare Wirklichkeit*," 2:1435–36.
153. Lazar, "In and Out of Palestine," 58, quoted in Hildesheimer, "*Die sichtbare Wirklichkeit*," 1: 228.
154. Lazar, "In and Out of Palestine," 59, quoted in Hildesheimer, "*Die sichtbare Wirklichkeit*," 1: 228.
155. Walid Khalidi in conversations with the author, Cambridge, MA, October 31, 2018.
156. Lazar, "In and Out of Palestine," 58–61, quoted in Hildesheimer, "*Die sichtbare Wirklichkeit*," 1:230 and 236–37. See, in parts, also Lazar, *Out of Palestine*, 83 and 87.
157. Lazar, "In and Out of Palestine, 1940–1948," 61–62, quoted in Hildesheimer, "*Die sichtbare Wirklichkeit*," 1:237.
158. Matiel E. T. Mogannam, *The Arab Woman and the Palestine Problem* (London: H. Joseph, 1937). See also Ellen L. Fleischmann, *The Nation and Its "New" Women: The Palestinian Women's Movement, 1920–1948* (Berkeley: University of California Press, 2003), 137, and "Matiel Mogannam," *Interactive Encyclopedia of the Palestine Question*, accessed May 28, 2023, https://www.palquest.org/en/biography/30018/matiel-mogannam.
159. Lazar, "In and Out of Palestine," page number not provided, quoted in Hildesheimer, "*Die sichtbare Wirklichkeit*," 1:233.

4. WOLFGANG HILDESHEIMER

160. Born in Budapest and educated in Vienna, he left for Palestine in 1926, and subsequently ran the office of Jabotinsky's Revisionist Party in Berlin, before he returned to Jerusalem as Middle East correspondent for the Berlin-based Ullstein Verlag in the late 1920s, which published a range of newspapers and periodicals in addition to books. Not mastering Hebrew well enough to embark on a journalistic career and find a place for himself in the Yishuv, he returned to Europe, where he joined Germany's Communist Party. In late 1933, he became a member of the Institute for the Study of Fascism (Institut Pour l'Étude du Fascisme), a Communist front organization, in Paris, where he likely met Walter Benjamin. Benjamin's essay "The Author as Producer" was written in spring 1934 to be presented as an address at the institute. A few years later, Benjamin wrote a detailed commentary to Koestler's 1937 *Spanish Testament*, which describes Koestler's experiences in the Spanish Civil War as a reporter and a prisoner sentenced to death by General Franco's Nationalist forces. See Susie Linfield, "Arthur Koestler: The Zionist and Anti-Semite," in *The Lions' Den: Zionism and the Left from Hannah Arendt to Noam Chomsky* (New Haven, CT: Yale University Press, 2019), 80–110; Michael Scammell, *Koestler: The Literary and Political Odyssey of a Twentieth-Century Skeptic* (New York: Random House, 2009), 62–63, 112–13, and 150; and Howard Eiland and Michael W. Jennings, *Walter Benjamin: A Critical Life* (Cambridge, MA: Belknap Press of Harvard University Press, 2014), 439.
161. Weizman quoted in Louis A. Gordon, "Arthur Koestler and His Ties to Zionism and Jabotinsky," *Studies in Zionism* 12, no. 2 (1991): 160.
162. Gordon, "Arthur Koestler," 163.
163. In Lazar, *Out of Palestine*, 86–87.
164. Hildesheimer, "*Die sichtbare Wirklichkeit*," letter 125, February 14, [1948], 369, and letter 128, March 30 [1948], 1:377.
165. Hildesheimer, "*Die sichtbare Wirklichkeit*," letter 102, [July 10, 1947], 1:271 and 1:311.
166. Wolfgang Hildesheimer, Letter to Eva and Ernst Teltsch, London, July 18, 1946, WHA 662.
167. Hildesheimer, "*Die sichtbare Wirklichkeit*," letter 102, [July 10, 1947], 1:271 and 1:273. See also Hilde Strobl, *Wolfgang Hildesheimer und die bildende Kunst: "Und mache mir ein Bild aus vergangener Möglichkeit"* (Berlin: Dietrich Reimer Verlag, 2013), 246, and Strobl, "Hildesheimers 'Zeiten in England,' " 56.
168. Wolfgang Hildesheimer, "Cornish Summer: Holiday-Makers Paradise," *Palestine Post*, October 23, 1946. See also Hildesheimer, "*Die sichtbare Wirklichkeit*," 1:273.
169. Hildesheimer, "The End of Fiction," in *GW VII*, 131. See also Hildesheimer, *Zeiten in Cornwall*, in *GW I*, 339–406; J. J. Long, "Time/Travel: Wolfgang Hildesheimer's Zeiten in Cornwall," in *Wolfgang Hildesheimer und England*, 17–30; and Karin Preuß, "Zwischen Wahrheit und Fiktion: Wolfgang Hidlesheimer in *Zeiten in Cornwall* und in seinen Briefen," in *Wolfgang Hildesheimer und England*, 31–52.
170. Hildesheimer, *Zeiten in Cornwall*, 406.
171. Hildesheimer, "*Ich werde nun schweigen*," 26.
172. Philippe Sands, "Nuremberg Trials Interpreter Siegfried Ramler: 'The Things We Saw Were Shocking,'" *Guardian*, October 22, 2014. See also Siegfried Ramler, *Nuremberg and Beyond: The Memoirs of Siegfried Ramler from 20th Century Europe to Hawai'i* (Hawaii: Islander Group, 2009).

173. Uwe Neumahr, *Das Schloss der Schriftsteller: Nürnberg '46: Treffen am Abgrund* (Munich: Beck, 2023), 8 and 17.
174. Neumahr, *Das Schloss*, 239.
175. Hildesheimer, "Mein Judentum," 163–64.
176. Wolfgang Hildesheimer, Letter to Eva Teltsch, Nuremberg, 1947, WHA 662.
177. For instance, in Hildesheimer, "*Die sichtbare Wirklichkeit*," letter 92, February 5, [1947], 278.
178. Hildesheimer, "*Die sichtbare Wirklichkeit*," letter 105, August 5, [1947], 1:317–18.
179. Hildesheimer, "*Die sichtbare Wirklichkeit*," letter 116, November 5, [1947], 1:346.
180. Hildesheimer, "*Die sichtbare Wirklichkeit*," letter 119, December 7, [1947], 1:354.
181. Hildesheimer, "*Die sichtbare Wirklichkeit*," letter 129, April 7, [1948], 1:379.
182. Hildesheimer, "*Die sichtbare Wirklichkeit*," letter 130, May 18, [1948], 1:383.
183. J.B.S. Jardine, Letter to Wolfgang Hildesheimer, London, April 15, 1949, unpublished correspondence, WHA 482.

5. JABRA IBRAHIM JABRA: "SPARK-PLUG" OF THE YMCA ARTS CLUB

1. Issa J. Boullata, *The Bells of Memory: A Palestinian Boyhood in Jerusalem* (Montreal: Linda Leith, 2004), 62–63. See also Issa J. Boullata, *Nafidha 'ala al-hadatha: Dirasat fi adab Jabra Ibrahim Jabra* (Beirut: al-Mu'assasa al-'arabiyya lil-dirasat wal-nashr, 2002), and Issa J. Boullata, "Living with the Tigress and the Muses: An Essay on Jabra Ibrahim Jabra," *World Literature Today* 72, no. 2 (2001): 214–23.
2. Sonja Mejcher-Atassi, "In Search of Jabra Ibrahim Jabra between Historical Figure and Literary Persona: On (Auto)Biographical Writing," paper presented at the workshop "Imagining the Future: The Arab World in the Aftermath of Revolution" organized by the Arab Fund for Arts and Culture in Berlin, June 9–10, 2018.
3. Ami Ayalon, *Reading Palestine: Printing and Literacy 1900–1948* (Austin: University of Texas, 2004), 16–17.
4. Elias Khoury, "Atlal al-bi'r al-thaniyya," *Mulhaq An-Nahar*, April 19, 2010. See also Majed al-Samarrai, "Dhakira thaqafiyya tunhar ma'a tafjir darat Jabra Ibrahim Jabra," *al-Hayat*, April 15, 2010.
5. Anthony Shadid, "In Baghdad Ruins, Remains of a Cultural Bridge," *New York Times*, May 22, 2010.
6. Jabra Ibrahim Jabra, *al-Bi'r al-ula: Fusul min sira dhatiyya* [1987], 2nd ed. (Beirut: al-Mu'assasa al-'arabiyya lil-dirasat wal-nashr, 1993), translated as *The First Well: A Bethlehem Boyhood*, trans. Issa J. Boullata (Fayetteville: University of Arkansas Press, 1995), xiii.
7. Jabra, *The First Well*, xvi–xvii.
8. Ahmad Dahbour, "Jabra Ibrahim Jabra," *Diwan al-'arab*, September 13, 2006, https://www.diwanalarab.com/جبرا-إبراهيم-جبرا.
9. Benny Morris and Dror Ze'evi, *The Thirty-Year Genocide: Turkey's Destruction of Its Christian Minorities, 1894–1924* (Cambridge, MA: Harvard University Press, 2019). See also David Gaunt, *Massacres, Resistance, Protectors: Muslim-Christian Relations in Eastern Anatolia During World War I* (Piscataway, NJ: Gorgias, 2006).
10. Mark Levene, "Harbingers of Jewish and Palestinian Disasters: European Nation-State Building and Its Toxic Legacies, 1912–1948," in Bashir Bashir and Amos Goldberg, ed. *The Holocaust and the Nakba: A New Grammar of Trauma and History* (New York: Columbia

University Press, 2019), 45. See also Eugene Rogan, *The Fall of the Ottomans: The Great War in the Middle East* (New York: Basic Books, 2015), 159–84.
11. Alexander Schölch, *Palestine in Transformation, 1856–1882: Studies in Social, Economic and Political Development* trans. William C. Young and Michael C. Gerrity (Washington, DC: Institute for Palestine Studies, 2006), 38. See also Adnan Musallam, "Bethlehem, Palestine Under the British (1917–23)," *Bethlehem University Journal* 3 (1984): 15–31.
12. Issa J. Boullata, "Jabrā, Jabrā Ibrāhīm," *Encyclopedia of Islam*, Three, ed. Kate Fleet et al., 2014, http://dx.doi.org/10.1163/1573-3912_ei3_COM_27617.
13. Issa J. Boullata in conversations with the author, Montreal, April 8, 2013.
14. Angelika Neuwirth, "Jabrā Ibrāhīm Jabrā's Autobiography, *al-Bi'r al-ūlā* and His Concept of a Celebration of Life," in *Writing the Self: Autobiographical Writing in Modern Arabic Literature*, ed. Robin Ostle, Ed de Moor, and Stefan Wild (London: Saqi Books, 1998), 115. As Neuwirth says, Jabra's first autobiography, *The First Well*, should be read in connection with his collected essays, published at around the same time as *A Celebration of Life: Essays on Literature and Art* (Baghdad: Dar al-Ma'mun, 1988) in a limited English-language edition on the occasion of the Mirbad Festival of Modern Arabic Poetry in Baghdad in 1988. The original Arabic-language version of the essays, and in one case the translation into Arabic, was published as *al-Fann wal-hulm wal-fi'al* (Baghdad: Dar al-Ma'mun, 1986; Beirut: al-Mu'assasa al-'arabiyya lil-dirasat wal-nashr, 1988).
15. Rashid Khalidi, *Palestinian Identity: The Construction of Modern National Consciousness*, 2nd ed. (New York: Columbia University Press, 2010), 19–20.
16. William Tamplin, "The Other Wells: Family History and the self-Creation of Jabra Ibrahim Jabra," *Jerusalem Quarterly* 85 (2011): 30–60.
17. Walid Khalidi in conversations with the author, Cambridge, MA, October 29–31, 2018.
18. Jabra, *The First Well*, 120.
19. Jabra, *The First Well*, 120, 139.
20. Paul Adalian Rouben, "Adana Massacre (1909)," *Historical Dictionary of Armenia* (London: Scarecrow Press, 2010), 70–71.
21. Jabra, *The First Well*, 140.
22. Rashid Khalidi, *Palestinian Identity*, 162.
23. Suja Sawafta, "Origin Stories: Tracing Jabra and Munif's childhoods in Bethlehem and Amman," *Arablit and Arablit Quarterly*, December 2022, https://arablit.org/2022/12/14/origin-stories-tracing-jabra-and-munifs-childhoods-in-bethlehem-and-amman/?fbclid=IwAR1V_k6eCs3FbEidXufHvWmu9VoOQeAvc8Ae1j_RhdEnd1JnlgXQ1_3tFWk.
24. Jabra, *The First Well*, 58.
25. Jabra, *The First Well*, 59–60.
26. Jabra, *The First Well*, 63.
27. Jabra, *The First Well*, 39.
28. Jabra, *The First Well*, 40.
29. Ayalon, *Reading Palestine*, 31; Neuwirth, "Jabrā," 116–17.
30. Jabra, *The First Well*, 47.
31. Jabra, *The First Well*, 53.
32. Jabra, *The First Well*, 124–31.

33. Jabra, *The First Well*, 108.
34. Rashid Khalidi, *Palestinian Identity*, 173–74.
35. Rochelle Davis, "Commemorating Education: Recollections of the Arab College in Jerusalem, 1918–1948," *Comparative Studies of South Asia, Africa, and the Middle East* 23, no. 1–2 (2003): 192, and "Growing Up Palestinian in Jerusalem Before 1948: Childhood Memories of Communal Life, Education, and Political Awareness," in *Jerusalem Interrupted: Modernity and Colonial Transformation 1917–Present*, ed. Lena Jayyusi (Northampton, MA: Olive Branch, 2015), 195.
36. A. L. Tibawi, *Arab Education in Mandatory Palestine: A Study of Three Decades of British Administration* (London: Luzac, 1956), 51.
37. Tibawi, *Arab Education*, 245–46.
38. Sadiq Ibrahim 'Odeh, "The Arab College in Jerusalem, 1918–1948: Recollections," *Jerusalem Quarterly* 9 (2000): 49.
39. 'Odeh, "The Arab College," 51.
40. 'Odeh, "The Arab College," 53–54.
41. Gudrun Krämer, *A History of Palestine: From the Ottoman Conquest to the Founding of the State of Israel*, trans. Graham Harman and Gudrun Krämer (Princeton, NJ: Princeton University Press, 2008), 267.
42. Jabra, *The First Well*, 185.
43. Jabra Ibrahim Jabra, "al-Ghramufun," in *'Araq wa-qisas ukhra* (Beirut: Dar al-Ahliyya, 1956), translated as "The Gramophone," in *Modern Arabic Short Stories*, ed. Denys Johnson-Davies, trans. Denys Johnson-Davies (London: Heinemann, 1976), 146–59. See also Ayalon, *Reading Palestine*, 103–08.
44. Jabra Ibrahim Jabra, "Shakespeare and I," in *A Celebration of Life*, 142. See also Margaret Litvin, *Hamlet's Arab Journey: Shakespeare's Prince and Nasser's Ghost* (Princeton, NJ: Princeton University Press, 2011), 30.
45. Such as Jan Kott's *Shakespeare Our Contemporary* (1974) which was published as *Shakespeare—mu'asiruna* by Dar al-Rashid in Baghdad in 1979. Jabra's translation of *Hamlet* was published by Dar majallat *Shi'r* in Beirut in 1960. His translations of Shakespeare's major plays and sonnets were issued in various publications, among them *al-Ma'asi al-kubra* (Beirut: al-Mu'assasa al-'arabiyya lil-dirasat wal-nashr, 1990).
46. "Successful 'Metric' Candidates of the Palestine Matriculation Examination," *Palestine Post*, August 18, 1937.
47. Salma Khadra Jayyusi, "Introduction: Palestinian Literature in Modern Times," in *Anthology of Modern Palestinian Literature*, ed. Salma Khadra Jayyusi (New York: Columbia University Press, 1995), 7–16.
48. Ishaq Musa al-Husseini, "al-Hayat al-adabiyya fi Filastin," *al-Adib*, May 1945, 47, quoted in Ibrahim M. Abdu and Refqa Abu-Remaileh, "A Literary Nahda Interrupted: Pre-Nakba Palestinian Literature as Adab Maqalat," *Journal of Palestine Studies* 51, no. 3 (2022): 23. A number of Jabra's short stories were published in *al-Amali*, among them "Ibnat al-sama,' " *al-Amali* 1, no. 44 (1939): 18–24, and *al-Amali* 1, no. 45 (1939): 20–25; "al-Hubb wal-junun," *al-Amali* 2, no. 9 (1939), 6–7; "Ghamra la tanjali," *al-Amali* 2, no. 13 (1940): 18–21, and *al-Amali* 2, no. 14 (1940): 13–15.
49. Abdu and Abu-Remaileh, "A Literary Nahda Interrupted," 36.

50. On the importance of translation in global modernism, see in particular Gayle Rogers, "Translation," in *A New Vocabulary for Global Modernism*, ed. Eric Hayot and Rebecca L. Walkowitz (New York: Columbia University Press, 2016), 248–62.
51. Emile Zola, "La Fée amoureuse," in *Contes à Ninon* (Paris: Hetzel et Lacroix, 1864), translated as "Rain Mines," in *Stories for Ninon*, trans. Edward Vizetelly (London: William Heinemann, 1895), and translated as "Jinniyyat al-gharam," trans. Jabra Ibrahim Jabra, *al-Hilal*, May 1, 1938: 805–08. Jabra probably translated from the English translation as the title of his rendition into Arabic suggests.
52. André Maurois, *Ariel ou la vie de Shelley* (Paris: Emile Paul Frères, 1924), translated as *Ariel: The Life of Shelley*, trans. Ella D'Arcy (New York: Appleton, 1924), and translated as "Qissat hayat Shelley: Ariel,", trans. Jabra Ibrahim Jabra, *al-Amali* 1, no. 15 (1938) to 33 (1939). Jabra probably translated from the English translation by D'Arcy.
53. Bashir Abu-Manneh, *The Palestinian Novel: From 1948 to the Present* (Cambridge: Cambridge University Press, 2016), 41.
54. Oscar Wilde, "al-Bulbul wal-warda," *al-Amali* 51, no. 1 (1939): 24–26; George Moore, "al-'Ashiq," *al-Amali* 52, no. 1 (1939): 23–25.
55. Taha Hussein, *Mustaqbal al-thaqafa fil-Misr*, 2 vols. (Cairo: Matba'at al-ma'arif, 1938), translated as *The Future of Culture in Egypt*, trans. Sidney Glazer (Washington, DC: American Council for Learned Societies, 1954); Albert Hourani, *Arabic Thought in the Liberal Age 1798–1939*, 9th ed. (1962; repr., Cambridge: Cambridge University Press, 1993), 328–29.
56. Sati al-Husri, "Hawl kitab *Mustaqbal al-thaqafa fil-Missr*," *al-Risalah*, vol. 7 (1939): 316–21. See also William L. Cleaveland, *The Making of an Arab Nationalist: Ottomanism and Arabism in the Life and Thought of Sati' al-Husri* (Princeton, NJ: Princeton University Press, 1971), 136–38.
57. Jabra Ibrahim Jabra, "Arab Language and Culture," in *The Middle East: A Handbook*, ed. Michael Adams (New York: Praeger, 1971), 177.
58. Jabra, "Arab Language and Culture," 178.
59. Jabra Ibrahim Jabra, *Shari' al-amirat: Fusul min sira dhatiyya* (London: Riyad El Rayyes, 1996), translated as *Princesses' Street: Baghdad Memories*, trans. Issa J. Boullata (Fayetteville: University of Arkansas Press, 2005), 6.
60. Jabra, *Princesses' Street*, 15–17.
61. Email correspondence with Alice Millea, Assistant Keeper of Oxford University Archives, Bodleian Library, February 26, 2018.
62. John Cleaver, ed., *Fitzwilliam: The First 150 Years of a Cambridge College*, with a foreword by David Starkey (London: Third Millennium, 2013). Many of Fitzwilliam's students from India were at the forefront of India's independence movement, among them Subhas Chandra Bose and Joseph Baptista.
63. A few letters written by Jabra as a student to Shire, relating to his studies, are held in the archives of Fitzwilliam College.
64. Held at the archives of Fitzwilliam College.
65. Email correspondence with Jacqueline Cox, Keeper of the University Archives, Cambridge University Library, February 26, 2018; source: UA Graduati 12/123.
66. Jabra, *Princesses' Street*, 16–17.
67. Jabra, *Princesses' Street*, 24–33.

68. Jabra, *The First Well*, 156–57.
69. Walid Khalidi in conversations with the author, Cambridge, MA, October 29, 2018.
70. Ussama Makdisi, *Age of Coexistence: The Ecumenical Frame and the Making of the Modern Arab World* (Oakland: University of California Press, 2019), 156–59. The notion of the Assyrian Affair was reinforced in "The Assyrian Affair of 1933 (I)" and "The Assyrian Affair of 1933 (II)" by Khaldun S. Husri, the son of Arab nationalist Sati al-Husri, published in *International Journal of Middle East Studies* 5, no. 2 (1974): 161–76 and *International Journal of Middle East Studies* 5, no. 3 (1974): 344–60. On the Assyrians in Iraq, see also Sargon George Donabed, *Reforging a Forgotten History: Iraq and the Assyrians in the Twentieth Century* (Edinburgh: Edinburgh University Press, 2015); and Sami Zubaida, "Contested Nations: Iraq and the Assyrians," *Nation and Nationalism* 6 (2000): 363–82.
71. Makdisi, *Age of Coexistence*, 159.
72. Elizabeth F. Thompson, *How the West Stole Democracy from the Arabs: The Syrian Arab Congress of 1920 and the Destruction of Its Historic Liberal-Islamic Alliance* (New York: Atlantic Monthly, 2020), 323.
73. Walid Khalidi in conversations with the author, Cambridge, MA, October 29, 2018. The gramophone is also mentioned in Jabra's short story "al-Ghramufun," quoted earlier (see note 43). Jabra gives a description of the house and the walks he took from it to school and into the city's different neighborhoods in "al-Quds: al-zaman al-mujassad," in *al-Rihla al-thamina* (Beirut: al-Maktaba al-'assriyya, 1968), 155–76, translated as "Jerusalem: Time Embodied," in *The Open Veins of Jerusalem*, ed. Munir Akash, trans. Issa J. Boullata, 2nd ed. (Arlington, MA: Jusoor, 2005), 245–65.
74. Tarif Khalidi in conversations with the author, Beirut, January 14, 2019.
75. Jabra, "Jerusalem: Time Embodied," 248–50.
76. Quoted in Rochelle Davis, "The Growth of the Western Communities, 1917–1948," in *Jerusalem 1948: The Arab Neighbourhoods and their Fate in the War*, ed. Salim Tamari (Jerusalem: Institute for Jerusalem Studies, 1999), 57–58.
77. "General Files. Annual and periodic reports, 1924–1945, 1947–1948." Box 18, Folder 8. Records of YMCA International Work in Palestine and Israel, Kautz Family YMCA Archives, University of Minnesota.
78. Hala Sakakini, *Jerusalem and I: A Personal Record* (Jerusalem: Habesch, 1987), 81–82.
79. Ayalon, *Reading Palestine*, 125.
80. Ayalon, *Reading Palestine*, 100.
81. Issa J. Boullata, *The Bells of Memory: A Palestinian Boyhood in Jerusalem* (Westmount, Quebec: Linda Leith, 2014), 62; Yusif Sayigh, *Arab Economist, Palestinian Patriot: A Fractured Life Story*, ed. Rosemary Sayigh (Cairo: AUC Press, 2015), 185. See also Kamal Boullata, *Palestinian Art: From 1850 to the Present* (London: Saqi Books, 2009), 93.
82. "General Files. Annual and periodic reports, 1924–1945, 1947–1948." Box 18, Folder 8. Records of YMCA International Work in Palestine and Israel," Kautz Family YMCA Archives, University of Minnesota.
83. "Social and Personal," *Palestine Post*, October 24, 1946. A couple of years earlier, Jabra published his essay "al-Adab al-inglizi al-mu'asir," *al-Muntada*, July 1, 1944: 15.
84. "Tambimuttu, 67, Dies; Indian Poet and Editor," *New York Times*, June 24, 1983.

5. JABRA IBRAHIM JABRA

85. Jabra, "Song," *Poetry London* 2, no. 10 (1944): 79–80.
86. Hamad Al-Rayes, "A Speculative Poetics of Tammuz: Myth, Sentiment, and Modernism in Twentieth Century Arabic Poetry," *Labyrinth* 22, no. 2 (2020): 156; and Neuwirth, "Jabrā," 306. Jabra's translation was first published as *Adunis: Dirasa fil-asatir wal-adyan al-sharqiyya al-qadima* (Beirut: Dar al-sira' al-fikri, 1957).
87. Jabra Ibrahim Jabra, "Fil-shi'r wal-shu'ara'," *Shi'r* 2, no. 7–8 (1958): 57–67.
88. The play was originally published by Matba'at Misr in Cairo in 1916, reissued in 1931, and translated as *Majnun Laila, A Poetical Drama in Five Acts*, trans. A. J. Arberry (Cairo: Lencioni, 1933). See Neuwirth, "Jabrā Ibrāhīm Jabrā's Autobiography," 122–23.
89. Jabra, *The First Well*, 182.
90. Michael R. Fischbach, "Tuqan (family)," *Encyclopedia of the Palestinians*, ed. Philip Mattar (New York: Facts on File, 2005), 495; "Ibrahim Tuqan," *Interactive Encyclopedia of the Palestine Question*, accessed May 28, 2013, https://www.palquest.org/en/biography/9721/ibrahim-tuqan .
91. Samia A. Halaby, "The Pictorial Arts of Jerusalem, 1900–1948," in *Jerusalem Interrupted*, 40.
92. Halaby, "The Pictorial Arts of Jerusalem," 54.
93. Reproduced in Kamal Boullata, *Palestinian Art*, 94.
94. Jabra, *The First Well*, 42.
95. Jabra, *The First Well*, 185.
96. Neuwirth, "Jabrā Ibrāhīm Jabrā's Autobiography," 124.
97. Reproduced in Hilde Strobl, *Wolfgang Hildesheimer und die Bildende Kunst: "Und mache mir ein Bild aus vergangener Möglichkeit"* (Berlin: Dietrich Reimer Verlag, 2013), WK 25–30.
98. Wolfgang Hildesheimer, *"Die sichtbare Wirklichkeit bedeutet mir nichts": Die Briefe an die Eltern 1937–1962*, ed. Volker Jehle, 2 vols. (Frankfurt: Suhrkamp, 2016), 1:272–73.
99. A. T. Tolley, *The Poetry of the Forties* (Manchester: Manchester University Press, 1985), 119.
100. Sandra Boselli, "Tambimuttu: Re-Inventing the Art of Poetry Illustration," *Electronic British Library Journal* 10 (2016), https://www.bl.uk/eblj/2016articles/pdf/ebljarticle102016.pdf.
101. "Jabra, Gabriel," Add MS 88907/7/12/1, British Library, accessed June 5, 2020, http://search.archives.bl.uk/primo_library/libweb/action/dlDisplay.do?docId=IAMS041-000001825&fn=permalink&vid=IAMS_VU2. See also Chris Beckett, "Tambimuttu and the *Poetry London* Papers at the British Library: Reputation and Evidence," *Electronic British Library Journal* 9 (2009), https://www.bl.uk/eblj/2009articles/pdf/ebljarticle92009.pdf.
102. "Jabra, Gabriel," Add MS 88907/7/12/1, British Library.
103. Jabra Ibrahim Jabra, "Fluctuations," Cambridge University Library, Department of Manuscripts and University Archives, MS Add.8403. The typescript is 88 pages long and includes a note saying that it was presented to the library by Muhammad Asfour in 1982.
104. Hildesheimer, *"Die sichtbare Wirklichkeit*," 1:231 and 1:423.
105. Jabra, "Fluctuations," 3.
106. Jabra Ibrahim Jabra, *Surakh fi layl tawil*, 2nd ed. (Beirut: Dar al-Adab, 1988).
107. Hildesheimer, *"Die sichtbare Wirklichkeit*," letter 88, [after May 24, 1940], 1:219–320.

108. Jabra, "The Palestinian Exile as Writer," 77.
109. Tamari, "Introduction," in *Jerusalem 1948*, 2.
110. Jabra, "The Palestinian Exile as Writer," 77–78.
111. Ilan Pappé, *The Ethnic Cleansing of Palestine* (Oxford: Oneworld, 2006), 60; Benny Morris, *The Birth of the Palestinian Refugee Problem Revisited* (Cambridge: Cambridge University Press, 2004), 66, 123.
112. "Spanish Consul Among Dead in Hotel Bomb," *Palestine Post*, January 1, 1948. On the Semiramis bombing, see also Larry Collins and Dominique Lapierre, *O Jerusalem* (New York: Simon and Schuster, 1972), 129–33.
113. Hala Sakakini, *Jerusalem and I*, 110–22. See also Khalil Sakakini, *Kadha ana ya dunya*, ed. Hala Sakakini (Jerusalem: al-Matbaʻa al-tijāriyya, 1955) and *Yawmiyyāt Khalīl al-Sakākīnī*, Vol. 8, *1942–1952: Al-Khurūj min al-Qatamūn*, ed. Akram Musallam (Jerusalem: Khalil Sakakini Cultural Center, 2010).
114. Itzak Levy quoted in Pappé, *Ethnic Cleansing*, 99.
115. Pappé, *Ethnic Cleansing*, 99.
116. Jabra, "The Palestinian Exile as Writer," 78.
117. Jabra, "The Palestinian Exile as Writer," 83–84.
118. Pappé, *Ethnic Cleansing*, 98–99.
119. Pappé, *Ethnic Cleansing*, 29–30, 39–41.
120. Based on his 1961 article on Plan Dalet, republished as Walid Khalidi, "Plan Dalet: Master Plan for the Conquest of Palestine," *Journal of Palestine Studies*, 18, no. 1 (1988): 4–33.
121. Morris, *The Birth of the Palestinian Refugee Problem*, 116 and 163–81; Pappé, *Ethnic Cleansing*, 90–91.
122. Walid Khalidi, "The Arab Perspective," in *The End of the Palestine Mandate*, ed. Wm. Roger Louis and Robert W. Stookey (Austin: University of Texas Press, 1986), 104–36; Khairiyya Qasmiyya, "Palästina in der Politik der arabischen Staaten 1918–1948," in *Die Palästina Frage*, ed. Helmut Mejcher, 2nd ed. (Paderborn: Schöningh, 1993), 123–88.
123. Born in Tripoli, in today's Lebanon, Qawuqji (1890–1977) had fought in the Syrian uprising against the French in 1925–1927 and in the Arab Revolt against the British in 1936–1939, when he commanded the Society for the Defense of Palestine, formed by Arab volunteers primarily from Iraq. In 1941, he participated in ʻAli al-Kaylani's coup against the British-backed government in Iraq. He subsequently fled to Nazi Germany. At the end of World War II, he was captured by the Soviet Army. He escaped to France, after which he traveled to Cairo. After the ALA's defeat in October 1948, he returned to Lebanon. See Laila Parsons, *The Commander: Fawzi al-Qawuqji and the Fight for Arab Independence, 1914–1948* (New York: Hill and Wang, 2016), and "Soldiering for Arab Nationalism: Fawzi al-Qawuqji in Palestine," *Journal of Palestine Studies* 36, no. 4 (2007): 33–48; Khairiyya Qasmiyya, *Filastin fi mudhakkirat al-Qawuqji, 1936–1948* (Beirut: PLO Research Center, 1975); and Fawzi al-Qawuqji, "Memoirs, 1948: Part I," *Journal of Palestine Studies* 1, no. 4 (1972): 27–58, and "Memoirs, 1948: Part II," *Journal of Palestine Studies* 2, no. 1 (1972): 3–33.
124. Benny Morris, *A History of the First Arab-Israeli War* (New Haven, CT: Yale University Press, 2008), 107, 235; Rashid Khalidi, *The Iron Cage: The Story of the Palestinian Struggle for Statehood* (Boston, MA: Beacon, 2006), 131–34.
125. Pappé, *Ethnic Cleansing*, 51.

126. Rashid Khalidi, *Iron Cage*, 132.
127. See in particular Avi Shlaim, *Collusion Across the Jordan: King Abdullah, the Zionist Movement, and the Partition of Palestine* (New York: Columbia University Press, 1988).
128. Quoted in Sonja Mejcher-Atassi, "Jabra Ibrahim Jabra's Suitcase: Carrying Modernism and Exile Across Borders from Palestine into Iraq," *Journal of Contemporary Iraq and the Arab World* 17, no. 1–2 (2023): 71.
129. Quoted in Mejcher-Atassi, "Jabra Ibrahim Jabra's Suitcase," 72.
130. Quoted in Mejcher-Atassi, "Jabra Ibrahim Jabra's Suitcase," 73.

6. BORDER CROSSING

1. Jabra Ibrahim Jabra, "The Palestinian Exile as Writer," *Journal of Palestine Studies* 8, no. 2 (1979): 77.
2. Rashid Khalidi, *Palestinian Identity: The Construction of Modern National Consciousness*, 2nd ed. (New York: Columbia University Press, 2010), 1.
3. This debate has recently been rendered as the subject of a children's book by Pei-Yu Chang, *Der geheimnisvolle Koffer von Herrn Benjamin* (Zurich: NordSüd Verlag, 2017).
4. Gershom Scholem, *Walter Benjamin: The Story of a Friendship*, trans. Harry Zohn, with an introduction by Lee Siegel (New York: New York Review Books, 2003), 280.
5. Quoted in Howard Eiland and Michael W. Jennings, *Walter Benjamin: A Critical Life* (Cambridge, MA: Belknap Press of Harvard University Press, 2014), 675. See also Michael Scammell, *Koestler: The Literary and Political Odyssey of a Twentieth-Century Skeptic* (New York: Random House, 2009), 189.
6. The poem was published in a collection of Darwish's poetry titled *Habibati tanhad min naumiha*, in *Diwan Mahmud Darwish*, in 10th ed. (Beirut: Dar al-'Awda, 1983), 342–51.
7. Mahmoud Darwish, *Madih al-zill al-'ali* (Beirut: Dar al-'Awda, 1983), 90 and 92.
8. Jabra, "The Palestinian Exile," 77.
9. Edward W. Said, "Reflections on Exile," in *Reflections on Exile and Other Essays* (Cambridge, MA: Harvard University Press, 2000), 178.
10. Said, "Reflections on Exile," 186.
11. Jabra, "The Palestinian Exile," 83–84.
12. Jabra, "The Palestinian Exile," 85–86. As Jabra says in his essay, he met Toynbee in 1957 in Baghdad, where Toynbee was on a lecture tour. During this tour, Toynbee also visited Palestinian refugee camps in the Gaza Strip. The same year saw the publication of his acclaimed *A Study of History*, vols. 7–10 in an abridged version by Oxford University Press. The lectures were published as *The Toynbee Lectures on the Middle East and Problems of Underdeveloped Countries* (Cairo: National Publications House, 1962) and *Four Lectures Given by Professor Arnold Toynbee in the United Arab Republic* (Cairo: Public Relations Department, 1965.)
13. Hannah Arendt, "We Refugees," *Menorah Journal* 31, no. 1 (1943): 69–77; republished in *Altogether Elsewhere: Writers on Exile*, ed. Marc Robinson (London: Faber and Faber, 1994), 110–19. See also Giorgio Agamben, "We Refugees," *Symposium: A Quarterly Journal of Modern Literatures* 49, no. 2 (1995): 114–19.
14. Jabra, "The Palestinian Exile," 84.

15. Wolfgang Hildesheimer, "Mein Judentum," in *Mein Judentum*, ed. Jürgen Schultz (Stuttgart: Kreuz, 1978), in *Gesammelte Werke in sieben Bänden* [hereafter *GW VII*], ed. Christiaan Lucas Hart Nibbrig and Volker Jehle (Frankfurt: Suhrkamp, 1991), *GW VII*, 163–64.
16. See Ingeborg Gleichauf, Hannah Arendt, und Karl Jaspers, *Geschichte einer einzigartigen Freundschaft* (Cologne: Böhlau Verlag, 2021).
17. Wolfgang Hildesheimer, "Mein Judentum," 164.
18. Wolfgang Hildesheimer, "*Ich werde nun schweigen*": Gespräch mit Hans Helmut Hillrichs in der Reihe "Zeugen des Jahrhunderts," ed. Ingo Hermann (Göttingen: Lamuv, 1993), 109.
19. Henry A. Lea, *Wolfgang Hildesheimers Weg als Jude und Deutscher* (Stuttgart: Hans-Dieter Heinz, 1997), 90–91.
20. Wolfgang Hildesheimer, *Tynset* (Frankfurt: Suhrkamp, 1965), in *GW II*, 7–153, translated as *Tynset*, trans. Jeffrey Castle (London: Dalkey Archive, 2016).
21. On Wolfgang's affinities with Joyce, see Maren Jäger, *Die Joyce-Rezeption in der deutschsprachigen Erzählliteratur nach 1945* (Tübingen: Niemeyer, 2009), 307–410, and Robert K. Weninger, *The German Joyce* (Gainesville: University Press of Florida, 2016), 75–76.
22. Hildesheimer, "*Ich werde nun schweigen*," 42.
23. See especially Kirsitin Gwyer, *Encrypting the Past: The German-Jewish Holocaust Novel of the First Generation* (Oxford: Oxford University Press, 2014), 182–204; Mary Cosgrove, *Born Under Auschwitz: Melancholy Traditions in Postwar German Literature* (Rochester, NY: Boydell and Brewer, 2014), 76–109; Henrike Walter, "Fern-Weh: Wolfgang Hildesheimer's Novels *Tynset* and *Masante* as Topographical Reflections of Exile Experience," in *Exiles Travelling: Exploring Displacement, Crossing Boundaries in German Exile Arts and Writing 1933–1945*, ed. Johannes F. Evelein (Amsterdam: Rodopi, 2009), 99–113; and Henry A. Lea, "Wolfgang Hildesheimer and the German-Jewish Experience: Reflections on 'Tynset' and 'Masante,' " *Monatshefte* 71, no. 1 (1979): 19–28.
24. Wolfgang Hildesheimer, *Masante* (Frankfurt: Suhrkamp, 1973), in *GW II*, 165.
25. Lea, "Wolfgang Hildesheimer," 20.
26. Deuteronomy 33: 27–28.
27. Walid Khalidi, ed., *All That Remains: The Palestinian Villages Occupied and Depopulated by Israel in 1948* (Washington, DC: Institute for Palestine Studies, 1992), 20.
28. Hildesheimer, *Masante*, 305.
29. Hans Helmut Hillrichs, "Der Dichter und die Eisenbahnen: Annäherung an Wolfgang Hildesheimer," in Hildesheimer, "*Ich werde nun schweigen*," 13.
30. Rolf Tiedemann, "Introduction: 'Not the First Philosophy, but a Last One': Notes on Adorno's Thought," in Theodor W. Adorno, *Can One Live After Auschwitz? A Philosophical Reader*, ed. Rolf Tiedemann, trans. Rodney Livingstone et al. (Stanford, CA: Stanford University Press, 2003), xv.
31. Wolfgang Hildesheimer, *Interpretationen: James Joyce. George Büchner. Zwei Frankfurter Vorlesungen* (Frankfurt: Suhrkamp, 1969), published as "Frankfurter Poetik-Vorlesungen," *GW VII*, 57. See also Hildesheimer, "*Ich werde nun schweigen*," 35–36. Hildesheimer visited Auschwitz in the early 1980s along with Walter Levin and Henry Meyer, both members of the LaSalle Quartet on the occasion of the quartet's concert in Kraków. See Stephan Braese, ed., *Jenseits der Pässe: Wolfgang Hildesheimer. Eine Biographie* (Göttingen: Wallstein, 2017), 529.

6. BORDER CROSSING

32. Giorgio Agamben, *Remnants of Auschwitz: The Witness and the Archive*, trans. Daniel Heller-Roazen (New York: Zone, 2002), 161.
33. Shoshana Felman, "Benjamin's Silence," *Critical Inquiry* 25, no. 2 (1999): 203.
34. Walter Benjamin, "The Storyteller," in *Illuminations*, ed. Hannah Arendt, trans. Harry Zorn (New York: Pimlico, 1999), 83–84.
35. Walter Benjamin, "Theses on the Philosophy of History," in *Illuminations*, ed. Hannah Arendt, trans. Harry Zorn (New York: Pimlico, 1999), 249. Benjamin bought Klee's little aquarelle at an exhibition of Klee's work in Munich in 1921 and it soon turned into his "most prized possession," as Eiland and Jennings point out in *Walter Benjamin*, 138.
36. Felman, "Benjamin's Silence," 227.
37. Hildesheimer, "*Die sichtbare Wirklichkeit*," letter 125, February 14, [1948], 1:369.
38. Volker Jehle, "Nachwort," in Wolfgang Hildesheimer, "*Die sichtbare Wirklichkeit*": *Die Briefe an die Eltern 1937–1962*, ed. Volker Jehle, 2 vols. (Frankfurt: Suhrkamp, 2016), 2:1492–93.
39. Hildesheimer, "*Die sichtbare Wirklichkeit*," letter 131, June 22, [1948], 1:386.
40. Pascale Casanova, *The World Republic of Letters*, trans. M. B. DeBevoise (Cambridge, MA: Harvard University Press, 2004), 29.
41. Margalit Fox, "Garry Davis, Man of No Nation Who Saw One World of No War, Dies at 91," *New York Times*, July 28, 2013.
42. Hildesheimer, "*Die sichtbare Wirklichkeit*," 1:421–22.
43. Hildesheimer, "*Die sichtbare Wirklichkeit*," letter 148, February 23, [1949], 1:420.
44. Hildesheimer, "*Die sichtbare Wirklichkeit*," letter 165, July 26, [1949], 1:461.
45. Hildesheimer, "*Die sichtbare Wirklichkeit*," letter 186, November 23 [or 24], [1949], 1:516.
46. Braese, *Jenseits der Pässe*, 149–50.
47. Both are mentioned in his letters to his parents, "*Die sichtbare Wirklichkeit*," letter 230, December 26, [1950], 1:604.
48. Hildesheimer, "*Die sichtbare Wirklichkeit*," letter 195, February 8, [1950], 544, and letter 236, February 4, [1951], 1:617.
49. Hildesheimer, "*Die sichtbare Wirklichkeit*," letter 273, February 4, [1952], 1:710.
50. On Gruppe 47, see Helmut Böttiger, *Die Gruppe 47: Als die deutsche Literatur Geschichte schrieb* (Munich: Deutsche Verlags-Anstalt, 2012); Stephan Braese, ed., *Bestandsaufnahme–Studien zur Gruppe 47* (Berlin: Erich Schmidt Verlag, 1999); and Hans Werner Richter, *Im Etablissment der Schmetterlinge: Einundzwanzig Portraits aus der Gruppe 47* (Munich: Hanser, 1986).
51. Hildesheimer, "*Die sichtbare Wirklichkeit*," letter 243, [March 26, 1951], 1:635; letter 261, October 24, [1951], 1:674; and letter 248, May 12, [1951], 1:644.
52. Hildesheimer, "*Die sichtbare Wirklichkeit*," letter 250, May 30, [1951], 1:647.
53. Hildesheimer, "*Die sichtbare Wirklichkeit*," letter 165, July 26, [1949], 1:461.
54. Hildesheimer, "*Die sichtbare Wirklichkeit*," letter 273, February 4, [1952], 1:709.
55. In his letters to his parents, Wolfgang mentions both Patricia Wood, to whom he refers as Patsy, who, like him, worked at the Nuremberg Military Tribunal, and Tena Carver, whose husband, Tom Carver, worked as a lawyer at the Office of Deputy Chief of Staff, Office of Military Government, United States (OMGUS) in Nuremberg. Hildesheimer, "*Die sichtbare Wirklichkeit*," letter 138, October 8, [1948], 1:399, and letter 178, [October 7, 1949], 1:495.

56. Hildesheimer, "*Ich werde nun schweigen*," 33
57. Braese, *Jenseits der Pässe*, 172–73.
58. Hildesheimer, "Mein Judentum," 160.
59. Jabra Ibrahim Jabra, Letter to Wolfgang Hildesheimer, Harvard, November 9, 1952, WHA 478,in Wolfgang Hildesheimer, "*Alles andere steht in meinem Roman*": *Zwölf Briefwechsel*, ed. Stephan Braese with Olga Blank and Thomas Wild (Frankfurt: Suhrkamp, 2017), 490–93.
60. Bashir Abu-Manneh, *The Palestinian Novel: From 1948 to the Present* (Cambridge: Cambridge University Press, 2016), 36.
61. Jabra Ibrahim Jabra, "The Rebels, the Committed and Others: Transitions in Arabic Poetry Today," in *Middle East Forum* no. 43 (1967), reprinted in Jabra Ibrahim Jabra, *A Celebration of Life: Essays on Literature and Art* (Baghdad: Dar al-Ma'mun, 1988), 73.
62. "The Libeskind Building: Architecture retells German-Jewish History," accessed June 10, 2020, https://www.jmberlin.de/en/libeskind-building.
63. Hildesheimer, "Mein Judentum," 160.
64. Jabra, "The Palestinian Exile," 84; Said, "Reflections on Exile," 178.
65. Elias Khoury, "Hiwar ma'a Jabra Ibrahim Jabra *Shu'un filastiniyya* 77 (1978): 176–92; republished as "Min al-furu' ila al-jusur," in *Yanabi' al-ru'ya: Dirasat naqdiyya* (Beirut: al-Mu'assassa al-'arabiyya lil-dirasat wal-nashr, 1979), 125.
66. "The Rockefeller Foundation: Personal History and Application for a Fellowship in Humanities," March 5, 1952, 1/4. Jabra Ibrahim Jabra, Box 297, Folder 4637, Rockefeller Archive Center.
67. Jabra Ibrahim Jabra, *Shari' al-amirat: Fusul min sira dhatiyya* (London: Riyad El Rayyes, 1996), translated as *Princesses' Street: Baghdad Memories*, trans. Issa J. Boullata (Fayetteville: University of Arkansas Press, 2005), 71.
68. Rockefeller Foundation RF 12, Box: John Marshall, Folder: Diaries, November 8, 1952, and May 5, 1953.
69. Yusif Sayigh, *Arab Economist, Palestinian Patriot: A Fractured Life Story*, ed. Rosemary Sayigh (Cairo: AUC Press, 2015), 235.
70. "The Rockefeller Foundation: Personal History and Application for a Fellowship in Humanities," March 5, 1952, 4/4.
71. Rockefeller Foundation RF 12, Box: John Marshall, Folder: Diaries, January 6, 1954. Marshall's report mentions "a friend, now in the Ministry of Interior" who helped with this. This reference might be to the Iraqi historian Abd al-Aziz al-Duri, who is listed as a reference in Jabra's application for a Rockefeller Foundation fellowship. Al-Duri is described by Jabra in "The Palestinian Exile as Writer" as the cultural attaché at the Iraqi Embassy in Damascus who gave him an Iraqi visa in August 1948, "though not much over thirty, with his bald head and large bright eyes, and a Peterson pipe which he kept smoking, he looked very academic" (81). Shortly thereafter, he became dean of the College of Arts and Sciences in Baghdad and translations and publications director at the Ministry of Education.
72. Robyn Creswell, *City of Beginnings: Poetic Modernism in Beirut* (Princeton, NJ: Princeton University Press, 2019). See also Dunia Badini, *La Revue Shi'r/Poésie et la modernité poétique arabe: Beyrouth (1957–70)* (Paris: Sindbad, 2009).

73. Creswell, *City of Beginnings*, 31–43; Elizabeth M. Holt, "Resistance Literature and Occupied Palestine in Cold War Beirut," *Journal of Palestine Studies* 50, no. 1 (2021): 3–18; and Elliott Colla, "Badr Shakir al-Sayyab: Cold War Poet," *Middle Eastern Literatures* 18, no. 3 (2015): 247–63. Not surprisingly, Koestler played a crucial role in the CCF's early days; he was the author of its founding manifesto, which was circulated in its meeting in Berlin in 1950. On the CCF, see especially Frances Stonor Saunders, *Who Paid the Piper? The CIA and the Cultural Cold War* (London: Granta, 2000).
74. Holt, "Resistance Literature," 12. See also Elizabeth M. Holt, " 'Bread or Freedom': The Congress of Cultural Freedom, the CIA, and the Arabic Literary Journal *Ḥiwār*," *Journal of Arabic Literature* 44, no. 1 (2013): 83–102; and Issa J. Boullata, "The Beleaguered Unicorn: A Study of Tawfīq Sāigh," *Journal of Arabic Literature* 4, no. 1 (1973): 69–71.
75. Walid Khalidi, "Hawla mawaqif al-gharb min al-qadiyya al-filastiniyya," *Hiwar* 9 (1964): 11.
76. Holt, "Resistance Literature," 6 and 11.
77. Yoav Di-Capua, *No Exit: Arab Existentialism, Jean-Paul Sartre, and Decolonization* (Chicago: Chicago University Press, 2018). See also Georges Khalil and Friederike Pannewick, ed., *Commitment and Beyond: Reflections on/of the Political in Arabic Literature Since the 1940s* (Wiesbaden: Reichert, 2015); and Verena Klemm, "Different Notions of Commitment (Iltizām) and Committed Literature (al-adab al-multazim) in the Literary Circles of the Mashriq," *Arabic and Middle Eastern Literatures* 3, no. 1 (2000): 51–62.
78. Marwan Buheiry, *Beirut's Role in the Political Economy of the French Mandate 1919–39* (Oxford: Center for Lebanese Studies, 1986), 5, 12–15.
79. Jabra Ibrahim Jabra, *Tamuz fil-madina* (Beirut, Dar majallat Shi'r, 1959), republished in *al-Majmu'at al-shi'riyya al-kamila* (London: Riad El-Rayyes, 1990).
80. T. S. Eliot, *The Waste Land* (New York: Boni and Liveright, 1922), translated as *al-Ard al-kharab* in *T. S. Eliot: Tarjamat min al-shi'r al-hadith* [T.S. Eliot: Translations of modern poetry], trans. Adonis and Yusuf al-Khal (Beirut: Dar majallat Shi'r, 1959).
81. Jabra Ibrahim Jabra. *al-Safina* (Beirut: Dar An-Nahar, 1970), translated as *The Ship*, trans. Adnan Haydar and Roger Allen (Washington, DC: Three Continents, 1985). Three excerpts of *al-Safina* were published in *Hiwar* 14, no. 2 (1965): 40–54. On *al-Safina*, see Roger Allen, *The Arabic Novel: An Historical and Critical Introduction*, 2nd ed. (New York: Syracuse University Press, 1995), 177–83.
82. Jabra Ibrahim Jabra, *al-Bahth 'an Walid Mas'ud*, 3rd ed. (Beirut: Dar al-Adab, 1978), 16, translated as *In Search of Walid Masoud*, trans. Roger Allen and Adnan Haydar (New York: Syracuse University Press, 2000), 5.
83. I borrow the notion of inherited exile from Etel Adnan, whose parents fled Smyrna during the Great Fire of Smyrna in 1922 at the end of the Greco-Turkish War—around the same time that Jabra's family fled Anatolia—to settle in Beirut, where Adnan was born in 1925. See Etel Adnan, *À propos de la fin de l'empire Ottoman* (Paris: Galerie Lelong, 2015); and the documentary film by Joana Hadjithomas and Khalil Joreige, dir., *Ismyrne/Ismyrna* (Lebanon: Abbout Productions, 2016).
84. Jabra, *In Search of Walid Masoud*, 14.
85. William Tamplin, "The Other Wells: Family History and the Self-Creation of Jabra Ibrahim Jabra," *Jerusalem Quarterly* 85 (2021): 47.

86. Zeina G. Halabi, "The Day the Wandering Dreamer became a Fida'i: Jabra Ibrahim Jabra and the Fashioning of Political Commitment," in *Commitment and Beyond*, 157–70. See also Zeina G. Halabi, *The Unmaking of the Arab Intellectual: Prophecy, Exile, and the Nation* (Edinburgh: Edinburgh University Press, 2017).

87. Jabra, *In Search of Walid Masoud*, 13. See my reading of the novel in "The Arabic Novel Between Aesthetic Concerns and the Causes of Man: Commitment in Jabra Ibrahim Jabra and 'Abd al-Rahman Munif," in *Commitment and Beyond*, 148–51.

88. See in particular Emile Habiby's 1974 novel *al-Waqa'i' al-ghariba fi ikhtifa' Sa'id Abi al-Nahs al-Mutasha'il* (Haifa: Manshurat Arabesque, 1974), translated as *The Secret Life of Saeed, the Ill-Fated Pessoptimist: A Palestinian Who Became a Citizen of Israel*, trans. Salma Khadra Jayyusi and Trevor LeGassik (Columbia, LA: Readers International, 1989), and Elia Suleiman's film *Chronicle of a Disappearance* (Israel: International Film Circuit, 1996). See also Emily Lucille Drumsta, "Chronicles of Disappearance: The Novel of Investigation in the Arab World, 1975–1985" (PhD diss., University of California, 2016), *eScholarship*, escholarship.org/uc/item/6tf2596b, and "Words Against Erasure: The Persistence of the Poetic in Jabrā Ibrāhīm Jabrā's *In Search of Walid Masoud*," *Middle Eastern Literatures*, 19, no. 1 (2016): 56–76.

89. Rebecca Carol Johnson, "The Politics of Reading: Recognition and Revolution in Jabra Ibrahim Jabra's *In Search of Walid Masoud*," in *Recognition: The Poetics of Narrative: Interdisciplinary Studies on Anagnorisis*, ed. Philip F. Kennedy and Marilyn Lawrence (New York: Peter Lang, 2009), 178. See also Halabi, *The Unmaking of the Arab Intellectual*, 103–08.

90. Jabra, *In Search of Walid Masoud*, 244.

91. Stefan G. Meyer, *The Experimental Arabic Novel: Postcolonial Literary Modernism in the Levant* (Albany: SUNY Press, 2001), 52. See also Samir Fawzii Hajj, *Maraya: Jabra Ibrahim Jabra wal-fann al-riwa'i* (Beirut: al-Mu'assasa al-'arabiyya lil-dirasat wal-nashr, 2005), 112; and Issa J. Boullata, "Living with the Tigress and the Muses: An Essay on Jabra Ibrahim Jabra," *World Literature Today* 72, no. 2 (2001): 219.

92. Emily Drumsta, "Words Against Erasure: The Persistence of the Poetic in Jabrā Ibrāhīm Jabrā's *In Search of Walid Masoud*," *Middle Eastern Literatures* 19, no. 1 (2016): 59.

93. Drumsta, "Words Against Erasure," 57.

94. Jabra, *In Search of Walid Masoud*, 201.

95. Tarif Khalidi in conversations with the author, Beirut, January 14, 2019.

96. *Hunters in a Narrow Street* was republished with an introduction by Roger Allen (Boulder, CO: Three Continents Book, 1997).

97. Tarif Khalidi in conversations with the author, Beirut, January 14, 2019.

98. Sonja Mejcher-Atassi, *Reading Across Modern Arabic Literature and Art* (Wiesbaden: Reichert), 51–63; Nathaniel Greenberg, "Political Modernism, Jabrā, and the Baghdad Modern Art Group," *CLCWeb: Comparative Literature and Culture* 12, no. 2 (2010): http://dx.doi.org/10.7771/1481-4374.1603.

99. Jabra Ibrahim Jabra, *Jawad Salim wa-nassb al-hurriyya: Dirasa fi atharihi wa-ara'ihi* (Baghdad: Ministry of Information, 1974). See also Jabra Ibrahim Jabra, *al-Fann wal-fannan: Kitabat fil-naqd al-tashkili*, ed. Ibrahim Nasrallah (Beirut: al-Mu'assasa al-'arabiyya lil-dirasat wal-nashr, 2000). Selim had worked on the restoration of Assyrian bas-relief at the Iraq Museum (founded by Gertrude Bell in 1926 and directed after her by the

Arab nationalist Sati al-Husri), before pursuing studies in London. He died before the completion of the monument. Jabra wrote the filmscript of a documentary in his memory, which was broadcast in his voice by Iraqi Broadcasting Television and Cinema in 1961. See "Jawad Salim bi-sawt Jabra Ibrahim Jabra," YouTube, accessed January 4, 2021, https://www.youtube.com/watch?v=1-Lh4hwazSY.

100. Trained in petroleum economics, Munif gained acclaim as an Arab novelist, in particular for his prison novel *Sharq al-mutawassit* (East of the Mediterranean, 1977) and his quintet *Mudun al-milh* (*Cities of Salt*, 1984–1989). See Sabry Hafez, "An Arabian Master," *New Left Review* 37, no. 37 (2006): 39–67; and Sonja Mejcher-Atassi, ed., "Writing a Tool for Change: 'Abd al-Rahman Munif Remembered," Special Issue, *MIT Electronic Journal of Middle East Studies* 7 (2007).

101. Muhsin Jassim al-Musawi, *al-Riwaya al-'arabiyya—al-nash'a wal-tahawwul*, 2nd ed. (Beirut: Dar al-Adab, 1988), 282.

102. Edward al-Kharrat, "The Mashriq," in *Modern Literature in the Near and Middle East 1850–1970*, ed. Robin Ostle (London: Routledge, 1991), 187. On the self-criticism of Arab intellectuals after 1967, see in particular Sadiq Jalal al-Azm, *al-Naqd al-dhati ba'da al-hazima* (Beirut: Dar al-tali'a, 1968), translated as *Self-Criticism After the Defeat*, trans. Geoge Stergios, with a foreword by Fouad Ajami, and an introduction by Faisal Darraj (London: Saqi, 2011).

103. T. Yousef, "The Reception of William Faulkner in the Arab World," *American Studies International* 33, no. 2 (1995): 42.

104. Mahmoud Alhirthani, "Jabra's Translation of Faulkner's *The Sound and the Fury*: A Critical Study," *Palestinian Journal for Open Learning and e-Learning* 6, no. 12 (2018): 9, https://digitalcommons.aaru.edu.jo/jropenres/vol6/iss12/9.

105. Esmaeil Haddadian-Moghaddam, "The Cultural Cold War in the Middle East: William Faulkner and Franklin Book Programs," Translation and the Cultural Cold War, Special Issue, *Translation and Interpreting Studies* 15, no. 3 (2020): 441–63; and Holt, "Resistance Literature," 11–12.

106. Haddadian-Moghaddam, "The Cultural Cold War in the Middle East," 443; and Holt, "Resistance Literature," 4.

107. Jabra Ibrahim Jabra, "Tahlil naqdi li-riwayat William Faulkner," *al-Adab* 1 (1954): 25–32. See Haddadian-Moghaddam, "The Cultural Cold War in the Middle East," 455.

108. Hilary Falb Kalisman, " 'A World of Tomorrow': Diaspora Intellectuals and Liberal Thought in the 1950s," *Journal of Palestine Studies* 50, no. 2 (2021): 1.

109. Jabra, *Princesses' Street*, 152–57.

110. Jabra, *Princesses' Street*, 156.

111. *Out of Place* is the title of Said's memoirs; Edward W. Said, *Out of Place* (New York: Vintage, 2000).

112. "A Founding Vision," Barenboim-Said, accessed January 4, 2021, https://barenboimsaid.de/about/history. See also Daniel Barenboim and Edward Said, *Parallels and Paradoxes: Explorations in Music and Society* (New York: Pantheon, 2002).

113. Wolfgang Hildesheimer, *Briefe*, ed. Silvia Hildesheimer and Dietmar Pleyer (Frankfurt: Suhrkamp, 1999). 44–45. See also Braese, *Jenseits der Pässe*, 204.

114. See WHA 205. It was broadcast on Süddeutscher Rundfunk and Bayrischer Rundfunk in 1953 in two parts, "Palästina und Griechenland" and "Auf einer Bank in Askalon,"

on Hessischer Rundfunk in 1953 as "Zwischen Florenz und Tel Aviv: Reisebericht," and on Nordwestdeutscher Rundfunk Hannover in 1955 as "Reise durch Griechenland und Israel." An extract was published in *Süddeutsche Zeitung* on November 12 and 13, 1955, under the title "Aufzeichnungen aus Israel," *Süddeutsche Zeitung* November 12–13, 1955, in *GW VII*, 652–56.

115. Hildesheimer, "Aufzeichnungen aus Israel," *GW VII*, 652.
116. After Israel's annexation of East Jerusalem in the 1967 War, it was renamed IDF Square.
117. Hildesheimer, "Aufzeichnungen aus Israel," 652–53.
118. Braese, *Jenseits der Pässe*, 200.
119. Hildesheimer, "Aufzeichnungen aus Israel," 655.
120. Khalidi, *All That Remains*, 134. See also Benny Morris, *The Birth of the Palestinian Refugee Problem Revisited* (Cambridge: Cambridge University Press, 2004), 529.
121. Morris, *The Birth of the Palestinian Refugee Problem*, 471; Khalidi, *All That Remains*, 82.
122. Morris, *The Birth of the Palestinian Refugee Problem*, 528–29.
123. Yochi Fischer, "What Does Exile Look Like? Transformations in the Linkage Between the Shoah and the Nakba," in *The Holocaust and the Nakba: A New Grammar of Trauma and History*, ed. Bashir Bashir and Amos Goldberg (New York: Columbia University Press, 2019), 182. Palestinian oral histories of ghettos, namely the ghetto of Lydda, have found their way into Elias Khoury's novel *Awlad al-ghitu: Ismi Adam*, vol. 1 (Beirut: Dar al-Adab, 2012), translated as *My Name Is Adam: Children of the Ghetto*, vol. 1, trans. Humphrey Davis (London: Archipelago Press, 2018). See also Adam Raz, "When Israel Placed Arabs in Ghettos Fenced by Barbed Wire," *Haaretz*, May 27, 2020.
124. Ben Knight, "Nuremberg Trials: An Important Step for Germany to Confront Its Nazi Past," Deutsche Welle, November 16, 2020, https://www.dw.com/en/nuremberg-trials-an-important-step-for-germany-to-confront-its-nazi-past/a-55617820; and Braese, *Jenseits der Pässe*, 198.
125. Noura Erakat, *Justice for Some: Law and the Question of Palestine* (Stanford, CA: Stanford University Press, 2019), 26.
126. Erakat, *Justice for Some*, 55–56. See also Hillel Cohen, "The First Israeli Government (1948–1950) and the Arab Citizens: Equality in Discourse, Exclusion in Practice," in *Israel and Its Palestinian Citizens: Ethnic Privileges in the Jewish State*, ed. Nadim N. Rouhana and Sahar S. Huneidi (Cambridge: Cambridge University Press, 2017), 73–102.
127. Braese, *Jenseits der Pässe*, 196–204.
128. Tania Tamari Nasir, "Introduction," in *Spring Is Here: Embroidered Flowers of the Palestinian Spring*, ed. Tania Tamari Nasir, flower design and embroidery Mary Jabaji Tamari, 2nd ed. (Beirut: Institute for Palestine Studies, 2014).

7. PUBLIC ENGAGEMENT IN WORLDS APART

1. Wolfgang Hildesheimer, *"Die sichtbare Wirklichkeit,"* letter 212 [late July 1950] and letter 213 [August 7, 1950], 1:573 and 575. Jehle dates these letters to 1950. However, Walid remembers visiting Wolfgang in Ambach in 1951, after having finished his master's degree and shortly before taking up a lectureship at Oxford. In his letters to his parents, Wolfgang mentions that Walid was offered a lectureship at Oxford. See also Stephan Braese, *Jenseits der Pässe: Wolfgang Hildesheimer. Eine Biographie* (Göttingen: Wallstein, 2017), 160.

2. Hildesheimer, *"Die sichtbare Wirklichkeit bedeutet mir nichts,"*: *Die Briefe an die Eltern 1937–1962*, ed. Volker Jehle, 2 vols. (Frankfurt: Suhrkamp, 2016), 1:399 and 1:409.
3. Quoted in Hildesheimer, *"Die sichtbare Wirklichkeit,"* 1:430.
4. Dan Teodorovici, "Sherban Cantacuzino (Paris 1928–London 1918)," *Studies in History and Theory of Architecture* 6 (2018), https://sita.uauim.ro/6/a/63/.
5. Hildesheimer, *"Die sichtbare Wirklichkeit,"* 1:575.
6. Hildesheimer, *"Die sichtbare Wirklichkeit,"* letter 250, May 10, [1951], letter 251, June 26, [1951], and letter 254, July 31 [and August 1, 1951], 1:648, 1:649, 1:657.
7. Hildesheimer, *"Die sichtbare Wirklichkeit,"* letter 215, 1 [- after 13] August [1950], 1:578.
8. Hildesheimer, *"Die sichtbare Wirklichkeit,"* letter 215, 1 [- after 13] August [1950], 1:579.
9. Hildesheimer, *"Die sichtbare Wirklichkeit,"* letter 217, August 31, [1950], 1:581. In German, he says, "Waleed hat etwas geniales." He adds that Patsy stayed with them at Oxford and that she, too, was very impressed by them.
10. Rasha Salam Khalidi, "A Non-Conformist Moslem Arab Woman: A Century of Evolution (1873–1976)," unpublished typescript, n.d.
11. Hadara Lazar, *Out of Palestine: The Making of Modern Israel*, trans. Marsha Pomerantz (New York: Atlas, 2011), 85.
12. Walid Khalidi in conversations with the author, Cambridge, MA, October 29–31, 2018.
13. The correspondence is preserved among Walid Khalidi's private papers.
14. Walid Khalidi in conversations with the author, Cambridge, MA, October 29–31, 2018. He contributed a number of articles based on his thesis to *Cassell's Encyclopedia of Literature I and II*, ed. S. H. Steinberg (London: Cassell, 1953 and 1955), including "Nabulsi, Abd al-Ghani."
15. "Israel-Jordan Border," *Times*, March 30, 1954; "Aiding Arab Countries," *Times*, January 3, 1955; "Contrasts in Cairo," *Times*, April 29, 1955; "Balance of Power in the Near East," *Times*, October 19, 1955; and "Israel," *Times*, December 21, 1956.
16. Anbara Salam Khalidi, *Jawla fil-dhikrayat bayn lubnan wa-filastin* (Beirut: Dar An-Nahar, 1997), translated as *Memoirs of an Early Arab Feminist: The Life and Activism of Anbara Salam Khalidi*, trans. Tarif Khalidi (London: Pluto, 2013), 161.
17. Tarif Khalidi in conversation with the author, Beirut, January 10, 2021.
18. Tarif Khalidi, *Ana wal-kutub* (Beirut: Manshurat al-jamal, 2018), 13, translated as "The Books in My Life: A Memoir," Parts I–III, trans. Tarif Khalidi, *Jerusalem Quarterly* 73 (2018): 63–78; 74: 30–47; 75: 115–31.
19. In my conversations with Walid Khalidi, he was not sure if the visit took place in 1955 or 1954. Brease quotes an email correspondence with Walid, in which Walid says that Wolfgang visited him in Oxford in 1954. Given that the Khalidis spent the summer of 1954 in Beirut and that Wolfgang refers to his visit to Oxford in letters to his mother after 1955, I assume that the visit took place in 1955.
20. Rasha Salam Khalidi, "A Non-Conformist."
21. Inge Geitner-Thurner in an email correspondence with the author, July 30, 2020.
22. Tarif Khalidi in conversations with the author, Beirut, January 12, 2019.
23. Hildesheimer, *"Die sichtbare Wirklichkeit,"* letter 343, September 11, [1955], 2:903, and letter 369, March 16, [1956], 2:968. Walid Khalidi in conversations with the author, Cambridge, MA, October 29–31, 2018.

24. Hildesheimer, "Die sichtbare Wirklichkeit," letter 343, September 11, [1955], 2:903.
25. Wolfgang Hildesheimer, Nachlese, in Gesammelte Werke in sieben Bänden [hereafter GW I–VII], ed. Christiaan Lucas Hart Nibbrig and Volker Jehle (Frankfurt: Suhrkamp, 1991), in GW I, 477.
26. Hildesheimer, "Die sichtbare Wirklichkeit," letter 343, September 11, [1955], 2:903.
27. Hildesheimer, "Die sichtbare Wirklichkeit," letter 325, December 7, [1954], 2:850–51. Some of Holme's translations of Wolfgang's plays and essays are preserved in the Taylor Institution Library, University of Oxford, Boxes MS.Fol.G27–29.
28. Hildesheimer, "Die sichtbare Wirklichkeit," letter 342, May 18, [1955], 2:899. One short letter from Sykes to Hildesheimer is preserved in the Academy of Arts, Berlin; see Christopher Sykes, Letter to Wolfgang Hildesheimer, London, June 18, 1957, unpublished correspondence, WHA 659, in which Sykes says that he will try to join Gruppe 47 again in September 1957.
29. Hildesheimer, "Die sichtbare Wirklichkeit," letter 380, [November 14, 1956], 2:999.
30. Wolfgang Hildesheimer, Letter to Eva and Ernst Teltsch, Ambach, March 6, 1955, WHA 663.
31. Benny Morris, "Survival of the Fittest, an Interview with Benny Morris," interview by Ari Shavit, Haaretz, January 9, 2004, reprinted in Journal of Palestine Studies 33, no. 3 (2004): 169.
32. Hildesheimer, "Die sichtbare Wirklichkeit," letter 345, September 25, [1955], 2:907. The book never saw an English translation. It was published in German as Die Welt der ungewohnten Dimensionen: Versuch einer gemeinverständlichen Darstellung der modernen Physik und ihrer philosophischen Folgerungen, foreword Werner Heisenberg (Leiden: Sijhoff, 1953).
33. Henry A. Lea, Wolfgang Hildesheimers Weg als Jude und Deutscher (Stuttgart: Hans-Dieter Heinz, 1997), 12.
34. Hildesheimer, "Die sichtbare Wirklichkeit," 2:912–13. A copy of the speech, which was delivered in Hebrew, is preserved in the Wolfgang Hildesheimer Archive at the Academy of Arts, Berlin.
35. Walid Khalidi in conversations with the author, Cambridge, MA, October 29–31, 2018.
36. Rashid Khalidi, "Khalidi, Walid," Encyclopedia of the Palestinians, ed. Philip Mattar, 280–84 (New York: Facts on File, 2005), 281.
37. See Simon C. Smith, Reassessing Suez 1956: New Perspectives on the Crisis and Its Aftermath (London: Routledge, 2016).
38. Adel Manna, Nakba and Survival: The Story of the Palestinians who remained in Haifa and the Galilee, 1948–1956 (Oakland: University of California Press, 2022), 11. See also Adel Manna, "Kafr Qasim, 1856: Israel's Army Massacres Its Own Peaceful Citizens," Interactive Encyclopedia of the Palestine Question, accessed June 1, 2023https://www.palquest.org/en/highlight/14334/kafr-qasim-1956.
39. Adel Manna, Nakba and Survival: The Story of the Palestinians Who Remained in Haifa and the Galilee, 1948–1956 (Oakland: University of California Press, 2022), 193.
40. Clifford Davies, "The Fighting Teacher Has a Secret!," Daily Mirror, November 26, 1956.
41. al-Maktab al-da'im lil-ittihad ghuraf al-sina'a wal-tijara wal-zira'a fil-bilad al-'arabiyya, ed., Israel: Khatar iqtisadi wa-askari wa-siyasi (Beirut: Dar al-'ilm lil-malayyin, 1952), 6.

42. Michael Johnson, "Political Bosses and Their Gangs: *zu'ama* and qabadayat in the Sunni Muslim quarters of Beirut," in *Patrons and Clients in Mediterranean Societies*, ed. Ernest Gellner and John Waterbury (London: Duckworth, 1977), 209 and 223.
43. Geoffrey Thursby, "Fight on the Rooftops Rocks a City: Beirut: Armoured Car Siege," *Daily Express* June 16, 1958.
44. Rasha Salam Khalidi, "A Non-Conformist."
45. They were first published in the now-defunct journal of the American University of Beirut's Alumni Office *Middle East Forum* and republished in the *Journal of Palestine Studies*: Walid Khalidi, "Why Did the Palestinians Leave, Revisited," *Journal of Palestine Studies* 34, no. 2 (2005): 42–54; "The Fall of Haifa Revisited," *Journal of Palestine Studies* 37, no. 3 (2008): 30–58; and "Plan Dalet: Master Plan for the Conquest of Palestine," *Journal of Palestine Studies* 18, no. 1 (1988): 4–33.
46. Samir Khalaf, *Civil and Uncivil Violence in Lebanon* (New York: Columbia University Press, 2002), 151.
47. Rosemary Sayigh, *Palestinians: From Peasants to Revolutionaries; A People's History* (London: Zed Books, 1979) and *Too Many Enemies: The Palestinian Experience in Lebanon* (London: Zed Books, 1993).
48. Walid Khalidi, "On Albert Hourani, the Arab Office, and the Anglo-American Committee of 1946," *Journal of Palestine Studies* 35, no. 1 (2005): 78.
49. Anis Sayigh, *Anis Sayigh 'an Anis Sayigh* (London: Riad El-Rayyes, 2006), 175. See also Elizabeth M. Holt, "Resistance Literature and Occupied Palestine in Cold War Beirut," *Journal of Palestine Studies* 50, no. 1 (2021): 12. Neither Sayigh nor Holt mention the novel's title. It may very well be *Dr. Zhivago*, which was published in Arabic translation by Maktabat Nobel/al-Mada Publications in Damascus in 1959. The book does not mention the translator's name. On the CIA's instrumentalization of *Dr. Zhivago*, see in particular Peter Finn and Petra Couvée, *The Zhivago Affair: The Kremlin, the CIA and the Battle Over a Forbidden Book* (New York: Pantheon, 2014).
50. Yusif Sayigh, *Arab Economist, Palestinian Patriot: A Fractured Life Story*, ed. Rosemary Sayigh (Cairo: AUC Press, 2015), 263.
51. Rashid Khalidi, "Khalidi, Walid," 280.
52. Sherene Seikaly, "In the Shadow of War: The *Journal of Palestine Studies* as Archive," *Journal of Palestine Studies* 51, no. 2 (2022): 1.
53. Hildesheimer, *"Die sichtbare Wirklichkeit,"* letter 377, [shortly after October 29, 1956], 2:992. See also letter 388, April 7, [1957], 2:1022.
54. Hildesheimer, *"Die sichtbare Wirklichkeit,"* letter 380, [November 14, 1956], 2:999. See also letter 388, April 7, [1957], 2:1022.
55. It also found its way into the memoirs of then–British Prime Minister Anthony Eden, *Full Circle: The Memoirs of Anthony Eden* (London: Houghton Mifflin, 1960), 559, quoted in Simon C. Smith, *Reassessing Suez 1956: New Perspectives on the Crisis and Its Aftermath* (London: Routledge, 2016), 1.
56. An early critic of Nasser was the Egyptian-French intellectual Anouar Abdel-Malek; see Anouar Abdel-Malek, *Egypt: Military Society* (New York: Random House, 1968).
57. Hildesheimer, *"Die sichtbare Wirklichkeit,"* letter 383 [December 22, 1956], 2:1007; Braese, *Jenseits der Pässe*, 212.

58. Hildesheimer, *"Die sichtbare Wirklichkeit,"* letter 415, May 5, [1958], 2:1093–96. On Richter's political engagement, see also Stuart Parkes, *Writers and Politics in Germany, 1945–2008* (Rochester, NY: Camden House, 2009), 34–35.
59. Hildesheimer, "Die vier Hauptgründe, weshalb ich nicht in der Bundesrepublik lebe," quoted in Braese, *Jenseits der Pässe*, 270. In a letter to his German literary colleague Heinrich Böll in 1953, Wolfgang wrote that he had accepted the offer to work as an interpreter at the Nuremberg Trials "because I wanted to convince myself of the much-cited collective guilt at the time, and not to return to Germany for good. I took this decision much later, when I was convinced that this collective guilt did not exist." Wolfgang Hildesheimer, *Briefe*, ed. Silvia Hildesheimer and Dietmar Pleyer (Frankfurt: Suhrkamp, 1999), 38.
60. Christoph Gunkel, "50th Anniversary of the *'Spiegel* Affair': A Watershed Moment of West German Democracy," *Spiegel International*, September 21, 2012.
61. Braese, *Jenseits der Pässe*, 271.
62. Wolfgang Hildesheimer, *Vergebliche Aufzeichnungen. Nachtstück* (Frankfurt: Suhrkamp, 1963), published as *Vergebliche Aufzeichnungen*, Mit acht Rastercollagen ("Textscherben") des Autors, in *GW I*, 275.
63. Henning Rischbieter, "Der Schlaflose: Gespräch mit Wolfgang Hildesheimer," *Theater Heute* 4, no. 4 (1963), 15, quoted in Braese, *Jenseits der Pässe*, 273.
64. The term was coined by Frank Thiess in 1945 in response to Thomas Mann, who addressed the subject of German guilt from his exile in the United States. See Braese, *Jeseits der Pässe*, 224–31.
65. Braese, *Jenseits der Pässe*, 226–27.
66. Wolfgang Hildesheimer, "Nachwort zu Djuna Barnes: »Nachtgewächs«," in Djuna Barnes, *Nachtgewächs*, trans. Wolfgang Hildesheimer (Frankfurt: Suhrkamp, 1971), in *GW VII*, 355.
67. Hildesheimer, "Nachwort," 358.
68. Hildesheimer, "Nachwort," 356 and 358.
69. Hildesheimer, "Nachwort," 356.
70. Wolfgang Hildesheimer, "Mein Judentum," in *Mein Judentum*, ed. Jürgen Schultz (Stuttgart: Kreuz, 1978), in *GW VII*, 160.
71. Hildesheimer, "Mein Judentum," 160.
72. Hildesheimer, *"Die sichtbare Wirklichkeit,"* letter 460, October 8, [1960], 2:1223. Titled *Déclaration sur le droit à l'insoumission dans la guerre d'Algérie*, the manifesto was published on September 6, 1960, in *Vérité-Liberté*, https://web.archive.org/web/20041030212203/http://www.lecri.net/liste_noire/manifeste_121.html.
73. Hildesheimer, *"Die sichtbare Wirklichkeit,"* letter 485, May 26, 1961, 2:1293.
74. Braese, *Jenseits der Pässe*, 266.
75. Braese, *Jenseits der Pässe*, 254.
76. Braese, *Jenseits der Pässe*, 245–55.
77. Theodor W. Adorno, *Aesthetic Theory*, ed. Gretel Adorno and Rolf Tiedemann, trans. Robert Hullot-Kentor (London: Continuum, 1997), 322.
78. Brease, *Jenseits der Pässe*, 459–66.
79. Hildesheimer, "Waren meine Freunde Nazis?," *Die Zeit*, November 9, 1979, in *GW VII*, 633–34.

80. Stuart Parkes, *Writers and Politics in Germany, 1945–2008* (Rochester, NY: Camden House, 2009), 70–87.
81. Rasha Salam Khalidi, "A Non-Conformist."
82. Rasha Salam Khalidi, "Non-Conformist."
83. Peter Weiss, "Der Sieg der sich selbst bedroht," published first in Swedish as "Seger som hotar sig själv," *Aftonbladet*, June 17, 1967, translated in the Zurich-based magazine *Die Tat*, July 1, 1967, 3; reprinted in *Rapporte 2* (Frankfurt: Suhrkamp, 1971): 70–72.
84. Hannah Arendt, *Eichmann in Jerusalem: A Report on the Banality of Evil* (London: Penguin, 2006), 49 and 135.
85. Hannah Arendt and Gershom Scholem, *The Correspondence of Hannah Arendt and Gershom Scholem*, ed. Marie Luise Knott, trans. Anthony David (Chicago: University of Chicago Press, 2017).
86. See Susie Linfield, *The Lions' Den: Zionism and the Left from Hannah Arendt to Noam Chomsky* (New Haven, CT: Yale University Press, 2019), 18 and 77–78; Enzo Traverso, *The End of Jewish Modernity*, trans. David Fernbach (London: Pluto Press, 2016), 75–77.
87. Wolfgang Hildesheimer, "Denken auf eigene Gefahr: Ein Offener Brief an Peter Weiss über den Nahost Konflikt," *Die Zeit* 30, July 28, 1967.
88. Hildesheimer, "Denken auf eigene Gefahr," 10.
89. Quoted in Hildesheimer, *Briefe*, 153.
90. Hildesheimer, *Briefe*, 152.
91. Hildesheimer, *Briefe*, 15. A reference to "Waren meine Freunde Nazis?"
92. Erich Fried, "Held Wider Willen," *Die Zeit* 33, August 18, 1967.
93. Wolfgang Hildesheimer, "Ist Nasser kein Faschist?," *Die Zeit* 35, September 1, 1967.
94. See in particular Tom Segev, *1967: Israel, the War, and the Year That Transformed the Middle East*, trans. Jessica Cohen (New York: Metropolitan Books, 2005).
95. Published as "Israel's 1967 Annexation of Arab Jerusalem: Walid Khalidi's Address to the UN General Assembly Special Emergency Session, 14 July 1967," *Journal of Palestine Studies* 42, no. 1 (2012/13): 71–82.
96. Rashid Khalidi, "Khalidi, Walid," 282.
97. Albert Hourani, *A History of the Arab Peoples* (London: Faber and Faber, 1991), 413–14.
98. Gil Z. Hochberg, "This City That Isn't One: Fragments on a Fragmented City," *Contending Modernities: Global Currents Article*, December 20, 2017, https://contendingmodernities.nd.edu/global-currents/fragmented-city/.
99. Nazmi Jubeh, "Patrick Geddes: Luminary or Prophet of Demonic Planning," *Jerusalem Quarterly* 80 (2019): 36.
100. Hochberg, "This City That Isn't One."
101. Rashid Khalidi, "Khalidi, Walid," 282.
102. Rashid Khalidi, "Khalidi, Walid," 282.
103. Walid Khalidi, "Thinking the Unthinkable: A Sovereign Palestinian State," *Foreign Affairs* 56, no. 4 (1978): 695–713.
104. Khalidi, "Thinking the Unthinkable," 706–07.
105. Wolfgang Hildesheimer, "The End of Fiction," in *GW VII*, 127.
106. Wolfgang Hildesheimer, "Aus einem aufgegebenen Roman," in *Aus aufgegebenen Werken*, ed. Siegfried Unseld (Frankfurt: Suhrkamp, 1968), 125–42; reprinted as "Hamlet. Ein Fragment," in *GW I*, 259–72.

107. Wolfgang Hildesheimer, "Zur Verleihung des Literaturpreises der Bayrischen Akademie der Schönen Künste," in *GW IV*, 266.
108. Wolfgang Hildesheimer, *Marbot: Eine Biographie*, in *GW IV*, 17; translated as *Marbot: A Biography*, trans. Patricia Crampton (New York: George Braziller, 1983), 8.
109. From T. S. Eliot, *Four Quartets*, quoted in Hildesheimer, "Zur Verleihung des Literaturpreises," 266.
110. Hildesheimer, *Marbot*, English translation, 113.
111. Hildesheimer, *Marbot*, English translation, 233–34.
112. Taylor Institution Library, University of Oxford, Box MS.Fol G27.
113. Mary Cosgrove, *Born Under Auschwitz: Melancholy Traditions in Postwar German Literature* (Rochester, NY: Camden House, 2014), 83.
114. Wolfgang Hildesheimer, *"Ich werde nun schweigen": Gespräch mit Hans Helmut Hillrichs in der Reihe "Zeugen des Jahrhunderts,"* ed. Ingo Hermann (Göttingen: Lamuv, 1993), 64.
115. Hildesheimer, *"Ich werde nun schweigen,"* 86–87.
116. From T. S. Eliot's "The Hollow Man," quoted in Hildesheimer, *"Ich werde nun schweigen"* 92.

EPILOGUE

1. Two letters by Wolfgang to Rasha dated March 20, 1984 and April 8, 1984 have been published in Wolfgang Hildesheimer, *"Alles andere steht in meinem Roman": Zwölf Briefwechsel*, ed. Stephan Braese with Olga Blank and Thomas Wild (Frankfurt: Suhrkamp, 2017), 497–500.
2. Wolfgang Hildesheimer, *Mozart*, trans. Marion Faber (New York: Farrar, Straus and Giroux, 1982). Reviewed by Alan Tyson, "Amadevious," in *New York Review of Books* on November 18, 1982.
3. Wolfgang Hildesheimer, Letter to Rasha Khalidi, Poschiavo, November 10, 1983, WHA 1642.
4. Walid Khalidi, ed., *From Haven to Conquest: Readings in Zionism and the Palestine Problem Until 1948* (Beirut: Institute for Palestine Studies, 1971), xxxv.
5. Khalidi, ed., *From Haven to Conquest*, lxxxiii.
6. Walid Khalidi in conversations with the author, Cambridge, MA, October 30, 2018.
7. Wolfgang Hildesheimer, Letter to Rasha Khalidi, Poschiavo, January 29, 1984, WHA 1642.
8. Rasha Salam Khalidi, Letter to Wolfgang Hildesheimer, Cambridge, MA, January 24, 1985, WHA 1642.
9. Wolfgang Hildesheimer, Postcard to Rasha Khalidi, Oxford 1984, WHA 1642.
10. In German, the sentence reads, "Eva sagt, W. hat das Buch nicht gelesen, sondern ihr gegeben und sie fand es verabscheuenswürdig und hat es, glaube ich, vernichtet."
11. Walid Khalidi, *Conflict and Violence in Lebanon: Confrontation in the Middle East* (Cambridge, MA: Harvard University Press, 1983).
12. Walid Khalidi, "State and Society in Lebanon," in *State and Society in Lebanon*, ed. Leila Fawaz (Cambridge, MA: Tufts University, 1991), 29. This very reference, and the impact of "the twin agonies of Palestine and Lebanon" on Walid's life and work is mentioned in Albert Hourani's foreword; see Walid Khalidi, *Palestine Reborn* (London: Tauris, 1992), ix.

13. Edward W. Said, "Permission to Narrate," in *The Politics of Dispossession: The Struggle for Palestinian Self-Determination, 1968–1984* (New York: Vintage, 1995), 254.
14. Wolfgang Hildesheimer, Postcard to Rasha Khalidi, Poschiavo, March 20, 1984, WHA 1642.
15. Wolfgang Hildesheimer, Letter to Rasha Khalidi, Poschiavo, April 8, 1984, WHA 1642.
16. Wolfgang Hildesheimer, Letter to Rasha Khalidi, Poschiavo, March 12, 1988, drawing Silvia Hildesheime, WHA 1642.
17. Wolfgang Hildesheimer, "Zur Verleihung des Bundesverdienstkreuzes," in *Gesammelte Werke in sieben Bänden* [hereafter GW I–VII], ed. Christiaan Lucas Hart Nibbrig and Volker Jehle (Frankfurt: Suhrkamp, 1991), in *GW VII*, 637. See also Stephan Braese, *Jenseits der Pässe: Wolfgang Hildesheimer. Eine Biographie* (Göttingen: Wallstein, 2017), 507–09.
18. Hildesheimer, "Zur Verleihung des Bundesverdienstkreuzes," 637.
19. Wolfgang Hildesheimer, Letter to Eva Teltsch, Poschiavo, January 14, 1990, WHA 675.
20. Braese, *Jenseits der Pässe*, 544–50.
21. Braese, *Jenseits der Pässe*, 546; Uwe Neumahr, *Das Schloss der Schriftsteller: Nürnberg '46: Treffen am Abgrund* (Munich: Beck, 2023), 254.
22. Wolfgang Hildesheimer, *Briefe*, ed. Silvia Hildesheimer and Dietmar Pleyer (Frankfurt: Suhrkamp, 1999), 375.
23. Hildesheimer, *Briefe*, 379.
24. Wolf Biermann, "Kriegshetze Friedenshetze," *Die Zeit*, February 1, 1991.
25. Paul Lewis, "After the War; U.N. Survey Calls Iraq's War Damage Near Apocalyptic," *New York Times*, March 22, 1991.
26. Philip Mattar, "The PLO and the Gulf Crisis," *Middle East Journal* 48, no. 1 (1994): 31–46.
27. Mattar, "The PLO and the Gulf Crisis," 31.
28. Mattar, "The PLO and the Gulf Crisis," 36.
29. Walid Khalidi, *The Gulf Crisis: Origins and Consequences* (Washington, DC: Institute for Palestine Studies, 1991), 20.
30. Mattar, "PLO and the Gulf Crisis," 44; Patrick Seal, *Abu Nidal: A Gun for Hire. The Secret Life of the World's Most Notorious Arab Terrorist* (New York: Random House, 1992).
31. Issa J. Boullata in conversations with the author, Montreal, April 8, 2013.
32. Samir al-Khalil [Kanan Makiya], *The Monument: Art, Vulgarity, and Responsibility in Iraq* (Berkeley: University of California Press, 1991), 68–78.
33. Issa J. Boullata, "Living with the Tigress and the Muses: An Essay on Jabra Ibrahim Jabra," *World Literature Today* 72, no. 2 (2001): 214–23.
34. Amatzia Baram, *Culture, History and Ideology in the Formation of Ba'thist Iraq, 1968–89* (London: Palgrave Macmillan, 1991), 49–50.
35. For the transcript, see Jeff B. Harmon, dir., "Saddam's Iraq," (Journeyman Pictures, 1991), https://www.journeyman.tv/film_documents/1181/transcript/. See also Kalisman, "'A World of Tomorrow'," 10.
36. Kanan Makiya, *Republic of Fear: The Politics of Modern Iraq*, updated ed. (Berkeley: University of California Press, 1998).
37. Gil Anidjar, *The Jew, the Arab: A History of the Enemy* (Stanford, CA: Stanford University Press, 2003), xvii.
38. Skype conversation with Matthew Pruen, May 6, 2021. Rüdiger Görner, "Obituaries: Wolfgang Hildesheimer," *The Independent* August 24, 1991.

39. Rashid Khalidi, "Khalidi, Walid," *Encyclopedia of the Palestinians*, ed. Philip Mattar, 280–84 (New York: Facts on File, 2005), 283.
40. Walid Khalidi, "The Ownership of the U.S. Embassy Site in Jerusalem," *Journal of Palestine Studies* 29, no. 4 (2000), 80–101.
41. Wolfgang Hildesheimer, "Zur Verleihung des Literaturpreises der Bayrischen Akademie der Schönen Künste [1982]," in *GW IV*, 267–68.
42. Bashir Bashir, "Interrogating Modernity and Egalitarian Binationalism in Palestine/Israel," *Contending Modernities* (blog), University of Notre Dame, August 26, 2021, https://contendingmodernities.nd.edu/theorizing-modernities/interrogating-modernity-egalitarian-binationalism; Michael Rothberg, *Multidirectional Memory: Remembering the Holocaust in the Age of Decolonization*, (Palo Alto, CA: Stanford University Press 2009), 313.

BIBLIOGRAPHY

ARCHIVES, LIBRARIES, AND ONLINE PORTALS

Archives and Special Collections Department, American University of Beirut/University Libraries
British Library, London
Cambridge University Library, University of Cambridge
Central Zionist Archives, Jerusalem
Fitzwilliam College, University of Cambridge
Harry S. Truman Library and Museum, Presidential Libraries, U.S. National Archives and Records Administration
Haus-, Hof- und Staatsarchiv (HHStA), Vienna
Institute for Palestine Studies, Beirut
Interactive Encyclopedia of the Palestine Question (PALQUEST)
Jewish Virtual Library
Kautz Family YMCA Archives, University of Minnesota
Middle East Centre, St Antony's College, University of Oxford
National Archives of the United Kingdom, Kew, Richmond
National Library of Israel, Jerusalem
New York Public Library, Manuscript and Archives Division
Palestine Land Studies Center, American University of Beirut
ProQuest Historical Newspapers
Rockefeller Archive Center, New York
Taylor Institute Library, University of Oxford
Times Digital Archive
Unilever Art, Archives and Records Management, Port Sunlight
Wolfgang Hildesheimer-Archiv (WHA), Academy of Arts, Berlin

Works by Wolfgang Hildesheimer

Hildesheimer, Wolfgang. "Aus einem aufgegebenen Roman." In *Aus aufgegebenen Werken*, ed. Siegfried Unseld, 125–42. Frankfurt: Suhrkamp, 1968.

———. *Bericht einer Reise*. Mit 17 Radierungen von Paul Mersmann. Nachwort von Michael Rumpf und Wolfram Benda. Bayreuth: Bear Press, 2002.

———. "Cornish Summer: Holiday-Makers Paradise." *Palestine Post*, August 23, 1946.

———. "Denken auf eigene Gefahr: Ein Offener Brief an Peter Weiss über den Nahost-Konflikt." *Die Zeit*, July 28, 1967.

———. *Gesammelte Werke in sieben Bänden* [hereafter GW I–VII]. Ed. Christiaan Lucas Hart Nibbrig and Volker Jehle. Frankfurt: Suhrkamp, 1991.

———. "Aufzeichnungen aus Israel." *Süddeutsche Zeitung* November 12–13, 1955. In *GW VII*, 652–56.

———. "Cornwall Interlude." *Palestine Post* April 20, 1945. In *GW VII*, 649–51.

———. "The End of Fiction [1975]." In *GW VII*, 125–40.

———. "Hamlet. Ein Fragment." In *GW I*, 259–72.

———. *Interpretationen: James Joyce. George Büchner. Zwei Frankfurter Vorlesungen*. Frankfurt: Suhrkamp, 1969. Published as "Frankfurter Poetik-Vorlesungen (1967)." In *GW VII*, 43–99.

———. *Marbot. Eine Biographie*. Frankfurt: Suhrkamp, 1981. In *GW IV*, 7–234. Trans. Patricia Crampton as *Marbot: A Biography* (New York: Braziller, 1983).

———. *Masante*. Frankfurt: Suhrkamp, 1973. In *GW II*, 155–366.

———. "Mein Judentum." In *Mein Judentum*, ed. Jürgen Schultz, 261–74. Stuttgart: Kreuz, 1978. In *GW VII*, 159–69.

———. *Mitteilungen an Max über den Stand der Dinge und anderes*. Mit einem Glossarium und 6 Zeichnungen des Autors. Frankfurt: Suhrkamp, 1983. In *GW I*, 407–55.

———. *Mozart*. Frankfurt: Suhrkamp, 1977. In *GW III*, 7–425. Trans. Marion Faber as *Mozart* (New York: Farrar, Straus and Giroux, 1983).

———. *Nachlese*. Frankfurt: Suhrkamp, 1987. In *GW I*, 457–88.

———. *Nachtstück in einem Akt*. Frankfurt: Suhrkamp, 1962. In *GW VI*, 561–99.

———. "Nachwort zu Djuna Barnes: »Nachtgewächs«." In *GW VII*, 355–58.

———. "On James Joyce." *Radio Week*, May 4, 1946. In *GW VII*, 273–75.

———. "Pansuun [1939]." In *GW VII*, 547.

———. *Tynset*. Frankfurt: Suhrkamp, 1965. In *GW II*, 7–153. Trans. Jeffrey Castle as *Tynset* (London: Dalkey Archive, 2016).

———. "Übersetzung und Interpretation einer Passage aus *Finnegans Wake* von James Joyce." In *Interpretationen: James Joyce, Georg Büchner: Zwei Frankfurter Vorlesungen*, 5–29. Frankfurt: Suhrkamp, 1969. In *GW VII*, 338–51.

———. *Vergebliche Aufzeichnungen. Nachtstück*. Frankfurt: Suhrkamp, 1963. Published as *Vergebliche Aufzeichnungen*. Mit acht Rastercollagen ("Textscherben") des Autors. In *GW I*, 273–302.

———. "Waren meine Freunde Nazis?" *Die Zeit*, November 9, 1979. In *GW VII*, 633–34.

———. *Zeiten in Cornwall*. Mit 6 Zeichnungen des Autors. Frankfurt: Suhrkamp, 1971. In *GW I*, 339–406.

———. "Zur Verleihung des Literaturpreises der Bayrischen Akademie der Schönen Künste [1982]." In *GW IV*, 265–68.

———. "Zur Verleihung des Bundesverdienstkreuzes [1983]." In *GW VII*, 637.

———. *"Ich werde nun schweigen": Gespräch mit Hans Helmut Hillrichs in der Reihe "Zeugen des Jahrhunderts."* Ed. Ingo Hermann. Göttingen: Lamuv, 1993.

———. "Ist Nasser kein Faschist?" *Die Zeit*, September 1, 1967.

Correspondence

Hildesheimer, Wolfgang. *"Alles andere steht in meinem Roman": Zwölf Briefwechsel*. Ed. Stephan Braese with Olga Blank and Thomas Wild. Frankfurt: Suhrkamp, 2017.
———. *Briefe*. Ed. Silvia Hildesheimer and Dietmar Pleyer. Frankfurt: Suhrkamp, 1999.
———. *"Die sichtbare Wirklichkeit bedeutet mir nichts": Die Briefe an die Eltern 1937–1962*. Ed. Volker Jehle. 2 vols. Frankfurt: Suhrkamp, 2016.
———. Letter to Eva Teltsch, London, 1938. WHA 661.
———. Letter to Eva and Ernst Teltsch, London, July 18, 1946. WHA 662.
———. Letter to Eva Teltsch, Nuremberg, 1947. WHA 662.
———. Letter to Eva and Ernst Teltsch, Ambach, March 6, 1955. WHA 663.
———. Letter to Eva Teltsch, Poschiavo, January 14, 1990. WHA 675.
———. Letter to Rasha Khalidi, Poschiavo, November 10, 1983. WHA 1642.
———. Letter to Rasha Khalidi, Poschiavo, January 29, 1984. WHA 1642.
———. Postcard to Rasha Khalidi, Poschiavo, March 3, 1984. WHA 1642.
———. Postcard to Rasha Khalidi, Poschiavo, March 20, 1984. WHA 1642.
———. Letter to Rasha Khalidi, Poschiavo, April 8, 1984. WHA 1642.
———. Letter to Rasha Khalidi, Poschiavo, March 12, 1988, drawing Silvia Hildesheimer. WHA 1642.
———. Letter to Christopher Holme, Poschiavo, September 3, 1981. Taylor Institution Library, University of Oxford, Box MS.Fol G27.

WORKS BY JABRA IBRAHIM JABRA

Jabra, Jabra Ibrahim. *A Celebration of Life: Essays on Literature and Art*. Baghdad: Dar al-Ma'mun, 1988.
———. "al-Adab al-inglizi al-mu'asir [Contemporary English literature]." *al-Muntada* July 1, 1944: 15.
———. "Arab Language and Culture." In *The Middle East: A Handbook*, ed. Michael Adams, 174–78. New York: Praeger, 1971.
———. *al-Bahth 'an Walid Mas'ud*. Beirut: Dar al-Adab, 1978. Trans. Roger Allen and Adnan Haydar as *In Search of Walid Masoud* (New York: Syracuse University Press, 2000).
———. *al-Bi'r al-ula: Fusul min sira dhatiyya*. 2nd ed. 1987. Reprint, Beirut: al-Mu'assasa al-'arabiyya lil-dirasat wal-nashr, 1993. Trans. Issa J. Boullata as *The First Well: A Bethlehem Boyhood* (Fayetteville: University of Arkansas Press, 1995).
———. "al-Fann wal-fannan [Art and artist]." *al-Amali* 2, no. 2 (1939): 17–19.
———. *al-Fann wal-fannan: Kitabat fil-naqd al-tashkili* [Art and artist: Essays in art criticism]. Ed. Ibrahim Nasrallah. Beirut: al-Mu'assasa al-'arabiyya lil-dirasat wal-nashr, 2000.
———. *al-Fann wal-hulm wal-fi'al* [Art, dream, and action]. Baghdad: Dar al-Ma'mun, 1986. Beirut: al-Mu'assasa al-'arabiyya lil-dirasat wal-nashr, 1988.
———. "Fil-shi'r wal-shu'ara' [On poetry and poets]." *Shi'r* 2, no. 7–8 (1958): 57–67.
———. "Fluctuations." Unpublished typescript, n.d. Cambridge University Library, Department of Manuscripts and University Archives, MS Add.8403.
———. "al-Ghramufun." In *'Araq wa-qisas ukhra* [Araq and other stories]. Beirut: Dar al-Ahliyya, 1956. Trans. Denys Johnson-Davies as "The Gramophone." In *Modern Arabic Short Stories*, ed. Denys Johnson-Davies, 146–59 (London: Heinemann, 1976).

———. "Ghamra la tanjali [An endless flood]." *al-Amali* 2, no. 13 (1940): 18–21 and no. 14 (1940): 13–15.

———. "al-Hubb wal-junun [Love and madness]." *al-Amali* 2, no. 9 (1939): 6–7.

———. *Hunters in a Narrow Street*. Boulder, CO: Three Continents Book, 1997.

———. "Ibnat al-sama' [Daughter of the sky]." *al-Amali* 1, no. 44 (1939): 18–24 and no. 45 (1939): 20–25.

———. "Jawad Salim bi-sawt Jabra Ibrahim Jabra [Jawad Salim in the voice of Jabra Ibrahim Jabra]." Iraq: Iraqi Broadcasting Television and Cinema, 1961. https://www.youtube.com/watch?v=1-Lh4hwazSY.

———. *Jawad Salim wa-nasb al-hurriyya: Dirasa fi atharihi wa-ara'ihi* [Jawad Salim and the Monument of Freedom: A study of his influences and opinions]. Baghdad: Ministry of Information, 1974.

———. *al-Majmu'at al-shi'riyya al-kamila* [The complete poetry collection]. London: Riad El-Rayyes, 1990.

———. "Modern Arabic Literature and the West." *Journal of Arabic Literature* 2, no. 1 (1971): 76–22.

——— "Mulahathat 'an al-adab wal-thawra al-filastiniyya" [Notes on Palestinian literature and revolution]." In *al-Nar wal-jawhar: Dirasat fil-shi'r* [Fire and essence: Studies in poetry], 157–65. 3rd ed. Beirut: al-Mu'assassa al-'arabiyya lil-dirasat wal-nashr, 1982.

———. *Mutawalayat shi'riyya: ba'duha lil-tayf wa-ba'duha lil-jasad* [Poetic sequences: Some for the specter some for the body]. Beirut: al-Mu'assasa al-'arabiyya lil-dirasat wal-nashr, 1996.

———. "On Interpoetics." Interview with Jabra Ibrahim Jabra by Najman Yasin. In *The View from Within: Writers and Critics on Contemporary Arabic Literature. A Selection from Alif: Journal of Comparative Poetics*, ed. Ferial J. Ghazoul and Barbara Harlow, 207–12. Cairo: American University in Cairo Press, 1994.

———. "al-Quds: al-Zaman al-mujassad." In *al-Rihla al-thamina* [The eighth journey], 155–76. Beirut: al-Maktaba al-'asriyya, 1968. Trans. Issa J. Boullata as "Jerusalem: Time Embodied." In *The Open Veins of Jerusalem*, ed. Munir Akash, 245–65. 2nd ed. (Arlington, MA: Jusoor, 2005).

———. *al-Safina* [The Ship]. Three excerpts. *Hiwar* 14, no. 2 (1965): 40–54.

———. *al-Safina*. Beirut: Dar An-Nahar, 1970. Trans. Adnan Haydar and Roger Allen as *The Ship* (Washington, DC: Three Continents, 1985).

———. *Shari' al-amirat: Fusul min sira dhatiyya*. London: Riyad El Rayyes, 1996. Trans. Issa J. Boullata as *Princesses' Street: Baghdad Memories* (Fayetteville: University of Arkansas Press, 2005).

——— [Jabra, Gabriel]. "Song." *Poetry London* 2, no. 10 (1944): 79–80.

———. *Surakh fi layl tawil*. 2nd ed. Baghdad: Matba'at al-'ani, 1955. Reprint, Beirut: Dar al-Adab, 1988. Trans. William Tamplin as *Cry in a Long Night and Four Stories* (London: Darf, 2022).

———. "Tahlil naqdi li-riwayat William Faulkner" [A critical analysis of William Faulkner's novel]. *Al-Adab* 1 (1954): 25–32.

———. *Tammuz fil-madina* [Tammuz in the city]. Beirut, Dar majallat Shi'r, 1959.

———. "The Palestinian Exile as Writer." *Journal of Palestine Studies* 8, no. 2 (1979): 77–87.

———. *Yanabi' al-ru'ya: Dirasat naqdiyya* [Sources of vision: Critical studies]. Beirut: al-Mu'assassa al-'arabiyya lil-dirasat wal-nashr, 1979.

Correspondence

Jabra, Jabra Ibrahim [Jabra, Gabriel]. Letter to Wolfgang Hildesheimer, Harvard, November 9, 1952, WHA 478. In Wolfgang Hildesheimer. *"Alles andere steht in meinem Roman"*: *Zwölf Briefwechsel*, ed. Stephan Braese with Olga Blank and Thomas Wild, 488–93. Frankfurt: Suhrkamp, 2017.

—— [Jabra, G. J. I.]. Three letters to William Sutherland Thatcher, Censor of Fitzwilliam House, University of Cambridge, Bethlehem, July 8, 1948, and Baghdad, October 11 and December 1, 1948, Fitzwilliam College Archives, University of Cambridge. In Sonja Mejcher-Atassi. "Jabra Ibrahim Jabra's Suitcase: Carrying Modernism and Exile Across Borders from Palestine Into Iraq." *Journal of Contemporary Iraq and the Arab World* 17, no. 1–2 (2023): 71–73.

WORKS BY WALID KHALIDI

Khalidi, Walid [El Khalidi, Walid A. S.]. "Aiding Arab Countries." *Times*, January 3, 1955.

——, ed. *All That Remains: The Palestinian Villages Occupied and Depopulated by Israel in 1948*. Washington, DC: Institute for Palestine Studies, 1992.

——. "The Arab Perspective." In *The End of the Palestine Mandate*, ed. Wm. Roger Louis and Robert W. Stookey, 104–46. Austin: University of Texas Press, 1986.

—— [El Khalidi, Walid A. S.]. "Balance of Power in the Near East." *Times*, October 19, 1955.

——. *Before Their Diaspora: A Photographic History of the Palestinians 1876–1948*. 4th ed. 1984. Reprint, Washington, DC: Institute for Palestine Studies, 2010.

——. *Conflict and Violence in Lebanon: Confrontation in the Middle East*. Cambridge, MA: Harvard University Press, 1979.

—— [El Khalidi, Walid A. S.]. "Contrasts in Cairo." *Times*, April 29, 1955.

——. "The Fall of Haifa Revisited." *Journal of Palestine Studies* 37, no. 3 (2008): 30–58.

——. "Fi filastin 15 hizban siyasiyyan yahudiyyan" [In Palestine: 15 Jewish political parties]. *Beirut al-masa'*, November 1, 1948; December 6, 1948; December 13, 1948; and December 20, 1948.

——, ed. *From Haven to Conquest: Readings in Zionism and the Palestine Problem Until 1948*. Beirut: Institute for Palestine Studies, 1971.

——. *The Gulf Crisis: Origins and Consequences*. Washington, DC: Institute for Palestine Studies, 1991.

——. "Hawla mawaqif al-gharb min al-qadiyya al-filastiniyya" [On the West's position in the Palestinian cause]. *Hiwar* 9 (1964): 5–18.

——. "The Hebrew Reconquista of Palestine: From the 1947 United Nations Partition Resolution to the First Zionist Congress of 1897." *Journal of Palestine Studies* 39, no. 1 (2009): 24–42.

—— [El Khalidi, Walid A. S.]. "Israel." *Times*, December 21, 1956.

—— [El Khalidi, Walid, A. S.]. "Israel-Jordan Border." *Times*, March 30, 1954.

——. "Israel's 1967 Annexation of Arab Jerusalem: Walid Khalidi's Address to the UN General Assembly Special Emergency Session, 14 July 1967." *Journal of Palestine Studies* 42, no. 1 (2012/13): 71–82.

——. "Khams maqalat 'an Filastin ashiyyat intiha' al-intidab al-britani" [Five articles on Palestine in the wake of the end of the British Mandate]. *Majallat al-dirasat al-filastiniyya* 133 (2018): 32–44.

——. "Kitab *al-Sayunizm aw al-mas'ala al-sahyuniyya* li-Muhammad Ruhi al-Khalidi [The book Zionism or the Zionist question by Muhammad Ruhi al-Khalidi]." In *Studia Palaestina: Studies in Honor of Constantine K. Zurayk/Dirasat filastiniyya: majmu'at abhath wudi'at takriman lil-duktur Qustantin Zurayk*, ed. Hisham Nashabeh, 37–82. Beirut: Institute for Palestine Studies, 1988.

——. "A Little Site." *Forum* 7, no. 17, April 14, 1944: 4.

——. "Nabulsi, Abd al-Ghani." *Cassell's Encyclopedia of Literature I and II*, ed. S. H. Steinberg, 1279. Vol. 2. London: Cassell, 1953.

——. "On Albert Hourani, the Arab Office, and the Anglo-American Committee of 1946." *Journal of Palestine Studies* 35, no. 1 (2005): 60–79.

——. "The Ownership of the U.S. Embassy Site in Jerusalem." *Journal of Palestine Studies* 29, no. 4 (2000): 80–101.

——. *Palestine Reborn*. London: Tauris. 1992.

——. "Plan Dalet: Master Plan for the Conquest of Palestine." *Journal of Palestine Studies*, 18, no. 1 (1988): 4–33.

——. *al-Quds miftah al-salam* [Jerusalem: Key to peace]. Beirut: Institute for Palestine Studies, 2017.

——. *al-Sahyuniyya fi mi'at 'am: min al-bika' 'ala al-atlal ila al-haymana 'ala al-mashriq al-'arabi (1897–1997)* [A hundred years of Zionism: From lamenting the ruins to dominance over the Arab Mashreq]. Beirut: Dar An-Nahar, 1998.

——. "State and Society in Lebanon." In *State and Society in Lebanon*, ed. Leila Fawaz, 29–46. Medford, MA: Tufts University, 1991.

——. "Thinking the Unthinkable: A Sovereign Palestinian State." *Foreign Affairs* 56, no. 4 (1978): 695–713.

——. "Why Did the Palestinians Leave, Revisited." *Journal of Palestine Studies* 34, no. 2 (2005): 42–54.

WORKS BY RASHA SALAM KHALIDI

Khalidi, Rasha Salam. "A Non-Conformist Moslem Arab Woman: A Century of Evolution (1873–1976)." Unpublished typescript, n.d.

Correspondence

Khalidi, Rasha Salam. Letter to Wolfgang Hildesheimer, Cambridge, MA, January 24, 1985. WHA 1642.

OTHER SOURCES

"39 Killed in Jerusalem Headquarters." *Times*, July 23, 1946.

"$1,000,000 Jerusalem Hotel Overlooks Biblical Territory." *New York Times*, December 21, 1930.

"A Founding Vision." Barenboim-Said Akademie. Accessed January 4, 2021. https://barenboim-said.de/about/history.

"A Senseless Outrage." *Times*, July 23, 1946.

A Survey of Palestine: Prepared in December 1945 and January 1946 for the Information of the Anglo-American Committee of Inquiry. 2 vols. and supplement. Jerusalem: Government Printer, 1946–47. Reproduced facsimile of Vol. 1. Washington, DC: Institute for Palestine Studies, 1991.

Abbas, Ihsan. *Ghurbat al-raʻi: sira dhatiyya* [The shepherd's exile: Autobiography]. Amman: Dar al-shuruq, 2006.

Abbasi, Mustafa. "The Fall of Acre in the 1948 Palestine War." *Journal of Palestine Studies* 39, no. 4 (2010): 1–22.

Abdel-Malek, Anouar. *Egypt: Military Society*. New York: Random House, 1968.

Abdul Hadi, Mahdi, ed. *Palestinian Personalities: A Biographic Dictionary*. 2nd ed. Jerusalem: Palestinian Academic Society for the Study of International Affairs, 2006.

Abboushi, W. F. *The Unmaking of Palestine*. Boulder, CO: Rienner, 1985.

Abdu, Ibrahim M., and Refqa Abu-Remaileh. "A Literary *Nahda* Interrupted: Pre-Nakba Palestinian Literature as *Adab Maqalat*." *Journal of Palestine Studies* 51, no. 3 (2022): 23–43.

Abowd, Thomas. " 'Diverse Absences': Remembering and Forgetting Arab-Jewish Relations in the Jerusalem of the British Empire." In *Jerusalem Interrupted: Modernity and Colonial Transformation 1917–Present*, ed. Lena Jayussi, 249–68. Northampton, MA: Olive Branch, 2015.

Abu-Lughod, Lila. "Palestine: Doing Things with Archives." Doing Things with Archives, Special Issue, *Comparative Studies of South Asia, Africa and the Middle East* 38, no. 1 (2018): 3–5.

Abu-Manneh, Bashir. *The Palestinian Novel: From 1948 to the Present*. Cambridge: Cambridge University Press, 2016.

———. "Sultan Abdulhamid II and Shaikh Abulhuda al-Sayyadi." *Middle Eastern Studies* 15, no. 1 (1979): 131–53.

Abusaada, Nadi. "Jaffa: The Rise and Fall of an Agrarian City." Institute for Palestine Studies, September 20, 2020. https://www.palestine-studies.org/en/node/1650539.

Achcar, Gilbert. *The Arabs and the Holocaust: The Arab-Israeli War of Narratives*. Trans. G. M. Goshgarian. London: Saqi Books, 2011.

"Action to Cope with Terrorists." *Times*, July 24, 1946.

Adnan, Etel. *À propos de la fin de l'empire Ottoman*. Paris: Galerie Lelong, 2015.

Adorno, Theodor W. *Aesthetic Theory*. Ed. Gretel Adorno and Rolf Tiedemann. Trans. Robert Hullot-Kentor. London: Continuum, 1997.

———. *Can One Live After Auschwitz? A Philosophical Reader*. Ed. Rolf Tiedemann. Trans. Rodney Livingstone et al. Stanford, CA: Stanford University Press, 2003.

Agamben, Giorgio. *Remnants of Auschwitz: The Witness and the Archive*. Trans. Daniel Heller-Roazen. New York: Zone, 2002.

———. "We Refugees." *Symposium: A Quarterly Journal of Modern Literatures* 49, no. 2 (1995): 114–19.

"Ahmad Samih al-Khalidi." *Interactive Encyclopedia of the Palestine Question*. Accessed May 28, 2023. https://www.palquest.org/en/biography/9833/ahmad-samih-al-khalidi.

Albert, Samuel D. "Egypt and Mandatory Palestine and Iraq." In *Architecture and Urbanism in the British Empire*, ed. G.A. Bremner, 423–56. Oxford: Oxford University Press, 2016.

Alcalay, A. *After Jews and Arabs: Remaking Levantine Culture*. Minneapolis: University of Minnesota Press, 1993.

Alhirthani, Mahmoud. "Jabra's Translation of Faulkner's *The Sound and the Fury*: A Critical Study." *Palestinian Journal for Open Learning and e-Learning* 6, no. 12 (2018): 10–19. https://digitalcommons.aaru.edu.jo/jropenres/vol6/iss12/9.

Allen, Roger. *The Arabic Novel: An Historical and Critical Introduction.* 2nd ed. Syracuse, NY: Syracuse University Press, 1995.
Alon, Shir. "No One to See Here: Genre of Neutralization and the Ongoing Nakba." *Arab Studies Journal* 27, no. 1 (2019): 91–117.
"Anbara Salam Khalidi." *Interactive Encyclopedia of the Palestine Question.* Accessed May 28, 2023. https://www.palquest.org/en/biography/9714/anbara-salam-khalidi.
Anderson, Benedict. *Imagined Communities: Reflections on the Origin and Spread of Nationalism.* London: Verso, 1983.
"Anglo-U.S. Talks Progress." *Daily Telegraph*, July 23, 1946.
Anidjar, Gil. *The Jew, The Arab: A History of the Enemy.* Stanford, CA: Stanford University Press, 2003.
Anton, Glenna. "Blind Modernism and Zionist Waterscape: The Huleh Drainage Project." *Jerusalem Quarterly* 35 (2008): 76–92.
Antonius, George. *The Arab Awakening: The Story of the Arab National Movement.* London: Hamish Hamilton, 1938.
Antonius, Soraya. *The Lord.* London: Hamish Hamilton, 1986.
———. *Where the Jinn Consult.* London: Hamish Hamilton, 1987.
"Arab Manifesto." *Times*, July 24, 1946.
Arberry, A. J. *Majnun Laila, a poetical drama in five acts.* Cairo: Lencioni, 1933.
Arendt, Hannah. *Eichmann in Jerusalem: A Report on the Banality of Evil.* 1963. Reprint, London: Penguin, 2006.
———. "Introduction: Walter Benjamin: 1892–1940." In *Illuminations*, ed. Hannah Arendt, trans. Harry Zorn, 7–58. New York: Pimlico, 1999.
———. *The Origins of Totalitarianism.* New York: Harcourt, Brace, 1951.
———. "To Save the Jewish Homeland: There Is Still Time [1948]." In *The Jewish Writings*, ed. Jerome Kohn and Ron H. Feldman, 388–401. New York: Schocken, 2007.
———. "We Refugees." *The Menorah Journal* 31, no. 1 (1943): 69–77. Republished in *Altogether Elsewhere: Writers on Exile*, ed. Marc Robinson, 110–19. London: Faber and Faber, 1994.
Arendt, Hannah, and Gershom Scholem. *The Correspondence of Hannah Arendt and Gershom Scholem*, ed. Marie Luise Knott. Trans. Anthony David. Chicago: University of Chicago Press, 2017.
"Arthur Ruppin (1876–1943)." *Jewish Virtual Library.* Accessed May 14, 2020. https://www.jewishvirtuallibrary.org/arthur-ruppin.
"Artist Biography: William Gear." Tate. Accessed May 20, 2020. https://www.tate.org.uk/art/artists/william-gear-1146.
al-Asad, Nasir al-Din. *Muhammad Ruhi al-Khalidi ra'id al-bahth al-tarikhi fi Filastin* [Muhammad Ruhi al-Khalidi: A leading figure of historical research in Palestine]. Cairo: Ma'had al-buhuth al-'arabiyya, 1970.
Assmann, Aleida. "One Land and Three Narratives: Palestinian Sites of Memory in Israel." *Memory Studies* 11, no. 3 (2018): 287–300.
Awad, Louis. "T. S. Eliot." *al-Katib al-misri* 4, no. 1 (1946): 557–68.
al-'Awdat, Ya'qub. *Min a'lam al-fikr wal-adab fi Filastin* [Figures of intellectual thought and literature in Palestine]. Jordan: Jam'iyyat 'ummal al-matabi' al-ta'awuniyya, 1976.
Ayalon, Ami. *Reading Palestine: Printing and Literacy 1900–1948.* Austin: University of Texas, 2004.
———. *The Press in the Arab Middle East: A History.* Oxford: Oxford University Press, 1995.

"Ayn Hawd and 'the Unrecognized Villages.' " *Journal of Palestine Studies* 31, no.1 (2001/2002): 39.
al-Azm, Sadiq Jalal. *al-Naqd al-dhati baʻda al-hazima*. Beirut: Dar al-taliʻa, 1968. Trans. Geoge Stergios as *Self-Criticism After the Defeat*. With a foreword by Fouad Ajami, introduction Faisal Darraj (London: Saqi Books, 2011).
Badini. Dunia. *La Revue Shiʻr/Poésie et la modernité poétique arabe: Beyrouth (1957–70)*. Paris: Sindbad, 2009.
Balint, Benjamin. *Kafka's Last Trial: The Case of a Literary Legacy*. New York: Norton, 2018.
Baram, Amatzia. *Culture, History and Ideology in the Formation of the Ba'thist Era 1968–89*. London: Palgrave Macmillan, 1991.
Barenboim, Daniel, and Edward Said. *Parallels and Paradoxes: Explorations in Music and Society*. New York: Pantheon, 2002.
Barnes, Djuna. Preface to *Nightwood*, by T. S. Eliot. London: Faber and Faber, 1958. Trans. Wolfgang Hildesheimer as *Nachtgewächs. Roman*. Einleitung T. S. Eliot (Pfullingen: Neske, 1959).
Bashir, Bashir, and Leila Farsakh. "Three Questions That Make One." In *The Arab and Jewish Questions: Geographies of Engagement in Palestine and Beyond*, ed. Bashir Bashir and Leila Farsakh, 1–22. New York: Columbia University Press, 2020.
Bashir, Bashir, and Amos Goldberg. "Introduction." In *The Holocaust and the Nakba: A New Grammar of Trauma and History*, ed. Bashir Bashir and Amos Goldberg, 1–42. New York: Columbia University Press, 2019.
Bashkin, Orit. *New Babylonians: A History of the Jews in Modern Iraq*. Stanford, CA: Stanford University Pres, 2012.
Beckett, Chris. "Tambimuttu and the *Poetry London* Papers at the British Library: Reputation and Evidence." *Electronic British Library Journal* 9 (2009). https://www.bl.uk/eblj/2009articles/pdf/ebljarticle92009.pdf.
Beinin, Joel. *Was the Red Flag Flying There? Marxist Politics and the Arab-Israeli Conflict in Egypt and Israel 1948–1965*. Berkeley: University of California Press, 1990.
Benhabib, Seyla. *The Reluctant Modernism of Hannah Arendt*. Rev. ed. Lanham, MD: Rowman and Littlefield, 2003.
Benjamin, Walter. "Franz Kafka: On the Tenth Anniversary of His Death [1934]." In *Illuminations*, ed. Hannah Arendt. Trans. Harry Zorn, 108–35. New York: Pimlico, 1999.
——. "The Storyteller [1936]." In *Illuminations*, ed. Hannah Arendt, trans. Harry Zorn, 83–107. New York: Pimlico, 1999.
——. "The Task of the Translator [1923]." In *Illuminations*, ed. Hannah Arendt, trans. Harry Zorn, 70–82. New York: Pimlico, 1999.
——. "Theses on the Philosophy of History [1940/1950]." In *Illuminations*, ed. Hannah Arendt, trans. Harry Zorn, 245–55. New York: Pimlico, 1999.
Benton, Michael. *Towards a Poetics of Literary Biography*. New York: Palgrave Macmillan, 2015.
Bernstein, Richard. *Hannah Arendt and the Jewish Question*. Cambridge, MA: MIT Press, 1996.
Biermann, Wolf. "Kriegshetze Friedenshetze." *Die Zeit*. February 1, 1991.
"Bomb Attack May Retard Peace Efforts." *Washington Post*, July 24, 1946.
Boselli, Sandra. "Tambimuttu: Re-Inventing the Art of Poetry Illustration." *Electronic British Library Journal* 10 (2010). https://www.bl.uk/eblj/2016articles/pdf/ebljarticle102016.pdf.
Böttiger, Helmut. *Die Gruppe 47: Als die deutsche Literatur Geschichte schrieb*. Munich: Deutsche Verlags-Anstalt, 2012.

Boullata, Issa J. "The Beleaguered Unicorn: A Study of Tawfīq Sāigh." *Journal of Arabic Literature* 4, no. 1 (1973): 69–93.

——. *The Bells of Memory: A Palestinian Boyhood in Jerusalem.* Westmount, Quebec: Linda Leith, 2014.

——. "Jabrā, Jabrā Ibrāhīm." *Encyclopedia of Islam, Three.* Ed. Kate Fleet et al. 2014. http://dx.doi.org/10.1163/1573-3912_ei3_COM_27617.

——. "Living with the Tigress and the Muses: An Essay on Jabra Ibrahim Jabra." *World Literature Today* 72, no. 2 (2001): 214–23.

——. *Nafidha 'ala al-hadatha: Dirasat fi adab Jabra Ibrahim Jabra* [A window on modernity: Studies on Jabra Ibrahim Jabra's literature]. Beirut: al-Mu'assasa al-'arabiyya lil-dirasat wal-nashr, 2002.

Boullata, Kamal. *Palestinian Art: From 1850 to the Present.* London: Saqi Books, 2009.

Bourmoud, Philippe. " 'A Son of the Country': Dr. Tawfiq Canaan, Modernist Physician and Palestinian Ethnographer." In *Struggle and Survival in Palestine/Israel*, ed. Mark LeVine and Gershon Shafir, 104–24. Berkeley: University of California Press, 2012.

Boyle, Susan Silsby. *Betrayal of Palestine: The Story of George Antonius.* Boulder, CO: Westview, 2001.

Braese, Stephan, ed. *Bestandsaufnahme—Studien zur Gruppe 47.* Berlin: Erich Schmidt Verlag, 1999.

——. *Jenseits der Pässe: Wolfgang Hildesheimer. Eine Biographie.* Göttingen: Wallstein, 2017.

"British Are Blamed for Ignoring Warning." *Washington Post*, July 24, 1946.

Brockelmann, Carl. *Geschichte der islamischen Völker und Staaten.* Munich: Oldenbourg, 1939. Trans. Joel Carmichael and Moshe Perlmann as *History of the Islamic Peoples* (New York: Putnam, 1947).

Brod, Max. *Franz Kafka: Eine Biographie (Erinnerungen und Dokumente).* Prague: Mercy, 1937.

Buchholz, Hartmut. " . . . ich wäre mir ohne sie gar nicht denkbar": Wolfgang Hildesheimer und die Psychoanalyse." *Luzifer-Amor: Zeitschrift zur Geschichte der Psychoanalyse* 41 (2018): 141–52.

Budeiri, Musa. *The Palestine Communist Party 1919–1948: Arab and Jew in the Struggle for Internationalism.* London: Ithaca, 1979.

Buheiry, Marwan. *Beirut's Role in the Political Economy of the French Mandate 1919–39.* Oxford: Center for Lebanese Studies, 1986.

Bulos, Afif Alvarez. *Afif Bulos Sings Songs of Lebanon, Syria and Jordan.* 1961. Reprint, Washington, DC: Smithsonian Folkways Recordings, 2007.

——. *The Arabic Triliteral Verb: A Comparative Study of Grammatical Concepts and Processes.* Beirut: Khayats, 1965.

——. *Classical Arabic Music: A Recital of Muwashahat with Afif Bulos and His Ensemble.* 1976. Reprint, Washington, DC: Smithsonian Folkways Recordings, 2007.

——. *Hajjeh Hilaneh: Stories from Palestine and Lebanon.* Foreword Edward W. Said. Beirut: Librarie du Liban, 1975.

——. *Handbook of Arabic Music.* Beirut: Librarie du Liban, 1971.

Bulos, Nassib. *Jerusalem Crossroads.* Beirut: Dar An-Nahar, 2003.

——. *A Palestinian Landscape.* Beirut: Arab Institute for Research and Publishing, 1998.

Bulos, Suhail. *The Church Bell on Sunday: A Memoir.* Beirut: Dar Nelson, 2016.

——. *Land of Dreams.* Beirut: Dar Nelson, 2016.

——. *Rue du Mexique and Other Stories.* Nicosia: Rimal, 2010.

——. *Seminar and Other Stories.* Beirut: Dar Nelson, 2018.

Burke III, Edmund, and David N. Yaghoubian, ed. *Struggle and Survival in the Modern Middle East*. 2nd ed. Berkeley: University of California Press, 2006.

Burton, Richard Francis. *The Book of the Thousand Nights and A Night*. London: The Burton Club, 1885.

Büssow, Johan. *Hamidian Palestine: Politics and Society in the District of Jerusalem 1872–1908*. Leiden: Brill, 2011.

Butler, Judith. "Who Owns Kafka?" *London Review of Books* 33, no. 5 (2011). https://www.lrb.co.uk/the-paper/v33/n05/judith-butler/who-owns-kafka.

Butros, Atef. *Kafka: Ein jüdischer Schriftsteller aus arabischer Sicht*. Wiesbaden: Reichert, 2009.

Cahill, Richard. "The Image of 'Black and Tans' in late Mandate Palestine." *Jerusalem Quarterly* 40 (2009): 43–51.

———. "Sir Charles Tegart: 'The Counterterrorism Expert' in Palestine (Part 1)." *Jerusalem Quarterly* 74 (2018): 57–66.

———. "The Tegart Police Fortresses in British Mandate Palestine: A Reconsideration of Their Strategic Location and Purpose (Parts 2)." *Jerusalem Quarterly* 75 (2018): 48–61.

Campos, Michelle. *Ottoman Brothers: Muslims, Christians, and Jews in Early Twentieth-Century Palestine*. Stanford, CA: Stanford University Press, 2011.

Casanova, Pascale. *The World Republic of Letters*. Trans. M. B. DeBevoise. Cambridge, MA: Harvard University Press, 2004.

Chang, Pei-Yu. *Der geheimnisvolle Koffer von Herrn* Benjamin. Zürich: NordSüd Verlag, 2017.

"Changing Jerusalem: A New Panorama of the Holy City." *Times*, January 17, 1931.

Charters, David A. *The British Army and Jewish Insurgency in Palestine, 1945–47*. New York: Palgrave Macmillan, 1989.

Cheikho, Louis. *Kitab 'ilm al-adab* [Book of literature studies]. Beirut: Jesuit Press, 1924.

———. *Majani al-adab fi hada'iq al-'arab* [Literature in the gardens of the Arabs]. Beirut: Jesuit Press, 1913.

Clarke, Thurston. *By Blood and Fire: The Attack on the King David Hotel*. New York: Putnam, 1981.

Cleaveland, William L. *The Making of an Arab Nationalist: Ottomanism and Arabism in the Life and Thought of Sati' al-Husri*. Princeton, NJ: Princeton University Press, 1971.

———. "The Worlds of George Antonius: Identity, Culture, and the Making of an Anglo-Arab in the Pre-World War II Middle East." In *Auto/Biography and the Construction of Identity and Community in the Middle East*, ed. Mary Ann Fay, 125–38. Berkeley: California University Press, 2001.

Cleaver, John, ed. *Fitzwilliam: The First 150 Years of a Cambridge College*. With a foreword by David Starkey. London: Third Millennium, 2013.

Cogen-Kattab, Kobi, and Shoval Noam. *Tourism, Religion, and Pilgrimage in Jerusalem*. New York: Routledge, 2014.

Cohen, Hillel. "The First Israeli Government (1948–1950) and the Arab Citizens: Equality in Discourse, Exclusion in Practice." In *Israel and Its Palestinian Citizens: Ethnic Privileges in the Jewish State*, ed. Nadim N. Rouhana and Sahar S. Huneidi, 73–102. Cambridge: Cambridge University Press, 2017.

———. *Year Zero of the Arab-Israeli Conflict*. Trans. Haim Watzman. Waltham, MA: Brandeis University Press, 2015.

Cohen, Michael J. "The Genesis of the Anglo-American Committee on Palestine, November 1945: A Case Study in the Assertion of American Hegemony." *Historical Journal* 22, no. 1 (1979): 185–207.

Colla, Elliott. "Badr Shakir al-Sayyab: Cold War Poet." *Middle Eastern Literatures* 18, no. 3 (2015): 247–63.

Collins, Larry and Dominique Lapierre. *O Jerusalem*. New York: Simon and Schuster, 1972.

"Correspondenzen." *Jüdische Presse*, May 5, 1897.

Cosgrove, Mary. *Born Under Auschwitz: Melancholy Traditions in Postwar German Literature*. Rochester, NY: Camden House, 2014.

Creswell, Robyn. *City of Beginnings: Poetic Modernism in Beirut*. Princeton, NJ: Princeton University Press, 2019.

Crossman, Richard. *Palestine Mission: A Personal Record*. London: Hamish Hamilton, 1947.

Crum, Bartley C. *Behind the Silken Curtain: A Personal Account of Anglo-American Diplomacy in Palestine and the Middle East*. New York: Simon and Schuster, 1947.

Dahbour, Ahmad. "Jabra Ibrahim Jabra." *Diwan al-'arab*. September 13, 2006. https://www.diwanalarab.com/جبرا-إبراهيم-جبرا.

Dalachanis, Angelos, and Vincent Lemire, ed. *Ordinary Jerusalem 1840–1940: Opening New Archives, Revisiting a Global City*. Leiden: Brill, 2018.

Damrosch, Leo. *The Club: Johnson, Boswell, and the Friends Who Shaped an Age*. New Haven, CT: Yale University Press, 2019.

Daniel, Clifton. "Palestine Chiefs Deny Accusations." *New York Times*, July 26, 1946.

———. "Palestine Paper Attacks Zionists: Hebrew Journal Says Boards Should Resign." *New York Times*, July 25, 1946.

———. "Terrorist Zionists Say They Set Bomb: Denouncing British." *New York Times*, July 24, 1946.

Darraj, Faisal. *Jabra Ibrahim Jabra: wujuh al-muthaqqaf al-rumansi* [Jabra Ibrahim Jabra: Faces of the romantic intellectual]. Doha: Hamad Bin Khalifa University Press, 2018.

Darwaza, Muhammad Izzat. *Durus al-tarikh al-mutawassit wal-hadith* [Studies in medieval and modern history]. Cairo: Matba'at al-Salafiyya wa-maktabatuha, 1930.

Darwish, Mahmoud. *Ahad 'ashara kawkaban* [Eleven planets]. Beirut: Dar al-Jadid, 1992.

———. *Akhir al-layl* [The end of the night] [1967]. In *Diwan Mahmud Darwish*, 165–248. 10th ed. Beirut: Dar al-'Awda, 1983.

———. *'Ashiq min Filastin* [A lover from Palestine] [1966]. In *Diwan Mahmud Darwish*, 77–163. 10th ed. Beirut: Dar al-'Awda, 1983.

———. *Habibati tanhad min naumiha* [My beloved rises from her sleep] [1970]. In *Diwan Mahmud Darwish*, 311–62. 10th ed. Beirut: Dar al-'Awda, 1983.

———. *If I Were Another*. Trans. Fady Joudah. New York: Farrar Straus Giroux, 2009.

———. *Madih al-zill al-'ali* [In praise of the high shadow]. Beirut: Dar al-'Awda, 1983.

Davis, Rochelle. "Commemorating Education: Recollections of the Arab College in Jerusalem, 1918–1948." *Comparative Studies of South Asia, Africa, and the Middle East* 23, no. 1–2 (2003): 190–204.

———. "Growing Up Palestinian in Jerusalem Before 1948: Childhood Memories of Communal Life, Education, and Political Awareness." In *Jerusalem Interrupted: Modernity and Colonial Transformation 1917–Present*, ed. Lena Jayyusi, 187–210. Northampton, MA: Olive Branch, 2015.

———. "The Growth of the Western Communities, 1917–1948." In *Jerusalem 1948: The Arab Neighbourhoods and their Fate in the War*, ed. Salim Tamari, 32–66. Jerusalem: Institute for Jerusalem Studies and Badil Resource Center, 1999.

Davies, Clifford. "The Fighting Teacher Has a Secret!" *Daily Mirror*, November 26, 1956.

"Death Roll of 123 Feared in Jerusalem." *Times*, July 25, 1946.

Defoe, Daniel. *al-Tuhfa al-Bustaniyya fil-asfar al-kuruziyya* [al-Bustani's masterpiece of Crusoe's travels]. Trans. Butrus al-Bustani. Beirut: American Press, 1860.

Delbanco, Nicholas. *Group Portrait: Joseph Conrad, Stephen Crane, Ford Madox Ford, Henry James, and H. G. Wells*. New York: Morrow, 1982.

Demichelis, Marco. "From Nahda to Nakba: The Government Arab College of Jerusalem and Its Palestinian Historical Heritage in the First Half of the Twentieth Century." *Arab Studies Quarterly* 37, no. 3 (2015): 264–71.

Deuchar, Hannah Scott. "'Nahda': Mapping a Keyword in Cultural Discourse." *Alif: Journal of Comparative Poetics* 37, no. 37 (2017): 50–84.

DeYoung, Terri. "The Disguises of the Mind: Recent Palestinian Memoirs." *Review of Middle East Studies* 51, no. 1 (2017): 5–21.

Di-Capua, Yoav. "Changing the Arab Intellectual Guard: On the Fall of the *udaba'*, 1940–1960." In *Arabic Thought Against the Authoritarian Age: Towards an Intellectual History of the Present*, ed. Jens Hanssen and Max Weiss, 41–61. Cambridge: Cambridge University Press, 2018.

———. *Gatekeepers of the Arab Past: Historians and History-Writing in Twentieth-Century Egypt*. Berkeley: University of California Press, 2009.

———. *No Exit: Arab Existentialism, Jean-Paul Sartre and Decolonialization*. Chicago: University of Chicago Press, 2018.

Diller, Edward. "With Paul Geheeb from the 'Odenwaldschule' to the 'Ecole d'Humanité.'" *Journal of Educational Thought (JET)/Revue de la Pensée Éducative* 17, no. 1 (1983): 23–28.

Docker, John. "Dissident Voices on the History of Palestine-Israel: Martin Buber and the Bi-National Idea, Walid Khalidi's Indigenous Perspective." In *Sovereignty: Frontiers of Possibility*, ed. Julie Evans et al., 1–29. Honolulu: University of Hawaii Press, 2016.

Dolev, Diana. *The Planning and Building of the Hebrew University, 1919–1948: Facing the Temple Mount*. London: Lexington Books, 2016.

Donabed, Sargon George. *Reforging a Forgotten History: Iraq and the Assyrians in the Twentieth Century*. Edinburgh: Edinburgh University Press, 2015.

Doumani, Beshara B. *Family Life in the Ottoman Mediterranean: A Social History*. Cambridge: Cambridge University Press, 2017.

———. "My Grandmother and Other Stories: Histories of the Palestinians as Social Biographies." *Jerusalem Quarterly* 30 (2007): 3–9.

———. *Rediscovering Palestine: Merchants and Peasants in Jabal Nablus, 1700–1900*. Berkeley: University of California Press, 1995.

"Dr. Weizmann Warns Jews." *Daily Telegraph*, July 29, 1946.

Drumsta, Emily. "Chronicles of Disappearance: The Novel of Investigation in the Arab World, 1975–1985." PhD diss., University of California, 2016. *eScholarship*. escholarship.org/uc/item/6tf2596b.

———. "Words Against Erasure: The Persistence of the Poetic in Jabrā Ibrāhīm Jabrā's *In Search of Walid Masoud*." *Middle Eastern Literatures* 19, no. 1 (2016): 56–76.

Durzak, Manfred. "Ich kann über nichts anderes schreiben als über ein potentielles Ich: Gespräch mit Wolfgang Hidlesheimer." In *Gespräche über den Roman: Formbestimmungen und Analysen*, 271–313. Frankfurt: Suhrkamp, 1976.

Eban, Abba. *An Autobiography*. London: Weidenfeld and Nicolson, 1978.

Eddé, Dominique. *Edward Said: His Thought as a Novel*. Trans. Trista Selous and Ros Schwartz. London: Verso, 2019.

Eden, Anthony. *Full Circle: The Memoirs of Anthony Eden*. London: Houghton Mifflin, 1960.

Eiland, Howard and Michael W. Jennings. *Walter Benjamin: A Critical Life*. Cambridge, MA: Belknap Press of Harvard University Press, 2014.

Eisenberg, Ronald L. *The Streets of Jerusalem: Who, What, Why*. Jerusalem: Devora, 2006.

Eliot, T. S. *The Waste Land*. New York: Boni and Liveright, 1922. Trans. Adonis and Yusuf al-Khal as *al-Ard al-kharab* in *T. S. Eliot: Tarjamat min al-shi'r al-hadith* [T. S. Eliot: Translations of modern poetry] (Beirut: Dar majallat Shi'r, 1959).

Ellenson, David. *Rabbi Esriel Hildesheimer and the Creation of a Modern Jewish Orthodoxy*. Tuscaloosa: University of Alabama Press, 1990.

Erakat, Noura. *Justice for Some: Law and the Question of Palestine*. Stanford, CA: Stanford University Press, 2019.

Faris, Hani A. "Israel Zangwill's Challenge to Zionism." *Journal of Palestine Studies* 4, no. 3 (1975): 74–90.

"Farm School Heads Released: Dr. Siegfried Lehmann and Colleagues." *Palestine Post*, May 9, 1940.

Faulkner, William. *The Sound and the Fury*. New York: Random House, 1929. Trans. Jabra Ibrahim Jabra as *al-Sakhab wal-'unf* (Beirut: Arab Institution for Research and Publishing, 1961).

Fawaz, Leila. "Albert Hourani (1915–1993)." *Middle East Studies Association Bulletin*. 2002. https://web.archive.org/web/20060218221244/http://fp.arizona.edu/mesassoc/Bulletin/36-1/36-1HouraniBio.html.

"Federal Plan for Palestine." *Daily Telegraph*, July 25, 1946.

Felman, Shoshana. "Benjamin's Silence." *Critical Inquiry* 25, no. 2 (1999): 201–34.

"Fine for School Heads: Ben Shemen Sentences Commuted or Reduced." *Palestine Post*, May 7, 1940.

Finn, Peter and Petra Couvée. *The Zhivago Affair: The Kremlin, the CIA and the Battle Over a Forbidden Book*. New York: Pantheon, 2014.

Fischbach, Michael R. "Arab Higher Committee." *Encyclopedia of the Palestinians*, ed. Philip Mattar, 28–29. New York: Facts on File, 2005.

——. "Khalidi, Husayn Fakhri." *Encyclopedia of the Palestinians*, ed. Philip Mattar, 279. New York: Facts on File, 2005.

——. "Safad." *Encyclopedia of the Palestinians*, ed. Philip Mattar, 430. New York: Facts on File, 2005.

——. "Tuqan (family)." *Encyclopedia of the Palestinians*, ed. Philip Mattar, 495. New York: Facts on File, 2005.

Fischer, Yochi. "What Does Exile Look Like? Transformations in the Linkage Between the Shoah and the Nakba." In *The Holocaust and the Nakba: A New Grammar of Trauma and History*, ed. Bashir Bashir and Amos Goldberg, 173–86. New York: Columbia University Press, 2019.

Fleischmann, Ellen L. "Mogannam, Matiel." *Encyclopedia of the Palestinians*, ed. Philip Mattar, 323. New York: Facts on File, 2005.

———. *The Nation and Its "New" Women: The Palestinian Women's Movement, 1920–1948*. Berkeley: University of California Press, 2003.

Flores, Alexander. "Judeophobia in Context: Anti-Semitism Among Modern Palestinians." Anti-Semitism in the Arab World, Special Issue, *Die Welt des Islams: International Journal for the Study of Modern Islam* 46, no. 3 (2006): 307–30.

Fox, Margalit. "Garry Davis, Man of No Nation Who Saw One World of No War, Dies at 91." *New York Times*, July 29, 2013.

Frazer, James. *The Golden Bough: A Study in Comparative Religion*. 2 vols. London: Macmillan, 1890. Trans. Jabra Ibrahim Jabra as *Adunis: Dirasa fil-asatir wal-adyan al-sharqiyya al-qadima* (Beirut: Dar al-sira' al-fikri, 1957).

Fried, Erich. "Held Wider Willen." *Die Zeit*. August 18, 1967.

Fuchs, Ron and Gilbert Herbert. "Representing Mandatory Palestine: Austen St. Barbe Harrison and the Representational Buildings of the British Mandate in Palestine, 1922–37." *Architectural History* 43 (2000): 281–333.

"Funduq al-malik Dawud [King David Hotel]." *al-Hayat*, December 21, 1931.

Furas, Yoni. *Educating Palestine: Teaching and Learning History Under the Mandate*. Oxford: Oxford University Press, 2020.

Furlonge, Geoffrey. *Palestine Is My Country: The Story of Musa Alami*. London: Murray, 1969.

Gabsi, Wafa. " 'Fiction and Art Practice': Interview with Larissa Sansour 'A Space Exodus.'" *Contemporary Practices* 10 (2012): 114–19.

Gaunt, David. *Massacres, Resistance, Protectors: Muslim-Christian Relations in Eastern Anatolia During World War I*. Piscataway, NJ: Gorgias, 2006.

Gavish, Dov. *A Survey of Palestine Under the British Mandate, 1920–1948*. London: Routledge, 2005.

"George Antonius." *Palestinian Journeys*. Accessed May 9, 2020. https://www.paljourneys.org/en/biography/6571/george-antonius.

Ghazoul, Ferial J., and Barbara Harlow. *The View from Within: Writers and Critics on Contemporary Arabic Literature. A selection from Alif: Journal of Comparative Poetics*. Cairo: American University in Cairo Press, 1994.

Gish, Amit. "Ownerless Objects? The Story of the Books Palestinians Left Behind in 1948." *Jerusalem Quarterly* 33 (2008): 7–20.

Glass, Joseph B. *From New Zion to Old Zion: American Jewish Immigration and Settlement in Palestine, 1917–1939*. Detroit, MI: Wayne State University Press, 2002.

Glazer, Steven A. "Language of Propaganda: The Histadrut, Hebrew Labour, and the Palestinian Worker." *Journal of Palestine Studies* 36, no. 2 (2007): 25–38.

———. "Picketing for Hebrew Labor: A Window on Histadrut Tactics and Strategy." *Journal of Palestine Studies* 30, no. 4 (2001): 39–54.

Gleichauf, Ingeborg. *Hannah Arendt und Karl Jaspers: Geschichte einer einzigartigen Freundschaft*. Cologne: Böhlau Verlag, 2021.

Glick, Thomas F. "From the Sarton Papers: Paul Kraus and Arabic Alchemy." *Cronos* 2, no. 2 (1999): 221–44.

Golani, Motti, and Adel Manna. *Two Sides of the Same Coin: Independence and Nakba 1948. Two Narratives of the 1948 War and Its Outcome*. Trans Geremy Forman. English-Hebrew edition. Dordrecht: Republic of Letters, 2011.

Gordon. Louis A. "Arthur Koestler and his Ties to Zionism and Jabotinsky." *Studies in Zionism* 12, no. 2 (1991): 149–68.

Gorman, Anthony. *Historians, State, and Politics in Twentieth Century Egypt: Contesting the Nation*. London: Routledge, 2003.

"Government and Army H.Q. Blown Up: Palestine's Worst Outrage." *Manchester Guardian*, July 23, 1946.

Green, Abigail. "Rethinking Sir Moses Montefiore: Religion, Nationhood, and International Philanthropy in the Nineteenth Century." *American Historical Review* 110, no. 3: 631–58.

Greenberg, Nathaniel. "Political Modernism, Jabrā, and the Baghdad Modern Art Group." *CLCWeb: Comparative Literature and Culture* 12, no. 2 (2010). http://dx.doi.org/10.7771/1481-4374.1603.

Gribetz, Jonathan Marc. *Defining Neighbors: Religion, Race, and the Early Zionist-Arab Encounter*. Princeton, NJ: Princeton University Press, 2015.

Gunkel, Christoph. "50th Anniversary of the 'Spiegel Affair': A Watershed Moment of West German Democracy." *Spiegel International*, September 21, 2012.

Gwyer, Kirstin. *Encrypting the Past: The German-Jewish Holocaust Novel of the First Generation*. Oxford: Oxford University Press, 2014.

Habiby, Emile. 1974. *al-Waqa'i' al-ghariba fi ikhtifa' Sa'id Abi al-Nahs al-Mutasha'il*. Haifa: Manshurat Arabesque, 1973. Trans. Salma Khadra Jayyusi and Trevor LeGassik as *The Secret Life of Saeed, the Ill-Fated Pessoptimist: A Palestinian Who Became a Citizen of Israel* (Columbia, LA: Readers International. 1989).

Haddadian-Moghaddam, Esmaeil. "The Cultural Cold War in the Middle East: William Faulkner and Franklin Book Programs." Translation and the Cultural Cold War, Special Issue, *Translation and Interpreting Studies* 15, no. 3 (2020): 441–63.

Hadjithomas, Joana, and Khalil Joreige, dirs. *Ismyrne/Ismyrna*. Lebanon: Abbout Productions, 2016.

Hafez, Sabry. "An Arabian Master." *New Left Review* 37, no. 37 (2006): 39–67.

Hajj, Samir Fawzi. *Maraya: Jabra Ibrahim Jabra wal-fann al-riwa'i* [Mirrors: Jabra Ibrahim Jabra and the art of narration]. Beirut: al-Mu'assasa al-'arabiyya lil-dirasat wal-nashr, 2005.

Halabi, Zeina G. "The Day the Wandering Dreamer Became a Fida'i: Jabra Ibrahim Jabra and the Fashioning of Political Commitment." In *Commitment and Beyond: Reflections on/of the Political in Arabic Literature Since the 1940s*, ed. Georges Khalil and Friederike Pannewick, 157–70. Wiesbaden: Reichert, 2015.

——. *The Unmaking of the Arab Intellectual: Prophecy, Exile, and the Nation*. Edinburgh: Edinburgh University Press, 2017.

Halaby, Samia A. "The Pictorial Arts of Jerusalem, 1900–1948." In *Jerusalem Interrupted: Modernity and Colonial Transformation 1917–present*, ed. Lena Jayyusi, 21–56. Northampton, MA: Olive Branch, 2015.

Halevy, Dotan. "Marginal Diplomacy: Alexander Knesevich and the Consular Agency in Gaza, 1905–1914." *Jerusalem Quarterly* 71 (2017): 81–93.

Halim, Hala. *Alexandrian Cosmopolitanism: An Archive*. New York: Fordham University Press, 2013.

Hallaq, Hassan. *Mudhakkirat Salim 'Ali Salam (1868–1938) ma'a dirasat lil-'alaqat al-uthmaniyya–al-'arabiyya wal-'alaqat al-firansiyya–al-lubnaniyya* [The memoirs of Salim 'Ali Salam (1868–1938) with studies of Ottoman-Arab and French-Lebanese relations]. Beirut: Dar al-nahda al-'arabiyya, 2013.

Halperin, Liora R. "Hebrew Under English Rule: The Language Politics of Mandate Palestine." In *The Routledge Handbook of the History of the Middle East Mandates*, ed. Cyrus Schayegh and Andrew Arsan, 336–48. London: Routledge, 2015.

Hammad, Isabella. "A Novel That Explores the Silencing of Palestinian Trauma." *New York Times*, June 21, 2019.

Hanley, Will. "Grieving the Cosmopolitanism in Middle Eastern Studies." *History Compass* 6, no. 5 (2008): 1346–67.

Hanssen, Jens. "Albert's World: Historicism, Liberal Imperialism and the Struggle for Palestine, 1936–48." In *Arabic Thought Beyond the Liberal Age: Towards an Intellectual History of the Nahda*, ed. Jens Hanssen and Max Weiss, 62–92. Cambridge: Cambridge University Press, 2016.

——. *Fin de Siècle Beirut: The Making of an Ottoman Provincial Capital*. Oxford: Oxford University Press, 2005.

——. "Kafka and Arabs." *Critical Inquiry* 39, no. 1 (2012): 167–97.

——. "Translating Revolution: Hannah Arendt in Arab Political Culture. *HannahArendt.Net* 7, no. 1 (2013). https://doi.org/10.57773/hanet.v7i1.301.

Hanssen, Jens, and Max Weiss, ed. *Arabic Thought Against the Authoritarian Age: Towards an Intellectual History of the Present*. Cambridge: Cambridge University Press, 2018.

——. *Arabic Thought Beyond the Liberal Age: Towards an Intellectual History of the Nahda*. Cambridge: Cambridge University Press, 2016.

Al-Hardan, Anaheed. "al-Nakbah in Arab Thought: The Transformation of a Concept." *Comparative Studies of South Asia, Africa and the Middle East* 35, no. 3 (2015): 622–38.

Harmon, Jeff B., dir. "Saddam's Iraq." Transcript. Surrey: Journeyman Pictures, 1991. https://www.journeyman.tv/film_documents/1181/transcript.

Hartman, Saidiya. *Lose Your Mother: A Journey along the Atlantic Slave Road*. New York: Farrar, Strauss and Giroux, 2006.

——. "Venus in Two Acts." *Small Axe* 12, no. 2 (2008): 1–14.

Hawas, May. "Taha Hussein and the Case for World Literature." *Comparative Literature Studies* 55, no. 1 (2018): 66–92.

Herzl, Theodor. *The Complete Diaries of Theodor Herzl*. Ed. Raphael Patai. Trans. Harry Zohn. New York: Herzl, 1960.

Hildesheimer, Arnold. *Die Welt der ungewohnten Dimensionen: Versuch einer gemeinverständlichen Darstellung der modernen Physik und ihrer philosophischen Folgerungen*. With a foreword by Werner Heisenberg. Leiden: Sijhoff, 1953.

Hildesheimer, Esriel. "Die Palästinafrage und ihre Geschichte (ein Vortrag)." In *Rabbiner Dr. Israel Hildesheimer, Gesammelte Aufsätze*, ed. Meier Hildesheimer, 180–217. Frankfurt: Verlag Hermon, 1923.

Hildesheimer, Hanna. Letters to Paul Geheeb, July 27 and October 7, 1933. Unpublished correspondence, WHA 891.

——. "Vier Generationen." Unpublished typescript, WHA 1639.

Hildesheimer, Henriette. "Memories of my Youth." In *Jüdisches Leben in Deutschland*. Vol. 2, *Selbstzeugnisse zur Sozialgeschichte im Kaiserreich*, ed. Monika Richarz, 77–86. Stuttgart: Deutsche Verlags-Anstalt, 1979.

Hildesheimer, Hirsch. *Beiträge zur Geographie Palästinas*. Berlin: Rosenstein and Hildesheimer, 1886.

Hillrichs, Hans Helmut. "Der Dichter und die Eisenbahnen: Annäherung an Wolfgang Hildesheimer." In *"Ich werde nun schweigen": Gespräch mit Hans Helmut Hillrichs in der Reihe "Zeugen des Jahrhunderts,"* ed. Ingo Hermann, 7–13. Göttingen: Lamuv, 1993.

Himadeh, S. B., ed. *Economic Organization of Palestine*. Beirut: American University of Beirut Press, 1938.

Hink, Christina. "Where East Meets West: Cultivating a Cosmopolitan London in the 1920s." *Altre Modernitsa/Otras Modernidades/Autres Modernités/Other Modernities* 20, no. 11 (2018): 38–52.

"History of the U.S. and Lebanon." U.S. Embassy in Lebanon. Accessed June 6, 2020. https://lb.usembassy.gov/our-relationship/policy-history/io.

Hochberg, Gil Z. *Becoming Palestine: Toward and Archival Imagination of the Future*. Durham, NC: Duke University Press, 2021.

——. *In Spite of Partition: Jews, Arabs, and the Limits of Separatist Imagination*. Princeton, NJ: Princeton University Press, 2007.

——. "This City That Isn't One: Fragments on a Fragmented City." *Contending Modernities: Global Currents Article*. 2017. https://contendingmodernities.nd.edu/global-currents/fragmented-city.

——. *Visual Occupations: Violence and Visibility in a Conflict Zone*. Durham, NC: Duke University Press, 2015.

Holme, H. Christopher. 1992. *Portrait*. Oxford: Text and Graphica.

Holt, Elizabeth M. " 'Bread or Freedom': The Congress of Cultural Freedom, the CIA, and the Arabic Literary Journal Ḥiwār." *Journal of Arabic Literature* 44, no. 1 (2013): 83–102.

——. "Resistance Literature and Occupied Palestine in Cold War Beirut." *Journal of Palestine Studies* 50, no. 1 (2021): 3–18.

Holtzman, Avner. *Hayim Nahman Bialik: Poet of Hebrew*. New Haven, CT: Yale University Press, 2017.

Höpp, Gerhard, ed. *Mufti-Papiere: Briefe, Memoranden, Rede und Aufrufe Amin al-Husainis aus dem Exil, 1940–1945*. Berlin: Klaus Schwarz Verlag, 2002.

Hourani, Albert. *Arabic Thought in the Liberal Age 1798–1939*. 9th ed. 1962. Reprint, Cambridge: Cambridge University Press, 1993.

——. "The Case Against a Jewish State in Palestine: Albert Hourani's Statement to the Anglo-American Committee of Enquiry 1946." *Journal of Palestine Studies* 35, no. 1 (2005): 80–90.

——. "Foreword." In Walid Khalidi, *Palestine Reborn*, ix–xii. London: Tauris. 1992.

——. *A History of the Arab Peoples*. London: Faber and Faber, 1991.

——. "Musa 'Alami and the Problem of Palestine, 1933–1949." In *Studia Palaestina: Studies in Honor of Constantine K. Zurayk/Dirasat filastiniyya: majmu'at abhath wuddi'at takriman lil-duktur Qustantin Zurayk*, ed. Hisham Nashabeh, 23–41. Beirut: Institute for Palestine Studies, 1988.

Hourani, Cecil. *An Unfinished Odyssey: Lebanon and Beyond*. London: Weidenfeld & Nicolson, 1984.

——. *An Unfinished Odyssey: Lebanon and Beyond: Books I and II*. Beirut: A. Antoine, 2012.

Hourani, Cecil, and Zelfa Hourani. *Fadlo Hourani: The Quiet Merchant of Manchester*. Beirut: Antoine, 2020.

al-Hout, Bayan Nuweihid. "The Palestinian Political Elite During the Mandate Period." *Journal of Palestine Studies* 9, no. 1 (1979): 85–111.

——. *al-Qiyadat wal-mu'assasat al-siyasiyya fi Filastin 1917–1948* [Political leaders and institutions in Palestine]. Beirut: Mu'assasat al-dirasat al-filastiniyya, 1986.

———. "Walid al-Khalidi wal-ta'rikh lil-nakba [Walid Khalidi and writing the history of the Nakba]. In *Mi'at 'am 'ala tasrih Balfour: al-thabit wal-mutahawwil fi al-mashru' al-kulunyali iza' Filastin* [Hundred years after the Balfour declaration: The invariable and the changeable in the colonial project towards Palestine], ed. Maher Charif, 7–26. Beirut: Institute for Palestine Studies, 2019.

Hughes, Edward. "Michael Sheringham Obituary." *Guardian*, February 12, 2016.

Hughes, Matthew. "The Banality of Brutality: British Armed Forces and the Repression of the Arab Revolt in Palestine, 1936–39." *English Historical Review* 124, no. 507 (2009): 314–54.

———. *Britain's Pacification of Palestine: The British Army, the Colonial State, and the Arab Revolt, 1936–1939*. Cambridge: Cambridge University Press, 2019.

Husri, Khaldun S. "The Assyrian Affair of 1933 (I)." *International Journal of Middle East Studies* 5, no. 2 (1974): 161–76.

———. "The Assyrian Affair of 1933 (II)." *International Journal of Middle East Studies* 5, no. 3 (1974): 344–60.

al-Husri, Sati. "Hawl kitab *Mustaqbal al-thaqafa fil-Misr* [On the book *The Future of Culture in Egypt*]." *al-Risalah* 7 (1939): 316–21.

Hussein, Taha. "Franz Kafka." *al-Katib al-misri* 5, no. 18 (1947): 197–213.

———. *Mustaqbal al-thaqafa fil-Misr*. 2 vols. Cairo: Matba'at al-ma'arif, 1938. Trans. Sidney Glazer as *The Future of Culture in Egypt* (Washington, DC: American Council for Learned Societies, 1954).

al-Husseini, Ishaq Musa. "al-Hayat al-adabiyya fi Filastin [Literary life in Palestine]" *al-Adib*, May 1945, 47.

Hysler-Rubin, Noah. "Geography, Colonialism, and Town Planning: Patrick Geddes' Plan for Mandatory Jerusalem." *Cultural Geographies*, 18, no. 2 (2011): 231–48.

"Ibrahim Tuqan." *Interactive Encyclopedia of the Palestine Question*. Accessed May 28, 2013. https://www.palquest.org/en/biography/9721/ibrahim-tuqan.

"Iqtirah irsal lajna wizariyya ila Filastin li-dars al-mawqif [A proposal to send a ministerial committee to Palestine to study the situation]." *al-Difa'*, July 23, 1946.

"al-Irhabiyun al-yahud yaqtarifun jarima wahshiyya . . . [Jewish terrorists commit a terrible crime]." *Filastin*, July 23, 1946.

'Isa, Marqus and George Sahhar. "Funduq al-malik dawud: shabaka min shibak al-suhyuniyyin [King David Hotel: A network among Zionist networks]." *Filastin*, December 20, 1931.

"Israeli Land Development Company." Accessed on May 16, 2020. https://www.ildc.co.il/en/category/company-profile.

"Izzeddin al-Qassam." *Interactive Encyclopedia of the Palestine Question*. Accessed May 28, 2023. https://www.palquest.org/en/biography/9837/izzeddin-al-qassam.

Jacobson, Abigail, and Moshe Naor. *Oriental Neighbors: Middle Eastern Jews and Arabs in Mandatory Palestine*. Waltham, MA: Brandeis University, 2016.

Jad, Islad. "From Salons to the Popular Committees: Palestinian Women, 1919–89." In *The Israel/Palestine Question: A Reader*, ed. Ilan Pappé, 186–204. 2nd ed. London: Routledge, 2007.

Jäger, Maren. *Die Joyce-Rezeption in der deutschsprachigen Erzählliteratur nach 1945*. Tübingen: Niemeyer, 2009.

Jardine, J. B. S. Letter to Wolfgang Hildesheimer, London, April 15, 1949. Unpublished correspondence, WHA 482.

Jawhariyyeh, Wasif, *The Storyteller of Jerusalem: The Life and Times of Wasif Jawhariyyeh, 1904–1948*. Ed. Salim Tamari and Issam Nassar. Trans. Nada Elzeer. Northampton, MA: Olive Branch, 2014.

Jayyusi, Lena, ed. *Jerusalem Interrupted: Modernity and Colonial Transformation 1917–Present.* Northampton, MA: Olive Branch, 2015.

Jayyusi, Salma Khadra. "Introduction: Palestinian Literature in Modern Times." In *Anthology of Modern Palestinian Literature*, ed. Salma Khadra Jayyusi, 1–80. New York: Columbia University Press, 1995.

Jehle, Volker. "Nachwort." In Wolfgang Hildesheimer. *"Die sichtbare Wirklichkeit": Die Briefe an die Eltern 1937–1962*, ed. Volker Jehle, 1492–93. Vol. 2. Frankfurt: Suhrkamp, 2016.

——. *Wolfgang Hildesheimer: Werkgeschichte.* Frankfurt: Suhrkamp, 1990.

Jenkins, Jennifer. *Provincial Modernity: Local Culture and Liberal Politics in Fin-de-Siècle Hamburg.* Ithaca, NY: Cornell University Press, 2003.

Johnson, Michael. "Political Bosses and Their Gangs: *zu'ama* and *qabadayat* in the Sunni Muslim Quarters of Beirut." In *Patrons and Clients in Mediterranean Societies*, ed. Ernest Gellner and John Waterbury, 207–24. London. Duckworth, 1977.

Johnson, Rebecca Carol. "The Politics of Reading: Recognition and Revolution in Jabra Ibrahim Jabra's *In Search of Walid Masoud*." In *Recognition: The Poetics of Narrative: Interdisciplinary Studies on Anagnorisis*, ed. Philip F. Kennedy and Marilyn Lawrence, 178–92. New York: Peter Lang, 2009.

Jolliffe, John. "Obituary: The Countess of Oxford and Asquith." *Independent*, September 6, 1998.

Joyce, James. *Finnegans Wake.* London: Faber and Faber, 1939. Trans. Wolfgang Hildesheimer as *Anna Livia Plurabelle* (Frankfurt: Suhrkamp, 1970).

Jubeh, Nazmi. "Patrick Geddes: Luminary or Prophet of Demonic Planning." *Jerusalem Quarterly* 80 (2019): 23–40.

Kafka, Franz. *Der Prozess.* Ed. Max Brod. Berlin: Verlag Die Schmiede. 1925. Trans. Willa and Edwin Muir as *The Trial* (London: Gollancz, 1937).

Kalisman, Hilary Falb. " 'A World of Tomorrow': Diaspora Intellectuals and Liberal Thought in the 1950s." *Journal of Palestine Studies* 50, no. 2 (2021): 1–16.

Kanafani, Ghassan. *Adab al-muqawama fi Filastin al-muhtalla 1948–1966* [Resistance literature in Occupied Palestine 1948–1966]. Beirut: Dar al-Adab, 1966.

——. *Rijal fil-shams.* Beirut: Manshurat al-tali'a, 1963. Trans. Hilary Kilpatrick as *Men in the Sun and Other Palestinian Stories* (London: Three Continents Press, 1983).

Kark, Ruth, and Michal Oren-Nordheim. *Jerusalem and Its Environs: Quarters, Neighborhoods, Villages 1800–1948.* Jerusalem: Hebrew University Magnes Press, 2001.

Karkabi, Waleed, and Adi Roitenberg. "Arab-Jewish Architectural Partnership in Haifa During the Mandate Period: Qaraman and Gerstel Meet on the 'Seam Line.'" In *Haifa Before and After 1948: Narratives of a Mixed City*, ed. Mahmoud Yazbak and Yfaat Weiss, 43–68. Dordrecht: Institute for Historical Justice and Reconciliation and Republic of Letters Publishing, 2011.

Kassir, Samir. *Histoire de Beyrouth.* Paris: Fayard, 2003.

Khalaf, Issa. *Politics in Palestine: Arab Factionalism and Social Disintegration 1939–1948.* Albany, NY: SUNY Press, 1991.

Khalaf, Samir, *Civil and Uncivil Violence in Lebanon.* New York: Columbia University Press, 2002.

al-Khalidi, Ahmad Samih. *Arkan al-tadris* [Pillars of teaching]. Jerusalem: Maktabat bayt al-maqdis, 1934.

———. "Filastin fi nusf qarn: Ra'aytuha tanhar [Palestine in half a century: I saw her disintegrate]." *Beirut al-masa'*, January 23 and 30; February 6, 13, 20, and 27; March 6, 13, 20, and 27; April 3, 10, 17, and 24; and May 1, 1950.

Khalidi, Anbara Salam. *Jawla fil-dhikrayat bayn lubnan wa-filastin*. Beirut: Dar An-Nahar, 1997. Trans. Tarif Khalidi as *Memoirs of an Early Arab Feminist: The Life and Activism of Anbara Salam Khalidi* (London: Pluto, 2013).

al-Khalidi, Hussein Fakhri. *Exiled from Jerusalem*. Ed. Rafiq Husseini. London: Tauris, 2020.

al-Khalidi, Muhammad Ruhi. *Muhammad Ruhi al-Khalidi al-Maqdisi (1864–1913): Kutubuhu wa-maqalatuhu wa-muntakhabat min makhtubatihi* [Muhammad Ruhi al-Khalidi (1864–1913): Books, articles, and selected manuscripts]. Ed. with an introduction by Mariam Saeed El-Ali. 2 vols. Beirut: Institute for Palestine Studies, 2021.

———. *al-Sayunizm aw al-mas'ala al-sahyuniyya: Awwal dirasa 'ilmiyya bil-'arabiyya 'an al-sahyuniyya* [Zionism or the Zionist question: The first academic study in Arabic on Zionism]. Ed. with an introduction by Walid Khalidi. Beirut: Institute for Palestine Studies, 2020.

Khalidi, Rashid. *The Hundred Years' War on Palestine: A History of Settler Colonialism, 1917–2017*. New York: Metropolitan Books, 2020.

———. *The Iron Cage: The Story of the Palestinian Struggle for Statehood*. Boston, MA: Beacon, 2006.

———. "Khalidi, Walid." *Encyclopedia of the Palestinians*, ed. Philip Mattar, 280–84. New York: Facts on File, 2005.

———. *Palestinian Identity: The Construction of Modern National Consciousness*. 2nd ed. New York: Columbia University Press, 2010.

Khalidi, Tarif. *Ana wal-kutub*. Beirut: Manshurat al-jamal, 2018. Trans. Tarif Khalidi as "The Books in My Life: A Memoir." *Jerusalem Quarterly* 73 (2018): 63–78, 74 (2018): 30–47, and 75 (2018): 115–31.

———. "A Family's History." Khalidi Library. 2020. http://www.khalidilibrary.org/en/Article/56/A-Family's-History—By-Tarif-Khalidi.

———. "Have I Seen This Movie Before? A Memoir." Unpublished typescript, Beirut, 2020.

———. *Images of Muhammad: Narratives of the Prophet in Islam Across the Centuries*. New York: Doubleday, 2009.

———. "Palestinian Historiography: 1900–1948." *Journal of Palestine Studies* 10, no. 3 (1981): 59–76.

———. "Unveiled: Anbara Salam in England 1925–1927." In *The Arabs and Britain: Changes and Exchanges*, 378–88. Cairo: The British Council, 1999.

Khalil, Georges, and Friederike Pannewick, ed. *Commitment and Beyond: Reflections on/of the Political in Arabic Literature Since the 1940s*. Wiesbaden: Reichert, 2015.

Khamsa wa-saba'un sana 'ala ta'sis al-kulliyya al-'arabiyya fil-Quds [Seventy-five years after the establishment of the Arab College in Jerusalem]. Amman: al-Bank al-'arabi, 1995.

al-Kharrat, Edward. "The Mashriq." In *Modern Literature in the Near and Middle East 1850–1970*, ed. Robin Ostle, 180–92. London: Routledge, 1991.

al-Khateeb, H. "Rūḥī al-Khālidī: A Pioneer of Comparative Literature in Arabic." *Journal of Arabic Literature* 18, no. 1 (1987): 81–87.

Khoury, Elias. "Atlal al-bi'r al-thaniyya [The ruins of the second well]." *Mulhaq An-Nahar*, April 19, 2010.

———. *Awlad al-ghitu: Ismi Adam*. Vol. 1. Beirut: Dar al-Adab, 2012. Trans. Humphrey Davis as *Children of the Ghetto: My Name Is Adam*. Vol. 1 (London: Archipelago Press, 2018).

———. *Bab al-shams*. Beirut: Dar al-Adab, 1998. Trans. Humphrey Davies as *Gate of the Sun* (New York: Archipelago Books, 2005).
———. "Foreword." In *The Holocaust and the Nakba: A New Grammar of Trauma and History*, ed. Bashir Bashir and Amos Goldberg, ix–xvi. New York: Columbia University Press, 2019.
———. "Hiwar ma'a Jabra Ibrahim Jabra [Conversation with Jabra Ibrahim Jabra]." *Shu'un filastiniyya* 77 (1978): 176–92. Republished as "Min al-furū' ilā al-jusūr." [From branches to roots] *Yanabi' al-ru'ya: Dirasat naqdiyya* [Sources of vision: Critical studies], 117–42. Beirut: al-Mu'assassa al-'arabiyya lil-dirasat wal-nashr, 1979.
———. "al-Nakba al-mustamirra [The ongoing Nakba]." *Majallat al-dirasat al-filastiniyya* 89 (2012): 37–50.
———. "Rethinking the Nakba." *Critical Inquiry* 38, no. 2 (2012): 250–66.
Khoury, Philip S. "Lessons from the Eastern Shore: 1998 MESA Presidential Address." *Review of Middle East Studies* 33, no. 1 (1999): 2–9.
Khuri, Yousef, ed. *al-Sihafa al-'arabiyya fi Filastin 1876–1948* [The Arabic press in Palestine 1876–1948]. Beirut: Institute for Palestine Studies, 1976.
Khuri-Makdisi, Ilham. *The Eastern Mediterranean and the Making of Global Radicalism, 1860–1914*. Berkeley: University of California Press, 2013.
"King David Hotel." YouTube, September 10, 2014, https://www.youtube.com/watch?v=QRaTKGiWjCk.
Klein, Menachem. *Lives in Common: Arabs and Jews in Jerusalem, Jaffa, and Hebron*. London: Hurst, 2014.
Klemm, Verena. "Different Notions of Commitment (Iltizām) and Committed Literature (al-adab al-multazim) in the Literary Circles of the Mashriq." *Arabic and Middle Eastern Literatures* 3, no. 1 (2000): 51–62.
Knight, Ben. "Nuremberg Trials: An Important Step for Germany to Confront Its Nazi Past." Deutsche Welle. November 2020. https://www.dw.com/en/nuremberg-trials-an-important-step-for-germany-to-confront-its-nazi-past/a-55617820.
Koestler, Arthur. *Darkness at Noon*. Trans. Daphne Hardy. London: Jonathan Cape, 1940.
———. *Spanish Testament*. London: Victor Gollancz, 1937.
———. *Thieves in the Night: Chronicle of an Experiment*. London: Macmillan, 1946.
Koselleck, Reinhart. *Futures Past: On the Semantics of Historical Time*. Trans. Keith Tribe. New York: Columbia University Press, 2004.
Kott, Jan. *Shakespeare, Our Contemporary*. London: Methuen. 1961. Trans. Jabra Ibrahim Jabra as *Shakespeare—mu'asiruna* (Baghdad: Dar al-Rashid, 1979).
Kotzin, Daniel P. *Judah L. Magnes: An American Jewish Nonconformist*. Syracuse, NY: Syracuse University Press, 2010.
Krämer, Gudrun. "Anti-Semitism in the Muslim World: A Critical Review." Anti-Semitism in the Arab World, Special Issue. *Die Welt des Islams: International Journal for the Study of Modern Islam* 46, no. 3 (2006): 243–76.
———. *A History of Palestine: From the Ottoman Conquest to the Founding of the State of Israel*. Trans. Graham Harman and Gudrun Krämer. Princeton, NJ: Princeton University Press, 2008.
Kraemer, Joel L. "The Death of an Orientalist: Paul Kraus from Prague to Cairo." In *The Jewish Discovery of Islam: Studies in Honor of Bernard Lewis*, ed. M. Kramer, 181–205. Tel Aviv: Moshe Dayan Center, 1999.

Kupferschmidt, Uri M. "Harari, Sir Victor Pasha and Ralph." *Encyclopedia of Jews in the Islamic World*. 2010. https://referenceworks.brillonline.com/entries/encyclopedia-of-jews-in-the-islamic-world/harari-sir-victor-pasha-and-ralph-SIM_0009300.

Lazar, Hadara. *ha–Mandatorim: Erets Yisra'el, 1940–1948*. 2nd ed. 1990. Reprint, Jerusalem: Keter, 2003. Trans. Marsha Pomerantz as *Out of Palestine: The Making of Modern Israel* (New York: Atlas, 2011).

Lea, Henry A. "Wolfgang Hildesheimer and the German-Jewish Experience: Reflections on 'Tynset' and 'Masante.'" *Monatshefte* 71, no. 1 (1979): 19–28.

——. *Wolfgang Hildesheimers Weg als Jude und Deutscher*. Stuttgart: Hans-Dieter Heinz, 1997.

"Leaders in Jail—Lunatics in Charge." *Palestine Post*, July 24, 1946.

Lehn, Walter. "The Jewish National Fund." *Journal of Palestine Studies* 3, no. 4 (1974): 74–96.

Lepore, Jill. "Historians Who Love Too Much: Reflections on Microhistory and Biography." *Journal of American History* 88, no. 1 (2001): 129–44.

"Lesser Evils." *Daily Telegraph*, July 22, 1946.

Levene, Mark. 2019. "Harbingers of Jewish and Palestinian Disasters: European Nation-State Building and Its Toxic Legacies, 1912–1948." In *The Holocaust and the Nakba: A New Grammar of Trauma and History*, ed. Bashir Bashir and Amos Goldberg, 45–65. New York: Columbia University Press.

LeVine, Mark, and Gershon Shafir. "Introduction: Social Biographies in Making Sense of History." In *Struggle and Survival in Palestine/Israel*, ed. Mark Levine and Gershon Shafir, 1–20. Berkeley: University of California Press, 2012.

Lewis, Paul. "After the War; U.N. Survey Calls Iraq's War Damage Near Apocalyptic." *New York Times*, March 22, 1991.

Likhovski, Assaf. *Law and Identity in Mandate Palestine*. Chapel Hill: University in North Carolina Press, 2006.

Linfield, Susie. *The Lions' Den: Zionism and the Left from Hannah Arendt to Noam Chomsky*. New Haven, CT: Yale University Press, 2019.

Litvin, Margaret. 2011. *Hamlet's Arab Journey: Shakespeare's Prince and Nasser's Ghost*. Princeton, NJ: Princeton University Press, 2011.

Lockman, Zackary. *Comrades and Enemies: Arab and Jewish Workers in Palestine, 1906–1948*. Berkeley: University of California Press, 1996.

Loeterman, Ben, dir. *1913: Seeds of Conflict, Early Encounters Between Jewish and Arab Nationalism*. Israel: Ben Loeterman Productions, Inc., 2014.

"London Matric Passes." *Palestine Post*, August 13, 1943.

Long, J. J. "Time/Travel: Wolfgang Hildesheimer's Zeiten in Cornwall." In *Wolfgang Hildesheimer und England: Zur Topologie eines literarischen Transfers*, ed. Rüdiger Görner and Isabel Wagner, 17–30. Bern: Peter Lang, 2012.

Lustick, Ian S. "Negotiating Truth: The Holocaust, *Lehavdil*, and al-Nakba." In *Exile and Return: Predicaments of Palestinians and Jews*, ed. Ann M. Lesch and Ian S. Lustick, 106–30. Philadelphia: University of Pennsylvania Press, 2005.

Makdisi, Ussama. *Age of Coexistence: The Ecumenical Frame and the Making of the Modern Arab World*. Oakland: University of California Press, 2019.

Makiya, Kanan. *Republic of Fear: The Politics of Modern Iraq*, updated ed. of 1989. Berkeley: University of California Press, 1998.

——— [al-Khalil, Samir]. *The Monument: Art, Vulgarity, and Responsibility in Iraq.* Berkeley: University of California Press, 1991.
al-Maktab al-da'im lil-ittihad ghuraf al-sina'a wal-tijara wal-zira'a fil-bilad al-'arabiyya, ed. *Israel: Khatar iqtisadi wa-askari wa-siyasi* [Israel: An economic, military, and political danger]. Beirut: Dar al-'ilm lil-ma'ayyin, 1952.
Mandel, Neville. *The Arabs and Zionism Before World War I.* Berkeley: University of California Press, 1976.
Manjapra, Kris. *Age of Entanglement: German and Indian Intellectuals Across Empire.* Cambridge, MA: Harvard University Press, 2014.
Manna, Adel. *A'lam Filastin fi awakhir al-'ahd al-'uthmani (1800–1918)* [The notables of Palestine at the end of the Ottoman era, 1800–1918]. Beirut: Institute for Palestine Studies, 2008.
———. "Kafr Qasim, 1956: Israel's Army Massacres Its Own Peaceful Citizens." *Interactive Encyclopedia of the Palestine Question.* Accessed June 1, 2023. https://www.palquest.org/en/highlight/14334/kafr-qasim-1956.
———. *Nakba and Survival: The Story of the Palestinians Who Remained in Haifa and the Galilee, 1948–1956.* Oakland: University of California Press, 2022.
Manning, Olivia. "Five Modern Artists." *Palestine Post*, December 23, 1942.
Mansour, Camille. "Zionist Operations Against the British Mandate Authorities 1944–1947." Accessed June 23, 2023. https://www.palquest.org/en/overallchronology?nid=139&chronos=139.
Mansour, Camille, and Leila Fawwaz, ed. *Transformed Landscapes: Essays on Palestine and the Middle East in Honor of Walid Khalidi.* Cairo: American University in Cairo Press, 2009.
Mara'ana, Ibtisam, dir. *Sajil ana 'arabi/Write Down, I Am an Arab.* Israel: Ibtisam Films, 2014.
Margalit, Elkana. "Social and Intellectual Origins of Hashomer Hatzair Youth Movement." *Journal of Contemporary History* 4.20 (1969): 25–64.
"Margarine Made in Palestine." *Palestine Post*, December 14, 1938.
Marnau, Fred, ed. *New Road: Directions in European Art and Letters* No. 4. London: Grey Walls Press, 1946.
Masalha, Nur. *Palestine: A Four Thousand Year History.* London: Zed Books, 2021.
———. *The Palestine Nakba: Decolonising History, Narrating the Subaltern, Reclaiming Memory.* London: Zed Books, 2012.
"Matiel Mogannam." *Interactive Encyclopedia of the Palestine Question.* Accessed May 28, 2023. https://www.palquest.org/en/biography/30018/matiel-mogannam.
Mattar, Philip. "al-Husayni, Amin." *Encyclopedia of the Palestinians*, ed. Philip Mattar, 213–18. New York: Facts on File, 2005.
———. "Khalidi, Walid." *Encyclopedia of the Palestinians*, ed. Philip Mattar, 280–84. New York: Facts on File, 2005.
———. *The Mufti of Jerusalem: Al-Hajj Amin al-Husayni and the Palestinian National Movement.* New York: Columbia University Press, 1988.
———. "al-Qassam, Izz al-Din." *Encyclopedia of the Palestinians*, ed. Philip Mattar, 408–09. New York: Facts on File, 2005.
———. "The PLO and the Gulf Crisis." *Middle East Journal* 48, no. 1 (1994): 31–46.
Maurois, André. *Ariel ou la vie de Shelley.* Paris: Emile Paul Frères, 1924. Trans. Ella D'Arcy as *Ariel: The Life of Shelley* (New York: D. Appleton, 1924). Trans. Jabra Ibrahim Jabra as "Qissat hayat Shelley: Ariel." *Al-Amali* 1, no. 15 (1938) to no. 33 (1939).

McCormick, Anne O'Hare. "Abroad: The Crisis of Palestinian Leadership." *New York Times*, July 24, 1946.
Meddeb, Abdelwahab, and Benjamin Stora. *A History of Jewish-Muslim Relations: From the Origins to the Present Day*. Ed. Abdelwahab Meddeb and Benjamin Stora. Trans. Jane Marie Todd and Michael B. Smith. Princeton, NJ: Princeton University Press, 2013.
Meiton, Frederik. *Electrical Palestine: Capital and Technology from Empire and Nation*. Oakland: University of California Press, 2019.
Mejcher, Helmut. *Der Nahe Osten im Zweiten Weltkrieg*. Paderborn: Ferdinand Schöningh, 2017.
——. *Imperial Quest for Oil: Iraq, 1910–28*. London: Ithaca, 1976.
——. "Palästina in der Nahostpolitik europäischer Mächte und der Vereinigten Staaten von Amerika 1918–1948." In *Die Palästina-Frage 1917–1948: Historische Ursprünge und internationale Dimensionen eines Nahostkonflikts*, ed. Helmut Mejcher. 189–242. 2nd revised ed. Paderborn: Ferdinand Schöningh, 1993.
——. "The Plight and Relief of God's Nation." In *The Struggle for a New Middle East in the 20th Century*, ed. Camilla Dawletschin-Linder and Marianne Schmidt-Dumont, 383–90. Münster: Lit Verlag, 2007.
Mejcher-Atassi, Sonja. "The Arabic Novel Between Aesthetic Concerns and the Causes of Man: Commitment in Jabra Ibrahim Jabra and 'Abd al-Rahman Munif." In *Commitment and Beyond: Reflections on/of the Political in Arabic Literature Since the 1940s*, ed. Georges Khalil and Friederike Pannewick, 143–55. Wiesbaden: Reichert, 2015.
——. "In Search of Jabra Ibrahim Jabra Between Historical Figure and Literary Persona: On (Auto)Biographical Writing," paper presented at the workshop "Imagining the Future: The Arab World in the Aftermath of Revolution" organized by the Arab Fund for Arts and Culture in Berlin, June 9–10, 2018.
——. "Jabra Ibrahim Jabra's Suitcase: Carrying Modernism and Exile Across Borders from Palestine Into Iraq." In *Journal of Contemporary Iraq and the Arab World*, 17, no. 1–2 (2023): 67–88.
——. *Reading Across Modern Arabic Literature and Art*. Wiesbaden: Reichert, 2012.
——. ed. "Writing a Tool for Change: 'Abd al-Rahman Munif Remembered." Special Issue. *MIT Electronic Journal of Middle East Studies* 7 (2007).
Mejcher-Atassi, Sonja, and John Pedro Schwartz, ed. *Archives, Museums and Collecting Practices in the Modern Arab World*. Farnham: Ashgate, 2012.
Menocal, Maria Rosa. *The Ornament of the World: How Muslims, Jews and Christians Created a Culture of Tolerance in Medieval Spain*. New York: Little Brown, 2002.
Mer-Khamis, Juliano, and Danniel Danniel, dirs. *Arna's Children*. Netherlands: Pieter Van Huystee Film and Television, 2004.
Mermelstein, Hannah. "Overdue Books: Returning Palestine's 'Abandoned Property' of 1948." *Jerusalem Quarterly* 47 (2011): 46–64.
Meyer, Stefan G. *The Experimental Arabic Novel: Postcolonial Literary Modernism in the Levant*. Albany, NY: SUNY Press, 2001.
Mirsky, Yehuda. *Rav Kook: Mystic in a Time of Revolution*. New Haven, CT: Yale University Press, 2014.
Mitchell, Timothy. *Colonising Egypt*. Oakland: University of California Press, 2007.

Moed, Kamal. "College Journals, Educational Modernism, and Palestinian Nationalism in Mandate Palestine: *Majallat al-Kulliyyah al-'Arabiyya*." *Journal of Holy Land and Palestine Studies* 20, no. 2 (2021): 180–98.

———. "A Memorable Educator from Palestine: Ahmad Samih al-Khalidi (1896–1951)." *Jerusalem Quarterly* 89 (2022): 78–87.

Mogannam, Matiel E. T. *The Arab Woman and the Palestine Problem*. London: Joseph, 1937.

Moore, George. *A Modern Lover*. London: Tinsley Brothers, 1883. Trans. Jabra Ibrahim Jabra as "al-'Ashiq." *al-Amali* 52, no. 1 (1939): 23–25.

Mordechai, Eliav, and Esriel Hildesheimer. *Das Berliner Rabbinerseminar: Seine Gründungsgeschichte, seine Studenten*. Ed. Chana Schütz and Hermann Simon. Trans. Jana C. Reimer. Berlin: Hentrich and Hentrich, 2008.

"More Illegal Immigrants: The Largest Load Greater Tension in Palestine." *Manchester Guardian*, July 30, 1946.

Morris, Benny. *The Birth of the Palestinian Refugee Problem Revisited*. Cambridge: Cambridge University Press, 2004.

———. *A History of the First Arab-Israeli War*. New Haven, CT: Yale University Press, 2008.

———. "Survival of the Fittest, an Interview with Benny Morris." Interview by Ari Shavit, *Haaretz*, January 9, 2004. Reprint, *Journal of Palestine Studies* 33, no. 3 (2004): 166–73.

Morris, Benny, and Dror Ze'evi. *The Thirty-Year Genocide: Turkey's Destruction of Its Christian Minorities, 1894–1924*. Cambridge, MA: Harvard University Press, 2019.

Morris-Reich, Amos. "Ruppin and the Peculiarities of Race: A Response to Etan Bloom." *History of European Ideas* 34, no. 1 (2008): 116–19.

"Muhammad Ruhi al-Khalidi." *Interactive Encyclopedia of the Palestine Question*. Accessed May 28, 2023. https://www.palquest.org/en/biography/9839/muhammad-ruhi-al-khalidi.

Munif, Abd al-Rahman. *al-Katib wal-manfa: Humum wa-afaq al-riwaya al-'arabiyya* [Writer and exile: Concerns and horizons of the Arabic novel]. 2nd ed. Beirut: al-Mu'assassa al-'arabiyya lil-dirasat wal-nashr, 1994.

"Musa Alami." *Interactive Encyclopedia of the Palestine Question*. Accessed May 28, 2023. https://www.palquest.org/en/biography/29920/musa-alami.

Musallam, Adnan. "Bethlehem, Palestine Under the British (1917–23)." *Bethlehem University Journal* 3 (1984): 15–31.

al-Musawi, Muhsin Jassim. *al-Riwaya al-'arabiyya—al-nash'a wal-tahawwul* [The Arabic novel—emergence and transformation]. 2nd ed. Beirut: Dar al-Adab, 1988.

Naguib, Hafiz. *Junsun wa-Miltun Tub* [Johnson and Miton Top]. Cairo: al-Maktaba al-tijariyya, 1922.

"Nahariya's Early Years 1934–1949." Lieberman House—Museum of the History of Nahariya. Accessed May 20, 2020. http://museum.rutkin.info/en/node/27.

Najm, Muhammad Yusuf, ed. *Dar al-Mu'allimin wal-kulliya al-'arabiyya fi Bayt al-Muqaddas* [The Teachers' Training College and the Arab College in Jerusalem]. Beirut: Dar Sadir, 2007.

al-Nashashibi, Muhammad Is'af. *al-Bustan* [The garden]. Cairo: Matba'at al-Ma'arif, 1927.

Nashashibi, Nasser Eddin. *Jerusalem's Other Voice: Ragheb Nashashibi and Moderation in Palestinian Politics, 1920–1948*. Exeter, NH: Ithaca, 1990.

Nashef, Khaled. "Tawfiq Canaan: His Life and Work." *Jerusalem Quarterly* 16 (2002): 12–26.

Nasser-Eldin, Mahasen, dir. *The Silent Protest: 1929 Jerusalem*. Creative Interruptions/AHRC, 2019.
Neumahr, Uwe. *Das Schloss der Schriftsteller: Nürnberg '46: Treffen am Abgrund*. Munich: C.H. Beck, 2023.
Neuwirth, Angelika. "Jabrā Ibrāhīm Jabrā's Autobiography, *al-Bi'r al-ūlā* and His Concept of a Celebration of Life." In *Writing the Self: Autobiographical Writing in Modern Arabic Literature*, ed. Robin Ostle, Ed de Moor, and Stefan Wild, 115–27. London: Saqi Books, 1998.
Niklew, Christiane. "Wolf Rosenberg." *Lexikon verfolgter Musiker und Musikerinnen der NS-Zeit*. Ed. Claudia Maurer Zenck, Peter Petersen, and Sophie Fetthauer. Hamburg: Hamburg University, 2015. https://www.lexm.uni-hamburg.de/object/lexm_lexmperson_00003149.
Noorani, Yaseen. "Translating World Literature Into Arabic and Arabic Into World Literature: Sulayman al-Bustani's *al-Ilyadha* and Ruhi al-Khalidi's Arabic Rendition of Victor Hugo." In *Migrating Texts: Circulating Translations Around the Ottoman Mediterranean*, ed. Marilyn Booth, 236–65. Edinburgh: Edinburgh University Press, 2019.
Norris, Jacob. *Land of Progress: Palestine in the Age of Colonial Development, 1905–1948*. Oxford: Oxford University Press, 2013.
"Obituary: Gideon Mer, M.D." *British Medical Journal* 2 (29 July 1961): 315.
'Odeh, Sadiq Ibrahim. "The Arab College in Jerusalem, 1918–1948: Recollections." *Jerusalem Quarterly* 9 (2000): 48–58.
"Palestine Outrage 'Insane Act of Terrorism.'" *Manchester Guardian*, July 24, 1946.
Pappé, Ilan. *The Ethnic Cleansing of Palestine*. Oxford: Oneworld, 2006.
——. *The Rise and Fall of a Palestinian Dynasty: The Husaynis 1700–1948*. Trans. Yael Lotan. Berkeley: University of California Press, 2010.
Parkes, Stuart. *Writers and Politics in Germany, 1945–2008*. Rochester, NY: Camden House, 2009.
Parsons, Laila. *The Commander: Fawzi al-Qawuqji and the Fight for Arab Independence, 1914–1948*. New York: Hill and Wang, 2016.
——. "Soldiering for Arab Nationalism: Fawzi al-Qawuqji in Palestine." *Journal of Palestine Studies* 36, no. 4 (2007): 33–48.
Powell, Eve M. Troutt. *A Different Shade of Colonialism: Egypt, Great Britain, and the Mastery of the Sudan*. Berkeley: University of California Press, 2003.
Preuß, Karin. "Zwischen Wahrheit und Fiktion: Wolfgang Hildesheimer in *Zeiten in Cornwall* und in seinen Briefen." In *Wolfgang Hildesheimer und England: Zur Topologie eines literarischen Transfers*, ed. Rüdiger Görner and Isabel Wagner, 31–52. Bern: Peter Lang, 2012.
Pugh, S. S. *Tales of Heroes and Great Men of Old*. London: Religious Tract Society, 1873. Trans. Ya'qub Sarruf as *Siyar al-abtal wal-'uzama' al-qudama'* (Beirut: American Press, 1930).
Pullan, Wendy. "Moments of Transformation in the Urban Order of Jerusalem." In *Routledge Handbook on Jerusalem*, ed. Suleiman A. Mourad, Naomi Koltun-Fromm and Bedross Der Matossian, 220–34. London: Routledge, 2019.
Qasmiyya, Khairiyya. *Filastin fi mudhakkirat al-Qawuqji, 1936–1948* [Palestine in al-Qawuqji's memoirs, 1936–1948]. Beirut: PLO Research Center, 1975.
——. "Palästina in der Politik der arabischen Staaten 1918–1948." In *Die Palästina Frage*, ed. Helmut Mejcher, 123–88. 2nd ed. Paderborn: Schöningh, 1993.
—— [Kasmieh, Khairieh]. "Rūḥī al-Khālidī 1864–1913: A Symbol of the Cultural Movement in Palestine Towards the End of Ottoman Rule." In *The Syrian Land in the 18th and 19th Century:*

The Common and the Specific in the Historical Experience, ed. Thomas Philipp, 123–46. Stuttgart: Franz Steiner Verlag, 1992.

al-Qawuqji, Fawzi. "Memoirs, 1948: Part I." *Journal of Palestine Studies* 1, no. 4 (1972): 27–58.

———. "Memoirs, 1948: Part II." *Journal of Palestine Studies* 2, no. 1 (1972): 3–33.

Ramler, Siegfried. *Nuremberg and Beyond: The Memoirs of Siegfried Ramler from 20th Century Europe to Hawai'i*. Kailua, Hawaii: Islander Group, 2009.

Ratzabi, Shalom. *Between Zionism and Judaism: The Radical Circle in Brith Shalom 1925–1933*. Leiden: Brill, 2001.

Al-Rayes, Hamad. "A Speculative Poetics of Tammuz: Myth, Sentiment, and Modernism in Twentieth Century Arabic Poetry." *Labyrinth* 22, no. 2 (2000): 156–76.

Raz, Adam. "When Israel Placed Arabs in Ghettos Fenced by Barbed Wire." *Haaretz*, May 27, 2020.

Raz-Krakotzkin, Amnon. "Binationalism and Jewish Identity: Hannah Arendt and the Question of Palestine." In *Hannah Arendt in Jerusalem*, ed. Steven E. Aschheim, 165–80. Berkeley: University of California Press, 2001.

Reinharz, Jehuda. "The Esra Verein and Jewish Colonisation in Palestine." *Yearbook of the Leo Baeck Institute* 24 (1979): 261–89.

———. "Ideology and Structure in German Zionism, 1882–1933." *Jewish Social Studies* 42, no. 2 (1980): 119–46.

"Responsibility for the Outrage." *Manchester Guardian*, July 24, 1946.

Richter, Hans Werner. *Im Etablissement der Schmetterlinge: Einundzwanzig Portraits aus der Gruppe 47*. München: Hanser, 1986.

Rischbieter, Henning. "Der Schlaflose: Gespräch mit Wolfgang Hildesheimer." *Theater Heute* 4, no. 4 (1963): 15.

Rivlin, Gershon, and Oren Elhanam. *The War of Independence: Ben-Gurion's Diary*. Tel Aviv: Ministry of Defense, 1982.

Rogan, Eugene, *The Arabs: A History*. New York: Basic Books, 2009.

———. *The Fall of the Ottomans: The Great War in the Middle East*. New York: Basic Books.

Rogan, Eugene L., and Avi Shlaim, ed. *The War for Palestine: Rewriting the History of 1948*. Cambridge: Cambridge University Press, 2001.

Rogers, Gayle. "Translation." In *A New Vocabulary for Global Modernism*, ed. Eric Hayot and Rebecca L. Walkowitz, 248–62. New York: Columbia University Press, 2016.

Rosen, Friedrich. *Oriental Memories of a German Diplomat*. New York: Dutton, 1930.

Roth, Mitchel, ed. *Encyclopedia of War Journalism*. 2nd ed. London: Grey House, 2010.

Rothberg, Michael. *Multidirectional Memory: Remembering the Holocaust in the Age of Decolonization*. Palo Alto, CA: Stanford University Press, 2009.

Rouben, Paul Adalian. "Adana Massacre (1909)." *Historical Dictionary of Armenia*, 70–71. London: Scarecrow, 2010.

Rouhana, Nadim N. "Decolonization as Reconciliation: Rethinking the National Conflict Paradigm in the Israeli-Palestinian Conflict." *Ethnic and Racial Studies* 41, no. 4 (2018): 643–62.

Rouhana, Nadim N., and Areej Sabbagh-Khoury. "Memory and the Return of History in a Settler-Colonial Context: The Case of the Palestinians in Israel." In *Israel and Its Palestinian Citizens: Ethnic Privileges in the Jewish State*, ed. Nadim N. Rouhana and Sahar S. Huneidi, 393–432. Cambridge: Cambridge University Press, 2017.

"Rudolf (Rudi) Lehmann." The Israel Museum. Accessed May 20, 2020. https://web.archive.org/web/20140813195201/http://www.imj.org.il/artcenter/default.asp?artist=280437.

Ruppin, Arthur. *Memoirs, Diaries, Letters.* Ed. Alex Bein. Trans. Karen Gershon. New York: Herzl, 1971.

Rush, Alan. "Princess Lulie Abul-Huda Fevzi Osmanoglu (1919–2012). Obituary." *al-Ahram Weekly*, December 26, 2012.

Sabbagh-Khoury, Areej. *Colonizing Palestine: The Zionist left and the Making of the Palestinian Nakba.* Stanford, CA: Stanford University Press, 2023.

Said, Edward W. "The One-State Solution." *New York Times Magazine*, 10 January 1999.

———. *Orientalism.* London: Penguin, 2003.

———. *Out of Place.* New York: Vintage, 2000.

———. "Permission to Narrate." *Journal of Palestine Studies* 13, no. 1 (1984): 27–48. Republished in *The Politics of Dispossession: The Struggle for Palestinian Self-Determination, 1969–1994*, 247–68. New York: Vintage, 1995.

———. *The Question of Palestine.* New York: Vintage, 1992.

———. "Reflections on Exile." In *Reflections on Exile and Other Essays*, 173–86. Cambridge, MA: Harvard University Press, 2000.

———. "The Return to Philology." In *Humanism and Democratic Criticism*, 57–84. New York: Columbia University Press, 2004.

Sa'di, Ahmad H., and Lila Abu-Lughod. *Nakba: Palestine, 1948, and the Claims of Memory.* New York: Columbia University Press, 2007.

Sakakini, Hala. *Jerusalem and I: A Personal Record.* Jerusalem: Habesch, 1987.

Sakakini, Khalil. *Kadha ana ya dunya* [So am I, o world]. Ed. Hala Sakakini. Jerusalem: al-Matba'a al-tijariyya, 1955.

———. *Yawmiyyat Khalil al-Sakakini.* Vol. 8, *1942–1952: al-Khuruj min al-Qatamun* [The diaries of Khalil al-Sakakini. Vol. 8, 1942–1952: Leaving Qatamon]. Ed. Akram Musallam. Jerusalem: Khalil Sakakini Cultural Center, 2010.

Salam, Saeb. *Qissat Imtiyaz al-Hula, 1914–1934* [The story of the Huleh concession, 1914–1934]. Beirut: self-published, 1976.

Salibi, Kamal. "Beirut Under the Young Turks, as Depicted in the Political Memoirs of Salīm 'Alī Salām (1868–1938)." In *Les Arabes par leurs archives (XVIe-XXe siècles)*, ed. Jacques Berque and Dominique Chevalier, 193–215. Paris: Centre national de la recherche scientifique, 1976.

Salih, Tewfiq, dir. *al-Makhdu'un* (*The Dupes*). Damascus: General Film Institute, 1972.

al-Samarrai, Majed. "Dhakira thaqafiyya tunhar ma'a tafjir darat Jabra Ibrahim Jabra [Cultural memory destroyed with the explosion of Jabra Ibrahim Jabra's house]." *al-Hayat*, April 15, 2010.

Sanagan, Mark. *Lightning Through the Clouds: 'Izz al-Din al-Qassam and the Making of the Modern Middle East.* Austin: University of Texas Press, 2020.

Sandqvist, Tom. *Dada East: The Romanians of Cabaret Voltaire.* Cambridge, MA: MIT Press, 2005.

Sands, Philippe. "Nuremberg Trials Interpreter Siegfried Ramler: 'The Things We Saw Were Shocking.' " *Guardian*, October 22, 2014.

Santiago, Silviano. "The Cosmopolitanism of the Poor." In *Cosmopolitanisms*, ed. Bruce Robbins and Paulo Lemos Horta, 21–39. New York: New York University Press, 2017.

Saud Alfaisal, Haifa "Liberty and the Literary: Coloniality and Nahdawist Comparative Criticism of Rūḥī Al-Khālidī's *History of the Science of Literature with the Franks, the Arabs, and Victor Hugo* (1904)." *Modern Language Quarterly* 77, no. 4 (December 2016): 523–46.

Saunders, Edward. "Introduction: Theory of Biography or Biography of Theory?" In *Biography in Theory: Key Texts with Commentaries*, ed. Wilhelm Hemecker and Edward Saunders, 1–8. Berlin: De Gruyter, 2017.

Saunders, Frances Stonor. *Who Paid the Piper?: The CIA and the Cultural Cold War*. London: Granta, 2000.
Sawafta, Suja. "Origin Stories: Tracing Jabra and Munif's childhoods in Bethlehem and Amman." *Arablit and Arablit Quarterly*, December 2022. https://arablit.org/2022/12/14/origin-stories-tracing-jabra-and-munifs-childhoods-in-bethlehem-and-amman/?fbclid=IwAR1V_k6eCs3FbEidXufHvWrru9VoOQeAvc8Ae1j_RhdEnd1JnlgXQ1_3tFWk.
Sayigh, Anis. *Anis Sayhig 'an Anis Sayigh* [Anis Sayigh about Anis Sayigh]. London: Riad El-Rayyes, 2006.
Sayigh, Rosemary. *Palestinians: From Peasants to Revolutionaries; A People's History*. London: Zed Books, 1979.
——. *Too Many Enemies: The Palestinian Experience in Lebanon*. London: Zed Books, 1993.
Sayigh, Yusif. *Arab Economist, Palestinian Patriot: A Fractured Life Story*. Ed. Rosemary Sayigh. Cairo: American University in Cairo Press, 2015.
Scammell, Michael. *Koestler: The Literary and Political Odyssey of a Twentieth-Century Skeptic*. New York: Random House, 2009.
Scheid, Kirsten L. *Fantasmic Objects: Art and Sociality from Lebanon, 1920–1950*. Bloomington: Indiana University Press, 2022.
Schleifer, Abdullah S. "Izz al-Din al-Qassam: Preacher and Mujahid." In *Struggle and Survival in the Modern Middle East*, ed. Edmund Burke III and David N. Yaghoubian, 137–51. Berkeley: University of California Press, 2006.
Schölch, Alexander. "Das Dritte Reich, die zionistische Bewegung und der Palästina-Konflikt." *Vierteljahreshefte für Zeitgeschichte* 30, no. 4 (1982): 646–74.
——. "Ein palästinensischer Repräsentant der Tanzimat Periode." *Der Islam* 57 (1980): 311–22.
——. *Palestine in Transformation, 1856–1882: Studies in Social, Economic and Political Development*. Trans. William C. Young and Michael C. Gerrity. Washington, DC: Institute for Palestine Studies, 2006.
Scholem, Gershom. *Walter Benjamin: The Story of a Friendship*. Trans. Harry Zohn, with an introduction by Lee Siegel. New York: New York Review Books, 2003.
Seal, Patrick. *Abu Nidal: A Gun for Hire. The Secret Life of the World's Most Notorious Arab Terrorist*. New York: Random House, 1992.
Sebestyen, Victor. *1946: The Making of the Modern World*. New York: Macmillan, 2014.
Segev, Tom. *1967: Israel, the War, and the Year That Transformed the Middle East*. Trans. Jessica Cohen. New York: Metropolitan Books, 2005.
——. *One Palestine, Complete: Jews and Arabs Under the British Mandate*. Trans. Haim Watzman. London: Little, Brown, 2000.
——. *The Seventh Million: The Israelis and the Holocaust*. Trans. Haim Watzman. New York: Holt, 2000.
——. *A State at Any Cost: The Life of David Ben-Gurion*. Trans. Haim Watzman. New York: Farrar, Straus and Giroux, 2018.
Seikaly, Sherene. "How I Met My Great-Grandfather: Archives and the Writing of History." Doing Things with Archives, Special Issue, *Comparative Studies of South Asia, Africa and the Middle East* 38, no. 1 (2018): 6–20.
——. "In the Shadow of War: The *Journal of Palestine Studies* as Archive." *Journal of Palestine Studies* 51, no. 2 (2022): 5–26.

———. "The Matter of Time." *American Historical Review* 124, no. 5 (2019): 1681–88.
———. *Men of Capital: Scarcity and Economy in Mandate Palestine.* Stanford, CA: Stanford University Press, 2015.
Sela, Rona. "The Genealogy of Colonial Plunder and Erasure—Israel's Control Over Palestinian Archives." *Social Semiotics* 28, no. 2 (2018): 201–09.
Shadid, Anthony. "In Baghdad Ruins, Remains of a Cultural Bridge." *New York Times,* May 22, 2010.
Shakespeare, William. *Hamlet.* Trans. Jabra Ibrahim Jabra. Beirut: Dar majallat Shi'r, 1960.
———. *al-Ma'asi al-kubra* [The great tragedies]. Trans. Jabra Ibrahim Jabra. Beirut: al-Mu'assasa al-'arabiyya lil-dirasat wal-nashr, 1990.
Shakry, Omnia El. "'History without Documents': The Vexed Archives of Decolonization in the Middle East." *American Historical Review* 120, no. 3 (2015.): 920–34.
Shammas, Anton, *Arabeskot.* Tel Aviv: Am Oved, 1986. Trans. Vivian Eden as *Arabesques* (New York: Harper and Row, 1988; New York: New York Review Books, 2023).
Shawqi, Ahmad. *Majnun Layla* [Layla and Majnun]. Cairo: Matba'at Misr, 1916.
Sherman, A. J. *Mandate Days: British Lives in Palestine 1918–1948.* Baltimore, MD: Johns Hopkins University Press, 1997.
Shirley, Dennis. *The Politics of Progressive Education: The Odenwaldschule in Nazi Germany.* Cambridge, MA: Harvard University Press, 1992.
Shlaim, Avi. *Collusion Across the Jordan: King Abdullah, the Zionist Movement, and the Partition of Palestine.* New York: Columbia University Press, 1988.
———. *Three Worlds: Memoirs of an Arab-Jew.* London: One World, 2023.
Shohat, Ella. "On Orientalist Geneologies: The Split Arab/Jew Figure revisited." In *The Arab and Jewish Questions: Geographies of Engagement in Palestine and Beyond,* ed. Bashir Bashir and Leila Farsakh, 89–121. New York: Columbia University Press, 2020.
Sinanoglou, Penny. "British Plans for the Partition of Palestine, 1929–1938." *Historical Journal* 52, no. 1 (2009): 131–52.
Smith, Daniella Ohad. "Hotel Design in British Mandate Palestine: Modernism and the Zionist Vision." *Journal of Israeli History* 29, no. 1 (2010): 99–123.
Smith, Simon C. *Reassessing Suez 1956: New Perspectives on the Crisis and Its Aftermath.* London: Routledge, 2016.
"Social and Personal." *Palestine Post,* December 4, 1941.
"Social and Personal." *Palestine Post,* May 6, 1942.
"Social and Personal." *Palestine Post,* July 18, 1945.
"Social and Personal." *Palestine Post,* May 3, 1946.
"Social and Personal." *Palestine Post,* October 24, 1946.
"Soskin, Selig Eugen." *Encyclopaedia Judaica.* Ed. Joseph Ben-Shlomo and Michael Denman. Accessed May 20, 2020. https://www.encyclopedia.com.
"Spanish Consul Among Dead in Hotel Bomb." *Palestine Post,* January 1, 1948.
Sparr, Thomas. *Grunewald im Orient: Das deutsch-jüdische Jerusalem.* Berlin: Berenberg Verlag, 2018.
Sperling, Edward J. Ezra [Th. F. M.]. "Chartres in Jerusalem." *Palestine Post,* January 17, 1940.
———. "The Judean Landscape." *Palestine Post,* December 27, 1939.
———. "Macbeth in Jerusalem." *Palestine Post,* May 5, 1943.

——. "Subjective Painting." *Palestine Post*, July 2, 1941.
Stark, Freya. *Dust in the Lion's Paw: Autobiography, 1939–1946*. London: Murray, 1961.
Sternheim Goral, Walter Lovis Arie. *Um Mitternacht*. Hamburg: Neue Presse, 1983.
Stoler, Ann Laura. *Along the Archival Grain: Epistemic Anxieties and Colonial Common Sense*. Princeton, NJ: Princeton University Press, 2008.
——. "Colonial Archives and the Arts of Governance: On the Content in the Form." In *Refiguring the Archive*, ed. Carolyn Hamilton et al., 83–100. New York: Springer, 2002.
——. "On Archiving as Dissensus." Doing Things with Archives, Special Issue, *Comparative Studies of South Asia, Africa and the Middle East* 38, no. 1 (2018): 43–56.
Stone, Lilo. "German Zionists in Palestine Before 1933." *Journal of Contemporary History* 32, no. 2 (1997): 171–86.
Strobl, Hilde. "Hildesheimers 'Zeiten in England' im Kontext des Surrealismus." In *Wolfgang Hildesheimer und England: Zur Topologie eines literarischen Transfers*, ed. Rüidger Görner and Isabel Wagner, 53–76. Bern: Peter Lang, 2012.
——. *Wolfgang Hildesheimer und die Bildende Kunst: "Und mache mir ein Bild aus vergangener Möglichkeit."* Berlin: Dietrich Reimer Verlag, 2013.
Strohmeier, Martin. *al-Kullīya as-salāhīya in Jerusalem: Arabismus, Osmanismus und Panislamismus im 1. Weltkrieg*. Stuttgart: Deutsche Morgenländische Gesellschaft/Franz Steiner Verlag, 1991.
"Successful 'Metric' Candidates of the Palestine Matriculation Examination." *Palestine Post*, August 18, 1937.
Sufian, Sandra M. *Healing the Land and the Nation: Malaria and the Zionist Project in Palestine, 1920–1947*. Chicago: University of Chicago Press, 2007.
"al-Suhuf al-britaniyya tanshuru al-maqalat haul al-taqsim li-ma'rifat al-saddaha [British newspapers publish articles about partition to find out its repercussions]." *al-Difa'*, July 23, 1946.
Suleiman, Elia, dir. *Chronicle of a Disappearance*. Israel: International Film Circuit, 1996.
Swedenburg, Ted. *Memoirs of Revolt: The 1936–39 Rebellion and the Struggle for a Palestinian National Past*. Minneapolis: University of Minnesota, 1995.
——. "Al-Qassam Remembered." *Alif: Journal of Comparative Poetics* 7 (1987): 7–24.
Sykes, Christopher. *Cross Roads to Israel: Palestine from Balfour to Bevin*. London: Collins, 1965.
——. *Evelyn Waugh: A Biography*. London: Collins, 1975.
——. Letter to Wolfgang Hildesheimer, London, June 18, 1957. Unpublished correspondence, WHA 659.
Tamari, Salim, ed. "The City and Its Rural Hinterland." In *Jerusalem 1948: The Arab Neighbourhoods and their Fate in the War*, ed. Salim Tamari, 74–91. Jerusalem: Institute for Jerusalem Studies, 1999.
——. *The Great War and the Remaking of Palestine*. Berkeley: University of California Press, 2017.
——. *Jerusalem 1948: The Arab Neighbourhoods and Their Fate in the War*. Jerusalem: Institute for Jerusalem Studies and Badil Resource Center, 1999.
——. "Lepers, Lunatics and Saints: The Nativist Ethnography of Tawfiq Canaan and His Jerusalem Circle." *Jerusalem Quarterly* 20 (2004): 23–43.
——. *Mountain Against the Sea: Essays on Palestinian Society and Culture*. Berkeley: University of California Press, 2009.

Tamari, Vera. "Tawfik Canaan—*Collectionneur par excellence*: The Story Behind the Palestinian Amulet Collection at Birzeit University." In *Archives, Museums and Collecting Practices in the Modern Arab World*, ed. Sonja Mejcher-Atassi and John Pedro Schwartz, 71–90. Farnham: Ashgate, 2012.

Tamari Nasir, Tania, and Mary Jabaji Tamari. *Spring Is Here: Embroidered Flowers of the Palestinian Spring*. 2nd ed. Beirut: Institute for Palestine Studies, 2014.

Tamplin, William. "The Other Wells: Family History and the Self-Creation of Jabra Ibrahim Jabra." *Jerusalem Quarterly* 85 (2021): 30–60.

"Tatawwur fil-janayat" [Development in crimes]. *al-Difaʿ*, July 23, 1946.

"Tawfiq Canaan." *Interactive Encyclopedia of the Palestine Question*. Accessed May 28, 2023. https://www.palquest.org/en/biography/14283/tawfiq-canaan.

Teodorovici, Dan. "Sherban Cantacuzino (Paris 1928–London 1918)." *Studies in History and Theory of Architecture* 6 (2018). https://sita.uauim.ro/6/a/63.

"The Earl of Oxford and Asquith." *Telegraph*, January 17, 2011.

Theilhaber, Amir. *Friedrich Rosen: Orientalist Scholarship and International Politics*. Berlin/Boston: De Gruyter, 2020.

Thompson, Elizabeth F. *How the West Stole Democracy from the Arabs: The Syrian Arab Congress of 1920 and the Destruction of Its Historic Liberal-Islamic Alliance*. New York: Atlantic Monthly, 2020.

Thursby, Geoffrey. "Fight on the Rooftops Rocks a City: Beirut: Armoured Car Siege." *Daily Express*. June 16, 1958.

Tibawi, A. L. *Arab Education in Mandatory Palestine: A Study of Three Decades of British Administration*. London: Luzac, 1956.

Tiedemann, Rolf. "Introduction: 'Not the First Philosophy, but a Last One': Notes on Adorno's Thought." In Theodor W. Adorno, *Can One Live After Auschwitz? A Philosophical Reader*, ed. Rolf Tiedemann. Trans. Rodney Livingstone et al., xi–xxvii. Stanford, CA: Stanford University Press, 2003.

"Time Presses." *Daily Telegraph*, July 24, 1946.

Tolley, A. T. *The Poetry of the Forties*. Manchester: Manchester University Press, 1985.

Toynbee, Arnold. *Four Lectures Given by Professor Arnold Toynbee in the United Arab Republic*. Cairo: Public Relations Department, 1965.

——. *A Study of History*. Abridgement of vols. 7–10. Oxford: Oxford University Press, 1957.

——. *The Toynbee Lectures on the Middle East and Problems of Underdeveloped Countries*. Cairo: National Publications House, 1962.

Traverso, Enzo. *The End of Jewish Modernity*. Trans. David Fernbach. London: Pluto Press, 2016.

Tugend, Tom. "A Grandson's Quest." *Jerusalem Post*. July 22, 1996.

"Two Funerals on Mt. Zion." *Palestine Post*, July 31, 1946.

Tyler, W. P. N. "The Huleh Concession and Jewish Settlement of the Huleh Valley, 1934–48." *Middle Eastern Studies* 30, no. 4 (1994): 826–59.

——. "The Huleh Lands Issue in Mandatory Palestine, 1920–34." *Middle Eastern Studies* 27, no. 3 (1991): 343–73.

Tyson, Alan. "Amadevious." *New York Review of Books*, November 18, 1982.

Virgil. "Dido's Passion." Part IV of the *Aeneid*. Trans. Walid Khalidi. *Forum* 6, no. 49 (November 26, 1943): 4.

Vogel, Manfred. *Ariel—ein Almanach fuer Literatur-Graphik-Musik*. Ed. Manfred Vogel. Jerusalem: Junge Dichtung, 1941.

Walid Khalidi: A Biographical Summary. Tunis: Arab League of Education, Culture and Sciences Organization, 2002.

Walter, Henrike. 2009. "Fern-Weh: Wolfgang Hildesheimer's Novels Tynset and Masante as Topographical Reflections of Exile Experience." In *Exiles Travelling: Exploring Displacement, Crossing Boundaries in German Exile Arts and Writing 1933–1945*, ed. Johannes F. Evelein, 99–113. Amsterdam: Rodopi, 2009.

Wasserstein, Bernard. 1992. *The British in Palestine: The Mandatory Government and the Arab-Jewish Conflict 1917–1929*. 2nd ed. London: Basil Blackwell, 1991.

Weiss, Peter. "Seger som hotar sig själv." *Aftonbladet* (Stockholm) June 17, 1967. Translated in *Die Tat* (Germany), July 1, 1967. Reprint, *Rapporte 2* (Frankfurt: Suhrkamp, 1971).

Weninger, Robert K. *The German Joyce*. Gainesville: University Press of Florida, 2016.

Wildangel, René. *Zwischen Ache und Mandatsmacht: Palästina und der Nationalsozialismus*. Berlin: Klaus Schwarz Verlag, 2007.

Wilde, Oscar. "The Nightingale and the Rose." In *The Happy Prince and Other Tales*. London: David Nutt., 1888. Trans. Jabra Ibrahim Jabra as "al-Bulbul wal-warda." *al-Amali* 51, no. 1 (1939): 24–26.

Wilmington, Martin W. *The Middle East Supply Centre*. Albany, NY: SUNY Press, 1971.

"al-Wizara al-britaniyya tabhath mushkilat Filastin. . . ." [The British ministry discusses the question of Palestine]. *Filastin*, July 23, 1946.

Woolf, Virginia. "The Art of Biography (1939)." In *Biography in Theory: Key Texts with Commentaries*, ed. Wilhelm Hemecker and Edward Saunders, 124–30. Berlin: De Gruyter, 2017.

——. *Orlando: A Biography*, ed. Michael H. Whitworth. Oxford: Oxford University Press, 2015.

Yazbak, Mahmoud. "Jaffa Before the Nakba: Palestine's Thriving City, 1799–1948." In *The Social and Cultural History of Palestine: Essays in Honour of Salim Tamari*, ed. Sarah Irving, 8–25. Edinburgh: Edinburgh University Press, 2023.

Yousef, T. "The Reception of William Faulkner in the Arab World." *American Studies International* 33, no. 2 (1995): 41–48.

Zangwill, Israel. "The Return to Palestine." *New Liberal Review* 2 (1901).

——. *The Voice of Jerusalem*. London: William Heinemann., 1920.

Ziyadeh, Nicola. "Ahmad Samih al-Khalidi (1896–1951): tarikh wa-dhikrayat [Ahmad Samih al-Khalidi (1896–1951): History and memories]." In *Dar al-Mu'allimin wal-kulliya al-'arabiyya* [The Teachers' Training College and the Arab College], ed. Muhammad Yusuf Najm, 181–97. Beirut: Dar Sadir, 2007.

Zola, Emile. "La Fée amoureuse." In *Contes à Ninon*. Paris: Hetzel et Lacroix, 1864. Trans. Edward Vizetelly as "Rain Mines." In *Stories for Ninon* (London: William Heinemann, 1895). Trans. Jabra Ibrahim Jabra as "Jinniyyat al-gharam. Qissa lil-adib al-faransi al-kabir Emile Zola." *al-Hilal*, May 1, 1938: 805–08.

Zubaida, Sami. "Contested Nations: Iraq and the Assyrians." *Nation and Nationalism* 6 (2000): 363–82.

Zurayk, Constantine. 1948. *Ma'na al-nakba*. In *al-A'mal al-kamila*. Beirut: Markaz al-dirasat al-wahda al-'arabiyya. Trans. B. Winder as *The Meaning of the Disaster* (Beirut: Khayat's CollegeBook Cooperative, 1956).

INDEX

1967 War, 71, 73, 78, 81, 112, 189, 217–18, 220–22

'Abd al-Hadi, 'Awni, 45, 62, 76
Abdel-Malek, Anouar, 294n56
Abdul Hamid II (Sultan of the Ottoman Empire), 56, 65, 66, 140, 144, 250n64
abstract art, 115, 119, 231, 273n113; Abstract Expressionists, 158
Abu Akleh, Shireen, 12
Abu Ali. *See* Salam, Salim Ali
Abul-Huda, Hasan, 250n64
Abul-Huda, Lulie, 2, 47–48, 77
Abul-Huda al-Sayyadi, 250n64
Abu-Lughod, Lila, 23
Abu-Manneh, Bashir, 71, 188, 259n90
Academy of Arts, Berlin, 26, 136, 160, 188, 225, 228, 269n42, 293n28, 293n34
Acre, 64, 79, 122, 262n140
Adab, al- (journal), 191
Adana Massacre 144
Adass Jisroel congregation, 104, 267n11
Adenauer, Konrad, 108, 200, 216
Adnan, Etel, 288n83
Adonis, 191, 192
Adorno, Theodor W., 178, 182, 216, 219
advertisements, 102, 118–19, *119*, *120*, *121*
Aeneid (Virgil), 67
Aesthetic Theory (Adorno), 216
Afghani, Jamal al-Din al-, 65

Agamben, Giorgio, 182
Age of Coexistence (Makdisi), 2, 154, 221, 225
Age of Entanglement (Manjapra), 225
Ahad 'ashara kawkaban (Eleven planets) (Darwish), 242n20
AHC (Arab Higher Committee), 8, 45–46, 76, 83, 114
Aichinger, Ilse, 185
Akhir al-layl (The end of the night) (Darwish), 242n19
al-Andalus, 178
'Alam bila khara'it (A world without maps) (Jabra, J. I., and Munif), 195
Alami, Musa, 45–46, 48–49, 77, 114, 116, 211, 256n56, 261n130
Alexandria Protocol (1944), 46, 235
Alexandria Quartet (Durrell), 79
Algerian Front de Libération Nationale (FLN), 216–17
Algerian War of Independence, 20, 191, 215–17
Aliya Hadassah (new immigration) Party, 107, 108
All That Remains (Khalidi, Walid), 18, 94
Allen, Roger, 144
Allenby, Edmund (General), 38, 132, 198
Alliance Israélite Universelle, Jerusalem, 64–65
Almansor (Heine), 271n83
Altmann, Samuel Paul, 269n40

Altmann Hottheiner, Elisabeth, 269n40
Amali, al- (weekly magazine), 151, 280n48
Ambache, Suzy, 258n88
American Friends School, Ramallah, 51
American University of Beirut, 25–27, 74, 77, 91, 192, 294n45; graduates of, 52, 79–80; as Syrian Protestant College, 37, 51–52, 64, 79, 85; teachers at, 49, 209, 274n132
Amman, 126, 137, 173, 192, 203, 275n136
Andersch, Alfred, 215
Angelus Novus (Klee), 183, 193
Anglo-American Committee of Inquiry, 49–50, 75–81, 123
Anidjar, Gil, 236
"Annals of Love, The" (Jabra, G.), 168
Ansari, Amin al-(Sheikh), 56
anti-Semitism, 21, 64–66, 93, 104, 135, 213, 244n42, 265n42
Antonius, George, 21, 46, 48–49, 116
Antonius, Katy, 48, 67, 76, 80, 132, 136, 178, 251n68
Antonius, Soraya "Tutu", 67
apartheid, 20
Aql, Ihsan, 55
Arab Awakening. *See* Nahda
Arab Awakening, The (Antonius, G.), 21, 46, 48
Arab College. *See* Government Arab College
Arab Cultural Committee, 150–51
Arab Higher Committee (AHC), 8, 45–46, 76, 83, 114
Arabic Thought in the Liberal Age, 1798–1939 (Hourani, A.), 21
"Arab Language and Culture" (Jabra, J. I.), 151–52
Arab League, 46–48, 151, 172, 211
Arab nationalism. *See* nationalism
Arab Office, Jerusalem, 100, 114, 211, 261n130; Albert Hourani and, 2, 48, 50, 75–76, 78, 205; Shukeiri and, 48, 50, 82, 212
Arab Revolt (1936–1939). *See* Great Revolt
Arab Revolt (1916–1918), Ottoman Empire and, 85–86
Arab Woman and the Palestine Problem, The (Mogannam, M. E. T.), 132

Arab Women's Information Committee (AWIC), 222
Arabian-American Oil Company (Aramco), 47
Arafat, Yasser, 48, 212, 222, 235
architecture, 58, 109, 123–24, 202–3, 274n132, 287n62
archives, 12, 18, 83, 88, 91, 112, 139–40, 152, 168, 231; colonial archives, 37; question of, 23–24; silences of, 228
Arendt, Hannah, 20, 61–62, 74, 106, 177, 179, 218–19, 244n42
Ariel (Vogel), 122
Ariel ou la vie de Shelley (Maurois), 151
Arkan al-tadris (Foundations of teaching) (Khalidi, A. S. al-), 52
Armenians, 4, 144, 156
Arna's Children (Mer Khamis and Danniel), 92, 265n32
Arp, Hans, 273n114
art. *See* modern art
artists, 11, 13, 16, 24, 50, 119–20, 133, 135, 157–58, 160, 168, 171, 179, 184, 192, 195, 229, 273
Arts Club, YMCA, 155–60, 199
Asfour, Muhammad, 282n103
'Ashiq min Filastin (A lover from Palestine) (Darwish), 242n19
Ashour, Issam Yusuf, 209
Askari, Bakr Sidqi al- (General), 154, 155, 189–90
Askari, Ja'far Pasha al-, 190
Askari, Lami'a Barqi al-, 155, 189, 190, 195
Askari, Muhammad Barqi al-, 189
Asmahan. *See* Atrash, Amal al-
Asquith, Julian (Earl of Oxford and Asquith), 57, 100, 202, 203, 206
Assmann, Aleida, 18
Assyrians, 144, 154, 281n70
Atrash, Amal al- (Asmahan), 48
Attari, Hamid, 152
Attlee, Clement, 49
Auden, W. H., 114
Aufbau (journal), 62, 256n48
Augstein, Rudolf, 214

Auschwitz, 182, 269n40, 285n31
"Author as Producer, The" (Benjamin), 276n160
autobiography, 28, 48, 68, 140, 144, 153; Arabic, 55
avant-garde, 179, 198
Awad, Louis, 73
AWIC (Arab Women's Information Committee), 222
Aydelotte, Frank, 260n117
Ayyam, al- (*The Days*) (Hussein, T.), 55
Azhar University, al-, 43, 56

Bab al-shams (*Gate of the Sun*) (Khoury, E.), 19
Bachmann, Ingeborg, 185, 216
Badran, Jalal, 148, 158
Baghdad, 71, 79, 138–39, 143, 169, 173, 170–90, 192–93, 195–96, 236, 287n71
Baghdad Group for Modern Art, 195
Baghdad Pact (1955), 208, 209
Bahth 'an Walid Mas'ud, al-. See In Search of Walid Masoud
Baker, James, 237
Balfour, Arthur James, 33, 59
Balfour Declaration (1917), 21, 63, 66, 80, 207; role of, 33, 56, 61, 65, 226
Ball, Hugo, 273n114
Baptista, Joseph, 280n62
Barbir, Kalsum. See Salam, Kalsum Barbir
Barenboim, Daniel, 197
Barenboim-Said Akademie, 197
Barker, Evelyn, 129
Barnes, Djuna, 181, 214–15
Bashir, Bashir, 19
Ba'th Party, 197
Baudelaire, Charles, 119
Bauhaus, 16, 95, 109
Beauvoir, Simone de, 215, 217–18
Beckett, Samuel, 17, 181, 196
Bedouins, 91, 118, 147
Beeley, Harold (Sir), 76
Beethoven, Ludwig van, 100, 109
Before Their Diaspora (Khalidi, Walid), 18, 64
Begin, Menachem, 7, 132, 240n24

Beirut, 82–84, 88, 91, 222, 261n134; siege of, 25, 101, 178, 229, 240n24; US Embassy in, 262n152. *See also* American University of Beirut
Beirut al-masa' (newspaper), 78, 205
Ben-Ami, Tamar, 15
Ben-Gurion, David, 46–47, 76, 106, 116, 207
Benjamin, Walter, 15, 60–62, 178, 182–83, 193, 260n112, 276n160, 286n35; Kafka and, 74–75
Ben-Zvi, Yitzhak, 60
Ben-Zvi Agricultural School, Jerusalem, 255n40
Berger, Jakob, 111, 112
Bergmann, Samuel Hugo, 60
Berlin, 46, 75, 102, 104–6, 122, 143, 199, 206, 207, 218, 267n11, 273n115, 273n116; Berlin Grunewald, 109; Berlin Wall, 216; Schloss Bellevue in, 234
Berlin Chronicle (Benjamin), 183
Berlin Rabbinical Seminary, 104, 105, 267n18, 269n49
Berlin Reichstag fire trial, 127
Bernadotte, Folke (Count), 61
Bethlehem, 26, 138–46, 193
Bevin, Ernest, 49, 207
Bialik, Hayim, 33, 80, 247n7
Bible, 147
Biermann, Wolf, 234
Bilad al-Sham (Greater Syria), 37, 86, 90
Bild-Zeitung (tabloid), 217
Biltmore Program (1942), 47, 106, 107
binationalism, 19, 270n65
binational state, 60–61, 111, 118
biographical writing, 14–15, 24, 71, 133, 138–40, 224
biography, 12–15, 26, 28, 223, 242n10
Bi'r al-ula, al-. See First Well, The
Black September, 78
Blenkinsop, F. W. G., 80, *81*
Bloom, Leopold, 215
Blue Band margarine, 102, 112, 119, *120, 121*
Blum, Ludwig, 221
Blumenfeld, Kurt, 105–7
Böll, Heinrich, 185, 197, 295n59

bombing, of King David Hotel, 25, 80, 133, 134, 156, 197, 238; Irgun Zva'i Leumi with, 3–5, 7, 22, 78, 132; media on, 5–10, 6, 9; witnesses, 10, 73, 155
bombings, 83, 100, 139, 155, 171
borders, 177–80, 192, 199–200
border crossing, 177, 193
Bose, Subhas Chandra, 280n62
Boullata, Issa J., 138, 154, 235
Bourguiba, Habib, 205, 251n75
Boustani, Emile, 52
Bowman, Humphrey E., 38, 40, 55, 66, 252n3, 255n45
Braese, Stephan, 273n125
Brandeis, Louis, 31
Brandt, Margarete, 121, 273n116
Bremen Literature Prize, 128, 181, 275n147
Breton, André, 71, 119, 195, 259n95
Briance, John, 81, *81*
British Army, 40, 49, 77, 92, 117, 118, 154, 255n38, 259n99, 265n31
British Mandate in Palestine, 106–7, 112, 116–17, 123, 131, 139, 148, 158, 190, 198, 200
British Zionist Federation, 7, 33
Brit Shalom, 60, 61, 107, 110, 114
brochures, 38, *39*, 40, *41–42*, *42–43*, 128, 222, 275nn146–47
Brockelmann, Carl, 62
Brod, Max, 73, 74, 75, 122, 260n112
Buber, Martin, 20, 60, 107
Bulos, Afif A., 78–80, *81*, 130, 151, *161*, 261n134, 262n137, 274n130
Bulos, David, 79, 80, 82
Bulos, Nassib, 79, 80, *81*, 100
Bulos, Suhail, 79–80, *81*, 258n74, 262nn140–41
Bulos, Suleiman, 262n140
Bundesverdienstkreuz, 233
Bushnaq, Abdul Rahman, 52, 150
Bustan, al- (The garden) (Nashashibi, M. I. al-), 147
Bustani, Abdullah al-, 85
Bustani, Butrus al-, 147
Buxton, Frank W., 260n117
Byron, George Gordon (Lord), 67, 80

Cahier d'un retour au pays natal (*Notebook of a Return to the Native Land*) (Césaire), 71–72, 259n95
Cairo, 96–97
Camp David Accords (1978), 240n24
Camus, Albert, 184, 192
Canaan, Leila Mantoura, 109
Canaan, Tawfiq, 124, 274n130
Canaan, Theo, 124, 228, 274n132
Cantacuzino, Sherban, 202, 203
Carver, Tena, 286n55
Carver, Tom, 286n55
Casanova, Pascale, 184
Catling, Richard, 81
Cattawi Bey, Joseph, 246n1
CCF (Congress of Cultural Freedom), 191, 196, 212, 288n73
Celan, Paul, 185, 216
Celebration of Life, A (Jabra, J. I.), 278n14
Central Intelligence Agency (CIA), 191, 196, 212, 294n49
Central School of Arts and Crafts, London, 113, 133, 215
Césaire, Aimé, 71–72, 259n95
Chaikin, Benjamin, 31, 33, 123
Chamberlain, Neville, 116
Chamoun, Camille, 210
Chiang Kai-shek, 129
Chehab, Fouad (General), 210
Chelico, Jabra, 143
Chichester, Richard, 81, *161*
children, 63, 92, 134, 147–48, 219, 252n4, 256n56
Christianity, 2, 34, 210 *See also* Young Men's Christian Association
Christians, 37, 40, 64, 66, 152, 156, 223
Church, Alfred J., 55
CIA (Central Intelligence Agency), 191, 196, 212, 294n49
citizenship, 112, 136, 183–85, 189–90, 197, 208, 233
citizen of the world, 184, 189, 233
Clark, Michael, 79, 196
Clarke, Thurston, 3–4
Clayton, Iltyd Nicholl (Sir), 49

coexistence, 2, 19–20, 40, 61–63, 118, 185, 197, 236
Cohen, Hillel, 44, 249n48
Cold War, 8, 47, 191, 196, 208, 212
colonialism, 4, 72, 138
Commentary (magazine), 62
communism, 92, 120, 136, 191, 202, 210, 276n160
Conflict and Violence in Lebanon (Khalidi, Walid), 228
Congress of Cultural Freedom (CCF), 191, 196, 212, 288n73
Cornwall, England, 114, 133–34, 197
cosmopolitanism, 37, 131, 248n27, 316, 317, 329; cosmopolitanism of affluence, 2, 31–40, 50; cosmopolitanism of the poor, 37, 248n28
Cotran, Naim, 37, 79
Covid-19 lockdown, 26
Crick, W. F., 260n117
Crossman, Richard H. S., 76–77, 260n117
Crum, Bartley C., 75, 76, 77, 260n117
Cry in a Long Night (*Surakh fi layl tawil*) (Jabra, J. I.), 71–73, 169, 170, 188, 195, 259n90
Cunningham, Alan, 5, 81

Daily Telegraph, The (newspaper), 5
Dajani, Burhan, 77, 209, 211, 261n130
Damascus, 9, 53, 95, 146, 173, 211, 264n10, 287n71, 294n49
Danniel, Danniel, 92, 265n32
Dar al-Adab, 169
Darkness at Noon (Koestler), 132
Darwaza, Muhammad Izzat, 147
Darwish, Mahmoud, 14–15, 178, 242n19, 284n6
Davies, Humphrey, 19
Davis, Garry, 184
Dayan, Moshe, 82, 112, 219, 220
Days, The (*al-Ayyam*) (Hussein, T.), 55
Defoe, Daniel, 147
De La Salle College, Jerusalem, 138, 190
decolonization, 20, 216
Deir Yassin Massacre, 94, 172, 209

democracy, 62, 151, 214, 263n5
Diary of a Palestinian wound ("Yawmiyyat jurhh filastini") (Darwish), 178
Difa', al- (newspaper), 9, 25, 80
Dillmann, Silvia. *See* Hildesheimer, Silvia
Dimashqiyya, Julia Tuma, 53
dispossession, 19, 37, 172, 298n13
Diwan Mahmud Darwish (Darwish), 242n19
Dos Passos, John, 134
Dovstoevsky, Fyodor, 192
Dr. Zhivago (Pasternak), 212, 294n49
Dupes, The (*al-Makhdu'un*) (Tewfiq Salih), 191
Duri, Abd al-Aziz al-, 287n71
Durrell, Lawrence, 79
Duzdar, Khalid, 35

Eban, A. S., 68, 71, 220, 258n88
Echo and the Pool (Jabra, J. I.), 259n91
Eckhart, Meister, 223
ecumenical circle, 12, 14, 25, 197; of friends, 1–5, 10–11, 13, 15–18, 20–21, 24, 26–28, 32, 37–38, 47, 50–51, 55, 57, 68, 72, 76–81, 81, 99–100, 124, 124, 125, 132–33, 154, 168, 192, 224, 228–29, 238. *See also* Hildesheimer, Wolfgang; Jabra, Jabra Ibrahim; Kassab, Sally; Khalidi, Rasha Salam; Khalidi, Walid
"ecumenical frame," 2
Eden, Anthony, 294n55
Editions Poetry London, 160, 168
education, 53, 108–10, 147–48
Egypt, 37, 47–48, 82, 96–97, 151, 172, 206, 208; Israel and, 199–200, 213, 218, 240n24; Syria and, 209, 212
Egyptian Hotels Limited, 31, 37
Ehrenburg, Ilja, 134
Eich, Günter, 185
Eichmann, Adolf, 218–19
Eichmann in Jerusalem (Arendt), 218–19
Eichmann Trial (1961), 216
Eilender, Margot, 124
Einstein, Albert, 106
Eisenhower Doctrine, 210
Eitington, Max, 121, 273n116
electricity, 95, 149

Eleven planets (*Ahad 'ashara kawkaban*) (Darwish), 242n20
"Eleven Sons" (Kafka), 75
Eliash, Mordecai, 61
Eliot, T. S., 2, 11, 73, 114, 192, 214, 223, 224
"End of Fiction, The" (Hildesheimer, W.), 134
end of the night, The (*Akhir al-layl*) (Darwish), 242n19
England, 16, 114, 133–34, 197. *See also* London
Eppstein, Hedwig, 269n40
Eppstein, Paul, 269n40
Epstein-Eilat, Eliyahu, 118
Erakat, Noura, 200
ethnic cleansing, 94, 140, 154, 171–72, 190, 207, 263n158
Ethnic Cleansing of Palestine, The (Pappé), 263n158
exile, 22, 23, 45, 59, 101, 185, 186–87, 199; Babylonian, 235; Palestinian exile 143, 177–79, 189, 193, 197

fascism, 115–16, 276n160
Facts (brochure), 222
Faisal I (King of Iraq), 86–87, *87*, 151, 154–55, 189, 254n32
"Fall of Haifa, The" (Khalidi, Walid), 117, 210
Farouk (King of Egypt), 208
Farrell, Jerome, 60, 66, 67, 147, 153, 154, 205, 252n3
Fathy, Hassan, 58
Faulkner, William, 17, 193, 196
Fawzi, Mahmoud, 61, 97
Felman, Shoshana, 182–83
fiction, 12, 14, 133–34, 150, 157, 195, 223, 237; dystopian fiction, 73; science fiction, 14, 62; works of, 13, 24
fictionality, 4
Field of Anemones (Jabra, J. I.), 158, *159*, 160
Filastin (newspaper), 8–9, *9*, 35
"Filastin fi nusf qarn" (Palestine in half a century) (Khalidi, A. S. al-), 205
Fil-shi'r al-jahili (On pre-Islamic poetry) (Hussein, T.), 55
Finnegans Wake (Joyce), 223

First Arab-Israeli War (1948–1949), 18–19, 23, 61, 88, 112, 172, 199–200, 220
First Intifada (1987–1993), 25, 92, 233, 265n32
First Well, The (*al-Bi'r al-ula*) (Jabra, J. I.), 28, 138–40, 143–47, 153–54, 157–58, 193, 278n14
Fitzwilliam House, University of Cambridge, 140, *141*, 143, 147, 152, 173, 189, 280n62, 281n63
Fleurs du mal (Baudelaire), 119
FLN (Algerian Front de Libération Nationale), 216–17
"Fluctuations" (Jabra, G.), 168–69
"Foam Dressed Riders, The" (Jabra, G.), 168
Forum (magazine), 67–68, 70, 134, 220. *See also* *Radio Week*
foster-brothers tradition, 63, 256n56
Foundations of teaching (*Arkan al-tadris*) (Khalidi, A. S. al-), 52
France, 46, 64, 97, 151, 178, 183–84, 213
Franco, Francisco, 127, 276n160
Franco-Turkish War, 17, 140
Franklin Book Programs, 196
"Franz Kafka" (Benjamin), 74
Frazer, James, 157, 158, 192
Freedom Fighters of Israel. *See* Lohamei Herut Yisrael
Freedom Theater, Jenin, 265n32
French Mandate for Syria and Lebanon, 86
Freud, Lucian, 115
Freud, Sigmund, 115, 121
Fried, Erich, 185, 219–20
friendship, 2, 10, 11, 13, 15–16, 20, 24, 27–28, 50, 61–63, 86, 99, 100, 128, 155, 169, 188, 195, 197, 206, 224–25, 227, 236–38
Frisch, Max, 215, 230
From Haven to Conquest (Khalidi, Walid), 18, 44, 59, 226
Froshaug, Anthony, 114, 133
Future of Culture in Egypt, The (*Mustaqbal al-thaqafa fi Misr*) (Hussein, T.), 151
Future of Palestine, The (Arab Office), 78, 261n130
Futures Past (Koselleck), 11

Gate of the Sun (*Bab al-shams*) (Khoury, E.), 19
Gaza Strip, 173, 200, 218, 222, 284n12
Gear, William, 120, 273n113
Geddes, Patrick, 33, 221
Geheeb, Edith, 108, 116
Geheeb, Paul, 108, 109, 116
Geitner, Christa, 205, 215, 216
Geitner-Thurner, Inge, 205
Gellhorn, Martha, 134
General Strike, 45, 113
genocide, 94, 140, 154, 171–72, 190, 207, 263n158
Georg Büchner Prize, 181
George, David Lloyd, 33
George, Stefan, 103, 275n152
Germany, 25, 66, 105–9, 115, 118, 180, 258n75, 276n160. *See also* Berlin; Hamburg; Mannheim; Nuremberg; West Germany
Ghazi (King of Iraq), 189
"Ghramufun, al-" (The Gramophone) (Jabra, J. I.), 150, 281n73
Gibb, Hamilton A. R. (Sir), 49, 50, 150, 204
Goethe, 109, 223
Golan Heights 81, 93, 218
Goldberg, Amos, 19
Golden Bough, The (Frazer), 157, 192
Goldino, Carlo, 108
Goldman, Nahum, 106
Goldschmidt, Jehuda "Leon," 103, 267n6
Goldschmidt, Salomon, 103
Goll, Claire, 216
Goll, Yvan, 216
Government Arab College, Jerusalem, 49, 55, 59, 60, 190, 205, 255n38; Ahmad Samih al-Khalidi as principal of, 17, 52, 57–58, 61, 67, 82–83, 148–49, *149*, 154, 252n3, 255n40; Khalidi family home at, *81, 124, 125*; students, 17, 52, 143, 146–52, *149*, 158, 193, 195, 196, 255n40; as Teachers' Training College, 52, 147
Gramophone, The ("al-Ghramufun") (Jabra, J. I.), 150, 281n73
Grands Moulins flour mills, 95
Grass, Günter, 185, 234

Great Britain, 21–22, 36, 43, 46, 58, 86, 94–95. *See also* England
Greater Syria (*Bilad al-Sham*), 37, 86, 90
Great (Arab) Revolt (1936–1939), 45, 113, 145, 150, 158, 245n54, 252n4, 283n123; Great Britain and, 21, 22, 36, 43, 58, 63, 93, 111–12; Walid Khalidi, 59–60
Greek Orthodox Church, 31, 38, 109
Greenpeace, 224
group portrait: archives question, 23–24; individual lives at heart of ecumenical circle, 11, 15–18, 20–21, 24, 28; methodological considerations, 11–15; spatial and temporal setting, 18–23
Gruppe 47, 16, 185, 197, 206, 215–19, 293n28
Guernica (Picasso), 195
Gulf War (1991), 25, 197, 234–35
Gush Emunim, 81

Haaretz (newspaper), 7, 207, 240n20
Habibati tanhad min naumiha (My beloved rises from her sleep) (Darwish), 284n6
Habimah Art Gallery, Tel Aviv, 120
Habimah Theatre, Tel Aviv, 74
Haddad, Yvette, 80
Haganah, 7, 62, 92, 95, 110–12, 229, 273n115; Irgun Zva'i Leumi and, 3, 8, 94, 171; Lohamei Herut Yisrael and, 3, 8, 22, 61, 94, 132, 171; with Plan Dalet, 117, 122, 172, 283n120
Haifa, 94–97, 117, 192, 210; German Colony in, 123; Mount Carmel in, 123
Haikal, Hassanein, 218
Hajj, Unsi al-, 191
Halaby, Samia A., 158
Hamas, 43
Hamburg, Germany, 16, 102–3, 107, 112, 213
Hamburger, Max, 35
Hamlet (Shakespeare), 114, 150, 153, 223, 279n45
Hanania, Malvina, 16, 125, 274n134
Hanania, Sotiri, 125, 126, 274n135
Handke, Peter, 185
Haram al-Sharif, Jerusalem, 56, 83
Harami, Shukri, 67
Harari, Ralph, 246n1, 259n99

Harari, Victor, 246n1, 259n99
Harmon, Arthur Loomis, 38
Harmon, Jeff B., 236
Harrison, Austen St Barbe, 58, 254n28
Hartman, Saidiya, 14, 36, 238
Haydar, Adnan, 144
hazima. See 1967 War
Hebrew University, Jerusalem, 33, 59–61, 75, 80, 91, 123
Heidegger, Martin, 214, 216
Heine, Heinrich, 115, 214, 271n83
"Held wider Willen" (Hero against one's will) (Fried), 219–20
Henein, Georges, 74
Hero against one's will ("Held wider Willen") (Fried), 219–20
Herzl, Theodor, 43, 64, 105
Highsmith, Patricia, 204, 227
Hilal, al- (journal), 151
Hildesheimer, Arnold, 110–11, 117, 207, 227, 269n49; with family, 102–3, 105, 107; Unilever and, 109, 112, 271n68
Hildesheimer, Esriel, 103–5, 267n18
Hildesheimer, Esriel Erich, 227, 269n49
Hildesheimer, Hanna Goldschmidt, 102, 103, 107, 109, 169
Hildesheimer, Henriette, 269n49
Hildesheimer, Hirsch, 104, 105, 227
Hildesheimer, Silvia, 185, 205–6, 213, 226, 228, *231*, 232–33
Hildesheimer, Wolfgang, 37, 69, 71, 102, *124*, 204, 213, 267n18, 270n59; with advertising agency, 119, *119*; Auschwitz and, 182, 285n31; in Cornwall, 114, 133–34, 197; cosmopolitan and, 103, 113, 130–31, 198; in ecumenical circle of friends, 2, 16–17, 26, 57, 68, 99–100, 133, 224; education of, 108–11, 113–14, 215; with Gruppe 47, 185, 197, 216–19; homelessness and, 103, 185, 189, 215; Jabra Ibrahim Jabra and, 130–31, 133, 158, 160, 162–67, 168–69, *170*, 171, *186*–87, 186–90, 192, 194, 197, 199, 201; in Jerusalem, 109–13, 123–32, 198–99; Sally Kassab and, 17, 122, 123–32, *125*, 136–37; Rasha Salam Khalidi and, 100–101, 123,
130, 136–37, 169, 202–6, 225–33, *230*, *231*–32, 237; Walid Khalidi and, 73, 130–31, 136–37, 202–6, 226–29, 291n1, 292n19; in London, 113–16, 133–34; with Mozart, 16, 100, 109, 212, 223, 225, 236; in Nuremberg, 169, 183–84, 189; at Nuremberg trials, 134–35, 180–81, 202, 216, 229, 234, 286n55, 295n59; PIO and, 67–68, 127, 128, *129*, 160; Bella Soskin and, 117–23, 185; as translator, 75, 134–35, 181, 214, 223; Wolfgang Hildesheimer Archive, 26, 136, 160, 188, 225, 228, 269n42, 293n28, 293n34; as writer, 13, 16, 112–13, 121–22, 128, 130, 133–34, 180–82, 194, 197–201, 206–7, 212, 214–15, 218, 220, 223–24, 228–31, 234, 236–37, 275n147; Zionism and, 74, 104–14, 116–19, 123, 130–32, 206
Hillrichs, Hans Helmut, 180, 182
Histadrut, 35, 76, 113
Histoire de Beyrouth (Kassir), 263n5
historical reconciliation, 19–20, 238
historiography, 5, 14, 18, 23
History of the Arab Peoples, A (Hourani, A.), 17
History of the Islamic Peoples (Brockelmann), 62
Hitchcock, Alfred, 204
Hitler, Adolf, 46, 106, 108, 115, 213, 234
Hiwar (journal), 191, 192
Hochberg, Gil Z., 24, 221
Hofmannsthal, Hugo von, 108, 114
"Hollow Man, The" (Eliot), 224
Holme, Christopher, 127–28, 132, 206, 224, 234, 275n140
Holocaust, 8, 19–20, 25, 49–50, 108, 181–83, 200
Holocaust and the Nakba, The (Bashir and Goldberg), 19
homelessness, 103, 185, 189, 215
Homer, 53, 55, 151
homosexuality, 78
Horace, 43, 67
Horkheimer, Max, 178
Hoss, Fawzi el-, 97
Hourani, Albert, 17, 21, 25–26, 47, 49, 71–72, 77, *81*, 297n12; at Arab Office, 2, 48, 50,

75–76, 78, 205; in ecumenical circle of friends, 2, 192, 224, 228; with *The Future for Palestine*, 261n130; on Anbara Salam Khalidi, 53; on 1967 War, 220
Hourani, Cecil, 49, 71, 205, 251n73, 251n75, 258n88
Hourani, George, 49, 80
Hourani, Zelfa, 251n73
"House of Shadows, The" (Jabra, G.), 168
Hovevei Zion (Lovers of Zion), 105, 267n18
Hufschmid, Gustave-Adolphe, 31
Huleh Valley, 90–94, 109, 264n21
Hundred Years' War on Palestine, The (Khalidi, Rashid), 22
Hunters in a Narrow Street (Jabra, J. I.), 195, 289n96
Husayni, Abd al-Qadir al-, 172
Husri, Sati' al-, 151
Hussein (Sharif of Mecca), 86
Hussein, Saddam, 197, 234, 235, 236
Hussein, Taha, 55, 73, 74, 151, 251n74
Husseini, Hajj Amin al-, 45–46, 48, 83, 147, 172
Husseini, Ishaq Musa al-, 150
Husseini, Jamal al-, 8, 76, 114
Husseini, Nimati al-Alami al-, 114
Husseini, Sirine al-, 114
Hutcheson, Joseph C., 260n117
Huxley, Aldous, 114
HW, 119, *119*

Ibn Arabi, 204
Ibn Khaldun, 57
Ibn al-Walid, Khalid, 51
Ibsen, Henrik, 127
identity cards, 10, 72, 184
IDF (Israel Defense Forces), 101, 110, 112, 199–200, 208
Idris, Suhayl, 191
If I Were Another (Darwish), 242n20
Illustrated London News (newspaper), 6, 7–8
Ilyad (Homer), 53
immigration, Jewish, 66, 83; from Germany, 106, 109, 118; to Palestine, 21–22, 45–47, 63–64, 92–94, 114, 117, 123
India, 22, 43, 95, 280n62

Indian Congress Party, 9
independence, Algerian 215; Arab national, 21 155, 283n123; of Lebanon, 82, 97, 210; of Iraq 154, 236; of India 280n62
Indigenous peoples, 7, 20, 65, 91, 96, 101, 172, 179
"In praise of the high shadow" ("Madih al-zill al-'ali") (Darwish), 178
In Search of Walid Masoud (*al-Bahth 'an Walid Mas'ud*) (Jabra, J. I.), 144–45, 192–95
Institute for Palestine Studies (IPS), 78, 211–12, 237, 294n45
intellectuals, 132, 198–99, 222, 229; Arab, 118–19, 139, 192; French, 184, 215–16; Palestinian, 179, 192–94, 196–97, 212
Iran, 123, 207, 208, 265n31
Iranian Revolution (1979), 209
Iran-Iraq War (1980-1988), 197, 236
Iraq, 47–48, 140, 154, 172, 189–90, 208–9, 211, 235–36
Iraq Revolution (1958), 190, 195, 209
Iraq War (2003), 139, 197, 228
Ireland, 205. *See also* Irish Rebellion
Irgun Zva'i Leumi (National Military Organization, Irgun), 8, 123, 171; with King David Hotel bombing, 3–5, 7, 22, 78, 132; with terrorism, 83, 94
Irish Rebellion (1919–1920), 43
'Isa, 'Isa al-, 9
'Isa, Marqus, 35
'Isa, Yusuf al-, 9
Islam, 2, 34, 55, 62, 66, 95, 151, 189, 204
Is Nasser not a fascist? ("Ist Nasser kein Faschist?") (Hildesheimer, W.), 220
Israel, 18, 74–75, 83, 92, 111, 173, 207, 246n69; Egypt and, 199–200, 213, 218, 240n24; establishment of state of, 19, 22–23; Lebanon invaded by, 25, 101, 178, 226, 229, 240n24; Eretz Yisrael (Land of Israel/ Greater Israel), 112
Israel Defense Forces (IDF), 101, 110, 112, 199–200, 208
Israeli-Palestinian conflict, 14, 20, 25, 229, 235
"Ist Nasser kein Faschist?" (Is Nasser not a fascist?) (Hildesheimer, W.), 220
Italy, 46, 91, 128, 181, 273n113, 274n134, 275n144

Jabiri, Saadiyah, 78
Jabotinsky, Ze'ev, 8, 95, 123, 132, 276n160
Jabra, Gabriel, 130, 157, 173. *See also* Jabra, Jabra Ibrahim
Jabra, Ibrahim, 139, 145
Jabra, Isa, 145
Jabra, Jabra Ibrahim, 3, *81*, *159*, *161*, 284n12, 288n83, 289n99; with book collaboration, 160–74; border crossings and, 177–80, 192; childhood in Bethlehem, 138–46, *193*; with destroyed house in Baghdad, *139*, 139–40; in ecumenical circle of friends, 2, 16–17, 26, 68, 72, 99–100, 124, 154, 224, 228; education of, 17, 52, 140, *141*, 143, 146–53, *149*, 158, 173, 189, 193, 195, 281n63; film and, 196, 235–36; *First Well, The* (see *First Well, The*); Wolfgang Hildesheimer and, 130–31, 133, 158, 160, 162–67, 168–69, *170*, 171, *186–87*, 186–90, 192, 194, 197, 199, 201; as Gabriel Jabra, 130, 157, 173; Walid Khalidi and, 27–28, 79, 144, 154–55, 194–95; *Princesses' Street* (see *Princesses' Street*); Rockefeller Foundation and, 140, *142*, 186, 189–90, 287n71; as translator, 17, 68, 71, 150–51, 157, 188, 192, 196, 214–15, 279n45, 280nn51–52, 282n86; as writer, 13, 17, 27–28, 68, 71–73, 79, 138–40, 143–47, 150–54, 157–58, 169, *170*, 177–79, 188–96, 215, 235–36, 259nn90–91, 278n14, 280n48, 281n73, 289n96; with YMCA Arts Club, 155–60, 199
Jabra, Maryam, 139, 144, 145
Jabra, Murad, 145, 148
Jabra, Sadeer, 190
Jabra, Susan, 68, 145
Jabra, Yasser, 190
Jabra, Yusuf, 145, 146, 148
Jabre, Adel, 35
Jackson, Robert H., 134
Jaffa, 9, 40, 42, 44, 46, 55, 59, 63, 83–84, 88, 93, 95, 106, 130, 211, 263n10; Palestine Office in Jaffa, 44; terrorist attacks in, 171
Jaffa Gate, Jerusalem, 33, 38, 59, 145, 154, 198–99

Jamali, Fadhil, 190
Jamal Pasha, 53
Janco, Marcel, 120, 273n114, 273n115
Jarallah, Hussam al-Din, 147
Jardine, B. S., 136
Jaspers, Karl, 180
Jawad Salim wa-nasb al-hurriyya (Jewad Selim and the Monument of Freedom) (Jabra, J. I.), 195
Jawhariyyeh, Wasif, 274n135
Jeanson, Francis, 215
Jehle, Volker, 118, 123, 128–29, 183, 270n59, 272n108, 275n144, 291n1
Jens, Walter, 185
Jerusalem, 10, 15–16, 20, 25, 31–40, 34, 74, 82, 88, 97, 101, 109–13, 120, 123–32, 153–55, 198–99, 237; character of, 23, 40, 77, 96, 171, 198, 199; Assyrian Quarter, 153–55; East Jerusalem, 78, 147, 199, 208, 218, 221–22, 291n116; German Colony, 10, 66–67, 267n18; Haram al-Sharif, 56, 83; Holy City, 31, 33, 38, 58, 246; Jabal al-Mukabbir, 58, 60, 62; Jewish Quarter, 63, 145, 267n18; map of, *32*, 55; Mughrabi (Moroccan) Quarter, 146, 221; New City, 38, 55, 58, 66, 155; Old City, 1, 3, 31, 38, 48, 51, 56, 58, 63, 83–84, 109, 132, 145, 198, 221, 267n18; as "ordinary city," 23, 40–47, 77, 171; Qatamon 10, 153, 155, 171; Rehavia, 109, 111, 155, 270n50; Sheikh Jarrah, 48, 51, 83, ; Upper Baq'a, 67, 80; Talbiya, 109, 131; West Jerusalem, 67, 199, 222; "years of fragile tranquility" in, 47–50, 72
Jewad Selim and the Monument of Freedom (*Jawad Salim wa-nasb al-hurriyya*) (Jabra, J. I.), 195
Jewish Agency, 7–8, 76, 83, 90, 107, 109, 118; UN and, 61; ZO and, 46
Jewish Museum, Berlin, 189
Jewish National Council. *See* Va'ad Leumi
Jewish National Fund (JNF), 43–44, 96, 110, 122, 258n75, 264n22
"Jewishness of M. Bloom, The" (Hildesheimer, W.), 215, 223

Jews, 4, 7, 10, 21, 35–37, 40, 45–46, 48, 58, 60–64, 66, 68, 76, 79, 81, 90, 101, 103–4, 111, 114, 115, 118, 131–32, 146, 156, 179, 189, 214–15, 221, 223, 226–27, 233, 236, 239n9, 256n56, American Jews, 31, Egyptian Jews, 31, German Jews, 106–7, 109, Jews of medieval Spain, 63, non-Jews, 7, 229
JNC. *See* Va'ad Leumi
JNF (Jewish National Fund), 43–44, 96, 110, 122, 258n75, 264n22
Johnson and Milton Top (Naguib), 147
Jordan (*formerly* Transjordan), 47, 78, 147, 173, 189, 209, 218
Jordan River, 93, 95, 207
Journal of Palestine Studies, IPS, 212, 294n45
Journal of the Arab College (*Majallat al-kulliyyah al-'arabiyya*), 52
Joyce, James, 73, 114, 130–31, 144, 181, 215, 223
Jubeh, Nazmi, 221
Judaism, 2, 34, 75, 105, 180, 215, 267n18
Jüdische Presse, Die (newspaper), 104, 105
Jumblatt, Kamal, 210

Kafka, Franz, 73–75, 131, 192, 260n106, 260n112
Kafr Qasim Massacre, 209
Kahn, Zadoc, 64
Kanafani, Ghassan, 191
Karami, Rashid, 210
Kassab, Aziz S., 123
Kassab, Sally (Selwa Pruen), 18, 71, 80, *124*, *126*, *161*, 202, 236, 275n136; in ecumenical circle of friends, 2, 16–17, 26, 57, 224, 228; Wolfgang Hildesheimer and, 17, 122, 123–32, *125*, 136–37
Kassir, Samir, 85, 263n5
Kästner, Erich, 134
Katib al-misri, al- (magazine), 73–74
Kaufmann, Richard, 109
Kaylani, 'Ali al-, 283n123
Keats, John, 67, 157
Kemal, Mustafa, 140
Kennedy, Gerald, 4
Khal, Yusuf al-, 190–92, 195

Khalaf, Salah (Abu Iyad), 222, 235
Khalidi, Ahmad Samih (b. 1948), 82, 97, 227
Khalidi, Ahmad Samih al- (1896–1951), 48–49, 62, 204–5, 225, 252n4, 253n8; with family, 51, 53, *54*, 56–58, 66–67, 82, 88, 90, 218, 254n32; as Government Arab College principal, 17, 52, 57–58, 61, 67, 82–83, 148–49, *149*, 154, 252n3, 255n40
Khalidi, al-Sayyid Muhammad 'Ali al-, 64
Khalidi, Anbara Salam, 17, 44, 131; with family, 53, *54*, 56–58, 60, 68, 72, 82, 85–90, *87*, 92–93, 97, 99, 204–5, 255n40; as translator, 55, 151
Khalidi, Fatima al-, 90
Khalidi, Hajj Raghib al-, 55, 56, 63, 83, 84, 88
Khalidi, Hussein Fakhri al-, 45, 55, 59, 83, 115–16, 227, 254n32
Khalidi, Ismail, 63
Khalidi, Karma (b. 1952), 27, 205
Khalidi, Karma (1940–43), 53, 68
Khalidi, Khadija al-, 56
Khalidi, Randa, 53, 61, 204, 205
Khalidi, Rasha Salam, 13, 18, 27, 28, 69, *81*, 89, 90–98, 222, 236; in ecumenical circle of friends, 1–3, 16–17, 26, 78, 124, 224; education of, 88, 97–99, 205; with family, 53, 57, 72, 81–82, 85–90, *87*, 96, *124*, 155; Wolfgang Hildesheimer and, 100–101, 123, 130, 136–37, 169, 202–6, 225–33, *230*, *231*–32, 237; Walid Khalidi and, 1, 3, 88, 99–101, 133, 202–6, 209–11, 217–18, 222, 225–28;
Khalidi, Rashid, 20, 22, 51, 93–94, 143, 144, 147–48, 177, 220, 237, 245n54;
Khalidi, Ruhi al-, 63, 65–66, 227, 257n71
Khalidi, Sulafa, 51, 53, *81*, *124*, *124*, 130, 202, 226; with family, 56–57, 90, 155, 203; Jabra Ibrahim Jabra and, 195
Khalidi, Tarif, 21, 26, 53, 57–59, 61, 67, 155, 206, 257n71; with family, 83, 85, *87*, 204–5; on Jabra Ibrahim Jabra, 194–95
Khalidi, Usama, 53
Khalidi, Wahida al-, 55

Khalidi, Walid, 24, 45, 48–49, 69, *81*, 82–84, 212, 235, 237, 261n130, 297n12; ancestors and role models, 63–75; Anglo-American Committee of Inquiry and, 75–81; in ecumenical circle of friends, 1–3, 16–17, 26, 57, 100, 124, 154, 224; education of, 51, 52, 66–67, 98, 204–5, 291n1; with family, 51, 53, 55–58, 60, 81–82, 84, 88, 90, 204; Wolfgang Hildesheimer and, 73, 130–31, 136–37, 202–6, 226–29, 291n1, 292n19; Jabra Ibrahim Jabra and, 27–28, 79, 144, 154–55, 194–95; Rasha Salam Khalidi and, 1, 3, 88, 99–101, 133, 202–6, 209–11, 217–18, 222, 225–28; poetic affinities and, 66–75; political awareness and, 51–63; as writer, 13, 15, 18, 44, 59, 64, 67, 68, 78, 82, 94, 117, 191, 210, 220, 222–23, 226, 228

Khalidi, Yusuf Diya al-, 63, 64–65, 227, 257n64

Khalidi Library, 56–57, 79, 204, 237, 257n71

Khalili, Amira, 56

Khalili, Muhammad al-, 56

Khamis, Saliba, 92

Khattab, 'Umar ibn al-, 58

Khayri, Khulusi al-, 251n75

Khouri, Mounah A., 190

Khoury, Elias, 19

Khoury, Philip S., 27

kibbutzim, 77, 111; Kibbutz Hanita, 111–12

Kinau, Johann "Gorch Fock," 267n6

King-Crane Commission, 263n10

King David Hotel, 31, 96, 123; brochures, 40, *41*, *42*, 42–43; ecumenical circle of friends at, 1–5, 11, 26, 38, 57, 77–78, 81, 99–100, 132–33, 154, 168; in media, 33, *34*, 34–36; workers at, 35–37, 50. *See also* bombing, of King David Hotel

King Fuad I University (Cairo University), 97, 98, 251n74

Klee, Paul, 183, 193, 237, 286n35

Knesevich, Alexander Anton, 255n36

Knesevich, Henry, 59, 82–83, 205, 255n36

Koestler, Arthur, 132, 178, 276n160, 288n73

Kook, Abraham Isaac (Rabbi), 33, 80–81, 247n8

Kook, Zvi Yehuda (Rabbi), 80–81
Koselleck, Reinhart, 11
Kotzin, Daniel P., 62
Krakauer, Leopold, 117
Krämer, Gudrun, 46, 245n51
Kraus, Paul, 49, 251n74
Kristallnacht, 115, 134
Kulliyya al-Salahiyya, 56
Kuwait, 234–35

Lac de Houlé, le (Onsi), 91, 264n26
land, 43–44, 90–94, 96, 109, 111–12, 122, 191, 264n21
Landauer, Georg, 107–8, 128
landlords, absentee, 178, 200, 264n22
Lanzmann, Claude, 217
LaSalle Quartet, 285n31
Lasker-Schüler, Else, 222
Lawrence, D. H., 115
Lawrence, Thomas Edward (Lawrence of Arabia), 86
Lazar, Hadara, 110, 130, 132, 160, 203, 229, 270n59
Lea, Henry A., 103, 181, 182
League of Nations, 21, 40, 44, 86, 154
Leavis, F. R., 153
Lebanese Civil War (1975–1990), 25, 82, 90, 92, 222, 228, 275n136
Lebanon, 17, 37, 47, 78, 86, 97, 140, 152, 208, 210, 211; Israeli invasion of, 25, 101, 178, 226, 229, 240n24; Syria and, 261n134, 263n5
Leggett, Frederick (Sir), 260n117
Lehi. *See* Lohamei Herut Yisrael
Lehmann, Rudolf, 120, 273n115
Lehmann, Siegfried, 110
Lepore, Jill, 12, 15
Levin, Walter, 285n31
Levy, Itzhak, 171
Libeskind, Daniel, 189
literature, 100, 103, 122, 134, 147, 150, 179, 184, 196, 198, 215; Arabic literature, 131, 138, 169, 191, 195, 237; English literature, 138, 152–54, 157, 160, 190, 223; English Romantic literature, 131; German

literature 131, 185, 194, 195, 214, 217, 229; German Jewish exile literature, 181; Palestinian literature, 150–51, 194; *Adab al-muqawama fi Filastin al-muhtalla* (Resistance literature in Occupied Palestine (Kanafani), 191; Western literature, 151; world literature 192
Lohamei Herut Yisrael (Freedom Fighters of Israel, Lehi, Stern Gang), 3, 8, 22, 61, 94, 132, 171
London, England, 6, 7–9, 136, 215; Wolfgang Hildesheimer in, 113–16, 133–34; University of London, 57, 66–67, 77, 80, 100, 150
lover from Palestine, A (*'Ashiq min Filastin*) (Darwish), 242n19
Lovers of Zion (*Hovevei Zion*), 105, 267n18
Lustick, Ian S., 246n69
Lydda, 44, 97, 95, 291

MacLeish, Archibald, 190
Mad about Layla (*Majnun Layla*) (Shawqi), 157–58
"Madih al-zill al-'ali" ("In praise of the high shadow") (Darwish), 178
Madrid Peace Conference (1991), 237
Maghout, Muhammad al-, 191
Magnes, Judah Leon, 20, 60–62, 74–76, 118, 225, 263n10
Magnolia (Kassab), 126
Mahfouz, Naguib, 236
Majallat al-kulliyyah al-'arabiyya (Journal of the Arab College), 52
Majnun Layla (Mad about Layla) (Shawqi), 157–58
Makassed Philanthropic Islamic Association, 53, 85
Makdisi, Ussama, 2, 154, 225
Makhdu'un, al- (The Dupes) (Tewfiq Salih), 191
Makiya, Kanan, 235
malaria, 91–92, 265n31
Malik al-shams, al- (Sun king) (Jabra, J. I.), 235–36
Malraux, André, 215
Manasca, Alfred, 246n1

Manasca, Felix, 246n1
Manifestoes of Surrealism (Breton), 71
Manjapra, Kris, 2, 225
Mann, Erika, 134
Mann, Thomas, 295n64
Manna, Adel, 209
Mannheim, Germany, 102, 107–8, 112, 128, 269n40
Manning, Olivia, 120, 132, 206
Manningham-Buller, Reginald E., 260n117
MAPAM (United Workers' Party of Israel), 111
Marbot (Hildesheimer, W.), 223–24, 234, 236–37
margarine, 102, 112–13, 119, *120*, *121*
"Margarinefabrik, Die" (The margarine factory) (Hildesheimer, W.), 112–13
Marnau, Fred, 75
Marshall, John, 190
Masante (Hildesheimer, W.), 181–82, 194, 214, 223
massacres, 25, 94, 154, 172, 190, 209. *See also* Deir Yassin Massacre; Kafr Qasim Massacre; Sabra and Shatila Massacre; Simele Massacre; Adana Massacre
Mattar, Philip, 234–35
Maurois, André, 151
"Mawtini" (My homeland) (Tuqan, I.), 158
McClintock, Robert, 62
McCormick, Anne O'Hare, 8, 134
McDonald, J. G., 260n117
Mears, Frank, 33
Mecca and Medina, 95
media, 20, 33–36, 134–35, 213–14; on bombing of King David Hotel, 5–10, *6*, *9*; journalists, 12, 25, 80, 85, 92, 119, 127, 276n160
Mehmed V (Sultan of the Ottoman Empire), 250n64
"Mein Judentum" (My Judaism) (Hildesheimer, W.), 180, 215
Meir, Golda, 76
Mejcher, Helmut, 25
Memoirs of an Early Arab Feminist (Khalidi, Anbara Salam), 17
memory, 4, 11, 18–20, 24, 62, 83, 133, 140, 144, 200, 203, 216

Memorandum of Arab Senior Government Officials to the High Commissioner (1936), 46
Mendelbaum, Izhak, 36
Men in the Sun (*Rijal fil-shams*) (Kanafani), 191
Mer, Gideon, 91–92, 265n31
Mer-Khamis, Arna, 91, 92
Mer-Khamis, Juliano, 92, 265n32
Messages to Max about the state of affairs (*Mitteilungen an Max über den Stand der Dinge*) (Hildesheimer, W.), 230–31
Meyer, Henry, 285n31
Michaux, Henri, 184
microhistory, 12, 15, 24, 238, 242n10
Middle East Centre, St Antony's College, University of Oxford, 38, 80, 205, 255n45
Middle East Forum (journal), 272nn95–96, 294n45
military tribunal, 72, 180, 202, 286n55
Miller, Alvah Leslie, 156
Mirbad Festival of Modern Arabic Poetry, 278n14
Mitchell, Timothy, 97
Mitteilungen an Max über den Stand der Dinge (Messages to Max about the state of affairs) (Hildesheimer, W.), 230–31
modern art, 16–18, 91, 115, 158, 192, 195
Modern Orthodox Judaism, 105, 267n18
modernism, 191; Arab, 17; European 158; global, 75, 144, 171, 191, 280n50; literary, 71, 196, 214
modernity, 73, 96, 103–4, 138; Arab, 9, 83; global, 38, 42
Mogannam, Elias Mogannam, 131
Mogannam, Matiel E. T., 38, 55, 131–32
Mommsen Theodor, 104
Mond, Alfred (Lord Melchett), 31, 35
Monnier, Adrienne, 184
Montessori, Maria, 52
Moon, Richard L., 125
Moore, George, 151
Morris, Benny, 18, 83, 94, 140, 207, 243n29
Morrison, Robert (Lord), 260n117
Moscheles, Serene, 63
Moses, Julius, 269n40

Mossad, 191, 235
Mosseri family, 31, 259n99
Motzkin, Leo, 269n40
Mozart, Wolfgang Amadeus, 16, 100, 109, 212, 223, 225, 236
Muhammad (Prophet), 26, 51, 58, 86
Mulka Trial (1963), 216
Munif, 'Abd al-Rahman, 195, 290n100
Muqtataf, al- (journal), 147, 251n68
music, 15, 57, 74, 100, 109, 116, 122, 146, 155–57, 179, 188, 192, 223, 260n105; Arabic, 151, 261n134; classical, 160
Muslims, 9, 36, 66, 86, 156, 187–90, 223; Jerusalem and, 40, 51, 65; Sunni, 64, 85, 210, 294n42
Mustaqbal al-thaqafa fi Misr (The Future of Culture in Egypt) (Hussein, T.), 151
My beloved rises from her sleep (*Habibati tanhad min naumiha*) (Darwish), 284n6
My homeland ("Mawtini") (Tuqan, I.), 158
My Judaism ("Mein Judentum") (Hildesheimer, W.), 180, 215
Myth of Sisyphus, The (Camus), 184

Nablus, 64, 84, 113, 158
Nabulsi, Abd al-Ghani al-, 204
Nachtstück (Nightpiece) (Hildesheimer, W.), 214, 215
Nadja (Breton), 195
Naguib, Hafiz, 147
Nahariya, 122–23
Nahda (Arab Awakening), 21, 40, 49, 52, 55, 138, 151; Afghani and, 65; with *al-Muqtataf* journal, 147, 251n68
Najm, Muhammad Yusuf, 196
Nakba, 139, 151, 183, 192, 202; Holocaust and, 19, 200; as ongoing, 19, 209, 229
naksa. *See* 1967 War
Nashashibi, Muhammad Is'af al-, 146–47
Nashashibi, Nasser Eddin, 248n37
Nashashibi, Ragheb al-, 45, 248n37
Nasser, Gamal Abdel, 208–9, 213, 219–20, 234, 294n56
National Defense Party, 45
National Library of Israel, Jerusalem, 23, 74

National Military Organization. *See* Irgun Zva'i Leumi
National Socialist German Workers' Party (NSDAP, *Nationalsozialistische Deutsche Arbeiterpartei*), 108, 269n40
nationalism, 77, 135, 185, 189, 196, 229, 233, 241n1, ethnoreligious 63, rise of 64, Jewish nationalism in Germany 104, Egyptian 151, Arab 151, 172, 189, 191, 283n123, Palestinian 253n6
Nazis, 16, 93, 103, 108, 116, 135, 200, 213, 216–17, 234; Germany, 45, 46, 61, 74, 128, 178, 182, 218–20, 256n48, 283n123; ideology, 115, 214, 265n42; with Reich Association of Jews, 267n11
Neske, Günther, 214
Neuwirth, Angelika, 143, 278n14
New York Times (newspaper), 8, 134, 191
Nicholson and Watson, 133, 160, 168
Nightpiece (*Nachtstück*) (Hildesheimer, W.), 214, 215
Nightwood (Barnes), 214–15
Nimr, Faris, 251n68
Nobel Peace Prize, 235, 240n24
Nobel Prize in Literature, 236
"Non-Conformist Moslem Arab Woman, A" (Khalidi, R. S.), 86
Notebook of a Return to the Native Land (*Cahier d'un retour au pays natal*) (Césaire), 71–72, 259n95
NSDAP (*Nationalsozialistische Deutsche Arbeiterpartei*, National Socialist German Workers' Party), 108, 269n40
nudes, 168–69
Nuremberg, Germany, 169, 183–84, 189; Race Laws, 112; trials, 134–35, 180–81, 200, 202, 216, 229, 234, 286n55, 295n59

Occupied Territories, 12, 37, 237. *See also* Gaza Strip; East Jerusalem; West Bank
'Odeh, Sadiq Ibrahim, 148–49
Odenwaldschule boarding school, Heppenheim, Germany, 108–10, 116, 184
Ohlendorf, Otto, 135
oil industry, 196

Omer Fevz (Prince), 250n64
one-state solution, 19, 20
"On James Joyce" (Hildesheimer, W.), 130, 223
On pre-Islamic poetry (*Fil-shi'r al-jahili*) (Hussein, T.), 55
Onsi, Omar, 91, 264n26
Operation Agatha, 5, 7, 76
Orell, Benjamin, 95
Orientalism, 76
Origins of Totalitarianism, The (Arendt), 62, 244n42
Orlando (Woolf), 13, 144, 228, 238
Oslo Accords, 19, 26, 235
Ottoman Empire, 56, 65–66, 85–86, 140, 144, 250n64
Out of Palestine (Lazar), 270n59
Owen, Roger, 97
Oxford, Anne Palairet, 57, 100, 202, 203, 206
Oxford and Asquith, Earl of. *See* Asquith, Julian

Palairet, Anne. *See* Oxford, Anne Palairet
Palestine, 7, 21, 33, 65, 75, 82–84, 104, 132, 144, 191, 205, 222, 243n28, 252n3, 270n59; ethnic cleansing of, 94, 171–72, 207, 263n158; *The Future of Palestine*, 78, 261n130; Jewish immigration to, 21–22, 45–47, 63–64, 92–94, 114, 117, 123; Jews purchasing land in, 43–44, 93, 96, 264n22; partition of, 21, 22, 59, 71, 83, 93, 108, 117, 136; *The Question of Palestine*, 25, 65, 76, 239n9, 240n24; Survey of Palestine, 32, 55–56; United States of Palestine, 61, 62, 263n10
Palestine Broadcasting Service, 55, 120, 150, 158
Palestine Edible Products, 112, 117, 271n68
Palestine Hotels Limited, 31, 35, 37, 259n99
Palestine Labor League, Histadrut with, 35
Palestine Land Development Company (PLDC), 92–93, 109
Palestine Liberation Organization (PLO), 25, 78, 226, 234, 237; Arafat and, 48, 212, 222, 235; Research Center, 211
Palestine Mission (Crossman), 76

Palestine Office, Berlin, 107
Palestine Office, Jaffa, 44, 46, 106
Palestine Police Force and Prisons Services, 43, 45
Palestine Post (newspaper), 7, 57, 66, 110, 117, 120, 122, 129, 133; Wolfgang Hildesheimer in, 168; HW ad, 119, *119*; Jabra Ibrahim Jabra in, 150; margarine and, 112, *120*, *121*; Semiramis Hotel bombing in, 171; YMCA in, 156
Palestinian Arab Party, 45
Palestinian Arab Reform Party, 45
Palestinian Arabs, 8, 21–22, 36, 43–44, 48, 53, 60, 114; Balfour Declaration and, 33, 61, 65; education of, 147–48; indigenous populations, 7, 65, 91, 96, 101, 172, 179; King David Hotel workers, 35, 50
Palestinian Authority, 26
"Palestinian Exile as Writer, The" (Jabra, J. I.), 177–79, 189, 195, 215
Palestinian Identity (Khalidi, Rashid), 177
Palestinian Independence Party, 9, 45
Palestinian National Liberation Movement (Fatah), 211
Palestinians, 12, 66, 210, 229; Afro-Palestinians, 36; refugees, 19, 78, 146n69, 192, 200, 205, 211, 237, 265n32, 275n136
Palmach, 92, 94, 112
Pappé, Ilan, 18, 22, 171, 172, 263n158
Paris Peace Conference (1919), 21, 86, 269n40
passports, 108, 113, 136, 140, 183
Pasternak, Boris, 212, 294n49
Peel Commission, 5, 21–22, 45, 59, 111, 114
Peres, Shimon, 235
"Permission to Narrate" (Said, E.), 229
"Perpetuum Mobile" (Hildesheimer, W.), 122
Personal Account of Anglo-American Diplomacy in Palestine and the Middle East, A (Crum), 75
Pessoa, Fernando, 144
Pestalozzi, Johann Heinrich, 52
PFLP (Popular Front for the Liberation of Palestine), 191
Phillips, William, 260n117
philosophy, 60, 100, 122, 206

Picasso, Pablo, 195
"Pieces of Poetical Reporting on Spain" (Holme), 127
PIO (Public Information Office), 67–68, 127–30, *129*, 160, 234, 275n140
Pirchan, Emil, 114
Plan Dalet, 117, 122, 172, 283n120
"Plan Dalet" (Khalidi, Walid), 210
plays, 13, 67, 127–28, 185, 206, 275n152, 293n27; Shakespeare's plays, 150, 196, 279n45
PLDC (Palestine Land Development Company), 92–93, 109
PLO. *See* Palestine Liberation Organization
poetry, 11, 13–14, 26, 68, 82, 130–31, 147, 150, 153, 155–57, 160, 168, 171, 182, 192, 216, 220, 224; Arabic, 157, 188, 195; English, 79, 188; English Romantic poetry, 1, 18; Expressionist poetry, 122; modernist poetry 2, 157, 171; pre-Islamic poetry, 55
Poetry London (periodical), 157, 168
Popular Front for the Liberation of Palestine (PFLP), 191
porteurs de valises, les (the suitcase carriers), 215–16
Poschiavo, Switzerland, 123, 213, 214, 226, 227, *230*, *231*, *232*, *233*, 236
Pound, Ezra, 195
Pouteau, Micheline, 215
Powell, Eve M. Troutt, 36–37
Princesses' Street (*Shari' al-amirat*) (Jabra, J. I.), 79, 138, 153, 188–90, 196, 259n91
Princeton University, 211, 261n134
Progress (magazine), 271n68
progressive education movement, in Germany, 108
Prometheus Unbound (Shelley), 151
Protestants, 9, 131, 147, 262n140
Pruen, John Belassis, 126, 275n136
Pruen, Matthew, 126
Pruen, Selwa. *See* Kassab, Sally
psychoanalysis, 115, 121
Public Information Office (PIO), 67–68, 127–30, *129*, 160, 234, 275n140
Pugh, S. S., 147
Pulitzer Prize, 8, 134

Qassam, Izz al-Din al-, 43, 96
Qawuqji, Fawzi al-, 172, 283n123
Question of Palestine, The (Said, E.), 25, 65, 76, 239n9, 240n24
Quran, 53, 56

Rabin, Yitzak, 235
Raddatz, Fritz, 234, 236
radio, 108, 116, 149, 185, 212; BBC radio, 218; German, 197
Radio Week (*Forum*) (magazine), 67–68, 70, 129, 130, 134, 220, 223
railway, 66, 135, 181, 213; Hejaz Railway, 66
Rais, George, 123, 124, 228, 274n132
Rais, Raja, 127
Rais, Wadad Kassab, 123
Ramallah, 51, 95, 99, 211
Ramler, Siegfried, 134
Rancière, Jacques, 24
Realität (reality), 223
reality (*Wirklichkeit*), 182, 184, 223
Rashidiyya Secondary School, Jerusalem, 147–48, 150, 154, 158, 178
"Rebels, the Committed and Others, The" (Jabra, J. I.), 188
Records in vain (*Vergebliche Aufzeichnungen*) (Hildesheimer, W.), 214, 224
"Reflections on Exile" (Said, E.), 179, 215
refugees, 154, 177–80; Holocaust survivors, 8, 49–50; Palestinian, 19, 78, 146n69, 192, 200, 205, 211, 237, 265n32, 275n136
Régence, La (restaurant), 1–2, 3, 40, 42–43
Reich Association of Jews, 267n11
Reich-Ranici, Marcel, 185
Reinharz, Jehuda, 104
religion 11–12, 107, 189, 228, 256n56
resistance, Arab, 44–45; anticolonial, 154; armed, 43, 222; French, 216; Palestinian, 222. *See also* literature
Resolution 181, UN (Partition Plan of 1947), 22, 71, 83, 93, 108, 117, 136
Resolution 186, UN, 61
"Return to Palestine, The" (Zangwill), 243n28
"Return to Philology, The" (Said, E.), 13
Revisionist movement, 8, 123

Richards, I. A., 153
Richter, Hans Werner, 185, 213, 216–17
Rihani, Amin al-, 92
Rijal fil-shams (*Men in the Sun*) (Kanafani), 191
Rimbaud, Arthur, 73
riots (1929), 45, 61, 145, 249n48
"Rita's Winter" ("Shita' Rita") (Darwish), 15, 175
"Rita wal-bunduqiyya" ("Rita and the Rifle") (Darwish), 14–15
Roberts, David, 59
Rockefeller Foundation, 58, 140, *142*, 186, 189–90, 287n71
Rogan, Eugene, 19
Roosevelt, Franklin D., 129
Rosen, Friedrich, 63
Rosen, Georg, 63
Rosen, Pinchas. *See* Rosenblüth, Felix
Rosenberg, Wolf, 73–74, 116, 184, 260n105
Rosenblüth, Felix (Pinchas Rosen), 105, 106, 107, 108, 207
Rosenfeld, Julius, 105, 106
Rothberg, Michael, 20
Rothschild, Edmund de (Baron), 31
Rothschild family, 64, 91
Rouhana, Nadim N., 20
Ruppin, Arthur, 44, 61, 92, 93, 106, 107, 265n42
Russia, 22, 63, 65, 66, 91
Rutenberg, Pinhas, 95

Sabra and Shatila Massacre, 25
Sadat, Anwar, 240n24
Saddam Literature Award, 236
Sadeh, Yitzhak, 112
Safad, 90, 94
Safina, al- (*The Ship*) (Jabra, J. I.), 192
Sahhar, George, 35
Said, Edward W., 59, 179, 185, 197, 215, 229, 235, 261n134; on literature, 13; on Palestine, 25, 65, 76, 239n9, 240n24
Said, Hassan Shakir Al, 195
Said, Nouri al-, 190
Saint George's School, Jerusalem, 51, 56, 59, 66–67, 79, 158

Sakakini, Hala, 9–10, 155, 156
Sakakini, Khalil al-, 10, 49, 59, 65, 147, 155, 171
Salam, Ali, 86, 99
Salam, Anbara. *See* Khalidi, Anbara Salam
Salam, Assem "Asid", 173, 228; architecture and, 130, 202, 203, 274n132; with family, *81, 90*, 124, *124*, 202–3
Salam, Fuad, 96, *96*
Salam, Haifa, *81*
Salam, Kalsum Barbir, 85, 88, 90, 96, 99
Salam, Malik, 96, *96*
Salam, Mohammad, 90, *96*
Salam, Rasha. *See* Khalidi, Rasha Salam
Salam, Saeb, 86, 90, 208, 210; archives, 91, 264n26; with family, 87, 92, 94, 96, *96–97*, 264n26
Salam, Salim Ali (Abu Ali, Salim Bey), 56, 85–86, *87*, 88, *96*, 210; archives, 91, 264n26; Huleh Valley and, 90–94, 109
Salam, Salma, *81*
Salam, Tammam, 264n26
Salama, Hasan, 172
Salam family archives, 91, 92, 264n26
Salibi, Kamal, 57, 90
Salih, Tewfiq, 191
Salim Bey. *See* Salam, Salim Ali
Samara, Hilmi, 152
Samuel, Herbert (Sir), 33, 44, 45, 59, 80, 252n3
San Remo Conference (1920), 86
Sansour, Larissa, 14
Santiago, Silviano, 37
Sarruf, Ya'qub, 147, 251n68
Sartre, Jean-Paul, 73, 184, 191–92, 215, 217–18
Saudi Arabia, 47
Saunders, Alan (Major), 40, *41*, *42*, 42–43, 45
Sayigh, Anis, 212, 294n29
Sayigh, Fayez, 212
Sayigh, Rosemary, 211
Sayigh, Tawfiq, 190, 191, 212
Sayigh, Yusif, 48, 211, 212, 261n130
Sayyab, Badr Shakir al-, 191, 192
Sayyadi, Abul-Huda al-, 250n64
Scherchen, Hermann, 116
Schiller, Friedrich, 103, 109

Schlosser-Glasberg Cabinet of Arts, Jerusalem, 119, 120
Schocken, Salman, 60
Schölch, Alexander, 25
Scholem, Gershom, 60, 74–75, 109, 178, 219, 260n112
schools, 33, 51–52, 56, 59–61, 64–67, 75, 79–80, 91, 123, 138, 147, 158, 190; *See also* American Friends School; Government Arab College; Odenwaldschule boarding school; Rashidiyya Secondary School, Al-Ummah school
Schopenhauer, Arthur, 223
Second Arab-Israeli War (Sinai War) (Tripartite Aggression) (1956), 112, 208–9, 212–13
Second Intifada (2000–2005), 12, 19, 207
security zones, in Jerusalem, 10, 72, 82
Segev, Tom, 36, 40, 110, 111, 118, 250n59
Seikaly, Sherene, 21, 37, 38, 212
self-determination, 19–20; Woodrow Wilson's principle of, 21–22; national, 131; Palestinian, 235, 298n13
Selim, Jewad, 195, 289n99
Semiramis Hotel, 83, 155, 171
settlements, 26, 44, 61, 92, 94, 112, 122, 182; Rosh-Pinna, 91, 94
settler colonialism, 19
settlers, Jewish, 19–20, 45, 63–64, 81, 91–93, 111–12
Seychelles, 45, 59, 114
Shadid, Anthony, 140
Shai, Haganah and, 62
Shakespeare, William, 17, 67, 131, 138, 157; influence, 153, 194, 223–24; theater productions, 108, 114, 127, 269n42; translations, 150, 196, 219, 279n45
"Shakespeare and I" (Jabra, J. I.), 150
Shanti, Ibrahim al-, 9
Sharett, Moshe, 76
Shari' al-amirat. *See Princesses' Street*
Shaw, John (Sir), 5
Shawqi, Ahmed, 157–58
Shelley, Percy Bysshe, 67, 80, 151, 157, 212

Shemen edible oil factory, 95, 107, 110, 113, 117
Shepheard's Hotel, Cairo, 31, 35
Sheringham, John, 80, *81*
Ship, The (*al-Safina*) (Jabra, J. I.), 192
Shi'r (journal), 190–91, 192, 197
Shire, Helena Mennie, 153
"Shita' Rita" ("Rita's Winter") (Darwish), 15, 175
Shlaim, Avi, 18
Shoah, 189
Shoah (Lanzmann), 217
Shukeiri, Ahmad, 48, 50, 82, 212
Shukri, Hassan, 84
Simele Massacre 154, 190
Sinai Peninsular, 181
Sinai War. *See* Second Arab-Israeli War
Singleton, John E., 260n117
Siraj, Sami al-, 9
Six-Day War. *See* 1967 War
slave trade, 14, 36
Smith, R. D. "Reggie," 120, 129, 132, 206
"Song" (Jabra, G.), 157, 168
Soskin, Bella, 117–23, 185, 273n121
Soskin, Selig Eugen, 122–23, 273n125
South Africa, 20, 68
Sound and the Fury, The (Faulkner), 196
Soviet Union, 123, 136, 208
Spain, 127–28, 271n83
Spanish Civil War, 128, 276n160
Spanish Testament (Koestler), 276n160
Special Emergency Session, UNGA, 71, 220
Sperling, Edward J. Ezra "Th. F. M.," 119, 272n111
Spiegel affair, 213–14
St James's Palace Conference (1939), 45
stage design, 113–14
Stark, Freya, 48
Stein, Gertrude, 16
Stephan, Stephan Hanna, 79, 262n137, 274n130
Stern Gang. *See* Lohamei Herut Yisrael
Stoler, Ann Laura, 24
Stone, Lilo, 106

"Storyteller, The" (Benjamin), 183
Strangers on a Train (Highsmith), 204
Strauss, Franz Josef, 213–14
Sudan, 36–37, 79
Sudanese workers, 1, 3, 35–37, 50
Suez Canal, 47, 96, 208
Suez War (1956), 112, 208–9, 212–13
Suhrkamp Verlag, 212, 214–15
suitcase carriers, the (*les porteurs de valises*), 215–16
Sun king (*al-Malik al-shams*) (Jabra, J. I.), 235–36
Supreme Court of Israel, 74, 75
Surakh fi layl tawil (*Cry in a Long Night*) (Jabra, J. I.), 71–73, 169, *170*, 188, 195, 259n90
Surrealism, 71–72, 74, 115, 116, 119, 131, 181
Sursuq (Sursock) family, 90, 264n22
Sursock Museum, Beirut, 91
Survey of Palestine, 32, 55–56, 264n21
Survey of Palestine, A (Government of Palestine), 123, 127
Switzerland, 116, 123, 155, 181, 204, 207, 227, 233, 235, 236
Sykes, Christopher Hugh, 206–7, 293n28
Sykes, Mark, 207
Sykes–Picot Agreement (1916), 21, 207
Syria, 37, 47, 86, 172–73, 209, 212–13; constitution of, 263n10; Lebanon and, 261n134, 263n5
Syrian-Ottoman Agricultural Company, 90, 92
Syrian Protestant College, 37, 51–52, 64, 79, 85. *See also* American University of Beirut

Tabet, Antoine, 123
Tamari, Salim, 23, 40, 171, 242n10, 274n130
Tambimuttu, Thurairajah, 157, 168
Tammuz fil-madina (Tammuz in the city) (Jabra, J. I.), 192
Tammuzi poets, 157
Tariq, al- (journal), 191
Tat, Die (magazine), 218
Taylor, Telford, 134

Teachers' Training College, Baghdad, 189
Teachers' Training College, Jerusalem, 52, 147. *See also* Government Arab College
Tegart, Charles (Sir), 43
Tel Aviv, 77, 83, 95, 106, 110, 118, 120, 197, 237, 247n7, 272n104
Tell, Wasfi, 77
Teltsch, Ernst, 117
Teltsch, Eva, 117, 118, 124, 133, 135, 202, 228, 229
Templars, German, 66, 258n75
terrorism: anti-, 81; Haganah with Zionist, 7, 61, 171; Irgun Zva'i Leumi with Zionist, 3–5, 7–8, 22, 78, 83, 94, 123, 132, 171; Lohamei Herut Yisrael with Zionist, 3, 8, 22, 61, 94, 132, 171
Thatcher, William Sutherland, 173–74
Theater of the Absurd, 181
Theresienstadt Ghetto, 269n40
"Theses on the Philosophy of History" (Benjamin), 183
Thiess, Frank, 295n64
Thieves in the Night (Koestler), 132
"Thinking the Impossible" (Khalidi, Walid), 222–23
Third River, The (Clark), 196
Tilbury, Pauline May, 114
Times, The (newspaper), 7, 8, 33, 34, 204
"Times in Cornwall" (Hildesheimer, W.), 197
"To Save the Jewish Homeland" (Arendt), 62
Totah, Khalil, 59
Toynbee, Arnold J., 49, 76, 151, 179, 284n12
"Tradition and the Individual Talent" (Eliot), 73
Trans-Arabian Pipeline, 47
Transjordan, 1, 118, 172, 250n64; Arab League and, 47; high commissioners for, 33, 44, 59, 81, 114
transportation, 59, 95
travel writing, 133–34, 197–201, 228–30, 262n137
Trial, The (Kafka), 74, 260n106
Triolet, Elsa, 134
Tripartite Aggression. *See* Second Arab-Israeli War

Truman, Harry S., 5, 82, 118
Tuqan, Fadwa, 52
Tuqan, Ibrahim, 52, 158
Tuqan, Nimr, 52
Turkey, 64, 140, 154, 193, 208, 245n51, 265n31
two-state solution, 19–20, 26, 222
Tynset (Hildesheimer, W.), 181, 214, 215, 218, 223, 275n147
Tzara, Tristan, 273n114

UAR (United Arab Republic), 209
UK. *See* United Kingdom
Al-Ummah school, Jerusalem, 67
UN. *See* United Nations
UNESCO (United Nations Educational, Scientific and Cultural Organization), 173, 183
UNGA (United Nations General Assembly), 22, 44, 71, 117, 220
UNWRA (United Nations Relief and Works Agency for Palestine Refugees), 205, 275n136
Unilever, 102, 107, 109, 112, 271n68
United Arab Republic (UAR), 209
United Kingdom (UK), 16, 33, 50, 67, 118, 207–8, 213; National Archives, 275n145; with White Paper, 22, 45–47, 116–17, 123, 128
United Nations (UN), 82, 132, 174, 206, 216, 222; Relief and Works Agency for Palestine Refugees (UNWRA), 205, 275n136; Resolutions, 22, 61, 71, 83, 93, 108, 117, 136
United Nations Educational, Scientific and Cultural Organization (UNESCO), 173, 183
United Nations General Assembly (UNGA), 22, 44, 71, 117, 220
United Nations Special Committee on Palestine (UNSCOP), 22, 71, 93
United Resistance Movement, 3, 7
United States (US), 22, 46–47, 66, 95, 208, 210, 222, 235; CIA, 191, 196, 212, 294n49; embassies, 134, 237, 262n152; Inter-Allied Commission and, 263n10

INDEX 355

United States of Palestine, 61, 62, 263n10
United Workers' Party of Israel (MAPAM), 111
Université Saint-Joseph, 37, 97
University of Cambridge, 46, 67, 72, 114, 124, 138, 202; Fitzwilliam House, 140, *141*, 143, 147, 152, 173, 189, 280n62, 281n63; Jabra Ibrahim Jabra at, 17, 140, *141*, 143, 147, 152–53, 173, 189, 281n63
University of Exeter, 17, 152
University of London, 57, 66–67, 77, 80, 100, 150
University of Oxford, 27, 38, 49, 80, 152, 205, 255n45
UNSCOP (United Nations Special Committee on Palestine), 22, 71, 93
Unseld, Siegfried, 214
'Uraysi, 'Abd al-Ghani al-, 53
US. *See* United States
Ustinov, Peter, 206

Va'ad Leumi (Jewish National Council, JNC), 7, 8, 107, 128
Van den Bergh, Sydney James, 102, 112, 207
Van Dyck, Cornelius, 147
veils, 53, 55, 89, 90
Vergangenheitsbewältigung, 217, 229
Vergebliche Aufzeichnungen (Records in vain) (Hildesheimer, W.), 214, 224
Verein Jüdischer Studenten Maccabaea (VJSt, Jewish student fraternity), 105
Verein für Palästinensische Angelegenheiten (Society of Palestinian Affairs), 104
Viertel, Berthold, 115
Vietnam War, 217, 218
Virgil, 55, 67, 68, 82, 151, 220
Vogel, Manfred, 122
Vogt, Emil, 31

WAAF (Women's Auxiliary Air Force), 57, 100
waqf, 56, 221, 237
Warburg, Felix, 31
Warburg, Otto, 92
Warburg, Paul, 106

"Waste Land, The" (Eliot), 2–3, 192
Wauchope, Arthur, 46, 114, 149
Waugh, Evelyn, 206, 207
Weidenfeld and Nicolson, 207
Weingarten, Mordecai, 63
Weiss, Peter, 185, 218, 219, 220
Weizmann, Chaim, 7, 33, 60, 71, 76, 107, 116, 132
Weizmann, Vera, 206
Weizsäcker, Ernst von, 234
Weizsäcker, Richard von, 234
"We Refugees" (Arendt), 177
West, Rebecca, 134
West Bank, 12, 78, 81, 84, 173, 218, 220, 222
West Germany, 185, 213–14, 216, 246n69, 260n105
Weston, Reginald "Reggie," *119*, 119–20
What is Literature? (Sartre), 184
White Paper (1939), 22, 45–47, 116–17, 123, 128
"Why Did the Palestinians Leave?" (Khalidi, Walid), 210
Wilbush, Nahum, 110
Wilde, Oscar, 127, 151
Wilson, Woodrow, 21, 245n51
Wirklichkeit (reality), 182, 184, 223
Witnesses of the century (*Zeugen des Jahrhunderts*) (TV series), 128, 180–81, 224
Wolfgang Hildesheimer Archive, Academy of Arts, 26, 136, 160, 188, 225, 228, 269n42, 293n28, 293n34
Women's Auxiliary Air Force (WAAF), 57, 100
Women's Social Endeavor Society, 250n64
Wood, Patricia "Patsy," 202, 203, 286n55, 292n9
Woolf, Virginia, 13, 144, 228, 238
Wordsworth, William, 67, 157
"World Ends, A" (Hildesheimer, W.), 206
World War I, 144, 183
World War II, 40, 47, 183
world without maps, A (*'Alam bila khara'it*) (Jabra, J. I., and Munif), 195
writers, 24, 50, 68, 73, 122, 134, 138, 140, 157, 160, 168, 171, 185, 191, 192, 197, 198, 214, 215, 229; modernist, 144, 151, 181
Wyatt, Woodrow, 209

Yarmouk River, 93, 95
"Yawmiyyat jurhh filastini" (Diary of a Palestinian wound) (Darwish), 178
Yaziji, Ibrahim al-, 49
Yellin-Mor, Nathan, 132
Yishuv, 21, 35, 44–46, 109, 117, 128, 229; Haganah and, 3, 7; members, 40, 130
Young Men's Christian Association (YMCA), 1, 38, *39*, 75, 127, 132, 154; Jabra Ibrahim Jabra and Arts Club, 155–60, 199; Wolfgang Hildesheimer and, 129, *129*
Young Turk Revolution (1908), 66
Youth Aliyah, 219

Zangwill, Israel, 243n28
Zaydan, Jurji, 151
Zeit, Die (newspaper), 218, 219–20
Zeiten in Cornwall (Hildesheimer, W.), 133–34
Zeugen des Jahrhunderts (Witnesses of the century) (TV series), 128, 180–81, 224
Ziegler, Adolf, 115
Zionism, 44, 46–47, 60, 61, 83, 240n24, 247n8, 259n99; Wolfgang Hildesheimer and, 74, 104–14, 116–19, 123, 130–32, 206; in Huleh Valley, 92–94; criticism of, 65, 74, 101, 111–12, 132, 206, 209, 243n28; cultural, 33; political, 18, 35, 43, 105; religious, 33, 80, 247n8; settlers, 19, 20, 45, 63–64, 81, 91–93, 111–12; support for, 8, 21, 33, 55, 82, 93
Zionist Congresses, 43–44, 105–6
Zionist Federation of Germany (ZVfD, Zionistische Vereinigung für Deutschland), 105–7
Zionist Federation of Great Britain and Ireland (British Zionist Federation), 7, 33
Zionist Organization (ZO), 7, 43–44, 46, 64, 71, 92, 106, 110; Zionist terrorists. *See* Irgun Zva'i Leumi; Lohamei Herut Yisrael
Zionist youth movement Blau-Weiss, 107
Zirikli, Khayr al-Din al-, 9
Ziyadeh, Nicola, 52, 53
ZO (Zionist Organization), 7, 43–44, 46, 64, 71, 92, 106, 110
Zola, Emile, 151
Zurayk, Constantine, 19, 211
ZVfD (Zionistische Vereinigung für Deutschland, the Zionist Federation of Germany), 105–7

Printed and bound by CPI Group (UK) Ltd, Croydon, CR0 4YY
15/10/2024